LEARNING TO TEACH,
TEACHING TO LEARN

3rd edition

LEARNING TO TEACH, TEACHING TO LEARN

A Guide for Social Work Field Education

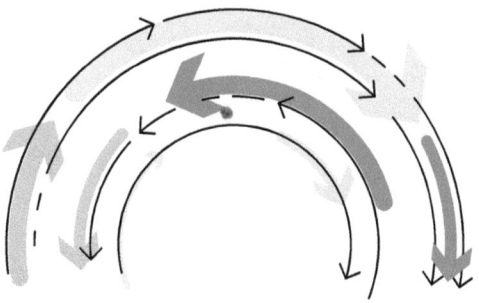

Jeanne Bertrand Finch, Ovita F. Williams,
Jacqueline B. Mondros, and Cheryl L. Franks

ALEXANDRIA, VA

Copyright © 2019, Council on Social Work Education

Published in the United States by the Council on Social Work Education, Inc. All rights reserved. No part of this book may be reproduced or transmitted in any manner whatsoever without the prior written permission of the publisher.

ISBN 978-0-87293-203-6

Printed in the United States of America on acid-free paper that meets the American National Standards Institute Z39-48 standard.

CSWE Press
1701 Duke Street, Suite 200
Alexandria, VA 22314-3457
www.cswe.org

CONTENTS

Foreword by Karina L. Walters .... *vii*

Acknowledgments .... *xi*

Introduction .... *xv*

PART ONE: *Advancing a Framework for Field Education*

➢ **CHAPTER 1.** Justice-Based Field Education 3
   The Bridge to Competence

➢ **CHAPTER 2.** Justice-Based Dialogues 42
   A Keystone for Field Education Supervision

➢ **CHAPTER 3.** Teaching Competency-Based Practice 101
   Rubrics, Assessment, and Evaluation

➢ **CHAPTER 4.** Adult Learning 141
   Thinking, Feeling, and Doing

vi Contents

PART TWO: *Clearing the Path for Learning*

> **CHAPTER 5.** Professional Values and Behavior 179
> *Self-Reflection, Self-Awareness and Self-Regulation*

> **CHAPTER 6.** Getting Started 223
> *Learning While Serving in Justice-Based Field Education*

> **CHAPTER 7.** Student Assignments 261
> *The Vehicles to Learning and Demonstrating Competency*

> **CHAPTER 8.** Promoting Reflection Through Recordings 301
> *Mirrors and Windows*

> **CHAPTER 9.** Shifting the Discourse 347
> *Beyond the Language of Problems*

> **CHAPTER 10.** Evaluations, Endings, and Taking Stock:
> Pulling it Together 401

PART THREE: *Moving Forward*

> **CHAPTER 11.** The Future of Social Work Education 437

APPENDICES

> **APPENDIX A.** Teaching Methods and Tools for Use
> in Supervision 475

> **APPENDIX B.** A Justice-Based Seminar in
> Field Instruction (SIFI) 493

References 505
Index 537
About the Authors 551

FOREWORD

> Creator I'm reaching out to you
> Tell them on the other side
> That they are alive within my soul…
> I hear Nigerian chains
> They say are buried real deep
> Tobacco fields, Trail of Tears
> Stolen people on stolen land
> Tell them, that I know…
>
> ("Going Home," by Pura Fe'/Ulali)

As the Ulali song lyrics above reflect, addressing societies' grandest challenges and eradicating human suffering in the United States cannot be understood without authentically unearthing and uprooting the legacy and ongoing manifestation of settler colonialism in the United States. As a country, we are still dealing with the atrocities of U.S. settler colonialism and White supremacy—as they are manifest in contemporary structures, policies, and everyday interactions—from structural racism supporting the prison-industrial complex to the expressions of everyday microaggressions. Moreover, as a society we continue to police bodies and equivocate about gender and LGBTQ+TS rights and equity among many, many other inequities. As a profession we still struggle at times to move beyond practicing as unwitting social control agents as we desperately plug holes and craft assistance in systems designed to leave people wanting and struggling. At a time when hate crimes are on the rise, the press and the media are under attack, and autocracy has become emboldened, social work's commitment to social justice is essential to creating liberatory practices and policies. However, the use of the familiar social justice social work approaches set within neoliberal policies and structures are simply inadequate because these approaches typically circumvent the larger colonial-based structural factors in which everyday interactions, including our field education approaches, are embedded. Refreshingly and just in time, this third edition of *Learning to Teach, Teaching to Learn*, unabashedly tackles and centers the role of *justice* in social work field education. Building on the second edition's human rights focus, this new edition provides a prescient justice-oriented framework for field instructors, field education, and social work as a profession.

I saw the potential for healing and liberation in the words of this new edition. It was thirst-quenching to read in a profession that sometimes struggles with arid neoliberal platitudes associated with diversity, cultural competency, and justice. Each chapter wrestles with the complexities of addressing intersecting injustices intrapsychically, interpersonally, and interprofessionally. They invite the social work profession—educators, supervisors, and practitioners—to dive deep into the justice struggles of our times as they manifest in intersecting positionalities embedded in the microcosm of the field instructor–student relationship, in the student practitioner–client relationship, and in the settings that all too often produce and reproduce settler colonial inequities. Importantly, the authors provide specific examples from the field with corresponding guideposts for fieldwork action and education.

One factor seldom addressed in field education is the culture in which practice, supervision, and field instruction take place—that is, the culture of the setting. The authors note that the norms, worldviews, and social scripts embedded in social work settings must be examined for justice-based education and practice. Indeed, settings can be conduits of settler colonial practices if the norms, pedagogies, and structures of practice remain unexamined. Specifically, their justice-oriented framework opens the door to examining the transmission of settler colonial individualism and associated normative "Whiteness" in social work field instruction. The settler colonial worldview is so pervasive in institutional settings that associated values, pedagogies, and practices are frequently assumed to be neutral and are presumed to naturally benefit social work trainees and clients (Walters et al., 2016). The internalization of this worldview by faculty members, field instructors, and trainees (on the up and the down side of power and privileged statuses) is emblematic in statements that might at first appear liberatory, but in fact problematize difference or diversity. Manifestations of settler-colonial ideology can be found in statements such as the need to accommodate diversity or address the diversity problem—thus problematizing diversity or the diverse individuals and not the system in which diverse individuals are working or training (Walters et al., 2019). As a result, social work trainees of color or clients of color, for example, are seen as objects to be managed or assimilated into the culture of the program or the agency. Opening the door to examining the culture in which social work training is embedded is a critical first step to a justice-based pedagogy and practice.

Additionally, the authors note the relevance and importance of examining reflexively the relationship between field instructor and trainee—creating the opportunity for a deeper dive into unpacking and addressing microaggressive encounters, attuning to settler colonial privileges (e.g., privilege checking), and building greater tolerance for ambiguity and comfort in examining racialized experiences. Importantly, their relational orientation sets the foundation to examine supervisor as well as trainee "settler moves to innocence" (Tuck & Wang, 2012, p. 10), the defensive maneuvers to restore power and equilibrium that tends to arise when confronted with intense emotions related race, sexuality, and gender, among other justice issues. In social work these can manifest sometimes as toxic applications of "calling out" others of one's same status (e.g., White student "calling out" another White student) to distance oneself from one's privileged status and reconcile settler anxiety. Settler moves to innocence can also manifest as minimization, anger, fear, guilt, tears, or outright flight from the situation (e.g., White fragility). Notably, the authors move toward calling us in—to examine unabashedly how power and privilege plays out in our relationships. Additionally, they provide cogent guidelines for engaging in challenging dialogues with openness and compassion and an eye toward building stronger justice-grounded practitioners, educators, and policy makers.

As a profession we need to look hard at our roles in supporting U.S. settler colonial structures and how we, as a profession, can more honestly move forward to justly serve the communities most affected by societal inequities and injustices. As professionals we need to examine our educational and field instruction systems to better train future generations of social workers to play an integral role in challenging and dismantling U.S. settler colonial structures. The final chapter concludes with a tantalizing note toward developing decolonizing practice strategies for the fourth edition of this book. Although a more in-depth look at decolonizing practices is warranted, this current edition provides ample opportunity to examine decolonizing and liberatory social work as a mandate of justice-based social work practice and field education. Like decolonization, justice should never be a metaphor—it is righteous equity (Latin-*Jūstitia*), it is sacred formula (Proto Italic-*jowos*), it is sine qua non for a liberatory social work ethic and practice for a truly just and healthful society. For once, I saw myself and my People in the text. Yakoke.

Karina L. Walters, PhD
University of Washington

ACKNOWLEDGMENTS

The first and second editions of this book serve as a foundation for the third edition. The work emerged from the Seminar in Field Instruction (SIFI) subcommittee of the Greater New York Field Education Consortium of Schools of Social Work. This consortium consists of all New York City Schools of Social Work and several schools from upper New York State, New Jersey, and Southern Connecticut. Their names appear below in association with committee members who have contributed to editions of this text. The SIFI subcommittee is responsible for teaching and orienting social workers for their roles as new field instructors and those whose work contributed to the earlier editions continue to deserve mention here. We acknowledge Naomi Pines Gitterman for her role in chairing the original SIFI subcommittee of the greater New York area directors of field education and leading the development of the New York State field instruction curriculum in the late 1970s. We are indebted also to Dee Livingston for her leadership on the subcommittee for more than 25 years. Their leadership created the structure still evident in SIFIs today.

We acknowledge the following field education directors and SIFI subcommittee members of the greater New York metropolitan area who shaped and inspired our work: Sidney Berengarten, Martha Bial, Ethel Catlin, Dan Gottlieb, Helen Graber, Alisa Hammerman, John Haynes, Reinhold Heckeler, Reva Fine Holtzman, Theodora Kaplan, Catherine Faith Kappenberg, Judith Lemberger, Eve Lodge, Maxine Lynn, Elaine Marshack, Jacqueline Mondros, Murray Raim, Cristy Ramirez, Michele Sarracco, Bea Seitzman, Georgiana Shephard, Selma Stevens, Carol Sturtz, Carlos Vidal, and Sylvia Weiss.

The first edition emerged from the contributions of the members of the SIFI subcommittee in 2005, who along with the authors of the first edition, included Barbara Stoker and Pat O'Dell, Rutgers University; Alice K. Wolson, New York University; Ruth Bigman, Yeshiva University; Mary Remito, Fordham University; and Beverly Feigelman, Adelphi University. Beverly Feigelman gave shape to the chapter on termination and contributed her time along with Elaine Marshack and Dee Livingston to carefully review the first edition. Betty-Jean Wrase, Stony Brook University, contributed educational materials, and Tanya Manvelidze, assistant librarian, Hunter College School of Social Work Library, helped with references. The 2005 greater New York metropolitan area directors of field education provided support and guidance throughout the development of the first edition. Jeanne Bertrand Finch was director of field education at Stony Brook University during the publication of the first edition and a special thank-you is extended to the other directors at that time: Peter Chernack, Adelphi University; Kathryn Conroy, Columbia University; Urania Glassman, Yeshiva University; Esther Howe and Minou Minchlip, Southern Connecticut State University; Catherine Medina, New York University; Jan Miner, Fordham University; Glynn Rudich, Hunter College, City University of New York; Bonita Sanchez, University of Albany, State University of New York; and Marjorie Talbot, Rutgers University.

The second edition was supported by the 2013 group of directors of field education and members of the SIFI subcommittee in the greater New York metropolitan area. Both groups demonstrated their commitment to furthering the improvement of field education and to the publication of the second edition.

As with the first edition, Betty-Jean Wrase, Stony Brook University, contributed materials for this third edition. The members of the current greater New York area SIFI subcommittee, including James Amato, Adelphi University; Richard Hara, Columbia University; Carla Parris, Fordham University; Abigail Miller Hunter College, City University of New York; Julie Aquilato, Lehman College; Renie Rondon-Jackson and Sabrina Brown, Long Island University; Virge Luce, New York University; Leslie Kulewicz, Stony Brook University; Susan Brot, Touro College, and Raesa Kaiteris, Yeshiva University, gave time to discuss their use of the second edition in the SIFI seminars offered by their programs. Their ideas and suggestions contributed to the improvement of the current edition. We thank them for their support and continued commitment in furthering the SIFI curriculum.

This edition, as the past two editions, builds on the significant knowledge base built over time in field education. Those who continue to develop field education pedagogy and engage in conducting research in this area play a critical role in the development of social work education. The extensive reference list at the end of this book attests to these contributions. SIFI teachers across the consortium of schools of social work within the tristate area of New York, New Jersey and Connecticut are a vital resource and support; their extensive experience in training new field instructors and their ongoing feedback on the use of the different editions of this book have helped to formulate this edition. Finally, the examples and scenarios in this text emerge from our work teaching SIFI, collaborations with field instructors and field liaisons, and our practice of teaching and supervising students. The commitment to teaching and learning demonstrated to us through these connections and interactions has enriched our vision for this text. A special thank-you to Garbena DaRosa, an advanced generalist practice and programming specialized practice-level student, who gave permission for a group process recording to be used and adapted for this book. All other scenarios were modified to protect identification and to clarify the lessons learned. All our students are remembered with fondness and gratitude for their inspiration and influence on our teaching.

Plans for a third edition began in 2015 while arrangements were being made for the adoption of the Council on Social Work Education's (CSWE, 2015a) Educational Policy and Accreditation Standards (EPAS) competency revisions. Carmen Ortiz Hendricks was chair of the CSWE's Commission on Accreditation (2013–2016) during the competency revisions; she saw the need for a revised edition of *Learning to Teach, Teaching to Learn* to better support these changes, but her illness postponed progress. Shortly after her untimely death in 2016, Ovita Williams and Jacqueline Mondros agreed to contribute their expertise as authors of this third edition. Williams brings her experience in field education and in conducting challenging dialogues, and Mondros brings her extensive involvement and leadership in social work education.

We hope this edition lends a vision and conceptualization that embraces the diversity of populations, social problems, service settings, and methods represented in field education and that the text's unifying framework illustrates the breadth of our profession. With this hope in mind, we provide a range of examples and scenarios that address core issues pertinent to our readers' interests and needs.

Dedication

We dedicate this edition to Carmen Ortiz Hendricks, author, colleague, dean and professor, National Association of Social Workers (NASW) Social Work Pioneer, SIFI teacher, field instructor, and loved friend. She guided the first and second editions of this text through publication. Her commitment to the advancement of human rights and to the development of standards and indicators for cultural competency (NASW 2001, 2015) has molded our work. Her voice and vision remain clear and vibrant. Read this edition carefully, and you will hear her calling us forward toward justice, equity, and liberation. ¡Ándele!

INTRODUCTION

This edition of *Learning to Teach, Teaching to Learn* builds on the successes of the preceding two editions and remains committed to supporting field instructors as they teach students in the current context of social work practice and education. Although primarily intended for new field instructors, the text will be useful to experienced field instructors and other field educators as they confront the challenges of teaching entry-level practice. Students will also benefit from the text as an introduction to field education supervision and competency-based social work education.

The first edition, published in 2005, compiled practice wisdom guiding field education and provided useful tools. Much has changed since this first edition, which predated competency-based education and field education's identification as social work's signature pedagogy. The second edition, published in 2013, incorporated the requirements for mastery of competencies outlined in the CSWE's (2008) EPAS and stressed field placement settings as important components of the implicit curriculum for student learning. The emphasis evident in the 2008 EPAS competencies regarding human rights and social and economic justice was integrated into the framework of the text. This was particularly relevant as the second edition was released during a worldwide recession that affected every aspect of service delivery locally and globally. Advances in learning theory were woven into the fabric of the second edition, and transformational learning perspectives provided an additional lens for viewing the field instructor's role as offering a vision of learning. A dual focus emerged: supporting competency-based social work education and introducing a human rights and social justice framework in field education.

The challenge laid out in the first two editions remains the same; that is, we train future social workers while we are rooted in the realities of present-day social work practice. Our focus needs to be on both—practice as it is now and practice that we can only visualize. Tackling this challenge, the third edition builds further on the foundation set down in the preceding editions by elaborating and enriching our dual purposes. This edition more clearly addresses responsibilities for educating for competency, and it presents a more cogent case for integrating a justice-based framework in field education. To achieve these goals, the material has been significantly revised. Before outlining the specifics regarding the organization of the book, we present its purposes.

The purposes of this text evolve directly from our professional mission and the realities of practice and social work education. Our professional mission and the resulting demands placed on us are intricately interwoven and combine to shape what we need to teach students, which is outlined clearly in the CSWE (2015) EPAS and in the structure of this text. Working for justice requires engagement with the issues of diversity, an ongoing commitment to advancing civil and human rights including tribal and indigenous justice, and economic, social, and environmental justice in every aspect of practice and, therefore, in our teaching. The importance of research, policy, and evaluation emerge as vital ingredients alongside efforts to effect change across multiple units of attention in a foundation of generalist practice. Field instructors prepare students for this work, and this text equips them with teaching strategies to meet the challenges of a quickly shifting demographic of social work students who are learning to practice in increasingly diverse communities.

More than a decade of working in competency-based education provides a strong base of experience to assist field instructors in their use of the CSWE (2015a) competencies for teaching and evaluating students. We address what competency-based education comprises, how it serves our teaching, how it serves students, and how we can use the competencies in supervision with students to improve their learning and our teaching. Addressing the other half of our aims, we consolidate the links between our core professional values and the EPAS (CSWE, 2015a) by providing a justice-based perspective for field education. We define what we mean by a justice-based framework and we call for facilitating challenging dialogues with our students on issues of social location, power, privilege, oppression, equity, and liberation as a necessity for their preparation for entry-level social work practice. We propose that excellence in field education demands this.

Competency in a Justice-Based Framework for Field Education

A justice-based framework in field education is rooted in civil and human rights, tribal and indigenous justice, and antioppression perspectives (here we mean to include antiracist theory, critical social theory, and critical race theory; empowerment models, ecological social theory, feminist and womanist perspectives, liberation theory, decolonization and strengths-based models of practice). The definition is not static and includes many forms of inclusive and equity-based forms of practice. This orientation directly addresses issues of justice as integral to our work and teaching. Practice that seeks to remedy social division and structural inequality so central to our professional goals and values also guides our teaching.

Advancing the fulfillment of basic human needs and achieving equity are deeply rooted key concepts of our professional mission. We find these precepts in the NASW (2018) Code of Ethics, the *Declaration of Human Rights* (UDHR; United Nations, 1948), the Declaration on the Rights of Indigenous Peoples (UNDRIP, United Nations, 2007) and the EPAS (CSWE, 2015a). These documents provide us with a moral compass for our practice and underpin our efforts to challenge oppressive policies and to promote strengths-based, inclusive, and democratic ways of working. These aspirations guide our practice, but the work is challenging.

Reisch (2013, 2017) points to the obstacles for social work and social policy to work toward justice in a society that does not credit the importance of human rights with at least the equal protection of property rights. These splits and connections to social work are not new. Reynolds (1942) recognized the associated challenges: "The philosophy of social work cannot be separated from the prevailing philosophy of a nation, as to how it values people, and what importance it sets upon their welfare" (p. 174). Likewise, Weick (2000) warns that "without an eye to protecting and creating a caring context, we may function only to uphold the inadequate structures that continue to place individuals at risk" (p. 402). In this vein, Walters et al. (2011) clarify that the expression of power in the United States as a settler colonial society remains pervasive and dangerous. The historical trauma experienced directly by indigenous peoples has "pernicious effects that persist across generations through a myriad of mechanisms from biological to behavioral" (p. 179). The ramifications reverberate from past to present. Becoming awake to these realities requires opening our minds and hearts not only to how we exercise power but also to how we evade, deny, or seek "moves to innocence" that perpetuate and negatively affect our interactions with each other (Tuck & Yang, 2012, p.10). Our approach to teaching students for entry-level practice requires strategies to meet these challenges. Otherwise, the danger is that we become part of the problem by perpetuating and benefitting from the divides that exist or that we create. More is involved than just students and ourselves. The increasing complex global context of practice and the forces impeding service delivery and social work education play their parts in the obstacles, challenges, and opportunities experienced in field education. A vibrant interchange is created that pushes and pulls for improvements and innovations in social work practice and education. In fact, understanding this is an important aspect of keeping our skills current and flexible to respond to emergent needs; however, the combination of these conditions places special strains on preparing students for practice. Past and present practice protocols and future trends exist simultaneously. Limitations of social policies become incorporated into practice and accepted as work factors; at the same time, a pulse is kept on the need for change, and we watch for research advances that indicate future trends and possible avenues for prevention. These varying pressures combine to strengthen our commitment to lifelong learning and to maintain our competence and improve opportunities for student education.

Recent examples point to the realities of pervasive societal violence and the effect of persistent microaggressions and violence on oppressed populations that need immediate attention in social work practice. For example, an increase in incidents involving police force in communities of color call for teaching students how to intervene in communities struck by persistent and recurrent racial trauma. Fears in communities regarding changing implementation of policies surrounding asylum seekers, refugees, immigration, and migrant worker employment require additional training on ways to advocate for and protect rights; access resources; form partnerships with invested stakeholders; and collaborate and mobilize with community and agency supports through ally and sanctuary networks. Increased othering in school bullying, gun violence, and sexual harassment call for special attention to emergent needs. Recurrent attacks on environmental protections, continuing gang violence and random shootings in our communities, including anti-Muslim and anti-Semitic hate crimes and murders of men and women with transgender experiences, perpetuate a climate of abuse, fear and turmoil. Persistent mistrust of reports of sexual misconduct, sexual assault, and sexual violence characterize societal responses, inhibit behavior change, and hinder healing. U.S. dominant values, expressed in privileged, cisgender, White male Protestant, straight normative worldviews and structures, are evident in policies, definitions of problems, and delivery of services. Social determinants of health outcomes continue to echo similar concerns. Dismantling and decolonizing these systems are mandatory for social work values. The power of voices advocating for change is emerging and being heard above calls to maintain the status quo, and it is our responsibility to keep pace with these changes and teach students to question the dominant discourse and advocate with communities toward change for justice.

These burgeoning issues need attention before we may have a clear strategy for change. Resulting concerns and constraints emerge in varying contexts of practice. Although global and local community chaos awakens societal outrage, the turmoil may cloud our vision regarding opportunities for healing that exist in these crises. Our strategies for appropriate interventions are challenged but provide avenues for reconciliation and positive outcomes. These are the recurrent conditions and future trends our students will be facing as they start their careers.

We propose that these challenges create a clear path forward. If we are serious about responding to the diverse needs and interests of the communities we serve, then we must activate approaches in our teaching to ensure that our students are adequately prepared. By modeling how to create mutual and collaborative relationships in situations of differential power and privilege, we create a climate and sanctuary for dialogues with our students. Field education supervision becomes the place where students enhance their self-awareness, capacity for self-reflection, and tolerance for the potential discomfort triggered by engaging in these conversations first with us and then in their work. Likewise, assisting our students' abilities to conduct analyses of power, privilege, and oppression places discussions about the work in a broader context. Students are given an opportunity to consider their perceptions and biases of why people are disadvantaged and how their perspectives may affect the people and communities served by the field placement. Of course, this involves discussing our position of power and authority over students and their own power and authority with those they serve, in the community, in the organization, and with us.

We propose that change starts by being honest with ourselves about our biases and our need for supports to manage the obstacles that prevent us from engaging in conversations about how power, privilege, and subjugated and intersecting identities affect our connections with one another. We need to commit to furthering our expertise in facilitating these dialogues and to advocate for schools of social work to provide training and developmental experiences to support this work throughout beginning and advanced SIFIs. We offer this book as a beginning guide toward greater awareness and increased ability to engage in authentic and effective relationships across difference as we work together toward justice-based field education.

Organization of the Text

This edition differs significantly from the previous two editions. The chapters are reordered in three parts. This restructuring supports our purposes and pays attention to overarching themes while focusing separately on the many practical aspects involved. Every attempt is made to assist the reader in applying the CSWE (2015a) competencies to supervisory practice. Other major changes reflect a commitment to strengthen what was begun in the second edition, that is, to consolidate links among our professional mission, competency-based social work education, and a justice-based model of field education.

The third edition builds on the strengths of the previous two editions while adding useful content connected to the current realities of social work practice. Multiple examples are used throughout the text and in chapter appendixes to illustrate how the competencies bolster our teaching. In addition, the application of challenging dialogues in supervision is illustrated, and examples are added that consider off-site field instruction, use of technology, practice across units of attention, interdisciplinary collaboration, and research-informed practice. Student scenarios are shown in shaded boxes to highlight them in the text.

Finally, the third edition maintains respect for the history of field education and those who have contributed to its knowledge base while also placing the lessons of this legacy in today's context. Attention is given to important advances in the realm of technology, including the revisions in the National Association of Social Workers (NASW, 2017) Code of Ethics. Group supervision of students and the use of task supervisors are also addressed. In this vein, we are compelled to address the calls to rethink the models of field education that reflect current forces emerging from practice and academe.

Part One: Advancing A Framework for Field Education

The four chapters in Part One address the themes of this book—a justice-based framework for field education, competency-based social work education, and the essential role of the field instructor in facilitating challenging dialogues in social work supervision and in teaching within the structure of the competencies. Part One presents how the mission of our profession is made real through the student's work in field education, the field instructor's part in shaping the students' perceptions of their role and how a justice-based framework sustains and guides that work, the place of competency-based education in the equation, and the theoretical perspectives that underpin our tasks as field educators. A clear emphasis emerges that envisions a justice-based perspective for field education bolstered by the competencies that guide our teaching to prepare social work students for the demands of entry-level practice.

Chapter 1. Justice-Based Field Education: The Bridge to Competence

The goals of this text are intricately woven together by introducing field education as a form of justice-based practice, addressing how to teach for the achievement of competence, and focusing this work through the multiple processes and details of field education within field education supervision. Chapter 1 begins by explaining what is meant by a justice-based framework for field education. We dare to define justice and how this vision sets our task for advancing competence in practice. We describe the context of competency-based education, what it involves, how it affects and supports our role as field instructors, and the implications for our roles as educators and partners in the academic enterprise.

The critical task of advancing our professional mission is addressed through consideration of the increasing diversity of students and the multiple dimensions we must address as we seek to achieve mutuality in the learning relationship. As we address the diverse learning needs and assets of our students through conversations in supervision, we are called on to assist them in managing conversations across difference, dominance, and oppression with those they serve. Engaged pedagogy is presented as the recommended approach to the task of inviting students to join us at the learning table.

Our aim is to provide a clear rationale for field education practices rooted in our professional mission and educating for practice that pursues justice and advances human and civil rights. The conclusion we reach supports an inclusive human rights and antioppressive perspective that we have coined as a justice-based framework. We emphasize the field instructor as an antioppressive educator and the field instruction relationship as the place where authenticity is reinforced around issues of social identity, social location, and inclusion. Additional implications include involving students as partners in the learning endeavor and similarly treating the people we serve as partners, collaborators, and political allies rather than as objects of rescue. The Chapter 1 Appendix includes two scenarios that examine establishing a reflective stance in supervision with an individual student and in a group supervisory session. Questions on these scenarios are provided for the reader's consideration.

Chapter 2. Justice-Based Dialogues: A Keystone for Field Education Supervision

This chapter links a justice framework to our teaching mandates in competency-based social work education and presents challenging dialogues on issues of race, power, privilege, oppression, and intersecting social identities as a foundational necessity for our work with students. This positions field education supervision as the place where critical dialogues on issues surrounding diversity and difference occur and where experience and rehearsal are offered to students in applying their acquired skills in their work. We propose the supervisory relationship as the space and sanctuary where students learn how their practice decisions and interactions can make a difference in dismantling injustice. Our conversations with our students start this work.

The commitment to justice-based field education is a pledge to a lifelong journey toward increased consciousness that proceeds in complex ways; the required knowledge and skills develop over time. This chapter outlines the journey by describing how we prepare for this work, we provide examples from field education and present a framework for facilitating challenging conversations that incorporates a justice-based approach. The content on facilitating challenging dialogues is strengthened to include explanations and examples. The knowledge, skills, and values needed are clarified, and main tenets are presented. Excellence in field education for today's practice does not exist without them.

The Chapter 2 Appendix includes tips on conducting challenging dialogues; a structured interview on dimensions of difference, identity, and social location; and scenarios to promote dialogue on various issues that regularly occur in supervisory relationships such as religious oppression, within-group differences and internalized oppression and privilege, race and racism, sexism, and ableism. Finally, a sample student recording of an interaction during a group session shows the student setting the climate for challenging dialogues to become part of the group's work.

Chapter 3. Teaching Competency-Based Practice: Rubrics, Assessment, and Evaluation

This chapter directly addresses how a competency-based framework supports our teaching throughout the field placement from orientation and assessment to evaluation and termination. The components of a rubric framework, used in most final evaluations, are explained as the tool that operationalizes our evaluations.

Identifying a learning focus is molded by the competencies and their associated performance outcomes; these are translated to the context of the setting and the student's assignments. The evaluation framework laid down in the program's formal evaluations shapes how we define the student's progress toward mastery. Students and field instructors together define what students know and need to know and determine how to develop collaborative learning plans that address learning needs and ensure that opportunities will be provided to demonstrate competence. The evaluative framework of a rubric makes this process transparent from the start so that it is possible to see where learning is headed. Three examples illustrate the use of the competencies along this evaluative process. The underlying components of the competencies—values, skills, knowledge, judgments, and cognitive and affective reactions—are used to demonstrate how each plays its part in forming a holistic evaluation of a student's progress toward competence. The Chapter 3 Appendix includes outlines for an educational assessment and a learning plan, questions to support preparation for the informal and formal oral reviews, and tips for completing the end-of-term evaluation.

Chapter 4. Adult Learning: Thinking, Feeling, and Doing

The chapter considers traditional theoretical contributions on learning and introduces developments that support our understanding of a student's journey toward proficiency in learning social work practice. Understanding these theoretical frameworks sheds light on the complex processes involved and supports our task to facilitate the integration of theory and practice. This includes consideration of adult learning theory, perspectives on environments conducive to learning, transformational learning theory, and promoting critical thinking and reflective practice. Information on learning styles, learning stages, perspectives on Kolb's (1984) model of experiential learning and Bloom's (1956) taxonomy of learning domains are summarized. As many of the current theoretical perspectives do not fully address how diversity and social location affect learning, to the greatest extent possible we have added consideration of how a student's social location and differing dimensions of identity affect the theoretical perspective presented. Together, these perspectives provide helpful views on the specific challenges facing students in field education—the context where learning practice is directly experienced, assimilated, and applied.

The Chapter 4 Appendix includes tips on individualizing our teaching approaches and four brief student examples for application. A summary of a group supervisory session examines the teaching approaches used; questions for the reader are provided for consideration of this example.

Part Two: Clearing the Path for Learning

Part Two contains six chapters that deal with the many practical processes and components of field education. This gives special place to ethical and professional behavior, orientation to field education, formulating the range of student assignments as contexts that provide opportunities for students to demonstrate their mastery of the competencies, using process recordings to support reflective practice, and teaching challenges and opportunities. The final chapter in this section examines transitions, terminations and evaluations, and the field liaison's role. It concludes with a review of the threads and themes of the text.

Chapter 5. Professional Values and Behavior: Self-Reflection, Self-Awareness and Self-Regulation

This chapter addresses the task of helping students scrutinize the inherent tensions often involved between personal and professional values and those that arise when students witness the pressures between societal values and the professional values that drive their work. Reinforcing students' capacities for mindfulness, self-reflection, self-awareness, and self-regulation is stressed as they work to determine how their values and assumptions influence their behavior. These processes are examined, and examples depict how self-reflection and self-awareness bolster students' curiosity to study how their biases and worldviews interact with the judgments and choices they make. Emphasis is given to the role of professional values in defining approaches to service and on the ethical dilemmas that arise through value conflicts, conflicts of interest, questions on confidentiality, and challenges of dual relationships.

Revisions to the Code of Ethics (NASW, 2017) are highlighted along with the special issues related to how technology may affect practice. Ethical dilemmas and scenarios are introduced, which involve exploring value conflicts on biased conceptions of the populations and communities being served, how agency practice influences student commitment to and views of service, and the special issues technology introduces in protecting confidentiality and the use of service options promoted on the Internet. The Chapter 5 Appendix includes eight brief ethical dilemma scenarios from the student's perspective and then from the field instructor's perspective for the reader's consideration.

Chapter 6. Getting Started: Learning While Serving in Justice-Based Field Education

This chapter addresses the practical components of orienting students to their new roles and preparing them for service in our profession, not just service in a specific setting. The information provides a structure that looks at the different aspects of getting started. This foundation involves preparing ourselves, our agencies, and students. Included are our attempts to create conducive environments, start dialogues for learning, and begin assessments of students' abilities to function and serve individuals and communities.

The placement setting and services it offers define the range of work that students will have access to for fulfillment of their practice requirements; therefore, care is placed on preparing our colleagues for what is entailed in hosting a student for placement. Equally, students need help in understanding the mission of the setting and in becoming familiar with the community where they will be working. Special consideration is given to growing concerns for students' safety in placement. The larger issues surrounding safety are explored, that is, what it means to be safe across identities, the biased assumptions about safe or unsafe communities, and implications for ensuring that agency-based procedures and protocols are in place.

Preparing ourselves for students enables us to focus on our students when they arrive and to help them understand what they can expect from us, what we will offer in field education supervision, how the competencies will be used to define performance expectations, and the role of engaging in challenging dialogues to create meaningful learning exchanges. Each of these elements helps prepare students for the assumption of their professional roles.

The Chapter 6 Appendix includes a supervisory scenario focused on the issues addressed in the chapter; it deals with the orientation of a student to a first assignment using the competencies. A summary outline of the various topics covered in the chapter also is provided.

Chapter 7. Student Assignments: The Vehicles to Learning and Demonstrating Competency

Assignments are the vehicles that provide students with opportunities to demonstrate their skill levels. It is therefore critical to give careful thought to crafting assignments. Special attention is given to the field instructor's role as architect and partner in designing a student's workload that encompasses the nine competencies and is geared to the student's level in the social work program. The potential challenges for off-site field instructors when assignments are allocated and crafted by a non-social-work task supervisor are considered. Possible assignments related to each of the nine competencies are outlined and examples of assignments show a range of opportunities to demonstrate skills across the competencies and across units of attention.

The Chapter 7 Appendix includes a sample assignment summary for a student at the advanced generalist specialized practice level and one for a generalist practice level student. Questions are provided for the reader's consideration. Additional suggestions for assignments are offered to prompt ideas and options when considering the broad range of possible assignment areas including policy, political social work, policy advocacy practice, and assignments across various units of attention for engagement, assessment, intervention, and evaluation.

Chapter 8. Promoting Reflection Through Recordings: Mirrors and Windows

This chapter presents the use of recordings in field education as a mechanism to promote self-reflection and prompt the development of self-awareness, which are so critical to competent social work practice. Despite our need to directly observe the work of students as we attempt to evaluate and measure competence, recordings continue to provide valuable information and support for the development of reflective practice. The use of recordings for micro to macro practice is presented followed by specific reference to process recordings for micro practice and logs, journals, and portfolios for macro practice.

Our reliance on traditional formats is adjusted to include focused recording formats to target and navigate the many different learning tasks involved in field education. Formats that attempt to incorporate several factors in one recording may dilute the need to highlight one or other of these important components. Several examples of focused recording formats are provided, for example, asking students to target a recording or reflection on one or another of the competencies provides an opportunity to incorporate questions related to the student's practice in an area that might otherwise be missed. Perhaps prompting students to identify institutional and structural barriers to service, to identify how issues of difference may affect service, to home in on issues of justice on a certain assignment, or to provide a recording that examines a challenging dialogue between the student and an individual receiving service gives these issues and interactions a special place for review. As students become familiar with the different ways of examining their work, they increase their abilities for self-review.

The Chapter 8 Appendix provides a justice-based perspective for a range of recording formats. A sample summary of a student recording is presented followed by the supervisory process recording of that session. Finally, a sample of a student's administrative log is also offered.

Chapter 9. Shifting the Discourse: Beyond the Language of Problems

From problems, opportunities emerge. This chapter attempts to alter perspectives on obstacles that arise as we engage in teaching and evaluating student performance to a more balanced view of the anticipated bumps in the road as individuals learn and test new capabilities. The challenges develop from a range of sources and may likely be related to the very nature of the complex tasks assigned and what we are attempting to achieve. The chapter discusses ways to examine possible underlying barriers to assist in discerning opportunities, talents, and strengths that indicate possible responses for resolution.

Situations are addressed that present special complications in field instruction and that may situate the student as the problem rather than acknowledge that the context may require adjustment. For example, the fact that our students experience challenges in performance should not surprise us. The persistence and pervasiveness of the challenges following our efforts to teach to these concerns should concern us. It is proposed that without examining the nature of the task, the context of the setting and our teaching responses, or seeking assistance from the program's field liaison, we may be missing a chance to find a way through the difficulties. Situations experienced as problems may be eased if additional organizational supports are present either from social work programs, from our settings, from task supervisors, or from student peer support groups. Additionally, building a community of field instructors where ideas and solutions can be shared might go a long way in helping to respond to situations that pose challenges in the normal course of our work with students. The chapter also provides guidance when marginal performance, failing performance, or discontinuance are an issue.

The Chapter 9 Appendix includes tips on overcoming students' resistance to inherent challenges experienced in learning, a list of components involved in creating educational learning contracts tailored for situations when obstacles emerge, and scenarios for review.

Chapter 10. Evaluations, Endings, and Taking Stock: Pulling It Together

This chapter assembles several remaining topics: terminations, transitions, and evaluation. The roles of field liaisons are reviewed and updated to include mediator and facilitator of challenging dialogues between field instructors and students. The reality of how changing field advising structures and current practice changes affect these roles is given some attention. The topic of supervision is returned to by encouraging a lifelong perspective on developing supervisory expertise. Additional theoretical perspectives and resources are provided to support exploration and development. Finally, the threads and themes of this text are presented as we conclude this section of the text and pave the way forward.

The Chapter 10 Appendix includes an outline on possible topics to cover during meetings with field liaisons, three termination scenarios from the field instructor's and student's perspective, a form to evaluate the field instructor's use of teaching techniques, a field instructor self-evaluation form, and a student self-assessment form.

Part Three: Moving Forward

This final section gives special attention to moving forward and looking to the future of social work education. As we wrote this text, we were struck with how much social work education has changed and how our own perspectives on our work have evolved. We saw that we could no longer just talk about the future of field education without breaking down the current silos of what is happening in the classroom, the administration of programs, and in service sectors to what is happening—and needs to happen—in field education. They are interconnected, and a change in one area affects the other. We are also prompted to think from a prospective position that considers the potentials in front of us rather than being protective of positions long held but not fully examined. As a result, we begin this conversation with a final chapter on the future of social work education and consider the road ahead.

Chapter 11. The Future of Social Work Education

This chapter considers current forces affecting service delivery, social work program admissions, changing population demographics, and economic, environmental and sociopolitical conditions and how they interact with each other to formulate what our profession's responses need to be. These forces are local as well as global. We consider four areas needing attention: our workforce, school environments and culture, the social work curriculum, and field education. The chapter provides compelling data to support our positions and summarizes trends that have begun, and efforts that show promise but need to be reinstituted or that need support. To achieve these recommendations, we need to examine long-held traditions, be prepared for experimentation, and find better ways to share and communicate with each other so that we might build more efficient and effective means to recruit and retain future social workers with our goal of improving our service and pursuit of justice.

Appendix A provides a list of methods and approaches we have found helpful in our own supervision of students and are offered as suggestions for field instructors to add to their growing repertoire of tools and techniques.

Appendix B describes Seminars in Field Instruction (SIFIs) and contains a sample outline based on the justice and competency framework presented in this book. The importance of facilitating challenging dialogues across differences with supervision is an essential component of justice-based practice and is given prominence throughout the SIFI. Sample assignments are also provided.

A Note on Language Used in the Book

To achieve inclusive and respectful writing, we adopted several literary devices such as the current usage of *Latinx* to represent an inclusive and gender-neutral alternative to Hispanic, Latino, Latina, Chicano, or Chicana. Except in quoted matter, we use alternative terms for *client* that more closely represent a mutual and collaborative relationship such as *individual, population, those we serve, service user, constituent,* or *consumer.* To avoid repeating an attempt at an inclusive listing of differences in social location and identity (such as race, color, ethnicity, national origin, age, gender identity or expression, sex, sexual orientation, marital status, religion or spirituality, language, immigration status, mental or physical ability, political belief, and geographic location) we abbreviate these isms with, for example, *multiple dimensions of identity, intersecting dimensions of identity, social location* or *positionality,* or *social dimensions of identity*. Our decision to use these inclusive phrases is purely stylistic and to help readability. It is not our intention to diminish any one dimension of identity or to imply we wish to wash away any aspect of a person's self-identity.

In the same vein we use the inclusive acronym LGBTQ+ to refer to a community of individuals who are united by gender identities or sexual orientations. Although not an exhaustive list, this includes gender ambiguous, gender nonconforming, gender variant, gender queer, androgynous, transsexual, intersexual, pansexual, asexual, and questioning. We add *Two Spirit* (LGBTQ+ Two Spirit or LGBTQ+TS) in reference to Two Spirit American Indian, Native Hawaiian, Alaska Native, and First Nation peoples whose identities and cultural contexts require recognition and respectful differentiation.

An inclusive reference to *indigenous* peoples is the broadest term used regarding the many unique relationships between tribes and the U.S. government including American Indian, Alaska Native and Hawaiian Native and Pacific Islanders. Also included in this term are First Nation peoples of Canada and other communities and populations across the globe. We sometimes spell these out in the text to provide space for these cultures in contrast to the usual invisible presence given to them; in other instances, we apply the term *indigenous peoples and populations* in respect for the local contexts that may apply to the reader. Although the data reported in Chapter 11 reports on Native Americans, a designation usually reserved for reference to populations throughout the Americas, we can presume the data reported is based on U.S. and Canadian schools of social work.

Field education is used as a broad generic term that includes all aspects of the placement internship and learning experience. In this context, the term *field educators* includes field instructors, field supervisors, field liaisons, field faculty, and task supervisors as part of the learning team. In addition, as we see field education supervision as a form of teaching, we use *supervision, supervisory practice, field education supervision, field instruction*, and *teaching* interchangeably. Likewise, we do not distinguish between a field instructor and a field supervisor. To reflect the current context of using a variety of sites for field education internships, we use the term *setting* in place of *agency-based* placement.

The book uses the structure of the CSWE (2015a) EPAS of generalist practice level competencies applied to BSW and first-year MSW students, distinguished from the specialized practice level competencies applied to second-year MSW students. Although the EPAS distinguish eligibility requirements for BSW and MSW field instructors, we simply use field instructor, implying this individual meets the appropriate requirements to supervise a BSW or MSW student. As the generalist practice level competencies apply to BSW and first-year MSW students, student scenarios of generalist practice level students refer to either BSW and first-year MSW students. The exception in the text appears in Chapter 11 when referring specifically to research pertaining to BSW or MSW students and in discussions of issues pertaining to BSW or MSW social work programs. Specialized practice level student scenarios apply to second-year MSW students.

Finally, although we address practice issues of global concern, we acknowledge that the text is rooted in U.S. social work education. Likewise, we recognize that local contexts introduce varying conditions and different regulations, and field education terms also differ across national and international boundaries. We hope our neighbors and international colleagues find the content easily applicable across borders, continents, and oceans. We look forward to engaging in a broader conversation about the issues and concerns we share and where our experience differs.

Part One

Advancing a Framework for Field Education

This first section introduces the main themes of the text: a justice-based framework for field education, competency-based social work education, and the essential role of the field instructor in facilitating a conducive environment for learning. The role of challenging dialogues in field education supervision for promoting work across differences in a justice-based framework is highlighted. This section stresses the importance of these overarching themes for guiding our teaching and assisting our goal of preparing social work students for entry-level professional social work practice.

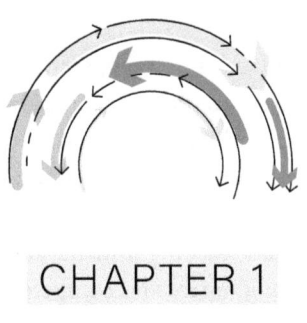

CHAPTER 1

Justice-Based Field Education

The Bridge to Competence

The primary mission of the social work profession is to enhance human well-being and help meet the basic human needs of all people, with specific attention to the needs and empowerment of people who are vulnerable, oppressed, and living in poverty. A historic and defining feature of social work is the profession's focus on individual well-being in a social context and the well-being of society. Fundamental to social work is attention to the environmental forces that create, contribute to, and address problems in living. . . . Social workers also seek to promote the responsiveness of organizations, communities, and other social institutions to individuals' needs and social problems (NASW, 2017, Preamble, para. 1-2)

Guided by a person-in-environment framework, a global perspective, respect for human diversity, and knowledge based on scientific inquiry, the purpose of social work is actualized through its quest for social and economic justice, the prevention of conditions that limit human rights, the elimination of poverty, and the enhancement of the quality of life for all people, locally and globally. . . . Competency-based education rests upon a shared view of the nature of competence in professional practice. Social work competence is the ability to integrate and apply social work knowledge, values, and skills to practice situations in a purposeful, intentional, and professional manner to promote human and community well-being. (CSWE, 2015a, pp. 5–6)

The mission of social work is to competently pursue justice, and social work education's role is to prepare practitioners who accomplish that task. The expansive and complex mission of social work requires a well-articulated examination of the human condition and what is just and fair, and the ability to act competently on that analysis. Educating social workers involves learning and teaching students about these two interdependent subjects—the mission of justice and competent practice. Together they frame the purpose of field education and are the basis of this book.

This chapter presents the aims of this book with a triple focus: introducing justice-based field education, addressing how to teach for the achievement of competence, and translating these concerns into the processes of field education. The first is our vision, which is to produce social workers whose every action advances justice. The second is our means to that end, or how we help students move competently toward our mission with the required critical consciousness and the knowledge and skills to do so. It is of no use for us to have a mission and hope without ensuring that our students are competent. Also, competence without mission is aimless. Third, these aims are supported at every juncture in the context and details of field education, and they are inextricably linked.

Introducing a Justice-Based Framework for Field Education

As our Code of Ethics evolves, each iteration targets aspects that require clarification or refinement to reflect changing contexts and understanding. For example, the National Association of Social Work (NASW, 2007b) called for a recommitment to the profession's mission to eradicate structural racism pervading our society as exemplified in policies that limit access to resources and in practices that exclude or benefit some groups over others. Beginning action steps included creating awareness, building knowledge, and becoming partners and allies in discussions "to share perspectives on how institutional racism is manifested in social work and to identify opportunities to create positive change" (p. 20). Language dating from the 1996 Code of Ethics in Standard 6.04(d) stresses that

> social workers should act to prevent and eliminate domination of, exploitation of, and discrimination against any person, group or class on the basis of race, ethnicity, national origin, color, sex, sexual orientation,

age, marital status, political belief, religion, and mental or physical disability. (NASW, 1996, p. 27)

Revisions in 2017 add "gender identity or expression" and "immigration status" to the already included isms and replace the term *disability* with mental and physical *ability* (NASW, 2017, Standard 6.04 d).

Revisions to the Preamble of the code in 1996 are reaffirmed again in 2017; that is, social work possesses a "unique purpose and perspective" (NASW, 2017 Preamble, para. 3). Our purpose is the promotion of core values embracing service, social justice, dignity and worth of the person, the importance of human relationships, integrity, and competence. Our perspective is that we focus on individuals and on their environmental contexts. Further, we execute our purpose collaboratively with individuals, families, groups, organizations, and communities, which means each and every one we serve. Our mission provides a framework and direction offering answers to questions about why we do what we do and why we choose to teach in any specific way; however, we also need a clear vision of what justice entails to guide our journey in its pursuit.

Our Code of Ethics (NASW, 2017) does not define justice and chooses instead to approach our responsibilities through consideration of injustice; the ethical principle associated to the profession's value of social justice declares "social workers challenge injustice." This has been stated as such since 1996 (NASW, 1996, p. 5). Standard 6, "Social Workers' Ethical Responsibilities to the Broader Society," (NASW, 2017) delineates more specific guidance, that is, social workers should

> promote the general welfare of society, from local to global levels, and the development of people, their communities, and their environments ...advocate for living conditions conducive to the fulfillment of basic human needs and...promote social, economic, political, and cultural values and institutions that are compatible with the realization of social justice (6.01)...engage in social and political action that seeks to ensure that all people have equal access to the resources, employment, services, and opportunities they require to meet their basic human needs and to develop fully...should be aware of the impact of the political arena on practice and should advocate for changes in policy and legislation to improve social conditions in order to meet basic human needs and promote social justice (6.04, a)...promote conditions that encourage respect for cultural

and social diversity within the United States and globally ... should promote policies and practices that demonstrate respect for difference, support the expansion of cultural knowledge and resources, advocate for programs and institutions that demonstrate cultural competence, and promote policies that safeguard the rights of and confirm equity and social justice for all people. (6.04, c)

We acknowledge that justice is as difficult to define as it is to achieve. Contention frequently exists regarding the various perspectives taken to capture what is meant by justice (Austin, 2014; Bangerjee, 2005; Funge, 2011; Hytten & Bettez, 2011; Reisch, 2011). Although different theoretical views in varying contexts and times yield disparate perceptions on what is essential, certain characteristics evolve from these views, including "fair play...fair shares...equal distribution...distribution dependent on unique individual needs...distribution based on status...and distribution based on compensatory principles to remedy past injustices" (Reisch, 2019, p. 18).

Achieving a more just society is generally seen as understanding how power, privilege, oppression, and dominance are sustained, how individuals are compensated for injuries, and how punishments are meted out; identifying who benefits and who is excluded from structures, resources, and systems; and devising strategies to alter these structures and barriers to ameliorate the inequalities and biases while empowering the voices of individuals, groups, and communities to seek and demand solutions. As a result, the concept of social justice is frequently used to embrace a sense of the profession's commitments. Barker (2014) defines social justice as "an ideal condition in which all members of society have the same basic rights, protection, opportunities, obligations, and social benefits" (p. 398). In search of greater clarity to support our practice and teaching, Reisch (2019) proposes

a revised vision of a socially just society that fits 21st century realities. This vision would emphasize both socially just means and ends. It would address both people's material needs and the non-material, often intangible assets they require to achieve what Martha Nussbaum and Amartya Sen refer to as their capabilities (Sen, 2009; Nussbaum, 2011). Finally, it would reconcile an approach based on the concept of universal human rights with respect for cultural diversity (Wronka, 2014). (p. 43)

We do not believe this goes far enough. A definition that embraces the different forms of justice—including social, economic, racial, political, legal, educational, and environmental—leads to a broader and stronger articulation of our mission and formulas for action. This view is based on the reality that a focus on one type of justice or issue experienced by individuals or specific populations does not adequately address the shared concerns across populations, the origins and structural causes of the issues, or more global expressions of the same concerns (Reisch, 2013; Steen, Mann, Restivo, Mazany, & Chapple, 2017). An individualized perspective ignores the role of privilege and the responsibility of the privileged to respond to how systems of injustice are maintained. This also ignores how the relationships between the oppressed and the privileged uphold systems of domination and lead to an unexamined total view of how some members of society become victims while systems of privilege are perpetuated. Likewise, keeping the various realms of injustice at the forefront enables our ability to search for liberating strategies in these multiple arenas. The quest for equality is also inadequate. Equity recognizes that some are disadvantaged more than others and thereby requires a different response to rectify this reality.

This text asserts that the mission of social work is to diligently and persistently pursue justice; every social work thought, and action, is calculated to advance justice. We use the word *justice* in a broader sense than *social justice*. That is, we include seeking justice in terms of the often-cited triad of social, economic, and environmental justice, but we recognize that this triad is not broad enough to capture the intent of a just society. We recognize that what we are pursuing is elusive and aspirational and that the goalpost moves according to the context and times. Still we dare to state that the quest for justice includes the following features:

> It is grounded in civil and human rights; including tribal rights that recognize and support tribal sovereignty, treaty obligations and environmental rights; and anti-oppressive perspectives (here we mean to include antiracist, critical social theory and critical race theory, empowerment models, ecological social theory, feminist and womanist perspectives, liberation theory, decolonization and strengths-based models of practice).
> It is informed by conceptions of positionality and intersecting identities (such as race, color, ethnicity, national origin, age, gender identity or expression, sex, sexual orientation, marital status, religion or spirituality, language, immigration status,

mental or physical ability, political belief, and geographic location).
- It seeks empowerment, and change, equity over equality, and pursues liberation, which addresses the causes of inequity and barriers that maintain it.
- It seeks to remedy social division and historical systemic structural inequality through an ongoing analysis of power.
- It is rooted in meaningful communication and authentic relationships characterized by honesty, openness, mutuality, and respect.
- It assigns responsibility to each of us to share power and apply our awareness of how power and privilege shape experiences.
- It incorporates awareness of the effects of historical and present-day trauma on current experiences.
- It confronts internalized and socialized thought processes.
- It pays attention to ameliorating the problems of broken systems of health, legal, education, and so forth, and seeks to provide the best care possible, even in these broken systems.
- It aims to undo endemic structures of marginalization, interconnections of oppression, and systems of dominance.
- It views problems as lodged in the environment and global context, not just within individuals or on a local level.
- It promotes those who experience injustice and harassment or discrimination based on race and other dimensions of identity to organize for action based on a justice analysis.

Justice includes considering how workers in human service settings interact with constituents and communities, how groups and staff are composed, what policies exist; and how to create policy proposals for change. It also includes engaging in challenging dialogues about justice that occur between field instructors and students and teaching the skills to have parallel conversations with those we serve—many examples of which we provide in this text. Engaged pedagogy and transformational and experiential learning theories reinforce the necessary supervisory approaches for this to occur. These perspectives challenge the neglect of issues of justice and human rights as part of our everyday concerns in practice and teaching. That is, practice that seeks to remedy social division and structural inequality is central to our professional goals and values and also guides our teaching.

Advancing Competence in Practice

Competence and professional mission are inevitably related. Social workers must be competent in their pursuit of justice. Every action by a social worker intended to advance justice and field education is designed to help students learn how to move competently toward that end. This requires us to constantly assess where our own competencies might fall short of advancing justice-based field education and to fill that gap in how we use our position and hold ourselves, our agencies, and our profession accountable.

The introduction of competency-based education is a response to the profession's search for agreed-on criteria to evaluate student preparedness for practice. This search reached a new threshold with the adoption of 10 competencies contained in the EPAS and applied across schools of social work accredited by the CSWE (2008). Their adoption marked a significant transition in social work education. By establishing a consensus on what constitutes competence, what social workers must be able to do, and what constitutes the fundamentals of social work, we establish a bar for effective entry-level practice. Those preparing students for professional practice are given an agreed set of required skills for all beginning professionals. The revised competencies in the EPAS (CSWE, 2015a) continue this trajectory, fine-tune what was begun in 2008 and combine with our professional mission to provide a cogent map for teaching and preparing students for professional practice. We can expect continuing revisions as experience, innovation, and shifting needs guide what entry-level practice requires.

Pre-competency-based social work education is characterized by field instructor driven content, agency-determined assignments and individualized field instructor assessment criteria. This contrasts with post-competency-based education which is characterized by accepted professional baselines regarding required skills to be mastered, assignments crafted to develop competence and approved measures and outcomes to guide evaluation of student performance. As opposed to searching our individualized practice repertoire to define the content needed to teach students, devising assignments related to that content and using an individualized sense of what good practice looks like, the CSWE (2015a) competencies provide principles, goals, and outcomes that determine competence.

Figure 1.1 lists the characteristics of competency-based social work education and illustrates the benefits derived directly from achieved consensus and professionally agreed baselines. Direction is given regarding which skills we are aiming to teach, and we are bolstered by the strength of the professional

Characteristics of Competency-Based Education
> Agreed professional baselines
> Assignments crafted to develop competence
> Set measures and outcomes to guide evaluation

Benefits
> Professionally agreed baselines for competence
> Direction for development of required skills
> Protection of professional standards

This promotes:
> Common language and agreed goals
> A mutual teaching focus
> Structure for student learning
> Active student learning toward proficiency

Figure 1.1 Characteristics, benefits, and implications of competency-based education

standards the competencies represent. By focusing our attention on the competencies, we provide clear targets for our students. The competencies give field instructors and students a common set of terms and a mechanism for talking about skills, knowledge, and professional values. These conversations encourage the ability to identify growing mastery and promote student reflection and self-awareness. As a result, students become more active in the learning-teaching process and as students seek proficiency, interventional choices evolve toward readiness for professional practice.

The revised EPAS contains nine interrelated generic competencies (CSWE, 2015a). They represent essential aspects of social work practice and together present a comprehensive set of capabilities required for entry-level professional social work practice, specifically, to demonstrate ethical and professional behavior, engage diversity and difference in practice, and advance human rights and social, economic and environmental justice, which are fundamental to all forms of practice. These competencies describe professional purposes and broad principles that guide and inform our work, whereas engaging in practice-informed research, research-informed practice, and policy practice refer to specific methods of practice—research and policy. At the same time, they represent elements that inform and enrich all facets of practice. Professional practice benefits from research findings, and research benefits from knowledge gained from practice. This reciprocal relationship ensures that our practice responds to innovations and remains effective. Equally, policy practice informs our efforts toward change. Research-informed practice, practice-informed research, and policy practice are required aspects across all levels of practice. Finally, the remaining CSWE (2015a) competencies delineate the stages of the helping process across various units of attention, that is engage, assess, intervene, and evaluate practice with individuals, families, groups, organizations and communities. These last four competencies stress the universality of the helping process across methods, and attention is paid to all units as we work toward change.

The interrelationships between and among these nine competencies are reciprocal and dynamic. Each is a required component; together they embrace the crucial ingredients of what future practitioners require to begin professional practice and the associated learning outcomes focus our attention on which behaviors offer evidence of student capabilities. In these ways, competency-based social work education focuses on professional performance goals and provides a compass for what we must teach.

According to the CSWE (2015a), "competence is perceived as holistic, involving both performance and the knowledge, values, critical thinking, affective reactions, and exercise of judgement that inform performance" (p. 18). These ingredients are the underlying components we look for as we work to help students improve their abilities in and across the competencies.

Recognizing that a student's cognitive and affective processes are involved in learning, a holistic view of competence includes how the student interprets and applies professional knowledge and values, abilities for critical thinking, and how affective reactions such as moods and feelings influence the student's work. These in turn affect judgments and decision making. Skills emerge as students choose to act based on their knowledge, values, and how they think and feel about the situation they are in. The associated components unite to present a picture of a student's capabilities in a distinct context while carrying specific responsibilities at a given point in time. Yet, determining competence involves a multifaceted and multidimensional holistic approach that considers performance across the competencies over time and in different contexts.

A further differentiation is made between two levels or types of competence; that is metacompetence and procedural competence (Bogo, 2016, 2018; Bogo et al., 2013). Metacompetence refers to general personal or professional aptitudes such as conceptual or interpersonal behavioral capabilities, which affect how students approach the task of learning, how they process information, and how decisions are made and implemented across all aspects of practice. Metacompetencies "consist of cognitive competence related to professional knowledge, relational competence with clients and colleagues, and personal and professional competence evident in qualities that facilitate practice in an organizational context, and ethics and values" (Bogo, 2010, p. 75). They represent actions and attitudes connected to philosophical approaches to helping and serving and include "characteristics such as self-awareness, compassion, motivation, and commitment to social justice" (Regehr, Bogo, Donovan, Anstice, & Lim, 2012, p. 307).

Procedural competencies involve skills, techniques, and approaches usually applicable to certain methods, units of attention, or interventions with certain populations (Bogo, 2018, 2016; Bogo, Katz & Regehr et al, 2013). Procedural competencies and technical or clinical competencies are actions and behaviors such as the ability to articulate and implement steps to attain program goals in macro practice (Bogo, 2018; Regehr et al., 2012). Understanding that we are teaching at meta and procedural levels of competence helps us to focus teaching strategies. In field education, the assessment of a student's skill attainment must occur on both levels.

For example, consider a student whose characteristic approach to new situations is to feel shy, awkward, and reticent. This student's skills related to the metacompetencies of self-awareness and self-regulation may provide needed antidotes and bolster an ability to stretch and meet the responsibilities of the role of outreach worker with for people who experience homelessness. Likewise, procedural competencies related to specific engagement and outreach skills would be assessed in this context, that is, the student's willingness to approach individuals in this situation with acceptance and respect to establish connections while also being able to negotiate clear parameters for safety and stabilization. Understanding that we are teaching at meta and procedural levels of competence helps us to focus teaching strategies. We assess a student's capabilities on both levels of competence—meta and procedural. One affects the other. The process of learning practice is complex. Students may struggle with a performance outcome and excel in other areas. In our experience, students often have the knowledge and values related to a competence before they develop the skill. They may gain early mastery in one area and not show progress in others. They may show mastery with a certain population and yet find themselves not able to work competently with others. For instance, we might see a student working well on joining and engagement except within mandatory conditions of service, being able to affirm strengths while not being able to withhold premature judgments, or being good at policy practice while not being able to engage with conflict. Examining how the student processes each of these components lets us assess overall competence. The skills we see are in the student's functioning in and across each element.

In this regard, assessing student performance and skill achievement presents challenges.

We assess these behaviors as a whole; this results in an evaluation of how these behaviors add up to demonstrate the achievement of overall competence. Evaluators assign a holistic rating, a single score, for any individual competency. For instance, the revised competencies address performance in general or on average across individual, family, group, community, and organizations in each phase of the helping process (CSWE, 2015a). This means that a student's engagement capabilities are assessed as a whole, including when uneven achievement is seen in and across various levels of service. This requires a judgment of the student's capability as an average across various assignments, using comments and examples to describe what was witnessed and to substantiate the rating chosen. In this way, the evaluative framework of a rubric aims to provide structure and lessen subjectivity.

A holistic perspective involves an inclusive outlook on these processes, which occur over time, in the context of how the student progresses across the nine competencies and in the various types of situations presented (Bogo, 2010, 2018). Knowledge, skills, values, cognitive and affective reactions, and judgment intertwine, and each contributes to an ability to demonstrate proficiency. Each plays a part. Depending on the context, some of these component ingredients may be more apparent than others, but often they exist together and contribute to the development of skills.

What we may observe is a student's effort to engage in critical thinking in response to our questions. Underlying this effort are a range of mood and feeling responses, judgments, and values not so immediately visible. To exhibit critical thinking, which leads to an analysis for action, the student is inherently using knowledge possessed and may be applying new knowledge gained; the student may also attempt to integrate an understanding of the emotions provoked by a value conflict prohibiting a response. These components evolve into judgments about interventions chosen and reveal themselves in the student's performance. Equally, time and context take their own parts in our being able to confirm that proficiency is consistently performed and perfected (Bogo, 2010, 2018; Gambrill, 2013). For example, a student recounts an interaction as follows: "Given what I know about the effects of anti-Semitism and feelings of marginalization and what I have learned in class, I should explore this mother's sense of trust of her doctors and health care professionals (knowledge). But I am unsure and nervous (affective reaction) because this individual already seems so depressed by her diagnosis (judgment). Although I should probably address the issue directly, I believe she will feel I am overstepping my role (judgment). Plus, I must pick up my child from school soon and addressing this issue might take longer than the time we have (personal and professional values in conflict). I also would like more help in knowing how to approach her. Therefore, I will not mention this today (decision making). Instead, I suggested that she try to relax today (action). I took time to gain her agreement, summarized what we talked about, and suggested we could pick up from here next time we meet (action)." Thus, competence is "multi-dimensional and composed of interrelated components. An individual social worker's competence is developmental and dynamic, changing over time in relation to continuous learning" (CSWE, 2015a, p. 6).

Figure 1.2 depicts the additive and interactive nature of the components embedded in skill performance. As shown in the preceding scenario, each dimension is discrete and available for evaluation. The process is dynamic and influenced by the context and situation where and when it takes place. In this way the nature of the placement and the situation itself affects abilities to use the knowledge we possess or manage the feelings involved. The figure depicts the relationship of the elements to one another and how they interact and affect each other. For example, the knowledge we possess includes procedural knowledge, knowledge acquired as social norms, and the meaning making of constructed social reality. This knowledge directly affects the values we form, and values influence how we filter the knowledge we obtain. In turn, the ability to think may be influenced by affective reactions to the situation. (Barnacle, 2009; Dreisbach & Böttcher, 2011). As knowledge, values, and affective reactions interact, it may become more possible to apply critical thinking and analytic skills that demonstrate a value-free consideration of the affective reactions involved. This takes place in relation to a specific situation and social context, which also influence the process of learning. These components affect judgments and decisions about interventions and actions chosen. Actions are activated, and the level of proficiency is demonstrated as skills. Any one action is affected by this process, and vice versa. Therefore, not only does this unfold over time but one action influences another. To advance the skill level of our students, we must include the various components in our discussions so that we can untangle them and facilitate navigation of the student's movements toward the achievement of improved practice. This helps to break the process into its component parts and enables consideration of elements to be strengthened or of those needing attention.

The end goal of competency-based social work education is demonstration of academic and professional performance. Professional performance in

CONTEXT AND SITUATIONAL FACTORS

- Critical thinking
- Values
- Knowledge
- Judgment
- Affective reactions
- Demonstrated performance SKILLS

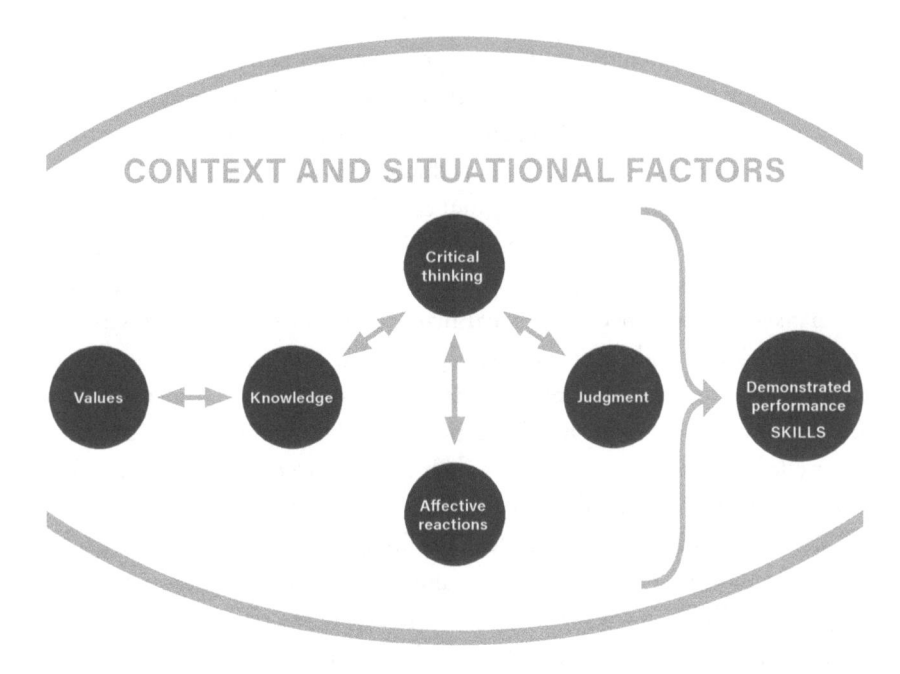

Figure 1.2 Competency components in the context and situational factors

field education is measured by observable behaviors, meaning the actions and skills performed by students in their efforts to gain competency.

These measures, or student learning outcomes, are determined by the social work program and are the activities or behaviors that represent the "observable components" (CSWE, 2015a, p. 7) we look for as we assess our students; they encompass the competency components of values, knowledge, judgments, and cognitive and affective reactions, which lead to and inform action. Examples of observable actions that demonstrate this integration are attached to each of the nine generalist practice level competencies, which are central to entry-level practice; in addition, program administrators are encouraged to specify learning outcomes unique to their mission and curriculum and to add specific competencies that are designed to coincide with the program's specialized practice level curriculum, concentration, or focus area (Pierce, 2016). Programs with an advanced generalist concentration may use the competencies similar to the nine generalist practice level competencies, but the advanced generalist concentration performance behaviors reflect greater depth, integration, or complexity. A program with a specialized practice year that concentrates or focuses on fields of practice, methods, or populations creates a set of curriculum-related competencies and performance behaviors geared to reflect the program's curriculum. The applicable generalist practice level or specialized practice level outcomes and associated behaviors are then used as measures on end-of-term field education evaluations.

One illustration are the behavioral components connected to the competency "Engage Diversity and Difference in Practice" (CSWE, 2015a, p. 7). One of the three listed components is "apply self-awareness and self-regulation to manage the influence of personal biases and values in working with diverse individuals and constituencies" (p. 7). This component is illuminated as we watch students in action. We witness self-awareness as students reflect on their work and reveal these reflections and their willingness to consider their effect on others, or we observe their attempts to develop this skill. This may include the extent to which a student engages in open and honest discussions regarding thoughts and feelings evoked by the work, the student's level of demonstrated ability to withstand an individual's anger and the corresponding ability to self-regulate emotional responses, to adapt engagement interventions to meet different needs and styles, to be a mindful and reflective practitioner examining the effect of power and privilege on interactions, or to recognize an oppressive policy and advocate for change. As we witness these actions, we can describe how the student incorporates these elements in practice and their influence on the development of meaningful work relationships. We may see that the student demonstrates varying levels of proficiency in any one skill over time and in different situations. Conversations between the student and field instructor about these behaviors promote the ability to assess and support the improvement of the skills involved. The scenarios throughout this book illustrate this process.

These behaviors are the learning outcomes students and field instructors are seeking; as we observe demonstrated abilities, we assess the extent to which the behaviors are mastered. To facilitate this task, guides of specific characteristics, components, and actions establish the path for learning. These guides delineate student learning outcomes; they make clear how practice competence will be measured. Throughout the internship, measurement is assessed on a continuum of competence. Competence grows as students perform the required skills more consistently, purposefully, and intentionally; generalize them to other aspects of their work; apply them in more complex situations; and increase their abilities to articulate what they are doing and why. Many end-of-term field education evaluation forms provide such continuums.

Field Education as the Signature Pedagogy

The third focus of this text is how teaching for justice and competency is translated into the complex context of field education and all that it encompasses. Part Two of this book examines the interconnected yet disparate components that combine to create field education. Here we introduce the importance of field education and the special role it plays within social work education.

In addition to the introduction of competency-based education, the EPAS (CSWE, 2008) identified field education as the signature pedagogy of social work education: "Signature pedagogy represents the central form of instruction and learning in which a profession socializes its students to perform the role of practitioner" (CSWE, 2008, p.8). Likewise, CSWE 2015 states "Signature pedagogies are elements of instruction and socialization that teach future practitioners the fundamental dimensions of professional work in their discipline—to think, to perform and to act ethically and with integrity" (CSWE, 2015a, p. 12). This designation challenges a bifurcated view of where and how learning for professional practice takes place. The predominant place usually given to the academic curriculum is shifted to acknowledge the vital roles of the field instructor and the field placement's culture and context in student learning and how "field education is positioned to influence program renewal and curriculum change" (Hunter & Poe, 2016, p. 79). Learning happens everywhere and all the time (Keeling & Dungy, 2004), but emphasis is placed on the function of field education. By implication, our role as field instruction supervisors elevates us to being an equal partner and educator with our colleagues in academe (Hunter & Poe, 2016).

Furthermore, the EPAS revisions introduced several field education standards (CSWE, 2015a). Of importance to us here is the one that requires social work programs to explain their provision of "generalist practice opportunities for students to demonstrate social work competencies with individuals, families, groups, organization and communities and ... how this is accomplished in field settings" (CSWE, 2015a, p. 13). This requirement, in agreement with our professional mandate, provides a vision that employs a generalist foundation for social work education.

It is proposed that these changes create challenges. The designation of field education as the signature pedagogy places a large share of the burden of assessing student performance and ensuring a generalist practice foundation on field instructors and on the settings where they are based. This requires programs to address generalist practice opportunities for all BSW and first-year MSW students and that field instructors, perhaps who are not used to thinking from this perspective, are helped to translate the required skills to their settings and chosen assignments. The competencies shape our focus, and we are required to pay attention to the identified areas as we educate students for the future of our profession. Areas of specialization, settings, and learning opportunities vary, but evaluating competence across these variations remains a constant (Pierce, 2016).

The Field Instructor as Educator and Partner

The beginning of this chapter considers how a focus on justice and competency affects our teaching role. In a similar manner, field education's designation as signature pedagogy places a center spotlight on the field instructor's roles as educator and partner. Other responsibilities derive from these major roles, which set the scene for establishing a teaching philosophy and perspectives on teaching for justice. Preparing students to pursue justice requires us to start from our own approaches to teaching and practice. In this way we demonstrate how growth is promoted by making use of power explicit, by sharing expertise and by learning together. We return to the special roles of educator and partner of field instructors throughout the text; what follows is an introduction to these roles and responsibilities.

Engaged pedagogy: A facilitative approach to teaching. According to hooks (2010), "Engaged pedagogy makes us better learners [and learner/teachers] because it asks us to embrace and explore the practice of knowing together, and to see intelligence as a resource that can strengthen our common good" (p. 22). Educating from this perspective means that we can no longer think of teachers as all-knowing authorities who pass on knowledge to passive recipients. "Supervision can be expressly considered a boundary space between the routine activity of the social worker and the experience of the student. It is therefore an ideal locus for the production of new ideas and new learning" (Fazzi & Rosignoli, 2016, p. 206). Field education supervision creates the conditions needed for new ways to consider responses to the work to emerge. We are shaped by and learn from each other.

Active and engaged learning is the preferred method (Danowitz & Tuitt, 2011; hooks, 1994, 2010; Roche, Dewees, Trailweaver, Alexander, Cuddy, & Handy, 1999; Shor, 1992). Our aim is not to merely transmit or share information but to facilitate learning and to promote and share in the well-being and growth of our students and ourselves. The concepts advocated by hooks (1994) are based on principles of critical pedagogy, as espoused by Paulo Freire (1993), which challenge the didactic, prescriptive, banking form of education, calling it oppressive rather than enlightening. Freire believed that a teacher-centered approach robs the learner of self-respect. He offered a theory of education as liberation, where teacher and students work toward mutual learning goals. Freire proposed the model of partner teachers in which students are encouraged to speak in their own active voices and to think for themselves as opposed to the traditional model of filling students up with the teacher's knowledge. Similarly, a feminist approach to "connected teaching" welcomes a diversity of opinions and considers that each of us has a unique perspective that is a valid representation of our reality and a worthy contribution for consideration (Belenky, Clinchy, Goldberger & Tarule, 1986, p. 214). Principles of shared power and privileging student voices emerge as important components in learning (Poole, 2010; Webb, Allen, & Walker, 2002). This approach constructs truth through consensus, feeling or sensing together, and bridging private and shared experience (Degges-White, Colon, & Borzumato-Gainey, 2012; Falender, 2009). Teacher and learner respect each other's differences; thus, they achieve goals of participatory learning, validation of personal views, and development of critical thinking capabilities.

However, the experience of some students may involve situations where learning "initiatives are experienced as too uncomfortable, too difficult, or simply too unwelcome and therefore resisted or rejected" (Hutchings & Quinney, 2015, p. 107). The students may be accustomed to and more comfortable in a situation where their teacher is the expert; they are reassured by having this expert give them directives, and they may need a different level of support before they can engage, or the level of independent learning expected demands more than they feel they are prepared for. Equally, they may be uncertain of what is expected of them and unfamiliar with democratic educational processes that are designed toward student-centered, active, autonomous, and in-depth experiential learning and teaching (Knight, 2016; Miller, Donner, & Fraser, 2004; Hair & O'Donoghue, 2009; Pease & Fook, 1999; Shen Ryan & Ortiz Hendricks, 1989).

Making clear what we expect of our students in our initial conversations forms the basis of a mutual contract. One approach is to introduce how we aim to create a teaching and learning partnership and how we will work together to succeed in this endeavor. Laird (2000) describes her approach as "informed not-knowing" (p. 102) to express the intricate relationship we have with our own expertise while recognizing that we not only do not know everything, we are never the expert on another's lived experience. We must challenge our "cultural and professional traditions that assume that 'truth' is discovered only by looking at underlying and often hidden meanings that only professional understanding and expertise can decipher and amend" (Blundo, 2001, p. 296). Once we accept this, we are available to make the shared journey of learning together through and with our students. We do not hand over or relinquish our power, authority, or expertise, we suspend them, keep them readily handy, and lend them to students as they develop their professional style and expertise.

By intentionally including a discussion regarding the learning relationship and implicit power and authority we share in the supervisory relationship, we embark on the journey together and create an analogous link to students' practice. It brings the parallels of the power of their position in relation to those they will serve to the foreground. For example, we control access to learning opportunities and feedback on student progress, and we hold the key to oral and final evaluations of student performance in the same way that students, as representatives of their settings, unlock access to resources and other forms of support through the assessments they conduct. In this way, how we manage the field education supervisory relationship is a model for students' practice with the people and communities they will work with. From a justice-based framework, what follows is a natural turn toward how working together may create positive social change and more humane structures supporting the people and communities we serve. Constantly bridging these concepts to the details of practice provides vivid examples of how the work of justice is rooted in developing authentic relationships that are based on openness, honesty, mutuality, and respect. This sets the stage for progressing on to other levels of change and deserves further comment. Chapter 2 addresses these issues, and we return to them throughout the text.

Acknowledging the power differentials operating within our relationships with students is an important facet of our partnership with them. Conceptions of supervision based on a traditional framework are challenged for lack of attention to considerations of culture and justice in supervisory practice (Chang, Hays, & Shoffner, 2003). An alternative framework supports the creation of a "conversational space to question the accepted knowledge and power relationships between supervisors and supervisees" (Hair & O'Donoghue, 2009, p. 84). From a justice-based perspective, we share power with students from the beginning of our work together (Bubar, Cespedes, & Bundy-Fazio, 2016; Bundy-Fazioli, Quijano, & Bubar, 2013; Hartman, 1997; O'Leary, Tsui & Ruch, 2013; Tew, 2006). This trains students for collaborative work, teamwork, and networking. This is particularly crucial in today's practice environment; for example, the complexity of behavioral health care delivery is just one area that requires social workers to work on interdisciplinary teams in the community as well as in institutions or organizations. Field education supervision is an optimal environment to model teamwork by applying an inclusive perspective to the work and achieving partnership in learning.

Introducing discussions about how oppression, dominance, and power and privilege are witnessed in the placement setting and in the community provide permission for these sometimes-difficult topics to be explored openly in supervision. Students quickly learn that these conversations are not only necessary but integral to their work. Helping students make sense of the ways these issues change when considered through a local, personal, political, or global lens allows students to practice conducting an analysis of how it happens that the privileged and oppressed maintain their roles and functions and how complex the work of change can be. This shared and transparent discussion makes clear what is to be learned and taught from the start, and this becomes the framework for the work (Lee & Kealy, 2018).

Advancing our professional mission as field educators. A justice-based perspective in field education requires us to incorporate inclusion and mutuality in preparing students for practice by involving them as partners and experts on their own lived experience and how this informs our work together. Ours is a profession based on relationships with individuals, families, groups, communities, and organizations. Our teaching must therefore use our relationships with our students to expand their understanding of how relationships can initiate change (Bisman, 2004). Chapter 2 examines this in more depth, but here we introduce the fundamental features of mutuality, which is key in how we demonstrate respect for individuals, and it is a means to teach our students the importance of this core professional value.

Consider the following ways mutuality affects our role as field educators:

> Achieving a mutual teaching and learning experience entails mutual evaluation. It invites students to evaluate us, not just including them in the discussion while inviting their comments about our evaluation of them. It involves maintaining a self-reflective posture, assessing our effectiveness with them, and seeking voices of those served in the evaluation of services rendered.

> Supporting students' control over their learning is crucial to their professional development and commitment to lifelong learning. Achieving active contributors in the process requires us to accept their essential role in shaping the learning agenda.

> Sharing power entails understanding the limits and inherent possibilities of shedding and distributing the power and authority of our role.
> Creating conditions for co-learning and collaborative teaching involves not only asking students to be attentive to our thoughts and suggestions but encouraging them to lead the discussion in supervision and listening to their concerns.
> Shifting from a focus on the individual to a person-in-environment perspective includes the community and the collective experience and calls for undoing the bifurcation between individual (micro) and community (macro) needs. This recognizes that they are interconnected and embraces the notion that problems also derive from the environment rather than merely from the individual.
> Learning how to communicate to others what to do and how to do it also means being prepared to provide a structure that supports listening and feedback.
> Accepting that others may not always follow our direction means accepting that the struggle may be as much about our being out of sync with their reality or experience.
> Peer learning and group supervision involves allowing students to learn from each other and permitting access to the power of collective learning.
> Training for collaborative work, teamwork, and networking involves providing the chance for students to engage in more than one-on-one case interventions; it means creating opportunities for students to become part of projects, programming, networking efforts, and policy formulations. It means working toward change with constituents.
> Learning collective leadership means that we provide a model for students to learn how to lead by providing opportunities for them to practice leadership.
> Supporting students to express their worldviews and examine their experiences of powerlessness and privilege requires us to take part in the same process.

What we are advocating is applying inclusive practice to field education, which means taking every advantage to purposefully acknowledge and respect multiple and intersecting layers of identity and to be responsive to the needs of all involved. Based on human rights and justice, this framework guides our relationships in supervision and our students' work in the field education setting.

The establishment of a trusting learner-teacher relationship is essential to this task (Bogo, 2010; 2015; Bogo & Vayda, 1993; Cohen, 2004; Fox, 2011; Kadushin & Harkness, 2002; Knight, 2016; Munson, 2001; Siporin, 1982), and it is in the field instructor–student relationship that students begin to examine their assumptions and expand their abilities. In a humanistic view of education, although "learning can and does occur without a teacher" (Jarvis, 1995, p. 102), often the relationship between the learner and the teacher promotes integration and facilitates learning and development. From a justice perspective, part of incorporating awareness of how power and privilege shape experiences in supervision is establishing a trusting relationship (Lusk, Terrazas, & Salcido, 2017). The construction of a favorable learning environment creates a space that is supportive and open and where it is possible to be creative, engages in the risk taking implicit in new learning, and examines efforts that fail (Bennett, 2008; Bogo, 2010; Bogo & Vayda, 1987; Drisko, 2000; Messinger, 2007). Our ability to build and maintain this space provides a model of professional behavior for students to follow (Barretti, 2007; Knight 2016).

Further, teaching for practice is understood to create potentially disorienting student responses (Butin, 2005a; Deal & Hyde, 2004; Garran, Kang, & Fraser, 2014; Jones, 2008). The content we are teaching, the often crisis-ridden, complex situations students are asked to respond to, probable conflicts between personal and professional values or viewpoints, and the fact that some students may face personal experiences like those of the populations they serve combine to create demanding teaching climates. They also create opportunities for transformative learning and growth. The task of educating students to work for change demands much of us and our students. It calls for us to explore how our students respond to this task and how to best facilitate and sustain their engagement in it. Wagner (2005) explores her experience of teaching from an antiracism perspective and acknowledges that promoting change in a student's ordinary way of thinking may evoke strong feelings. The same can be said about the field educator who is reluctant to consider alternative teaching and practice approaches. Often "what is most significant intellectually is not where we end up, but how we go about getting there" (p. 263). The process matters.

Facilitative and reflective field educators model self-awareness and mentor students in recognition of how values and experiences affect our work with each other, those we serve, and our colleagues. Reflective practice holds that "nothing is truly unusual and that preparation for the unexpected must be incorporated into the mental stance of the learner. . . . Providing this mental orientation may even reduce students' hunger for 'quick fixes' and easy-to-follow rules of practice" (Papell & Skolnik, 1992, p. 22). However, this takes time and is an ongoing process throughout one's career. Examining beliefs and assumptions may take a lifetime of unlearning; the environments we aim to create support a commitment to the work of lifelong learning. We need to be patient. Learning is cumulative, it may not be instantaneous, it often takes circuitous paths, and it occurs over time. As students recognize that we grapple with many of the same issues, they are reassured and empowered to overcome obstacles. This is often directly related to their growing ability to think critically and to practice with growing self-awareness; it is also related to our ability to model self-reflection and self-awareness (Lee & Kealy, 2018).

We have noted the importance of creating an environment conducive to learning and a learning relationship built on trust. The establishment of trust is directly connected to producing conditions for learning, and our approach to teaching involves building collaborative activities that promote an atmosphere where conversations about learning may occur (Bogo, 2015; Carroll, 2010a, 2010b; Knight, 2016). This is especially true as we teach for competence. One does not master something quickly. There are usually obstacles, a need for repetition, assimilation, and broadening the learning to new experiences before competence is consistently achieved. These learning conversations are possible in each step of the field education process. They include clarifying competency standards for field performance to chart the learning course ahead and being prepared to individualize the conditions we create for this student in this context at this time. Each step of the process, from preparing for field education conferences to sharing and exploring values, beliefs, ethics, and motivations, provides opportunities for dialogue and open and honest feedback and for learning to occur. Not only does this facilitate a spirit of inquiry, it provides direct experience of sharing power and authority, so important in social work practice. The model proposed here builds on emancipatory education principles and critical pedagogy, which advocate for mutuality, to provide students with an alternative view of authority and where they are given opportunities to experience the power of their views and voices (Hughes, 2013; Morley, 2013; O'Neill & del Mar Fariña, 2018; Roche et al., 1999; Van Soest & Garcia, 2008). In this way, we offer our students a direct experience of how they may approach their work to encourage participation in social transformation.

Responding to our students' diverse needs. It is important for us to look at whom we teach as much as what and how we teach, because who, what, and how intertwine in complex ways. Students are diverse in age, experience, practice method and practice orientation, their place in their educational program, age, race, ethnicity, color, class, nationality, gender identity, sex, ability, sexual orientation, religion, spirituality, geographic location, language, and goals and aspirations. This list, although long, is not exhaustive. It simply reflects the myriad ways students mirror the diversity among us and the challenges we face in shaping individualized responses. The following examples illustrate this diversity and ways field instructors can supervise from a justice-based perspective.

A, a 22-year-old Black woman with a BA in psychology and some work experience with emotionally disturbed children in a summer camp is a first-generation student and ecstatic about her newfound profession and her desire to work with inner-city children in an elementary school. She expected her 2 years of full-time graduate education to be like her undergraduate education, but she soon finds working several days a week, attending classes, and completing her course work is more difficult and exhausting than she expected. She is also finding that the trauma experienced by many of the children she serves affects her more than she anticipated. She finds their experiences reverberate with her own growing up in an underserved inner-city community where educational and career planning for girls were ignored and where many became pregnant before finishing high school. The student is intellectually curious but is being told she lacks self-awareness and that her writing skills need improvement. Although she is finding the reality of graduate education challenging, her enthusiasm and purpose sustain her hopes. Her field instructor is White, has 7 years of work experience, and this is her first student. The field instructor recognizes her student's anxiety in response to the initial feedback she provided. The field instructor realizes she may be making assumptions based on her White privilege grounded in White supremacy culture and worldview; that is, she may be overly focusing on the ability to verbalize self-reflections and relying on standard Eurocentric writing skills while ignoring her student's experience in the field and other attributes. She sees that her student has considerable strengths, and her previous work experience will provide a good foundation for this setting. The field instructor examines her assumptions and involves her student in a dialogue that includes her student's thoughts and feelings. They engage in a discussion that considers the student's strengths and skills alongside her need for improved capability in written and verbal articulation. The discussion gives voice to the student's and field instructor's experiences with power, powerlessness, and the effects of sexism and racism. The field instructor recognizes a more balanced approach is needed. They decide to focus first on helping the student adjust to her new role with this population; they also agree strengthening the student's written and verbal expressions will be a longer-term goal they will work on together through the academic year.

B, a 30-year-old generalist practice level Latinx student comes into an advanced-standing program with 2 years of undergraduate social work classes, one field work experience, and 2 years of employment in an inpatient psychiatric unit; she has chosen administration as her specialization. A great deal is expected of her as a bilingual, bicultural student in a community-based setting in a predominately Dominican neighborhood. She comes from a wealthy Peruvian family and has a hard time understanding the poverty that afflicts the community served by her field placement. She is also a lesbian and is having personal problems related to her family's rejection of her sexual orientation and partner. Her graduate education will be over in 9 months of full-time study, but she is already feeling burned out after just 3 months in her placement. Although she is being praised for her professional demeanor, she is beginning to doubt her decision to pursue an MSW at this point in her career. Her field instructor is of Dominican descent and has been living and working in this community for several years. She has noticed her student's changed attitude and diminishing receptiveness over the past few weeks but is not certain what might be causing this change. She decides to raise her observations during supervision to open a dialogue incorporating each of their identities, backgrounds, and shared and differing professional goals as a start to achieving greater connection.

C, a 29-year-old student of Orthodox Jewish background has several years of experience in a child welfare agency and little formal education in social work. He is a work-study student and is attending a part-time program. He is eager to learn more of the theory behind direct practice, especially as a group worker. He struggles to unlearn his previous approaches and relearn professional social work practice; he finds himself defensive at times when his field instructor asks him to explain why he chose a certain intervention. His current placement is in a child welfare prevention program of his agency that serves a diverse population of predominantly immigrant families from Mexico, Ecuador, and West Africa. His field instructor is a Black woman who is an experienced social worker and has worked in this setting for 2 years. She asked her student to reflect on what it is like for him as a White Jewish Orthodox man to work in this multicultural community with so many immigrant single mothers on his workload and to consider how this might inform his practice. As they proceed in this discussion, the field instructor asks if race, gender, or ethnicity have come up in the parent groups he is running. He replies that he is not clear why he needs to discuss this in his parent groups or even why he needs to bring up the obvious fact that he is a White Orthodox Jewish man, and further, this has never been requested of him before in supervision. Used to being identified as Orthodox, he is less comfortable in acknowledging the issue of privilege associated with being a man and White. He expresses his frustration and feeling as if his experience, skills, and knowledge are constantly being called into question. His field instructor acknowledges the discomfort her questions have caused, especially as this had not been requested of him previously. She continues to encourage his reflection on why his ascribed identity and its influence on his work might be important. She raises the obvious fact that she is a Black woman and invites a conversation about how this may be affecting their conversation. The field instructor is bolstered by the mandates of the competencies to examine diversity and difference in practice as they proceed to discuss this further and to expand her student's awareness and capabilities.

D, a 40-year-old dual-degree student of southern Italian American background is married with one child. Pursuing MBA and MSW degrees simultaneously, she represents an elite group of students who are accepted into full-time 3- or 4-year dual-degree programs that require negotiation of two new professional identities. She previously worked in the film industry for 15 years and has the money and time to complete the dual-degree course of study. She has functioned in a highly competitive and sexist work environment and prides herself on her survival skills and her bottom-line approach. Her goal is to open her own agency someday to serve autistic children. She has very little prior knowledge of, or experience in, social work and is challenged by her field instructor's expectations for self-reflection and examination of her decision making. Her field instructor is an American man of Irish descent who is a new field instructor. Although he has extensive experience as a community worker, he is younger than his student. He recognizes the shifts and adjustments required of his student and views her as being challenged by what is being required of her. He chooses an assignment that will require her to organize a community meeting with various stakeholders regarding a proposal to develop a new community center. He explains this assignment in relation to the skill set that will be needed, and together they begin to outline the goals for the project and goals for her learning. During this discussion the field instructor uses the competencies and associated components to identify self-awareness and self-regulation as important components of practice. He acknowledges the differences that exist between them in terms of gender, age, and experience, how their own experiences of power and privilege might be different from and similar to those experienced by the people who live in the community they serve, and he points to the differences and similarities between her previous work experiences and this assignment. He opens a dialogue that includes how these differences and similarities will support and enhance their learning together.

E is a 22-year-old generalist practice level student. She is placed in a youth development organization where she provides after-school programming. The field instructor is an experienced supervisor, and he has been working in this setting for 7 years. From the moment the student started, the youths have asked E whether she is a boy or a girl; she brings this to the attention of her field instructor who asks how she may want to answer these questions and expresses understanding that the questions may place her in a difficult position. The field instructor had been aware that this might be a difficult conversation because of the population served and their lack of understanding about transgender experiences. E explains that she is not offended by the youths' curiosity as she is used to this kind of questioning, but she wants to know how to disclose her gender identity in this setting and when or whether it is advisable. The field instructor is unsure how to respond, and his instinct is to tell the student there is no need to say anything either way. Instead, he raises his question as an opportunity to engage his student in her thoughts and feelings about how she would like to proceed. A conversation develops in which the student shares her feelings and experiences about coming out. Through this discussion it becomes clear to him that saying to his student that she does not have to respond either way would be simplifying the issues and perpetuating oppression. He realizes he was approaching the situation from his own worldview and only considering this situation from the lens of cisgender privilege. Instead, he and his student talk about self-disclosure in practice and how he can use his positionality and social location to promote a more open atmosphere in this setting around genderism and transphobia. They consider what might be involved in these macro and structural changes and how together they might intervene with the youths for a discussion about sexual orientation and gender identity.

It is a challenge to respond to the learning needs of such a diverse group of students, to aid their professional development, and to consider the larger justice implications for service delivery. In the group described, multiple social identities within and between group issues are identified, and each holds different consciousness of these identity dimensions (Baxter Magolda, 2009; Bertrand Finch, 2016). The ways these identities intersect in students' broader contexts are critical factors that affect teaching and learning (Braxton, 2009; Jones, 2008; King, 2009; Mattsson, 2104; Yorks & Kasl, 2009).

Responding to our evolving roles. It should be clear now that we share Rogers's (1995) image of field instructors "as being at the heartland, a vital and solid place, balanced at the nexus of practice, education, profession and personhood." (p. 34). It is through this lens that we approach our alliances with academe, colleagues, and students and where quality field education emerges. The call is for field instructors to join this collaboration as equal partners.

Becoming a field instructor requires several different types of role changes that create expected stresses and possible tensions, but these role changes also involve professional growth and development. We must be prepared to act as educators, mentors, models, facilitators, capacity builders, gatekeepers, evaluators, and "empathetic provocateurs of learning" (Mezirow, 1991, p. 206) while also maintaining our positions as administrators and service representatives of our settings. The role of field instructor is different from the role of an agency staff supervisor, yet field education supervision does entail the components of staff supervision, which are characterized by administrative, supportive, and educative functions. The difference resides in how the educative role becomes primary to the other functions and the additional responsibilities of supporting our students' growth and development. One of the main transitions for us involves shifting from being in the direct line of service provision to secondhand management of service delivery; we work through students to meet consumer needs. This involves sharpening our focus on the student's professional development while maintaining a balance that keeps the target system and task in mind (Reynolds, 1942). Our lens must be adjusted to include all three supervisory functions: educative, administrative, and supportive. This is accomplished by starting where the student is and by being prepared to individualize the assessment of each student's capacities so that they are channeled for action. Being one step removed from service adjusts our focus on the organization as a training site, not just as a service site; provision of services performed through the eyes and voices of students gives us a new way of viewing the services offered. This lens often identifies needed changes.

We have added the following shifts in our role changes listed by Aptekar (1966), which reflect current demands and the context of social work education:

> From supervisor to partner-educator with field liaisons and classroom professors

> From worker to colleague of other social work educators and collaborator with social work program faculty and staff
> From being allocated work to architect of student assignments
> From employee to advocate for organizational change to secure a conducive learning environment and to expand service delivery to meet learning needs
> From technician to theoretician, that is, balancing the technical aspects of practice to becoming a competent conveyer of theory and practice principles and an interpreter who promotes integration between practice and theory
> From doer to explainer and exemplar of competency-based practice requirements
> From being on the sidelines of the academic endeavor to provider of feedback and contributor to improvements in the social work program
> From consumer of social work education to evaluator and gatekeeper
> From helper of those in need to teacher and mentor of future colleagues

The role of mentor extends our understanding of our responsibilities to our students. Mentorship, in Schön's (1987) terms, is a type of coaching, that is, facilitating reflective practice by providing guidance while promoting the acquisition of needed skills. Pomeroy and Steiker (2011) define our role as mentor in the following:

> mentoring... is more than providing adequate supervision to a student or an employee. It involves extending oneself and genuinely sharing those inner qualities that can assist mentees as burgeoning professionals.... Their interest lies in assisting the mentee in becoming the best he or she can be. Good mentoring involves making mistakes and being wrong and not being afraid to discuss those errors.... Mentors must also be able to manage crises that inevitably occur as mentees struggle with their own growth as individuals and professionals.... They must be aware of the power they hold over their mentees and be sensitive to the position they hold in their mentees' lives. Treating mentees with the utmost respect for their hard work and desire to develop is sacrosanct. Mentees are people who work not for a mentor but, rather, beside a mentor.... Good

mentoring involves knowing when to let go and allow mentees to fly on their own. (pp. 197–198)

Developing supervisory skills. The progression in the development of supervisory skills occurs step by step over time; we often begin by being thrown into the role with little preparation, and in this situation, we rely on models we have experienced or observed (Dearnley, 1985). As the role begins to feel more comfortable and confidence builds, we draw on our repertoire of practice skills and apply them to the supervisory relationship. Seeking support from colleagues and seeking additional knowledge are common in our search for increased competence. Finally, there is the

> development of a sense of credibility ... a freedom "not to know" and to be more open, by imaginative association, to the worker's [student's] explicit and implicit material. ... One discovers one's own style, becomes more comfortable with it, and creates and refines a framework of knowledge in which to operate. (p. 62)

In this conception, it is assumed that learning how to become an effective field instruction educator will improve with experience and exposure to a variety of students with varying learning needs and cultural backgrounds. It is true that as we progress in our work with students, we influence and are influenced by these interactions over time. Supervisory competence is achieved. However, practice perspectives advance, new challenges emerge, or behaviors may become set. Field education, much like social work practice, is an ever-evolving search for increased competence and effectiveness. Each situation presents different twists, and we need to remain open to extend our repertoire of skills. These realities prompt our need for lifelong learning.

Best practice standards, jointly developed by the NASW and the Association of Social Work Boards (ASWB, 2013) "provide a general framework that promotes uniformity and serve as a resource for issues related to supervision in the social work supervisory community" (p. 5). Although the standards do not specifically address student supervision, the issues explored apply.

Several studies have looked at qualities and types of teaching that social work students want from their field instructors (Hartung, 1982; Knight, 1996; Kanno & Koeske (2010); Ketner, Cooper-Bolinskey, & VanCleave, 2017; Lazar & Eisikovits, 1997; Miehls, Everett, Segal, & du Bois, 2013; Navari, 1993; Rosenblatt & Mayer, 1975; Solas, 1990; Van Soest & Kruzich,

1994). Interestingly these qualities remain consistent over time. Knight (2000) wrote:

> The supervisory skills that have been evaluated by students as particularly helpful are those that contribute directly to their learning and provide students with structure and direction in their work. Field instructors who are supportive, as well as those who actively involve their students in the learning process, provide instructive feedback to their students, and encourage their students to be autonomous, self-critical, and link the classroom to the field also have been evaluated as effective. (p. 174)

Ten years later Bogo (2010) similarly noted:

> The following educational principles are presented as generic and the foundation for quality field teaching: 1) field education takes place within an available and supportive relationship; 2) learners benefit from a balance between structure and autonomy in practice and learning; 3) learners need to develop reflective and conceptual capacity; and 4) observation, reflective discussion and the provision of constructive feedback facilitates mastery of skills. (p. 105)

Each of these elements are closely associated to those listed in NASW and ASWB's (2013) best practices in supervision; however, the emphasis here is placed on the student's special place in the process of learning and our responsibilities to begin at the beginning. It is agreed that the task is to release the learner's potential. This effort is helped by building an alliance based on trust, confidence, and fairness, while also finding the balance between the right time to push or pull back. The aim is to broaden the capacity to move beyond comfort zones and to other ways of knowing, learning, and doing. In fact, important learning often happens when we are most uncomfortable and challenged to tolerate the ambiguity of practice. In summary, our credibility as field instructors is rooted in knowledge, theoretical familiarity, and experience. But more is involved, such as identifying aspects of what it was like being supervised and evaluated, and the feelings evoked as we assume the role of field instructor to expand our notion of success from student satisfaction to a more significant evaluation of the student's demonstrated progress and achievement (Baum, 2006). It requires individualizing our methods and exploring ways to reach for each student's potential.

For example, a field instructor supervising three students built in an ongoing group supervisory session for the three students on their group work assignments. As the term progressed, it became clear that one of the students had previous experience in running groups. She demonstrated well-developed group work skills, whereas the other two students were less experienced. The task involved for the field instructor was to manage the implications of these differences for each of the students and providing for their effective use of group supervision. The challenge was to achieve a balance between acknowledgment and affirmation of the more experienced student's expertise while also encouraging the other students to participate and extend their skill levels. The process included respecting each of the student's capabilities while involving them in trusting their abilities to enhance each other's development. Soon all three were actively engaged in attempting to incorporate new methods and techniques. The field instructor's own skills were enhanced by rethinking intervention strategies to further each student's learning. The student with previous experience was assigned to cofacilitate a group with a staff member who had no group experience. The field instructor created a differentiated response enabling the students to increase expertise while providing an environment in which each student was helped along in their professional development.

Group Supervision, Learning Teams and the Task Supervisor's Role

We have predominately talked about field education supervision from the perspective of the dyad of field instructor and student. Although perspectives have shifted in how we deliver services and how we organize models for field education placements, the current context of delivery of field education supervision remains rooted in the one-to-one ratio of field instructor and student. This historical perspective on the central position of a one-to one ratio remains persistent in today's practice, despite growing recognition that alternative models for field education are frequently used and offer advantages in addressing workforce realities and students' needs. Access for student placements in otherwise unavailable settings due to a lack of eligible field instructors at the placement setting is often pursued by using off-site field instructors; group supervision is sometimes introduced as a method of teaching if multiple students are involved in these situations (Alschuler, Silva, & McArdle, 2015; Knight, 2014; Wayne, Bogo, & Raskin, 2016).

Although a running dialogue regarding the value of group supervision exists in the literature, group supervision currently remains a support or supplement to individual supervision (Sussman, Bogo, & Globerman, 2007; Walter &Young, 1999; Wayne et al., 2016). On the other hand, group supervision is recognized as a powerful method for learning (Heffron, Reynolds, & Talbot, 2016; Gitterman & Knight, 2016; Gitterman & Miller, 1977). Groups allow students to talk with other students and provide a potent atmosphere for learning. As field instructors, our perspectives on the work are not the only perspective of importance. Even if there are only two or three students in a placement, bringing students together provides a forum for learning. Certainly, if there is a student unit, it is a lost learning opportunity not to offer some form of group supervision. Peers may more easily challenge each other to think outside their usual frames of reference, and small-group discussions can challenge assumptions and add or expand perspectives as members learn to give constructive criticism to each other (Bertrand Finch & Feigleman, 2008; Gitterman & Knight, 2016; Heft LaPorte & Sweifach, 2011; Wayne & Cohen, 2001; Wayne et al., 2016).

Group supervision sessions are focused on the students' development of skills. This includes an in-depth examination of actions taken and a focus on shared themes and topics of concern relating to the students' work. Although it is sometimes challenging to apply learning from someone else's work to one's own, seeing the success of an approach for a peer provides courage for students to apply the learning in their own work. In this way students understand that although their work assignments are completely different, practice principles apply across units of attention, problems, and issues. In a similar manner, introducing issues or topics provides the opportunity to examine related themes, skills, or methods; relevant research; organizational and policy implications; or justice issues in the context of their assignments and implementation of suggested strategies. As students become a resource to each other, they progress in their ability to learn the material while also learning how to lead a discussion and to teach (Coulshed, 1993; Oşvat et al., 2014; Wayne & Cohen, 2001). They learn about group dynamics and stages of group development as they experience the group, and they experience the power of mutual aid as they help their colleagues think about the work and help themselves through their own articulation of the practice principles underpinning the interventions they suggest. Group supervision also provides opportunities to practice and model challenging conversations on race, gender, and intersecting identities with their peers. Using the diversity of the student group can sustain ongoing dialogue related to existing differences and similarities; in turn, this dialogue can serve to deepen understanding while furthering students' skills.

In addition to the groups we may form, students can independently form into peer groups for support or to research specific topics. One method of peer group supervision asks students to research issues in an assignment and then analyze, collate, present, and evaluate their findings. Peer groups can be empowering learning experiences that increase students' confidence and sense of independence as they voice concerns about their learning or validate the field placements' strengths and limitations (Golia & McGovern, 2015). Sometimes the students present their findings to other staff members, and other staff can be used to contribute to the peer group's learning by offering expertise on a special area of practice.

Despite these benefits, caution has been suggested on moving too quickly and on the lack of careful attention for when and how group supervision is used. Caution for a greater examination of the skills needed and increased training for this supervisory modality are recommended (Bogo, Globerman, & Sussman, 2004). Several important factors for successful group facilitation that have also been noted are (a) the availability and supportive nature of the group leader, (b) clarity of the rationale for the group and formation of a conducive group climate, (c) competence of the group leader, and 4) involvement of the members in processing the group's dynamics (Bogo, 2010).

Emerging models that expand the traditional structure of one student to one field instructor involve a field education learning team that includes a task supervisor who may or not be a social worker but who is assigned to assist in the supervision of a student on a specific assignment or task. An example includes task supervision in a specific method of practice. In these situations, task supervisors provide additional support and add an important component of expertise to the learning team. The field instructor maintains the primary role in field supervision of the student and may or may not be situated at the same work site as the task supervisor.

A shared supervisory model is where task supervision is combined with off-site field education supervision; this model is used frequently when the placement setting does not have an on-site social worker eligible or available to provide supervision and is also used in international field settings. In these models, task supervisors often "assigned cases, guided students through agency policy, and helped students with service provision" (Wayne et al., 2016, p. 42).

Abram, Hartung, and Wernet (2000) note the wide range of arrangements regarding these situations; they warn that unclear roles and responsibilities for those involved may blur the boundaries between task supervision and field instruction. Yet this sharing of roles may also result in joining forces to contribute to the student's learning and progress (Wayne et al., 2016). At the same time, the student may be introduced to working with professionals from other disciplines and interdisciplinary practice. The difference in these effects relate to the relationships and communication forged between and among those involved and an understanding that although the roles are differentiated, each member has much to offer the student as part of the learning team. The off-site field instructor supports the placement of the student at the site, carries primary responsibility for completion of program requirements and evaluation, and if the task supervisor is not a social worker, the field instructor is responsible for ensuring that a social work perspective on the work is provided. The task supervisor provides needed accessibility and guidance at the site and a different perspective and direct observation of the student at work, which broaden evaluation of performance.

Other models introduce co-supervision arrangements when supervision of a student is shared by two or more colleagues (Coulton & Kimmer, 2005). This may work well for part-time workers who would not otherwise have time to take on a full-time student.

Each of these models rely on transparent and open communication, perhaps different types of technological communication formats, coordinated and articulated agreement on responsibilities and roles, and collaboration between and among those involved to result in the intended benefits of providing adequate support, access to differing learning experiences, and clarity on student performance and supervisory expertise (Cohen & Garrett, 1995; Cooper-Bolinskey & Ketner, 2016; Coulton & Kimmer, 2005; Golia & McGovern, 2015; Henderson, 2010; Maynard, Mertz, & Fortune, 2015; Oșvat, Marc, & Makai-Dimeny, 2014; Wayne et al., 2016).

Wayne et al. (2016) provide a guide to shared and individualized responsibilities for the task supervisor and field instructor, which are summarized here. We are reminded that the task supervisor and the field instructor both have a part in developing an educational learning plan. This is especially important when the task supervisor has the primary responsibility of allocating work to the students. Likewise, as the task supervisor is often on site with the student, task supervisors share evaluative responsibilities, and the task supervisor's observations of the student should be shared and included as part of the student's overall evaluation. The task supervisor meets regularly with the student to oversee administrative issues and issues related to service, supervision of tasks and assignments, management and allocation of new assignments, and to provide general feedback and guidance related to the student's performance. The field instructor remains responsible for the final agreements on the educational plan; maintaining communication with the task supervisor and student regarding assignments, review, and supervision and evaluation of student process recordings; conducting evaluations on performance; and maintaining a social work focus on the student's progress in achieving competence.

It is likely that we will see an increasing use of these and similar innovative models. They respond to the power of group learning, peer-to-peer learning, and the promising outcomes of shared supervisory models that open new venues for placement settings.

Summary

As field instructors, we draw on our experience, practice wisdom, and the supervision and field education literature to inform our supervisory practice. Our aims include encouraging "a safe place for examination of multiple truths and stepping out of the expert role can become a powerful way to teach about oppression, power and diversity" (East & Chambers, 2007, p. 822). Achieving this provides a solid ground for students to grapple with the mandates of our professional mission. In this context, East and Chambers (2007) refer to three guiding philosophic principles: We teach who we are, that is, how we think about the content, what we feel about it, and how we connect with the topic and those we teach; teaching and learning are acts of connectedness and relationship, that is, we are connected to the material and to each other as we find relationships with what we are attempting to learn and teach; and community is essential to teaching and learning, that is, creating community fosters diverse perspectives and increases consideration of alternative views of the issues.

The CSWE (2015a) competencies contribute to the development of our teaching by codifying the principles of social work practice into learning outcomes that encapsulate our professional mission. In this way, we are provided with a framework for our teaching. The competencies define the required content and provide a clear goal that gives us a focus. Further, field education is recognized as the playing field where the knowledge, skills, and values of our profession are transmitted. It is the place to understand, apply, and integrate theory and practice and where fundamentals of practice, policy, justice, human behavior, and research taught in the classroom are tested and consolidated. It is in this context that educational principles are balanced with the realities of community-based practice and the demands of service delivery to a range of diverse systems. The bedrock is the field instructor and field education context where the student is assigned.

CHAPTER 1 APPENDIX

This appendix includes two recordings that provide examples of establishing a reflective posture early in the field placement experience. Although setting a climate for learning is addressed in Chapter 4, and the importance of a reflective posture is addressed in more detail in Chapter 5, the following scenarios introduce the reader to these issues, which are critical to beginning. How we begin the work of supervision shapes the relationships we form with our students and the work that follows. (See Chapter 8 for a full discussion of recordings for use in field education supervision.)

Establishing a Reflective Stance in Justice-Based Field Education

The following is a field instructor's reflection on a supervisory interchange early in the academic year with a generalist practice level student.

Setting and Practice Context

The people served in this medical outreach program either are ill themselves or have a member of their family who is being seen at the clinic attached to this program. They are seen for a range of issues related to the patient's illness including difficulties in their relationships with their partners or families. This recording describes a supervisory session after the third meeting between a generalist practice level student and a widower, Mr. M., age 70, who suffers from heart disease and is experiencing difficulties with his new live-in partner. It is also the third meeting between the student and her field instructor. The student has not worked with adults before; her previous work experience has been serving young children in a residential group home setting. The student, field instructor, and individuals served are White.

Supervision of a Student Session

The student reported finding Mr. M. upset upon her home visit. When she asked what had upset him, he reported that no one was helping him, although he had been asking for months. He and his live-in partner had another fight. The student acknowledged Mr. M's frustration and his desire to find a solution to his problems. She reminded him of the steps they had begun to take together over the past few weeks and recounted what they had achieved and what they had identified and agreed on as next steps that could be taken. Mr. M. continued to express his irritation and stated that he had to do everything himself.

In supervision, the student expressed her disappointment. She had assessed they were working well together, and she was somewhat annoyed by Mr. M's dismissal of her efforts and the work they had done together. Before discussing the nature of the fight between Mr. M. and his live-in partner, the field instructor stated she would like to understand the interchange better and asked the student to describe in greater detail what it was like being with Mr. M. while he was expressing anger and frustration. The field instructor explained she was asking for clarification, so they could examine the underlying affective reactions operating within this interchange. She clarified they could then examine the engagement issues before discussing the fight between Mr. M. and his live-in partner. The student agreed and replied she was taken off guard, but she knew she had done all that she could. She had worked hard to go at his pace, not hers. She expressed frustration in not knowing how to respond next. The field instructor acknowledged there are often no good solutions. Those we work with sometimes feel frustrated, and we sometimes do, too. The field instructor provided feedback that the student had self-regulated her annoyance and that it did not seem to interfere with her ability to empathize and acknowledge Mr. M's frustration. Did the student agree? The student stated that she tried to do just that! The field instructor noted the student's attempt to neutralize Mr. M's anger. The student stated, "Yes, but, this only enflamed him more."

The field instructor and student continued to process the student's session and decided to move on from the specific interaction to consider the broader context to gain a different perspective and to enhance their understanding of Mr. M and his situation. They spent time considering Mr. M's medical condition and circumstances, asking how the external surroundings of Mr. M's situation affect his reactions to his situation and how these factors affect what he believes about being older, sick, and facing life alone;

what might underlie his attack and perceived failure of efforts being made; what he was attempting to communicate in his expression of powerlessness and feeling on his own; how the differences in age and gender between them might influence this feeling; and where the fight with his partner fit into all this.

The field instructor then asked the student to contrast her work with Mr. M. to that of another individual with whom she is working. The other individual, a middle-age woman whose sick son lives with her, is seeking support because of the challenges related to this son's care. The student's work with this woman has involved identifying alternative resources and introducing additional supports to the mother's care of her son. The comparison of the work with these two individuals enabled looking at the levels of support not yet explored with the first, older, more emotionally distant man, who possessed very different expectations and responses to receiving help. Questions posed included the following:

> What is Mr. M. experiencing in the face of difficulties in this live-in relationship and the possibility of living on his own once again? What other issues have been unaddressed that may contribute to either untapped resources or additional barriers for resolution? What worries might he be carrying but not expressing?
> How might the student's age and gender be affecting her ability to facilitate their work and her ability to gain his trust? Had the student let him down, like others had before?
> How might she better understand his frustration and the implications for their work together?
> What thoughts did the student have about the ease of her relationship with the mother compared to the challenges of working with Mr. M assist the student? How might the joint work with the mother and her son or the community connections provided to the mother and her son be models for the work with Mr. M?

The student successfully worked with her field instructor to consider alternative ways to look at her beginning work with these individuals. She felt heard by her field instructor and not rejected for the frustration she experienced and expressed. Instead, these factors were seen as being related to the work and used to further her thinking about how to better approach both situations. Her affective reactions were used as material to think critically about the engagement process and to discern next steps. Efforts to consider the details of the interaction were balanced with considerations of what external issues might be influencing the interaction; for example, what being old, ill, and alone mean to Mr. M. in his current context. What might asking for help mean to Mr. M., and what assistance was not being asked for or responded to? The supervisory session ended with the field instructor commenting on the work they had done to identify important skills and possible issues that could improve the student's engagement and interventional approaches. A relevant reading that would further the student's thinking about her work was provided.

Discussion

Although this interchange is brief and early in the year, it demonstrates that the field instructor created a reflective posture in supervision that allowed looking at the work from different angles that enhanced their work. Issues of difference and power were addressed. Responding to Mr. M's frustration is an opportunity for reflection on what he is attempting to communicate rather than confirmation of his being difficult, resistant, or challenging. The student is encouraged to think beyond the immediate interaction to consider the broader issues involved.

The student responds by attempting to look at the needs of those involved and the ways their differing responses to receiving help affected the work. Further, she is encouraged to consider her assumptions and those of the individuals she is serving regarding dimensions of identity and how these also may affect the work. The beginning of trust, acceptance, and stretching the student's participation in new perspectives is evident. Practice principles of engagement, critical thinking, and self-regulation are identified to increase the student's awareness and understanding of her developing practice (Deal, 2003). The tone is set for a relationship where an honest appraisal of potential blocks and answers to complex questions are explored. The student's internal affective reactions are used to examine the interaction but do not cloud or consume the external realities that also need to be examined. The student is referred to readings that will increase her knowledge and confidence, and a model for increasing curiosity, reflection, problem solving and risk taking is provided.

Consider the following questions:

› How was a reflective stance achieved in this supervisory session?
› What did this supervisory session accomplish?
› What competencies and performance behaviors were focused on?
› How does the field instructor explore differences in worldview and identities that may influence the relationship, expectations, intervention, and assessment? How might the field instructor include additional dialogue on self-awareness, power, and privilege? How might the field instructor extend connections to broader issues and social concerns affecting Mr. M?
› Going forward, what actions and skills might illustrate improved practice?

Establishing a Reflective Stance in Justice-Based Field Education: A Group Supervisory Session

A group of six specialized practice level students are engaged in weekly group supervisory sessions during the academic year. They also receive individual supervision from the group supervisor, and they are assigned a task supervisor in their settings. Each is placed in a different department of a large institution, and they also vary in their chosen area of specialization. Their assignments range from predominately administrative to predominately micro-level individual counseling.

This interchange occurs in the first three weeks of the fall term, and the group was beginning to learn about each other. Two of the group members graduated from the same undergraduate program, and two others knew each other through membership at the same gym. These connections created an automatic sense of familiarity and friendliness among the group members. Those not known previously were easily brought into this circle of students. They had begun to share their shared and differing worldviews in their responses to group discussions. They represent a range of social dimensions of identity; three are White, one is of Chinese descent, and two are Black; there is one man in the group.

Following the group field instructor's question regarding how things were progressing in field, one intern immediately responded, "I need help." Encouraged to go on, she described an assignment she had just received. Her department was contacted by a local high school guidance counselor who asked for help in presenting the aims and purposes of a new ally campaign to support LGBTQ+ TS students in the high school. The request involved creating and delivering a presentation that would be given twice to two different groups of students at the high school. Each session would have about 10–50 students. The precise number of participants was not known as this would be a voluntary session. The intern was asked to create an outline for the presentation, to help deliver the content, and to include two high school students involved in the project who could help in the presentation. This request was made of her on Friday. She was expected to present her ideas to her task supervisor and colleagues in her department on that following Monday, the afternoon following her group field education supervisory session. The presentation was scheduled to be held at the local high school that following Friday one week from the initial request.

The intern presented this assignment and was met with a resounding gasp from her peers. They felt this task was overwhelming. The intern laughed and said, "That's exactly how I felt when I was asked to do this!" She shyly stated that she had begun to put things together in a PowerPoint presentation and asked the field instructor whether she could share it with the group. As this session was during the first few weeks of the fall term, the group was still developing its way of working together. The intern's presentation of this assignment was the first piece of work to be discussed in depth.

The field instructor's response to the intern's request was to turn to the others in the group for their opinions. Each of the group members stated in varying ways that they were excited to begin their work together and were eager to get started. The field instructor suggested that before playing the PowerPoint presentation, perhaps the intern could explain more of what she understood of the high school's expectations, who her audience will be, and what her own goals are for the presentation to help the field instructor and group members connect with the goals of the presentation and provide a context for providing feedback. She asked if there was other information the group would like before viewing the presentation. One student asked if anything is known about the school's context and history with LGBTQ+TS inclusion.

As the intern began to respond to these aspects, the group had their own questions that furthered understanding of the target system, its expectations, mutual goals, and the purposes of the assignment. The intern stated that it felt like a tremendous responsibility to help high school students consider equity and inclusive practices, and it was also very important to her to do a good job. Group members listened intently and affirmed the intern's declaration. They demonstrated their shared views by considering what would be involved in facilitating a discussion about this topic with high school students. The field instructor prompted discussion of their experiences in high school and of the current context of bullying among youths. They considered the milieu of this high school, the demographics of the population of students, and the larger social conversation regarding inclusion and marginalization. A range of goals were identified including, supporting the two high school students already involved in the campaign and developing their leadership and presentation skills.

By the time the intern began to go through the presentation, the group had a clear vision of the intern's role and purposes to be achieved. They were ready to provide feedback, and to help create an engaging and pertinent presentation. The initial gasp heard from them had shifted to curiosity over how to meet the challenge of this interesting learning opportunity and a shared commitment to intervene to make a difference for these youths. The prepared material was perfectly pitched to the audience, the visuals were engaging, and the intern had also begun to consider her role in supporting the students identified to help lead the presentation. It was clear that this intern possessed considerable skills and passion suited to this task. The field instructor acknowledged that the presentation demonstrated how carefully the intern approached this task and that it would be clear to her audience that she is committed to providing a thoughtful session on the aims and importance of the project. The group discussion turned to how our views and feelings influence—and are visible—in how we approach a topic or task.

Following the initial review of the presentation, the field instructor asked the group to consider the skills and aspects of the helping process they were discussing. Together they pieced together a focus on tuning in so that they might engage the potential audience. They identified their attention on group process, setting a structure to achieve the stated goals and analyzing the many ways the activity might be experienced from places of privilege or powerlessness and marginalization.

During this discussion, the intern asked for additional help regarding what kind of activity she could use to connect her audience to the content. She was concerned about how to pitch the activity given her lack of knowledge of the population, the nature of the content embedded in the mission of the project, and her desire to ensure that meaningful dialogue on inclusion and sexual identity could occur. She was reassured by her peers that there was a lot she did not know about her potential audience, but at least she knew that they would be voluntary participants and that the high school was invested enough to offer this opportunity. They reminded her that even if students were not invested in the topic and went only because their friend was going, or they were curious, she could still count on those there as wanting to learn about the project. One student asked, "After all, how likely was it that the students were there to set up a rejection of the project? Or that they would engage in bullying right then?" The intern's worst fear was confronted and given voice.

Discussion

The intern's commitment and readiness to tackle this topic conveyed itself, but she had never led this sort of group presentation before. In this regard, her peers shined. Group members shared experiences in their high schools of exclusionary practices, the difficulty of rallying support, and their view on the importance of establishing a community of allies. The conversation shifted from creating and editing a PowerPoint presentation to a discussion about the importance of this assignment. Together the group members worked at reconsidering the goals that had been initially set and then designing some activities to support these adjustments. They came up with two ideas. One for a group of 10 students and one for a group of 50 students. By the end of this group session, the intern felt supported. She was armed with a clear focus and tools that she could apply to the challenge presented to her. Her initial effort was applauded as a more than adequate start, her hopes and fears were validated, she had practice in addressing challenging questions on the topic, and viable strategies were identified. The field instructor ended the session by acknowledging and summarizing the work the group had achieved together and identified the required aspects of professional practice they had considered.

Consider the following questions:

> What did this group supervisory session accomplish?
> How was a reflective stance achieved in this supervisory session?
> How might this have been different if the supervisory session was an individual session? What would have been gained? What would have been lost?
> What competencies and performance behaviors were focused on? Should others have been added?
> How does the field instructor explore differences in worldview and identities that may influence the relationship,

expectations, intervention, and assessment? How might the field instructor include additional dialogue on self-awareness, power, and privilege?

> Going forward, what performance behaviors might illustrate improved practice?

CHAPTER 2

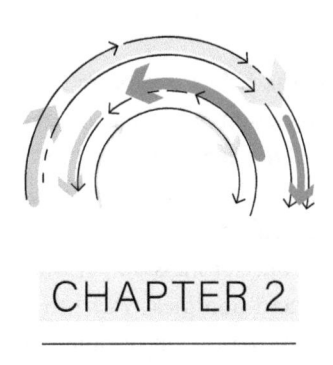

Justice-Based Dialogues

A Keystone for Field Education Supervision

How can I dialogue if I always project ignorance onto others and never perceive my own? How can I dialogue if I regard myself as a case apart from others—mere "its" in whom I cannot recognize other "I"s [*sic*]? How can I dialogue if I am closed to—and even offended by—the contribution of others? How can I dialogue if I am afraid of being displaced, the mere possibility causing me torment and weakness? At the point of encounter there are neither utter ignoramuses nor perfect sages; there are only people who are attempting, together, to learn more than they now know. (Freire, 1993, p. 78–79)

And let us acknowledge that such work is not easy.... Listen hard, listen generously, risk making a mistake, risk being made uncomfortable, risk forgiveness. Learn from one another. (Harvard President Drew Faust, as cited in Rosenberg, 2015)

This chapter is central in meeting the book's aim of linking the primary focus of seeking justice in social work practice to field education. We introduce what it means to place justice in the foreground of field education, why it is important, and how it serves our field education supervisory role. The supervisory relationship is proposed as the space where students learn how their practice decisions and interactions can make a difference in dismantling the injustices that afflict and harm the populations and communities we serve. Our conversations with our students start this work, specifically, conversations that acknowledge existing multiple layers of identity and the differences and similarities that separate and connect us. The commitment to providing justice-based field education supervision is a pledge to a lifelong journey toward increased consciousness on personal, social, and global levels that proceeds in complex and nonlinear ways; the required knowledge and skills develop over time. This journey is outlined by describing how we prepare ourselves for the work involved, providing field education examples, and presenting a framework for facilitating challenging conversations with students in field education supervision that incorporate a justice-based approach to their practice.

There are at least three levels for consideration. First, we bring ourselves into the conversation; we model how to navigate dialogue across multiple dimensions of identity so that issues of diversity, equity, and inclusion can be tackled. Second, we introduce issues of justice related to all aspects of student assignments. Third, we prepare students for entry-level practice to recognize injustice, form partnerships for change, and gain skills that challenge systemic structures of oppression and dominance locally and globally.

To achieve these goals, this text addresses the processes that operate on the micro level between field instructors and students and how these processes influence and prepare students. The work of justice begins on the personal level. This includes developing conscious use of self, self-reflective practice, mindfulness, self-regulation, and self-awareness (Sensoy & DiAngelo, 2014). With these skills, it is possible to approach others in intentional and purposeful interactions and dialogue around issues of justice for the creation of collaborative, mutual partnerships to effect change. The work between field instructors and students sets the stage for the work undertaken with individuals, groups, families, organizations, and communities; provides a justice lens for each phase of the helping process at all levels of intervention; and offers strategies and skills that support paths toward justice.

Educating for justice includes key concepts of "meaning, power, history, context and possibility" (Finn, 2016, p. 32). These concepts and processes are grounded in work using a strengths-based perspective for empowerment. A critical lens is applied using conceptions of positionality, intersecting identities, and cultural equity and liberation to view problems as being located beyond the individual and to examine structural barriers existing in the environment and context. Finn (2016) asks us to consider the following questions related to these concepts.

How do we give *meaning* to the experiences and conditions that shape our lives? How do structures and relations of *power* shape people's lives and their choices for individual and collective action? How might *history* and a historical perspective help us grasp the interplay between sociopolitical structures and human agency, the ways in which struggles over meaning and power have played out, and the human consequence of those struggles? What are the *contexts* in which those experiences and conditions occur, and how might context limit or expand possibilities for actions? How might an appreciation of these struggles help us claim a sense of *possibility* for transformative social work practice? (p. 33)

This book provides guidance and examples for field instructors to apply justice-based teaching methods. Questions are suggested that prompt student reflections on how issues of justice affect the problems and issues faced by the individuals, groups, and communities they will be working with. The aim is the development of student awareness that awakens the commitment to challenge injustice and to prompt action when human and civil rights are blocked. We recognize that the conversations we initiate are not the end goal, the goal is to fine-tune the lens through which students view the problems and solutions they address. In this way, issues of diversity, equity, and inclusion are brought forward for attention. Yet interventions on the micro, local level alone cannot achieve the change required, skills to pursue change at other levels for other units of attention on regional and global levels are also needed (Reisch, 2002, 2011, 2016).

Advancing Practice Competence for Justice-Based Field Education

Advancing the fulfillment of basic human needs and achieving equity are deeply rooted in the social work profession and are key concepts in the *Universal Declaration of Human Rights* (UDHR, United Nations, 1948), the *Declaration on the Rights of Indigenous Peoples* (UNDRIP, United Nations, 2007) and the NASW (2017) Code of Ethics. The United Nations declarations align with the values and purposes of our profession and are vital resources for our work and teaching. Basic human needs

> are inherent in our nature and without which we cannot live as human beings. Human rights and fundamental freedoms allow us to fully develop and use our human qualities, our intelligence, our talents and our

conscience to satisfy our spiritual and other needs. (United Nations, 1948, Preamble, para. 1)

These precepts provide us with a moral basis for our practice, underpin our efforts to challenge oppressive policies and promote strengths-based, inclusive, and democratic ways of working. The aspirations guide our practice, but the work is challenging. Current civil discord centering around divisive language, exclusive policy initiatives, and biased responses have become actualized in negative discourse and actions that intensify fear. Communities are experiencing hate crime incidents and inadequate community protections. The fear seeps into our lives whether it comes from television coverage or from actual direct experience. Those we serve bring this exposure with them as they walk into hospitals, schools, or placement settings and are fearful of accessing resources because of restrictive policies and practices or being turned away from services no longer available.

These issues are directly addressed in the CSWE (2015a) competencies, for example, in the description provided on engaging diversity and difference in practice:

> Diversity and difference characterize and shape the human experience and are critical to the formation of identity. The dimensions of diversity are understood as the intersectionality of multiple factors... as a consequence of difference, a person's life experiences may include oppression, poverty, marginalization, and alienation as well as privilege, power, and acclaim. Social workers also understand the forms and mechanisms of oppression and discrimination and recognize the extent to which a culture's structures and values, including social, economic, political, and cultural exclusions, may oppress, marginalize, alienate, or create privilege and power. (p. 7).

The competency description for advancing human rights stresses understanding for action:

> Social workers understand the global interconnections of oppression and human rights violations and are knowledgeable about theories of human need and social justice and strategies to promote social and economic justice and human rights. Social workers understand strategies designed to eliminate oppressive structural barriers to ensure that social goods, rights, and responsibilities are distributed equitably, and that civil,

political, environmental, economic, social, and cultural human rights are protected.... regardless of position in society, every individual has fundamental human rights such as freedom, safety, privacy, an adequate standard of living, health care, and education. (p. 7).

It seems clear that for students to apply their understanding of these competencies, they must see the connection between our mandates for justice and the need to protect these basic rights. This demands that we expand their awareness and understanding of how human rights and justice apply to their work, increase their tolerance for the ambiguity and complexity involved, and provide strategies and tools to assist them. We set the tone for dialogue about these issues, and together we frame the discourse.

The descriptions and delineated components of the competencies dealing with engaging diversity and difference in practice and advancing human rights guide our teaching of what this entails, and by implication, what is involved in confronting internalized and socialized thought processes. The development of student self-awareness and the ability to converse across the divides, communicate understanding, and achieve a learning stance in students' relationships with others are critical (Finn, 2016; Jani, Pierce, Ortiz, & Sowbel, 2011). Our work involves explaining the importance of our approach to others "as learners" and the role of self-awareness and self-regulation in handling "biases and values in working with diverse clients and constituencies" (CSWE, 2015a, p. 7). We also are required to explain how issues surrounding human rights arise in the lives of those the students will be working with, and how the field education setting addresses these issues.

Understanding should not remain on the individual level; social and global interconnections also need attention as they directly affect personal levels of experience. Inquiring about how the social work education program introduces students to this material facilitates integration of the content. For example, some programs provide students with professional development and self-awareness training at orientation; others have required courses on justice, diversity, and race, or the content is interwoven throughout the curriculum. Knowing how a student is exposed to and is assimilating this material supports our role as field instructor. We can build on these curriculum efforts by using some of the same exercises, readings, and content in supervision to ensure continuity and integration in student learning.

Awareness of injustice strengthens our determination to support students in their preparation for professional practice and acting on this awareness presents some of the richest, yet most difficult, challenges for us as social work educators and practitioners. Our education and experiences may not have prepared us to have conversations related to race, oppression, dominance, and intersecting multiple identities, especially in mixed company. In fact, given the historical legacy of racism and other isms, we are encouraged not to have them (Hardy, 2016; Smith, Foley, & Chaney, 2008). Too often, the typical response is to avoid, divert attention, or simply argue and speak over the opposing view to shut the conversation down and avoid discomfort or conflict.

The inherent challenges of field instruction are multifaceted and intricately connected to the increasingly diverse communities that surround us and the existing structural divides connected to race and other social dimensions of identity that engulf our work. People of color often have conversations with friends and family members about their experiences with racism and the effect it has on them; in fact, it may be an essential outlet for their survival. Many may have less exposure, opportunity, or tolerance in having these conversations in racially integrated spaces, especially with Whites. In a similar way, Whites do not often have conversations about race in mixed company. They may not have had opportunities to relate authentically with people of color about issues of racial identity and oppression, much less have a conversation about what it means to be White in the United States, discuss issues of White privilege and advantage, or consider their global implications (Pathy Solett, & Koslow, 2015). The literature on White racial identity development states that in general Whites do not discuss their race, let alone racism, because of their privilege (Blitz, 2006; McIntosh, 1989). Certain stages of White racial identity development prohibit these conversations because Whites do not see that racism exists, feel guilt and shame that prohibits their consideration that it does, or live in racial and social bubbles that perpetuate boundaries that do not support or encourage cross-racial interactions except on superficial levels. However, these conversations are critical to building authentic cross-cultural relationships that are based on openness, honesty, mutuality, and respect. This is particularly pertinent for field education, for developing sanctuaries to promote supervisory relationships and for modeling ethical professional practice. Increasingly, schools of social work embrace their responsibility to train students on how to engage in these conversations, and curriculum content includes dialogues on sexism, racism, diversity, human rights, and antioppressive issues. Similar content for field educators can be found at social work conferences or at seminars provided by the social work program's orientations for field instructors. Additionally, specialized training programs exist, and state licensure requirements provide incentives to participate in continuing education on such issues.

Practitioners outside these education circles are influenced by contemporary media's language and intent that such conversations should occur while rarely covering how they should be conducted. More is focused on descriptions of the cautions involved than the means to achieve dialogue. As a result, when issues such as race or sexual orientation surface in mixed company, fear, caution, and panic emerge. We fear we might say the wrong thing, offend, or be viewed as incompetent, racist, anti-Semitic, or homophobic, or we fear that we might have to represent our whole group or be stereotyped or experience bias. Familiarity with the concepts of microaggressions and microinsults seems to increase our concerns that these conversations may provoke further harm, estrangement, and pain, and place us in danger of being misunderstood or attacked. A lack of training or support for our efforts further limits our confidence to engage in these dialogues. So although we know we should engage in these challenging conversations or acknowledge that our role as educators requires us to facilitate them, we just do not know how. We move away from them, ignore what our profession demands, and discount what the possibility of a truly authentic professional relationship involves. We are immobilized so we move on, sensing we have left something significant on the learning table in the room, perpetuating continued separation, disconnection, and lack of engagement with these critical issues. This occurs despite the continued disparities between those who serve and those who are served and the current social discourse addressing the consequences of these divides.

Being prepared for these conversations in field instruction is affected. A student might be upset by the state of current affairs and raise this in a supervisory session. Others may experience a retriggering of historical trauma that affects their ability to be open about their reactions to these same issues. Our own reactions are also part of the mix (Walters et al., 2011). Clearly the playing field is not level, and it is our job as field instructors to anticipate these reactions and work toward equity. In a justice-based approach, equity (custom building supports to remove barriers and ensure equal access) is desired over equality (everyone benefits from the same support regardless of identities and social location). The next goal post is liberation, that is, addressing the causes of inequity and taking down systemic barriers and structures that privilege or oppress. Whether at the micro, mezzo, or macro level, our work must be grounded in the aim for liberation so that those we serve are free to realize their potential. Finn (2016) said, "The everyday struggle for social justice demands ongoing vigilance, resistance, and courage. It demands ongoing crucial reflection on our practice as social workers" (p. 20). As we reach towards each level of increased awareness, another level is on the horizon. Tuck and Yang

(2012) awaken those of us, as settlers, to the "unsettling" (p. 36) demands of decolonization in a settler colonial society; they call for the voices of indigenous peoples in the growth of science, research, knowledge production and in creating liberatory spaces of possibility. Applying these visions to field instruction enables conversations that support just practice and delivery of just services.

Together, we can learn to initiate and sustain these dialogues and do a better job of using human rights and justice to inform our practice, scholarship, and teaching (Dessel & Rodenborg, 2017; Funge, 2011; Miller, Hyde, & Ruth, 2004; Witkin, 1998). We start by acknowledging that nothing has prepared us to have conversations in mixed company about race, color, sexual orientation, special abilities, supremacy, oppression, and their intersections, so we should not expect that we should just know how. It is something we must learn. It takes a body of knowledge, skill, work, and willingness specifically focused on increasing our capacity to engage in these conversations. This approach honors the work.

Challenging Dialogues: A Keystone for Justice-Based Field Education and Practice

The ability to increase our awareness of what separates and connects us, and how this operates in supervisory relationships, is vital to beginning competence in facilitating challenging conversations in field education. Theoretical advances aid understanding, such as critical race theory (Constance-Huggins, 2012; Crenshaw, 2011), antioppressive practice (Dominelli, 2017; Mullaly, 2010), and conceptions of intersecting identities (Bowleg, 2012; Manuel, 2008). These perspectives help to shift our lens to legitimize alternative voices and differing ways of viewing the world, they emphasize cultural equity in the delivery of services to a wide range of diverse constituents, and they put varying social work roles and levels of service into a unified, holistic, and global view of practice. These are essential ingredients in a justice-based framework. Our supervisory conversations provide space where this understanding is applied to the context of practice and where increased skills move the student's work forward.

A picture of several scenarios that illustrate the diverse group of students we serve and how this diversity becomes a critical and necessary part of the work in field education was presented in Chapter 1. Now consider a Black man who attends a session with his social work intern having had a difficult journey traveling to their meeting that day. He sits down while the space between them holds a history of slavery, take over, genocide, pain, resilience, and "dogged strength" as Du Bois (1903, p. 3) describes. Whether the intern is also Black, or White, Asian, Latinx, American Indian, Alaska Native, Native Hawaiian or Pacific Islander, or a First Nations individual, it may or may not be possible to acknowledge or respond to the differences and similarities that exist between them. Their identities might advance or limit understanding; for example, issues may interfere with meaningful communication, such as color, internalized racial oppression (Pyke, 2010) or stage of racial identity development (Helms, 1995). They may not be aware of the differences between them, and they may assume their experience is the same or that these realities are not relevant to their work together. Yet each of these factors influences how their relationship develops and how the context will support the climate needed for learning and healing. Will the relationship end up as a sanctuary from microaggressions, or will collusion, denial, and avoidance perpetuate more trauma, discomfort, uncertainty, and pain? How will field education supervision prepare the intern for the awareness and sensitivity needed to engage in meaningful conversations across these differences and similarities? Will interventions be crafted that include the influences of meaning, power, history, and context to offer possibilities and solutions that confront assumptions and promote change on multiple levels?

Preparing students for this work requires a collaborative learning environment based on mutuality and transparency, and as with all discussions across difference, it is essential to create a climate where diversity, inclusion, and equity are discussed openly and freely and viewed as a normal and regular part of the field instruction agenda. This includes considerations of difference and similarities not only between the student and the individuals and communities they serve, but also between students and us as their supervisors. Educational assessments specifically ask questions that require us to describe and assess differences and similarities that exist between us and our students and between those served and staff in the setting. We are asked not only to identify these factors, we must consider how they influence the learning relationship and their influence on the student's experience in field education.

Much attention has been placed on helping students explore the world of the individuals and communities they work with. Less attention has been paid to how the influence of existing parallel differences and similarities in our supervisory relationships modulate or promote the goal of justice-based practice. Likewise, it is accepted that differences should not connote *better than* or *less than* but simply *different from*, but we have less understanding of how to manage the possible similarities that may exist between us. According to Pinderhughes (1989), "Attention only to similarities without attention to differences reinforces the orientation that all people are the same and invites ignoring or denial of difference. Attention only to difference without attention to similarities reinforces distancing, separation, and barriers between people" (p. 27). The demands of our times and the changing demographics of our student population and communities we serve require us to continue to heighten our awareness of these issues.

For example, although we know that the past shapes the current social, economic, racial, cultural, and political state of affairs, we must acknowledge that this past history also exists in the present. We cannot escape the fact that our work is influenced by this history and that current events evoke remnants of this legacy. These factors are in the room in all our supervisory sessions. They are in the space between us, the space that separates us. This also applies to relationships between students and the individuals and communities they serve. What specifically is held in this space? It holds our journeys, our histories, our current experiences as we move through supervision, and it is in this space that the work of teaching, learning and healing must be done. Practice competence begins with empathy and engagement, yet this cannot be achieved if we do not attend to what may separate us. The relationship is cemented when both parties have an understanding and compassion for the history that is brought with us into this space, the ancestors who exist in this space, the micro- and macroaggressions contained in this space, and the experiences we have of moving through the world without giving voice to the infringements of human rights that are also in this space. The climate we create begins from the start of the supervisory relationship, it communicates explicitly that race, oppression, power, and privilege are something we talk about in here. It needs to be made clear that given our country's legacy, we will not talk about it unless we intentionally commit together for these conversations to happen. It is important that this is seen as crucial, yet at the same time as ordinary, just something we do as social workers. Talking about identities, equity, and inclusion becomes as natural as breathing, and we consider it at every juncture in the student and field instructor relationship. This serves as a model for how students work with individuals and with the systems that provide barriers and supports to their work. Anything less clear says that this is something we don't talk about in here. The resulting implication is that we are asking our students and those they serve to leave a part of themselves at the door.

There are many teaching moments to use. For example, student reflections and recordings at all levels of practice are full of illustrations of potential value conflicts arising from differences or similarities in gender, sex at birth, sexual orientation, race, ethnicity, color, gender expression, social class and status, age, abilities, or religious and spiritual beliefs; therefore, it is important to encourage students to include their reactions, thoughts, and feelings as a regular part of their recordings and discussions. Yet we know that discussions on race and other dimensions of difference or social location often go unaddressed even when they emerge in student recordings or in supervisory sessions. A study of field instructors' responses to this question noted that field instructors were adept at describing diversity factors but hesitant to discuss how they would teach about issues of diversity (Marshack, Ortiz Hendricks, & Gladstein, 1994). Likewise, in a review of field instruction sessions, Maidment and Cooper (2002) identify challenges for field instructors in assisting students to acknowledge instances of diversity and oppression in their work and to recognize the global influences that may be operating. The field instructors used several methods to facilitate awareness of socially constructed understandings of difference but "made no overt references to aspects of power, inequity, oppression or exclusion" (p. 406). A diversity training model delivered to field instructors aimed to address "gaps in the ability of instructors to directly address cultural concerns with student supervisees" (Armour, Bain, & Rubio, 2004, p. 27) reports that following this training, improvements in field instructor attention to diversity issues were encouraging, and the authors argue for continued training. They call attention to the limitations of the pilot study and recommend replication. Clearly, replications of these studies are overdue.

At the same time, whether explicitly present or not, diversity issues and issues of difference and social location manifest themselves as the elephant in the middle of the room. Another way of describing this dynamic is to consider the piece of furniture in the middle of the room that we ignore, deny, and walk around even as it remains positioned in an awkward place, obstructing the flow and creating barriers for movement (Williams, 1991). Instead, we aim to put our hands on that obstruction and slowly move it to a place where it is most useful, enhancing the flow and eliminating barriers for movement and connection. This is our goal as we increase our capacity to engage in these critical dialogues. These conversations are the key to understanding; they bridge the distance between us and our students, and they promote a meaningful and authentic relationship in supervision.

Challenging Dialogues: Starting With Ourselves

According to Hardy (2016), "Being a good steward of effective racial conversations requires one to 'know thyself,' particularly in terms of the relative power and privilege that one holds in a relationship" (p. 139). As we undertake the role of field instructor, we are committing to increasing our consciousness about the total human experience; however, we need to begin with ourselves. Acknowledging where we stand in relation to our experiences of initiating these conversations or in facilitating them includes being honest about how comfortable we are in these situations and what we will do to increase our abilities to ride the wave of uncertainty often created. This may involve embracing the opportunity to learn alongside our students, committing to tackling the next issue that arises, seeking support, or embarking on new learning (Southern Poverty Law Center, 2017).

Identifying the obstacles that prevent us from initiating these conversations involves self-reflection and techniques of mindful practice, which promote tolerance of the ambiguity and discomfort often associated with this work. For example, Brookfield (2014) describes a collaborative of White educators he meets with to educate one another about White supremacy; they discuss how to recognize it and how to change and challenge it once it is recognized. The questions the group members pose to each other provide some guidance to us here:

> (a) How is racism learned from dominant ideology? (b) How do racist impulses continue to manifest themselves in actions? (c) What are ways to identify these? (d) How are our racist leanings interrupted by disruptive experience? and (e) How do we challenge and push back against them? (p. 90)

We must be patient with ourselves, admit to our privileged and subjugated selves and commit to strengthening our resolve to progress for ourselves, our students, and those we serve.

Supervisory conversations that promote growth in this area are linked to how skilled the field instructor is in facilitating the dialogues that occur; therefore, we need to commit to consider the previous questions, expand our knowledge, and keep our skills in this area current. To stress this point, much has been written about how students of color or LGBTQ+TS students experience microaggressions when the classroom professor is not skilled (Dentato, Craig, Lloyd, Kelly, Wright & Austin, 2017 Franks & Yoshioka, 2008; Messinger, 2007; Sue, 2010). Microaggressions can occur at any time and are more common in a situation (likely in many field placements) where the student is the only student of color, a member of the LGBTQ+TS community, or is from an otherwise unrepresented religious community or population.

Microaggressions may be experienced from actions by our colleagues in the field placement or by our own actions.

> Consider a 45-year-old Puerto Rican student who is placed in a community setting addressing a range of issues in a politically conservative rural community. She has worked as an office manager in a family business, and she approaches her work and education with sincerity and maturity. Her White field instructor has provided successful field education to a range of students over many years. The staff is composed of predominantly White workers; the population served ranges from White middle-class to a mixed population of low-income and unemployed constituents.
>
> The student was assigned a project to research statistics regarding youth opioid substance abuse in the community to provide information for a board meeting that was reviewing threatened services to the agency's adolescent substance abuse program. The student created a presentation, which after review by the field instructor, was accepted to be used at the board meeting. Asked when the presentation would take place, the field instructor stated it would happen on a day the student was not in placement, and the student was not required to be there. Although the student felt dismissed, she asked whether she could attend and if she would be allowed to present her work. The field instructor responded that of course she was welcome to attend; she went on to say that the board was very demanding, and she herself would make the presentation. She added that the student should feel free to add any comments during the meeting.
>
> The next day the student discussed this situation in class and was guided by her classroom professor to discuss her concerns with her field liaison. The student remembered her field liaison's facilitation of a session on issues of diversity, power, and privilege, so she was comfortable approaching her. In their meeting the student was clearly ambivalent, upset, and angry. Should she go to the board meeting? If she went, would she be able to contain her anger while her work was being presented by someone else? Would her comments be invited, or would she have to butt in? Did her field instructor have so little confidence in her abilities that she preferred that she not be there? Did the field instructor use the term *demanding* to diffuse concerns that the student is Puerto Rican and not up to the challenge? If she presented the research, would it place the program's future in jeopardy? Was she being too sensitive? Was she feeling

> this way because she felt her work was not being recognized, or was it the racial and ethnic overtones? Could she continue to work with this field instructor for the remainder of the year?

In this example, the questions and concerns are addressed openly between the field liaison and the student. The field liaison asked the student how she would like to proceed. They talked about the student's different levels of concern and how the student could discuss them with the field instructor or how they could approach this together. The student did not feel able to bring her concerns to the field instructor either alone or with the field liaison. Instead, together they decided that the liaison would connect with the field instructor to understand this situation more clearly. They agreed on how she would discuss the student's concerns. This discussion allowed the student to edit and frame how her voice would be represented.

The field liaison had her own questions. The field instructor seemed to be focused on the program and was not seeing how her behavior might affect the student and be experienced as a microaggression. Further,

> Was this field instructor unable to serve this student?
> Was the setting blind to the implications of having a Puerto Rican student in this otherwise White organization? Other students of color had been placed there before; did they experience similar problems but remained silent rather than raise concerns?
> Would the field instructor respond to requests to include this student in the presentation? Could the student continue in this learning situation?
> How should field education faculty and staff address disproportionate racial representation in placement settings and the effects on students? This issue may be included in the SIFI for new field instructors, but what needs to be done for experienced field instructors? What more should field education faculty and staff do to support students of color who are placed in settings that employ predominantly White staff and serve predominately White populations?

This situation was resolved in the best possible manner. The student felt supported in recounting her experience. She felt empowered and protected by lending her voice to the field liaison. The field instructor responded with humility at her insensitivity. She saw that she missed an opportunity to reflect and critically think about her hesitancies and the effect this had on her student, who already was experiencing some marginalization in a predominantly White office environment. She was eager to engage in a conversation about this incident with her student and acknowledge that although she may have been acting to protect her student, she was doing so without explicitly discussing this with the student, and that she was not holding her setting and board accountable for the existing pervasive dominant worldviews that may be more oppressive than helpful for staff and the community served. She was ready to introduce changes in how the presentation would be managed.

The student was included in the presentation in a plan mutually agreed on that also involved acknowledging the student's role in preparing the material; however, the field instructor needed the intervention of the field liaison to fully respond to the student. The student's responses to this situation needed attention whether the field instructor initially responded because of a conflict of interest between meeting her responsibilities to her setting and to her student, whether she was protecting the student from potential difficulties from a challenging, mostly White board, whether she was avoiding engaging in significant work with the board regarding their oppressive structures, or whether she simply missed the significance of the situation. The field liaison's involvement was indispensable to the creation of space for the dialogue to occur and to secure the possibility for future learning for all involved.

> Consider another example in which an intern asks a youth she is working with what pronoun she should use when referring to the youth. The youth says *she*. Despite this, the intern continues to slip and say *he*. The intern mentioned this in passing to her field instructor, not understanding the full weight of what she was sharing. The field instructor recognized the importance of this communication and prompted a discussion in supervision with the student to consider the possibility of the youth experiencing this as a microaggression. Among the questions posed, the field instructor asked how the youth might experience the intern's slip of the tongue. Is it a signal to the youth that it is impossible for her to be accepted as she? Is the intern signaling her lack of acceptance or respect for the youth? Is the youth adding this interchange to the many others she experiences? The discussion proceeds to consider how the intern might address validation of and respect for the youth's identity.

> The ensuing discussion acknowledged that simply apologizing and saying "I am sorry" is inadequate. The intern is assisted in seeing that her continued use of *he* assaults the youth's identity. She needs to commit to slowing down her conversations to help her become more mindful and intentional as she demonstrates the respect she intends to show to this youth. This discussion offers an opportunity for a meaningful conversation with the youth that invites understanding of the youth's experiences. They can agree that the youth can hold the intern to a higher standard of demonstrating respect now that they have openly shared and discussed this.

These examples illustrate how easily such dialogues on difference, historical trauma, and microaggressions can be shut down and submerged. The second example shows the field instructor's recognition of a teachable moment in which they discuss the skills and renewed awareness the intern will need to return to interaction with this youth. It also provides an opportunity for the field instructor to educate her student on heteronormative values and binary gender norms. The intern is supported in exploring her awkwardness in failing to affirm the youth's gender identity and commits to becoming more mindful and conscientious to establish a stronger foundation, so engagement and trust can ensue.

In the first example, the student felt unable to express her thoughts and feelings directly to her field instructor. These conversations were not part of their ongoing supervision, and therefore the student did not have any experience in how her concerns might be taken. She could not trust that her voice would be heard in the way she intended. Also, at any step along the way, the student's expression of confusion or anger could have been stifled or explained away. The classroom professor might not have responded to the student's concerns. Either the professor or field liaison might have responded dismissively, saying, for example,

> Perhaps your field instructor did not require your attendance and wanted to protect your time. Do you think you might be oversensitive to your field instructor's remarks? After all, services are being cut in that area, and your field instructor may be deciding based on her experience and the delicacy of the program's future.

Any number of responses from any of the actors might have created a very different outcome. It is important to note the field liaison's role in facilitating challenging conversations and their part in paving a path for the student. As committed players in this work, we move it forward and invite others to join us.

The development of trust will be hampered if field instructors do not invite these discussions and if students feel they either need to put parts of themselves aside or that these issues are not important (Garran & Rasmussen, 2014; Knight, 2016). Bringing multiple dimensions of identity into the room helps to build a relationship where openness and trust can emerge, and the ability to think through diversity dilemmas can occur naturally. The link to the purposes of our professional mission commits us to the task and ensures a responsive approach that moves us toward the removal of barriers that perpetuate obstacles to the achievement of equity. Justice-based field instruction creates a climate in which these issues are discussed openly and are viewed as a normal and regular part of the supervisory process because they are integral to practice, and students are given the support and skills to seize the opportunities for these conversations to occur with those they serve. We are all products of socialization; we hold prejudices, biases, and racist and homophobic attitudes that are reinforced by families, friends, neighbors, the media, and so on throughout our formative and adult years. Because racism and privilege are inherent in our society, we cannot be blamed for learning what we were taught but we do have the responsibility to learn more about our role in maintaining systems of dominance and oppression and the role we undertake in undoing them as social workers. This is especially significant in a profession where the majority of those we serve are people from historically marginalized populations, and most of those serving them are White. To move forward, we must be accountable to, and authentic with, ourselves and others; this includes a continual examination of how our profession contributes to benefiting from and perpetuating oppressive systems. This requires us to intentionally discuss power, privilege, and systemic racism at every opportunity to move the discourse forward and support our students' abilities in this arena.

An analysis of power adapted from the People's Institute for Survival and Beyond (Chisom & Washington, 1997) focuses on understanding what racism is, where it comes from, how it functions, why it persists, and how it can be undone. The Undoing Racism training (www.pisab.org) helps us think critically and reflect on the key question of why people are poor and discuss the subsequent implications for our profession and professional role. Likewise, the structural analysis of power provides an antiracist lens that examines power and privilege historically and in the present. It examines the role we all play as gatekeepers in maintaining the social arrangements that maintain racism.

Challenging Dialogues: Starting the Conversation

So what does a conversation on diversity, equity, and inclusion look like? If this is not something we already do, it can be difficult to see how we might interject issues of identity, power, and privilege into a conversation. At first it may feel artificial or awkward. Even small steps start the process, and there are many ways to begin.

We have already suggested that field instructors must not wait for students to raise these issues or wait for what seems to be the perfect moment. We must initiate challenging dialogues regarding justice with students from the beginning of the placement experience, not just when an obvious need arises (Armour et al., 2004; O'Neill & del Mar Fariña, 2018). Chapter 1 introduces the indispensable part mutuality plays in field education supervisory relationships and how we can act to incorporate it. Mutuality sets the stage.

A public syllabus statement from the Harriet W. Sheridan Center for Teaching and Learning (2018) at Brown University, which offers extensive useful information on teaching, provides an example. Borrowing from this outline, starting with an acknowledgment that although we aim for a more just world where the effects of injustice are ameliorated, the world we live in contains many intractable obstacles associated to biases and prejudices that affect us and the individuals and communities we serve. We might then say, "together we can build our relationship on our aspirations and aims. I will raise diversity and issues of justice as we work together, and I would like you to do so also. It is important to me that we work at this together so that we create an environment that supports our learning and that we might grow in our comfort and expertise to talk about these issues, especially on how they affect the work we will be doing together and the work that you will be doing within this setting."

This introduction sets the tone for the seriousness of our intention to provide practice, experience, and development of skills in having these conversations so that students gain greater confidence and comfort in talking with us and others about these issues.

To achieve an environment that supports challenging conversations, we must reconsider what we mean by safety, challenge normative constructs of safe spaces, and act on these different meanings for students from historically marginalized groups and less privileged social locations (Arato & Clemens,

2013; Garran & Rasmussen, 2014, Sensoy & DiAngelo, 2014). However, being safe is not the same as being comfortable. The work we do often causes discomfort (Hardy, 2017) and requires a sense of bravery and courage (Arato & Clemens, 2013). This means that safety and comfort need to be continually assessed for ourselves, our students, and the individuals and communities we serve. We have the responsibility for setting ground rules and clarifying expectations (Arato & Clemens, 2013). At the same time, we need to increase our tolerance and that of our students for the discomfort and help with the management of feelings, fears, and projections that emerge in such socially circumscribed discussions (Pinderhughes, 1989). The aim is to affirm facilitation that prepares those involved for the bravery and courage required to engage in conversations across difference (Arato & Clemens, 2013), conversations that our culture, social norms, and history have ill prepared us for. In this way, we model how to apply our self-awareness and self-regulation to the work and how to create a climate for such discussions with those we serve. More important, we ensure that our students apply this learning in their work and that we monitor their applications to enable the development of increased skills.

Further, the concept of safety implies that safety is a realistic goal or that only conversations on social justice are dangerous, when in fact people of color may experience situations of learning generally as potentially hostile places and especially so when the topic is justice or race. These nuances are linked to the differences in positionality between students and field instructors in supervisory relationships that resemble authoritarian frameworks in which power differentials exclude subjugated voices (Sensoy & DiAngelo, 2014).

We aim to foster what Freire (1993) refers to as a problem-posing approach to education, in which

> people develop their power to perceive critically the way they exist in the world with which and in which they find themselves; they come to see the world not as a static reality, but as a reality in process, in transformation. (p. 83)

In this way, and by supporting conversations and practice that incorporate a justice-based framework, students are encouraged to consider themselves as activists and change agents, locally and globally, to eliminate systems of oppression affecting people's lives. They experience how the power of reconstructing what we know changes harmful and brutalizing systems of oppression (Anderson & Collins, 2015; Dominelli, 2017; Finn, 2016; Mullaly, 2002, 2010; Tuck & Yang, 2012). Once we embrace the fact that many parts of ourselves exist at the same time and that we can be privileged and subjugated and possess dominant and nondominant statuses, we inherently crush the barriers between these sides of ourselves, and we are ready to engage and promote dialogues that address the implications of this analysis for others (Adams, Bell, Goodman, & Joshi, 2016; Crenshaw, 1993; Yan & Wong, 2005).

When students question the importance of this discussion, as they might, we explain that just as it is important to understand the perspective of family-centered practice whether or not we see whole families, our professional value of the importance of human relationships requires us to keep a relationship perspective in our work. Similarly, it is as important to possess a justice framework as a lens and perspective for approaching those seeking help in a society that often marginalizes and oppresses those in need. It is a lens that helps focus our attention on issues we might otherwise skip or miss, often stemming from our own worldviews and privileged statuses; the more we fine-tune our view on these issues, the more likely we will target them for change. We remind students of our profession's commitment to the ecological systems theory that includes a person-in-environment perspective, which taken together responds to human need and social reform; problems are often rooted in the context and environment surrounding individuals. This stresses that these concerns should not be polarized, and they will be examined and discussed in field education supervision.

> Consider an example in field education that involves a White generalist practice level male student, who is working with youths in a mixed community youth agency. The field instructor notices that the intern's work with a Black high school student lacks empathy for her dilemma; she is wondering whether she should drop out of her high school step dance team as she is struggling academically. Rather than exploring this dilemma, he affirms her inclination to drop out of the team and comments that it would certainly give her more time to study. In supervision, the field instructor asks him to consider this interaction more closely. She asks what step dancing might mean to this young woman. He responded that she enjoys the activity, but she recognizes how much time it takes from her study time. As the conversation continued, the field instructor sensed some disconnection in the intern's remarks. As their discussion progressed, she asked how his being White and male might affect his work with this youth. He responded, "Well why should it? It

makes no difference to me whether she is Black or White or whatever. It doesn't matter that I am working with a man or woman, I treat everyone the same." The field instructor asked, "What would it mean to you if you found out it does make a difference? Is the goal to treat everyone the same? What if it matters to her?" The field instructor continues to explore, interspersing the discussion with questions such as the following:

> What supports does she have, and what messages is she receiving from these supports on this issue?
> What if being on the step dance team means more to her than the time involved? What would she be losing if she drops out? What connections with friends are involved? Is participation a means to achieve acceptance? Being free to express herself? What does doing well academically mean to her?
> How can your effort to help her think about what is important to her represent something different in her experience when a White man in a position of power may help her consider the options in front of her or instead assume his values over hers? What would your problem-solving look like with attention to these issues?

This example aims to increase the understanding of how issues of identity affect our work. The aim is to enhance understanding to facilitate change in the way the student intervenes.

> Consider the following example for use within supervision to discuss interventions on the micro level while thinking about the broader systemic issues that may bolster or hinder any efforts toward change. Johnny, age 8, is referred for individual counseling because of underperformance in his classes. His social functioning is causing concern, and he is increasingly socially isolated from peer interaction. Johnny is a child of small stature and slim build; he presents as quiet and shy. Lately he has often been tired and falls asleep during class, and other students have begun to laugh at him and call him Sleepy Eyes. His teachers are worried because this picture is a contrast to Johnny's previous performance. You learn that his father is an undocumented immigrant from Malaysia who

is being charged with driving without a license and is under threat of deportation. For safety, he is living with family members in a different state, and Johnny's mother now works nights at a local factory.

During discussion, you ask how your student understands the presenting problem. You introduce concepts of ecological systems theory and take your student beyond understanding how to bolster Johnny's ability to function in his environment and assessing his resiliency to which structural components of his situation need adjustment and change. In addition, consider

> How does your student's reflections on power, privilege, and oppression influence the way this situation is viewed, or what interventions are prioritized?
> What thoughts does your student have regarding the responsibility of Johnny's school in providing supports for Johnny? What possible interventions might be needed on the individual, family, school, community, and interstate levels? What possible societal structures and cultural assumptions are creating challenges to a resolution of Johnny's performance and functioning? Are global issues and policies influencing this situation? How might your student work with Johnny, his classmates and parents to tackle the larger macro issues that are influencing or perhaps creating this micro situation?
> How does your student view Johnny's experience of isolation from his peers? What knowledge or experiences are your student drawing from regarding understanding of bullying in school and interventions that may be used? What responsibilities are identified regarding other students struggling with similar challenges? What interventions are needed to address Johnny's classmates' treatment of him? How can the school provide support and education on racial slurs, hurtful behaviors, and acceptance?
> What are the racial components in the nickname Sleepy Eyes? How can your student begin to broach these issues in discussions with Johnny? How would the discussion change if the social work student is a student of color? White? A woman or a man?

In this example, the services offered may not incorporate programs that meet all of Johnny's and his family's needs. A justice-based perspective to field education demands us to consider the gains that can be achieved by inspiring and generating student attention on the larger solutions regarding the lack of support to youths whose families are broken because of inadequate health care, the type or lack of employment, bullying in school, or immigration policies such as in this scenario. Enabling the student's consideration of these local and global issues spark greater understanding of Johnny's situation but they are also meant to inspire interventions that address more than the individual work that is undertaken with Johnny.

These two examples illustrate that the conversation can be introduced in a variety of ways, over a variety of issues. Expanding our lens to include an ecological perspective with a vision for working for equity and deconstruction of barriers to rights and justice ensures that situations and conditions are addressed when they previously were excluded from view.

Tasks and Responsibilities in Conversations Across Difference

Dr. Kenneth V. Hardy (2016, 2017), an expert in racial trauma and how to participate in and facilitate dialogues on race, outlines a "Privilege and Subjugated Task (PAST) Model" (2016, p. 125) that offers communication paths across the polarization created by the power of racial privilege. The model acknowledges the reality of these divides and assigns differing tasks for those in privileged positions from tasks assigned to those in subjugated positions.

Generic tasks for everyone might include being the expert in your own experience, not that of others; creating space for telling your own story; and making space for thoughts and feelings. Hardy's work is an essential contribution for preparing ourselves and our students. A suggested supervisory session would entail presenting his work, focusing the session on reactions to his conceptualizations, and then reaching for implications and applications.

Tasks of the privileged can be summarized as follows:

> Intentions are not the same as consequences. Acknowledge the effect and consequences of your actions. Intentions are the province of the privileged. Consequences are relegated to the subjugated. Focus the discussion on the consequences experienced.
> Resist false notions of equality. It is not helpful to equate suffering.

> Challenge the ahistorical approach; the past does affect the present; the privileged cannot understand the subjugated out of context. Validate the effects of history.
> Do not become a FOE (framer of others' experiences).
> Develop a thick skin; do not give up on connections with the subjugated even if initially rebuffed; continue going back and back, continue to try.

Following are tasks of the subjugated:

> Overcome learned voicelessness and advocate for oneself; unlearn the belief that it is not worth it to speak up.
> Learn to exhale the negative messages that have become internalized and lead to toxicity.
> Overcome the addiction to protect, educate, or change the privileged.
> Deal with one's own rage, channel it appropriately, rather than eradicating it. Shame is a major stumbling block for the privileged. Rage is a major stumbling block for the subjugated.

For example, a White student continues to use the word minority in her sessions with a Latinx mother she is seeing. The mother experiences this as "a punch in her gut" each time she hears it. All the mother hears is *minor*, but she says nothing. The student noticed some discomfort one day and remarks that the mother seemed troubled and asked if it was something she said. Instead of letting the student know how she felt or engaging in a conversation that could lead to increased understanding, the mother minimized the student's concerns. She chose to protect the student from the truth that it is offensive and hurtful to her to being continually referred to as a minority.

The student has a good working relationship with her field instructor, and when asked how things are going, the student lets her field instructor know that she is confused by the mother's discomfort during sessions. They examine the recent interaction more closely in the process recording and wonder together whether it is the student's use of the term minority and lack of exploration of the mother's lived experience as Latinx. The field instructor encourages her student to have a more direct conversation with this mother, and they role-play how the student might engage in the conversation. They used Hardy's (2016, 2017) tasks and responsibilities in challenging conversations on diversity-related content as a guide. The student was struck by the tasks for Whites especially, "Differentiate between intentions and consequences"

(Hardy, 2016, p. 127). It was as if a light bulb went off. The student told her field instructor that it wasn't her intent to say anything to hurt the mother, but she was able to acknowledge the effect of her actions on the mother. She understood Hardy's explanation that explaining intentions are an indulgence only permitted to the privileged, whereas the resulting consequences of miscommunication are usually borne by the subjugated (Hardy, 2017). They continued to talk about this and what was required of her to let go of her intent and allow herself to consider the experience of the mother that would not trigger an apology or minimize the effects on the mother.

The student felt armed with understanding and a commitment to act on this in her next meeting with this mother. She brought her understanding and her desire to move back so they could move forward together. She shared her wonderings and reflections on their work together. The mother listened and responded with tears in her eyes, thanking the student for an opportunity to talk about her struggles and to be acknowledged for more than her race.

Concepts of Power and Powerlessness

As can be seen above, the issues of power and powerlessness as expressed in privilege and subjugation, require special attention. Freire states that praxis is critical consciousness and social action; that is, we reflect and act on the world to transform it (Ginwright & Cammarota, 2002). To practice critical consciousness, we move through three stages of awareness: self, social, and global. Together these stages embrace issues of identity but also a historical and systemic analysis of issues of power and privilege and their effect on human interaction and connection. This includes an examination of (a) our social identities and their potential advantages and disadvantages; (b) our positionality and the way our multiple identities intersect, interact, and provide us with power, privileges, or powerlessness and limited privileges in a socially structured society; and (c) our assumptions and often one-dimensional and self-referenced view of the world (Adams, Bell, & Griffin, 2007). Engaging in these levels of critical self-awareness and self-reflection paves the way for justice-based field education.

Power in supervisory relationships. Power in supervisory relationships, or lack of it, exists for everyone to varying degrees (Tew, 2006). The reluctance to admit to the power we possess, the discomfort that is embodied in unequal power relationships, the compulsion to defend oneself against power and powerlessness, and the problematic behaviors that are used to maintain these defenses are all issues that make it difficult to manage dynamics in cross-cultural encounters and in field education. Understanding the degrees of power, its nuances, and how it differs, or is the same, for individuals can help students become aware of their own power. By becoming aware of issues of power and difference operative in our relationships with students, we move toward creating an environment where these issues can be discussed. By exploring our perceptions of the world, we give voice to alternative and indigenous perspectives and move beyond understanding and awareness to engage in action (Finn, 2016). Through this process we acquire the skills and strategies for engaging in and facilitating dialogues across difference and creating a capacity to affirm meaningful conversations that move toward change.

At the same time, just by the nature of field instruction supervision, our students are caught in a position of traditional subservience to us as the experts and evaluators, which we must actively work to balance. Of course, we are both these things, and our students also share these roles. They evaluate us, and they are experts on their own experience. Their voices and views matter; therefore, although the field instructor and student relationship is founded on power and authority (Foucault, 1980), a reframing of this learning relationship moves toward equality, mutuality, and co-learning. Opportunities for more honesty, collaboration, and sharing in learning shifts the power dynamic inherent in this relationship; this is also achieved by seeking opportunities to use and activate the student's expertise.

Likewise, as students are in a position of power over the people and communities they serve, that also requires balancing. They must learn to follow while learning to lead. These apparently contradictory stances are two sides of the coin. Students need support to assume their legitimate power in the learning relationship so that they may form similarly authentic professional relationships with those they serve. Helping students experience the power of followership while also assuming power in seemingly unequal relationships provides potent learning experiences (Kellerman, 2007). We model applying student expertise in the supervisory relationship, and students use a teaching and learning model of practice (Finn, 2016) to seek opportunities that engage others to use their own expertise and power.

We know the field instruction relationship is only a part of the internship experience. Often the context itself plays a huge part, and students may feel challenged in settings that are not deconstructing systems of racism or oppression; this is accentuated if the field instructor's role to model and create spaces for dialogue do not have agency-wide support. In these situations, the burden is on field instructors to raise awareness and teach and assist students in naming the structural systems of racism and other oppressive practices. The aim is to produce social workers who possess a structural lens that informs their views of challenges that go beyond simplistic explanations of individual characteristics, that is, a lens that sees how individuals are "constrained and shaped by structural factors" as well as by individual and interpersonal factors (Metzl & Hansen, 2014, p. 132). In this way, the student is supported to be actively engaged in analyzing and devising a response rather than complicit in ignoring the need.

> Consider the following example that offers a glimpse into the ways this might be achieved. A student returns to placement and finds her room reassigned to a new member of the staff. The student is told she must now share a desk with other part-time members of the staff. The director simply announced a change in the student's room assignment mid-year to a much smaller office without a phone that was shared by several personnel. The move occurred suddenly, without explanation to the field instructor or the student. In supervision the student stated that she felt unimportant and ignored. The field instructor saw her student's surprise and recognized this situation as an opportunity for learning about power and powerlessness. The field instructor assisted the student's extraction of the organizational implications of the room change from her emotional reaction to it and supported the student's wish to discuss the way it was handled with the director of the agency.

In this example a seemingly ordinary part of organizational life was incorporated into the student's educational experience, and the field instructor modeled how communication can occur with those in authority. Reminiscent of assertiveness training, the aim was not to achieve reassignment to the larger room or a move to another more private space but instead to facilitate the student's ability to explain the consequences of the director's decision and to advocate for how room assignments for students could be handled in the future. The field instructor assisted the student in exercising her power in gaining insight into the institution's decision-making processes. The student did not enter the conversation with winning as her goal, and she felt better for voicing her views and being heard (Bertrand Finch, Bacon, Klassen, & Wrase, 2003).

This field instructor recognized the situation as an opportunity to learn about power by directly addressing feelings of powerlessness. Unfortunately, a field instructor's own lack of power in the organization or existing political undercurrents often prevent this from occurring. More often such incidents pass without comment, or the student is told to accept the difficulties associated with institutional life and, by implication, to accept the powerless position of student status. In this manner, opportunities to facilitate learning regarding organizational structure and negotiating within hierarchical decision-making processes are often lost. Instead, this student was encouraged to consider her experience of powerlessness from the perspective of how it translates to the student's work with those she serves. At the same time, the field instructor modeled how it is possible to acknowledge, validate, and address feeling powerless while also providing an experience of empowerment and having one's voice heard.

The student was able to understand the importance of discussing her experience and finding words to move the discussion up through the agency's structure. Consider the learning opportunities missed if the actors in this situation were unable to recognize the importance of this seemingly ordinary part of organizational life from the student's point of view. If students retreat to intellectualization ("Oh, it doesn't matter") or to tangential material ("I know of other students who have had similar experiences"), we can respond in a respectful but firm manner that steers the discussion back to the emotional plane, for example, "Let's consider your position as a student in this situation. How does this play into your thoughts and feelings about not being consulted or informed about the pending move? Equally, how does your position affect opinions of what might be a legitimate response now, what might be possible in the future, or how you might work with an individual who is affected by a similar experience?"

How does this example change if we add dimensions of the actors' social identities in this situation? Imagine the director as a White man and the student as a Black woman, an American Indian woman, or an Asian woman? What if the director is a Black woman, and the student is a White man? How do the different identities at play affect the conversations and issues being managed and the learning that is at stake? How might these varying identities be used to enhance the learning for the student involved?

Power in communities. In addition to addressing the inherent issues of power in the supervisory relationship and in our settings, it is essential to examine the external issues of power that exist in the communities we serve. Our goal is to support students' understanding of structural oppression and systemic forces of domination that exist in the communities we serve and to recognize systems of inequity and how they continue unobstructed by our actions and service delivery in these communities (Finn, 2016). Global influences are not beyond the scope of consideration. These discussions provide opportunities for students to fully comprehend the intent of engaging in diversity and difference in practice and of advancing human rights. Simply discussing the populations and communities served by the placement setting is an engaging way of bringing students into the context of the work they will soon begin; that is, who is served by the setting and who lives in the community surrounding the agency. A conversational bridge can explore the student's understanding of the community and how it is that parts of the community are thriving, and others are marginalized, oppressed, or discriminated against. Finally, consider the possible consequences of these circumstances for the populations—and the multiple nations they may represent—likely to be served during the field education experience. Attending to how these realities affect the student's experience walking into supervision, the community, and the setting is also part of this work.

This introduces an opportunity to discuss the work being done to address the historical and current trauma experienced by populations served by the field placement setting. The intention is to make a justice-based lens directly applicable to the work undertaken. It also introduces tools and strategies for rights-based assessments and interventions that include stakeholder and constituent participation as a necessary and integral issue for discussion. For instance, discussing the skills and strategies needed to facilitate conversations that include constituent views about poverty, discrimination, lack of political power, oppression, and unequal opportunity in this community provides a platform for how field education supervision will contribute to the student's skill development. Equally, pointing to the realities of the existing current social and global context introduces additional components to the equation, for example, asking the student, "How might the larger societal debates and international conversations about unaccompanied minors, asylum seekers, refugees and immigrants affect the community and population we serve?" and " "Do you imagine that the people you will be working with might be curious about your own position on these issues?"

Concepts of Identity Theory and Intersectionality

It is proposed that discussions of diversity, difference, social location, and related content are integral to all teaching and practice efforts. Capability includes several significant factors, such as the capacity to develop authentic relationships and an ability to understand and value differences for their potential for dialogue and connection. Connection is characterized by working alongside or behind individuals and communities, learning to follow, guiding not directing movement toward change, lending and sharing our privilege and power, and acting as learners from our and others' lived experiences. This also requires an ability to recognize institutional arrangements that maintain racism, oppression, internalized oppression, dominance, and privilege (Franks & Riedel, 2008), and to recognize the costs of internalized dominance, privilege, and othering. It embraces a will to apply this understanding toward change.

Identity theory, including racial and sexual orientation identity (Franks, 2001; Helms, 1990; Pathy Solett & Koslow, 2015; Simoni, Meyers, & Walters, 2001; Sue & Sue, 2012), is key in developing an understanding of these complex levels of worldviews. Racial identity theory aids our ability to see what is involved in being authentic in cross-racial relationships. For example, early stages of White racial identity correlate with feelings of anxiety and discomfort, anger, and fear in our interactions with people of color, or feelings of guilt and shame manifest themselves in behaviors and attitudes that are expressed as wanting to help those poor victims, and which often translate into helping them be more like us (Franks, 2001; Helms, 1990). Early stages of identity in people of color imply an overidealization and identification with the dominant culture and may cause conflicts with other people of color who are at more advanced stages in their development where they have worked through these foundational stages and statuses and may have achieved more self-actualized places in professional relationships. In the way we integrate the work of such psychological theorists as Bowlby, Erikson, or Kohlberg in our consideration of case assignments, we need to familiarize ourselves with theories and models of White, Black, and Latinx racial identity, and sexual orientation identity (Cross, 1978; Helms, 1995; Simoni et al., 2001). This extends to an understanding of how these identities intersect, cultural dimensions as part of personality and human development (Carter, 1995), and consequences of racism and other forms of oppression and dominance on the beneficiaries as well as on the victims of these systems (Jones, 1997; Bowser & Hunt, 1996). This enables integration of these perspectives in our discussions with students.

The concept of intersectionality allows us to explore how our multiple social identities interact and connect, as well as how the effects of societal and cultural structures shape and influence us (Adams et al., 2016; Crenshaw, 1993, 2010; Mattsson, 2014). This concept examines race and class, two identities that have been hotly debated as one having more prevalence and importance than the other when, in fact, intersectionality examines the effect of race on class and vice versa. For example, a Black man and a White man who both identify as gay, experience homophobia, but their experiences cannot be assumed to be the same. An understanding of how racism affects the Black gay man leads to a deeper understanding of his identity and marginalization. Although the White gay man may experience White privilege and advantage in the form of higher paying jobs, better housing options, and acceptance in many circles, the Black gay man may experience oppression in the forms of racism and homophobia.

Exploring our privileged identities requires something different from us. It is often easier and more comfortable to explore those dimensions that place us in the oppressed, nondominant status; this relates to living in a world that obscures privileged statuses. Our aim is to increase our students' capacity to recognize and explore both dimensions of identity—the dominant and privileged and the nondominant and oppressed (Adams et al., 2016). A focus on one diminishes how these markers of identity interact and make us whole. Likewise, it may also occur that two or more subjugated aspects of our identities pull us in different directions, causing splits within ourselves instead of the potential of mitigation for each other (Crenshaw, 1993; Manuel, 2008).

Intersectionality supports the premise that we give up nothing of our oppressed selves to also hold and embrace our privileged selves and vice versa. In fact, to be truly human we need to do both—to hold all aspects of our identity. For example, White women might be proud and affirmed by their gender or sex and its rich history, struggle, and defining elements. They give up nothing of this essential identity to also embrace their dominant identity as White. However, when it comes to White women, a leap over their dominant status of race often occurs to get to their nondominant status of gender or sex; the work is to increase the capacity to hold both, to explore both, to identify with both. Manuel (2008) proposes that a bifurcation of identities challenges the links that are possible, for example, between Black women and White women over shared concerns such as sexual abuse or gun violence in our schools and communities. Likewise, Black and Latinx men are defined by their dominant male privilege and by their race and ethnicity. They might hold on to this male privilege even in a context that does not acknowledge their privilege and advantage because of the predominance of the nondominant status of their race and ethnicity (Franks & Riedel, 2008; Simoni et al., 2001). Their privilege provides power and is a buffer to their being disregarded.

To engage in this process is to be true to ourselves. We can then bring our whole selves into the cross-racial interaction; in field education this means a truly authentic professional relationship. Otherwise, we are in danger of sending the message that we are not open to hearing what others might wish to share. The same applies to any dimension of identity that places us in the dominant status; these are often more difficult to explore because exploration is not supported. Therefore, the challenge is to create opportunities for this to occur so the goal of analyzing intersectional identity is achieved. Because this is not something we are used to doing, it takes our full attention to increase our students' tolerance for the inherent ambiguity and discomfort. We do this while we continue to learn, grow, and seek support for ourselves (Franks & Insel, 2008).

A Changing Landscape of Terms

The NASW's (2015) *Standards and Indicators for the Achievement of Cultural Competence in Social Work Practice* combines two previous independent documents that address standards (NASW, 2001) and indicators for the achievement of these standards (NASW 2007a). The resulting document provides a useful guide for creating goals and objectives on cultural competence. One of the challenges in this work relates to the evolving understanding of terms and their limitations in reflecting changing contexts that shape their use.

For example, although it is widely accepted that the term *cultural competence* has been a helpful tool (NASW, 2001, 2015; Pinderhughes, 1989), it is also viewed as insufficient to address current understandings of what is involved (Abrams, & Moio, 2009; Almeida, Hernandez-Wolfe & Tubbs, 2011; Jani, Osteen, & Shipe, 2016; Kohi, Huber, & Faul, 2010). That is, we accept that competence in cultural understanding and practice is ongoing, and we are unlikely to ever be finished or deemed competent. We see that it is impossible to fully know another culture and that the term does not allow for the multiple complexities inherent in ever changing cultural values and experiences. Further, the term implies that once we know how a community behaves, acts, and thinks, we can apply our understanding to everyone in that group. This promotes stereotypes of groups of people and tends to place communities into categories. It is argued that the construct of cultural competence not only leads to generalization and stereotyping, it also presumes that cultural competence exists in a sphere of the other; that is, that cultural competence is required only in those situations where *that* culture is different from one's own, whereas cultural differences apply in every encounter. We all grow in different worlds with different experiences, and all therapeutic alliances require an analysis of existing oppressive systems while providing support for individuals in "challenging, resisting, and questioning the debilitating effects of privilege, power and oppression in their own lives and the lives of others" (Almeida et al., 2011, p. 50).

Although acknowledging that cultural competence is an ongoing enterprise, the NASW (2015) standards and indicators maintains the use of cultural competence and supports the goal of achieving competence. Standard 1.05, Cultural Awareness and Social Diversity, of the NASW's (2017) Code of Ethics substitutes for the term *cultural competence* with *cultural awareness*. The term *cultural awareness* subsumes cultural sensitivity and cultural humility and has been adopted as a descriptor that more closely identifies the modest stance required in the face of the intricate and multiple identities and realities people encounter. These terms imply a lifelong journey and address the false assumption of achieving cultural competence.

This causes some confusion as the terms suggest different points of view and seem in opposition to one another, or at least incomplete without the other. On the one hand, understanding that the concept of cultural competence is unclear and possesses limitations, greater clarity or other terms need to be used to avoid the associated pitfalls (Jani et al. 2016). On the other hand, the term continues in use, thus perpetuating its limitations. Replacing the term with cultural awareness, cultural humility, or cultural sensitivity is also inadequate. Awareness, humility, and sensitivity are essential precursors to achieving an empathetic approach to our work; however, they are inadequate on their own to work toward justice and to achieve the undoing of the endemic structures of marginalization and oppression.

Leading an alternative wave of understanding, the concept of cultural equity is used to guide our responses to the complexities of multiple identities across personal, social, and institutional locations (Almeida et al., 2011). Seeking cultural equity involves creating individualized supports that remove barriers that limit or prohibit access to resources; thus, working for cultural equity directs our attention toward change. The concept of cultural equity takes us beyond seeking humility and sensitivity in our practice. It implies more than just being aware of our values, attitudes, and worldviews and relies on the personal attributes of awareness, humility, and sensitivity. It presupposes an understanding of how multiple and interlacing dimensions of identity influence all stages and levels of practice (Franks et al., 1996). It calls us to action and it means we take a stand. Striving to achieve cultural equity involves breaking down the structures and systems that oppress, alienate, and divide.

Cultural equity, however, also is not enough. Liberation is what we are aiming for. Liberation represents sweeping change; it is undoing the effects and prompting the transformation of the causes of social oppression. The undoing and transformation must occur at the institutional level as well as at the level of group and individual interactions. Liberation involves changing oppressive behavioral patterns and eliminating oppressive attitudes and assumptions (Belkin-Martinez & Fleck-Henderson, 2014). Transformative processes include depathologizing others, acknowledging the effects of the environment, and encouraging self-awareness and self-actualization.

Belkin-Martinez & Fleck-Henderson (2014) present a model of practice based on concepts of liberation that moves to a holistic vision that is micro and macro. It acknowledges that people are affected by the different isms and forms of oppression in their daily lives, and it examines the personal, cultural, structural, and global factors that define and aggravate the nature of their problems. From this perspective, field instructors may ask students to define the problem at the three levels of awareness—individual, social, and global—and find solutions in each of these realms. For example, the work with a survivor of domestic violence who is approaching family court for an order of protection and who is fearful that her children may be taken away includes an analysis of the court system's control over communities with limited resources, an understanding of the court's treatment of women, a perspective of the powerlessness of people who are scrutinized for their mothering choices, and an understanding of interpersonal violence from a broader perspective than our own local societal lens. It leads to a conversation that is not focused on one person's inadequacies but on the inadequacies of local and global social structures and the consequences of viewing others as objects. It also promotes the possibility of the mother's and her community's self-actualization and ability to act in their own liberation. In this way, field education assignments generate understanding of these processes and may include active intervention in systems of oppression. Students gain experience in identifying how oppression is expressed in institutional life, cultural norms, and personal beliefs and behaviors and how global contexts and perspectives also play a part (Adams et al., 2007).

Our vision of what is involved in working across difference is affected by the terms and concepts at our disposal. Students are taught how to examine a situation from these different perspectives and from a critical analysis of the barriers facing those served. Seeking cultural competence is enhanced by our development of awareness, humility, and understanding. These attributes are applied to promoting cultural equity and creating a society based on liberation from the structural and institutional barriers that perpetuate inequality. Social change becomes integral to effective practice.

Summary

A justice-based approach to field education positions us next to or behind the people and communities and students we serve. We lead from behind or alongside; we support, lend, and share our access to resources, power, and privilege (Finn, 2016). As Narayan (1997) suggests, this approach enables us to treat people not as objects of rescue but as intellectual collaborators and political allies. This is a goal that is often hard to achieve, especially for those who carry privileged (often unexamined or unexplored) statuses attributed by society. Sharing and shedding the power and authority granted to us as helpers in this society are skills that need to be taught and monitored as a part of developing successful and authentic professional relationships from a justice-based perspective (Finn, 2016).

It is impossible to prepare students for the competencies of "engaging in diversity in practice," (CSWE, 2015a, p.7) and "advancing human and social, economic and environmental rights" (CSWE, 2015a, p.7) without increasing their capacity to engage in dialogues that tackle movement toward cultural equity and liberation. Challenging dialogues on the issues of identity, power, and privilege are critical to a justice-based model of field education (Chang et al., 2003; Green & Dekkers, 2010; Hair & O'Donoghue, 2009). Yet as we have declared throughout this chapter, little instruction on how to have these conversations is offered, and faculty members and field instructors themselves may not know how to facilitate them. So what does it take, and where do we begin?

We begin by admitting that nothing has prepared us to have these conversations especially in mixed company, that is with individuals who have different power statuses from our own. We just do not know how. In fact, given the legacy of racism, slavery, genocide, and settler colonialism in this country, we have been encouraged not to. We do not have models for how to manage them, we have not been taught how to begin, and social barriers prevent many of us from having contact with those different from ourselves and engaging in meaningful conversations with them. Even conversing about these dimensions of our identity with those we share similarities with is not easy.

Acknowledging this seems to be more difficult for those of us who feel that we should just somehow know how to begin these conversations. A resistance to admit that we do not know often results. This is followed by the reality that these conversations just do not happen. When difficult issues regarding identity, power, and privilege emerge, we move away from them, rather than move toward them. We do not have the capacity for the ambiguity and discomfort inherent in this work, so we stay away from it. However, these dialogues are essential. It is critical not only for competency in social work practice but for the possibility of a real connection and change to occur. There is no engagement without it; our interventions fall flat if we do not talk about what makes us similar, what makes us different, and how issues of power, privilege, oppression, and dominance shape how we came to be in the room together at a certain moment in time.

This work takes a body of knowledge, will, and skill to learn how to engage in challenging dialogues on diversity and justice-related content in mixed company (Sensoy & Di Angelo, 2014; Garran et al., 2014; Hardy, 2016). When we focus on learning, we can get better at it. When we talk to students about what happens in the classroom and field education with an open ear to the signals of how powerlessness and power influence interactions, we see how to put a voice to these dynamics. We often must take the lead. Once the first step is taken, it becomes possible to take the next step and then the next.

We propose the previous discussion as a beginning conception of facilitating challenging dialogues in field education supervision. The discussion presumes several conditions. First, that one's willingness to engage in this work is embedded in an ongoing and lifelong commitment of developing critical consciousness to achieve greater self-awareness and a willingness to engage in an analysis of power and privilege that includes understanding their effects on human interactions. Second, understanding safety is different from being comfortable, and conditions for feeling safe may be different for those from historically marginalized and less privileged social locations. Third, as these dialogues are not only challenging but often taboo, we must be prepared to manage the barriers within ourselves that define these conversations as off limits. Resources exist to help us including training programs and educational offerings from social work programs and offices of field education.

Once we acknowledge that we are not fully prepared with the skills required, we search our heart for our will to proceed. Both are needed—the commitment and the skill. Our professional skills go a long way in helping us move forward. The strength of our determination carries us over the hurdles. Finally, honesty with those we engage in dialogue creates a bridge for the conversation to occur and continue.

Emphasis on field instructor training to facilitate these challenging conversations is necessary. Some offices of field education are paving the way in teaching field educators to engage in the dialogues and conversations that emerge when one teaches according to a justice-based model. Increasing student capacity for this work certainly requires faculty members and field educators to be better prepared to teach in the context of shifting paradigms of a both/and worldview and to increase tolerance for the inherent ambiguity and discomfort involved. That is, not to just talk about it but to model it across the curriculum and in field education.

A collaboration between social work programs and placement settings to create training sessions would be a powerful means to achieve progress. These trainings could occur at centrally located settings to accommodate personnel and to include staff from across different locations. Sessions led by a trained facilitator that focus on the promotion of critical consciousness and self-awareness and are based on a joint commitment to student education will push the profession and service delivery forward. Most important, incorporating an antiracist framework will also add to the purpose and work of the organization (Carten, Siskind, & Pender Greene, 2016; Miller & Garran, 2017). Even if the field instructor is alone in this vision, it can still be possible to offer insights and discussions with students to support a justice-based work ethos that will influence the way students treat and serve community members (Soheilian, Inman, Klinger, Isenberg, & Kulp, 2014).

Although schools of social work in Britain, Australia, and Canada are further advanced in their inclusion of justice-based perspectives in teaching and practice than those in the United States (Reisch, 2011), U.S. schools of social work are increasingly framing their curricula to include courses on antiracism, antioppression, and decolonizing social work. We look for support from wherever we can find it; the school's field liaison or director of field education, outside training, the local NASW chapter are some familiar resources. The call for additional supports can have a ripple effect as seen across schools of social work; students' requests for antioppressive education filter down to classrooms and involve administrative changes in policy, hiring of faculty, websites, and curriculum changes that espouse commitment to inclusive and antioppressive practices. The response cannot just be at the individual social work school level. Placement settings and field instructors must be a part of the interventions and the strategies to deconstructing these oppressive systems (Carten et al., 2016; Miller & Garran, 2017). Social workers must demand from our profession that we and our institutions are held accountable for incorporating justice-based principles in our work and demand that we incorporate the voices of our scholars, activists, and neighbors from many communities that have been erased, silenced, and misappropriated by colonizing worldviews. This accountability should be evident in our licensing exams, in moving competencies past cultural competence, and using diversity and human rights in the practice of justice including restorative justice, equity and liberation.

Familiarizing ourselves in the way the social work program introduces this content provides a bridge for us and our students as we gain experience and knowledge in this educational shift. Additionally, we can build on these experiences by developing assignments, recording formats, tasks, and dialogues that emphasize a justice-based framework. Each opportunity provided for students to act on their growing understanding of these issues provides an incremental synthesis and integration in their application to practice and to their capacity to advance justice for others and themselves.

CHAPTER 2 APPENDIX

Building on the content of Chapter 2, this appendix contains several summaries and tools. The first is a summary based on Pinderhughes' (1989) seminal work. Next, tips on conducting challenging dialogues is provided. This is followed by an outline for a structured interview that can be conducted with your student, or for self-review and reflection. Five scenarios are presented on religious oppression, within-group differences and internalized oppression and privilege, race and racism, sexism, and ableism. Finally, an extract from a student group process recording that shows the student's efforts to promote a discussion on microaggressions is included.

Basic Assumptions

Power touches all levels of functioning for the oppressed and the privileged alike. This means that students may experience oppression and feel powerless related to their status as students and our relationship to them requires us to facilitate discussions about their power and privilege. The seminal work of Elaine Pinderhughes, *Understanding Race, Ethnicity and Power* (1989), continues to offer guidance and inspiration in support of a justice-based framework to social work education and practice. Although conceived in an earlier time, her wisdom remains pertinent. Her discussion of basic assumptions (pp. 212-213) that underly her approach to cross-cultural interactions inform our work. We have benefited from her insights and provide excerpts here applied to our work with students.

> Students "need to feel predominately positive about their cultural identity and group connectedness, although some ambivalence is to be expected." (p. 212)
> "Clarity concerning values, including value conflicts... enhances functioning." (p. 212)
> "When persons of different cultural backgrounds interact, they need validation and acceptance of their cultural

identity. However, this carries a risk, since values may differ and learned perceptions of the other may represent distortions and bias." (p. 212)
- "Distortion and bias take on greater significance when they are used to justify power arrangements that oppress and exploit victims, as in the case of class and racial categorizations, discrimination, and other forms of oppression." (p. 212)
- Students need us to support their reflection on generalities and specifics and on sameness and difference to encourage their critical analysis of these issues. This requires us to tackle complexity and ambiguity, values, cultural identity and group connectedness to protect against concrete thinking, generalization, and oversimplification of multifaceted issues of social identity and diversity.
- Therefore, we must assist our students to "transcend distortions and biases because they are destructive to effective work, and they undermine the values and goals of service delivery." (p. 212)
- Our work with students seeks to understand "internalized distortions and preconceptions, their etiology, and the purposes they serve" (p. 212). We also have a responsibility to seek change of these distortions and biases and the societal structures they justify.
- A relationship where "there is trust and support enables the self-examination necessary to clarify values, confront racial and other cultural biases, and to understand their etiology, purpose and benefits, including costs to beneficiaries and victims." (p. 213)
- "Emotional growth occurs through self-confrontation and interaction with others" (p. 213). If managed with sensitivity and respect, conflict promotes growth.
- Understanding one's power, or lack of it, "deepens self-understanding in the social context and offers an opportunity to avoid embracing power for destructive or selfish purposes" (p.213).

Some Tips on Having Challenging Dialogues in Justice-Based Field Instruction

The following list of tips are derived from the text of Chapter 2 and provide a reminder and support to the task of conducting challenging dialogues in field education supervision.

- Neutralize the anxiety that is aroused by interactions across difference. Initiate dialogue about the meaning of diversity identity, social location, attitudes about culture, and the psychological damage and uses of maintaining biases.
- Recognize that conversations on race require certain tasks and responsibilities for the privileged and the subjugated. Familiarize yourself with your tasks and responsibilities as defined by Hardy (2016) and summarized in Chapter 2.
- Support awareness of your student's identities and positions of power and powerlessness. Increased awareness of one's background and intersecting identities foster more effective cross-cultural interactions.
- Explore how dimensions of identity and issues of power and powerlessness influence the various levels of human functioning. Focus on how behaviors, feelings, and assumptions influence decision- making and service delivery.
- Support your student in conducting a structural analysis of oppression and dominance. Discuss the implications of historical and current trauma and daily microaggressions for an understanding of the communities they serve. Compare this knowledge to where the student lives. Examine how global perspectives influence this analysis.
- Model the importance of these discussions. By conducting these conversations in supervision, with your colleagues in the hallway, with individuals in waiting rooms, with community leaders and constituents, and in staff meetings and training, you model these conversations as being essential to social work practice.
- Craft assignments and discussions that engage students in practicing their skills including, reflections, articulation, and action, on several levels. Much of what is presented

here begins in the supervisory relationship with the aim to prepare students to apply this knowledge and understanding to their work.

A Structured Interview on Dimensions of Difference, Identity, and Social Location

The structured interview guides a self-examination process that we all must go through. For individual reflection, in pairs, in small-group discussions, or with your student, review the following questions and reflect on how you would answer them. The aim of this interview is to promote consideration of the various dimensions of difference, identity, and social location.

1. How would you define your cultural heritage? Who are your ancestors? How important are they in your everyday life? Include as many dimensions of your heritage and identity as possible, such as multiple generations, race, ethnicity, social class, nationhood, color, religion, sexual orientation, gender, sex at birth, languages spoken, abilities, national or regional affiliation, mental and physical abilities and immigration experience. Organize this information on a genogram or family tree. The student and field instructor can do this together in an early supervisory session as part of establishing discussions of these issues as part of the day-to-day work of supervision.
2. What were the values, norms, beliefs, and behaviors you grew up with? For example, what were your family of origin's structure and norms of behavior? How do you define family? What was the approach to child rearing, and how were you disciplined? Were there other relatives around during your childhood? What role did your grandparents play in your family of origin?
3. What is your primary reference group identity at this stage of your life? Include as many dimensions as possible in your identity, such as generation, gender, race, ethnicity, social class, religion, sexual orientation, languages spoken, and abilities.
4. When did you first become aware of yourself as different and unique from others? As similar?
5. What messages did you receive from others (e.g., parents, teachers, religious and community leaders, peers) about

these dimensions of your identity? How were these messages delivered?
6. What are the most affirming and empowering aspects of your identity and why? What do you like most about this identity? What parts of your identity give you joy?
7. Which dimensions of your identity are the most troublesome and difficult to manage and why? Are there any painful experiences associated with your heritage that continue to affect you today?
8. Have you ever tried to ignore, deny, or reject any dimension of your identity, and if so, why? Which dimensions of your identity do you need to work on and why?
9. What generalizations do people make about you that reflect their misinformation about some aspect of your group identity? What would you like to teach people who are not of your group about your heritage and identity?
10. What would your life be like if you did not have some of these dimensions of your identity (e.g., your race, religion, color, sexual orientation)?
11. Which dimensions of your identity are most helpful and least helpful to you as a social worker?
12. What are the implications for your identification as a social work professional? How does this affect your ability to practice from a justice-based framework?

Student Scenarios to Promote Dialogue in Field Instruction

The following five scenarios deal with different situations dealing with religious oppression, within group differences and internalized oppression and privilege, race and racism, sexism and genderism, and ableism. They provide a glimpse into sometimes difficult situations and provide questions to support the readers' consideration of the issues raised.

Religious Oppression

A White woman student is running a group for parents. A Black group member has been talking more and more about his religious views and beliefs. In a recent session this man talks about ways to use prayer to ease pain and anxiety and begins to pray in the group. Two group members join him in prayer, and other group members look uncomfortable. The student interrupts, saying, "We understand that your faith is very important to you, but we are here to talk about ways to raise our children and not to pray." The group member says that one cannot raise healthy children without a belief in God. He asks group members whether they agree with him.

The student is uncomfortable and distressed by this confrontation, and she is not sure how to proceed. She feels her leadership in the group is being challenged; she has never faced this situation before, and it is confusing. The student was raised in a religious family, but she is now nonreligious and a little conflicted about the place of religion in her life as an adult. She responds to the group that sharing religious beliefs is important, but they have come together for help with being parents. The student asks the group whether they should get back to their common purpose for being together. Everyone agrees, including the member who had led the group in prayer. No one challenges whether a discussion on religion is part of the group's common purpose. In a subsequent session a parent says that her adolescent son has just found out that his girlfriend is pregnant. The member who previously led the group in prayer tells the parent that abortion is a sin and urges her to put her faith in God. The group erupts into a heated discussion about the pros and cons of abortion. The group member dramatically claims that he cannot go against his religious beliefs and that he will have to quit this "sinful" group.

Consider the following issues raised by this scenario:

> If you are the field instructor, what are your immediate reactions to this scenario based on your own beliefs and positionality?
> How can the field instructor support the integration of the competing demands witnessed in this scenario with the student? How might a dialogue about difference and similarities create pathways to possible solutions for the student in supervision and her work with this group?
> What issues of group contracting are influencing the student's success as a group facilitator? What skills are required of her to be supportive to the group's development?
> What issues of power and privilege are operating? How are these issues shaping this situation?

› What are the justice, rights, and ethical issues in this situation? What history or larger contexts need to be considered? Are any issues of historical or current trauma or microaggressions relevant to explore? What are the potential obstacles in engaging in a dialogue about the issues in this scenario?
› What literature might support the work required in this scenario?

Within-Group Differences and Internalized Oppression and Privilege

A 54-year-old student with 10 years of baccalaureate-level social work experience is assigned to a homeless shelter for her field placement. She was raised in Ecuador, educated in Europe, and has been living in the United States for 12 years. She is fully bilingual in English and Spanish. The setting staff is thrilled to finally attract a Latinx student to intern in the homeless shelter serving mostly Puerto Rican and Dominican families. The shelter director and field instructor is a 27-year-old White man with 3 years of postmaster's experience. He was concerned initially about the age and background differences between him and his student but is pleased to have a student.

After a few months of placement, the field instructor finds himself deferring to the new student's opinions, believing that she is an expert on the Latinx community. He gives the student all the cases involving Spanish-speaking people, and staff use her as an interpreter. He fails to confront the student when she does not follow through on certain assigned tasks and notices value-laden and judgmental statements coming through the student's records, such as "weak, unfit mother," "dirty, ill-mannered child," and "low-class parents." When those she serves begin to miss appointments with her, the field instructor brings his concerns to her attention.

She complains vehemently about the futility of engaging such difficult individuals in therapeutic relationships. She says she is being expected to work miracles with low-functioning women and to meet unrealistic demands from him. She also tells him that her interviews are better in Spanish, and that the English translations make her sound more judgmental than she really is with the individuals she sees.

The field instructor is beginning to suspect that the student is not culturally sensitive or self-aware. He still feels inadequate in supervising such an experienced Latinx student, and he is concerned with how she is responding to the needs of those she serves.

Consider the following issues raised by this scenario:

> If you are the field instructor, what are your immediate reactions to this scenario based on your own beliefs and positionality?
> How can the field instructor support the integration of the competing demands witnessed in this scenario? How might a dialogue about difference and similarities create pathways to possible solutions for the student in supervision and in her work?
> What issues of power and privilege are operating? What are the practice and diversity issues and dilemmas confronting the student? How are these issues shaping this situation?
> What skills are required of the student and field instructor for the next steps to be taken?
> What are the justice, rights, and ethical issues in this situation? What history or larger contexts need to be considered? Are any issues of historical or current trauma or microaggressions relevant to explore here? What are the potential obstacles in engaging in a dialogue about the issues in this scenario?
> What literature might support the work required in this scenario?

Race and Racism

The student is a highly experienced White woman who is culturally sensitive and aware of the importance of creating a climate where race and ethnicity can be openly discussed in the helping relationship. The program participant, a Nigerian woman, is in the middle of a career transition, and has financial and relationship difficulties. The student and this individual have been meeting together weekly for 6 months in an employee assistance program where most of the professional staff is White and most of the individuals served are people of color, mainly African American, African and Latinx.

In their individual sessions, the student has discussed the importance of identity issues in the participant's life and has raised the issue of racial and ethnic differences between them and how this might affect their work together. The student feels that she has modeled openness in discussing these sensitive issues. However, despite the student's encouragement, the individual refrains from joining her in these discussions and stops short of expressing how race or racism affects her problems at work or in relationships. Rather than pursue the issue, the student decides to wait until the individual is comfortable enough to voluntarily raise these issues.

One day on her way to the waiting room to meet this woman, the student overhears her and another person of color talking animatedly about a racial incident covered in the media that day and that "Whites still think they rule this country." The individual she is working with goes on to say that her White boss was so condescending she felt totally incompetent, stating, "She even had the nerve to talk about my accent. That's why I want to leave there. I am stressed out trying to act White." The student is confused, hurt, and angry that this woman does not trust her sufficiently to discuss these matters with her.

Consider the following issues raised by this scenario:

> If you are the field instructor, what are your immediate reactions to this scenario based on your own beliefs and positionality?
> How can the field instructor support the integration of the competing demands witnessed in this scenario? How might a dialogue about difference and similarities create pathways to possible solutions for the student in supervision and in her work?
> What issues of power and privilege are operating, and what practice issues and dilemmas are confronting the student? How are these issues shaping this situation? How can the field instructor support the student's understanding about how these dynamics shape what is going on in the working relationship? What organizational issues are affecting the relationship?
> What skills are required of the student for the next steps to be taken?
> What are the justice, rights, and ethical issues in this situation? What history or larger contexts need to be considered? Are any issues of historical or current trauma or microaggressions relevant to explore here? How do these connect to potential obstacles in engaging in a dialogue about the issues in this scenario?
> What literature might support the work required in this scenario?

Sexism and Genderism

A generalist practice level female student is placed in a local high school. Two male students are also placed in this setting. The task supervisor, guidance officer, and principal are also men. Her field instructor, a woman, is in the same district but in a different school. The students receive weekly group supervision and meet with their field instructor individually on a biweekly basis. The task supervisor allocates assignments to all three students and is accessible daily for any questions or concerns relating to the work. The female student notices that the two other students are given assignments involving complex assessment responsibilities and that she is often asked to help with filing and to call students' homes for attendance check-ups. She also notices that the guidance officer and task supervisor often tell jokes to each other and stop talking when she enters the room. She feels awkward and finds herself attempting to avoid them. On several occasions one of the other students communicates on the task supervisor's behalf. One day he said: "I was asked to mention the school's dress code. You know, this is a high school and you have to be careful not to appear too trendy." She was embarrassed and did not say anything in return. She felt growing discomfort and feelings of anger developing. The student talked to a student friend placed in the same school district but in a different school. This friend tells the field instructor what the student shared.

Consider the following issues raised by this scenario:

> If you are the field instructor, what are your immediate reactions to this scenario based on your own beliefs and positionality?
> What are the first steps to be taken? What should the field instructor say to the student who divulges her friend's situation?
> What are the issues involved? How is the dialogue about sexual microaggressions, sexism, and genderism acknowledged and discussed? What should the field instructor be prepared to do and say? To whom?
> What issues of power and privilege are operating, and what issues and dilemmas are confronting the students? How are these issues shaping this situation? How can the field instructor support the students' understanding about how these dynamics shape what is going on? What organizational issues are affecting the relationship?

> What if anything should the field instructor do or say to the task supervisor?
> Should the field instructor contact the field liaison?
> What literature might support the work required in this scenario?

Ableism

The student is a 36-year-old White man who has had cerebral palsy since childhood. The field instructor is an able-bodied White woman, 5 years his junior. She has never supervised a student in need of reasonable accommodations, nor has the setting ever hosted an intern or employee needing accommodations. The student uses a wheelchair, has good control of his upper body motor activity, communicates well verbally, and is adept at using a word processor. He is currently interning as a specialized practice level direct practice student in the setting. He presents as a capable, intelligent, personable, and easygoing person who makes jokes about his abilities. He lives at home with his mother, an aunt, and a younger sister.

The field instructor is having trouble engaging this student in a supervisory relationship because he is always joking around with her and acting like her friend rather than her student. The field instructor is getting conflicting messages from him, at times he is seductive or flirtatious and at other times he behaves in a way that seems to mask enormous rage and dependency needs. The student states that he is getting a great deal from his supervisory sessions with the field instructor, but he is often late arriving for supervisory appointments, noting transportation difficulties. He canceled three successive supervisory sessions with the field instructor, stating fatigue and transportation problems. The field instructor is reluctant to confront him about his behaviors because, she says, "He always has an excuse ready or just talks circles around me." The field instructor feels she is getting nowhere. Frustration has increased to the point where she is asking to have this student reassigned to another field instructor.

Consider the following issues raised by this scenario:

> If you are the field instructor, what are your immediate reactions to this scenario based on your own beliefs and positionality?
> What issues of power and privilege are operating, and what practice issues and dilemmas are confronting the student?

How are these issues shaping this situation? How can the field instructor support the student's understanding about how these dynamics shape what is going on in the supervisory relationship? What organizational issues are affecting the relationship?
- How can the field instructor support the integration of the competing demands witnessed in this scenario? How might a dialogue about difference and similarities create pathways to possible solutions for the student in supervision and in his work?
- What skills are required of the student for the next steps to be taken?
- What are the justice, ethical, and rights issues in this situation? What history or larger contexts need to be considered? Are any issues of historical or current trauma or microaggressions relevant to explore? How do these connect to potential obstacles in engaging in a dialogue about the issues?
- What supports from the agency, the field liaison, or the office of field education might the field instructor use to provide more just and equitable field education?
- What literature might support the work required in this scenario?

Process Recording: Managing a Challenging Dialogue

The following is an extract from an intern group process recording that focuses on an interchange between the intern and a college sophomore (CS) in the group. The intern shares thoughts that highlight her affective reactions and concerns about her management of the content and group process. The setting is a community college academic support center; the group's purpose is to support student members through their transition to their second year of studies and to support their academic success. This session takes place in week three of the semester; the eight group members represent a diverse group of students. The interaction takes place at the start of the group meeting in response to the intern's prompting a discussion on the adjustments required of them for this new academic year. One group member responds as follows:

CS: I used to live in an area with people who looked like me but now I live with a lot of White people. I feel uncomfortable, especially when they look at me. They are always looking at me. I feel like they are judging me.

Intern: What do you think they are assuming or judging when they look at you?

CS: I think they are trying to figure out what I am. Or, what is a Latina girl doing here in their neighborhood.... I think they are also trying to figure out if I am Latina or Black. Especially when I am with my parents, they are always looking at us because my dad is dark, and my mom is very light.

Intern: It sounds like you are you feel uncomfortable and are internalizing how they are looking at you. Are you saying that you feel like you don't belong there, and this is making your adjustment harder?

CS: Yes, I feel so uncomfortable. I feel like I am in their world and I shouldn't be. I don't think I belong there because of all the looks I get. It makes me feel like I am not enough.

Intern's Thoughts and Reflections: Oh! I feel like this is going to bring up racial tensions for everyone. The looks that CS is receiving from White neighbors is causing her to feel like something is wrong with her. CS is starting to internalize the problem and blaming herself. It seems like CS is having a hard time adjusting to being surrounded by a predominantly White population. This is also her first time living near White people. I wonder if CS is experiencing culture shock and/or internalizing microaggressions or oppression? I wonder if she is questioning if she belongs here, at college, too. I wanted to ask CS what she assumes those "looks" mean. As a Black woman, I know what they would mean to me, but let me not assume that it is the same for her. I tried to give CS the language for her emotional experience and some healing space to process what is coming up for her. I don't want to assume the other group members' experiences either, so I hope I went about it correctly by telling CS that it seemed like she was internalizing the microaggressions she experienced. How should I be managing the group? It is hard to think of them and her! Did I respond correctly? I am having difficulty thinking what else I could have done.

Intern: It sounds like you are internalizing a lot of what is occurring to you. You know, internalized oppression occurs when people of color take in the messages of the dominant group (i.e., White people). It sounds like when they make weird facial expressions or constantly look at you, it makes you question your racial appearance, which then is making you feel like you are not enough.

CS: That's it. That's exactly how it happens in my brain. Their looks and living with them makes me feel like I am not good enough.

Intern's Thoughts and Reflections: I was not sure if I should have gone into depth about the historical context of racism or just ask the other group members how we can be supportive. My gut told me that CS would benefit more if the group could be supportive rather than me giving a lecture on why those microaggressions are occurring. I felt conscious of wanting to include the others.

Intern: What can I and the rest of the group do to support you?

CS: Honestly, I just need to talk about it with someone. Talking to you about it is making me feel better.

Intern: To the group: Is it okay if we give CS the space and support to share her experiences? The rest of the group agrees and states that she should share how she feels with us.

Intern: It sounds like the rest of the group is open and willing to make room for you to express yourself. Please feel free to share anything that comes up for you with us. People of color carry a lot of emotional weight in their hearts and body, which weighs them down and makes them super stressed and tense, so know that we can help you carry that burden. And when you are ready, we can learn different self-care practices that we can exercise to remove any negativity from your heart and body.

CS: Thank you, I feel better already.

Intern: How about everyone else? Does CS' experience make you think about anything that has happened to you?

Intern's Thoughts and Reflections: I think by asking the group for its support makes the entire group responsible for each other's healing rather it being solely on me and CS. At first, I felt as if CS was taking away time from the others in the group, but her experience opened up the conversation about race and racism. After CS shared about this experience, another student shared how someone said something racist to her on the train. Then, other students of color spoke about how they feel "constantly having to be on" by having only White professors. Even though I felt like CS was taking time from the others, I think I did the right thing by allowing the conversation to flow and by asking for other input. They responded well to CS and contributed to the discussion. Next time I will emphasize that I and everyone else in the group are here for everyone to discuss racism, how it affects us, and how we will support each other.

Discussion

The intern demonstrates her efforts to be mindful about how to manage the individual and the group. Her thoughts and reflections are open and honest and demonstrate her feeling torn over how to deal with this material and how to manage the group at the same time. The intern stays with CS's distress and struggles with how to balance CS's needs while being mindful of the group and the power of support in the room beyond what the intern may be able to offer.

As the field instructor,

- What part of this interchange would you comment on in supervision?
- What skills do you observe, and what are the next steps for the student's growth and development?
- How would you continue to support this intern's work in furthering the development of group process?
- How would you continue to support her work in facilitating challenging dialogues?

CHAPTER 3

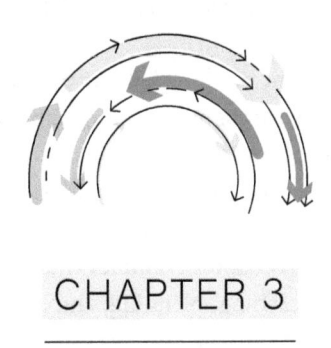

Teaching Competency-Based Practice

Rubrics, Assessment, and Evaluation

A hallmark of competency-based education is that it begins with the end point—the program expresses the competencies as educational outcomes.... This focus and emphasis on competency—what graduates are able to do—means that evaluation of student learning and performance in field education is even more crucial than in previous accreditation frameworks. (Bogo, 2016, p. 155.)

Rubrics orient us toward our goals as teachers. We use them to clarify our learning goals, design instruction that addresses those goals, communicate the goals to students, guide our feedback on students' progress toward the goals, and judge final products in terms of the degree to which the goals were met. (Andrade, 2005, p. 27)

The essential benefit of competency-based education is that the CSWE (2015a) competencies establish a baseline of knowledge and skill, a common vocabulary, and a core standard for performance. Further, the competencies enable social workers to identify, articulate, describe, and demonstrate what they value and know, how they behave, why they do so, and most important, what actions and interventions they can perform. The competencies promote transparency about what is to be taught and what is to be learned. They even the playing field so that expectations for outcomes are clear.

In each chapter we point out how field instructors and students can enhance student competency through discussions and activities. In this chapter we describe how the use of rubrics establish the expectation for discussions about the competencies, set the context for such discussions, and discuss how this evaluative framework serves as a road map for learning and ongoing assessment. In particular, this chapter examines the ways this framework supports our approaches to teaching, planning, and evaluations; it assists us in establishing goals, planning content, and measuring outcomes.

According to the EPAS (CSWE, 2015a) at least one assessment of each competency must be demonstrated in real or simulated practice situations. This means that in many if not most social work programs, primary measures of competence will be lodged in field education. Consequently, if we are to ensure the competence of social work graduates, the competencies must become central to learning and teaching in field education. Discussion of the competencies must be deeply embedded in every aspect of student training. Advancing competence, the goal of everything the student learns in field education, will be purposefully included in every interaction between the student, the field instructor, and the field placement setting. Students learn to say, for example, "Here I am using research to inform my work with this individual." Field instructors assigning work on a voter registration drive frame it as building competence in policy practice. The administrators of the setting review the agency's waiting list procedures as a way of demonstrating ethical behavior. Competencies are taught and learned directly through supervision and absorbed through the setting's learning environment or "implicit curriculum" (CSWE, 2015a, p. 14; Petracchi & Zastrow, 2010a, 2010b).

Practice principles and their components are defined in the competencies in the EPAS (CSWE, 2015a); these components describe what competence looks like in action and specify what we look for as we witness our student's actions and skill development. The task of teaching another person what we do as social workers and how we do it involves first being able to understand the competencies and the practice baselines and principles they represent. Then we translate this understanding to the context of our setting and the work assigned, and finally we must recognize and illustrate these principles demonstrated in practice.

We can start the conceptualization of our teaching task from identifying required outcomes associated with the nature of the work, or we may begin by translating our context through the learning opportunities offered. As Figure 3.1 illustrates, no matter how we begin, we must journey through the competencies before we attempt to teach. This means that although the context of our

Translate placement context ⇄ Understand competencies ⇄ Identify performance behaviors

Figure 3.1 The process of field teaching in a competency-based framework

work shapes our role, function, and approach to the foundational skills of the helping process, essential practice principles such as diversity and difference in practice, advancing human rights and justice, engaging in research-informed practice, practice-informed research, and understanding the contribution of policy also need to be taught, and student performance in these areas must be examined in relation to defined outcomes. Competency-based education expands our lens to include how the placement context and assignments fit into the range of defined social work competencies and required professional performance for entry-level professional practice.

As discussed in Chapter 1, teaching in the context of competency-based education requires a shift from teacher-driven views of what should be taught to defined outcomes of what students should learn and be able to demonstrate. This shift has important implications. Prior to competency-based social work education, we approached teaching students from our view of what was important for students to learn in relation to the work they were assigned. For example, working in a hospital emergency room requires us to teach students how to manage crisis situations in a host setting. The helping process is experienced through a fast-paced, and often stressful, environment; proactive engagement and assessment is essential. Whereas if we are working in a grassroots community context serving unaccompanied minors or recent immigrants, although engagement and assessment remain vital, the skills and attributes needed in this context may be focused on another phase of the helping process, determined by a different pace and with different concerns regarding the importance of community engagement. Within these contexts and functions of our role, defining what we teach relies on our view of the approaches, skills, and knowledge that are required. Competency-based education adds an additional component—defined performance outcomes irrespective of the context.

Using a Rubric Framework

Comprehending the overarching substance and details involved in the competencies is required to comprehend the associated student learning outcomes. Our understanding of these components forms the basis of our supervisory agenda and shapes the credibility for students to begin to trust that their learning goals will be achieved. A rubric framework takes these component parts and places them in a format that defines and illustrates how the desired performance behaviors are demonstrated on the road to proficiency. The items associated with each competency presented in formal evaluation formats mold a learning focus. The transparency and clarity of the criterion help students prepare and organize themselves according to stated expectations. An example of such a framework in an advanced generalist specialized practice final evaluation is provided later in this chapter.

In addition, an associated rating scale describes the trajectory and provides guideposts to aid the student's path and our teaching focus. The items associated with each competency are rated by linking the student's performance to the definitions and examples that exemplify the behavior according to the scale used. The scale shapes our judgment of student progress toward mastery. A student's performance becomes a gauge, or indicator, of the outcomes we are seeking, and it becomes possible to determine what behavior or actions are required for the next skill level. In this way, in combination with the program's evaluation, a rubric rating scale helps us evaluate performance according to the degree of quality observed, or how capably, fittingly, consistently, or fully the student has mastered the learning goal. The rating scale in Figure 3.2 uses a 5-point Likert scale consisting of the following categories: advanced competence, competence, beginning competence, uneven progress, and insufficient progress. The levels of performance indicate the reliability that the skill will be demonstrated on two dimensions; that is a growing depth of understanding and increasing sophistication and breadth of its application in a variety of situations across methods or units of attention. The range from 5 to 1, as shown in Figure 3.2, indicates a student whose actions represent (5) an advanced ability to articulate understanding and to effectively and consistently integrate the demonstrated competency into practice in a variety of complex situations across methods or units of attention, (4) a growing depth of understanding and consistence in applying the behavior in most situations, (3) a beginning understanding that is demonstrated in continued and increased consistency in application, (2) a beginning understanding with struggles and uneven implementation, and (1) insufficient understanding to support application or rare demonstration of the behavior despite opportunities. An additional option indicating that there have been limited opportunities to practice or discuss the skill or learning outcome could be a signal that the setting, assignments, or discussions in supervision may need fine-tuning to provide opportunities for the student's learning in the areas identified.

5	4	3	2	1
Advanced competence	Competence	Beginning competence	Uneven progress	Insufficient progress

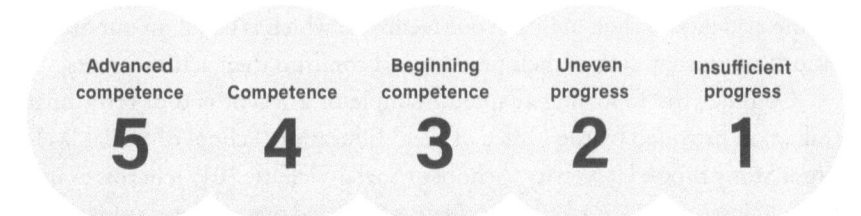

Figure 3.2 Example of a rubric rating scale

The stepwise progression in the rating scale lays down the steps toward mastery, and the progression provides guidance for what is ahead. Anticipating what is required next is an important part of the learning process. Over time, students' attempts to demonstrate and communicate how their practice reflects the competencies become more pronounced. Ongoing assessment, provision of feedback, and evaluation are integral.

Although clear demarcations are the aim, even with precise definitions, levels may overlap or be difficult to discern given the variability of skills across populations or methods. Further, as the rating calls for an overall holistic assessment, there are interlocking areas. Although the CSWE (2015a) competencies are listed as if they are discrete, in practice they interconnect, and one informs the other. Yet we may approach the rating process as if we teach and evaluate the competencies individually.

Despite these in-built challenges, the rubric provides a learning map; the outcomes are a set of standards and descriptions that are available to the evaluator and the learner from the start of their journey. These learning outcomes are associated with the competencies, listed in final evaluations, and illustrate what is being measured. A student's performance is viewed over time through a continuum of achievements and through various contexts. Expectations for students in their generalist practice year differ from those in the program's specialized practice level curriculum. The continuum recognizes that capability often grows over time as one learns to perform a skill more consistently and more capably and as application of the behavior is transferred to a diverse set of situations and modalities. Planning and active engagement moves the process toward mastery; as students and field instructors review the student's actions together, they recognize the move toward competence (Brookhart, 2013).

Introducing the evaluative framework offers additional guidance. As we familiarize students with the baselines and observable practice actions attached to the competencies, they are given language and tools to name and define their skills, theories, and approaches to practice. Their work and actions are the evidence of their abilities; our feedback, which is based on our observations and review, shapes their practice and confirms their achievements.

Consider the following adapted example of a recent end-of-term final evaluation provided by the Office of Field Education, School of Social Welfare at Stony Brook University (School of Social Welfare, 2017). In this example, field instructors are asked to evaluate specialized practice level students in an advanced generalist practice sequence under the competency of engaging in policy practice. The format offers examples that illustrate the competency in action and that are followed by performance behaviors that further delineate behaviors associated with the competency. Each performance behavior is rated individually on a scale similar to the one presented in Figure 3.2. A total score is then achieved for each competency.

> Advanced generalist students evaluate the relationship between social policies at all levels and the provision of social work services to individuals, families and groups and in communities and organizations. Students discuss the impact of policies at all levels affecting those they are working with and advocate for changes where needed.

Consider these examples:

> - A student placed in community medical clinic accompanies the field instructor to a HIV planning council meeting and learns how new federal funds are being allocated. The student works with 2 HIV positive individuals and uses what she has learned to access previously unavailable services.
> - In working with her case load, an advanced generalist student recognizes an agency procedural issue affecting most of the individuals she is assigned. She presents this information at a staff meeting with strategies to address this issue.
>   Rate your student on each of the following performance behaviors according to the rating scale continuum provided. The student:
>   A. Develops, promotes and advocates for policies that affect social change for individuals, families, groups, organizations, and communities.
>   B. Critically analyzes and evaluates the relationship between social policy at all levels and the provision of social work services.

    C. Critically assesses policies at multiple levels (agency, local, state and/or federal) in supervision and their effects.
    D. Engages collaboratively with organizational and community interests to formulate and amend policies that improve the effectiveness of service delivery. (School of Social Welfare Office of Field Education, Stony Brook University, (2017), *Competency 5, Engage in Policy Practice*.)

This evaluation example includes performance behaviors (A–D) that are chosen by the social work program in connection with the program's mission and curriculum and are used to focus attention on evaluation of student performance. Meta competencies and procedural competencies are included. Each student learning outcome is rated separately according to the continuum provided on the rating scale depicted in Figure 3.2, which then produces a cumulative score for the competency.

The defined dimensions of practice listed on the end-of-term evaluation combined with the trajectory illustrated by the rating scale are used as cornerstones of teaching and learning. The competencies as set out in the program's evaluation forms may be used in a variety of ways. We may (a) review the practice items associated with each competency and the continuum of mastery with our students; (b) explain the concepts in relation to the work and assignments chosen; (c) specifically point to illustrations of the items being measured in our conversations with students about the work we have reviewed or observed; (d) refer to the progression in mastery when reviewing student process recordings, logs, and journals; and (e) use the behaviors and observed proficiency levels to prepare for feedback, assessments, and evaluations. Additionally, students can be asked to review the actions described in their recordings, for example:

> As this individual was sharing his situation, I was assessing the setting's eligibility policies at a range of levels. I am more aware of how this policy affects this individual and how it may affect others. I don't think I would have heard what he was trying to tell me before, and I have a clearer sense of what I would like to present to staff about how this issue affects service users' rights to service. I would like to discuss this further in supervision.

This statement provides evidence for at least a few performance behaviors and point to the student's willingness to collaborate and advocate for policy review that advances human rights and justice, the student's use of supervision to further the integration of policy and practice and to reflect on progress being made, and an ability to critically analyze policy implementation and its applicability to influence service. We confirm the student's skill level through the review of these actions and the evidence their actions provide on their depth of understanding and consistency of application.

As our familiarity develops, how the competencies embed themselves in practice situations across varying scenarios and modalities becomes clearer. It becomes possible to recognize how they interrelate and intersect, what practice situations are more likely to provide opportunities to exercise abilities, what competencies are rooted in the context of our conversations and dialogues about practice, what observable behaviors illustrate their achievement, and what gaps exist. Using the evaluative framework regularly also encourages students to become increasingly conscious and articulate about their practice and their level of proficiency and skill development. The field instructor and student can agree on areas of strength and where additional skill is desired; it is then possible to discuss what improved practice might look like.

The Ongoing Educational Assessment Process

The competencies, and the framework that encircles them, are part of the ethical requirements of our evaluative role as field instructors. We assess students in a "manner that is fair and respectful" (NASW, 2017, Standard 3.01 d). We achieve this by ensuring that the topics of assessment and evaluation are included from the very start of our work together. We explain that assessment is based on observed behaviors as outlined in the performance expectations associated with the competencies, and we describe how these behaviors are rated on the program's rating scale. Making it clear that we engage in evaluation during every discussion we have about the work lets students see that evaluation is integrated throughout their experiences and that it is a fundamental part of the process of learning. The ongoing process of assessment and evaluation should not be something that happens to students; they participate in this process together with us.

Working together prepares students for what to expect from an ongoing evaluation process, how the competencies shape expectations, what specific criteria the social work education program uses for generalist practice and specialized practice level students, and what students' responsibilities are in achieving these outcomes. In this way, students see the direct link to a fair and respectful process that aims at clear expectations and transparency. The call for student active participation in self-review acts as a commitment to competence.

Preparing students for what to expect from field performance appraisals enables them to be more fully equipped and to participate as equal partners in the process. Each program delineates outcomes and associated performance behaviors specific to the program. As in the previous example, the formal end-of-term student evaluation is based on criteria that specify the generalist level practice competencies and the program's expression of its specialized practice curriculum. Although the following questions were written to be used alongside the review of the school's established criteria before the CSWE competencies, they continue to serve as useful prompts (Horejsi & Garthwait, 2002). We have added competency language to the questions to act as a bridge to the current context.

> How clearly do I understand the description of what the student must demonstrate in practice and on which competencies, terms or specific performance behaviors do I need additional guidance?
> What questions arise when I attempt to apply these criteria and behaviors to my agency's context?
> In what ways are the competencies connected to the work in this setting and what competencies will require special attention to ensure that they will be part of the student's assignments?
> Are there aspects of the student's assignments or performance that do not seem to fit into the competencies or specified performance behaviors?

Field liaisons provide support to us as we attempt to address these questions; they act as resources as we familiarize ourselves with how the competencies are contextualized by our setting. The tempo of the academic year also offers support for ongoing assessment benchmarks. Programs may differ in the titles of the general assessment benchmarks; however, generally for programs on a two-semester academic year schedule, at least five points during the academic year are marked for review and evaluation. Figure 3.3 provides a table depicting these benchmarks. They include (a) a midterm review or sixth- to eighth-week educational learning review and plan; (b) an oral review 1 month prior to the end of term, which begins formal preparation for the first term final evaluation; (c) the first semester end-of-term final evaluation; (d) an oral review 1 month prior to the end of the second term final evaluation;

Student Practice Level	Weeks 6–8 Midterm Review or Plan	1 Month Before End of First Term	End of First Term	1 Month Before End of Second Term	End of Second Term	As-Needed Meetings With Field Liaison
Generalist practice	Educational learning plan	Oral review	Final evaluation	Oral review	Final evaluation	General review, problem resolution, or establish a learning contract
Specialized practice	Educational learning plan	Oral review	Final evaluation	Oral review	Final evaluation	General review, problem resolution, or establish a learning contract

Figure 3.3 Evaluation benchmarks and time frames

and (e) the second-semester final evaluation. Additionally, other opportunities for review may surface on an as needed basis with the field liaison.

Contacts with the program's field liaison may be scheduled at any point during the academic year to review the student's progress; these contacts may take the form of face-to-face meetings and need not be focused on problem resolution. They are an opportunity for general review (see the Chapter 10 Appendix for a sample topic outline). If problems emerge, and there is a need to establish a specific review and response, a formal process for establishing an educational plan is conducted on an as-needed basis with the field liaison. An educational plan under these conditions is differentiated from a general educational learning plan and called an *educational learning contract* in this text. Formulating this educational learning contract involves the field instructor, the student, the field liaison and any other members of the learning team as needed (see the following section on educational learning contracts and Chapter 9 for a full discussion of learning contracts).

The first formal review requirement occurs around the sixth or eighth week of placement and is often called the midterm review or the sixth-week educational learning review or plan. This review may require completion of a program form or it may be conducted by an oral review. A formal verbal appraisal during the month before the final evaluation marks an opportunity to begin the preparation for the final formal term evaluation. The end-of-term evaluation is the culmination of the ongoing assessment and evaluative process. Each social work program recommends its own format for these required review and evaluation points, which can be found on the school's website or in the school's field education manual. The competencies and collaborative feedback are used throughout the process to further student understanding of how they are progressing toward mastery.

Educational Assessment

An educational assessment is different from an end-of-term evaluation. It aims to identify student strengths and learning needs and assess how these will be matched with the assignment opportunities in the setting. This assessment helps to structure our thoughts about how we will meet our student's learning requirements. Our educational assessments are ongoing; they begin as soon as the placement is confirmed, continue throughout the placement, and culminate at the end of each term's final evaluation. Along the way, the feedback we provide based on these assessments offers students reference points to help determine their talents and to focus their learning.

For the initial educational assessment, information is gathered to examine students' skills and talents. This involves an appreciation of past experiences, intellectual capacities, personal strengths, distinctive ways of learning, identified worldviews and dimensions of identity, and stated professional goals. Identified learning goals are affected by characteristics of the student, placement setting staff, population served, and field instructor.

The educational assessment is refined as an environment conducive to adult learning is established; the sixth to eighth week of the first term marks an opportunity to reshape and define our initial impressions and assessment. In this atmosphere students become comfortable in fully contributing to define their learning needs and abilities. Although the educational assessment process is ongoing, benchmarks throughout the academic year are used to shape and reformulate this assessment and the strategies defined to reach goals. This dynamic process provides opportunities to contextualize and individualize the student's experience based on proven talents and untapped potential. Repetitive patterns materialize over time, and therefore we reserve our judgment until evidence emerges. It is in the identification of these patterned responses that educational assessments are formulated and inform our choice of teaching interventions.

Engaging in an educational assessment, whether it is formally written, composed of our notes, or thought through orally with the student, promotes self-reflective practice through the involvement of students as active participants in the ongoing formulation and review of their skill development and their learning needs in relation to the competencies. As the uniqueness of each student's approach to learning is discerned, the selection of learning opportunities, teaching techniques, and methods leads to the creation of an individualized learning plan within the framework of program goals, competencies, and aimed-for outcomes. Over time our beginning impressions are enriched through direct exposure to the student's practice, deepening our assessments and shaping our final evaluations.

Educational Learning Plans

Educational learning plans are components of and based on the educational assessment; they are intimately tied to the learning goals and objectives we set. Learning plans guide our choice of assignments and teaching strategies. They individualize the experience for students, foster partnerships between students and field instructors, and specify what work a student will be assigned in a given period.

Learning goals are generally described as broad concepts with long-range purposes, such as helping students become effective advocates, group workers, or program planners. Learning objectives are more specific and involve an outcome that can be measured; student learning outcomes in competency-based education are defined by the CSWE (2015a) competencies. The learning activities defined in the plan are tasks and situations undertaken to achieve the identified learning objectives; these activities are the student's assignments. The teaching focus and strategies evolve from the student's behaviors we witness as the student engages in these assignments either directly witnessed or reviewed through recordings, discussions, or reflections. The learning plan, therefore, identifies essential elements of students' learning needs, indicating short- and long-term objectives, major teaching methods used, and types of assignments planned to advance learning. Specifying learning outcomes sets the context upon which we will base the conclusions of the end-of-term evaluation (Bogo, 2016; Bogo & Vayda, 1987; Boitel & Fromm, 2014; Drisko, 2014; Fox & Zischka, 1989; Lemberger & Marshack, 1991; Poulin & Matis, 2015).

The context for learning is an integral part of these considerations. The learning plan notes the types of populations served, problems addressed and methods available. In this context, educational learning plans outline the path and strategies to achieve goals, objectives, and outcomes. If task supervisors are used to allocate work to students in the setting, it is essential to include this member of the learning team in formulation of the learning plan. To be maximally useful, educational learning plans are developed mutually with students (Boitel & Fromm, 2014; Fox & Zischka, 1989; Hamilton & Else; 1983). Field education relationships that include trust, respect, and a spirit of mutual collaboration are essential for this to occur (Knight, 2016). In this way, educational learning plans parallel contracting with those we serve.

Questions that establish and shape the student's learning plan are the following:

> What learning strengths, learning needs and learning goals have been identified? What patterns exist in how the student approaches new learning? What additional assignments are needed to help with the achievement of learning goals? What teaching strategies are suggested to address identified learning needs? Are shared and individual responsibilities made explicit?
> What skills have been demonstrated through supervision, recordings, or direct observations? Have obstacles to learning been defined? What action is planned to address them?
> Have each of the competencies been part of the discussion? To what extent is there a shared vision of next steps in the progression toward increased competence? How clear has it been made to the student what needs to be accomplished to get where the student needs to be?

This process promotes explicit agreement on the learning goals and learning needs that will be tackled in the context of the setting and the opportunities available. Directly linking the assignments to the student's learning, models how to engage in planning based on identification of need, mutual collaboration, constructive feedback, and ties assessment to performance and growth.

Informal and Formal Oral Reviews

These are ongoing dialogues about progress toward achieving learning goals and objectives. Informal reviews occur on an ongoing basis throughout the academic year and give us the opportunity to take stock of the progress being made. These reviews may lead to new or more challenging assignments and needed changes in teaching methods may also be identified. If oral reviews are done well, they will include the feedback students require and they will have greater comfort and confidence in the evaluation process. They will understand the benefits of mutual feedback and will be prepared to become active participants in the learning process. They will be given direction on the incremental performance expectations, and in this way, they are empowered to assume responsibility for their professional development.

Taking responsibility for learning is a prerequisite for students to become active learners and active evaluators of their work. Each supervisory conference is viewed as an opportunity to progress toward this learning goal. This promotes development of self-awareness and the ability to describe, illustrate, and evaluate progress through explicit examples; identify emerging themes and gaps in skill development; and identify similarities and differences of performance across units of attention.

The baseline established in the initial learning plan discussed at the beginning of the field placement also serves as a reminder of early issues. The baseline includes the knowledge, skills, and values students brought to the learning situation and the overall abilities and talents they possess. By the time of the midsemester review at the sixth or eighth week of placement, it is possible to identify how far students have come in achieving learning goals. Suggested questions for review at this stage include the following:

› What new skills have students acquired or consolidated? What new knowledge has been incorporated? What patterns have emerged that help the student approach new learning?
› What professional behaviors, values, and ethics have been discussed and demonstrated?
› Have assessments and practice included a range of skills across the CSWE's (2015a) nine competencies, including an analysis of structural elements that create and perpetuate inequality or barriers to receiving or using resources?
› Where have students met expectations? In what areas do they excel? Where is further progress needed, and what next steps need to be taken?

If not already discussed, the review offers an opportunity for a more general check in with how students experience their assignments, supervision and the feedback being provided. The expectation is that we will build in ongoing opportunities for review and feedback. (See the appendix to this chapter for possible questions to assist in this review.)

In addition to the formal midterm review between the sixth and eighth week of a placement, a formal oral review 1 month before the due date of the end-of-term evaluation provides a chance to prepare for the work of final evaluation. Just as we prepared students for their midterm review, we should also have a date set for the formal oral end-of-term review. As the date approaches, we can remind students to review their work binders, and we can also review the student's written recordings, case records, field conference notes, and agendas. If field instructor journals are kept, these provide additional information. If task supervisors are part of the learning team, their views and observations should be included at this stage so that their contributions to the student's evaluation are part of the process.

A typical review during the month prior to the end-of-term evaluation often goes something like the following:

> When we initially met together to confirm your generalist practice level placement I explained that as we are a community-based agency, initially you will be learning outreach and engagement skills with this hard-to-reach population and that this term will be focused on project planning and group assignments. During the first half of the term you were actively engaged in outreach. There were struggles in finding ways to approach the youths, but you demonstrated considerable determination, creativity, and ability to adapt to the different ways they required you to adjust your approaches. This illustrates your consistent and commendable performance in several areas including professional behavior and understanding of your role, applying your understanding of the importance of differentiating your approaches to the various needs of this population, and your empathetic approach to the engagement phase of your work. Your previous experience and innate determination to serve this population seemed to bolster your efforts. The second half of this term has given you the chance to develop regular individual contacts with the youths. You have made good progress in developing some group projects with them and in your ability to address how the youths experience your efforts to engage with them. This will encourage their involvement in the groups, and meaningful work with these individuals will follow. I have noticed how frustrating it has been for you not to have developed a regular workload with individual youths more quickly. This has given us an opportunity to examine an additional skill—your ability to self-regulate your disappointment and frustration involved in outreach. You used supervision well to process these affective reactions, and this allowed you to proceed in creative ways, including research of best practices used with this population. Let's talk about your experience of these assignments, whether you agree with what I have just described, what you identify as the areas where you have learned most, and whether there are adjustments we need to consider. Can you give some examples from your practice when you displayed some of these skills?

The oral evaluation concludes by establishing new or expanded learning goals and objectives for the next step in the student's progress toward graduation and entry-level practice. This paves the way for students to take a more active and mutual role in their final evaluations.

Educational Learning Contracts: When Obstacles Occur

The preceding scenario describes educational learning assessments as supportive to students in the development of focused self-directed learning early in the academic year and in formulating a learning plan that is used as a baseline and refined throughout the year. When obstacles occur that signal that a student is struggling, programs have processes that ensure opportunities are available to assess the problem and to devise strategies that attempt to reduce the difficulties experienced in the learning situation. A specific educational learning contract is used to outline the issues, define goals for each student's experience, give focus and direction to the choice of assignments, and devise strategies to improve the likelihood of success.

The elements mentioned earlier in an educational learning plan are part of a learning contract when obstacles arise, however, as these situations frequently indicate potential barriers in meeting program competency expectations, the written formulations become part of the student's academic record. The student's field liaison is consulted and usually takes part in the discussions seeking resolution. This partner provides balance to the discussion, offers another perspective on the learning obstacles identified, and often presents possible alternative teaching approaches and potential avenues for growth. As with the other opportunities to define learning assessments and plans, if a task supervisor is involved, this member of the learning team also has an important contribution to make in the success of any learning contract. The process provides direction and structure, which are useful targets for identified priorities to increase the possibility for change and success (Fox & Zischka, 1989; Raymond & Sowbel, 2016). (See Chapter 9 and the Chapter 9 Appendix for a continued discussion of learning obstacles, educational learning contracts, and student scenarios).

End-of-Term Evaluations

The formal end-of-term evaluations are sent to the social work program and become part of the student's academic record; they define measures of success and identify areas for further growth. They mark goal attainment, provide examples of accomplishment, and summarize student achievements and growth points. As noted earlier, competency-based education uses evaluation formats that contain a rating scale indicating the student's level of proficiency in each of the competency areas; however, field instructors should be prepared for ambiguity as each rating involves some level of interpretation over what represents competence despite stated demarcations. Although the aim is to be objective and to form value-free judgments based on evidence, this is not always easy to achieve. The criteria are often phrased in abstract or general terms, and it is sometimes difficult to determine an overall rating if performance is uneven.

The broad competency categories may not provide adequate and specific feedback to the student. This disadvantage may be partly ameliorated by our ability to translate the criterion into the context of the students' assignments and through our comments attached to each rating that offer specific examples in support of the rating choice. Providing ongoing feedback and illustrating specific evidence of professional performance provide the clarity required, and evaluations usually offer space for commentary, so examples can be given that point to the rating chosen. Students benefit from specific feedback that articulates evidence linked to actual practice. Therefore, the most useful end-of-term evaluations contain individualized, balanced, and clear statements as opposed to generalized statements that fit any student. The statements may say how the student can improve performance or address a specific learning need or provide examples of how the student demonstrated the level of mastery rated.

A performance expectation associated with engaging diversity and difference in practice states that the student should apply "self-awareness and self-regulation to manage the influence of personal biases and values in working with diverse clients and constituencies" (CSWE, 2015a, p. 7). To indicate a rating of uneven performance without linking it to actual practice misses an opportunity to make it clear to the student how the rating was chosen. Providing this information also gives the social work program additional information on its students. A clarifying statement is recommended, such as,

> the student has had difficulty establishing meaningful working relationships with some individuals. Work with an introverted and isolated 12-year-old child and her family exemplifies these challenges. Although a good relationship has been established with the child, difficulties of maintaining a balanced working relationship with the child's family have persisted. The persistently neglectful parental behaviors exemplified by

the child's father have affected the student's ability to work alongside this parent on the child's behalf. This is an agreed area for focus; plans for deepening understanding of ways to engage with this parent are being discussed. Although progress is currently uneven, signs of shifting toward improved practice exist.

In this way, the rating of an uneven performance is balanced by examples of the range of performance demonstrated and the context of the identified learning goals. Providing clear guidance on how performance can be improved in working with this family gives focus to the work ahead and promotes the possibility that additional growth can be realized. Further, it is rare to have a student who has not demonstrated any strengths or positives, and a student who is excelling should also understand that improvement is an ongoing learning goal. By providing these examples, the criterion is specific, real, and balanced. Students play an important role in identifying illustrations from their practice, recordings, and supervisory discussions. Direct observations of the student's work provide additional material for examples. Discussion of these examples should occur throughout placement so that when it comes time to write the evaluation, examples are easily selected.

Extenuating circumstances that have affected experiences in the placement should be mentioned (e.g., illness, inadequate assignments, union strikes, a change in field instructor, policy changes, natural disasters, or traumatic events). These situations contextualize challenges and provide an important perspective on the work undertaken and the learning attained.

In most social work programs, field instructors submit the student's evaluation, but the field liaison or director of field education issues the grade for field performance. In this way, the end-of-term evaluation represents a collaborative exercise based on trust between students and field instructors and field liaisons, who are representatives of the program's field education department. Our role is to provide evidence to students and social work programs that support our recommendations for the levels that represent the student's proficiency. Students are actively engaged in completion of their evaluations, and many programs require a student statement on the evaluation as confirmation of this involvement.

Identifying a Learning Focus Using the Competencies

We have stressed the importance of understanding the competencies and the practice principles they represent for us to complete a comprehensive holistic assessment of our students and to devise an appropriate learning plan. The following examples illustrate the implications of our confusion regarding the meaning and place of the competencies for student learning.

> A field instructor in a mental health clinic says her students do not have the opportunity to advance human rights in her setting. This prompts a discussion with her field liaison, who asks her to describe some of her students' assignments to help identify avenues for introducing this content. In the description, the field instructor mentions a project that promotes examination of the use of pronouns on organizational forms. The field liaison noted that the field instructor did not make the connection of this assignment to advancing human rights and justice and engaged the field instructor in a discussion about the ways this project provides opportunities for the students to examine and apply their skills in this area. Similarly, another field instructor in a foster care agency states that the students placed there do not engage in policy practice. Yet child welfare practice is deeply affected by policy. The initiative to understand disproportionality and advance human rights and justice in child welfare requires comprehending the forces impinging on policy implementation. As in the previous example, the field liaison provides links that clarify how policy practice can be made real to the students.

What are the implications of the field instructors' lack of clarity about these issues for the students' learning? How will the students be helped to understand the relevance of advancing human rights in either of these situations? How will their understanding of their professional responsibilities to engage in policy practice in their work be affected? How will their skill development in these areas be assessed? It is proposed that in grasping the specific details of each competency, learning opportunities are more easily addressed and translated into teaching that equips students for the real-world of practice. Yet this is not always straightforward.

Students' assignments are the vehicles used to apply learning and demonstrate skills. In the preceding examples, how our work advances human rights or how policies contribute should be part of our discussions. If not, we must ask ourselves how is it that these elements are not included, and we must consider how to build them into our discussions and examine how they apply to students' work. Enabling our students to reflect on how they will advance human rights is a critical component of practice. We teach in response to a student's initial lack of clarity about how human rights might apply, how they analyze appropriate strategies, and how they proceed in intervention. As we teach, we watch for the student's growing understanding and proficiency. This is the heart of our work. It begins with understanding the principles and the way they exist in practice in a specific context through the assignments we choose.

Balanced feedback based on these assessments shape student self-review and self-correction and allow us to work together on the journey to mastery across the competencies. We use assessment tools of student recordings, our experiences of talking with students about their work, direct observations of students as they interact with constituents and colleagues, and our own experience of working with students in forming our opinions and judgments regarding their proficiency. However, gaining the ability to recognize and name behaviors and skills that signal achievement and attempting to more accurately measure the level of performance mastery achieved remains a challenge as we move from assessment to evaluation. To facilitate this task, three examples show use of the competencies in the ongoing assessment process that culminates in the end-of-term formal evaluations. These examples illustrate how the competencies and their six component parts—values, skills, knowledge, judgments, cognitive reactions, and affective reactions—contribute to a holistic evaluation of a student's progress toward competence and how we use them in our supervisory practice with students.

> A specialized practice level student comments on what she perceives as an increase in unemployment rates among the agency's population served, especially among youths. The field instructor engages the student in a discussion regarding employment in the community and asks her to examine the Articles in the UDHR (1948) and UNDRIP (2007) in preparation for their next supervision. Seeing an opportunity to build research into the learning, the field instructor suggests that the student also explore data to verify her hunch, not just for the agency's target population but for the community where the setting is located. Over the next week, the student's hunch is confirmed. Next, the field instructor asks if the student is interested in examining the community supports and resources for youth job training. The student pursues this line of inquiry and finds none. As the student's interest increases, she asks if it would be possible to lead a discussion that explores this reality with staff to pool

> their experience of working on this issue with the youths on their workloads. Additionally, she asks if she could create a workshop for youths regarding challenges they face finding employment and provide them with information to address this situation.
>
> Consider what competencies are being addressed in this scenario? How do they interconnect? Even from this short description, what performance behaviors is the student beginning to display?

In this example the field instructor first recognizes the student's conceptual ability to connect the dots between how the issues in one case leads to identification of action and advocacy required for the cause the issue represents. This student's philosophical approach and values that underpin her understanding of her role in advancing social and economic justice are demonstrated as part of her work. The field instructor spots an opportunity to incorporate an unanticipated assignment that asks the student to research her perceptions further and to deepen her understanding of the issues. When the student reports her findings, the field instructor prompts additional new areas to expand exposure to the community and to link the student's interest with an assessment of the presence or absence of structural community supports for this issue. The student's interest increases and prompts a request to pursue discussion with staff and to offer workshops for youths.

The student displays other skills for evaluation. Her exploration of the importance of this issue activates her passion to advance opportunities for youths and to garner staff support. The student engages in writing a proposal for approval to involve youths. The field instructor sees these efforts as effectively responding to research-informed practice, as advancing human rights and social and economic justice, and as intervening to improve organizational understanding. These were not part of the original learning plan but emerged in response to service needs and to the student's interests and drive.

The discussion with staff and the workshop proposal could come to fruition only in a supportive field education environment that encourages an evaluation of the structural environments that surround the agency's target population, a consideration of assets and needs, and the creation of possible responses. This presumes that the field instructor identifies the proposal as essential for social work practice and as an opportunity to exercise skills in related and required competency areas. It also presumes that the administrators of the setting are willing to accept this as an opportunity for student learning and improved service delivery. Implementation would then enable the student to be evaluated on engagement, assessment, intervention, and on several levels of practice including community, organizational, and group. Learning about organizational life and factors affecting adoption of new proposals for service may materialize when a student prepares a well-conceived proposal, but learning and demonstrated student proficiency occur whether or not the plan is implemented.

> The following scenario is presented as an example of using the competencies in field instruction supervision for assessment and evaluation of skill development. Consider a generalist practice level White student who is having difficulty engaging a reluctant 15-year-old of Mexican descent who has been referred for counseling because of her frequent physical outbursts in the classroom. This youth came for a second session with the student, but as she did in the first session, she sat in the chair, arms crossed, looking down at the floor, hair covering her face and was unresponsive to the student's attempts to engage her in conversation. The student recounts her frustration and desire to say, "You don't need to come for counseling, and you can return when you want help!" The student asks her field instructor how she is supposed to help her when she doesn't want help?
>
> Consider what competencies are being addressed in this scenario. How do they interconnect? Even from this short description, what performance behaviors are the student beginning to display and what behaviors indicate the need for increased proficiency?

This example details the situation of a student who is willing to share her thoughts and feelings but is stuck by frustration and suggests terminating her contact with a youth rather than trying to manage the struggle. The student and field instructor must decide what they are trying to accomplish with and for the youth. Together they acknowledge, "We are certainly flexing our engagement and assessment muscles!" The field instructor must attempt to help the student make sense of this situation, begin a plan for the work, connect with her empathy for this youth, expand her view beyond the youth's perceived rejection of help and continued refusal to talk, and gain social empathy for the youth's situation (Austin, 2014). This is a partial list of the behaviors associated with skills the student will require, but they are a beginning to assess this student's abilities to respond to this assignment.

This situation presents the student as struggling with several competency areas: defining her role, how to engage this youth, and the implications of the issues of diversity and difference in practice. These competency areas are distinct, but they also interconnect. Being clear about her role will help the student define the boundaries surrounding her relationship with this youth. Having greater understanding of the engagement phase in the helping process and how to apply this knowledge differentially will enable the student to approach the situation with increased confidence, understanding, and direction. The behaviors embedded in these areas, which have been demonstrated, are the student's openness and willingness to share her frustration and uncertainty of how to proceed in supervision. The student is also able to display self-awareness of her frustration and her attempts to self-regulate her display of this frustration in her sessions with the youth. The extent of her frustration is a measure of how upsetting it is not being able to work effectively. It matters to this student that she was not able to connect with this youth.

The field instructor is looking for performance that shows empathy for the youth's situation, a willingness to explore a range of possible explanations of the youth's reluctance to engage in discussion, an ability to tune in to possible factors of importance, a critical review of the referral and what is known about the presenting problem and the youth's physical outbursts that precipitated the referral, a willingness to explore literature on engagement with reluctant youths, consideration of the social climate of the youth's school and class, openness to self-reflect and present the interaction from the perspective of what actually happened in the session and what was being communicated nonverbally between the lines, and an ability to examine this youth's possible ambivalence on being sent for or obtaining help. The field instructor also notes that although the youth returned for a second session, this positive sign is not acknowledged by the student.

The components of the CSWE (2015a) competencies, which act as a checklist of the areas that need to be addressed, include values, knowledge, judgments, affective reactions, cognitive reactions, and skills. A critical step is to identify how to manage these interconnected issues in conversation with the student, define the role and goals for work, and test the student's ability to reflect on her interactions to guide next steps.

Each of these component areas are addressed separately below; questions are suggested to prompt the conversation in supervision and to aid the field instructor's assessment of the student's learning needs; help the student dissect her thought processes, awaken reflections, promote greater understanding of the decisions and judgments involved; enhance her skill level to further the work; and provide evaluative material on the student's capacities.

Social work values. The field instructor might begin the conversation as follows:

> Let's talk about the social work values that are involved in this situation. Are you aware of any value conflicts in this situation? If so, what are they and how might they be resolved? For example, let's consider what wanting help means to you and what it might look like for this youth.
> How would you define your role in this situation? How might this youth define your role?

Social work knowledge. Questions concerning this category might include the following:

> What do we know about the engagement process that applies in this situation? Let's try to consider what this youth's behavior is saying.
> Let's identify some theoretical perspectives and intervention approaches you used or might use in this situation. If we take a strengths perspective, what might we see? Using an ecological systems perspective, what factors are important to consider in your work with this youth?
> What understanding of the youth's needs assisted you in this interaction? Can you point to the social work literature that supports your knowledge?
> How might this youth's heritage affect our considerations? What do we know about this school district and the issues for Mexican youths in this community?
> How do the human rights involved in this situation guide our work? For example, which Articles of the UDHR (1948) and UNDRIP (2007) address education and what do they say about educational rights that might inform how we are considering this discussion?

Cognitive and affective reactions. Thoughts and feelings evoked by the work require attention. The following prompts aim to tackle cognitive and affective reactions.

> What were you hoping to achieve here? Let's talk together about the frustration in the room for both of you.

> Let's examine how these feeling reactions affected the actions and responses for both of you. What might have happened if you chose to sit with the silence for a while? What might have happened if you were to talk while engaging in an activity with her?
> How might you give voice to your desire to understand what she has been expressing and experiencing at school? What do you think might have happened if you spoke to her feelings of being sent for counseling?
> Consider the issues of power and powerlessness between you and this youth, what implications might these considerations have on your work? Given the cross-racial tensions in today's context, why wouldn't it be normal for her not to want to talk to you? How might you address the unspoken differences that exist between you and how this might affect your work together?

Examining judgments made. This component is often difficult to discern because students feel that one thing simply leads to another and they are challenged to break down the process and make connections in their thought processes to their choice of action. The field instructor might ask the following questions:

> You made some decisions about what to say and how to approach this youth. Let's try to unpack what might have been influencing these decisions. What thoughts do you have about what is going on for this youth?
> You seem to be equating talking and responding to your questions with wanting help. What assumptions might you have been making and how did this affect your actions? What else did this youth do that might be an indication of wanting help? What did her posture and looking down at the floor mean to you?

Social work skills. Reviewing the competencies will help the student gain familiarity with them and ensure that the field instructor is not just picking obvious skills and missing others the student is developing. Later, it may be useful to review the other competencies to see whether others apply in this session.

> Let's see whether we can recognize the competencies that underpin the work you did in this session. I recognize engagement, diversity and difference in practice, and professional

behavior as important. g. How are they connected? Can you identify an intervention that illustrates these competencies in your work? Let's consider the competencies together to see if there are some hints on what we might be missing.

> Let's consider the phase of the helping process you are in and how this affects the skills you might need to focus on. Let's identify a few specific skills you used. What seemed to be more effective? Do other approaches than those you used come to mind that might be useful in this situation, and did you think of interventions at the time, but decided not to try them?

> We identified skills you are demonstrating in your work with this youth, now let's talk about the skills you are working to improve and what a next step might be. What are your thoughts on what a next step might be?

The questions in the previous sections attempt to use the competencies in a natural manner while reviewing the work. Often, as we begin to use the competencies, they feel artificial because they may be new to us, it may seem we are forcing them into the discussion, or they get in the way of how we normally approach the work of supervision. As we grow to see the importance and relevance of the competencies, we become more accustomed to their role in our teaching.

The questions point the discussion to a range of professional behaviors that are stressed in the competencies. This approach uses the competencies and components of practice as a support to our work with students and requires a clear vision of how the competencies and their components support the development of competent entry-level professionals. It grounds the mutual work between field instructor and student and focuses it on identifiable themes and practice concerns. It also focuses the student's attention on what practice skills are being honed and acquired while staying the course with the difficult work involved, takes the conversation to a different level beyond what to do next, and offers a firm and mutual ground for a conversation that addresses essential components of our work. How the student responds to these considerations helps clarify the direction forward.

Consider the following example of a generalist practice level Black student who is working in a residential facility for predominately White adults between the ages of 70 and 98. The student is 29 years old, has an undergraduate degree in English, and has been working since graduation as a journalist. Her desire to work with elders relates to her own relationship with her grandparents, who raised her. She currently lives at home with her grandfather, works part-time, and presents as a serious, somewhat shy individual. The field instructor is a White experienced staff supervisor, and this is her second student in placement.

In preparation for this supervisory session, the field instructor reminded the student that they would be reviewing the term together before tackling the end-of-term evaluation which was due in a month's time. She told the student that they would go over her assignments and her learning, and based on this review, they would consider her hopes for next semester so that they could begin to shape her assignments. She asked the student to give this some thought before their meeting.

The field instructor prepared herself by reviewing the student's assignments and noting the areas of strength and the learning they had been focusing on during the term. The identified areas of strength were the student's commitment to her work, her desire to learn, and her willingness to try new things. Another area of strength was her written expression shown in the e-mails she wrote and in other written aspects of her work. The student's practice was uneven. It was clear that this student experienced the residents' issues deeply, and although she was earnest in her efforts, she seemed somewhat frozen and constrained. She was reticent to share her thoughts in supervision, inconsistent in producing recordings, and constrained in her interactions with the adults and with the other staff of the unit; however, some progress was shown as issues repeated themselves. The student showed greater comfort in dealing with these issues as they reappeared with different individuals. Once she had experienced a situation, she was less anxious on the next occurrence. The field instructor approached the final evaluation with concerns; she felt torn in wanting to move at the student's pace, but the term was quickly coming to an end. Although there was growth in the student's comfort and familiarity with what was required, the growth was slow and uneven in areas of engagement, assessment, and use of supervision.

The areas of focus had been on developing the student's understanding of her role, abilities to engage with the adults, use of supervision and demonstration of self-awareness and self-reflection. The student's lack of submitting recordings was reducing their ability to examine and respond to the detail of the student's interventions. The student explained that her failure to produce recordings was because of her inability to recall the detail of the interactions. The field instructor shared her commitment to work with the student to find ways to take one step at a time together. As a result, the field instructor suggested changing the requirement of a process recording to a reflection on what the student could recall. They discussed the importance of increasing the student's comfort level in supervision and providing an avenue to build her abilities to reflect on her work—an essential skill required for her development. The following reflection submitted was intellectualized and detached.

The formal oral review meeting in preparation for the final evaluation began by the student and field instructor listing the range of assignments for the past term. Assignments were reviewed in terms of the major learning areas each provided: program planning, engagement with residents, group development, assessing group dynamics, engaging diversity and difference in practice, and understanding policy practice. The student was then asked to identify her greatest learning areas and comment on whether she noticed differences in her performance.

The student began by saying she recognized that her discomfort in this new role affected her more than she realized. She stated that as she reflected on the semester she could see she has grown most in her understanding of what was required of her and how different this is from what she expected or what has been required of her previously. She gave examples of how her first meetings with the residents were "tight," "somewhat forced," and "awkward." Now, she approached them differently. "I feel like I know what they are going to be asking and talking about. I am not so concerned about my ability to respond. I see that I need to respond more naturally. I know I have further to go, but I don't feel so much in my own way." She followed this with, "Is that a competency?"

The field instructor understood the difference these statements represented in the struggles over the semester and experienced relief that this student was able to demonstrate self-reflection and self-awareness and express that she felt some growth in several areas of concern. This was central to all the other concerns about this student's abilities. The field instructor was able to point exactly where these insights were in the competencies and noted each of the times self-awareness and self-reflection were noted. She went on to reaffirm how important this was to their work in supervision and in the student's ability to gain competence in practice.

The conversation turned to providing specific examples on both ends of the spectrum from beginning examples to more current examples of her practice. This illustrated the nature of the progress made and provided a baseline for next steps toward progression. Areas were also identified where insufficient and uneven progress existed. They then turned to the month ahead, discussing each other's hopes for next steps in the learning, naming specific goals and devising strategies for moving forward with a focus on the areas where the student was experiencing progress and the greatest challenges.

They identified some of the adults whom the student had begun to connect with and arranged a time they could devote to discussing next steps for each. A discussion regarding process recordings or reflections resulted in the student choosing to try a return to the process recording format. She agreed that the reflections were too much like a class assignment and that she needed to tackle her difficulties in recall. A new assignment was devised that would use the student's written capabilities by creating a Home Newsletter. Several of the more active residents were identified as possible helpers. The student was energized and commented, "Yes, I might have jumped in too deep here. Everything was so new, I found myself sinking into writing papers for my courses rather than trying to produce any sort of recordings. I would love to create a Home Newsletter with some residents!" The month ahead provided time to observe continued movement forward; clear goals and strategies were set for next steps.

This example shows the progression of an ongoing evaluative process. Each discussion provides a foundation for next steps in the evaluative process. The field instructor attempts different approaches to test whether these might shift the student's ability to participate more fully in the learning process. The ratings for this student will reflect the need for continued progress and will be based on appraisal of the culmination of progress made; the additional comments provided by the field instructor on the evaluation will provide feedback about the areas that show greatest movement and those where work is needed. The next few weeks will provide evidence of the student's ability to maintain progress, demonstrate capacity for relationship building in the assignment shaped more closely to her strengths, and determine whether a meeting with the field liaison might facilitate a clearer path forward.

Summary

Competency-based social work education requires an evaluative framework for assessment. A rubric provides this structure. The competencies, their components, and specific items identified on evaluation forms establish performance expectations; the rating scale clarifies how performance will be measured. By specifying outcomes and performance criteria and establishing levels of proficiency, this evaluative format moves toward more objective measurement. Performance criteria are observable and are clearly described so that measurement is less influenced by individual judgment. As such, the rubric is much more than a mere grading tool. The competencies and the program's framework used to measure competence combine to set clear objectives for teaching and student learning.

As we approach assessing and evaluating students, one of our initial tasks is to be clear about what each competency contributes to the development of professional skills, understand how certain actions are linked to the competencies, and recognize the myriad ways these behaviors exhibit themselves in practice. We need to identify what we have seen our students accomplish that relates to the competencies before we can clarify this for them, before we are able to compare behaviors that consolidate evidence, and before we can help move students to a more advanced level of practice.

Our task is to understand the competencies in their fullest complexity and the various steps students take as they tackle gaining expertise. We are then on the lookout for signs of behaviors that guide how we may actively help students progress and develop in these essential areas of practice. Bogo (2010) reminds us that if we rely on the competencies merely as learning objectives, we are in danger of translating them in a mechanistic manner. In fact, the challenge is to understand the competencies from the complex nature of practice and the "various dimensions of competence" (p. 75). Bogo calls on us to consider the competencies from our professional values and mission, how the competencies interact and combine, and how they are experienced as we learn our craft.

Furthermore, seeing the student's responses and actions allows us to witness their integration and application of what we are attempting to teach. For example, we may assess our student as lacking in professional demeanor or being insensitive to requirements regarding dress codes, absences, or timeliness. However, if we do not attempt to teach professional behavior and codes of professional conduct, we are only assessing attributes the student brings into placement instead of evaluating the students' ability to acclimate to expectations, demonstrate identification with their professional roles, and master control of personal preferences in a professional context.

Our students' responses and actions inform our understanding, and they help reformulate our approaches. As in the last example, the student expresses understanding of how her performance had been affected and constrained, which provided an opportunity to create strategies to test whether this newfound awareness can be channeled into action. Our evaluations of performance are shaped by this continual and ongoing explicit process. In this way, we aim to shape our assessment into a "transformative process that engages both the teacher and the learner and results in an even better educational experience.... [It is] not a product or an end—it is a process that leads to enhanced teaching, learning and informed decisions" (Wehlburg, 2010, pp. 5–7).

Conducting an educational assessment identifies learning needs and assists in developing individualized learning plans for students. These plans are dynamic and develop over time, are derived from a shared experience, and we do them jointly with students to promote mutual participation. Once a meaningful working alliance is established, both parties agree on mutual purposes that are geared to promote learning and to push into new areas of learning. The plans evolve through ongoing feedback and frequent review of where students are in relation to these mutually established goals and objectives, which form the basis of the final evaluation. This is all done with the competencies at the center of our discussions. The plans link professional knowledge to be acquired with performance objectives defined by the competencies and specializations or focus areas of the student's social work education program. Familiarity with the program's field practicum manuals and established evaluation criteria for student performance is therefore essential to this task.

Chapters 1 through 4 address the foundational tools and theoretical perspectives needed for assessing students. Our educational assessments play an incremental role in identifying progress made toward achievement of the specified required learning outcomes and, as such, propel and guide the learning forward. We propose that the rubrics of competency-based education in combination with the time frames offered by the benchmarks of each academic term provide the necessary structures to aid our ongoing assessments and evaluations of students. The theoretical frameworks of engaged pedagogy, learning theory, and attention to how students implement professional values and our professional mission provide the necessary perspective and compass. We turn to these topics in the next chapter.

CHAPTER 3 APPENDIX

The items in this appendix relate to the processes of creating an educational assessment and learning plans and preparing for oral reviews and end-of-term evaluations. The first item is an outline for an educational assessment, the second is an outline for an educational learning plan, the third provides questions to consider when preparing for an informal or formal oral review, and the last item provides tips for completing an end-of-term evaluation.

Outline for an Educational Assessment

This outline highlights the areas needing consideration when conducting an educational assessment. These areas include the student's life experiences, skills and professional attributes; pertinent demographic characteristics of the student, field instructor, setting staff and those served; the student's characteristic learning patterns; the learning opportunities that exist within the setting; emerging learning goals and objectives; and a developing learning plan.

Student's Life Experiences, Skills, and Professional Attributes

Consider the student's prior educational, employment history and other experiences relevant to learning. Highlight strengths for further professional development.

Demographic Characteristics

Consider similarities and differences in culture, ethnicity, race, gender, class, age, sexual orientation, immigration status, religion, and abilities between the student and field instructor, between the student and program staff, and between the student and populations served. Consider the following:

- What are the implications of these differences on the work, teaching, and learning?
- What are the student's strengths and learning needs regarding sensitivity to cultural issues? How is the student's self-awareness of diversity demonstrated? How is understanding of the role of culture in human development expressed? How does the student demonstrate understanding of issues of diversity, power, privilege, dominance, and oppression in professional relationships?
- Does the student engage in an antioppressive analysis of issues and problems? Does the student understand the roots of poverty and oppression? How aware is the student about global influences on these issues?

Student's Characteristic Learning Patterns

Evaluate the student's pattern of responses to the learning situation, including understanding of the learner's role. Note the student's strengths and any obstacles to learning that impede the student's professional performance, including the type of learner and implications for teaching.

- To what extent does the student use supervision and consultation? Begin by noticing how the student directs or responds to topics raised for discussion. For example, consider what questions are raised more frequently and what issues regularly appear on the student's agendas.
- Consider to what extent the student is self-preoccupied and concerned how performance is viewed. Does the student use reflection and self-regulation in these situations?
- To what extent are questions posed for immediate answers and direction, or to what extent is ambiguity and uncertainty tolerated? To what extent are questions focused on how the problems presented by those served represent larger social problems experienced in the community?
- Identify the ability to engage in self-reflection and to what extent the student considers practice theories and how they are applied.

Learning Opportunities

Consider the range and nature of learning opportunities in the setting, including available assignments and other resources for learning. Link these opportunities with the competencies.

- How will the helping process be experienced in relation to the assignments in this placement? How will policy practice be incorporated? What human rights are associated? What specific professional behaviors or skills are required in this context? In other words, in what ways will the competencies merge with the work of this setting for the student to practice mastery? How do these opportunities match with what the student needs to focus on to meet the criteria established by the social work program for the student's chosen practice method and level of professional education?
- Refer to the program's field education manual for guides related to the competencies and performance expectations.

Learning Goals and Objectives

Consider how opportunities will be provided to offer involvement across the competency areas. Give examples to support your statements. It is useful to describe assignments and how they respond to the student's learning goals.

- How do the assignments made available to the student relate to the social work program's curriculum? What learning opportunities are likely to emerge from the context of these educational experiences? How will students be introduced to opportunities to engage in an analysis of the issues and contexts surrounding service delivery by this setting?
- In addition to the specific populations, methods, and issues addressed, what opportunities exist for students to integrate these perspectives into broader professional considerations of practice and identification of areas targeted for potential structural change?

Initial Strategies to Achieve Learning Goals

The teaching plan evolves from all the information obtained from the previous questions and in consultation with the student. Consider the timing and sequencing of assignments, teaching methods chosen, and priorities set.

An Outline for Educational Learning Plans

Educational learning plans emerge from an educational assessment. The plan identifies essential elements of the student's learning needs, indicating short- and long-term goals and objectives and the types of assignments planned to advance learning. The essential characteristics of an educational learning plan include

- mutual participation, that is, parties agree on a mutual purpose geared to promote learning and therefore, questioning, review, and evaluation are inherent;
- reciprocal accountability by encouraging taking responsibility for learning so that field instructors, task supervisors, field liaisons, and students have individual, complementary, and shared, although not necessarily equal, responsibilities; and a working alliance that establishes permission to push into new areas of learning.

Expectations are made explicit so that

- what there is to learn and the best way to teach it are identified;
- a baseline is established, progress can be assessed, and gaps can be identified (i.e., gaps in learning and in teaching);
- self-evaluation is encouraged so that all involved assume a professional stance when identifying and resolving problems.
- priorities are formulated; what is possible is defined; hopes, expectations, and opportunities are identified.

Learning plans are

- constrained by time,
- bound by the realities of the context, and
- based on the learning opportunities available,
- formulated for the possibility of success, and

- dynamic, dependent on recurrent review, renegotiated, and redefined over time.

Preparing for Informal and Formal Oral Reviews

- Formal reviews occur at least five times during the academic year, at the midterm or sixth week review, 1 month prior to each end-of-term evaluation and during the preparation for each end-of-term evaluation. Informal oral reviews are part of each supervisory session. They are the opportunities we take to provide ongoing feedback on our students' progress to competency. Consider the following questions as prompts for discussion with your student:
  - Is the range of assignments you are carrying providing adequate work for you?
  - Are there ways we need to adjust your schedule?
  - What areas of practice embedded in the competencies are unclear to you?
  - What new areas of practice are you interested in?
  - What areas do you want to improve in?
  - Are there ways we can improve on the arrangements with your task supervisor?
- How are you experiencing the way we are working together in supervision? How are field education supervisory conferences meeting your learning needs? What alternative methods might be helpful to you?
- What is most helpful in supervision? What is least helpful? Do I provide enough feedback to help you know how I think you are doing? Do I give you enough guidance on how to improve your efforts? Do you feel you have enough space in supervision to tell me when I am going too fast or too slow or not hearing what you are trying to tell me? You have had difficulties in providing weekly recordings. Let's talk about this so that we can decide whether an alternative format might help you become more comfortable with this requirement.
- Are we spending adequate time balancing your need for discussion on your interventional choices with needing to expand your understanding of how to advance human rights

and justice, how to work with diversity and difference, policy and research implications for your work, and understanding your professional role in this context? In what ways does your work in field education relate to what you are learning in your courses?
- How comfortable are you in managing the technology required in this setting? What populations, issues, problems, tasks, or systems do you believe you work with best? What populations, issues, problems, tasks, or systems do you find most challenging? What new areas of practice are you interested in? What areas do you want to improve in?
- Do you need help in identifying theoretical perspectives in your work? How effective do you feel in your attempts to critically analyze your work? How comfortable are you in your abilities to reflect on your work and to self-regulate?
- Are there issues of concern that have not been addressed?

End-of-Term Evaluations

The end-of-term evaluation requires attention to several factors. The following summary provides suggestions for completing end-of-semester evaluations:

- Competency-based evaluations require rating proficiency. Underlying these ratings are three components: What is the skill being rated in the context of the opportunities and assignments available, is progress witnessed over time, and how do students' attitudes toward learning, learning patterns, and examples illustrate the skill in context?
- Even when a final evaluation form uses rating scales of performance, written comments or summaries provide evidence and valuable feedback.
- In addition to being ongoing, evaluations are dynamic; we invite students to participate and take ownership of assessing their performance throughout the placement experience.
- Evaluations should be comprehensive, but they also focus on specific areas of learning. They should be personal and individualized and identify what is unique to the student in the ways practice and learning are approached and demonstrated.

- Setting descriptions and assignments are brief and focus on the specific context of practice that shapes learning assignments (e.g., short-term crisis intervention with a runaway youth that requires collaboration with a variety of service organizations and outreach services to families.)
- Despite mutuality and collaboration in the evaluation process leading up to the written evaluation, field instructors have overall responsibility for final evaluations; however, students should have ample time to read, digest, discuss, give feedback, and contribute to their evaluations.
- Final evaluations build on prior reviews and are summaries that mark the end of each academic term; therefore, new information or critiques are not added until discussion has occurred.
- If task supervisors are part of the learning team, arrangements are made to include their observations and comments as part of the final evaluation.
- Ensuring a chance to read and absorb evaluations before signing them builds in assurance of due process. This offers another occasion to model mutual and collaborative feedback.
- Mutual feedback includes allowing students to express their disagreement with the substance of a statement, wording, or a rating. Disagreements may reflect miscommunication or deeper differences of opinion about field performance. A formal evaluation conference set aside to review the final evaluation provides time to consider and make any needed changes.
- The review is an opportunity to clarify or modify our opinion of the student's skill level, consider additional evidence, and agree on the words to express concern about a student's continuing lack of progress that is balanced by acknowledgment of progress made.
- Despite prior verbal discussions, students may react as if it were the first time they heard our concern or critique. In these circumstances faculty field liaisons are available for consultation or feedback on the wording or handling of potentially complex or delicate situations.
- Evaluations include goals for future learning in the student's next term, placement, or job. In this way, evaluations

contribute to professional development and provide the opportunity to emphasize a teaching point or to restate a learning goal.
› Evaluations are signed by the field instructor and student, become part of a student's record, and are the basis for field performance grades.
› Because a signature does not mean that both parties agree with everything stated in the evaluation, some programs ask students to write addenda to evaluations. It is expected for field instructors to have access to students' comments.
› Timely submission of evaluations is important for several reasons: students benefit from written feedback to navigate the next steps in the achievement of their learning goals, fieldwork grades are withheld and cannot be submitted without proper documentation, and for graduating students, the timely submission of grades determines eligibility for licensure exams and employment. Finally, it models good professional practice.
› Evaluations are most useful to students; therefore, it is important to ensure they receive a copy.

CHAPTER 4

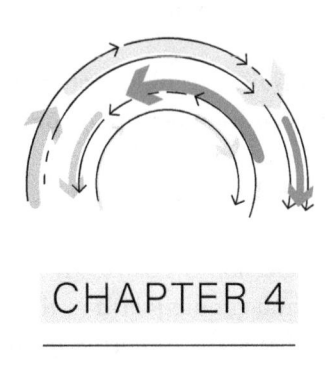

Adult Learning

Thinking, Feeling, and Doing

Fostering transformative learning is much more than implementing a series of instructional strategies with adult learners.... It is also not an easy way to teach. It means asking yourself, Am I willing to transform in the process of helping my students transform? This means taking the position that without developing a deeper awareness of our own frames of reference and how they shape practice, there is little likelihood that we can foster change in others. (Taylor, 2008, p. 13)

Educators should make the attempt to become aware of their own cultural presuppositions about learning. They should openly share these presuppositions and engage their students in a dialogue about learning.... By drawing upon knowledge of their students' and their own past experiences and history of participation, instruction can be designed to bridge what is familiar and comfortable to less developed or practiced areas of learning. In other words, both students and instructors can be encouraged to work from the known to the lesser known. (MacCleave & Eghan, 2010, p. 245)

This chapter considers theoretical contributions that support our understanding of a student's journey toward proficiency in learning practice from a justice-based framework. These theoretical frameworks are central to the aims of this book, and they shed light on the complex processes involved in teaching for justice in competency-based social work education.

Competency-based education is particularly well suited to adult learners; field instructors and students are joined in the mutually desirable goal of achieving competence. Using the competencies and the rubrics that surround them make teaching and learning more equal and transparent with both parties participating in shared goals; this sets down essential conditions for environments conducive to learning. This chapter builds on these foundations and considers the guidelines suggested in adult learning theory for establishing a conducive learning environment. Additionally, transformational learning theory provides important insights into how learning may promote critical analysis, reflective practice, and establish a climate for teaching for justice. Strategies emerge for managing reactions to learning how privileged statuses may affect interactions. Information on learning styles, developmental learning stages, Kolb's (1984) model of experiential learning and Bloom's (1956) taxonomy of learning domains are summarized; they offer additional information to guide our supervisory responses. These perspectives offer helpful views on the specific challenges facing students as they negotiate their quest for competence through their field education experiences, the context where learning practice is directly experienced, assimilated, and applied.

Justice-Based Conducive Learning Environments: Adult Learning Theory

Adult learning theory, andragogy, promoted by Malcolm Knowles is the art and science of helping adults learn (Knowles, 1972, 1975, 1984; Knowles, Holton, & Swanson, 1998). It sets forth principles for shaping adult learning situations. Adult learning theory presupposes that adults benefit from knowing what will be taught, how it will be taught, and why it is important to learn. As an individual's self-concept shifts from dependency to self-direction, motivation to learn is viewed as increasingly internal rather than external (Bransford, Brown, & Cocking, 2004; Jarvis, 2009), and adult learners' experiences, needs, and objectives are viewed as primary (Goldstein, 2001). Our orientation and readiness to learn are progressively related to the demands of our social roles and become more problem centered and connected to an inherent wish and need to apply new knowledge. Additionally, our experiences increasingly serve as a resource for learning (Carpenter-Aeby & Aeby, 2013; Cox, 2015; Knowles et al., 1998; Smith, 2002).

These guidelines drive the approach to teaching adult learners; being clear about what is to be learned, how best to teach it, and its effect on the learner provides an approach to our role as a facilitator of student learning (Bogo, 2010; Knowles et al., 1998; Moen, Goodrich Liley, & Dennis, 2016; Rogers, 1995). We also need to be prepared to prompt new ways of thinking about interactions and experiences (Carroll, 2010b; Mezirow, 1997; Taylor, 2006). This active role requires being aware of the multiple and complex factors involved in social work practice that may present barriers to students' abilities so that we might anticipate potential stumbling blocks, be intentional and purposeful in our teaching, and create an environment of challenge and support to promote learning.

Research confirms that the context in which learning occurs is a powerful influence on how we learn. Context refers to more than the conditions of the physical place; it includes the extent to which the environment is centered on the learner and the knowledge conveyed, the ways learning is assessed, how this information is used to individualize learning and the way the community is used to promote learning (Bransford et al., 2004). Knowles (1972) connects the environment for learning directly to the quality of learning achieved. Not surprisingly, the learning environment is included in the CSWE's (2015a) EPAS and defined as the *implicit curriculum*; it is described more fully later in this chapter.

Creating such an environment is also associated with the nature of the alliance established between the learner and the supervisor (Bogo, 2016). Chapter 2 positions the relationship between the field instructor and student as crucial for enabling challenging conversations to occur and for the promotion of critical thinking and self-reflection (Deal, 2003; Plack & Grennberg, 2005; Postma, 2015). Based predominately on the provisions espoused by Knowles (1972, 1975, 1984), the following section expands on characteristics linked with favorable learning environments: informality, respect, decision making and collaboration, openness, authenticity, curiosity, physical comfort, and trust.

Informality equalizes the differential power that exists between field instructors and students. The way we define and enact our role may lessen the inherent power differential between us and invites a more reciprocal relationship. This must be handled in a manner that creates comfort, promotes mutuality, is responsive to students' feelings, and is consistent with cultural expectations.

Respect involves possessing an inclusive perspective and responding to students with dignity and concern, which in turn promotes the development of mutuality. Inclusivity involves responding to the range of backgrounds, approaches to learning, and abilities represented by our students, which contributes to feeling valued and accepted. For example, we address the use of pronouns early and straightforwardly, the culture of the context is explained in a manner that conveys that the student is welcome, and the student's own unique potential contribution is explored. We communicate respect by acknowledging lived experiences and helping students integrate past achievements with current learning. For example, a student who has experience working with older adults but is now placed in a foster care agency may benefit from assignments that involve working with groups of grandmothers who are kinship foster parents. The familiarity from previous experience acts as a link to new areas of work and new roles. This links the unfamiliar with the familiar. Providing such connections demonstrates respect for the past and communicates that although the new learning presents challenges, prior experience and learning can be transferred to new areas (Boitel & Fromm, 2013).

Decision making about learning is a shared and collaborative process. Are students asked to participate in making decisions on issues that directly concern them? For example, shared decision making is promoted by how clear the decision-making process is made surrounding assignment choices and how often students are engaged in reflective discussions that promote dialogue. Other activities that contribute to shared decision making revolve around agenda building for supervision, setting priorities for learning, inviting open discussion of what we expect of students and what they expect of us, and including students' views on our evaluations of their performance. Collaboration rather than cooperation often emerges from a shared decision-making process related to opportunities to help plan learning experiences. This partnership builds on the mutual respect that exists in the relationship and involves shared planning. In this way, students are invited to own their learning, develop motivation, and increase self-direction and autonomy.

Openness involves direct, frank, reciprocal, and genuine dialogue. In addition to receiving feedback, students are encouraged to give us feedback about learning environments, conditions, contexts, and assigned tasks on an ongoing basis. Eliciting student reactions encourages a dialogue about learning and allows expression of possible confusion. Providing such opportunities models respectful dialogue. This openness also reinforces a sense of inclusiveness and mutuality. Openly sharing and being willing to examine how our experiences, supervisory styles, expectations, needs, social dimensions of identity, and issues of power, privilege, and oppression affect the learning process promote dialogue.

Authenticity is achieved by open, mutual, honest, and respectful responses to student questions by providing sincere appraisals and by tuning in to student concerns. This means that we are straightforward in our approach to learning issues that need attention. Feedback contains a balance of pointing out strengths, achievements, and deficits. Conflict is not avoided, and meaningful dialogue results.

Curiosity demonstrates interest in our students as people and as learners. One way to achieve this is a detailed assessment of learning needs, which implies that we are inquisitive about the effectiveness of our teaching and that we want to know how our efforts are experienced. It means we take time to be clear and to adjust the pacing of our teaching accordingly.

Physical comfort is achieved by providing rests, breaks, and changes in pace that give students time to absorb new learning. The structure of the physical environment includes having a space for students to call their own, which in turn increases their sense of belonging and belief that their presence in the setting matters. This can be a challenge in the current context of practice where space is a scarce commodity. Acknowledging this reality and providing some accommodation such as schedules that indicate when space is free for the student to use or providing a locker where belongings may be kept go a long way in helping the student adjust to the reality of space constraints. Physical safety combines with physical comfort to create conditions conducive for learning. Minimizing risk and unsafe conditions requires ongoing attention (Lyter, 2016). Ensuring that students are prepared and informed about safety practices contributes to their ability to manage obstacles related to anxiety and discomfort. The work of Sensoy and DiAngelo (2014) points to the complexity of creating safety for the risk taking involved in learning. As safety means different things to different individuals, the work is more about being sensitive to this reality than promising comfort and ease; safety for learning includes promoting tolerance for ambiguity and inviting multiple perspectives.

Trust and a lack of defensiveness emerge when students believe their opinions will be heard, when they see that attempts are made to meet their needs, and by viewing learning as experimentation rather than as doing the right or wrong thing or success or failure. Dialogues about learning achievements and growth points that occur in a nonjudgmental manner promote risk taking and progression toward the achievement of goals and objectives. This involves encouraging interest about, and experimentation with, new ways of thinking (Bogo, Rawlings, Katz, & Logie, 2014). Likewise, conveying a belief in the process of education communicates a belief in the individual's capacity to change. This provides hope.

In addition to the above characteristics of a conducive learning environment, attention to our use of time, space, title or status, information sharing, and access to resources are concrete ways that demonstrate our intentions to promote environments conducive to learning. The way we exercise our power in relation to each of these areas demonstrates respect and achieves mutuality. Following are considerations for each dimension:

> Time: Schedule consistent, private, and uninterrupted field instruction supervisory time, which allows students to plan and provides a prism for viewing students' abilities to use and organize time. Consider when supervision is scheduled in relation to the work assigned.
> Space: Consider the physical setting for instructional conferences. Are chairs on different levels or different heights? Do students and field instructors face one another? Is the office or meeting place private? Do our offices include items that symbolize a variety of worldviews? Will students recognize their culture is being valued through the artifacts represented?
> Title or status: How do we choose to be addressed? How do we choose to address students? How does this fit with the setting's social norms? How quickly is this issue settled? How is the use of pronouns handled?
> Information sharing and access to resources: How accessible is information about routine aspects of field placement settings? Are we the only person students can turn to for information or to obtain resources? How quickly do students receive bathroom keys or find out where office supplies are located? How do we ensure students know it is possible to make requests of us?

Learning as Change: Transformational Learning

There are specific challenges connected to teaching social work practice. Goldstein (2001) reminds us that "given the noble mission of social work, we need to discover how learners begin to appreciate and contend with the [historical and] deep-set social injustices, prejudices, and other inequities that engulf their clients" (p. 5). As working for justice and challenging the status quo frequently involve examining new and different perspectives, we can anticipate responses that sometimes include rejection of the material presented; additionally, the reactions may vary depending on the student's social location (Butin, 2005a; Davis, Mirick, & McQueen, 2014; Garran & Rasmussen, 2014; hooks, 2010; Jones, 2008; Kumashiro, 2004; Shor, 1992; Sullivan & Johns, 2002).

For those from marginalized backgrounds, responses may be linked to feeling their voices have been silenced, perhaps their hidden identities are ignored or purposefully protected, or they may feel they have been made an object of ridicule or misrepresentation (Davis et al., 2014). The work of Garran and Rasmussen (2014) identifies our responsibility to create "a holding environment" (p. 408) for greater inclusion and awareness of the possible challenges for everyone involved.

Those from privileged backgrounds may experience something different. Their rejection of the material may be a reaction against a clash of value conflicts that produces confusion and conflicting emotions. These responses provide evidence about our students' readiness to tackle new or disquieting perspectives, they provide clues on how to steer our responses and hint to possible larger issues. These responses are resources for further engagement with the issues (Mildred & Zuniga, 2004); they point the way forward and are described as a process of identity reconstruction (Butin, 2005b). Jones (2008) explains that this identity reconstruction is connected to the process of "maintaining and reformulating a sense of self." (p. 70). From a transformative learning perspective, the process of reconstruction gives students a chance to "shift from resisting challenges to their position of power and privilege to resisting the very structures that produce systems of oppression, and privilege." (p.78).

Transformational learning theory (Merriam, 2008; Merriam & Caffarella, 1999; Mezirow, 2000) proposes that education transforms ways of thinking about the world and ourselves. Mezirow (1978) calls this a "perspective transformation," (p. 100) which is prompted by disequilibrium and which results from exposure to a disorienting event, a critical incident, or an accumulation of transformations in our meaning schemes over time. Further, a perspective transformation is

> the process of becoming critically aware of how and why our assumptions have come to constrain the way we perceive, understand, and feel about our world; changing these structures of habitual expectation

to make possible a more inclusive, discriminating, and integrating perspective, and finally making choices or otherwise acting upon these new understandings. (Mezirow, 1991, p. 167)

Thus, the disorienting dilemma promotes an ability to expand our frames of reference. It stimulates being open to new learning, and it has the potential of transforming our points of view and habits of mind.

The experience of psychological and cognitive disequilibrium produces feelings of internal dissonance that are revealed as uncertainty and sometimes as conflict and retreat (Sanford, 1967). According to Dalton and Crosby (2008),

> it is the experience of such dissonance that opens the possibility for learning and growth because it nudges students into confronting and considering new ways of understanding, thinking, and acting that help to unsettle the old and integrate it with the new.... It is essential for students' learning and growth to have challenging stimuli and experiences of positive restlessness because these provide the creative disequilibrium and intellectual stimulation that drives personal exploration and development. (pp. 1–2)

Facilitation of transformative learning requires us to understand and be willing to critique the learner's assumptions. We provide practice in examining these assumptions and biases, which leads to different ways of viewing and experiencing the situation or issue. This process helps redefine the problem. We also need to provide the opportunity for discourse. As Mezirow (1997) stated,

> discourse ... is a dialogue devoted to assessing reasons presented in support of competing interpretations, by critically examining evidence, arguments, and alternative points of view.... We learn together by analyzing the related experiences of others to arrive at a common understanding that holds until new evidence or arguments present themselves. (pp. 6–7)

Although early work in transformative learning theory stresses cognitive and rational processes, the current understanding includes a holistic view that incorporates "the body, the emotions, the spirt as well as the mind" and shifts from a focus on the individual learner to making connections to "the learner in context" (Merriam, 2008, p. 95). This includes what has already been described in creating a conducive environment for learning and how perspectives affect learning and knowing (Merriam & Kim, 2008). Additionally, a review of research on transformative learning theory notes methods of instructional support that assists the application of new understanding; communicating new perspectives alone is not adequate. Specific steps and directions may be needed to ensure students have the practical knowledge and know-how to manage what is required of them (E. W. Taylor, 2007).

These perspectives on teaching for change show promise of clarifying how lived experiences frame a perspective transformation. At present, understanding what is involved in transformative learning stresses the changes that emerge from the recognition that old ways of doing, seeing, or feeling must give way to newer, more relevant views or ways of being. This "awakening change in perspective" adds to our understanding of the processes that affect the often-challenging task of prompting learners "to consider alternative perspectives on their personal political, work, and social lives" (Knowles et al., 1998, p. 106). It provides a theoretical perspective to the aha moments often encountered in field education learning.

Facilitating the development of "a sense of trust in the process" and helping "students to live with some discomfort while on the edge of knowing" are critical components (E. W. Taylor, 2007, p. 187). This requires our being cognizant of a student's readiness for new learning and often involves negotiation, being authentic, and balancing challenge with support (E. W. Taylor, 2006).

Daloz (1986) applies Sanford's theory of challenge and support (1967) as pertinent to how effective mentoring relationships promote growth and development. Based on Daloz's depiction, Figure 4.1 demonstrates how challenge and a response of supportive stimulation, as described by Sanford (1967), interact in a learning situation. Challenge is presented as a developmental crisis or situation that involves tackling new learning in the service of growth and development, whereas support is described as a response that "holds" and "provides vision" for the learner so that learning and development may occur (Daloz, 1986, p. 212).

Figure 4.1 shows that the learning situation characterized by low support and low challenge results in nothing changing; the learner does not experience adequate challenge or stimuli (Sanford, 1967) and without the interaction between developmental challenges and a supportive "holding response" (Daloz, 1986, p. 212), things remain the same, new learning is not tackled, and "stasis" results (Daloz, 1986, p. 213). Situations of high challenge matched with low support result in frustration and retreat from the learning. This contrasts with providing high challenges matched with the appropriate

150 Part One: Advancing a Framework for Field Education

	HIGH	
CHALLENGE	Retreat	Growth
	No Change	Confirmation
	LOW	HIGH

SUPPORT (A HOLDING RESPONSE)

Figure 4.1 Challenge and support
(*Source:* Adapted with permission from Daloz [1986].)

high levels of support needed by the learner to meet the challenge and for that learner to grow, develop, and learn. Those situations characterized by high support and low challenge interestingly may produce learning, but this is described as learning that confirms what the learner already knows and that does not take the learner beyond thresholds already achieved. In a sense, the deeper learning is stymied (Daloz, 1986; Dalton & Crosby, 2008; Sanford, 1967). This understanding underscores our need to provide learning challenges and to match challenges with appropriate levels of support that hold and bolster students' abilities to meet the inherent challenges associated with new learning. The reality is that some students need more support than others to get started, some students require more challenge than others to feel they are learning, and the conditions change given the task. The work is to assess student readiness and needs and to aptly respond.

The development of transformational teaching and supervisory techniques support student learning and personal growth (Carroll, 2010b; Fazio-Griffith & Ballard, 2016; Slavich & Zimbardo, 2012). The tenets of this approach include creating a collaborative learning experience that offers opportunities for combining challenging learning while providing support and individualized responses. The teaching strategies aim to examine assumptions while providing ample opportunities for reflection. Teachers are instructional coaches who facilitate active student learners in the acquisition of new knowledge while also encouraging positive attitudes on the process of learning (Slavich & Zimbardo, 2012). The link to our purposes is clear.

Experiential Learning: Models, Styles and Stages

Experiential learning examines interactions with experience and the process of converting that experience into knowledge (Sternberg & Zhang, 2000). "Experience is grasped and transformed into knowing" (Kolb, 1984, p. 68). This is important given what students experience in field education and our aims to facilitate their ability to make meaning from these encounters. Understanding these processes has implications for teaching, individualizes our approach, increases awareness of the complex needs of students, and propels the search for ways of adapting teaching methods and structuring assignments to improve learning.

This section addresses several theoretical aspects of experiential learning that guide our assessment of learners and strategies for teaching. We examine Kolb's (1984) four-stage learning cycle and the resulting four learning patterns or styles. These styles guide assessment of learners and strategies for teaching. Bogo and Vayda's (1993) model depicting the integration of theory and practice (ITP) is based on Kolb's learning cycle and Schön's (1983, 1987) understanding of educating for reflective practice. This ITP loop is described to assist understanding of the processes involved. This section ends with a consideration of developmental stage models that describe the natural learning trajectories expected for students.

Kolb's Learning Cycle, Bogo and Vayda's ITP Model

Recent adjustments to Kolb's (1984) model contribute to our growing understanding of the complexity of how we learn. For example, Jarvis (1995, 2009, 2015) assesses Kolb's learning cycle as simplistic and sets forth an alternative dynamic model to reflect the complexity of learning. Likewise, Miller, Kovacs, Wright, Corcoran, and Rosenblum (2004) report on an exploratory study that builds on the work of Jarvis with groups of social work students and field instructors to examine the field learning process. Interesting modifications of Kolb's learning cycle include appreciation of the role emotions play in learning; feelings, intuition, and imagery also offer vital contributions (Jarvis, 2015; Yorks & Kasl, 2002). Despite these modifications, Kolb's foundational framework continues to provide direction for work with students and is therefore important to include here (Carroll, 2010a, 2010b; Moen et al., 2016).

Likewise, although research on Kolb's (1984) learning cycle is often applied in different academic disciplines and professions, and even though Kolb's model is frequently applied to field education (Moen et al., 2016), research on applying the model in social work is limited. Berengarten (1957) and Papell (1980) are early proponents of the importance of understanding learning styles of social work students, and continuous applications of Kolb's learning theory to identify learning styles illustrate its ongoing relevance to our work (Bogo & Vayda, 1993; Cartney, 2000; Massey, Kim, & Mitchell, 2011; Moen et al., 2016; Williams, Brown & Etherington, 2013; Wolfsfeld & Haj-Yahia, 2010).

Bogo and Vayda (1987, 1991, 1993, 1998) and Bogo (2010, 2018) provide a conceptual map of points in the learning process when it becomes possible to increase student awareness and how reflection progresses through experience, linking, and reflection. Bogo and Vayda (1993) illustrate this process as an interactive and ongoing loop of learning as we manage thoughts and reactions (http://www.socialwork.utoronto.ca/wp-content/uploads/2014/08/Bogo-and-Vayda-The-Practice-of-Field-Instruction.pdf). In this way we prepare and reflect for action. The process moves back and forth in a manner that conveys interaction and interrelation. A picture of how actions are influenced and linked by knowledge, values, thinking, reflections, and cognitive and affective reactions and judgments emerges. Bogo and Vayda (1993) suggest the process begins with the

> retrieval of the factual elements of a practice situation. The next step, reflection, focuses on the effectiveness of the retrieved interaction or intervention as well as the identification of personal values, attitudes and assumptions which modify the retrieved facts. These processes are then linked to professional knowledge that explain or account for the findings of the preceding steps. This leads directly to the selection of a professional response to the initiating action that began the loop.... A response or action is selected, and its effect then becomes the focus of the same process. (pp. 3–4)

The ITP model involves learning through retrieval, reflection, and linkage, and explains where a professional response emerges. In this knowing in action and reflecting on action, we learn new ways of doing and being.

This understanding is based on Schön's description of various types of knowing and reflection involved in the skillful art of decision making in practice (1983); Schön explains "knowing in action" (p. 50) as situations where we act without thinking; we may not even be aware of where or when or how we learned or knew what to do. "Reflection in action" (p. 54) is, as it implies, reflecting even as we are acting; this reflection provides insight and guidance for action. In reflection-on-action we become cognizant of needing to puzzle through a situation. Bogo and Vayda's ITP model uses Kolb's and Schön's concepts to clarify the processes and assist our understanding of how these functions work together as we attempt to build and improve our practice.

Kolb's Four Dominant Learning Patterns

Kolb's (1984) model proposes that an individual learner enters the learning cycle from any one of four distinct positions. The positions connect with each other as opposite ends on two axes, or continuums: how we approach a task and how we respond, think, or feel about the task (Sternberg & Zhang, 2000).

In addition to focusing on ways we process and perceive learning, Kolb's (1984) model introduces predominant learning styles. A learning style refers to characteristic ways of approaching learning tasks and of tackling new learning situations or contexts (Bogo, 2010; Burack-Weiss, Coyle & Brennan, 2013; Cartney, 2000; Knight, 2016). These predominant and preferred ways of approaching learning signify how adult students can best learn and be taught to experiment with the application of new concepts.

For example, some students will state their preference to develop broad conceptual frameworks about problem areas before meeting service users. They often comment, "I don't feel I understand enough. I wish I could read an article about this problem before meeting this individual." Others want to meet the person before giving thoughtful attention to facts about the situation. A familiar statement from these students is, "I will be better able to answer that question after I have met the person." Still others prefer to rehearse their practice approaches by role-playing or modeling their early interventions on observations of more seasoned practitioners. Understanding a student's preferred response to new learning can help guide choices of teaching to enhance a student's approach to the task.

Structuring assignments also requires attention to how students learn and understanding how information is most easily processed. As above, introductions to any planned assignments or learning experiences may be viewed from different perspectives. Likewise, realizing that the student could benefit

154 Part One: Advancing a Framework for Field Education

Feeling and Watching: (Divergers) Summary

Characteristics	Teaching Response
Watches and reflects before acting	Arrange an observation of an interview
Provides accurate observations	Arrange group learning situations
Open-minded and able to reflect and consider a variety of influences to broaden their assessments	Build on perceptions to increase comfort in discussion of theory
	Brainstorming or heartstorming to generate ideas
Feeling oriented	Discuss reflections, add reflective journals/logs

Thinking and Watching: (Assimilators) Summary

Characteristics	Teaching Response
Thrives on learning theoretical approaches, reading, and theoretical discussions	Select pertinent readings
	Start with thinking about cases, move to feelings
Tends toward question-and-answer interviewing	Assign to read canned cases or sample case files
Analytical in approach to new learning	Develop a diverse caseload to diffuse generalization
Logical in approach to problem solving	Practice open-ended questions and exploration
	Build on analytical and planning skills

Thinking and Doing: (Convergers) Summary

Characteristics	Teaching Response
Action oriented	Provide assignments that require immediate action
Takes risks and jumps in	
Learns from recurring activity	Discussion of work is easier after experience
Problem-solving abilities	Build on hunches
Anticipating problems or possible outcomes does not come easily	Explain the slow process of change
	Offer supportive links of theory to practice
	Provide videos or simulations

Feeling and Doing: (Accomodators) Summary

Characteristics	Teaching Response
Uses senses and personal experience	Recordings give opportunities to reflect separately from the feelings evoked
Connects easily with people	
Learns in the context of the here-and-now	Review several sessions to identify patterns of behavior, and enable stepping back from feelings involved
Leads with senses and intuition	
Has a good ear for latent content	Help make conscious what comes intuitively
Often creative and able to respond to a range of clients and problems	Arrange group learning situations
Is interested in the end goal	

Figure 4.2 Kolb's four learning positions and teaching responses

from a different type of experience from which to bridge new learning, we arrange for this exposure and involvement for better integration of the material.

Figure 4.2 summarizes the dominant learning positions identified by Kolb and their corresponding learning styles; these are presented alongside corresponding possible teaching responses. These summary characteristics are compiled from Kolb (1984) and Sternberg & Zhang, (2000), whereas the corresponding teaching responses are summarized from Urbanowski and Dwyer (1988), and Wolfsfeld, Haj-Yahia (2010).

Adult Learning Styles and Individualized Learning Approaches

Although considerable attention is placed on learning styles, it is important to note there is debate on whether matching learning styles with assignments improves how an individual learns; however, it is generally agreed that adults approach new learning in different ways, and evidence is growing that there are methods of teaching certain subjects that match the content better than others (Pashler, McDaniel, Rohrer, & Bjork, 2008). Similarly, increasing evidence linked to how multiple intelligences affect learning point to the need to individualize our teaching approaches and to introduce a variety of methods to assist the learner (Gardner, 2011). In these views, instructional practices are individualized, varied and flexible. Matching teaching strategies to learner needs is not presented as a panacea; it is a means to respect the complexity of learning and teaching, a way to respond to the diversity of our learners and the demands of specific learning tasks, and for thinking about how to facilitate growth and development given the variations in the ways we learn.

This point seems particularly important given the range our students represent in their developmental stage of life. It also supports the use of similar supervisory practices with BSW students and first-year MSW students who are measured on the same generalist practice level competencies. Of course, first-year MSW students differ from BSWs because they survived and achieved an undergraduate degree. This is an important difference, but emphasis should also turn to individualized assessments of our students' learning needs and adapting our supervisory approaches to these needs with the identified competency outcomes as goals.

Developmental Stages of Learning

In addition to appreciating the individualized needs students exhibit given their diversity, stage of life, and preferred approaches to learning, it is helpful to identify the student's level or stage of learning. Applying stage models of skill development adds another dimension to our teaching strategies.

Identifying what stage of learning is operating facilitates the assessment of what students may need for their adjustment to new learning situations (Bogo, 2010; Solo, 2018); stages of learning also provide a gauge for understanding the pace of the student's learning. Awareness of these elements provides guideposts to the potential stumbling blocks along the way. We often see this progressive movement when students grasp a threshold concept such as start where the person seeking help is. Until the student understands the importance of working alongside and at the individual's pace, efforts toward change will be stymied. Likewise, until the student understands that helping does not mean doing for but doing with, the door will remain closed to grasping their role and to understanding the deeper meanings of empowerment. Crossing these thresholds signal reaching for a different stage in learning (Bain & Bass, 2012). Developmental stage models also suggest how learning key constructs and complex concepts signify attaining higher levels of thinking about an issue or identifying ways to manage the issue; they offer perspectives on student progression from novice to proficient practitioner and corresponding recommendations for supervisory responses. Stage models also predict potential challenges. According to Everett, Miehls, DuBois, and Garran (2011), developmental models... presume that (a) student professional development follows a series of sequential, hierarchical stages from less to more competent; (b) as they proceed through these stages students struggle with developmental issues or concerns such as competence, use-of-self, and identity; and (c) appropriate supervision interventions differ at each stage of development. (p. 252)

Although developmental stage models provide guideposts, they describe a linear progression toward mastery, as if it were reliably predictable. However, the actual progression may not easily fit into the parameters described. Progress may differ in acquiring understanding of a certain skill to being able to apply this same skill and to gaining insight on the demands and challenges involved (Carroll, 2010a, 2010b; Granello, 2010). Still, the models are important contributions to our growing understanding of what we might expect along the way.

For example, Reynolds (1942) developed a five-stage model addressing the stages of learning in social work that continues to offer useful insights. These stages can be viewed as the journey to greater confidence in fulfilling the student's role and function in the placement setting. Reynolds asserts that there is movement back and forth between stages, learning does not occur in a linear fashion, and returning to earlier stages is normal and expected as the learner is faced with new facets of tasks to be mastered. She stresses keeping a focus on what is happening to the learner and recommends beginning where the student is, using what the situation yields, building on the student's experience, and supporting new learning to facilitate integration, assimilation, and application. Her five-stage model is the following.

Stage 1 is *acute consciousness of self*, which is characterized by feelings that students do not have the capacity to succeed. Students respond by fight or flight, paralysis, feelings of inadequacy, feeling stupid, keeping silent, using self-deprecating humor, using aggression to mask anxiety, or becoming increasingly verbal. In this stage we need to help students find solid ground in the personal adequacy they already possess. This stage is normal, expected, and usually short lived. If students remain frozen in this stage beyond the fourth week of placement, it may be a cause for concern that should be brought to their attention and, if appropriate, discussed with the field liaison. However, it is not unusual for students to return to this stage of learning over the course of the placement whenever they are faced with another new or difficult task or situation.

In Stage 2, *sink or swim*, students are aware of expectations but can barely keep up with the demands. Approval-seeking and dependence characterize this stage. We can help by supporting identification of spontaneous or intuitive responses that further the work. We are responsible for acknowledging strengths while providing balanced and constructive criticism.

Understanding a situation without the power to control one's own actions or activity in it is the third stage and involves freedom from preoccupation with the self and freedom to study the situation as it is, for example: "All at once it came to me. I thought I understood what it was all about, but now I know I have been in a fog all this time." Although students may be performing well, and a sense of confidence is achieved in this stage of learning, disillusionment quickly occurs when there are setbacks or when students find themselves regressing to previous stages of learning. This is a stage of progress and of regression. Reynolds advises us to anticipate this ebb and flow so that we do not get disillusioned along with our students and lose confidence in our own teaching performance. Many students typically achieve this stage of learning before graduation but may remain in this stage as they consolidate proficiency.

In Stage 4, *relative mastery*, students can understand what is involved and control the activity required. This stage is characterized by the integration of theory and practice. Confidence is gained, and students know they can deal with what is required of them. The activities become second nature to them, and they can autonomously analyze their own performance. In this way, students have achieved autonomy and a level of professionalism where they can apply knowledge to solving practical problems and use themselves as instruments with their acquired skills. Not all students achieve this level of consolidation across all aspects of learning before graduation. It is common that the first 2 or 3 years after graduation are years of consolidation and attainment at this stage of learning.

Stage 5, *learning to teach what one has mastered*, acknowledges that once learners achieve more comprehensive mastery, they are often called on to offer consultation and to teach others. As new teachers enter this stage, they concomitantly return to the stage of acute self-consciousness and the expected anxieties faced when in a new role. New field instructors often remark they feel acutely self-conscious of themselves as field instructors, which brings the process full circle back to Stage 1. At this point, returning to the beginning provides a platform for refined expertise and continued professional development (Granello, 2010; Urdang, 1999).

Saari (1989) uses Reynolds's model to formulate student progression of symbolic capacity. She describes beginning stages as involving a shift from an undifferentiated and general sense of problems, a tendency to provide advice and reassurance, and looking for the magical right words and formulas to an eventual development of understanding of the helping process and an ability to formulate self-direction.

Deal (2002, 2003) integrates several developmental stage models from psychology and social work for application to field education. Deal's framework describes three stage points (Deal, 2000; Deal & Clements, 2006). The first stage identifies a novice who is anxious, dependent, and focused on self and who engages in concrete undifferentiated thinking that leads to concrete interventions. By the end of the generalist practice year, an advanced beginner in the second stage emerges with greater understanding, an ability to engage in theoretical discussion, and a drive for greater autonomy. Increased understanding is evident, although there may be unevenness in the student's ability to assess performance accurately, often either overestimating or underestimating skill performance. By the third stage, the student achieves a decrease in concrete thinking, is more aware of the complexity of practice, and is more able to consider underlying factors and issues, and a possible dependency-autonomy crisis may emerge that is connected to a need to demonstrate competence. Finally, there is increased ability to understand and apply learning.

Deal (2002) notes shifts in student attitudes in several areas, including students' recognition of and attention to "interpersonal processes occurring between themselves and their clients," distinctions in "their personal and professional selves," and their "receptive capacities without intruding or imposing their own thoughts or ideas" (pp. 124–125). These shifts parallel those noted by Benner (2001) who applied the Dreyfus (1980) model to the development of expertise in nursing practice. Benner describes a learner's movement along at least three critical aspects of performance:

> shifts from reliance on formalized abstract principles as prescriptions for action to the use of experience and transfer of learning from one situation to the next,
> shifts in the learner's ability to see the situation in its full complexity with an ability to discern some aspects as more critical than others, and
> shifts in the learner's level of self-preoccupation and greater engagement that yields improved performance (Altmann, 2007; Benner, 2001; Jarvis, 2009).

The developmental progressions in these models are like the pathways described in the scaling gradations spelled out in the program's rubric outcome measures. The path is tracking the road to competence and proficiency along critical performance thresholds, signifying growing mastery and preparedness for entry-level practice.

Supervisory models use the developmental stages of student growth to frame supervisory interventions (Benner, 2001; Deal, 2000, 2002; Everett et al., 2011; Stoltenberg, 1981). For example, because beginners are often likely to have little previous employment experience in the human services, they must be taught specific policies and procedures to guide actions. Yet policies and procedures are limited guides for the context-specific situations and judgments needed in the real world of practice; therefore, we must aid the beginners' ability to transfer knowledge and skills from previous situations while supporting their acquisition of new knowledge. Beginners start to see that more is needed than simply applying their own life experience or what has worked in somewhat similar situations. They see that change is not achieved simply by telling an individual what to do. Impetus emerges to apply learning principles of practice in their new role and context of practice. Support and feedback prompt growth in self-confidence and result in progress. Deal (2002) explains how our supervisory responses take this movement into account:

> A student... might benefit from the field instructor's initiating a discussion of how their jumping in too quickly affected the interview. "When you broke the silence so quickly, the client had less opportunity to direct the course of the interview. What meaning did this appear to have for this particular client?" This supervisory response stands in contrast to one recommended for a more advanced student who is ready to reflect on their [sic] own behaviors and motivations: "Have you noticed that you have difficulty tolerating silences with this client. Why do you think that is?" (p. 132)

Moving along developmentally includes the student's ability to plan for next steps. This implies being aware of the complexities of the problem to be solved; we need to be in tune with the student's need for clear direction or need for exploration. Growing self-confidence produces a desire to demonstrate competency, but in the face of continuing complexities, a potential crisis brews regarding students' ability to accept critical feedback (Deal, 2002) and the desire to try it their way. Sustaining the working alliance is critical at this stage. Advancing skill level is exhibited as the student begins to gain self-confidence, anticipate what growth is required, and manages the inherent anxiety and ambiguity involved. Eventually what emerges is the ability to respond to more complex situations and problems with growing comfort and critical judgment.

Developmental stages are also applied to multicultural learning (Deal, 2004). Deal (2004) uses a similar stage model as noted earlier, and implications for multicultural learning are provided that parallel characteristics along cognitive, behavioral, and affective domains. In this model, we see movement from unsophisticated ways of viewing cultural information, awkward responses, and anxiety over how best to deal with the material to an ability to explore and become increasingly open. This increased receptivity however does not necessarily translate into increased ability to differentiate "culture-specific from unique characteristics of clients" (Deal, 2004, p. 77). Mastery is sustained by balancing challenges with adequate support. We select assignments that increase students' abilities to reflect on the work and identify what worked and what did not work. This type of analysis is difficult for beginners, but in time it is possible to see evidence of increasing understanding of their professional role and responsibilities (Solo, 2018) and in their abilities to evaluate and analyze their approaches (Anderson & Krathwohl, 2001; Bloom, 1956; Deal & Hyde, 2004; Granello, 2010; Simmons & Fisher, 2016).

Each of the developmental models offers guidance about what is normal and anticipated during field education learning. Each presents a somewhat different glimpse into experiences and needs as students pass through initial, middle, and specialized stages of learning. Understanding these models aids our teaching in the framework of competency-based social work education. Although not specifically stated, the population of students most likely described in these models are White. As a result, we must be mindful of the limitations of these models in helping us consider the experience of historically oppressed or marginalized student populations. Research with more diverse student populations is overdue.

Bloom's Taxonomy and Critical Thinking

Bloom's (1956) taxonomy has been widely applied to teaching and scaffolding learning opportunities that build students' abilities to learn. The taxonomy distinguishes and defines learning activities in three domains of learning: cognitive, affective, and psychomotor. It delineates progressive movement through each domain as the learner strives for more and more complex mastery. One level sets the foundation for the next. Practice is needed at all levels in the domain to move forward and gain increased proficiency. The domain frequently used, and of interest to us here, is the cognitive domain.

Descriptions are easily found on many universities' teaching center websites. Two such centers are the Princeton University McGraw Center for Learning (https://mcgraw.princeton.edu/) and the Vanderbilt University Center for Teaching (https://cft.vanderbilt.edu/guides-sub-pages/blooms-taxonomy/).

Revised in 2001 by Anderson and Krathwohl, the cognitive classification devised by Bloom remains largely the same except for the two highest levels of learning, which have been reversed; that is, the levels are currently *evaluating* and *creating* rather than the other way around. The taxonomy offers a way of viewing the complexity of learning and the various steps we engage in as we achieve understanding and reach for critical thinking skills. Here we present the cognitive domain and its uses as an introduction to a discussion on critical thinking.

Bloom's Taxonomy

Bloom's taxonomy is a tool that steers how teaching is pitched; it assists the assessment of the student's level of understanding and the creation of assignments that prompt development. The cognitive domain consists of six categories: remembering, understanding, applying, analyzing, evaluating and creating. These categories form a litany of increasingly complex learning skills and abilities. It is easier to recite or define an individual's symptoms from memory (knowledge) than to critique the accuracy of a diagnosis (evaluation). In fact, understanding the definitions of the diagnostic criterion is essential before we can critique and evaluate the accuracy of the diagnosis, and to formulate or propose an alternative. Likewise, it is easier to describe an after-school program than it is to synthesize this information and devise improvements or propose new solutions to programmatic problems. The incremental steps inherent in acquiring adequate understanding to analyze, evaluate and synthesize or create are important ingredients for our teaching. That is, we need to pitch our teaching appropriately and balance our approaches.

If we remain on the level of providing information without moving to stimulate higher levels of learning, we limit what students can achieve. Or if our questions are formulated to seek descriptions or meaning without moving to requests for comparisons or new formulations, we limit our requests for student development of the critical analytic skills that practice demands. Equally, if we intend for all assignments to be at higher levels of learning without providing an adequate foundation, we are setting students up for skewed or negative feedback on their abilities. If our assignments are geared to lower level abilities without attention to reaching for higher levels, we limit our student's quest for increased competence. For example, we limit students' attainment of skills by assigning predominately information-seeking tasks, review of cases, or observational tasks without direct exposure to interventional opportunities that expand and test students' abilities.

In the revised hierarchy (Anderson & Krathwohl, 2001), what we often call critical thinking is found in the higher levels of each domain. It involves increasingly complex processes that integrate sometimes opposing or conflicting affirmations or beliefs and it is recognized as a complex type of thinking that takes practice. Accordingly, effective teaching entails some understanding of how and when to engage students in higher order skills so that they may practice and be stimulated to think, respond, and act in more complex ways. We intervene to increase capacity to manage the complexity of social work practice, and we design our interventions to stretch those boundaries. We are referring to a developmental process of increased mastery that involves managing something learned through an educational and lived experience.

Plack and Greenberg (2005) provide useful questions aligned with Bloom's (1956) cognitive domain that are summarized here. They propose that we facilitate the process toward higher levels of thinking by posing questions geared to each level of learning. The knowledge and comprehension levels require questions that ask students to describe their encounters, organize the information they have obtained, recount their knowledge of the factors involved in the situation, describe what they may anticipate based on this knowledge, and describe what feelings are evoked by this situation. Questions geared to analysis and application are posed to identify any other factors that might be involved, whether some factors have been ruled out as pertinent and why, what plan has been devised, and what feelings have been evoked in this situation and how might they be affecting the encounter. Finally, questions geared to evaluation and synthesis or creation focus on the conclusions that may be drawn from the student's analysis, the differential diagnosis that might be operating, prediction of the outcome of the plan, formulation of goals in this situation, and the prognosis anticipated.

Critical Thinking

Thinking critically about what we believe, feel, and do is essential for competent practice. Uncertainty and ambiguity are unavoidable; our aim is to decrease their immobilizing effects. Being clear about what research can tell us, understanding theoretical advances, and being open to discover how our personal views affect our decisions are all ways to increase our effectiveness.

Review takes courage, and critical thinking can help (Gambrill, 2013). As noted previously, asking who, when, what, and where are straightforward, important descriptive aspects that aid in understanding a situation. Asking why a response or reaction emerged gives an additional layer of information to be able to analyze the situation. Likewise, asking how a different response from a different theoretical perspective might have affected the situation and what difference this choice might have had provide an even deeper level of analysis. Providing answers to what might make a difference going forward provides a level of evaluative analysis required for future action.

Critical thinking is the direct result of reflection. As we progress in our curiosity and questioning on how to improve our effectiveness, we exercise and practice our critical thinking skills. In other words, critical thinking uses the analytic process of reflection to extract deeper meaning from experience. Reflection provides a means to step back, trace our thoughts, emotions, and actions and to reconsider and disentangle how we recall events to reveal other perspectives that spark awareness and guide next steps (Brookfield, 1987).

As much of our work is complex, examining situations from multiple perspectives aids problem solving; old ways of explaining or viewing a situation may not work or do not always apply, and this stimulates a need to search for new ways of viewing and thinking about a situation. This is particularly true when attempting to change attitudes or to alter an individual's perceptions and biases. It is not surprising that critical thinking, self-awareness, self-regulation, or reflection are specifically mentioned throughout the practice components of the competencies. According to the CSWE (2015a),

> social workers ... apply principles of critical thinking to those [ethical decision making] frameworks in practice, research, and policy arenas; use reflection and self-regulation to manage personal values and maintain professionalism in practice situations; apply self-awareness and self-regulation to manage the influence of personal biases and values in working with diverse clients and constituencies; apply critical thinking to engage in analysis of quantitative and qualitative research methods and research findings; apply critical thinking to analyze, formulate, and advocate for policies that advance human rights and social, economic, and environmental justice; use empathy, reflection, and interpersonal skills to effectively engage diverse clients and constituencies; apply critical thinking to interpret information from clients and constituencies; understand theories of human behavior and the social environment, and critically evaluate and apply this knowledge in the [engagement and] assessment of

diverse clients and constituencies, including individuals, families, groups, organizations, and communities; critically choose and implement interventions to achieve practice goals and enhance capacities of clients and constituencies; and critically analyze, monitor, and evaluate intervention and program processes and outcomes. (pp. 7–9)

The range of these applications clarifies the multiple ways critical thinking and reflection affect how we classify problems, how we assess the information we gather, and how we evaluate solutions. In addition, the promotion of critical thinking with a focus on power and privilege is central to justice-based field education.

Having an eye on systems of power and oppression while seeking pathways for equity ties these processes to our profession's mandate to advance human rights and to advocate for change (Allan, Pease, & Briskman, 2009; Dominelli, 2017; Finn, 2016; Fook, 2008; Fook & Gardner, 2007; Jani & Reisch, 2011; Lavoie, 2012; Mullaly, 2002; Pimpare, 2011; Powers & Faden, 2006; Robbins, Chatterjee, & Canda, 2012). The intent is to give students ample opportunity to practice critical analysis, increase their capacity to tolerate ambiguity, and guide their engagement in critical reflection to consider how global contexts affect local configurations and how power and privilege affect problem definitions, service delivery, and solutions.

Chapter 2 argues for applying critical social perspectives to our thinking, analysis, and reflections. In this perspective critical thinking discerns and analyzes social structures and power relationships; the aim is to engage understanding in the service of change and to use critical thinking and reflection to seek remedies to conditions of oppression and the misuse of power. The glossary provided in the CSWE's (2015a) EPAS defines critical thinking as an included aspect of cognitive processes: "Critical thinking is an intellectual, disciplined process of conceptualizing, analyzing, evaluating, and synthesizing multiple sources of information generated by observation, reflection and reasoning" (p. 20). This definition focuses on the broader purposes of critical thinking that enable the capacity to think analytically and facilitate self-awareness through the process of reflection in and on action. These differing definitions of critical thinking do not conflict with one another. It is more a matter of choosing where to place a focus on social change—in the foreground or the background. From a critical social theory perspective, critical thinking and critical reflection place understanding for change in the foreground; that is, the aim is to apply understanding for change. Much of what we have been discussing here regarding how we learn involves understanding how we think and the influences on our resulting actions. Applying understanding to effect change simply encases the effort in our commitment to justice.

Critical thinking is acknowledged as being difficult; as seen in Bloom's (1956) taxonomy, it is recognized as a higher order thinking skill, which implies that a foundation of other lower order abilities is needed to achieve a critical level of analysis. Yet, possessing lower order abilities does not guarantee the ability to think critically. After all, "compared to your ability to see and move, thinking is slow, effortful, and uncertain" (Willingham, 2009, p. 5). Based on this understanding, critical thinking is not a set of skills; instead it is a "type of thought... very much dependent on domain knowledge and practice." (Willingham, 2007, p. 8). This means the topic we are thinking about affects the process of puzzling over it and that being able to think critically in one situation may not easily transfer to another. Perhaps we just do not have enough knowledge; or we need more practice and repetition; similarly, feelings associated with a situation or issue affect our ability to think straight; perhaps the context is new and our confidence is shaken (Adams, 2001; Van Gelder, 2005; Willingham, 2009).

Our attempts to facilitate critical thinking, reflection, and regulation require us to support our students' efforts and abilities through several stages. First, to bring previous experience and knowledge forward, identify assumptions and then challenge these assumptions through the introduction of alternative perspectives. This involves helping students consider the importance of the context on the issue, encouraging their creativity, exploration, and developing their curiosity to foster appropriate skepticism on seemingly straightforward situations. This entails provoking and assisting our student's thought processes, that is, challenging preconceived assumptions and supporting new ways of understanding familiar circumstances and adding the lens of justice to the equation (Brookfield, 1987; Carroll 2010a, 2010b; Daloz, 1986; Dalton & Crosby, 2008; Gambrill, 2013; Sanford, 1967).

We achieve this by providing the support needed to navigate the challenges. We begin by prompting a review of what the intentions were in an interaction, examining what occurred, deciphering what went well or not so well, identifying what was learned in this situation, considering what we might choose to do differently, considering what unfinished business might exist, and proposing a possible next step. Alongside this review, we use a range of methods to prompt sensitivity to how differential power is witnessed in the situation and how issues of justice underlie the presenting problems. Methods such as modeling, engaging in brainstorming and heart storming activities, reviewing and reframing the situation, and posing questions that promote reflection and linking one idea to another facilitate these considerations. Furthermore, by identifying themes, patterns, and metaphors we provide a means to view the situation from different points of view. These efforts aid students' understanding and appreciation of experiences as different from their own and provides a view into the complexity of the situation and its relationship to our pursuit of justice (see Appendix A: Teaching Methods and Tools for Use in Supervision for an explanation of these methods, and see www.criticalthinking.org for resources on the promotion of critical thinking in education).

Summary

Learning is a process, and growth occurs on a continuum. We have been describing the various theories and perspectives that support a holistic view of competence. Growth is individualized and may proceed straightforwardly, but it is also likely to occur in leaps and bounds, with the occasional plateau and possible regression to earlier stages. Progress varies with the task to be learned, familiarity with that task, the context, when it is to be tackled, and the level of initiative involved. Approaches to new learning evolve as we develop; this means students' learning needs change as they progress.

From these perspectives, traditional and more current, the different ways of knowing combine for whole-person learning where experience is a state of being and a felt encounter that incorporates more than what we do. Experiential learning is a process of experiencing what we do and how that encounter is used to further our understanding. Thus, it is an interaction and a process (Yorks & Kasl, 2009). This is an important distinction, given what we are aiming to teach and what students are aiming to learn. How judgments and actions are influenced and linked by knowledge, values, thinking, reflection, and affective reactions is made clear.

The identification of similarities or differences in learning preferences between us and our students provides insight into how these preferences might interact in field education. For example, if the field instructor and student are conceptual learners, they may enjoy reading all there is to know about an issue or population and delay assignment of cases. If both are operational learners, they may jump in and get the work done, leaving little time for reflection. Dissimilar approaches to learning pose other combinations. An operational learner and conceptual teacher may clash over who wants to act and who wants to think or reflect as the first step. Yet, in a similar fashion, these differences can enrich the interchange by broadening the approaches to learning and problem solving. What is most important is an awareness of these approaches and a supervisory process that allows discussion and curiosity about the similarities and variances and their effects on the supervisory relationship and skill mastery.

Learning and teaching interact in complex ways, and this interaction is an essential component in adapting teaching techniques to suit individual learning needs. Collaborative teaching requires an atmosphere where honest and straightforward discussion of these issues can occur. In this way, adult learners are given the opportunity to accept responsibility for their own learning. Students can then begin to integrate their personal selves into their professional selves and engage in self-appraisal. Being asked to consider new ways of looking at an issue also requires collaborative methods and depends on the extent to which supervision is experienced as a learning dialogue, a conversation that poses questions and promotes curiosity with an invitation to wonder about other possible meanings and solutions.

Recent developments in learning theories propose that we are more alike in our approaches to learning than different and that chronological age or levels of maturity may carry less significance in explaining how learning occurs than other factors such as culture, personality, or political beliefs (Bransford et al., 2004; Brookfield, 1995; Jarvis, 2010; Jarvis 2015; MacCleave & Eghan, 2010; Willingham, 2009). The advisability of attempting to espouse adult learning theory as discrete and unconnected to how we learn as children or as adolescents is questioned. Identified areas for further research into adult learning include appreciating the interaction of emotions and cognition, understanding the role of gender in learning, giving full weight to whole-person learning rather than placing selected emphasis on experience and doing, and giving social context and lived experience their proper place in understanding how adults approach learning (Brookfield, 1995). These cautions made by Brookfield in 1995 have guided the way forward for developments and research; we have much further to go in fully understanding the implications of these complex issues on learning and how we teach.

Additionally, developmental models provide helpful reminders that our students' journeys pass through increasingly complex levels of thinking and proficiency. They add value to our efforts in refining our supervisory techniques (Bogo, 2010; Deal & Clements, 2006; Diambra, Cole-Zakrzewski, & Booher, 2004; Solo, 2018). Each stage represents varying levels of competency, and varying teaching responses are needed to facilitate progression to the next plateau and eventual mastery. Although stage models imply a linear progression, it is accepted that we recycle through these stages when confronted with new knowledge or even with a somewhat different application or context. Finally, transformational learning provides understanding on the ways learning for practice engages the whole person and the role reflection plays in how we build knowledge. Critical thinking and reflection are the mediums our students use to attain this goal. Carroll (2010b) wrote,

> In transformational learning, supervisees critically reflect not just on their experience but the way they construct their experience. In doing so, they open themselves up to new transformational learning, which creates new mental maps or meaning-making frameworks that help interpret their experience, learn from it and go back to their work with new insights and new behaviors. (p. 17)

Our emotions add another layer to influence our thinking and actions and how we exercise our judgment. According to Robbins, Coe Regan, Williams, Smythe, and Bogo (2016), "Critical thinking, judgments, and decision making are powerfully affected by our emotions. Emotional reactions are in turn related to meanings individuals derive from their personal and professional lives that are internalized and influence subsequent cognitive appraisals and guide interactions" (pp. 391–392). The conditions and learning activities that prompt perspective transformations require critical thinking and reflection to support deeper level learning (Gambrill, 2013). Whole-person learning that combines cognitions and emotions requires a single view of mind and body rather than a bifurcated or dualistic lens that separates these aspects of our experience. It is the whole person, not just the mind or our emotions that are affected by learning (Jarvis, 2009, 2015).

As we engage in learning dialogues with our students, we encourage them to examine multiple sides of the issue, and this provides opportunities for critical thought and reflection. Critical thinking involves more than intellectual competence or understanding of the subject at hand. It necessitates awareness of our "intrinsic tendencies toward illusion, distortion and error" (Van Gelder, 2005, p. 45). We naturally tend to seek evidence to support our beliefs. However, the demand for critical analysis requires an ability to accept evidence that provides alternative perspectives on our views and opinions. This practice entails awareness of personal blind spots, otherwise referred to as belief preservation (Van Gelder, 2005). In this way, critical thinking and the willingness to reflect are interconnected. Each of these aspects contributes to an explanation of the processes involved in achieving a holistic view on the development of competence.

CHAPTER 4 APPENDIX

The items in this appendix highlight the importance of understanding what is involved in helping our students learn how to learn, provide an exercise in applying Kolb's (1984) learning style to possible teaching strategies linked with the characteristics of each style, and present a group supervisory session to illustrate the use of learning theory approaches.

Supporting Our Students in Learning How to Learn

Students require our support in expanding their understanding of how to learn. This includes stretching their repertoire of learning methods, facilitating the accessibility of learning, being aware of possible pitfalls, and guiding understanding of the nature of learning.

> Stretch students' repertoire of learning methods: Practice situations often call on students to shift and use different ways of approaching new learning. We can focus our support as students test new and less familiar means of learning by assessing students' inner resources and providing learning opportunities that stretch their capabilities. It is possible for students to experiment with new ways of learning when the challenge is balanced with responses that support their functioning.

> Recognize the potential pitfalls of a one-method-fits-all approach: Identification of similarities and differences in preferred ways of learning and teaching provides a rich interchange that broadens understanding of methods for tackling new learning and problem solving, or it can explain tensions that cloud the educational task. For example, a rigid approach to how students tackle new learning may heighten student anxiety. The discomfort we observe may reflect a mismatch of approaches rather than indicating the student's abilities.

> Make learning more accessible: We can shape assignments to accommodate students' preferences and usual ways of approaching new learning while also facilitating experience with new modes and methods for learning. For example, assignments that require students to jump in might be started by arranging for students to observe before performing tasks or vice versa. Likewise, offering readings that apply to the work is an option that might suit some students' learning needs or help others experience the benefits of seeking support from relevant literature.

> Guide understanding of the nuances and evolving nature of learning: Approaches to learning change over time, and learning is a process. Learners' needs are influenced by past experiences, traditions and current contexts; our teaching strategies need to adapt to these realities. Stretching our own use of varying teaching approaches and methods can facilitate student learning.

Teaching and Learning Approaches: Four Student Examples

These examples provide an opportunity to consider which teaching methods might be useful in view of the students' approaches to learning. Following consideration of your own style of teaching and learning, consider the teaching approaches you might use with each of the following students.

Student A is a natural problem solver. She is drawn to helping with tasks and assignments that recur so she can refine her approaches. She is eager to be busy and often approaches you for additional work. She is ready to jump into whatever you ask. She has more difficulty when you ask her to anticipate what might be a problem or possible outcome of a certain intervention or approach. She seems easily frustrated when confronted with complex situations that do not go the way she thought they would. You are aiming to slow her down, to increase her reflective capacity, and to improve her ability to think more deeply about her work.

Student B enjoys discussing theories. She also shows abilities for logical reasoning. She has been working to develop a theory of identity development on the population of youths she is serving and has been slow to pick up the two individuals you recently assigned. She excels at comprehending a range of information and can organize it into a logical format. She is always reading and shares the information she is learning in her classes. She feels best prepared for action when she has a grasp of the information she needs. You also notice that she tends toward a question-and-answer probing format in sessions with the youths. You are aiming to improve this student's flexibility in responding to the immediacy of the situation. She is quick to provide advice and to generalize a specific concern, and you are trying to improve her ability to empathize and tune in to the issues presented to her by the families she is working with.

Student C is a hands-on learner, who often uses intuition to tackle problem solving. She enjoys challenges and is not afraid to take on a new assignment. She is adept at thinking on her feet and responds well to changing situations. She is action oriented, and she demonstrates strength in her ability to connect with a range of individuals. She is not keen, however, to use recordings. She seems to rely on her intuition and uses her own experience as a ruler for her decision making. You are aiming to move this student from her reliance on her own life experiences as a source for guidance on how she might intervene. You would like her to develop her ability to support the individuals she is working with to find their own solutions to the problems they are experiencing.

Student D looks at things from a variety of perspectives. She tends to be innovative and imaginative in her approach, to be feeling oriented, and prefers to watch than to do. She enjoys feedback, and when in group supervision she often contributes by bringing the group to the big picture. She often wants time to reflect on her work before acting. When asked to recall an interaction, she provides good recall of the interaction on multiple levels, and she can distinguish between essential and trivial information. She keeps an open mind and reserves judgment until she feels she has gathered all the information she needs. She is able to look at many points of view. Your aim is to support this student's ability to reflect on the affective reactions operating within her decision making. You would also like to lessen her generalizations about situations and to tune in more deeply to the situations presented to her.

Applying Adult Learning Theory and Transformational Learning Theory in a Group Supervisory Session

This scenario describes a group supervisory session of eight generalist practice level students of varying approaches to learning and talents engaged in a discussion of how to intervene in a support workshop for adults who are maintaining sobriety following completion of an in-patient treatment program. The workshop aims to provide a transitional experience for participants. The student who presented her work is cofacilitating the workshop; she is concerned that some members are silent, whereas one member persistently interjects views over the others' efforts to speak. The workshop will run for 6 weeks, this was its second meeting.

The student asked the members of her supervisory group for help on how to affirm all members in the workshop while also attempting to balance contributions. She did not want to offend the one member who was contributing in a manner that precluded others, and she wanted to encourage the silent members to speak up. Other students in group supervision nodded in agreement that this was something they had also found challenging. The field instructor noted that this is a common issue as groups begin to form their norms and develop a group culture for their work. Looking to draw on the experience in the room, the field instructor asked if anyone had experience of achieving balance or in observing an effective intervention.

The students looked at each other for someone to respond. Hesitatingly, one student said that in her experience, setting group rules in the beginning helps. The student was encouraged to expand on her statement, and she gave an example of how time spent in the beginning on expectations about group participation might support the facilitator's need to intervene when this group rule was not being supported. She stated she found a helpful approach was repeating the rules or asking the members how they felt they were doing in maintaining their agreement. The student who initially presented the problem stated that no group rules had been set and said, "I am just a student and a co-facilitator in the group, if the other facilitator doesn't see it as a problem, there is nothing I can do about it." All the other students nodded in agreement. The field instructor asked if the student felt that her cofacilitator saw the developing group's way of communicating as a problem, the student stated that she and the cofacilitator did feel the same way about it but differed in the way to manage moving forward. For example, the student suggested moving the group members' seats the following week to "mix it up," but the cofacilitator responded that they could watch this behavior again this coming week before intervening in this way. The student felt dismissed, and she gave up attempting to present her views. It seemed her desire to mold the group process was overridden by her sense of being disempowered and unaffirmed.

Aiming to tap into the student's desire to learn and to improve the workshop's group climate, the field instructor interjected that the cofacilitator seems to be choosing to move more slowly than the student would about a seat change intervention. Perhaps she wanted to observe a little longer, whereas the student wanted to act now. Perhaps the student might intervene in another way, like the one suggested about discussing group rules, or perhaps attempting to clarify the other facilitator's reasoning for choosing not to intervene might provide a way to continue the conversation. The field instructor then asked, "Perhaps we ought to start by clarifying whether we should first examine how to intervene to influence the group culture, or whether we should first consider how to increase collaboration with the cofacilitator on this issue." The student responded that she gets on well with the cofacilitator, but she cannot make her see it the way she sees it. Here, the other students became more active, saying things such as, "Right, we are only students, it is not worth rocking the boat." "It is early in the term. Give it time." "Yes, you will be able to say more later." "Yeah, we are just the new person in the room." "We don't have any authority."

This led directly into a discussion about the authority and power they do and do not have, the differences between legitimate and ascribed authority, and the earned authority derived from knowledge and expertise. The group was not buying it and continued to express frustration in their student status. "She can't just overstep the cofacilitator. She's not staff." The field instructor attempted to reframe the discussion, first by asking whether there might be steps along the way before an attempt was experienced as overstepping the cofacilitator, then by pointing to the power the student holds by looking at the power associated with her role as learner and through the role assigned to her in the group. "Do we agree that your role in this group carries responsibilities—responsibilities that give you authority to act to fulfill them?" The reframe shifted the group's attention. Several students nodded, as if to say, "Well yes, but—" This was enough for the student who presented the problem to respond: "I am there only as a support to the other facilitator." The field instructor asked her and the group to break that down into what activities and responsibilities are involved even if it was just only as a support to the other facilitator. Activities emerged such as helping to deliver the material, sharing the review of the written reflection assignments required of the participants, filling in when the cofacilitator could not be present, and helping the group members get something positive out of the experience. As soon as "helping the members get something positive" was said, the group laughed. One student remarked, "We have come full circle." The field instructor asked, "Yes, we've come full circle, but are we in the same spot? Has anything changed in how we are viewing this situation?"

> Consider what aspects in this scenario are supported by adult learning theory, experiential learning theory, transformational learning theory, possible learning approaches to learning, transformational teaching methods, developmental learning stages, critical thinking, and conducive learning environments.
> In what ways is the issue of power discussed or experienced in this scenario? In what ways could the field instructor intervene to support the students' assumption of power in this situation to act for greater group member cohesion or for better collaboration with the cofacilitator?
> What issues are important for the field instructor to consider in managing the student's practice and in managing the issues that have emerged for all the students in this group supervisory session?
> What actions and skills demonstrate competency? Which competencies are being developed? What next steps might indicate progression toward mastery?

Part Two

Clearing the Path for Learning

This section of the text gives attention to the many practical aspects of field education that need to be addressed before and throughout the academic year. The chapters consider teaching professional and ethical behavior, providing orientations to field education, crafting student assignments, the use of recordings, teaching opportunities in the face of challenges and preparing for transitions, terminations and evaluations.

CHAPTER 5

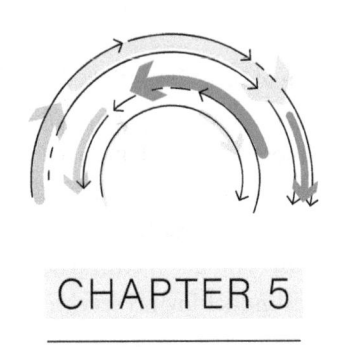

Professional Values and Behavior

Self-Reflection, Self-Awareness, and Self-Regulation

[Unless students] learn to examine themselves and what they really value, their command of ethical theories and their ability to think about ethics from diverse perspectives are not likely to bring them any closer to being willing and able to do the right thing. (Marino, 2004, p. B5)

Ethics and values are at the heart of the social work profession. Although there has been considerable stability in the core values of the profession, the day-to-day ethical issues that social workers encounter have not remained static. On the contrary, applications of core values in social work have undergone substantial change over the years in response to social, political, and economic developments. (Mizrahi & Davis, 2008, p. 143)

A justice-based framework asks us to be watchful that our practices and policies do not perpetuate injustice and violate core social work values. Teaching ethics from this framework emphasizes the examination of personal values and worldviews as directly related to ensuring equity for the individuals and communities we serve. Without critical self-reflection, we run the risk of imposing our personal views on others, and unexamined practice places us in danger of perpetuating inequalities in the services we deliver. Therefore, professional behavior is linked to ethical decision making. Critical reflection of personal values assists our abilities to honor the views of others and to engage in discourse focused on social change.

Promoting a critical analysis of the values that underpin policies that might be marginalizing communities rather than creating practices for equity and justice support an inclusive model of ethical decision making (McAuliffe & Chenoweth, 2008). This model invites service recipients to become full partners in the decision-making process so that their voices are represented. Inclusive ethical decision making embraces these opinions in some form, even if our own values are in conflict. Translated to supervisory discussions, rather than tell a student that is just the way we do things, we find ways to include their voices in the decision-making process.

"Demonstrate Ethical and Professional Behavior" is the first of nine competencies in the EPAS (CSWE, 2015a, p. 7). The fact that demonstrating ethics is the first on the list perhaps indicates its importance in the practice of all social workers. Competence in this area has several components: Students in field placements must understand and put into practice the ethical obligations in our Code of Ethics, they must learn how to manage the tensions between competing interests, and finally they must learn to take ethical stands on some of the vexing ethical issues inherent in the agency's specific domain of practice. This layered and complex learning occurs throughout the internship. These potentially difficult and upsetting situations require that students comport themselves ethically and professionally, and it is often this learning that is most profound and enduring.

Field education supervision builds students' abilities to examine their personal values and worldviews in the context of their assumptions about the profession they are choosing; this supports their abilities to manage the tensions that inevitably emerge among competing societal, professional, and personal values. Field instructors are tasked with supporting the development of mindfulness, self-reflection, self-awareness, and self-regulation as students engage in this work. In fact, field instructors are charged with encouraging the student's abilities for critical analysis of their decision making and prompting curiosity about how their biases may affect their work. To support the field instructor's role in fulfilling these responsibilities, this chapter examines the inherent tensions involved between personal and professional values and the stresses that may also arise when students are confronted with conflicts between personal, societal, and professional values that drive their work, that is, altruistic values of respect for individual choice, the importance of human relationships, a commitment to service, the desire to pursue and advance social justice and human rights, and the importance of seeking competence and maintaining integrity in all that we do.

Recognizing the complex interchanges involved in facilitating the development of a professional identity, this chapter also lays out possible paths for student learning that promote mindful and reflective practice in a specific placement context while also keeping an eye on ways to place this in the broader context of the profession. The roles of self-reflection, self-awareness, and self-regulation in facilitating consideration of the potential tensions between personal and professional values are examined. Self-care is presented as integral to ethical professional behavior, and safety issues are part of this review. Given the importance of our professional Code of Ethics (NASW, 2017), standards pertaining to student education and new standards regarding technology are summarized, and examples are provided to illustrate implications for field education. Understanding these differing but interlaced components informs how students comprehend their roles and acquire their professional identities.

Advancing Professional and Ethical Behavior in Field Education

U.S. society is currently shaped by White-dominant Eurocentric cultural values. Although professional values shape our practice, it follows that U.S. social work practice, the development of service programs, and the establishment of human service institutions are influenced by the culture that surrounds them. For example, at the beginning of our profession, those in social work services were much more concerned about the morality of the individuals served than about the morality of practitioners or in the development of an ethical code. Services were delivered in the context of discerning the deserving poor, and policies drove the separation of children from their parents because of conditions of poverty. Parental and children's rights activists were successful in changing views, and this separation was judged to be unjust and an inadequate sole measure to justify removing children from their parents. However, fragments of the underlying philosophy morphed into differing conditions that continued family disruption related to conditions of homelessness, separations related to substance abuse, incarceration, and the current tests being made related to immigration status.

Although societal values evolve over time, change is slow, and philosophical remnants often linger. Bisman (2014) reminds us that, "Just as their knowledge base is continually in development, professional occupations are continually in formation, being shaped by their history and by contemporary social norms" (p. 11). Interpretation of social issues and implementation of policies are also bound by time and place; our enduring professional values remain as guides, our ethical standards provide direction, but the tensions and how to advocate for the implementation of just social policies continues as an ever-present challenge. Changing circumstances, economic globalization, definitions and demands for protections of human rights across the globe have their effects on developing practice responses. A current example is work with unaccompanied minors, asylum seekers, and refugees who bring the world to our doorstep in explicit ways.

U.S. definitions of family are shifting but remain valued as heteronormative, that is, a heterosexual, cisgender, two-parent-headed household of working adults with a basic education. Social service agencies are shaped, and service delivery is funded, by policies that express this view. Equally, allocation of benefits is frequently made to those families who depict this philosophy. When families deviate from these dominant definitions, human service organizations and programs are in danger of responding in punitive, disapproving, and dismissive ways. Currently, child welfare cases are filed under the mother's name, assuming an absent father. There is limited to no space in domestic violence shelters for transgender individuals who experience relationship violence. Programs that serve mothers with substance abuse histories and their children are often nonexistent, and when they are funded, services to children are often time limited and restricted to infants and toddlers. Initiatives that serve custodial fathers are also limited. Immigrant families are torn asunder when facing deportation and then often punished by not being granted aid for the family members who remain behind.

Value conflicts inevitably arise between students and those they serve. Each time an individual meets with a student, that individual's world is brought into the room, and the student is obliged to listen with an open mind and heart to the stories that may challenge the student's own lived experience. This may be illustrated by students who are stunned by the strength of an individual's homophobic expressions; perhaps a student recounts astonishment that a young adult still living at home does not stand up to her parents and assert independence, or perhaps it is we who are shocked by the strength of our student's bias and its effect on the student's ability to empathize with the youth who has just learned she is pregnant.

The exposure to direct work confronts students with the complexity of these issues, the effects of societal stratification and oppression, and the importance of acquiring a justice-based approach in their work. This exposure fosters an awakening to the injustices our profession attempts to address and our responsibilities in developing awareness of how our values affect our perspectives and judgments. The meaning of professional accountability to our professional values is clarified against these contrasts. Our professional mission sets aspirational goals to end discrimination, poverty, and other forms of injustice; to enable people to strengthen their capacities and address their needs; and to promote the responsiveness of organizations, communities, and other social institutions to these issues. These purposes and perspectives are essential to our profession. Our responsibility lies in increasing students' understanding of the often inadequate responses to existing pervasive and oppressive social conditions. The foundation we provide will follow them to wherever their career path takes them.

The CSWE (2015a) competency that addresses ethical and professional behavior requires students to become cognizant of our professional values, ethical standards, and the relevant laws and regulations that affect their work on multiple levels. It is also important to note that students are expected to apply their understanding, self-refection, self-awareness, self-regulation, and critical thinking to inform decision making in the service of maintaining professional standards and in demonstrating a commitment to lifelong learning. Field supervision is where students seek consultation to guide judgments and to seek alternative responses.

Comprehension of the purposes for supervision is illustrated by a student's respect and use of supervisory time, a growing ability to prepare an agenda for work, reflection on supervisory discussions and comments on recordings, and how these discussions, comments, and reflections manifest themselves in subsequent actions and practice choices. This includes applying knowledge in a purposeful, planned, problem-solving manner; acquiring a repertoire of specific practice strategies and techniques; and promoting the development of meaningful relationships. It is not unusual for students to benefit from direction on how to use supervision; likewise, some may need practice in creating work agendas, and still others may require clear stated expectations on the importance of recordings for supervisory sessions before a rhythm of regular submissions occur. Despite an expected trajectory from less to greater autonomy, students are expected to demonstrate an early and clear commitment to the importance of discussion and reflection throughout their time in placement. The atmosphere we set is critical in aiding their ability to reflect, reveal their insights, and share sensitive information about such conflicts that occur between their personal and professional values (Dunn, Callahan, Farnsworth, & Watkins, 2017; Knight, 2016).

Personal and Professional Values: Managing the Tensions

An ethical dilemma is when two or more divergent values are in conflict, and the path to a decision is difficult to discern. Some studies suggest that personal values may interfere with or even prevent the adoption and practice of professional values (Bisman, 2004, 2014; Clark, 2006). Clearly, we often witness conflicts playing out in this way. Students' desires to serve may drive their quest for education, but they may not fully understand the implications of this choice for themselves. Personal values may clash with those of the profession before students understand how this new set of guides for behavior collide with older, more ingrained and comfortable ways of understanding the world and their place in it. These tensions and potential conflicts are expected; the relationship between societal values and social work's mission often involves sorting through conflicting philosophies and ways to respond; it also happens that personal values win over the emotions produced and create confusion over what to do.

Often we are in the best position to have discussions with students about how our core professional values arise in the day-to-day realities of practice by framing practice dilemmas in these terms (Haynes, 1999; Osteen, 2011). By providing nonjudgmental, reflective forums for discussion of ethics and values in field education, we help our students deal with dilemmas honestly and directly. We model how to handle conflicts in practice and what professional behavior looks like (Barretti, 2007; Congress, 2002; Dunn et al., 2017; Knight, 2016).

It is helpful if we discuss common value conflicts that occur in the context of our setting before they happen and support students in confronting them when they do. Anticipating the "professional dissonance that arises from the conflict between professional values and job tasks" is a vital contribution to the student's understanding of practice demands (M. F. Taylor, 2007, p. 89). We begin by giving students permission to raise concerns about contradictory values and beliefs and letting them know that together we will figure out the most appropriate professional stance in each situation. However, some conflicts arise in practice unexpectedly or with little warning, and we are called on to respond in the moment. It is precisely the nature of being taken off guard and not having had adequate preparation that makes value conflicts and ethical dilemmas difficult to handle (Bisman, 2014; Black, Hartley, Whelley, & Kirk-Sharp, 1989). For this reason, it is vital to ensure supervisory opportunities to discuss how personal values may supplant those of the people and communities we serve or be imposed on them. In these dialogues students experience how personal values may cloud vision, negate the benefits of multiple and diverse values, and delay consideration of how power, privilege, and inequality play a role.

Students are generally willing to intellectually identify with and commit to uphold fundamental professional values such as respect for the individual; however, an unsettling encounter with a consistently assertive individual may create frustration and confusion over how to maintain professional composure. Likewise, students may not fully understand the limits or constraints on an individual's right to confidentiality or self-determination.

Common examples regarding an individual's right to self-determination are often illustrated by a person's desire to live independently in the face of the family's desire to have the individual admitted to an assisted living facility. This leads to discussion about the individual's understanding of the risks and rights involved, the possible sense of frustration created in the face of the student's earnest attempts to help, or being caught between the desires of the individual and the legitimate concerns of the family. Persisting and offering a second invitation to services or seeking clarification on the initial response may not be viewed as possible or may be viewed as disrespecting the individual's statement. The opportunity for continued review of the options may be lost ("He said he didn't like the idea of having services. He has a right to choose, doesn't he?"). Or an assurance of confidentiality may be made before the student fully understands the limits placed on this promise. Even if breaking confidentiality is required for the safety of the individual, the student may feel that the person's privacy is being invaded, the student is being asked to betray her integrity, and this individual will never trust the student again.

These core professional concepts may further test the student's understanding when working across difference and with diverse populations (Bain & Bass, 2012). If we do not place discussions about these values in the context of the service user, we miss an opportunity to discuss the influence of oppressive environments and contexts on our practice. That is, how do our practice responses demonstrate respect for confidentiality or self-determination while acknowledging understandable self-protective and safeguarding behaviors related to oppressive histories in the face of the authority we represent? It is our responsibility to initiate these discussions so that students are given an opportunity to consider how these differing frames influence engagement approaches with historically oppressed populations, immigrants, and indigenous peoples.

Consider how a generalist practice level student who possessed a strong ethic of helping those in need and always making good on a promise struggled with understanding how she could complete an assignment that involved engaging constituents in a discussion of the services they would like developed for their community. She resisted the assignment and beginning a conversation about it. The field instructor saw the student's procrastination in getting this assignment started. One reason turned into another, and the delays were finally impossible to ignore. When the field instructor mentioned her confusion about the student's continued reluctance to begin the task, the student said, "You are asking me to set them up. I have no way of knowing who, if anyone, would follow up on this, and I won't begin a conversation I can't finish." She argued that doing otherwise would be "unethical"; "I can't promise that any of the services would be developed. I would be setting them up for disappointment."

In this example, the strength of the student's statement about her dilemma in this scenario was a surprise to the field instructor and the student. The field instructor acknowledged the force of the student's statement and responded that she heard the student's anger, but she also heard that the student was worried about setting up constituents. The field instructor's wondering about the underlying worry this student was expressing was followed by a request for the student to put more words into her statements so that they might better understand what the student was experiencing. This led to an honest discussion regarding the student's feelings of distrust and disappointment in her placement setting, which she experienced as disorganized and understaffed.

This student's disenchantment with the setting and its perceived lack of professionalism translated into the student's wish to protect service users from similar disappointment. She was unable to see beyond her dissatisfaction to consider her professional role and responsibilities. Even starting the assignment seemed to promise that desired services would be provided and only served to strengthen her feelings of being powerless in creating an immediate solution. She lacked an understanding of how involving community participants in developing and prioritizing needed services could support fulfilling their needs. Her discontent hampered beginning the steps of engaging community members in the improvement of community resources. Instead, she saw the approach as inappropriate: "The community has so little, how could anyone expect them to do what you are asking?" The interchange precipitated an honest conversation regarding the student's strong reactions to the agency's mission and her increasing level of frustration with the placement, which she had not previously shared with the field instructor. What was first seen as avoidance of a service assignment was revealed as a more complicated situation regarding the student's expectations of what helping involves and her inability to identify community strengths. The assignment challenged her perceptions of her role and responsibilities. The field instructor responded by revisiting the agency's mission and aligning it with our professional mandates of service, principles of collaborative practice, and community empowerment. An opportunity was presented to talk about positionality, power and privilege or lack of either, the student's social location, and how all these might play a role in her reactions. For example, community members cannot ignore the needs of their community, yet the student's privilege gives her the opportunity to avoid doing anything. The discussion about community assets and her biases toward this community provided an opportunity to enhance the student's self-reflection and awareness. The tenets of the liberation health model (Belkin-Martinez & Fleck-Henderson, 2014) were given attention as a theoretical basis for their discussion. Reengagement with the student on her role and stance on issues of community empowerment became critical for resolution.

In this example we see a student stuck in disillusionment over her placement's inadequacies. The student was unable to move forward toward discussion with her field instructor or in seeking greater understanding of her potential role in responding to community needs. Was the student concerned that her field instructor would not hear her views? Was the field instructor viewed as part of the problem? Did the student fully understand the agency's mission and the implications for the social worker's role in this setting? Or was she feeling this task was beyond her abilities? Once the problem could no longer be ignored, the student's voice needed to be heard to discern what the best action and next steps could be. The field instructor's willingness to consider the student's perceptions was critical to move ahead. Furthering the student's understanding of what was required of her, organizational change, participatory practice, and clarifying her role as a change agent participating with community members were critical for this student's learning.

In each situation, discussions about value conflicts aid the students' reflection on the various levels of complexity and ambiguity regarding what initially may seem to be a straightforward situation or issue. By seeking permission to explore these value conflicts and placing these situations in the context of the student's professional role and responsibilities, the student is given a way to see the value conflict in different terms and to consider an alternative response. Acts of reflection prompt self-awareness, and an alternative response can be activated (Dunn et al., 2017). The lessons learned are often heartfelt. Sandars (2009) proposes that

> at the heart of reflection is the challenge, and subsequent change, in perspective that can inform future action. The most significant experiences that result in the greatest challenge and change are usually those that are associated with the presence of strong emotions. (p. 688)

Promoting Reflective Practice

The demands of field education involve dealing with the unexpected; this entails thinking on one's feet, and in Schön's (1983, 1987) terms, this is a prime factor for reflection in and on action. Reflective practice requires openness and a willingness to take the risk of exposing underlying thoughts and feelings, but reflection for action (Schön, 1987) requires an appraisal that inspires application, action, and change (Moen et al., 2016). Our ability to be self-aware of how our personal views and reactions affect our judgments and behavior requires us to engage in this examination. Emotional responses associated to information and experiences affect our thinking and decision making. The links between and among these processes emphasize the inherent power they exercise individually and together; "doing and thinking are complementary" (Schön, 1983, p. 280). These processes can become ingrained and are often challenging to untangle; reflection is the key (Bisman, 2014; Mishna & Bogo, 2007; Bogo et al., 2014).

Self-reflection and self-awareness also are connected. Self-reflection is our ability to turn inward and engage in an examination of ourselves, to take time to be curious, and to wonder at what just happened, or what we just felt or thought. Self-awareness evolves from self-reflection and involves our ability to assess how we react to the outside world, to acknowledge our emotions and motivations, and to consider how the outside world reacts to us. Self-awareness and self-reflection alone, or together, may not be sufficient in leading a student to new ways of looking at a situation, questioning one's normal way of reacting, or acting differently, but they are catalysts for this to occur (Aronson, 2010). Both are personal attributes, and both may be developed and enhanced.

> Consider a self-confident and independent learner who was assigned to work with a mother with a substance abuse disorder. The mother recently had been discharged from a rehabilitation facility for mandated services while attempting to reestablish contact with her four children in foster group home care. The student went to the reception area of her agency to collect the mother for her first individual session. The waiting area was packed, but she saw only one woman waiting, so rather than call out the mother's name, the student decided to approach her. The woman was sitting in a corner, her appearance was disheveled, and she looked dejected. The student introduced herself and asked the woman if she was Mrs. W. The woman looked up and said "No." The student was surprised and apologized and then looked around to reconsider the waiting area. A petite, well-groomed woman, whom the student had not noticed before, approached the student. She said, "Excuse me, but I overheard you introduce yourself, I believe you are looking for me." The student understood immediately that she had seen the unkempt individual in the corner and assumed this was the woman she was looking for; so strong was her assumption, she overlooked the only other woman in the room. She was shocked by the bias revealed in this incident.
>
> The student was self-reflective enough to notice the behavior, and she was self-aware enough to understand that there were implications for her practice and that she may need to work on the assumptions and prejudice evident in this incident in field education supervision. The student thanked the mother for identifying herself, and they went together to the interviewing room. The student was able to talk to the mother straightforwardly about her mistake. "I am sorry for the confusion. I did not see that there was another woman in the room." The mother responded, "That's OK." The student was embarrassed and unsure of what to say and moved on to the reason for their meeting. Bothered and shaken by the incident, the student expressed her worries to her field instructor about possible lingering effects on her work with this mother; she asked whether she should return to this incident and, if so, how she should approach the topic with the mother.

Stage 1 Self-Reflection Initiation or Stagnation	Stage 2 Engaging Self-Awareness	Stage 3 Achieving Self-Awareness
Comfort and acceptance of uncertainty and change	Values self-reflection and is open to review	Willing to engage in ongoing self-review
Creative and reflective thinking	Supportive environment that encourages reflection	Commitment to professional development
Supportive environment that encourages reflection Missing the above conditions leads to stagnation		Understanding that reflection is connected to professional integrity and competence Humility and empathy
		The acceptance of ambiguity

Figure 5.1 Stages and Conditions for Self-awareness

This example illustrates how self-reflection and self-awareness combined to prompt consultation over the incident and possible needed action. It also highlights the nature of implicit bias and its implications for possible microaggressions that can be discussed in supervision and provide an opportunity for authentic dialogue. The path to self-awareness that prompts action has been conceptualized by Pompeo and Levitt (2014) as occurring in three stages and dependent on certain conditions. The stages are initiating self-reflection or stagnation, engaging in self-awareness, and achieving self-awareness. A description of the stages defined by Pompeo and Levitt (2014) follows; based on this description, Figure 5.1 summarizes essential characteristics of these stages.

The first stage, "initiating self-reflection or stagnation" (p. 81), involves a "potential opportunity" (Pompeo & Levitt, 2014, p. 83), which may or may not trigger self-reflection, such as in the preceding scenario. The event provides the potential for self-reflection, but individual cognitive capacities and personality and environmental conditions influence whether the trigger event becomes a critical incident that results in reflection. Reflection may not occur, and instead stagnation results.

The identified conditional factors include personal comfort in accepting uncertainty and change, the ability to think in a creative and reflective manner, and an environment that is supportive of the reflective process. In the previous scenario, the student was awakened in a way that she felt she could not ignore; perhaps if the emotions provoked were not as strong, she could have avoided thinking of how to bring up the situation with the mother or raise it for discussion in supervision. The second stage in Pompeo and Levitt's (2014) model, "engaging in the self-awareness process" (p. 84), is characterized by participating in ethical decision making based on the identification of personal values and professional experience. Again, the environment is a powerful influence on whether self-reflection and self-awareness occur. A supportive environment is influential, but the action is also reliant on the individual's valuing self-awareness and being open to review. In the previous example, we see the student wanting to learn from this incident; she feels that professional behavior required her to bring it forward in her discussions with the mother and field instructor. The final stage of Pompeo and Levitt's model, "achieving self-awareness" (p. 85), signals development of empathy and a willingness to engage in ongoing self-review. Humility is identified as an important trait; it is related to the commitment to professional development and acceptance of ambiguity. The outcomes of this process include meeting new critical incidents with readiness to engage in self-reflection, recognition of the necessity to reflect, and understanding its place in the development of professional integrity and competence. This incident points to the openness and maturity often required in these situations. The student was shaken and embarrassed, but her commitment to developing her professional skills provided the self-regulation required to override these emotions and seek improved action. She was unsure of how or whether to use this incident with the mother in the moment, but she was clear about her desire to bring this up for discussion in supervision. Field education supervision was identified as an opportunity for this incident to be examined.

The implications relate to the importance of setting a conducive environment for reflection, prompting opportunities for reflection to occur, and building on students' efforts so that increased acceptance of ambiguity and the rewards of reflection and self-awareness may be experienced. Clearly, the meta competencies of self-reflection and self-awareness are integral for the development of other proficiencies, Pompeo's and Levitt's work (2014) provides hope that these attributes may be honed and nourished in a supportive context for reflection and review.

As students develop their self-awareness, they are expanding their concept of themselves as social workers at the same time. As students are introduced to social work principles and values, they engage in reflection that leads to developing skills that represent accepting the values as their own. As students display empathy for others and their situations, concomitantly, they are influenced in an interactive process. Likewise, as they engage in diversity and difference in practice, their ability to show respect for others is expanded. Those they work with are also influenced and changed (Miehls & Moffat, 2000). One student, reflecting on her evolution, described it this way: "I get it now. I understand what the strengths perspective means when I am with people. I see that I was beginning an interaction without a clear view of my role or purpose or how I should approach my work. That was affecting how I saw everything. It's different now. I am different now. I see that it requires something different of me. When I am with people, I get what it feels like to treat people with respect. It feels intentional and purposeful, and I see their response to how I talk to them and how they respond to me."

Promoting Mindfulness

In recognition of the rich history of mindfulness in Eastern traditions, Epstein (1999) presents its applications to medicine in support of encouraging a nonjudgmental attitude, critical self-reflection, "moment-to-moment self-monitoring" (p. 833), listening attentively, and examining deeply held values. Mindfulness practices are used to support tuning in and "being present" (p. 833) to issues and concerns. Likewise, the benefits from mindfulness for critically self-reflective social work practice are related to its promotion of centering ourselves and focusing on the here and now in mind, body, and spirit. The benefits of mindfulness practice for students in field education are acknowledged as assisting their ability to pay close attention to what is evolving in their practice and in consciously examining feelings, thoughts, and physiological reactions to improve abilities to pre-engage, engage, and intervene with individuals and communities they serve (Lee & Himmelheber, 2016).

Enabling students to take time to create time and space to tune in to their inner selves creates an environment for mindfulness practice, which deescalates and reduces anxiety, increases thoughtfulness, and encourages positivity about the tasks ahead (Lee & Himmelheber, 2016). According to Epstein (1999), "Although mindfulness cannot be explicitly taught, it can be modeled by mentors and cultivated in learners" (p. 833). We can use ourselves as guides and models of practice that look inward and tune in to experiences while creating a nonjudgmental space that examines these experiences anew.

In this way we model curiosity, examination of our values and in what ways they affect how we define problems, resolve issues, work with individuals, and "see the world as it is rather than how one would have it be" (Epstein, 1999, p. 838). By taking a deep breath, closing our eyes, counting to 10 and back again, we center our thoughts and emotions for the work ahead of us.

Mindfulness practices can also increase awareness of the ways we *otherize* people. For example, the person who has sexually assaulted a woman or who has been arrested for intimate partner violence also has a narrative, one we may dismiss and ignore because of the way we hold on to deserving and undeserving biases. (See the following for a related scenario.) Quiet moments, meditation, visualization, and appreciation of what is around us open us to tuning in to ourselves, others, and the space around us. Mindfulness exercises are used to create space where everyone starts from a place of conscious awareness so that we can move on to the difficult conversations. In a similar manner, field instructors may want to allow moments of mindfulness before individual or group supervision, staff meetings, workshops, or training sessions to center participants to the work of the moment and to enable their ability to remain present and self-aware. Students can also practice mindfulness through recordings and reflective journals by centering their attention on what people are not saying, which matters just as much as what was verbalized.

> Consider this example: A student begins field education getting to know the placement setting and community needs. The placement setting offers weekly mindfulness exercises for all staff; the student and her field instructor attend regularly and frequently share their experiences of this group.
>
> The student's first assignment is reviewed; the person's history, current mental health status, medical history, living conditions, and reason for referral are explained. Progress notes written by the previous worker and the referral notes state that this person has served time in prison for murder. The student asks her field instructor whether it is possible to refer this individual to someone else. The field instructor uses this as an opportunity to assist the student with tuning in to herself, considering her values, and attempting to raise awareness about judgments that are surfacing. The field instructor purposely creates a space for reflection on the student's reactions, judgments, and assumptions and asks her to be present on her thoughts and feelings about this assignment. She explains

that this may aid their evaluation of and differentiation between what the student thinks is known and what the person's reality is.

To promote reflective practice and to establish an appropriate disposition on this assignment, consider the following questions:

> How might we be influenced by files and records? What meaning and context might the person attach to his own experiences? (Finn, 2016). How might the individual view how the realities of the past are perceived by others? What information might the person use to judge the student?
> To what extent will the student's bias impede her ability to help? Is it bias, or are there other factors that prompt her concerns? What may shape how the student engages with this individual? How will uncertainty be tolerated?
> Given this review, what might emerge as possible next steps?

Promoting Self-Regulation

Self-awareness, self-reflection, and mindfulness contribute to self-regulation. For example, the concept of self-regulated learning (Postma, 2015) considers the individual's ability to set learning goals, display strategic thinking, and monitor and evaluate performance and effectiveness. In this model, a student is involved in forethought, self-efficacy, and goal setting. This is followed by performance, characterized by attention, focus, and self-monitoring activities. Self-monitoring triggers a process of self-reflection and self-judgment that results in causal attribution and reactions that trigger action. The progression is not always in the direction of a positive path forward. Sometimes a choice of "handicapping behaviors" (p. 203) is made that does not further learning but is viewed as a way to protect and enhance self-esteem. That is, the individual makes a choice to slow down, step aside, or step back. In these situations, causal attributions are made external to the individual, or a choice is made that protects the individual from future blame, for example, "I couldn't raise the fact that she was ignoring her child's needs. After all, that would be disrespecting her parental choice," or "He was yelling so loud, there was no way for me to intervene. After all, I could not have yelled louder than he was and be heard."

Consider these examples: A student encounters a man at a weekly free lunch in the community center of her agency. Each week after his lunch, this man asks if he can take another plate of food with him as he is leaving the center. The first week, the student met the man's request. She then checked with the director of the center and was told that guests are not allowed to take food home with them and that the student should explain the policy to him or to any other guest who makes this request. Each week the same man approaches the student to ask to take some food with him, and each week she explains the center's policy but usually gives in to his continued requests for food. She feels beaten down by him and is conflicted by his need for food and her need to abide by the setting's policies. Each week the student becomes more active in avoiding him. One week she notices him approach a new volunteer. She sees that he has finished his lunch and that he and the volunteer are engaged in a long conversation. The student senses her rising anxiety. She thinks to herself, "Here we go again. Now he is trying to get food from someone else. It is bad enough that I have difficulty managing him, now he is trying this on a new volunteer." In that moment she stridently approaches the pair. When she hears the conversation and her assumption is confirmed, she senses her body tense up, and as she begins to speak, she recognizes that her voice is becoming stern. At this point, the student is aware of how angry she is. Her self-awareness is awakened, and her ability to reflect on her professional role initiates her thinking that she must make a choice between modulating her reactions, turning away from interaction, or moving forward in her anger.

The student chooses not to proceed in anger or to turn away from the interaction. Instead, with awareness intact, she decides to take a deep breath, relieve the new volunteer of the burden of dealing with this man, engage in a conversation with him again about the policies of the center, and remind him of their previous interactions. This leads to a different conversation with him. He tells her about his wife who is at home and is physically unable to come to the center for lunch. The student learns that he is more than his assertive behavior and that his food insecurity extends beyond himself. She sees that her responses of giving in to what he was asking for prevented her from talking to him about his need; she sees she was protecting herself from her confusion over his refusal to accept the center's policies and the conflict she felt when responding to him. A new stage for service was set for this man and his wife through her ability to self-regulate and reengage with increased understanding of his situation.

The supervisory discussion reviewed the student's ability to self-regulate her emotions. The student was proud of her ability to modulate her response but was shocked to discover the real reason behind the man's continued requests for more food. By focusing her attention on the new volunteer and centering herself, she was able to manage her interaction with the man differently. She saw how her frustration had prevented her from exploring this before. Her insight and willingness to bring this up for exploration in supervision was reinforced. Although it was important to review how the student's frustration over the man's persistence affected her ability to engage with him, it was also important to consider how the policies created to guard against misuse of the center's resources resulted in a conflict for this student's ability to serve this man. This conflict prevented her from exploring the policy further with her field instructor and finding a better resolution in this—and potentially other similar—situations. The conflict also blocked her ability to respond to the man as an individual with unmet needs. Had this man complied with the policies as outlined by the student, she would have been saved from the frustration of being in the middle. The agency's policies would have been upheld, but the couple's needs would not be met. The continuing conflict and buildup of emotions prompted a different response that resulted in increased self-awareness, self-regulation, changed attitudes and behaviors and improved service.

Another student placed in a youth program, where she was the only Black student intern, recounted an incident with a group of adolescents who were talking to each other at cross-purposes. As their conversation became louder, the student heard a White youth shout, "Well, all lives matter and this stuff about 'Black Lives Matter' is a sham." At that moment the student stopped advancing toward the group and turned back. On reflection in supervision, she stated, "I knew I should intervene but what was I supposed to say or do? Me, a Black woman, is expected to face that? No way! If it was a group of peers, I would have just jumped in. But I am responsible for these kids." After a pause she said, "I felt terrible. I knew I should respond. I knew that is why I am here. I knew it was my role and purpose for being there. I failed to intervene. I still feel awful. I didn't want to go in storming and I didn't know how else to act, so I turned away."

In supervision the student described how she felt over her inability to intervene. She shared her experiences as a Black woman and anger at the inherent racism she faces and how the youths' comments made her react. She prides herself on her normally unabashed willingness to act in similar situations but in this instance, she didn't trust herself to contain her anger. The field instructor affirmed the student's decision to hold off intervening until she was clearer about what response was needed. The field instructor also validated the student's lived experiences as a reality, which may have influenced how she decided to intervene or not in the situation. Was she choosing not to respond given her experiences of racial microaggressions? They attempted to craft an approach the student might have used. None felt right to the student. The field instructor, who is White, asked if she felt the field instructor was "just not getting what it felt like to be a young Black woman faced with this situation." The student hesitated then responded in a serious tone "I think you may be right. Now what?" Together they decided to take time to talk more about their own identities in the field supervisory relationship, to think more about the situation, and to return to the topic. They both agreed that ongoing discussions about dimensions of identities and worldviews could lead to greater understanding and a way to move forward. The student stated she would like to observe the youths the next week for more information on who they are individually and as a group. The field instructor supported how the student would like to proceed and decided to move at the student's pace. They agreed to continue discussions about ways for the student to manage responding to the youths out of the heat of the moment; they also agreed to consider other levels of interventions that may be possible for the youths that involve education, discussions, or workshops on the existing racial undercurrents and to spend time sharing the student's own reactions to these same images and messages. Their discussion turned to the larger issues regarding cross-racial tensions within the community and in their program, and how this incident represents work that needs to be tackled in ways that extend beyond the student's interactions. They agreed to return to this topic the following week.

These examples illustrate how two students used the incidents to prompt self-reflection and move toward self-awareness (Pompeo and Levitt, 2014). Both were able to review their experiences in the supportive environment of field education supervision. This made it possible to examine their reactions and responses in more detail. Each situation was sparked by a different initiating event, but similar ingredients were involved. The students were caught off guard and experienced feelings of anger, frustration, fear, and discomfort. Each situation involved a sense of unease, but a desire to learn emerged. Each situation required the student to step back before moving forward. Responses depended on where the incident was placed in the student's priorities of professional and personal values, how clear the issues were to the student, and what abilities existed to control emotions and provide a sense of environmental support and a desire for clarity of what was required of them in their role in the situation. The result was an attempt to self-regulate toward goals of learning professional practice instead of choosing an action that was doing what they normally would. The complexity involved demonstrates the journey to achieving professional behaviors that represent ethical performance of our responsibilities. Each student was prompted to clarify professional expectations and to seek guidance on how they might respond next time. Had these students not been mindful, they may not have used supervision to explore these disorienting situations, and the learning opportunities may have been lost.

One thing leads to another, and although we often see the thing that results, we must search for the events that led up to the final situation. Ethical dilemmas are similar. Events and situations often lead up to a dilemma or critical incident that consumes our attention. These scenarios illustrate the attention needed to explore values and assumptions that underpin understanding of our role and responsibilities. Each situation required the field instructor to respond to the learning on all levels of practice—the individual interactions that began the concerns, the repercussions on the micro and mezzo level, and how macro-level issues of policy implications and definitions of professional roles and justice applied. Remaining on micro and local levels are an inadequate response.

Placement settings may offer a well-defined protocol of expectations on how students perform their professional role; however, this may not protect them from the confusion and challenges that emerge. Other situations provide less guidance, such as when the student is the only social worker in the setting, or the role is challenging and there is a lack of professional models to follow. Attention to these underlying issues provide space to help resolve the crisis and point the way for interventions that take us beyond the immediate issue on the micro level. This paves the way to consider the mezzo, macro, and global components that are involved and therefore must be considered in the resolution (Lee & Himmelheber, 2016).

Teaching Students About Self-Care and Safety

The passage through this journey can be arduous. The communities, groups, families, and individuals we serve are often plagued by surmounting unmet needs that produce a range of feelings including, fear, frustration, anger, and desperation. Oppressive structures create barriers and challenges for community members, and as students of varying backgrounds begin to witness these systems and continued marginalization, they may themselves feel overwhelmed or unable to act. These realities may just as likely infect our students with secondary trauma, compassion fatigue, and elements of vicarious trauma, leaving them susceptible to burnout. Any student is vulnerable, but those who may have already been exposed to trauma or those with few supports in their lives may be particularly at risk from incidents experienced as triggers or microaggressions. Their student status may further aggravate the situation because they have not yet developed adequate self-reflective practices or do not have adequate preparation or instruction in self-care methods.

Newell (2017) reminds us that NASW policy statements address the importance of educating students about the role of self-care practices and their links to our responsibilities for teaching and educating students. Our task is to teach students how to effectively engage in work while also defining what self-care means and learning how to balance and respect their needs; maintaining competence as a professional social worker depends on these abilities (Berger, Thornton, & Cochrane, 1993; Newell & Nelson-Gardell, 2014).

The issues, social problems, and the individuals we encounter often represent circumstances that provoke stress. These trauma-infused conditions yield pernicious effects on individual lives and on those who seek to assist them. Teaching skills of empathetic listening and understanding require students to tune in to challenging and painful personal stories and social situations; these stories and situations leave their mark on students, and we are required to pay attention to this fact. Even if empathy is an infinite personal resource, "It needs to be nurtured and replenished through the practice of self-care, self-compassion, and self-regulation" (Newell, 2017, p. 114). Our students need skills and tools to allow them to remain open to the work. As professionals we understand that the consequences of remaining open to human suffering may leave us vulnerable; we accept that part of being professional means taking care of ourselves for the long haul. Our students have this to learn and they need resources to guide them. Newell (2017) provides materials for students and professionals to create a self-care plan. In addition, the University of Buffalo School of Social Work (2019) provides a Self-Care Starter Kit, developed by students, along with exercises and tools for self-care.

Teaching self-care involves preparing students for the reality of practice and developing their ability to recognize signals of stress while providing them with tools and antidotes. For example, we need to connect offering respect, compassion, and empathy to diffuse anger with paying attention to the emotional residue involved (Bressi & Vaden, 2017). Also, when students demonstrate self-regulation, we need to applaud them while also giving them time to examine what this level of self-regulation has demanded of them. Helping students develop the ability for self-assessment and paying attention to their needs for sustenance is part of teaching them how to maintain their professional skills. The need to attend to issues of self-care are not related only to work connected with crisis or trauma.

> Consider these examples. A student who is eager to contribute to work in placement during the day was angered by an e-mail she received from a task group member after hours requesting a copy of the proposal she was working on. Angrily she commented to her field instructor, "There was no way I was going to take time to reply, I had other things that needed to be done. It's not really expected of me to respond when I am not in field placement, is it?" Her question suggested that she was inviting a conversation, but her tone and nonverbal physical manner indicated her anger over the intrusion and request for contact.
>
> Another student put on his agenda "self-care." When this item was addressed by his field instructor, he recounted how difficult he is finding his journey coming to placement. The previous week he witnessed harassment of a man who was begging for food. That morning he witnessed a mother abusing her toddler. He didn't know what to do, and he said he can't stop thinking about these incidents, asking, "What could I have done? How should I have responded?" On the one hand, he thinks it would be easier if these had been assignments, then at least he would have had a role to play; on the other hand, he didn't feel equipped to handle either situation.
>
> The field instructor did not know how to respond and instead listened and waited. The student talked more about his feelings and the

> impressions of these incidents. The conversation turned to the broader context of societal tolerance of incidents of harassment and violence in contrast to the profession's stance against them. The field instructor listened and said that she was not sure how to help, but that it seemed important to talk about this and that field education supervision was a space where he can talk about it. He responded that he felt powerless. She asked that he continue to let her know when she might support him in managing the emotions aroused by these and similar traumatic scenes we witness; scenes where we may be powerlessness—even when in the role of social worker—to protect individuals from abuse and the conditions that produce marginalization and pain.

In these examples the students' comments contain appeals for recognition of their needs as they develop clarity on the limits of their professional roles and responsibilities. The first student questioned whose needs were more important and, by implication, how far the limits and boundaries of service extend. Her presentation of the situation seems blunt and seeks confirmation of her own view rather than inviting reflection. In contrast, the second student's self-awareness and openness to share his feelings provide an opportunity to have his story heard and feelings validated. He felt powerless and vulnerable. He was not left alone with the horror of the images and his panic over not knowing what to do; the field instructor was given an opportunity to explore options and to talk about what is involved in managing the emotions aroused by bearing witness. Both field instructors were tasked with recognizing that the growing awareness of the realities these students were experiencing differently through their professional training would require ongoing discussions to monitor their needs for self-care while they develop professional efficacy and commitment to intervene to make a difference in people's lives. Sometimes our own feelings prevent us from fully seeing the impact on our students.

> Consider a specialized practice level student who was placed in a special county project serving young adults who are diagnosed with severe and persistent mental illness. The field instructor was keen to have the student work on several shifts during the week to cover the week's programs as much as possible and provide the student with access to a

range of learning opportunities. The student lived nearby and agreed to a schedule that would make it possible for her to take advantage of several unique programmatic offerings; she worked her job and class schedule around her placement. As the fall term got under way, the student became ill and missed several days in placement. She began to appear late for supervision and was irregular in producing reflections or recordings on her work. When asked about this, the student commented that she was adjusting to her new schedule and would "do better."

In supervision, the field instructor asked whether they should attempt to consolidate the student's hours so that she was not spread so thin and made some suggestions on how her schedule could be rearranged. The student resisted, stating that she was used to working hard and gave reasons why she felt she would be losing important learning if she dropped any of the assignments she was currently carrying. The field instructor acquiesced. The student continued to strive for excellence, but the tardiness, irregular submission of required recordings, and frequent illnesses continued; a sense of stress characterized her demeanor. Although the field instructor was aware of the potential overload that the placement schedule was creating, their shared value of working hard to gain as much learning as possible and the field instructor's conflict of interest between protecting programmatic coverage and her student's learning experience blurred the need to address this student's ongoing problems.

We cannot expect students to learn professional values and ethical standards automatically. If a student exhibits inappropriate behavior such as judgmental remarks or ongoing violations of confidentiality, we might move too quickly to our gatekeeping function and rush to request that a student be removed from the placement before considering whether we taught the expected behaviors in a clear, deliberate, and precise manner. In this example, does the student's behavior reflect lack of knowledge and experience and a continuing inability to function in a professional manner, or have we given proper attention to teaching what professional and ethical behavior entails? Teaching professional conduct is part of field education learning. Even how to manage lateness or unexpected absences are behaviors that students must consider in the context of their professional role and responsibilities. Framing these discussions as part of developing mindful practice and self-reflection supports awareness of how their behavior affects others.

The student who was angered by the task group member's e-mail may be judged wrongly if we have not prepared her for appropriate limit and boundary setting, the need to educate those she works with about the limits on her availability, how to manage the realities of e-mail accessibility, and how she will accommodate demands outside placement time. If we do not discuss how to balance her needs with those of the people she serves, we miss an important opportunity to discuss how ethical behavior and professional expectations intermingle with our personal selves and identities. A more realistic field education schedule was not provided to the student, who was assessed as operating under stress and applauded for going over and above expectations. She was unassisted in achieving a more balanced learning environment, and an opportunity was lost to teach her principles of self-care.

The emphasis placed here on how we assist students in self-care practices is not meant to release our responsibilities from assessing inadequate protective structures. Personal self-care is an important but inadequate answer to ingrained meager institutional supports (Bressi & Vaden, 2017).

Resolving Conflicts of Interest: Examples From Field Education

The following example concerns conflicts that may emerge between deeply held personal beliefs and professional duties and may express themselves as conflicts of interest.

> Consider a 45-year-old Haitian woman who is working with a 30-year-old Puerto-Rican mother of a 10-year-old boy and 8-year-old girl who have been in foster care for 9 months because of their mother's history of a substance abuse disorder and alleged neglect of the children. The mother wants her children returned to her care and plans for her mother to come from Puerto Rico to help care for the children. However, due to the devastation her mother experienced following Hurricane Maria, this plan is no longer feasible, and her mother's needs have become an additional burden; nor has she followed through with mandated drug treatment. In addition, she has failed to keep several visitation appointments. The preventive services agency staff is demanding that a permanency plan be made for the children. Because the children cannot be returned to their mother, they want the children to be placed for adoption. The student is conflicted about this plan and believes that the mother needs more help

> to achieve her goals. She feels that the mother must turn her life around in a snap without resources and that she will be unjustly deprived of her children.

In discussing this example, the development of the student's awareness of personal values about single mothers of color, substance abuse, child neglect, and the developmental needs of children needed to be examined. This examination occurs in the context of our responsibilities to individuals, colleagues, and practice settings as professionals; and our examination of responsibilities to our profession and the broader society. Values that emphasize individual self-determination and that focus on practicing according to social policies, laws, and regulations are critical considerations; the safety of the children is paramount, permanence is the goal, and definitions of adequate parental abilities are controversial and often unclear. In addition, the student and mother are women of color, and they have similar and different cultural values and ethnic and racial life experiences. The issues of this assignment require the student to be sustained while working through conflicting values of keeping the family system's best interests in mind and managing being caught between the needs of the children and those of the mother. The way ahead is to support attention to these conflicts on several levels including personal, individual, familial, societal, cultural, and professional.

Helping the student look at structural levels of oppression at play—racism, sexism, immigration status, economic injustice, disproportionality among children of color in the child welfare system, and the effects of global environmental devastation on possible familial resources—adds a justice lens that provides a clearer view for decision making. The resolution takes place over the course of the student's work with the mother and the preventive services agency. The student learns a great deal about her personal beliefs and her new role from this single case assignment. She is helped to consider her role in relation to the mother and to the children. She works with the mother to set specific goals and engages in clear boundary setting for the work ahead. As her work with this mother develops, more realistic expectations are achieved. The aim is to help the mother consider her children's needs, the consequences of her substance abuse, and examine her continued choices while supporting solutions that address the larger systemic issues.

Consider another example that involves a specialized practice level student, a former police officer, who was placed in a setting that provides advocacy and support services regarding employment discrimination and rights of immigrants and migrant workers. The student's placement immediately preceded a terrorist attack in the community where the setting is based. Several local policemen were killed as well as several civilians. The terrorists were not caught, and the community was on heightened alert.

The student experienced a conflict in allegiances, including his commitment to civil protection, loyalty to ex-colleagues who had lost their lives while on duty, and his commitment to pursue his social work degree versus loyalty to his current placement, which advocated for protective policies for immigrants and migrant workers in an immediate postevent atmosphere of fear. His assignment involved facilitating a community discussion of provisions for immigrants and migrant workers in the face of discrimination and community responses that included increasing intolerance. The student and field instructor identified anticipated obstacles to a balanced community discussion for decision making given the range of opinions and attitudes likely to be represented in the meeting. The student expressed the strength of his feelings about the need for tightening rather than loosening protocols dealing with either unaccompanied minors, asylum seekers, refugees, migrants, or immigrants after the recent terrorist attack. He felt conflicted and lacked confidence in his ability to remain nonjudgmental at the meeting. His field instructor did not attempt to change the student's mind, nor was the question raised over giving this student a different assignment or placing him elsewhere. Rather, the student was praised for his honesty, and the situation was viewed as an opportunity to work with the realities of these issues.

In this example the student's views and values were seen as a reflection of existing global, national, and local societal and community values; the issue was translated as a practice problem, that is, which skills and tools does this situation require and could the student be helped to see how to manage his role in this situation without betraying his own views? Could the discussion regarding how to resolve value conflicts assist this student?

Together the field instructor and student brainstormed about the voices that might be present at the community discussion meeting, goals and purposes that should be set, the strategies that might facilitate achievement of these goals, and the lessons that could be learned by examining the range of community responses in these situations on national and international levels. Time was given to examine the differing inherent personal and professional values present in this situation and the student was supported in this exploration. Next steps were devised to enable the student to take on this task. The student was helped to see that the community discussion about next steps was the focus and that his personal views could be held in check so that he could facilitate the community meeting on the issues.

The NASW Code of Ethics

We have been examining helping students grapple with the inevitable tensions between personal and professional values to support the development of professional and ethical practice. We are currently protected by a comprehensive code of ethics for the profession and the emergence of a significant body of literature focusing on ethics-related malpractice and liability risks, practical risk management strategies designed to protect consumers, and the prevention of ethics complaints and ethics-related lawsuits (Barker & Branson, 2000; Houston-Vega, Nuehring, & Daguio, 1997; Mizrahi & Davis, 2008; Reamer, 2013a, 2013b). These help us manage the complexities of practice. In addition, the NASW website contains useful information on current topics, ethical considerations, challenging dilemmas, and literature resources. For example, such topics as social media or termination of services are contained in the section titled "Ethical Standard of the Month" (NASW, 2019).

The revisions in the Code of Ethics (NASW, 2017) primarily reflect the implications of technological advances. Whereas the code's Preamble and Ethical Principles remain unchanged, 19 new standards address the effects of technological developments on ethical professional practice. The purpose of the code contains supportive language that defines what is meant by technology-assisted social work practice, stipulating that social workers should keep up to date on emerging advances in the use of technology and how various standards of the code may influence or be influenced by these applications. Other changes include replacing the term *disability* with *ability* throughout the document and replacing *cultural competence* with *cultural awareness* in Standard 1.05. These changes, although seemingly minor, signify the power of language to reflect current inclusive practice trends that are focused on justice practice.

The Revised Code of Ethics and New Ethical Standards

The revised NASW (2017) Code of Ethics addresses various ways technology has entered the practice arena and considers the implications in specific areas. The 19 new standards clarify how existing obligations such as informed consent, competence, cultural awareness and social diversity, access to records, evaluation and research, conflicts of interest, boundaries and dual relationships, and privacy and confidentiality apply when technology is used (Barsky, Reamer & Hobdy, 2017). Minor additions include added language to existing standards that clarify how technology affects the standards. Minor but significant changes also have been included on how long records should be maintained, limits to privacy and confidentiality regarding disclosure to prevent harm to others and those served, and protection of an individual's right to privacy by not allowing solicitation of private information from sources except for compelling professional reasons. This includes, for example, searching for information on those served via the Internet without their consent (Barsky et al., 2017).

We are expected to discuss policies concerning the use of technology in provision of services, adapt our informed consent protocols when using technology, assess the suitability of these services for those we serve, possess the necessary knowledge and skills in the use of these services, and comply with applicable laws governing their use. Awareness of how different populations access and use electronic technology is critical in determining how technological services may need to be adapted. Likewise, we must be watchful for potential conflicts of interests, dual relationships, privacy and confidentiality protections, and potential boundary confusion when using technology and social media.

The demands and potential uses of technology require us to consider how technology may influence our students' practice. For example, the many advances made possible through technology, such as ease of contact and increased accessibility, create opportunities for communication and outreach but also include areas for caution for maintaining appropriate protections. Although online communications may not be the prime mode of contact, they may quickly become part of the interchange and require consideration (Berzin, Singer, & Chan, 2015; Mishna, Bogo, Root, Sawyer, & Khoruy-Kassabri, 2012, Reamer, 2013a). In the past, students were often concerned about professional boundaries being affected by giving out their personal telephone number, whereas today we are mindful to discuss the implications of texting, the availability of personal information through Web searches and being invited to be Facebook friends with individuals we serve. As students may use their personal cell phones for accessing e-mail from work, they may be easily tempted to call or reply using these devices without considering the implications that may ensue regarding confidentiality and privacy issues.

Technologies are powerful resources but often vulnerable to lost information or to being hacked. The reliability of available information is variable, and it may be difficult to confirm credentials of service providers or the credibility of the information obtained. In their eagerness to serve and provide information, students may put too much trust in the information gained. On the other hand, the use of technology has been an important resource in advocacy, sociopolitical change, the potential for increasing outreach, and making service and supports widely available. It has been used to influence participation in elections and circulate information on marches and demonstrations, which have rapidly affected involvement from around the world.

The growth of social media and technology demands a parallel growth in related standards for professional behavior. Given our responsibilities for ensuring that our students understand the new Code of Ethics (NASW, 2017) and achieve competency in relation to advances in technology, the practice standards collaboratively created by the NASW, ASWB, CSWE, and Clinical Social Work Association (CSWA) (2017) are a helpful additional resource in clarifying new directions and innovations as well as identifying potential dangers. Four main sections include providing information to the public; designing and delivering services; gathering, managing, storing, and accessing information; and educating and supervising social workers.

Section 4 of this document deals with social work education and supervision. The first standard (4.01) addresses the ethical use of technology as appropriate for a specific context and purpose to enable students to master core and essential professional skills. It states that we should "adhere to best practices...and teach students to think critically about the potential benefits and risks of using technology in social work practice" (p. 47). We are advised to ensure that students have access to technological support to assist them with questions or problems that arise (Standard 4.08). Educator and student boundaries are the focus of Standard 4.10, which considers the appropriate use of personal devices or accounts and the protections needed to ensure maintaining boundaries. Standard 4.11 stresses that we should discuss the ways technology is used in the setting including protocols regarding access to records, examination of settings, and social work program media policies, use of personal and professional social media outlets, and compliance with relevant laws and policies to protect confidential information.

Six Main Standards

The NASW (2017) Code of Ethics contains standards for social workers who are responsible to the following: clients, colleagues, practice settings, professionals, the social work profession, and society. Each standard provides specific ways our core values apply to these categories of responsibility. The six standards intertwine with one another; for instance, our commitment to those we serve may be affected by our responsibility to the larger society or by legal obligations. Discussions about the meaning of these standards and the kinds of ethical dilemmas students can expect to see in their work aids to integrate ethical values, principles, and standards.

Standard 1, Social Workers' Ethical Responsibilities to Clients, examines areas such as professional commitment, self-determination, informed consent, competence, cultural awareness and social diversity, conflicts of interest, and privacy and confidentiality. The final standard of the code, Standard 6, addresses our responsibilities to the broader society (NASW, 2017). We quoted this standard on p. 4 in Chapter 1 for its specific reference to how we act to realize, promote, and confirm social justice; here, we return to our code's special call to our responsibilities in social and political action. The implications of this standard require us to assist our students' recognition of their role in identifying gaps in services that fail to meet individuals' needs. Students should not be shielded from in-depth discussions examining practices that are not responsive to all community members; rather, we should support them to think about ways to provide care under existing policies, and most important, to challenge themselves to find strategies to advocate for change. Sources and systems that perpetuate and sustain exclusion are often taken as a given; challenging this position requires permission to question the status quo, and it requires using a floodlight to search for systemic root causes for a reexamination of the situation and a new understanding that ignites an impetus for change.

The aim is to first enable students' awareness of these issues, nourish a desire to intervene, and then facilitate the acquisition of skills that sustain efforts toward change. Students need to acquire knowledge of the issues and a sense of their ability to effect change. To achieve a sense of efficacy, they need to have an experience of themselves as leaders, collaborators, and critical thinkers (Johnson, 2005). Shulman (2012) aptly acknowledges a student's fear of groups, which is often related to the growing number of dynamics needing attention in groups, so we can surmise that students similarly fear attempting to create change on macro issues ("Current social problems are so complex. I just can't get my head around how to begin. Everything is so interconnected and complicated."). Likewise, as group work assignments are not made available as widely as desired (Gitterman & Knight, 2016), Reisch (2016) cites CSWE annual statistics indicating that "only 6% of MSW students were placed in macro-oriented placements, that is, placements that emphasized community development or planning, administration, advocacy, or social policy." (p. 259).

Whether a student is placed in a setting that is predominately oriented to micro interventions, building an understanding of the mezzo and macro components that affect situations on the micro level increases competent practice. Having an eye on the influences of the global context on the issues is equally important. Helping to clarify students' value assumptions so they are open to enhancing and enriching these views leads to an acceptance that alternative perspectives may exist. The work of field education presents students with realities of social problems of inequality, disproportionality, exclusion, and privilege as well as examples of reformative change. Identifying systemic causes leads the way for strategies and proposed responses that might lead to solutions. Understanding the slow process of change is essential. Finding opportunities for students to experiment and use their creative ideas while under our supervision is essential. These ingredients combine to create ethical practice and competent social change agents (Johnson, 2005; Reisch, 2011, 2016).

Standard 3.02 Education and Training

Since 1996 the Code of Ethics has specifically mentioned supervision and consultation, education and training, and performance evaluation under Standard 3, Social Workers' Ethical Responsibilities in Practice Settings. The revised Code of Ethics (NASW, 2017) adds a statement to remind us that as educators we should not engage in any dual or multiple relationships with students, including those that may arise while using social networking sites or other electronic media.

It is important to uphold and model adherence to boundary issues between ourselves and our students. Our adherence is analogous to what the students must observe in their work. Although boundary violations in the field instructor-student relationship may involve more subtle differences than boundary issues in situations with those we serve, they are similar in that consumers are similarly dependent on students for service and access to resources. We should not engage in any dual or multiple relationships with students when there is a risk of exploitation or potential harm. This involves being aware of our positionality and its potential effect on students. White field instructors supervising students of color need to be sensitive to this power differential and be vigilant of microaggressions as a dynamic at play in the supervisory relationship. The same sensitivity and awareness are required for heterosexual field instructors supervising LGBTQ+TS students or for men supervising women.

Students who complete field education requirements while employed in a different department of their placement setting fall under specific CSWE policies and standards that aim to protect students from any dual relationships that may exist, but it sometimes happens that students have current or previous relationships with the setting where they are placed. For example, they may be a current or previous worker, they may have received services from the agency, or they may have a relative who is employed there. In most cases, the social work program has policies that address these issues, which are most frequently handled during the placement process; when these relationships are revealed after a placement is arranged, consultation with the field liaison may be warranted.

Dual relationships with students, particularly as they pertain to educational policies on sexual harassment, are generally included in field education manuals. Beyond sexual harassment, we need to be aware of our own tendencies to use covert or overt power to control students or their behavior. We are responsible for setting clear and appropriate boundaries with students. Maintaining these boundaries can seem even more complicated as we espouse mutuality and being prepared to openly share information about ourselves with our students to balance power and to encourage students to share information with us. It is a balance that should always be about the learning and the work (Knight, 2016). Building authentic relationships maintains boundaries while offering powerful discussions about ourselves in supervision.

This is all to say that we must guard our role as educators and avoid any possibility of inappropriateness such as becoming a friend, therapist, romantic or sexual partner, or employer of our students. Some of us, highly sensitive to power differentials, may overcompensate by abdicating our power and authority and establish relationships with students based on rules of friendship or collegiality. The worst-case scenarios are field instructors who engage in personal or sexual relationships with students. Students are aware of their vulnerability in instructor-student relationships, and the reality of being evaluated by us places students at a further disadvantage. They may feel dependent on our good wishes or integrity. Students are not able to choose this relationship in a truly voluntary way because of the power we hold over them—possessing the authority of granting their grade (Bogo, 2016; Bonosky, 1995; Bubar et al., 2016; Bundy-Fazioli et al., 2013; Congress, 1996, 2000, 2002; Foucault, 1980; Jacobs, 1991; Kagle & Giebelhausen, 1994; Knight, 2016).

There is a clear difference between teaching and treating students, but field instructors becoming counselors for their students occurs more often than we want to admit. From a justice-based perspective, we need to consider this discussion from the standpoint that students may be stretched to their limits resulting from experiences in field education. They may be confronted by the consequences of White supremacy, racism, sexism, and other forms of oppression in practice and in their lives, and we have an ethical responsibility to address these situations and their repercussions. That is not to say we should become their therapists, but we do carry responsibilities to hear their stories and to consider the implications for them, their learning, and for us and our settings.

Another area covered in Standard 3.02, Education and Training, of the Code of Ethics (NASW, 2017) deals with taking "reasonable steps to ensure that clients are routinely informed when services are being provided by students." (Standard 3.02c). Adhering to this requirement confirms the need for transparency and creating an open and honest mind-set for students to approach their work (Miller & Rodwell, 1997). It diminishes fear or guilt related to trying to be someone they are not. Assisting students' comfort in acknowledging their student status may require more attention than simply introducing this subsection of the standard. An opportunity is presented to discuss how students should introduce themselves and raise the issue as an ethical responsibility to accurately tell service users exactly who is providing services. It is important to provide adequate time for discussion of the underlying intent and implications involved.

Standard 3.02 also states that field instructors "should provide instruction only within their areas of knowledge and competence and should provide instruction based on the most current information and knowledge available in the profession." (Section 3.02a). We need to interpret the meaning of this standard for ourselves and our students. New field instructors may read too much into this standard, fearing that they do not have enough experience with a specific consumer need or practice method to meet a student's learning needs. We do have expertise and knowledge gained from education and years of practice, yet if we identify areas where our students require additional expertise, this standard supports availing ourselves of opportunities to expand our knowledge and skills as professionals or use task supervisors to supplement opportunities for our students. Social work education programs are additional sources of support, including field liaisons whose role is to support us in our role as teachers of social work students. A variety of orientation sessions and seminars in field education may be offered by the academic program. Advanced seminars and workshops expand our skills and keep us updated on new trends in practice and teaching. Additionally, many states require continuing education credits to maintain licensure, which may be used to enrich our supervisory skills and practice knowledge.

Other Ethical Considerations

This section introduces two areas of ethical and professional practice that often require special attention in field education supervision. We consider issues regarding privacy, confidentiality, and privileged communication and follow with a discussion on dual relationships and boundaries.

Privacy, Confidentiality, and Privileged Communication

Students need to learn about the relationship between the law of privileged communication (protection of communication in certain relationships) and the ethics of confidentiality (our ethical commitment to confidentiality, which is limited by laws such as Duty to Warn). This helps them answer questions about what to say about confidentiality and how this is affected by using electronic communication or technology in service delivery.

Confidentiality is usually introduced at the beginning of field education when students are informed about the importance of maintaining confidential records of all case materials. Classroom professors and field educators emphasize the need to disguise case materials when writing papers or recordings or when making case presentations that involve real people and their life situations. Students, in turn, need to consider measures to protect field education materials or information they share with others for professional purposes, classroom discussions, or casual discussion. As future practitioners, students need to be made aware of their rights and responsibilities under the laws of the state where they practice. The laws are often very specific about the limitations on confidentiality. The Health Insurance Portability and Accountability Act (HIPAA) regulations and protections provide a useful example. (See U.S. Department of Health and Human Services, 2003, for a summary of the HIPAA privacy rule.)

Although schools of social work may administer required HIPAA training for all students prior to their beginning field education to ensure introduction to the federal privacy regulations regarding the use and disclosure of individually identifiable health information (protected health information), clarification may still be required on whether any other policies regarding HIPAA affect practices in the setting. This includes such policies on review of records and removing recordings or records from the site and policies and procedures on electronic records and communications.

Students may find that disclosure of their student status and their responsibilities for supervisory disclosure to constituents places their authority under question, but like the requirement of reflecting their status honestly, addressing their supervisory accountability also protects them by not falsely representing presumed levels of authority and confidentiality. Although protecting those we serve is the major goal underlying confidentiality, students cannot promise absolute confidentiality, and they are required to share information with us to ensure their work is monitored, best service is rendered, and individual and public safety is protected. Additionally, as noted previously, in this modern technological age, there are many limitations that make confidentiality difficult to uphold.

We are advised to protect the confidentiality of electronic communications, yet the slip of a finger or being unclear of the boundaries of e-mail communications may place confidentiality in jeopardy. A simple example involves the use of the blind carbon copy (Bcc) option in e-mail communication, which protects identification and e-mail addresses when sending an e-mail to multiple addressees; however, not all technological communications include this feature, and some students need to be educated about them to protect against unintended disclosure. The premises of confidentiality in relation to technological communications need to be made clear so that students may review practice protocols in accordance with potential constraints.

Social workers are obligated to prevent harm to those they work with or to others, such as in cases of child abuse, suicide, or homicide. Students often feel inept in assessing suicidal risk or conflicted when reporting child abuse incidents. This is understandable. Organizational and professional guidelines or protocols are not always well defined or clear in these situations. It is incumbent on us to explain policies in such cases, to prepare students for what may occur, help them determine what should or should not be kept confidential, and actions to take when confronted with these circumstances.

A typical example arises when a student learns of a potentially harmful situation reported by a parent, but the student does not recognize it as a reportable incident to child protective services. When the information is disclosed in supervision, the student's failure to see its seriousness and its implications may be viewed as a deficit or lack of professional behavior or as an indication of overidentification with the parent. It may also indicate a need to educate the student about how judgments are influenced by values and feelings. However, the opposite may also occur. Sometimes students report suspicion of abuse or neglect prior to seeking advice or regardless of advice given against it. This reinforces ensuring that these discussions transpire prior to a crisis occurring.

Confidentiality between field instructors and students or between students placed in the same setting should also be stressed. Sharing office space may make keeping confidentiality and privacy for each student challenging. We also need to be clear about what information we will need to share with task supervisors, field liaisons or our own supervisors about what takes place in student supervision.

Dual Relationships and Boundaries

Earlier, we briefly addressed the challenges of dual relationships between students and field instructors under Standard 3.02 of the Code, Education and Training. Here we consider dual relationships and boundaries between students and those they serve. Students need help in thinking about self-disclosure, gifts offered to them, invitations to be friends on a social networking site, or invitations to attend events. How to manage running into service users in the normal course of our daily lives outside work is another recurring dilemma. This is especially true in rural communities where personal and professional circles often intertwine. Technology introduces the added dimension of the prevalence and availability of information online. A useful exercise is to help students search their names online to examine what information about them is publicly available. Students may choose to edit and elect to restrict this information. As tempting as it may be to explore material about service users online, the code warns against this practice as an unethical invasion of privacy, except for compelling professional reasons. Likewise, it is not unusual for students to slip into personal conversational talk with service users in their efforts to learn new skills and as they begin to engage and connect with them.

> Consider a specialized practice level White student, a naturally vivacious and sociable individual, who was placed in a therapeutic group

home for latency-age youths for her generalist practice level placement. Her specialized practice level placement was serving Black young adults who were seeking to obtain their general education degrees and career advancement services. The role in this setting required supporting the young men in their assumption of increased adult responsibilities. The student found herself sharing information of her own life and providing advice, often starting with, "Well, when I was struggling with this problem, I—" or "Perhaps you need to try—I have done this when I was in the exact situation and found it very helpful." In supervision, the field instructor asked the student to clarify her purposes for this choice of intervention.

The student responded that she wanted to share her own experiences to let the young men know that she understood their context and problems. She was looking for a way to let them know that she had experience to offer. The field instructor translated the student's intent as seeking to establish rapport and communicate understanding and empathy; she invited the student to consider how the issue of gender, race, and age might be at play. She assisted the student to consider ways to convey personal and social empathy and understanding while also maintaining some personal distance for clearer professional boundaries in the relationship. The student asked, "What's wrong with sharing what has worked for me?" When the field instructor took the conversation beyond exploring alternative ways to engage and directly addressed the continuum of maintaining boundaries and dual relationships from being a close friend at one end and a distant professional on the other, this student began to work on what the differences were and what her ethical responsibilities were in this setting. It was then possible to move the conversation to consider how age, gender, and race affected her interventive choices.

In this example, taking the conversation directly to the demands of ethical and professional behavior provided a different context to the discussion. The student began to see what it meant to make service users' interests primary, how assuming her solutions would be their best solutions might be experienced, and how protecting the men's interests to the greatest extent possible might be achieved in this setting. She was able to compare her role and relationship with the younger children in the group home setting with her role in this new setting and how a different demeanor was necessary. The student moved forward to engage in meaningful conversations with the men so that they could experience her authentic, vivacious, and sociable nature while also understanding that her concern was about them; to find their solutions in a working relationship that supported their growth; and using every minute possible for them, not her. She saw how the realities of her social location, race, age, and gender provided important ingredients for opportunities for meaningful discussions and reparative experiences with these men to give space to hear their own voices, discuss their own experiences, and move toward their empowerment, which is the goal of this program.

Summary

Demonstrating professional and ethical behavior are tied together. Professional values are solidified by ethical standards; together they offer guidance for action to fulfill our mission. Therefore, teaching students about professional values is central to a justice-based framework for field education. The ability to promote growth in students' understanding of the demands of professional behavior relies on what we teach them about professional values and how we push this dialogue beyond expectations surrounding the concrete determinants of how our values are employed in this role or in this setting. Students need to be oriented to their specific roles and responsibilities in the culture of their placement setting while also being provided opportunities to consider these responsibilities in the broader context of the profession. Each plays its part. Students need to know what is required of them, what is unique to this context and field of practice, and what translates to their professional obligations wherever they may be employed.

The path to this understanding involves promoting mindful practice, self-reflection, and self-awareness. Growth occurs over time, and students are shaped by prior life experiences and what they anticipate social work to be. Often, challenging conversations on professionalism and ethical decision making are rooted in dominant discourse and tensions between perceived acceptable values and interpretations of professional conduct. Students are influenced by the formal, dominant, and privileged socialization process provided by the content and structure of the social work program and what is taught about professional values, ethics, and human rights through didactic and experiential teaching techniques. They are also influenced by us as role models for ethical practice (Boyd Webb, 1988; Knight, 2016). The forces that shape the development of professional identity reflect myriad personal, cultural, and global perspectives. Knowledge, skills, values, attitudes, and developing professional identity interconnect and interact as students move toward graduation. Finally, students continue their journey and crystallization of their professional identity as they enter and progress in the workforce (Barretti, 2004; Miller, 2010; Osteen, 2011).

The demands of ethical practice have increased alongside the growing complexities of social life and interactions. Perhaps they have not increased; perhaps it is the nature of ethical challenges and that as the world changes, we are faced with new and unfamiliar situations and contexts that test our values and assumptions. Clearly, one of the difficulties for us as field instructors is that our students are building their social work identities and career paths in a time that is different from when we were entering the profession.

Although there are certain consistent ethical rules that are unquestionable, such as not exploiting those we work with or not having sexual relationships with students, vague areas remain, and new situations will arise. Broadening global interconnections and influences create ambiguities and complexities that require self-awareness and critical consciousness—that is, being open to examining the complications of history, power, and oppression in ethical decision making. We cannot allow students to move into the profession with a myopic or solely local view of how personal, professional, and societal values intertwine, interact, and often conflict in our decision-making processes. As situations arise, new opportunities emerge that provide the chance to highlight the ethical dimensions of our practice. Discussions and learning dialogues about these issues and introducing differing international perspectives and solutions provoke students to become competent practitioners.

Students are held to the standards of professional behavior in the NASW (2017) Code of Ethics, and we reinforce our students' understanding of the Code so they might be in a better position to apply its standards. Reading the code with students and having initial discussions on any questions about the profession's values, principles, and standards that apply specifically to the setting and population of the field placement is a useful strategy. Translating the code to our own relationships with students is another way to bring the material alive to them. Bringing the values of our profession to field education supervision by reading the code together with students, substituting the *field instructor* for *worker* and *students* for *constituents* focuses the document through the direct lens of how it applies to the student and creates a potent teaching method (Lewis, 1987). Although common themes emerge during field education, including conflicts of interest, confidentiality, dual relationships, and boundary issues, the context and how these issues emerge may change depending on the unit of attention, population served, and setting.

The best teaching points about professional ethics emerge from students' practice experiences, but it is often helpful to anticipate common ethical dilemmas related to the work of the placement setting. These discussions reinforce the common base of our professional values, which permeate different practice methods. This is particularly important considering the ethical dilemmas posed by the challenges in social work practice today. Helping students with the emotions evoked in practice responds to the vulnerability they experience; but without connecting their experience to our professional mandates, we provide only half of the perspective needed. If we are successful in making connections with them, it will prepare them for compassionate concern and ethical decision making that may produce a more self-aware, developing professional stance regarding power in relationships. They will be better prepared to "engage in practice that is sensitive both to the needs of service users, and to conflicting demands of agencies and others" (Clifford & Burke, 2005, p. 680).

CHAPTER 5 APPENDIX

The items in this appendix provide parallel scenarios for field instructors and students to consider from their various roles and positions. The first item presents the scenarios from the field instructor's perspective, whereas the second item presents similar situations from the student's perspective.

Ethical Dilemma Scenarios for Field Instructors

The following ethical dilemmas in field instruction are presented as scenarios that may be used to stimulate reflection on these issues.

- You are having a party for your son's graduation and are inviting many of your colleagues from the agency. Do you invite your specialized practice level student? If yes, why? If no, why not?
- Your student presents you with an expensive gift at the end of the field placement. Do you accept the gift? If not, how do you handle this situation? What are the cultural issues involved?
- Your student invites you to join in the student's Facebook or YouTube community. How do you respond?
- A few weeks into the placement your student notices the pride flag on your wall, shares that he is gay and wonders whether you are also. How do you respond?
- Your student is going through a painful divorce and custody battle and mentions it to you during a field instruction conference. How can you be helpful and supportive to the student? Would you encourage discussion of your student's mental and emotional state with this situation? What is involved in maintaining objective, professional boundaries?
- Your student is assigned to work with a group of teenagers at a community center. He makes a comment in supervision

about how cute the teenagers are and refers to one girl as having nice biceps and a cute butt. How do you respond?
> You and your student are both women of color of the same age, have the same number of children, and are Seventh-day Adventists. You sense that the student is eagerly looking for ways to make you a friend rather than deal with you as her field instructor. Your student is also avoiding responsibilities in the field placement and jokes when you request recordings or question her work management skills. How do you maintain a professional working relationship without appearing uncaring?
> Your student asks that you text her rather than use her e-mail. The only way you would be able to respond to this request is to use your cell phone to send a text. What issues do you discuss with your student?

Ethical Dilemma Scenarios for Discussions With Students

The following ethical dilemmas are presented as scenarios that field instructors might use to prompt discussion with students.

> An adolescent is having a graduation party and enthusiastically invites the social work student to attend. How do you help the student discuss the pros and cons of accepting or rejecting the invitation?
> An individual presents the student with an expensive gift at the end of the field placement. How do you help the student handle this situation?
> An adolescent invites the student to join in the youth's Facebook or YouTube community. How do you help the student respond to this request?
> A few weeks into the placement, your student asks you whether he can tell this one individual that he is gay because he thinks it would help the individual be more comfortable in coming out to the student in their work together. How do you respond?
> Your student is running a group for women dealing with domestic violence. She discloses to you that she is a survivor

of domestic violence. How can you be helpful and supportive to the student in dealing with the painful memories that the group evokes in her? Do you discourage the student from connecting her experiences with those of the women in her group? Do you encourage the student to discuss her mental and emotional state at the time of the domestic violence as a way of preparing her for the work anticipated in this group?

› A woman student is working with a man; both are of similar age, from similar middle-class backgrounds, and both are Italian Catholics. In recordings, you sense that the student is trying to be objective and distant from this individual, and she has established very rigid boundaries in their work together. This behavior is strikingly different from how she works with others. The student mentions that the individual makes comments about her hair and she is aware staff often comment on his good looks. Do you ask the student whether she feels a physical attraction to this person or whether she senses that he is physically attracted to her? How do you help the student maintain a professional working relationship while allowing her to connect with the similar life experiences between them?

› Your student is assigned to work with another student to co-lead a group of teenagers at a community center. The student, a man, makes a comment about how cute the teenagers are and refers to one girl as being attractive and provocative. How do you respond? How might your response be affected by the possible different gender identities of those involved?

› An individual has been difficult to engage. She finally comes in to see your student. She tells the student that she never responds to e-mails and that she prefers to be texted. The only way your student would be able to respond to the youth's request is to send a text from a personal cell phone. What issues do you discuss in supervision?

CHAPTER 6

Getting Started

Learning While Serving in Justice-Based Field Education

In the field, students are personally involved in learning to think and to act like a social worker and to incorporate social work values.... Involvement with "real life" clients, communities and social issues provides experiences, immediacy, and activity through drawing students into the concerns of others and offering meaningful opportunities to be helpful or to bring about change—likely the very factors that motivated students to choose social work as a career. (Bogo, 2010, p. 88)

Professional education is not education for understanding alone; it is preparation for accomplished and responsible practice in the service of others. It is preparation for "good work." Professionals must learn abundant amounts of theory and vast bodies of knowledge. They must come to understand in order to act, and they must act in order to serve. (L. Shulman, 2005, p. 53) earning to serve requires a framework that embraces justice. Likewise, engagement is the base for the process of change and is a core competency required of all social work students. At the beginning of any relationship, whether with a person, a community, or organization, understanding our role and function begins the relationships we form and shapes the ongoing work. Building trust, establishing rapport, creating a space that is open, honest, mutual, and respectful builds authentic partnerships that reduce potential obstacles of strife, distrust, and ambivalence. Likewise, our first connections with students lay the foundation for a relationship in which we can work together to achieve competent practice. These beginning processes are critical in setting the tone for teaching and learning.

Field instructors introduce students to competency-based education during the earliest days of field education. It is perhaps ironic that competence is the stated goal of the internship and is introduced at the very moment when students feel the most incompetent; however, it is critical for the field instructor to specifically and wholeheartedly commit to be the student's partner in introducing and enhancing the student's capacities in each area. Each of the nine CSWE (2015a) competencies should be briefly explained, telling the student how they will appear in assignments and how the field instructor and student will work together to strengthen the student's capacity. If the student is studying a specialized area of practice, the competencies related to the specialization should be reviewed.

It is also important for the field instructor to expect the student to identify, define, and describe learning and challenges in competence terms. This provides evidence, even at the very beginning of the internship, that the student is active in defining and assessing learning. But the student cannot feel alone in this work. The field instructor is the coach, mentor, and cheerleader in the process of mastering these areas. A justice-based framework creates the means to support student growth and learning from the start; it promotes the genesis of a relationship that is grounded in mutuality and equity, encourages dialogue, bears witness to people's stories, and sets a positive space for learning to occur (Finn, 2016).

Getting Started: Setting the Stage for Justice-Based Learning in Field Education

The epigraphs at the beginning of this chapter point to the vibrancy of learning while serving others. Direct work with individuals and the communities where they live introduces students to social work's mission and values and provides real-life experiences to enhance classroom learning. This combination—classroom learning and field placement experiences—forms the basis of social work education. It introduces students to the significance of their role, exposes them to the consequences of their actions, and shapes their professional development.

This chapter examines how we prepare ourselves and our settings for working with students and how we set the context for our students' abilities to start on firm ground, so they are prepared to serve as they learn. We address the practical components of helping students become oriented to their new roles and preparing them for service in our profession, not just service in a specific setting. In this way, the chapter demonstrates how introducing students to competency-based education sets the stage for justice-based field education. The information provides a structure that attends to the many different aspects of getting started. Without this basic structure in place, everything else can collapse. Our attempts to create conducive environments, dialogues for learning, assessments of students' abilities to function in settings, and their abilities to serve individuals and communities depend on this foundation. Chapter 2 addresses preparing ourselves for our role; in this chapter we continue and add preparing our setting and students.

Differing expectations exist among the staff in the placement setting, the social work program, and students, and these expectations affect decisions about what form the beginning will take. Although each setting and student may need a somewhat different approach, the beginning phase can be enhanced by paying attention to some basic and universal factors, such as addressing orientations to field education supervision and the competencies, assignments, setting, organizational life, and importance of a justice-based lens to field education. Orientations are helpful ways to provide specific and incremental information to propel students toward success. This is not to recommend a fixed approach to the beginning phase. On the contrary, orientation to field education should move at a guided but individualized pace to allow the process to unfold. According to Towle (1954),

> the educational task ... [involves] balancing giving and demanding, taking care not to give too much at once in too great detail. This entails giving first things first, with a realistic expectancy that they be mastered. It also implies helping the learner put them to use and holding him [or her] accountable for doing so. (p. 33)

The initial concerns brought by students depend on several factors including differing social dimensions of identity. Our journeys of moving through the world prepare us differently, including our actual journeys to the setting. For example, what was the student's experience when first entering the setting? Was the student welcomed? Looked at suspiciously? Was identification or going through a metal detector required? A student who wears a hijab in today's current political and social climate might have a completely different journey and welcoming experience. Given these concrete realities, students come with differing levels of trust, curiosity, and hesitation about beginning their internships. It is critical for us to tune in to these realities and have the capacity to address them early and consider what staff preparation is needed to host students.

This perspective has roots very early in our professional traditions. Reynolds (1942) refers to this entry period of field education as "the vestibule to learning" (p. 214). She proposes that beginning the field education relationship requires different skills and attitudes from those needed later when the foundation has been established. Although support and guidance remain essential throughout, as initial anxiety and uncertainties diminish, interactions will naturally shift in response to our students' changing needs and demands. Because apprehension is expected (Gelman, 2004), it is possible to manage this dynamic through anticipatory planning and preparation. Grounding ourselves in our aims places us in a good position to plan how we will prepare for our student's entry to the placement. Also, understanding basic expectations required for field education prepares students for what is ahead.

Just as some individuals seeking service have limited understanding of the helping process and unrealistic expectations of social work services, social work students may be unclear about the process of field education; they may have unrealistic expectations of us as field instructors and of the settings where they will be working. Likewise, many of the concerns students have are not dissimilar from our own as field instructors. Anxiety and potential unease are natural responses to any role change and can be expected when evaluating and being evaluated are involved. Immediately, issues related to power and privilege emerge. Unsurprisingly, questions surface from these varying perspectives, such as, "What will be expected of me, and how will I be evaluated?," "Will I meet my own expectations and achieve my goals?," and "Will I be able to meet the demands of this setting, those I serve, this field instructor—or, this student?"

Before the Student Arrives: Starting With Ourselves

Setting the stage for learning entails pairing and balancing expectations with realistic goals. The way the placement starts sets the tone and affects how next steps are taken (Dettlaff, 2003; Knight, 2016; Nelson, 1974; Nisivoccia, 1990). How we prepare ourselves, the setting, and students has a far-reaching effect on how students understand what is required of them in their tasks and responsibilities. It stands to reason that just as it is good social work practice to teach students to tune in to beginning processes, there are similar positive effects on learning when we prepare ourselves and the placement setting using this same technique for educating students (Shulman, 2012).

Understanding our own reasons for agreeing to supervise students is an important component. Our reasons may impose unrealistic expectations on us, the setting, and students. For example, we may not have chosen to have a student in placement and instead are required to do so by our own supervisor, we may be motivated by boredom from our job and wish to inject new life into our work, or we have a genuine desire to contribute to a student's professional development. All three may play a part, and each affects our intentions and attention to the demands of the task.

Drawing on our own experiences and recalling what it was like when we began our field placement or started new jobs is a helpful way to tune in to the issues involved. Also, understanding how our experience might be similar or different from our student's experience aids this tuning in. However, it often happens that only after the first experience of working with a student can we fully appreciate what hosting a student requires of the setting and us. Only then may we fully understand what supports we need in dealing with the increased demands on our time. Therefore, it is important to identify who we can rely on if the demands affect our capabilities to manage. If possible, discussions with more experienced field instructors are a useful way to pool expertise. Field liaisons perform important roles in this regard. Field education seminars, often called SIFIs, bring new field instructors together and are another important additional resource (Fishbein & Glassman, 1991).

Tuning in to what we know and do not know about the student's social dimensions of identity aids our preparation for how we might introduce the student to the issues and work of the setting and prepare a path for the student within the setting. For example, we can consider whether the student is the only person of color among an all-White staff or the only Muslim among an all-Jewish or all-Christian staff. Examining the student's résumé provides information about whether this is the student's first experience of working in a human service setting. These are potentially important considerations that extend to other aspects of difference. For example, emerging literature provides a glimpse into the special stressors existing for LGBTQ+ students and the need for thoughtful preparation and ongoing work to create and advance an inclusive environment (Dentato, Craig, Messinger, Lloyd, & McInroy, 2014; Messinger, 2007; Newman, Bogo, & Daley, 2009).

Before the Student Arrives: The Setting

Our responsibilities for becoming field instructors begin with the need to assess and intervene on an organizational level to determine the elements required to host students. For example, it is not the responsibility of a social work program to match a student with the population served by the setting; students are placed where learning can occur.

> Consider the example of a Black student who is placed at an organization with Russian-speaking staff members who identify as Jewish. The staff members speak Russian to one another, thereby excluding the student. So that she can be a part of the conversation, the student asks them to speak in English, but they dismiss her. During discussion in supervision, the student expresses feeling angry and being uncomfortable with the staff members. The field instructor shifts the conversation, implying that perhaps the student is being too sensitive because the staff members have been used to conversing in Russian for years. The staff members feel disrespected, the field instructor feels stuck between her staff and her student, and the student feels ignored, stressed, and marginalized.

For this example, consider these questions: What if the tables were turned? Which is more likely—a Russian American Jewish student placed in a predominantly Black setting or, as in this example, a Black student in a Russian American Jewish setting? Are the expectations any different in either scenario? Is the purpose for students to learn how to practice in any environment with any community? Of course, but some communities and placement settings may be less sensitive and less tolerant of the differences between the student and staff or the population served. The staff representing the community may be perpetuating systems of exclusion and oppression. Further, what are the implications for the student in this example when the field instructor implies that the student is too sensitive? Will this response result in feelings of being in a hostile environment, an increased sense of exclusion, and a possible experience of racial microaggression?

This example raises questions about what field instructors must do to better prepare staff for welcoming students. Being placed as the only student in an established work environment is a potentially isolating and marginalizing experience. Without the field instructor doing the necessary preliminary work, it is difficult to assess the receptivity of staff and the setting as an appropriate placement for students where they may learn to their full potential. Without this assessment, we may be setting up the learning to be about preparing students for work in isolating work environments.

We have the responsibility to address issues of racism, sexism, and other forms of oppression that exist in our settings (Carten et al., 2016; Miller & Garran, 2017), and this responsibility certainly applies when we invite unknowing students into these environments. To begin, assess the external and internal features of the settings and how they may affect the student's experience; these features make up the real-life situations students will encounter in their work and deserve attention before the student arrives.

Although external conditions may be beyond the control of the organization, certain responses to these conditions affect the internal work climate and which learning opportunities are available to students. The concept of an implicit curriculum introduced in the CSWE (2008) EPAS describes the potent influence of the milieu on student learning. Although this concept is often described in terms of the academic program's role, the setting's climate and staff have equal roles to play in student learning. Discussions with the social work program's field education liaison may be useful in determining a plan for hosting students. Any concerns that emerge about the placement site should be discussed so the external and internal realities may be placed in the context of learning opportunities for students.

Students are quick to spot flaws in the educational program's offerings and in the placement's service delivery system. They spot professional burnout often present when staff turnover is high and staff morale is low, and they are keen observers of inadequate efforts to redress societal inequities, poor administrative choices, and oppressive policies or procedures. The populations and communities served may be faced by conditions such as growing unemployment, increasing economic hardship, and escalating violence. Similarly, the current climate of fiscal cutbacks in human service fields and the fear of additional losses mean that many social service agencies are experiencing organizational problems resulting from reduced funds to support adequate staffing levels. These external factors may shape the setting's view of students as potential resources to help fill these gaps. It is important to consider how these differing factors affect the creation of a conducive environment for learning.

Likewise, internal organizational factors affect learning opportunities. For example, staff members' morale and their willingness to host students will affect the student's sense of belonging. Whether staff members will play a role in the student's assignments; whether the student is supervised by an off-site field instructor, is only social worker in the unit, or will be guided by a task supervisor; and the perspective and approach a task supervisor takes to the work all contribute to the student's overall experience and learning.

Students are introduced to a strengths-based model of working with those they serve in their classes, and they will be supported or hindered in their ability to work with this approach based on what they observe in the setting's work methods. The questions students raise often prompt a new understanding of service, igniting an incentive toward change. In this way, students provide a new set of inquiring eyes that enable us to view the status of our approaches to service from a justice-based perspective. Students also can be the impetus for change, even as seemingly small as requesting to initiate gender-inclusive intake forms. Such a change will affect delivery of just services, build awareness, and promote conversations about improving inclusive practices.

Sometimes the idea and anticipation of having a student differ from the realities of this responsibility. The first time a student is placed in the setting, it is important to establish what kind of commitment exists to provide professional training. Inevitably, hosting students requires cooperation from staff. We can prevent some of the difficulties that arise by talking about the implications of having students, such as students should attend staff meetings and assume more than an observational role, and they need space and resources to do their work. This includes an orientation to the setting, policies, and procedures; an introduction to how technology is used; and assignments that reflect the student's method of study or program year and extend capacities while promoting achievement of competence. Each of these ingredients may accommodate students' learning needs, positively affect daily operations, and offer opportunities to support and extend services.

The answers to the following questions help determine what will be needed in creating conducive learning environments for students.

- Will students be seen as professional staff in training or as outsiders? Will students be accepted as potential new recruits to the social work profession for whom this setting will play a role in shaping their professional identity or will students be seen as an additional burden on an already overburdened work environment?
- What has been the experience of hosting students in the past?
- Will more than one student be placed in the setting? If so, what arrangements may be made to incorporate shared learning experiences? Could a group for student supervision be offered? Does sharing an assignment provide additional learning opportunities? How do the student's special attributes combine with the characteristics of the staff and population served or issues addressed?

Before the Student Arrives: The Social Work Education Program

Requirements of social work education programs are best anticipated well before the student arrives. Gaining understanding of the social work program's philosophy and mission as well as information on practical concerns are generally spelled out in the program's field education manual. Examples of some practical concerns include field education time and workload requirements, selection of assignments, addressing competencies, formats used for written field education recordings, time frames for assessments and evaluations, and collaboration with field liaisons. Several suggestions follow that aid further examination of how the program's philosophy and mission are implemented.

How are students oriented to field education? Understanding what the program provides as an orientation to field education identifies issues stressed by the program as important and may highlight areas the setting needs to offer or enhance. Does the program begin by acknowledging students' use of pronouns that show awareness of gender identity, or are these issues not addressed? How does the program introduce students to the competencies, and what are the school's expectations about how competencies are evaluated in field education?

How does the program's curriculum support integration of field practice? Become acquainted with the program's organization of the curriculum and its relationship to field teaching and expectations. The social work program's mission and goals are often ways to understand each program's special emphasis and curriculum. Likewise, elective and specialization or concentration choices reflect the program's practice orientation.

How are field assignments shaped by program requirements? Clarify how curriculum structures and expectations as expressed in specialization or concentration choices affect student assignments. Advanced standing, work study, reduced residency, specialized practice curriculum concentrations, part-time options, or dual degree programs often have certain requirements attached. They determine requirements for a student's learning focus, and they define the program's competencies and learning outcomes.

Discussions with the program's field liaison about the learning opportunities available and connections to the development of required competencies must begin early because they shape the choice of assignments and set the context for the educational plan and appropriate learning experiences. Consider which assignments have been used in the past, for example, by asking the following questions: Which have been most successful? Which have failed? and, What skills and competencies are likely to predominate in this setting?

How does the program administer field education? Consider the program's defined general and respective responsibilities, including

> defined roles and responsibilities of field liaisons;
> rights and responsibilities of students, field instructors, task supervisors and agencies;
> the social work education program's calendar and holidays, religious holidays (including holidays the student might observe that the setting does not) sick leave policy, end-of-semester evaluation due dates, and relevant policies that affect field placements; and
> description of student learning outcomes assessment; and
> seminar or conference opportunities for field instructors.

Learning While Serving in a Justice-Based Model

This section continues examination of beginning processes that promote learning in a justice-based model; the aim is to stimulate student engagement with the role and responsibilities they will carry. Student orientations are presented as more than a single event; they continue in varying formats and foci throughout the student's experience in the setting. Suggestions regarding student orientations to their setting are made including planning the student's first day or week; and introductions to the setting's staff and services, the community served or issues to be addressed, and issues of safety. This is followed by orientation to the student's role and functions within the internship. Orientation to field education supervision includes ways to discuss the context and goals for supervision as well logistics surrounding supervisory sessions. Clarifying shared expectations, fears, and hopes, and clarifying issues of safety are also critical components. Finally, ways to begin orientation to the competencies are proposed.

Learning While Serving: Orientation to the Setting

Orientations help students develop a sense of belonging and identification with the mission and goals of their placement setting. Orientation to the setting is an ongoing process that begins during the first few weeks in placement and continues throughout the academic year as the student is introduced to different aspects of organizational life. Depending on the size or complexity of the placement site, some orientation programs are agency-wide formal programs organized by field instructors and administrators. Some include a welcoming breakfast, structured lectures, tours, meetings with key personnel, and handouts that include manuals and other literature. Still other orientation programs are less formal and consist of the field instructor and student walking through the setting, going to a staff meeting together, having the student shadow a worker for an afternoon, or taking a walk through the community neighborhood. Each provides another glimpse into the culture of the setting.

Students need to understand the setting they will be based in, but much of this understanding comes with time and exposure. Instructing students to read the policy manual without including other activities is not recommended. Policy manuals often are written in formal language that may alienate students rather than acclimate them. Instead, information should be broken up into what is needed to manage the placement, the role students will play, their assignments, and how all this relates to the social work profession and a justice-based approach to field education and practice. This requires us to consider these aspects in advance and to gather relevant information associated with identifying the setting and the services it provides, the population and community served, the setting's place in the continuum of services offered to this population and community, and how the issues addressed are affected by broader forces such as those that apply on national and international venues.

The variability of settings used as field placement sites may require flexibility in considering how students are introduced to the services provided and to how service users experience these arrangements. Students may assist at or join an event to observe how service users experience the setting.

If asked to observe service delivery in a waiting area, considering how phone intakes occur, or participation in a program is offered, students should be asked to expand on their observations, feelings, and assessments. The following questions provide an opportunity for broader discussions about the setting and its philosophy of service delivery. For example, ask the following:

> What did you notice?
> What do you think it is like for someone to approach for help in this setting? Can you give an example that helped you to form this opinion?
> How does the setting represent the community and populations served?
> What seemed to be working in the program or activity you observed? What needs adjustment?

Orientation to the community being served or where the placement is located helps students connect to the context of service. A tour, walk, or drive through the community with students, or arranging such a tour, gives them a broader view of the community and provides a context for understanding accessibility of resources, the culture of the community, and the setting's place in the community. For these reasons, community engagement expanding beyond the walls of the setting is strongly encouraged.

Some neighborhoods are labeled unsafe or safe based on prejudices, media information, and personal biases. It may be that a community is viewed as unsafe because of assertive police scrutiny, anti-Semitic graffiti, differing political views about gentrification, or transphobic policies and actions that influence community tensions. In response to these realities, we aim to balance personal safety discussions and the student's perceptions before the student begins work with community members and their surroundings.

Many students will not know the community where their internship is located, or they may base their knowledge on what others have told them about the location or what they have read in the media. Even if they are familiar with the community, quite possibly as a resident, they will experience it from a different lens as an intern. Traveling through the community provides an opportunity for the student to see it with fresh eyes. This excursion can be planned as a sort of scavenger hunt that examines differing perspectives relating to the setting's service agenda. For example, this may include finding where the schools, parks, banks, medical resources, and churches are located and seeing the types of housing and their relation to available transportation systems.

A set of reflection questions can be prepared to help focus students' interest on aspects related to their work, such as the following:

> What did you learn about the population, issue, or community that changed or clarified your preconceived expectations? Who lives here? What resources exist? What resources seem to be missing? In what ways did the community seem to lack essential resources or qualities?
> Did you feel like you want to be part of this community? Why or why not? How comfortable did you feel during this exploration? What contributed to the way you felt? Were there aspects that represented strength, vibrancy, and a sense of belonging?
> In general, what impressions are you left with, and what do these impressions suggest about the population or issues you will be encountering in placement? How did this experience contribute to your understanding of the issues, population, or community you will be working with?

Similar concerns relate to familiarizing students about the population or issues addressed in the field education placement. Orientation requires addressing what students know about the population served, how they understand the problems and issues of concern, and what aspects of these preconceived notions need to be tackled. Thought should be given on how to introduce students to these issues and on providing information that can facilitate thoughtful consideration of their preconceived ideas about the service agendas that will be assigned.

Have a plan for the student's first week and first day. There is a great deal for students to absorb in the beginning, and we should take a moment to consider the first week in its totality. How balanced will the first week be between didactic material, activities, student observations, and active participation? Even if a brief group field education meeting of students is planned, meeting individually with students on the first day goes a long way toward establishing the student and field instructor relationship. This meeting confirms that field education supervision is a safe harbor in the middle of all that students are trying to manage.

Balance how much information to provide to the students and in what form. In the beginning, it is best not to overburden students with too much information too quickly. The aim is to give enough information supported with dialogue that students feel included and clued-in to their role in the setting and can start their placement with a sense of direction. This can be achieved by selecting the most important information for students to have on the first day of placement, the first week, the second week, and so on. During the first few days of placement, students mostly want to know what they will be doing, what is expected of them, if they will they fit in, if there are people there like them, and if they belong in the setting. Addressing these questions translates functions and procedures into the work students will be doing, the support they will encounter and how the work culture will affect them.

Deciding which pieces of information are useful in discussions as opposed to prepared handouts is another way of breaking up the flow of information. Agency brochures, website information, and mission statements are useful guides. Having such concrete items and information ready for students, supported by dialogue that addresses what is often hidden between the lines, is an easy way of letting them know their arrival has been prepared for, and their adjustment to the setting and their role is important. If the setting has a history of receiving student interns, establishing a network of past and current students is helpful. This natural network maintains links with previous students and provides a network for current students. Sometimes these networks extend across the United States and to international students from countries around the world.

Specific, understandable explanations about their social work role, purpose, focus, and goals of the placement can be used to gradually introduce students to their responsibilities. Brief descriptions of the setting, populations served, the role of social work, funding sources, and rules and regulations are all helpful pieces of information. An organizational chart that shows the student's relation to others in the agency is another way to demonstrate the student has a place in the setting. Organizational charts also identify staffing patterns and prompt discussions of leadership and community representation. Explaining significant procedures that the student will need to know, such as rules and norms, formal and informal communication systems, dress codes, and lunch break details, are important. Do not forget essentials such as bathroom keys, supplies, mailboxes, a list of telephone extensions, identification or name tags, an overview of technology, and safety precautions. How to answer the telephone and how to sign e-mail communications also help to prepare the student. These necessary elements provide the information students will need and prevents them from having to ask for them.

Ensure that students are introduced to staff, from the maintenance workers to the department head or executive director. If there is a reception area or main telephone receptionist, make sure the student's name, office location, and schedule of placement hours are provided. Introducing students to the department head or executive director reminds this individual of the importance of the student program in the setting and acknowledges the field instructor's and task supervisor's roles in supporting this component of service. Likewise, introducing students to those who work in the setting ensures they will be on more firm footing and move forward with a sense of belonging and acceptance. Including introductions at the highest and lowest levels of power in the setting emphasizes to the student that everyone in the setting deserves acknowledgment, no one is ignored, and they also will not be ignored. The aim is to avoid situations in which students are left to fend for themselves or feel that they or others are either not important enough to be recognized and named or too important to be approached.

Keep a pulse on how the orientation is progressing to introduce students to evaluation processes from the very start of placement. Asking how students are experiencing the orientation process reveals the type of information they need, and in what form, to adapt to the setting and to their role. Be mindful that the student's response might also be reflective of how well a job the field instructor and staff have done in creating a climate of affirmation, safety, and beginning levels of trust. As students become more familiar with the setting—its culture, its services, and its philosophy toward service delivery—asking them to comment on observed strengths and gaps provides them with the chance to practice critical thinking skills and to shift the power differential from field instructor as expert to student as a provider of expert analysis (Pinderhughes, 1983). As making links to broader perspectives may be difficult, it is important to help them make these connections. This includes pointing to national and international news and policies affecting the agency's population or service agenda. Students may be asked to keep a reflective journal on what they observed in terms of issues of justice-based perspectives, which introduces the notion that all activities in the placement are sources for reflection, analysis, and learning. These formulations help students move from a specific setting perspective to a professional stance regarding service provision and provides an early indication of the student's reflective capacities.

Legitimate questions to ask new student interns include the following:

> How is orientation to this setting and role going? What is working and what was useful? What did not work and what might be done differently?
> Did the orientation meet your needs? If so, what was helpful?
> How did the first day go? How did the first individual meeting or group meeting with students go? Did anything unanticipated occur?

› How are we doing in engaging in the dialogue that explains how a competency and justice-based model of field education supports your work?
› What questions remain unanswered? What needs have not been met?

Such specific questions address whether students have the information and resources they need to begin their assignments or whether aspects of their role remain unclear. Responses provide information on the progression of the work and their learning ahead. These early opportunities for review and feedback establish a model of field education in which mutual feedback, collaboration, and critical reflection are legitimate and expected. The answers to these questions also provide useful information for future orientation programs. Students provide a different view of the setting, which offers new insights. For example, ask each year's students to revise the orientation manual to be used for the following year's cohort of students. This might take the form of a program planning assignment that introduces student voices for the continuation of support for student placements.

Learning While Serving: Orientation to the Student's Professional Role

Building on what has been provided as an introduction to the setting, its mission, and services, gather useful information that will facilitate adjustment to social work practice in the setting. A glossary of terms and articles on practice considerations regarding the populations served or issues addressed are examples of items to include. Providing a clear definition of the student's role places a student's performance on firm ground.

Clarity about the student's role also yields rich material for discussion about our professional purposes and how we communicate these in varying ways to those we serve. Ideally, we should describe their functions in jargon-free, operational terms, as shown in the following conversation.

> "We provide help to people who have experiences with drug abuse, have been recently discharged from an inpatient psychiatric hospital, and who need housing, psychiatric clinic follow-ups, and counseling," rather than simply, "We provide intensive case management to mentally ill and chemical-abuse patients."

> "You will be helping us reach out to unemployed migrant men in this community so we can ask their opinions about which services they

and their families may need. You will also assist a task group currently working on revising a questionnaire that has been previously used," rather than, "You will be involved in conducting a needs assessment."

Having work ready for students ensures that time will not be lost. As mentioned previously, it is important for students to have access to work during the first week, and ensuring an adequate flow of work provides structure for the placement. This helps reduce anxiety over how they will be able to contribute, learn, and serve in the setting. Explaining why these early assignments are chosen and connecting them to learning objectives, as in the following example, promotes purpose and direction:

> This setting serves families with a wide range of needs. One of the ways to get a sense of how this affects the work is by working on telephone intakes, where you will have exposure to the broad range of requests we receive for services. This will give you an opportunity to practice your engagement and assessment skills. So I am planning to assign you to a weekly morning intake session. Let's talk about what this task involves and what your role will be.

This open discussion helps students understand the reasons for our request to try something new or to put aside old ways of approaching situations. It promotes student curiosity about methods and approaches. Students often think all they will do the entire year is the same thing they were told to do at the beginning of the placement. Setting an expectation for how the assignments will develop provides students with a vision for what is ahead and an understanding of how their exposure to assignments will grow throughout the year. Specifying the roles and responsibilities that will be required helps students orient themselves to these expectations.

The approach to assigning new cases for generalist practice level students may include instructions and role plays on how to make contact and set up appointments before learning how to conduct initial sessions. Help students practice how to introduce themselves as social work students. Introducing themselves as students directly connects to the professional Code of Ethics regarding honesty and the prohibition against misrepresentation of skills (Feiner & Couch, 1985; Miller & Rodwell, 1997). Likewise, helping students practice introductions of their role is a useful exercise to see how well they can verbalize their understanding of their responsibilities and function.

Building on the orientation to the community being served or the issues being addressed by the setting continues the work of helping students identify similarities and differences between themselves and the communities they will be serving and the issues they will be working on; that is, how the community is viewed and how the student will be viewed or how the issues of concern are viewed by society and how they affect the student. Asking for students' continuing reactions to the field placement helps them trust that they will be listened to. They will experience how understanding comes with openness and dialogue. Providing space to reflect on how their individual attributes will contribute to their work while also considering what obstacles they may face ensures meaningful consideration of these issues that are often avoided. Likewise, seeking opinions and feedback on students' experiences validates their input and demonstrates the mutuality of the learning experience. It also sets the expectation that they will be curious about what they see and experience. It communicates that they have a voice, and we are interested in hearing their perspectives and in helping them appraise their reflections and articulate their views.

Provide access to the various types of records students are required to complete. Explaining the uses of required records, the amount of time allocated for recording and plans for their review are all important pieces of information. Examples of completed forms and the technology required also link functions with the student's professional role. The discussion however, should also embrace the broader place of these requirements in our professional responsibilities. We need to explain how the forms and technology used relate to our professional tasks of assessment, eligibility determination, and professional terminology and how they relate to privacy and confidentiality, professional accountability for public funds, and professional integrity and competence. These are ways we can help students identify with their professional role to act accordingly and place these responsibilities in the professional value of service. In other words, we are helping them to understand what is involved in demonstrating ethical and professional behavior. An understanding of the many practical aspects of their role is essential for students' success, but how these practical components combine with broader goals and purposes in their journey to professionalism will sustain their commitment to serve. At the same time, helping students critically assess what is missing in these recording formats, whose voice is privileged, and whose voice is absent, and then making recommendations for greater inclusion is a good example of advancing justice.

Not all students are beginning-level students. Orientations for more experienced students may be handled differently and adapted to their needs, but it cannot be assumed that these students do not need an orientation or that they will not benefit from discussing their changing professional roles. Students who have had other careers or who are returning to school after working in human service settings have developed skills and knowledge over time. They may need support to translate this experience to their student status and new social work role.

Likewise, students currently employed in the setting may not need an orientation to the organizational structure but will need an orientation to their new student role and to their role in a new department or assignment. For work–study students it is important for written educational plans authorized by the social work program and the placement administrator to address field assignments and field education supervision to avoid potential conflicts of interest. All parties (students, work supervisors, field instructors, task supervisors, administrators, and the social work program) should agree about placement expectations and the field instructor's roles and responsibilities before the placement begins.

For a student who has had previous work experience, it may be helpful to provide an explanation of possible differences, such as in the following:

> "Our approach to working with families may differ from the work you have done previously. Let's see if we can identify the similarities and differences. We begin by acknowledging the parents' efforts in caring for their children and our shared concern for their family's survival. We have found a focus on their past failures to be an unproductive way of starting. Let's talk about this approach as it relates to your role here and the way you are expected to engage families in this program. First, how is this approach different from what you expected?"

Again, by explaining service delivery, the discussion can flow in ways that consider professional theoretical approaches. Likewise, a student who is switching to macro practice from a more micro perspective may benefit from a discussion of the links and shifts involved. Identifying the similarity across the helping process will help the student recognize that it is possible to transfer skills previously acquired. For instance, engaging a family in mandated services is similar to and different from attempting to engage in community outreach. Explaining the similar and differing skills required in both situations helps make connections. In addition, we can ask students to link these approaches to what is being covered in class.

These examples require bridging or transferring learning from one situation to another. Drawing attention to the nature of the current learning task in relation to previous life and work experiences reassures students that they will not be viewed as blank slates but instead will be valued for what they bring with them to this new field education experience. Open discussion of students' previous paid or volunteer work or placement experiences encourage the development of an individualized learning plan. In addition, some social work education programs provide a summary, placement planning forms, or other written materials that shape educational assessments and ideas about possible assignments. Directly discussing this information with students lets them know that their learning needs will be mutually discussed, and assignments will be shaped in relation to their interests, learning needs, and program requirements.

Safety issues should be presented in a straightforward, clear, and caring manner. We have referred to the issue of safety several times throughout this discussion to stress its importance in helping students navigate their way through their placement. Students need to be introduced to discretionary practice protocols as they relate to safety in the placement and in the community. These discussions must begin with a larger discussion of the complex meaning of safety, including what is safety, how who is safe changes depending on the location and the individual, and whether safety is a privilege or a right. Included in this discussion is a consideration of who the student is, who lives and works in the neighborhood where the placement is based, and the reality of conditions of the areas where the student will be working. If the student is interning in a neighborhood where a high level of crime is reported, discussing the realities of practice and the specific implications for work in this setting gives students the information they need to protect themselves and exercise appropriate discretion. Understanding how issues of safety will be managed in regular supervisory sessions provides another means to hold ourselves accountable for these discussions to occur (Criss, 2010; Walters et al., 2011). Above all, we should provide an atmosphere where it is permissible to consider a balanced and justice-based discussion of these circumstances. The issues of feeling uncomfortable in a setting or community are different from feeling unsafe, but both need attention. No matter what the characteristics are of the neighborhood, students need to understand that families live and work there, and often students are guests in people's homes. Issues of safety and how it is defined and perceived extend to them as well. These conversations offer opportunities to discuss the context of the setting's work and the risks and challenges we and the communities we serve face. Here are some useful questions to prompt these conversations:

› What are the student's associations with this district? Is the student a member of this community? How does the student's neighborhood differ from this location?
› Is the student walking or using a car? Are students expected to use their car to transport service users, and if so, what are the policies surrounding this? Does the setting and social work education program have policies on home visits? Will the student make home visits alone or with another staff person? What safety measures are in place for off-site or late-night meetings?
› What useful tips can other workers or staff provide? Are these tips void of bias, prejudice, and racism? What stories circulate about the community and its inhabitants? How do people we serve talk about or consider the meaning of safety?

Likewise, it is never too early to discuss worst-case scenarios or special situations that may arise during work in placement. This gives students permission to express their fears, anxieties, and biases, and to devise problem-solving skills in certain situations. What is the procedure to be followed when individuals threaten to hurt themselves or others? How should students handle illnesses or emergencies of their own? Lines of communication should be clarified, and students should know whom to contact in our absence. Introducing anticipated ethical dilemmas that may emerge related to the work offers the chance to consider these situations in advance and outside a crisis. Such conversations enable recognition of these scenarios and the ability to manage them more successfully if they do occur. A secondary purpose is to identify preconceived bias, prejudice, and racism that may hinder students' abilities to learn and serve.

Learning While Serving: Orientation to Field Education Supervision

Introducing the place of field education supervision in social work education and the goals for learning provides an important context for students. Sharing our hopes and expectations for the year ahead and asking for similar input from students sets a beginning agenda for the work.

We tune in to students' hopes and fears about field education by remembering how it felt to be a student and how our learning was facilitated as students. These are important components for tuning in to the inherent anxiety associated to beginnings but asking students directly about their expectations and hopes is key. Equally important is understanding how this might differ across social dimensions of identity. For example, if students need accommodations to match their abilities, what provisions have been put in place and what does it mean for a student to ask for help to access these accommodations? If the student is a new mother, what arrangements can be made for her to express milk? What arrangements can be made regarding the comfortable use of restrooms and how is the question on the use and identification of pronouns integrated into field education supervision and practice?

If students have had previous placements, gaining a sense of what worked or didn't work for them gives us a perspective on what their previous experiences have been. Likewise, sharing our own reasons for entering the profession and supervising students gives a sense of our intentions and motivations. Sharing our experience of field education supervision lets our students know what we are attempting to duplicate or avoid. Telling our students what our experience has been in the profession provides additional information that helps students understand what they may be able to rely on from us. Using self-disclosure that supports reciprocity and mutuality serves to level the playing field and contributes to building trust and safe spaces for learning.

Explain what we mean by *authentic dialogue* and why it is crucial to justice-based field education and practice. As we have prepared ourselves in considering what our own expectations and hopes are for the learning experience, we invite students to explore this with us. We set the stage for this conversation from the beginning by explaining that getting to know each other is important to trusting and forming a relationship based on mutuality. Beyond what we have already told them about our experiences with supervision and our hopes for their learning, sharing something about ourselves that is not immediately visible, that is, a hidden part of our identity, provides a foundation for connection, for example, telling them why social justice is important to us, when we first became aware of our commitment to justice, when we first noticed that not everyone is regarded the same, how the community we grew up in affected our lens of equity, or how our avowed or achieved identity affects our commitment to our professional mission. The aim is to describe an aspect of ourselves that directly affects our passion and professional commitment to service, our profession, and to social work education.

Once we have revealed something about ourselves, ask the student to do the same. The conversation then can turn to how these sides of ourselves may have become less visible and the importance of understanding that we possess many selves, and hidden or not, these selves influence our views and actions. For example, during the first meeting or even during orientation, the field instructor may introduce the Structured Interview on Dimensions of Difference, Identity, and Social Location (see the Chapter 2 Appendix, p. 85). These activities begin to bring parts of the student and field instructor into conversations, normalize discussion across differences, and send the message that the space is respectful of multiple ways people identify. This leads naturally into a discussion regarding the delicacy and importance of exploring invisible dimensions of identity and the challenge of being able to make this exploration possible and safe.

We make it explicit that field education supervision is where these issues will be discussed to ensure development of the student's professional sense of self, self-awareness, and ability to reflect on thoughts, feelings, and behaviors. Likewise, openly acknowledging the inherent power differential between us as evaluators and students as learners gives voice to the often-unspoken barrier of power and authority. This acknowledgment provides a climate for ongoing openness and, in turn, increases confidence that needs will be met. Field supervision becomes a sanctuary for professional learning and growth.

We can connect this to the mission of the setting and to our professional goals while making it clear that how we engage in supervision directly influences the growth of students' professional skills. This leads to consideration of what is involved in sustaining an authentic supervisory relationship based on openness, mutuality, respect, and trust (L. Shulman, 2005). The manner we accomplish this serves as a model for how students can develop authentic relationships with the individuals, families, and communities they serve. The more we encourage crossing boundaries of our own power and privilege, the more we encourage an examination of how we serve community members and the more students have a visceral experience of what it means to examine who has power and who does not, who is considered deserving and who is not, and what systems continue to affect people's lives and how we take part in them (DiAngelo, 2018).

In addition, students need clues on how to assess danger, awareness of safety measures, useful phone numbers, and knowledge that enables access to advice and support. Protecting students through adequate safeguarding practice policies and ensuring that students have the information they need to exercise discretion are essential (Lyter, 2016). Each of these factors goes a long way in keeping our students and service users safe, and each provides a means for a broader discussion about the profession they are choosing, the means we possess to ameliorate consequences of the conditions that confront us, how to develop resilience in the face of challenge, and how to prevent danger from occurring or escalating.

Students expect us to be available to them, frequently in the beginning and less frequently as the placement proceeds. The pace and gradual decrease of immediate need helps us assess the student's movement toward greater professional autonomy. Movement in this direction is aided by intentional and purposeful supports (Deal, 2002, 2004; Deal, Hopkins, Fisher, & Hartin, 2007; Everett, Miehls, DuBois, & Garran, 2011). Given the inherent uncertainties connected with adjusting to new contexts, students may need help to express the many concerns and uncertainties they experience in this early phase. Providing links between their previous successful experiences and this new situation eases anxiety and provides encouragement to move forward. Expressing interest in their work and life experiences gives reassurance that they will not be assessed separately from their strengths, achievements, and abilities.

Normalize and validate the anxiety and nervousness that most students experience at the start of a new placement through a direct and supportive response. We may try a variety of ways to support students in the beginning, but we simply need to balance recognizing the expected anxiety with giving students time before assessing their apprehension as excessive (Deal, 2004; Gelman, 2004; Grossman, Levine-Jordano, & Shearer, 1990; Rosenthal Gelman, 2011; Rosenthal Gelman & Lloyd, 2008). During this initial phase, we aim to use affective reactions and relevant assessment skills and tools as sources of information to identify student strengths and learning needs. Anxiety that remains high over several weeks takes on a different dimension and must be examined as part of the educational assessment. A prime concern is to determine the student's capacity in tolerating the ambiguity inherent in the work and to provide incremental interventions and ongoing feedback aimed to increase that capacity.

Set clear parameters on field education supervisory times to support the student's ability to manage the responsibilities in placement. In some fast-paced settings, securing a regular uninterrupted time for supervision seems an unrealistic goal. In these situations, it may be possible to arrange shorter periods for supervision more frequently through the week instead of the traditional hour or hour and a half per week. This may also support the student's learning needs. However, even in these situations interspersing longer sessions throughout the academic year protects time for the development of thoughtful reflection rather than providing only short spurts of supervision that too often model a quick fix on practice concerns. Other issues include how students' learning needs shape decisions for field instruction, the lines of communication regarding emergency questions or issues that arise between supervisory sessions, and whether other sources of learning are available for students. The ideal setting balances students' taking advantage of as many resources as possible and protecting time for their direct exposure to work.

If task supervision is used, collaborative relationships must be established. Task supervisors may or may not be social workers who teach the student some task or impart a special expertise (e.g., grant writing, lobbying activities, group work, antiracism training, family therapy, or welfare rights information). In situations where the field instructor is not on site, task supervisors may be the person the student turns to for on-the spot-guidance and instruction. Three-way meetings with task supervisors should occur periodically to review how students are doing, to incorporate this aspect of the learning experience into the student's overall performance and learning goals, and to align the work with a justice-based approach for field education. Field education faculty and staff can be supportive in offering mini seminars or workshops to support and acknowledge the essential role of task supervisors (for a discussion of task supervisor responsibilities, see Chapter 1).

The structure of students' time in the placement—specific days, location, and length of field education meetings—include consideration of the days and times most important in terms of learning. For example, it is important to determine which staff meetings or discussion groups are essential for student participation, and which must be built in to students' field education experience. Asking oneself what the necessary components are for a healthy and stimulating learning experience in this setting initiates consideration of the essential ingredients and practicalities of the placement. It also offers a perspective on what else should be incorporated into the learning experience. Making explicit what opportunities exist in the setting that respond to specific competencies provides a more informed choice of which experiences should be included for students. Additionally, involving the student in decisions on opportunities and choices supports their participation as active learners.

Learning While Serving: Orientation to the Competencies

Ensure that students comprehend how the competencies relate to their field education experience. Students will be introduced to competency-based education by their social work program. This may be accomplished in several ways, through their course outlines, classroom discussions, and introduction to field education manuals, orientations, and recording formats. Despite these mechanisms, it is essential for us to assume responsibility of guaranteeing that our students grasp exactly how the competencies will affect their learning and evaluation when in placement. We can use the materials provided by the social work program, but we also need to find our own ways of translating the competencies and ways to assess performance into the context of the work in the placement setting.

Use a first assignment to illustrate how the competencies apply; the following steps provide some suggestions for beginning this conversation. Refer to the orientation scenario in the Chapter 6 Appendix for a more thorough presentation of these steps.

1. Begin by explaining competency-based education as outcome-focused learning. Explain its importance to teaching and learning by ensuring the student understands the components, principles embedded in the competencies, and the rubrics used to support evaluation. This includes breaking down the competencies into categories, or differentiating those that represent the helping process (engagement, assessment, intervention, and evaluation) through different units of attention (individual, group, community, and organization), that are fundamental components of professional practice (demonstrating ethical and professional behavior, engaging diversity and difference, and advancing human rights and social, economic and environmental justice), and that represent two distinct methods while also representing essential aspects that contribute to all aspects of our work (research-informed practice, practice-informed practice, and policy practice).
2. Choose a beginning student assignment. Select different learning outcomes related to a few competencies that represent the work in this assignment. Examine the competencies through the lens of this assignment for a focused discussion. Use the social work program's final evaluation or refer to the CSWE (2015a) EPAS.

Summary

Setting the stage for field education involves understanding the expectations of students, field instructors, and social work education programs. We need to be clear about the social work program's expectations for our role and responsibilities. Reviewing the program's materials before the start of a student's placement is recommended as well as preparing staff for the student's arrival. Setting the stage for a good start to the placement involves welcoming and orienting students to their new setting, introducing them to the social work profession and practice competencies, and prearranging appropriate assignments. It involves preparing, paving the way ahead, and anticipating obstacles.

The orientation process begins with our first contact with students, and it involves students in learning relationships that entail mutual exchanges and open dialogue. The tasks and activities in the orientation process are vehicles toward a deepening understanding of professional roles and expectations and professional values and goals. If not seen as directly connected to our professional values, the orientation will be experienced merely as an orientation to a specific setting. Presenting the student's role and function as interwoven with our professional mission and values, we powerfully and purposefully introduce our students to the overarching values that drive our work: service, justice, dignity and worth of the person, importance of human relationships, integrity, and competence.

CHAPTER 6 APPENDIX

The two items in this appendix are (1) using an example of a first assignment to orient a generalist practice student to the competencies and (2) a summary listing of issues covered in Chapter 6.

Orientation for a First Assignment Using the Competencies

A 37-year-old, cisgender, single, non-Spanish-speaking Dominican generalist practice level student is placed on a medical service in a large city hospital. He does not live near the community where the hospital is situated and has not yet ventured into the community beyond getting to and from the hospital. He is placed with a new field instructor, who is in her early 30s, single, cisgender, French-speaking Haitian with 6 years of social work experience.

On his first day, the student and four other students toured the hospital and the floors where they will work. They were given an orientation to medical charts, the technology that supports chart materials, access to a Web-based medical dictionary, and a tour of patients' rooms. The students were also briefed about the role of the social worker in the hospital, the sources of referrals, and what to expect when interviewing in a patient's room. Later, he was introduced to medical and nursing staff on his ward and shown how to locate the doctors and nurses caring for his patients. The field instructor told him she would go over this information again with him because she knew it could be a lot to absorb at once.

The field instructor identified a first assignment for her student on the second day of placement. The patient, Ms. B, a 41-year-old, cisgender, Black, divorced, mother of two, was referred to the social work department for help with financial problems by her doctor. Ms. B. was admitted the previous day because of renal failure, secondary to systemic lupus erythematosus, a rheumatic autoimmune disease characterized by complex and changing disease manifestations (Ortiz Hendricks, 2013).

Using an assignment as an opportunity to orient the student to social work competency-based education, consider the following steps:

1. Begin by ensuring understanding of competency-based education as outcome-focused learning.
2. Examine the competencies and select several (at least one) relevant to a chosen assignment. Include an explanation of the learning outcome or skills associated with the chosen competencies.
3. Discuss the assignment and chosen competencies and one or two relevant learning outcomes or skills associated to the work anticipated in this assignment.

The field instructor begins by explaining that they will start the work of this first assignment by looking at it alongside the competencies. She explains they will have an opportunity to examine how the student will begin this assignment in more detail, but she first wants to illustrate the relevance of competencies to their work in supervision.

She asks the student to comment on his understanding of the competencies; she fills in and adds information as needed to ensure that he has foundational knowledge about the role of the competencies in defining the focus of teaching required skills, how they relate to evaluation of performance, and a beginning acquaintance with the practice components and principles they represent. She explains that they will not look at all of them at once but will focus on several that are pertinent to starting this assignment.

Together they use a hard copy of the CSWE (2015a) competencies to keep their discussion focused. The field instructor explains that the initial task in this assignment will be to establish rapport and engage with this patient so that he can explain his role, gain consent and agreement on the possible work needed, and gather information to assess her needs and how he might be helpful. They review the student's role in this situation by beginning with demonstrating ethical and professional behavior. She shares her plan to turn to engagement of individuals and then to assessment of individuals to help the student understand this assignment through the stages of the helping process. She tells him that diversity and difference in practice and human rights and social, economic, and environmental justice will be considered that day because of their importance in engagement, but they will leave the other competency areas until after his first session.

They start with demonstrating ethical and professional behavior. The field instructor explains this competency requires him to apply his understanding of his role as a social work intern in the hospital and his responsibilities as a member of the health care team. She draws on the student's orientation to assess which parts of the explanation of his role he understood. The student replies that although the orientation explained that he is a support to the medical team by obtaining information regarding how external factors might affect the patient's recovery, he adds that this is his first experience in a hospital, and he does not have knowledge about this patient's medical diagnosis. The field instructor acknowledges he correctly recalls how the role was explained, and that she understands this new experience may influence his feelings about beginning. She reassures him that she will provide access to the resources he needs and that she has already selected an article about this patient's condition that may be helpful. She asks what he remembers about the discussion of other important roles directly related to the patient rather than to the medical team. This leads into a discussion about his responsibilities as a patient advocate, liaison to the medical team on behalf of the patient, link and broker to needed resources, and advocate in helping the patient develop a discharge plan. The student, says, "Oh, yes. I remember. I guess there was a lot to take in."

She nods in agreement and reminds him that the details he needs to know about the patient are available on the computerized data system the hospital uses, but that right now she wants to focus on his understanding of his role and purpose for meeting this patient. She asks if he feels he needs more information about the purpose of his meeting with this patient before meeting her. From his body movements, the field instructor notes that the student seems anxious. The student asks whether all charts are similar. The field instructor responds that most are. He continues with several questions about the notes, especially abbreviations and medical jargon. She notes that it is OK to be anxious about all the information, and states that his anxiety shows her that this is important to him. She indicates that she hopes that going through what is expected of him and explaining the purpose of this first meeting might allay some of the nervousness. She stresses her commitment to help him understand what is expected of him as a social work intern and that she will check in with him once they review this material to make sure he is feeling prepared to begin. They also arrange a time when they can meet once he has seen the patient. She makes a mental note to herself to make sure that he can articulate his role.

Still considering ethical and professional behavior, they choose to consider "use supervision and consultation to guide professional judgment and behavior" (CSWE, 2015a, p. 7). This prompts discussion on the place of supervision in managing the questions he has regarding how to proceed. The field instructor remarks on his already demonstrated ability to ask the questions that are on his mind. She indicates pleasure that this is the beginning of their work together. They talk more about their shared views of supervision.

They turn next to the task of engagement and focus on two aspects identified associated with this competency: "apply knowledge of human behavior and the social environment, person in environment, and other multidisciplinary theoretical frameworks to engage with clients and constituencies, and use empathy, reflection, and interpersonal skills to effectively engage diverse clients and constituencies" (CSWE, 2015a, p. 9). She says, "That seems like a lot. Let's break it down."

Together they review the patient's medical illness and medical record. She asks the student, "From your knowledge of human behavior and the social environment, what information from the patient's record do you find pertinent?" He responds that he noticed she is unemployed and has had numerous hospital stays. The field instructor says, "Yes, the referral states the patient has financial problems, and you have identified two indicators that may be associated with this problem." They discuss this further and note that the patient is receiving benefits. The student adds that she is divorced, and that might contribute to her financial problems. The field instructor replies, "OK, you are making links with the material that is connected to other knowledge you have about potential causes of stress and financial strain for divorced women." She praises the student for making these connections and notes that he has already begun to make the competencies real. She asks him if he understands what she means, and he says that he is not sure. The field instructor says that this component of the competency is asking us to consider relevant person-in environment (that is, biological, sociological, ecological, and psychological) factors from a theoretical base rather than from our own knowledge, experience, intuition or, interest. They discuss some of the issues raised and then link the content of his courses to add to his understanding of these issues. The field instructor encourages him to bring this knowledge and his questions to their work together.

The field instructor asks whether there is other information about the patient's situation that may be important. He mentions that the admission sheet notes she has young children; he comments that it must be hard for her to be away from them. The field instructor notes that is a good observation and another example rooted in theoretical perspectives that could help his understanding about what the patient and her children are experiencing. She asks whether he would ask the patient about her children. He replies, "I don't know." Rather than respond to this uncertainty, the field instructor asks if the student understands how the expression of empathy works to promote engagement and whether he has thoughts about how he might go about using empathy to engage this patient. The student replies, "Perhaps I could ask how she and her children are managing during this hospital stay." As they discussed this, the field instructor notes that his reflections are appropriate and directly related to the skills pointed to in this competency.

She notices that he became anxious again, and he began to ask questions about what he should say and how he should say it. The field instructor assures him that they will discuss how to get started and asks him to jot his questions down so that they can return to them later. She suggests that they move forward to consider assessment and then return to setting priorities regarding how to address what he could say to introduce himself and what questions would be important to ask. She commented that it is important for them to spend time on what he is aiming to achieve as this affects the questions and conversation he will have.

They see that they already started to cover some of the required aspects surrounding assessment. They consider what other required information he might need to collect to ensure that he explores the patient's needs alongside her strengths and resources in her situation.

To engage diversity and difference in practice, they choose to discuss "present themselves as learners and engage clients and constituencies as experts on their own experiences" (CSWE, 2015a, p. 7). This discussion addressed some of the student's concerns about how he should proceed and his discomfort in asking questions. Seeing himself as a learner and the mother as the expert provided a perspective that helped him realize he will need to let her tell her story to be of service to her. The field instructor notes the complexity of having to ask and having to listen to the patient's concerns and questions.

The field instructor encourages the student to use his own hesitation in asking questions of the mother to tune in to what the patient might be feeling. They discuss that they do not know how the doctor explained the referral to the mother, but we do know that the student is single, younger than the patient, and he will be interviewing the patient by her bedside. These factors introduce issues of power, privilege, and choices that may influence the conversation. In addition, the field instructor refers to their earlier discussion about racial, ethnic, and gender factors and the fact that the student is a man and Dominican, whereas the patient is an African American woman. She added, "Of course, I am a Haitian single woman, so there will be ample opportunities for us to consider the role of gender, race, and other dimensions of identity as they relate to our work together and your work with this patient." In this way she starts to create a climate where these realities may be openly considered as part of their ongoing work.

Before returning to his concerns about how to proceed with questions for his first contact, the field instructor suggests that they review human rights and social, economic, and environmental justice. The student states that he finds this competency confusing. The field instructor reassures him by pointing out that he will have an opportunity to exercise this competency as the UDHR (United Nations, 1948) identifies the "right to a standard of living adequate for health and well-being" as a human right (p. 52). She suggests that he has already begun to demonstrate an understanding of the issues of justice that may be involved for this mother as she is divorced, unemployed, and with a severe chronic illness who may be burdened by challenges in accessing resources and having her and her children's needs met. He smiles and states that he has been reassured about opportunities to work at the skills required for this competency.

The discussion provided additional professional perspectives on his role. Together they return to his unanswered worries regarding what he should ask and how he might phrase his questions. They address the importance of establishing rapport and on gathering information that will further an assessment of this mother's definition of the issues needing attention. They set a time when they can consider this in more depth, and the field instructor asks the student to reflect on how he will introduce himself and what he might say to explain the reason for his meeting the mother. She explains that his first responsibility will be to clarify that he is meeting with her at her doctor's request and that he understands she had expressed financial concerns. The field instructor asks him to compose some points of conversation and questions that he would like to consider as important for this first session. They confirm a time when they will continue their discussion. The field instructor gave the student the article that addresses the mother's illness to build his knowledge of the difficulties she may be facing.

The field instructor and student went together to the patient's floor so that they could go over the medical chart together. Everything the student needed to know about the patient was available on this computerized data system. The student was left to review this material, and he was reminded to go over his thoughts on how he might approach this first patient when they meet.

Discussion

We have the complex task of orienting students to the setting, simultaneously preparing them for a first assignment and their professional role while also broadening the student's perspective to consider the requirements of competency-based education and issues of justice. In this scenario the field instructor provides basic support for the student and ensures that an incremental approach to the different types of information needed is taken for the student to begin. She also uses the opportunity to model the competencies in her role as field instructor and what their future supervisory sessions will be like.

Giving students adequate information and ample time to consider the expectations of their role and function in the setting is necessary. Reviewing this case through the lens of the competencies provides a structure to consider perspectives that take this student beyond what he needs to do next, what he will say, and how he will say it. The field instructor does not ignore the student's request for information but stays with the structure provided by the competencies and builds in another session to review the student's reflections of what was covered to help him prepare for how he will handle the assignment. How he manages this request will guide the field instructor's decision on whether the student would benefit from first observing an interview, whether they need to role-play the initial contact, or whether he is equipped to proceed on his own.

Consider your own reactions to this scenario and its applications to your work with students. What would you have liked the field instructor to add to the supervisory session and dialogue with her student? Although it is not proposed to consider every case using the competencies in this manner, what are the pros and cons of using this approach?

Getting Started: Setting the Stage for Justice-Based Learning in Field Education

The sections in this outline summarize the suggestions covered in Chapter 6. Considerations include work that occurs before the placement begins and the tasks associated with different components of orientation after the student arrives.

Before the Student Arrives: Starting With Ourselves

The field instructor prepares to receive a student by examining reasons, goals, and expectations associated with the role of field supervisor and by considering what is known about the student in relation to what will be expected in the performance of assigned role and responsibilities.

> Tune in to our own expectations
> Tune in to what we know of the student's dimensions of identity and how they may affect the placement.

Before the Student Arrives: The Placement Setting

The field instructor engages in a review of the placement setting's readiness to host students for placement before the student arrives. This involves the following ingredients.

> Assess external and internal organizational factors that will affect the placement
> Assess how the field education site will react to having students
> Clarify that everyone in the setting has a role to play in the student's educational experience.

Before the Student Arrives: The Social Work Education Program

Acquainting oneself with the mission of the social work program and requirements of field education is an essential part of preparing oneself for receiving the student and being able to respond in accordance with program expectations. Some of the tasks involved include the following components.

> Understand how students are oriented by the school and by the Office of Field Education to enter their field education placement
> Be familiar with the organization of the curriculum and its relationship to field teaching and expectations
> Be familiar with the administration of field education, the organization of the Office of Field Education, and everyone's defined general responsibilities

› Clarify program structures and expectations that affect student assignments

Learning While Serving: Orientation to the Setting

After the students arrive, orientation to a range of issues and tasks will help them develop a sense of belonging and identification with the setting's mission. The following components should be considered for initial orientation as well as for aspects that may require ongoing attention.

› Help place the setting and its mission in broader professional terms including influences of global policies and international practice perspectives that relate to the population and issues addressed.
› Arrange for observation of some aspect of service delivery and how service users experience it.
› Orient the student to the community where the placement is located, which helps students connect themselves to the context of service. Introduce ways to engaging with the community that identify resiliency and strengths as well as challenges and deficits.
› Have a plan for the student's first week and first day.
› Balance how much information to provide and in what form.
› Use specific understandable explanations about the purpose, focus, and goals of the placement setting to gradually introduce students to the setting's mission and program of services.
› Ensure that students are introduced to staff, from maintenance workers up to the department head or executive director.
› Be aware of how the orientation is progressing to introduce students to evaluation processes from the very start of placement.

Learning While Serving: Orientation to the Student's Professional Role

In addition to an orientation to the setting, special attention should be paid to ensuring that the responsibilities associated with the student's role and functions are understood. The following components provide ways to engage in these discussions.

- Explain the student's role in this setting and provide structure for the student's time in placement.
- Have work ready for students to ensure that time will not be lost.
- Help students practice how to introduce themselves as social work students.
- Help students identify similarities and differences between themselves and the communities they serve, that is, how the community is viewed and how the student will be viewed.
- Provide access to examples of the various types of required records students will need to complete.
- Remember, not all students are beginning-level students, but all require attention to the responsibilities associated to their new role.
- Introduce safety issues in a straightforward, clear, and caring manner.

Learning While Serving: Orientation to Field Education Supervision

One of the more important aspects of beginning is taking adequate time to orient the student to field education supervision. Various components involved in this task are presented in the following list.

- Tune in to students' hopes and worries about field education, but asking them directly is key.
- Introduce the place of field education supervision in social work education.
- Explain what we mean by authentic dialogue and why it is critical to justice-based field education and practice.
- Engage your student in a discussion that considers each other's worldviews, assumptions, and choices of social work as a profession. Consider how power and privilege may affect field education supervision.
- Normalize and validate the anxiety and nervousness that most students experience at the start of a new placement through a direct and supportive response.

> Clarify the structure of the student's time in the placement—types of meetings and specific days and times most important in terms of the learning opportunities available. Set clear parameters on field education supervisory times to support the student's ability to manage assigned responsibilities in placement.

Learning While Serving: Orientation to the Competencies

Introducing the competencies in relation to the work undertaken provides a vibrant way for the competencies to become real and integral to the student's learning.

> Ensure that students comprehend how the competencies relate to their field education experience.
> Use a first assignment to illustrate how the competencies apply.
> Choose at least one competency and at least one learning outcome or skill that applies to the assignment chosen.

CHAPTER 7

Student Assignments

The Vehicles to Learning and Demonstrating Competency

If the [field education] supervisor chooses cases based only on service needs (selecting those clients who are in greatest need of help) the intern may be ineffective and discouraged by professional expectations beyond his [sic] capacity.... If the supervisor chooses cases based only on learning needs (selecting cases because they are "interesting" or "not too difficult" or offer broad exposure to the field) the assignment will not reflect a real situation—and it is a real practice situation for which the interns are preparing. (Burack-Weiss & Coyle Brennan, 2008, p. 102)

If we want to nurture the capacities within our students to contribute constructively to their communities and to the larger society, we must take responsibility for the ways in which we influence our students.... We can provide opportunities to explore the potential of serving others. We can help them develop a more complex and nuanced understanding of the world. We can ultimately nourish the realization that they have the power to help transform social institutions and create a more just and compassionate world. I encourage you to embrace this potential through the mindful reconstruction of your ... interactions and your selection of assignments. (Johnson, 2005, p. 55)

These quotes capture the aims of this chapter and how directly connected our choices of assignments for students are to social work's pursuit of justice and competence. Assignments are the venues through which competencies are taught and learned. Although assignments have traditionally been constructed through an educational planning process that emerged from the program's requirements, needs of the agency, and student learning needs and interests, competency and justice-based perspectives present a more mindful process of selecting and developing assignments to increase the awareness of students on issues of justice and on seeking competence. Everything the student does in the internship is in some way (and sometimes in many ways) linked to one of the CSWE's (2015a) nine competencies. Engagement with diversity and difference occurs with every service contact. Every intervention is either linked to practice research or can be raised as a research question. Every policy area affects consumers of service, and any individual request for service has implications for policy change.

The selection, range, and sequencing of assignments has a significant influence on teaching and learning for justice and competence. Through engagement with field education assignments, students demonstrate their values, understanding, and skills; assignments provide the situations for students to interact and respond to real-life experiences and reveal their abilities. Measuring competence is then achieved through our discussions with students, observing their interactions, and reviewing their written reflections on these assignments.

This chapter addresses the various factors that shape assignments. It provides guidance for the field instructor's role as architect of a student's workload, describes possible assignments related to each of the competencies, and offers examples to support crafting assignments that provide a range of opportunities to demonstrate skills across the competencies and offer opportunities to consider issues of justice. It is certainly true that one cannot gain mastery in a vacuum. How do you get to competence? Practice, practice, practice.

A Competency and Justice-Based Framework for Designing Assignments

Well-crafted assignments that represent the work of the placement and are geared to the student's level in the social work program are essential early in the field placement, even before we fully understand who our students are and what they can do. Often the initial contacts with students offer opportunities to define initial assignments, even if in broad terms. As experience increases,

Program Mission and Curriculum

Curriculum focus area, specialization, student learning needs

Educational Policy and Accreditation Standards

(EPAS, CSWE, 2015a)

Generalist and specialized practice competencies

Setting Mission

Field of practice, methods, units of attention, theoretical approaches, setting, pace, staffing, and services

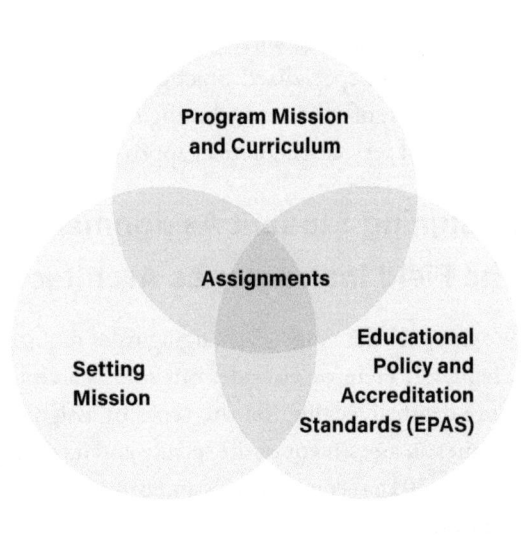

Figure 7.1: Components in every student assignment

students have greater input into designing assignments, but it is important to anticipate and prepare a range of activities that will help students start working as soon as they begin placement. Early assignments help direct students' energy to the work, focus their efforts to demonstrate abilities (Pierce, 2016), and assist our ability to measure each student's initial learning needs.

The generalist practice and specialized practice competencies provide the bedrock and structure for the range of actions and skills students will be expected to demonstrate. These competencies presume there is a unified perspective on the work assigned and support an integrated approach to units of attention, processes, and methods. The mission and curriculum of each social work program shape requirements for student assignments. These distinctions reflect historical, philosophical, and theoretical positions that emphasize certain curriculum content or approaches over others; the program's mission also governs the type of settings sought for field education placements. In turn, each placement context determines the type of assignments available for students. Assignments also are shaped by the realities of agency-based practice; any one setting may not provide the full range of assignments discussed here. The aim is to develop assignments that keep the competencies in mind and that are balanced to meet educational levels of study, course work requirements, and the student's chosen method of practice. In summary, Figure 7.1 depicts these various components of every student assignment. They include the social work program's mission and curriculum, the CSWE 2015 EPAS generalist and specialized practice competencies, and the setting's mission and program of services, including the setting's field of practice, context and methods of service, theoretical approaches, and staffing patterns.

Designing Student Assignments:
The Field Instructor as Architect

We consider the range of changing roles required of us as field instructors in Chapter 1. Here we consider our role as architect of student assignments in more depth. Deciding on the types of assignments the placement can offer requires an assessment of the setting and its range of services in relation to the CSWE (2015a) competencies and program requirements. An interesting task resulting from discussions on preparing the setting for student placements is discerning existing criteria or preconceptions of what constitutes an appropriate case or project for students. This may take us into a new sphere of responsibility and requires shifting our lens to examine the setting from the perspective of professional education. If we rely on other departmental managers or task supervisors for student assignments, our changed perspective may place us in a position of potential conflict with them. Also, our assessment of what will benefit the student's learning may challenge the existing criteria of what determines a student assignment, and ongoing collaboration may be required.

Whether we are responsible for defining assignment criteria, or they have been set by others, it is important to reflect on their degree of fit with the competencies and the student's and social work program's prerequisites. However, the context often shapes what and how we teach and how students are introduced to practice. In general, many settings provide work from a certain theoretical framework and may also offer services geared for a specific population or related to a specific issue. Still, exposure to diversity, consideration of the pace of work, problem focus, and method are helpful aspects to consider in what might seem to be a homogeneous service setting. In a setting or with a type of service, there may be opportunities to expand the parameters of service delivery to stretch the student's practice exposure. This is especially important for students who are bilingual and may often feel ambivalent about only being given assignments that rely on their language ability. They may experience this as a microaggression or typecasting as they are not given the same opportunities as their peers, and their learning is curtailed. Balance is crucial. It is also a labor issue. Students should not be used to fill a labor gap that the organization has a responsibility to cover.

Creating an intentional student-centered focus in the allocation of work requires a conversation about what can be learned from assignments. This may result in redefining approaches and rethinking practices that challenges the status quo. In a student-centered approach, field instructors plan assignments according to program requirements, students' past experiences, level of competency, and areas of interests. On the other hand, an organization-centered perspective might focus on transferring individuals to students to lighten staff workloads or reassign problems or case types that have become part of students' workloads. In these instances, students are viewed as resources that reduce the burden on other workers. The administrators may believe that the student's fresh attitude will introduce a new viewpoint on how to intervene or that the student's special attributes, such as language ability or identities similar to the populations served, provide opportunities to fill gaps in the range of services offered. Rethinking assignments from the perspective of student learning exposes students to a diverse group of service users.

For example, the generalist practice competencies presume the students have been exposed to assignments that prepare them for the demands of today's practice environment, which often requires moving in and out of a variety of roles and activities involving a repertoire of skills and knowledge for intervention in complex systems to provide support, advocate for services, and effect change (Arditti, 2005; Kirst-Ashman & Hull, 2015; Netting, Kettner, McMurtry, & Thomas, 2017). Creating assignments that offer a broad range of these activities presents special challenges when we are immersed in one aspect of practice over others or when the setting is limited in the range of services provided. Without question most social workers choose to focus on developing clinical skills to help individuals, families, and small groups; yet, exposing students to experiences that transfer skills to a range of modalities and units of attention breaks the bifurcation between micro and macro practice and opens the prospect of seeing skills and attributes as applicable across these sometimes seemingly unconnected aspects of practice. Skills detected in one sphere may enable a student to gain the confidence to apply these skills in a different aspect of work. For example, students able to facilitate a family meeting may shift and expand this skill to group work or to facilitating a committee meeting, assignments that are not initially included in the student's workload.

Sometimes administrators of a predominately clinical setting will assign students a more macro task such as planning a holiday party for consumers and staff. This assignment can become a series of tasks experienced by the student as helping out, unless the student is shown the assignment's relationship to the competencies, that is, it provides the student with opportunities to build a sense of community for consumers and staff, augment consumer partnerships in planning the event, build coalitions with community businesses that may donate resources, and lead, delegate, and recruit volunteer partners. Following the event, an evaluative process may be built in to facilitate future planning. In this way, the student experiences how skill development occurs across methods and units of attention.

Exposure to a diversity of populations, problems, or needs may provide a mix of ages and ethnicities as well as complex problem situations for student interaction. Work with different time dimensions, such as crisis intervention, intakes, short-term contacts versus longer term contacts, or case management services offer students the chance to identify the special issues related to service over time. The focus of intervention offers a range of opportunities regarding the depth and range of work, such as collateral contacts, interdisciplinary collaboration, information and referral, assessment and multiaxial diagnosis, intervention planning, advocacy and empowerment, or mandatory substance abuse monitoring. Intervention may include work in the community such as home visits, community board meetings, case conferencing, interagency collaboration, researching community resources, community outreach, and community organizing. Each broadens the types of contexts for students to experience and provides a different vantage point for student mastery. A range of examples follow.

A crisis-oriented service that provides short-term work may be able to assign an individual who is scheduled for a return visit; it may be possible to facilitate continuity on readmittance, or there may be an opportunity to provide a longer-term group experience for family members of those who have used the crisis service. A group home for adolescent girls between the ages of 10 and 17 may normally assign several girls to the social work intern for individual sessions, in addition to the collateral work needed with the girls' families and other tasks related to group home management that involve contact with the other girls in the house. Allowing the student to facilitate or cofacilitate a group, assist in intakes, participate in staff selection interviews, or participate in other aspects of the work provides a more rounded experience and gives the student a greater assortment of experiences to consolidate knowledge and skills.

A hospital emergency room setting requires students to perform rapid assessments and hold their own as part of an interdisciplinary team. Still, it is also often possible to provide different experiences by pairing the student with another social worker on the unit for conjoint assessments with families in crisis or by allowing the student to follow a patient to the next level of care at the hospital. Rather than saying there are no opportunities for that type of arrangement, we may need to expand our views, create opportunities, establish collaborations, or use the field liaison to consider how it might be possible to enhance the assignments to better fit the student's learning needs. Assignments should be examined individually for the range and type of learning involved and how they combine to form a well-balanced workload. Consider the following:

> What roles and responsibilities will the student be expected to fulfill? What skills and what knowledge will the student likely learn through this assignment? Which competencies are explicitly and implicitly associated with the assignment?
> To what extent does the assignment fit into the field instructor's expertise, have the setting's support and sanction, meet the student's learning needs and fit with educational or life experiences that prepare the student for this assignment?
> Does this assignment combine with other assignments to create a range of opportunities related to different populations, issues, conditions, methods or units of attention? Does the social work program's curriculum support the assignment?
> Are the assignments increasing the student's experience in dealing with diversity and differences in practice and in advancing justice and human rights? Research? Policy practice? Evaluation?
> Are there broader issues associated to the assignment that extend the student's exposure or understanding of how international practice applies or how global policies influence approaches to the population or issue?
> To what extent will this assignment expand service delivery?

The last question presents challenges: identifying student assignments that meet educational and service delivery goals while also possessing the potential to enrich and reach for future trends that prepare students for practice and expand service. This is not a required aspect of assignments, but it is important for us to be flexible; our role as architect involves considering current as well as new modes of practice and new frontiers of service that expand our student's and the setting's abilities to meet ever changing needs. We are educating for the profession as it exists today but also for the future. Again, balance matters. Our students represent a resource to placements that may help push boundaries to provide a type of service that the setting administrators have been considering but have not been able to offer because more information is needed or resources are insufficient.

> Consider the following examples: A local union's members' assistance program was moving from a long-term psychodynamic focus in its work with employees to short-term time-limited treatment and preventive and educational models of practice. Social work students traditionally were used in clinic services, and a well-tested field education site had been created. The move to more short-term services was under way but needed additional attention and build-up time to become fully functional. The site worked with the director of field education to create a unit of specialized practice level students, whose chosen method in their social work program was advanced generalist practice with a focus on programming, supervision, and short-term models of treatment. They were assigned a field instructor, and together with a new director who was committed to this change, they helped to transform the unit. The students were assigned direct clinical cases while also providing helpful resources for the development of staff procedural manuals, the creation of educational workshops, and the development of new brochures for outreach and referral sources and to educate the community about the changes in service.
>
> Another example involves a program serving graduating high school students. The guidance program administrators wanted to introduce voluntary mindfulness meditation into seminars for these students but did not have the resources to research best practices and, if appropriate, devise a pilot program incorporating it into seminars for seniors. As part of the social work student's assignment, research into best practices of mindfulness meditation for high school seniors was completed, an introductory pilot project was developed for the school's guidance center committee to consider, and the pilot program was implemented by the student during the school's spring semester seminars. An evaluation of this implementation was completed for further attention by the committee.
>
> Likewise, social service settings are becoming more attuned to the need for interventions and programming to support cross-cultural staff relations and cultural equity among the diverse communities served. Conducting training promotes staff development and community en-

gagement efforts. Including students in these initiatives introduces them to these developing areas of service.

The assignments in these examples span each of the competencies, provide exposure to a range of roles and responsibilities, meet the requirements for the students' chosen specializations, extend the settings' range of service options, and explore the benefits of different practice approaches for the populations served. Involving students in helping organize such services or workshops supports exposure to the forefront of practice trends. Our aim is to create assignments within a context where we can evaluate the full range of strengths and potential of our students. We search for the methods that provide a path to that purpose, and thus assignments are individualized. The task requires creativity, a willingness to shape assignments for learning, and the understanding that a variety of approaches may enhance this effort.

Competencies and Assignments

Thus far, the CSWE (2015a) competencies have been presented as the background and overarching framework for crafting assignments. This section focuses on designing optimum learning assignments for students that link to specific competencies. In addition, this section explains the potential for students to demonstrate ability across competencies in a single student assignment. Any one assignment might offer greater potential in relation to one or more of the competencies, but opportunities exist to bring the other competencies forward through discussion or as an additional piece added to the work.

We begin by considering each competency. We then consider various units of attention, and possible assignments are suggested that elucidate the varied roles students engage in as they develop and expand their skills and knowledge base. The examples are not intended as an exhaustive list; rather, they are presented to stimulate ideas for additional, innovative assignments. Some assignments are specific to certain levels of practice, and others are appropriate for all levels of practice.

Our view is that together the competencies provide a way to examine skills required in any student assignment. The assignments provide the ingredients that combine to create an integrated view of what it is we do, that is, the processes we engage in as we proceed toward change, the knowledge we consider, the skills we apply, and the values that guide our work. At first glance, it may appear that one or more of the competencies predominate in any one assignment. After a closer look, it emerges that other competencies have their role to play. It also becomes clear that the competencies have not been sculpted in isolation. They are not discrete, they intersect, and they are meant to build on one another. For example, how do we discuss conducting oneself professionally without thinking about ethical principles, critical thinking, professional judgment, and how research, policies, and issues of diversity, human rights, and social and economic justice apply? The overlap becomes evident as we gain experience in working with the competencies and as they are given life in the supervisory process. As we apply the competencies, seeing their links to our professional mission and values further guide their use.

Demonstrate Ethical and Professional Behavior

Examined in detail in Chapter 5, the competency calling us to demonstrate ethical and professional behavior (CSWE, 2015a) is considered here through the lens of preparing students for their assignments. Although each assignment requires us to discuss actions and behaviors in an ethical and professional context, students are often confused over how they will demonstrate competency in this area. They may feel awkward as they attempt to adopt a professional stance before they truly understand the full ramifications of their role; they may think it means they must acquire a certain type of demeanor or behave totally different from normal. They may say, "But, I have not experienced an ethical dilemma in my work" as if this were all that is involved in this competency area. Whether they have experienced a specific ethical dilemma during their interactions, their conversations and manner of approaching their work gives witness to their understanding of our professional values. In fact, how we enact professional roles prevents many ethical dilemmas from occurring, or at least prepares us for how to manage them. Even their interactions with us and other students demonstrate their mastery and application of the skills required in putting our values to work. Making these behaviors explicit helps students recognize how their values become actualized into professional ethical behaviors.

Discussions in supervision provide space for students to reflect on their role and the ethical considerations associated to it. Their demeanor and professional stance demonstrate understanding. This often occurs naturally, but some students need our help to adjust their personal style to fit more closely with their professional role and function in the context of their placement. Helping students articulate the choices they make in responding to the demands of their roles brings these decisions forward. This promotes self-awareness and further hones and develops their professional selves. In addition, some assignments provoke special ethical considerations and dilemmas that emerge as the work proceeds, which provide openings to deepen understanding and consolidate professionalism.

Our conversations naturally involve questions regarding how the NASW (2017) Code of Ethics, the UDHR (United Nations, 1948), and the UNDRIP (United Nations, 2007) prescribe and guide our actions and interventions, whether with an individual in a counseling relationship or as a member of a community team when planning a public hearing. These questions require helping students think critically and facilitating their consideration about the larger mission of our profession and where their settings and assignments fit in relation to these larger concerns. If we simply introduce our students to the listing of the standards or articles incorporated into these documents, we do not provide an adequate foundation for how our work is informed by these values and inalienable rights, how they apply to the populations or issues assigned, or how we expect the documents to inform our clinical formulations.

For example, what do these documents tell us about how we should conduct ourselves professionally? What do they tell us about professional roles and responsibilities in relation to a specific context and in relation to specific assignments?

> What dominant values and worldviews are inherent in the ethical standards? How is this service setting perpetuating privileged values? How do the UN documents inform practice in this setting? How might an analysis of power and powerlessness in the community served help the student's understanding of these views and implications for their roles?
> How do we understand our relationships with those we serve? How are our responsibilities to individuals and the communities we serve defined by the setting?
> How do we view the work of this assignment? How closely aligned is this definition with our professional and personal values?
> What boundary issues with families or community members might exist in this assignment or group of assignments? What typical ethical scenarios might emerge? What expectations do we have regarding handling these conflicts and dilemmas?

> What reassurance is needed for students to begin to tackle an approach to these situations? In what ways will this assignment allow the student to function on an increasingly responsible and independent level?

Engage Diversity and Difference in Practice

Engaging diversity and difference in practice (CSWE, 2015a) includes understanding concepts of intersectionality and multiple dimensions of identity, involves grasping the myriad ways these factors affect identity development and shape human experience; and involves understanding that the interconnectedness of world economies and cultures require a global awareness to transcend local and insular perspectives. Issues of diversity and difference may be explicitly obvious in the assignments we choose; however, students may need help to recognize these features and need guidance on how to apply and communicate their understanding in action. It is also not unusual for students to take some time in fully engaging individuals and communities as experts on their own experiences.

Students may also believe that this competency is addressed by seeing the differences between themselves and the people they are serving or by their innate abilities to appreciate different approaches they apply in their dealings with people. They may need help to more deeply explore their work across difference and diversity. Chapters 2 and 5 examine ways to facilitate our students' participation in the examination of their personal biases. A means to assess the student's progress in these areas may be to engage in a review of the different choices the student has made in engagement or interventions across assignments. Perhaps a review of the issues involved in an assessment may provide equally important insights on how justice-based knowledge and skills affect our practice. Contrasting assignments bring opportunities for these conversations to the forefront and promote a critically reflective approach to practice and learning (Bay & Macfarlane, 2011; Finn, 2016; Fook, 2008; Schön, 1983, 1987).

For example, in anticipating the need to ease the path for our students we might consider which obvious dimensions of identities exist in this assignment and how they should be managed in the work. The following questions present other considerations:

> What are the less obvious areas of difference or similarities between the student and the population or service issue?

› What expectations do we hold regarding the student's exploration and handling of areas of similarities and difference? What reassurance is needed for students to tackle the explicit and implicit multiple dimensions of identity that inevitably exist?
› How might this assignment involve the student in identifying strengths and resiliency of the population or community? How might this assignment provide discussion of the ways individuals and communities served are affected by the existing myriad forms of oppression?
› What opportunities exist in this assignment for students to engage in honest dialogue about themselves and their assumptions, values, and judgments of the people they will be serving?
› What opportunities are there for the student to exercise inclusive and mindful practice?

Advance Human Rights and Social, Economic, and Environmental Justice

Advance, the active verb used to introduce this competency, calls on us to make progress and press forward in the areas of rights and justice (CSWE, 2015a). It does not specify how large a leap forward we must make, but the expectation is for each student to demonstrate abilities in making headway in applying their understanding to tackle human rights and justice issues with and on behalf of the individuals and communities they serve.

Students are introduced to our professional values and aims through the assignments we choose, and this competency demands engaging our students in discussions that invite an analysis of how power and privilege affect the issues and problems involved. This competency also demands taking our students beyond consideration to the application of their understanding in their work. Keeping an eye on justice is critical. Discussing how issues of tribal and indigenous justice and human rights relate to the problems and issues in the population served by this setting brings the issues alive and legitimizes student advocacy in these areas. Each assignment and placement experience provides this opportunity.

> Consider a specialized practice level student who noticed that the transgender woman she had been working with was taking considerable

time when taking a restroom break. The student was concerned that this individual was not well and approached her about her health. The individual revealed that the reason it took her so long was because she had to walk to an all-gender restroom elsewhere in the building. She went on to explain that she had received several negative comments from other people in the setting's restroom and no longer felt comfortable using the facilities there. The student was initially paralyzed by what she had learned. What could she say? What could she do? Who could she discuss this with? She brought her concerns to her field instructor, who validated her student's concerns, and the student was empowered to talk with her field instructor about the injustice experienced by this individual. An analysis of cisgender privilege was part of their dialogue as they considered how dominant views influenced their sense of how to proceed. Bolstered by her student's commitment and concern, they devised a plan of action to advance the rights of this individual and work together to move toward justice. The student had the support of the field instructor to talk with the person she was seeing, seek permission to recount her experiences to the director of the setting, and ask if she wished to be involved. The woman was relieved that her experience was being taken seriously; she did not want to be present at any discussions but asked to be kept informed of any progress. Together the field instructor and student met with the director to begin conversations about how to effect change.

This example shows that, as with the competency on ethical and professional behavior, issues related to human rights are intricately woven with justice and supervisory discussions to highlight the knowledge, values, and skills needed to address these issues in any assignment. Certain assignments may provoke the emergence of injustice as a central issue given the nature of the work involved, others may require an emphasis on the effects of oppression needing attention. Infringement of rights may be obvious, as in this example, and just as likely, they may be less clear and complexly layered. Critical consciousness about the implications of human rights and diversity and difference in practice is required for learning in this arena to occur (Almeida et al., 2011; Freire, 1993; Ginwright & Cammarota, 2002). This necessitates a connection between self-awareness and an appreciation that lived experiences provide bridges as well as barriers to their work.

When considering assignments, we ask ourselves the following questions:

> How does this assignment illustrate opportunities for justice-based practice?
> Which human rights, tribal and indigenous rights or civil rights issues are involved? Which issues emerge after review of the articles within UDHR (United Nations, 1948) or UNDRIP (United Nations, 2007)?
> Beyond the identification of the rights involved, how might the justice issues unfold in the work of this assignment? How does the infringement of one right affect others? Are rights violated on multiple levels?
> How might we support students' abilities to question and challenge issues such as police brutality in communities of color, lack of educational resources, limited housing, and the many other structural barriers affecting a community's access to resources? At the same time, how can students be helped to identify community strengths and resilience in the face of these forces?

Engage in Research-Informed Practice and Practice-Informed Research

Some assignments will focus on a research question, and students will be clear that they are working on this CSWE (2015a) competency. It is proposed, however, that each assignment provides an opportunity for students to demonstrate abilities in this competency. Achieving competency in research-informed practice requires us to understand the importance of evidenced-based and evidence-informed knowledge, actively apply this developed knowledge to inform our practice interventions and see the relevance to the effectiveness of our work and skill development. Also, improving research and evaluations involves infusing practice knowledge into these efforts.

Students need to be exposed to research not only in the classroom but also to experience research in their field placements. Research assignments are appropriate for each practice method and across all units of attention; designing such assignments emphasizes the significance of practice research in all aspects of social work.

Ultimately the question is how do we maintain our commitment to lifelong learning without using research to improve our efforts? What access to literature, studies, books, and scholarship in our areas of practice are available? How might we access such information? One way would be to encourage students to conduct a literature review regarding the population or issue they will be focused on as part of their student assignment and to use supervision to review the findings.

For example, given the growth of research relevant to practice and ease of access to this information, students can explore which best practices are discussed in the literature regarding the issues faced with any assignment. Likewise, if assigned work involves planning a program, students can research best practices for these programs. We can share articles regarding the population or community that highlight research findings and applications, and students can collate these resources for future students. Addressing applicable evidence-based practices is also important. Examining the role practice wisdom plays in the setting can be undertaken along with how this practice wisdom might inform research efforts. Issues that arise in one assignment can be pursued as concerns that may be more broadly affecting others; students can poll staff or lead a focus group discussion about the issue. Additionally, the interventions being applied to the work and the theoretical frameworks they fall under can become topics for discussion in supervision.

In addition to asking students to seek research articles regarding a certain practice issue or population, we can engage our students in direct research on their practice. Asking students to notice changes in their service user's behavior and to figure out what these changes are related to is critical to monitoring work efforts and effectiveness. By introducing this as part of the supervisory agenda, students are engaged in seeking responses to these questions and reporting back in supervision. This begins their experience and commitment to incorporating research-informed practice into their work and to using tools to introduce practice-informed research into their thinking. This competency is closely aligned with the expectation that students engage in evaluation across units of attention and demonstrates how closely aligned these competencies are. Following are some possible research assignments; the reader may find additional examples under the suggestions for evaluation assignments in the Chapter 7 Appendix.

Micro research assignments. Instead of the usual process recording in a clinical session, students can be instructed on using a single-system research design. Identifying change or progress in achieving goals may be pursued by gathering data, which could include a simple application that attempts to evaluate the efficacy of a problem or behavior that can be measured and can be observed over time. Rapid assessment instruments may be used to aid the collection of the information. If the question posed attempts to track whether there was improvement after an intervention, the use of a single-system research design may be applied (Thyer, Artelt, & Shek, 2012). Attempting to show evidence of this or to prove that the improvements were directly related to the social work intervention would require more research rigor. Sticking with the simpler option here, the student can track chosen behaviors over time, or if a rapid assessment instrument is applied, the person served may be required to complete a release form and the instrument for more complete information on the behavior. A baseline is obtained on the occurrence of the behavior, which is followed and tracked following the introduction of a chosen intervention. The design may be adapted, and the articles from Cooper (2006) and Thyer et al. (2012) give direction on how to proceed.

Group work research assignments. A research project may be designed to assess the effectiveness of a series of time-limited, educational workshops offered to an identified population. For example, youths in foster care who are starting their first job are invited to attend a series of educational workshops to support their adjustment to work. Research on issues that help with time management or how to balance various new responsibilities can be conducted, and workshops on these topics may be designed to target certain behaviors and attitudinal change. Either a pretest and posttest or a time series design could be applied to track change in these areas.

Community organization research assignments. Students can design and test a questionnaire to help tap into the opinions of a select constituency or community stakeholders to determine the feasibility of a program (e.g., day care center) or community project (e.g., reclaiming a park). Focus group discussions also may be introduced.

Policy analysis research assignments. Track the legislative response to a social problem at the city, state, and national levels. Locate and analyze survey data on the prevalence of a specific social or health problem, the populations affected, and the scope of the problem for a specific zone or area. Students could also conduct surveys to evaluate staff or community support or opposition to program reform, elimination, or expansion. Students can do this in a participatory fashion with the individuals and communities they serve.

Organizational research assignments. Choose an issue that has been identified as affecting organizational productivity. For example, the field instructor is aware that several departments have requested additional help on the issue of sexual harassment. Because of the current emphasis on this topic and the setting's desire to be proactive, the field instructor instructs the student to research literature on areas associated with responding to the perpetuation and occurrence of organizational sexual harassment. Existing policies on sexual harassment or gender discrimination may be compared with policies at other organizations to examine ways to improve the expression of inclusion and respect for others in organizational life. The student might also assess the training that is being offered and propose new models or ways to support what currently is in place. The results are reported to identify best practices or to point to areas for attention and possible further training. In addition to providing exposure to organizational research, this type of assignment often involves meaningful learning experiences in collaborative teamwork.

Engage in Policy Practice

Not all students will focus primarily on policy analysis in field education, but all students need an introduction to the importance of policy in professional practice, and all need to understand the importance of policy analysis as critical to social and political change. Students might begin understanding the importance of policy to their assignments by first discussing the setting's mission and service delivery goals and objectives and then connecting them to their assignments. This entails being clear on what policies at the local, state, and federal levels apply. Too often these various levels of policy seem so far in the background that students are unaware of the mandates that frame their work. Current political debates have brought issues of health care and immigration to the surface, which are only two examples of how bringing policies to attention provide focus on how our work is affected by policy development and implementation.

Less overt examples include existing eligibility requirements that affect the population served. For instance, exploring who is served implicitly includes consideration of who is not served. This level of policy is often taken for granted and not explored as a determinant of the context of work. Students working in a shelter for people insecurely housed can take note of policies related to length of stay, such as who can stay, who cannot, and for how long. Students often wish to focus on which intervention to consider next or how to best respond to specific circumstances. Discussing the broader considerations of how situations can be viewed in terms of policies that create, perpetuate, influence, or impinge on the individual's life provides a vibrant conversation on the power of policy to shape practice. Global considerations are an important additional component.

The following questions are provided to guide supervisory discussion regarding policy implications to promote mastery in this competency. Examples of policy practice assignments can be found in the Chapter 7 Appendix.

> In what ways does this assignment support the student's understanding of the origin and intent of policies that affect this population's problems and the policies' goals and objectives toward meeting population system needs?
> Are the policies (local, state, or federal administrative demands and operating mandates) affecting this assignment inherently justice-based?
> Are the policies surrounding the issues associated with this assignment in need of reform? If so, are there opportunities to prepare policy documents that are responsive to the issue, and how clear is the process for developing the policy or changes to the policy?
> What opportunities exist to engage the student in the implementation of a new policy or review of how the implementation of an existing policy matches the original intent? What work with constituents and stakeholders is possible to integrate their voices into policy making, evaluation, and monitoring outcomes?
> What global influences require attention?

The discussion of policy presents opportunities for students to demonstrate critical thinking and to consolidate a justice-based framework into their practice. For example, discussions in supervision with a specialized practice level student involved understanding federal and state policies relating to student success initiatives in higher education. Understanding the intent of these policies, the student questioned why workshops and supports in the department were geared only to students with a cumulative grade point average (GPA) below 2.0, the minimum requirement for graduation. Her initial question was, "Could you explain why the program is not aimed at students whose GPAs were below 2.5 rather than 2.0?" In her discussion she pointed out that once a student receives a GPA below 2.0, the chance of increasing the GPA is so much harder. "Don't students lose their federal funding if their GPAs drop below a 2.0? Wouldn't an intervention prior to that catastrophe be wiser? Why wouldn't it make more sense to provide services when there is a chance for the intervention to make a difference and help the student succeed as the program mission states?" Two days later, the department issued a revised policy that offered services to students to include those whose GPA had dropped below 2.5. This example is unusual as the simple posing of considered questions provoked change; on the other hand, it demonstrates that sometimes educating a student on the issues and enabling the student to craft pointed questions to the person with authority for change is all that is needed.

Placements with a greater focus on policy may offer assignments that involve policy analysis and development. This requires a range of activities, such as recognizing how a social condition comes to be viewed as a social problem; collecting and analyzing data measuring the extent and consequences of a social problem; identifying and analyzing prior policy efforts aimed at solving a social problem; identifying, analyzing, and assessing alternative policy options; and developing and presenting policy recommendations before legislative or community groups.

Students may be asked to consider whether individuals are treated as objects of rescue or as intellectual allies and political collaborators (Narayan, 1997). Any part of this process may be applicable for a range of assignments as policy practice requires a multidimensional lens to deal with policy deliberations and external realities (Jansson, 2018; Medina, 2010). Equally, these activities and related questions form the basis for possible community work. For example, how are the people and communities served woven into every step of the policy planning process and what does it take to do this? As policy planners and analysts, do we stand next to or behind those we serve? That is, do they lead while we follow, using our power, privilege, and resources to support their efforts; if not, what would it take to practice in this way? How can we as field instructors aid in understanding these critical aspects of professional practice?

Engage, Assess, Intervene, and Evaluate Practice

These four CSWE (2015a) competencies—engage, assess, intervene, and evaluate—place attention on students' abilities across units of attention and across phases of the helping process. They remind us that each of the levels of our work—micro, mezzo and macro—uses the same helping process to move toward change. Assignments in these units of attention may look different and require special considerations, but the knowledge, values, and skills are similar, remain constant, and are applied across all units. Their application to certain systems, populations, and issues requires content-specific knowledge and skills including the evidenced-based and evidence-informed treatments and interventions that apply to specific populations or diagnoses.

The following section considers first micro, mezzo, and macro assignments and is followed by the phases of the helping process. Each section contains assignments that fall under the various phases of the helping process;

additional assignments are provided in the Chapter 7 Appendix. As suggested earlier, the assignments under one unit of attention may spark ideas for assignments in a different area. For example, outreach to individual veterans to explore what resources they may require, may be a useful micro-level assignment; this same assignment may be integral to the formation of a group for veterans or a research focus group seeking to learn about ways to better serve this population. Although the assignments are discrete, they are not exclusively relevant to one level of practice. In fact, they may serve to inspire other assignments across units of attention.

Micro level practice. Most social work students are given assignments to work with individuals, pairs, or families. The range of problems can include personal problems (e.g., mental or physical illness, substance abuse, financial problems, developmental crises, trauma, friendship or peer relationships, work or education problems), family-centered problems (e.g., marital conflict, domestic violence, divorce, addiction, parent-child conflict, or illness of family members), and problems lodged in the social environment (e.g., unemployment, discrimination, oppression, inadequate housing, health care and education, or the effects of other limited societal resources). Students are often required to move freely among these interrelated categories. In addition to cases that require ongoing concrete services, case management, and clinical services, students benefit from a range of assignments that expand their perceptions of their roles and interventions and their understanding of how context affects human development (Arditti, 2005).

Group work assignments. Most placements provide the opportunity or potential for work with a variety of groups, including educational, socialization, recreational, self-help, problem-solving, milieu, discussion, mutual aid, and task-centered groups (Garvin, Gutiérrez, & Galinsky, 2004). Groups also vary in structure from open-ended to closed membership and have different time frames, from single-session to long-term ongoing treatment. Although the type and character of intervention in these groups may differ, the opportunity for group work practice introduces students to the process of the group as a system. This exposure offers the chance to experience and appreciate the power of group work (Northern & Kurland, 2001). In fact, working with the power of mutual aid is an important ingredient to add to a student's repertoire of skills. According to Gitterman and Knight (2016),

> group modality is the most natural and effective modality to promote client resilience.... Resilience and adversarial [or post-traumatic] growth are fostered by the multiple helping relationships that exist between

members, augmented by the relationship between the members and the leader. (pp. 448, 451)

Certain core skills and knowledge are essential for students to learn as they begin to study and work with groups, including the facilitator's role; cofacilitation of groups; stages of group development; group process; roles of members; dealing with conflict, tension, and silence; facilitating challenging dialogues; promotion of mutual aid; use of activities; and assessment and evaluation. To the greatest extent possible, opportunities for student group work assignments should be considered even if groups are not a regular institutionalized modality of service in the setting.

Creating group work assignments requires sensitivity to the fact that students often have trepidations about taking on a group. The "fear-of-groups syndrome" (Shulman, 2012, pp. 284–285) relates to generalized worries about performance; these worries are connected to the complexity of groups. According to Shulman (2012), "After all, there are so many more of them and only one of me!" (p. 284). The fear is also related to the possibility that whatever occurs among members will be out of the group leader's control. Lack of exposure to groups may account for some of this fear, but even if the student has some experience with groups, the next group is different. Enabling the exposure to group work offers the chance for students to be comfortable with different personalities in each group, the vast array of information that emerges, and how to set the climate for the work (Wayne & Cohen, 2001).

Several variables may influence the educational experience of suitable group assignments for students. For instance, students may be assigned to a new group, an existing group, a student-developed group, or they may begin their exposure to groups through co-leadership experiences. The experience of planning and developing a group provides students with a very rich, often neglected, aspect of group-work practice (Goodman & Munoz, 2004; Wayne & Cohen, 2001). Planning a group allows students to learn about group purpose, composition, duration and meeting patterns, membership norms, physical environment, and use of group activities. However, it may be preferable for students to be assigned to groups that are already formed rather than to develop groups solely based on students' interests. Good learning can occur if the student explores the interest that motivates the development of a group; however, there may be insufficient response unless the issue meets a real need, and consumers are engaged in the development of groups that align with their concerns.

Community practice assignments. Interventions aimed at the community level of macro practice usually begin with identifying the target community's physical boundaries, its self-identification, and the community's structure, including demographic characteristics, values, power, economic structure, and the government service system (Hardina, 2013; Landon & Feit, 1999). *Community organization* generally refers to practice in the following distinct areas:

> Organizational or group development for democratic collective action on economic, social, and community problems affecting health and well-being and advocacy for change or the creation of laws, policies, and programs to better meet human needs; assignments include providing technical assistance, preparing community needs assessment, constituency development through self-help or mutual support groups, coalition building, and social action campaigns.

> Planning and program development for involvement of professionals and service constituents in the coordination of existing services and the development of a new collaborative or program; assignments include resource development, fact finding, interagency coordination, proposal writing, program evaluation, policy and legislative analysis, and lobbying.

> Community education and leadership development for the acquisition of human and legal rights, self-actualization, self-determination, social cohesion, and community empowerment; assignments include developing information and referral services; educating and training staff, consumers, and volunteers through workshops or conferences; preparing newsletters; organizing speakers' bureaus; community outreach; and community-building events with stakeholders and organizing community coalitions.

Essential skills for community practice include understanding the use of influence in group decision making and facilitation of group processes. Like administration, community organization and planning require the development of skills in the areas of needs assessment and budgeting as well as an ability to "bring groups of people and organizations together...to foster community change using both collaboration and confrontational methods." (Hardina, 2013, p. 6). These assignments provide unique opportunities for students to develop coalition-building, advocacy, and empowerment skills in cross-cultural practice (Hardina, 2013; Richan, 1989; Wendt & Seymour, 2010).

Administration and organizational assignments. Social administration or management of organizations provides students with macro experiences in organizational dynamics. Exposure to administrative skills regarding such aspects as supervision of volunteers, program structure and design, leadership development, motivation and control, and resource acquisition also include issues such as "stress management and conflict resolution and employee assistance" (Tsui & Cheung, 2009, p. 155).

Engagement across units of attention. Demonstration of skills in the engagement phase requires assignments that call on the student's ability to show empathy on a personal and a social level (Austin, 2014) and use active listening skills and other skills that serve to enhance and build trust. Assignments that require outreach are a useful way for students to practice engagement skills; the use of technology in expanding outreach is a growing area that students could usefully gain exposure to. The ability to articulate the student's role and to formulate the purposes of contact and making this understandable to service users provides another means to evaluate a student's competence in this phase of the helping process. Some assignments to provide student experience in engagement are provided in the Chapter 7 Appendix.

Assessment across units of attention. Micro practice focuses on an assessment of the biopsychosocial and spiritual needs of individuals and their families. It applies social work theory and methods to the treatment and prevention of psychosocial dysfunction, ability, or impairment, including emotional and mental disorders. It is based on knowledge of one or more theories of human development in a psychosocial and ecological context. The perspective of person in environment is central. This means that the assessment includes the strengths people bring to the work and the potential barriers that exist. Part of the student's assessment of an individual includes an assessment of whether the services offered in this setting adequately address needs and expectations. Questions for consideration include how issues of marginalization, oppression, and privilege affect this situation.

Although the skills necessary for family-centered practice encompass similar considerations, they take on greater complexity when applied to work with families (Ho, Rasheed & Rasheed, 2003). For example, what was an assessment of a person's readiness to discuss feelings becomes an assessment of the individual's readiness to reveal feelings in the presence of other family members. It is important to assess the role this may play in the dynamics of family intervention. Likewise, assessment in mezzo and macro practice involves increasingly larger systems for consideration. See the Chapter 7 Appendix for some assignments.

Intervention across units of attention. The varying units of attention involve different types of interventions geared to the specific goals and outcomes sought. Skills of intervention are linked to certain models of treatments and to specific units of attention. For example, understanding the appropriate uses of cognitive behavioral therapy or dialectical behavior therapy builds the student's repertoire of skills and abilities across their many different formal and informal interventions with the individuals they will be serving.

Students may need assistance in understanding that interventions may be used across the matrix of systems but that they may be termed differently. For example, work with individuals uses many skills including active listening, clarification, exploration, probing, reframing, normalizing, and contracting. These same skills are used in our work with groups, communities, and organizations but may be more frequently termed as fostering cohesion, scanning, universalizing experience within groups, consensus building, mediation, or coalition building in a community, business, or organizational meeting. Building these links for students to see what their goals are for any intervention helps to bridge, build, and consolidate their interventional repertoire.

Evaluation across units of attention. In addition to introducing students to the importance of engagement, varying methods of assessment, and expanding their range of interventions, students also need to consider the range of appropriate evaluation methods for their work. This competency in combination with research-informed practice and practice-informed research provides a vibrant example of how the competencies complement each other and intertwine to create a powerful means for students to gain familiarity and comfort with the professional skills supported by the competency framework.

Enabling our students to consider how they will evaluate their own work is a critical component. We teach in response to witnessing a student's initial lack of clarity about appropriate methods of evaluation, how to phrase questions, or how to analyze the results. As we teach, we watch for the student's growing understanding and proficiency. For example, how do we ensure that our students engage in the assessment and review of their practice? How do we help our students prepare for evaluation of their work with individuals, families, groups, organizations, and communities they serve? What exposure might be given to creating evaluation forms for the programs they conduct or is it possible to introduce a focus-group evaluation of certain assignments? How might we promote student involvement in the evaluation of service delivery?

Summary

Selecting assignments is at the core of our work and begins with understanding the competencies and practice principles embedded in the assignments, the way these principles exist in practice, and how they are expressed in the specific context of the assignments we choose. Additional assignment suggestions can be found in the Chapter 7 Appendix.

CHAPTER 7 APPENDIX

In this appendix, two samples of assignments demonstrate the range of opportunities available to facilitate work across all competency areas; one example is provided at the specialized practice level and one at the generalist level of education. The third item provides examples of assignments in specific competency areas including policy, political social work, and policy advocacy practice; and assignments across various units of attention for engagement, assessment, intervention, and evaluation.

Sample Assignment Summary: A Specialized Practice Level Student Placed in a Food Pantry

A specialized practice level student in a generalist social work program was assigned to a macro placement in a grassroots community food pantry. The food pantry has existed for 4 years through the efforts of two local community leaders and a range of volunteers who manage access to food for the guests who use its services. Individual supportive and preventive work with the guests of the food pantry was part of the assignment as was creating a strategic plan, developing operating procedures, and drafting a volunteer manual.

In addition to forming links with the guests of the food pantry, the fall semester was focused on researching what a strategic plan involves, what process should be followed, and what form the plan might take. Interviews with stakeholders took place to gather relevant information. In addition to creating these documents, the student was assigned to manage two food pantry sessions and supervise the volunteers. This part of the assignment provided a means for the student to experience the issues involved in the daily operations of the food pantry as well as adding group work with the volunteers to the student's assignments. It soon became clear that the work with volunteers would provide opportunities to assist their understanding of their roles and how they could improve their interactions with the food pantry's guests rather than just keeping the shelves full and handing out bags of food. Discussions with the volunteers evolved into dialogues about food insecurity and perceptions, meanings, and consequences of food insecurity in their community.

As the placement progressed, other ideas for needed interventions emerged, including revamping the facility, making it more presentable, adding posters and a suggestion box, and creating handouts with useful community information. Another aspect of the student's assignment included collaboration with a local community college for the student to cofacilitate a seminar on food insecurity. This assignment provided yet another role for the student and for experience in public speaking. Tours of the food pantry were incorporated as part of this seminar, and guests of the pantry were invited to participate in conducting the tour and providing information in some of the seminar sessions. Additionally, several students in this seminar asked to become volunteers.

Encouraging the student to assess the various systems and the issues of justice involved in this placement required the student to engage in researching food insecurity in general and how it is experienced in the context of this setting and community. The student began to consider what she might be able to contribute in addition to what was originally conceived as her assignment. For example, rather than solely defining the target of her intervention as the guests of the food pantry, she sought to understand the community where the pantry was located. She contacted a local food bank, which resulted in their staff holding a food stamp information session for guests of the food pantry and opening it to the community. As the community and guests largely consisted of new immigrants, she conversed with them about their experiences in managing adjustments to U.S. food and finding access to more familiar foods. As a result, handouts regarding community markets and international food resources and how to understand American food labels were provided to the guests, and these handouts were distributed in the community. The student became better informed about the effects of inequality on people's access to healthy foods and the resulting impact on health outcomes. She worked with local farmers and produce sellers to advocate for improved access to these items as additional offerings at the pantry.

By the end of the academic year, the student maintained regular supportive counseling with several of the guests, was successful in changing volunteers' view of their role, completed the documents originally assigned, developed a volunteer orientation, added a suggestion box to the food pantry, and distributed an evaluation feedback survey to all volunteers for an end-of-year assessment of how the pantry may better serve its volunteers and guests. The student attended community leadership meetings to present updates and developments at the food pantry and to seek stronger links in the community. The range of tasks and roles provided ample opportunity for this student to demonstrate competency across all nine CSWE (2015a) competencies and to implement a justice agenda in her work.

Sample Assignment Summary: A Generalist Practice Level Student Placed in a Tutoring Program With Academically At-Risk Youths

A generalist practice level student was placed at a local after-school program for tutoring high school students from a community that experiences high levels of economic stress and crime. The main task for the intern was to provide outreach to sophomores on academic probation as a means of encouraging them to use the tutoring center resources. Referrals were received from the guidance office. The intern was assigned to conduct outreach for 25 students who were in danger of academic failure. It was planned that working with this cohort would provide support to the students and a range of individual and group counseling contacts for the intern. As the program staff were experiencing challenges in reaching this student cohort, the intern was encouraged to consider alternative approaches to reach them.

The intern decided to organize a study group for the students, and she was given a budget to provide pizza. Despite active outreach, none of the invited students attended. Several more attempts were made but without success. The intern was asked to do some research on outreach methods and interventions that might aid the program's efforts with these students. In addition to researching the community and demographics of the identified youths, the student uncovered the promising approach of using a *success coach* program based on peer-to-peer interventions similar to mentorship programs, which have proven effectiveness. The student developed a framework for the program that was supported by the high school social work and guidance office staff. The proposal included involving students in the high school to act as success coaches. The guidance office staff worked to identify potential student leaders, and as names of interested students emerged, guidance officers and the intern interviewed them for inclusion. The intern then created a program announcement and introduction to the program to attract more than the previously identified students to benefit from the program. As students responded, the intern matched them with success coaches. The students initially identified as needing support were also individually invited to participate. The student's dedication and vision were communicated to the success coaches, the peer-to-peer intervention captured the energy and leadership skills of the successful students, and the newly formed program was advertised in a manner that reduced the stigma for any student who wished to participate, including the students initially identified as the target population.

Responsibilities included in this assignment involved meeting all students in both cohorts to make appropriate matches. The student also met with the success coaches on a regular basis to support them in their role and assess how they were managing contacts with their peers. Several pairs required additional follow-ups to help manage the stresses that arose. This aspect of the work provided an opportunity for the intern to problem solve and to offer additional mediation and supportive counseling. This work assisted the coaches in their leadership development and resolution of the problems presented. It also helped to retain the students in the program who had been seeking mentorship.

The setting already had a program of mandated educational workshops for students considered to be at academic risk, but these also were not well attended. The social work intern collaborated with program staff to alter the focus of these workshops to invite all students involved in the newly created program and have the success coaches attend with their matches. In this way, the coaches were supported, the pair could attend together, and the mentees had a partner to accompany them—a win-win for all. Additionally, the intern developed and conducted three workshops through this series of seminars. The topics arose from her ongoing sessions with the success coaches. One session was on decision making; another was focused on the challenges of balancing school, family, work and fun; and the third was on finding purpose and setting goals.

This revised assignment gave the social work intern exposure to work on all levels of practice and provided a solid foundation for the development of skills across units of attention. As important, the implementation of this program created a more effective means to reach and support students in need, as well as those who displayed leadership skills. The intern's beginning understanding of how the students identified as at risk felt marginalized, and her attempts to create a more inclusive community for students to succeed, created an alternative response to the problem presented to her. This setting was ready for an alternative approach and was rejuvenated by this intern's passion to create a difference in students' lives. The intern interacted with 15 of the 25 initially assigned students plus 30 success coaches and an additional 15 students who requested an opportunity to increase their academic effectiveness by working with a success coach. The remaining 10 students of the original 25 received more targeted individualized outreach services.

Additional Assignments: Policy Practice, Engagement, Assessment, Intervention, and Evaluation

The following policy practice assignments include policy analysis, development, and implementation.

Policy Practice Assignments

- Following are suggestions for policy practice assignments. Provide relevant local, state, or federal policies that affect the work of at least one assignment. Consider the problems and issues in relation to the identified policy. How does the policy affect the issues presented? Consider the global issues or policies that may influence the work of this assignment. What aspects of the issue are not addressed? Are there problems with the limitations of the policy or its implementation and what recommendations emerge?
- Conduct interviews with key stakeholders, including constituents and community leaders, to gather and compare alternative perspectives on the extent and consequences of a social problem or condition.
- Learn about the constituents and community being served; gather demographics that characterize the community. Complete a stakeholder analysis that identifies key individuals and organizations, their bases of legitimacy and power, and their interests in the problem or issue.
- Research the legislative history of an existing or proposed program, including prior attempts to solve the problem or address the identified issue.
- Complete a cost-benefit analysis comparing two or more policy alternatives.
- Critically review a policy or program proposal to identify potential implementation challenges and generate possible

solutions. Following this review, contact legislative or bureaucratic decision makers to explain and advocate for a policy.
› Identify and contact groups and individuals to solicit support for a policy reform. Include constituents at every stage of the policy planning process.
› Present the policy analysis and recommendations at a community meeting with constituents; organize and facilitate advocacy and lobbying efforts with constituents.
› With constituents, prepare and present public testimony in support of a policy or program reform for legislative or budgetary hearings or board meetings.
› Track and critically analyze the progress of a legislative or administrative reform.

Political Social Work and Policy Advocacy Assignments

Creating assignments distinct from general policy practice in the areas of political social work and policy advocacy may include asking the student to do the following:

› Participate in voter registration drives with community members, labor unions, and other groups.
› Participate in voter education programs focused on issues that will appear on an upcoming ballot.
› Research a legislative issue, write a legislative brief on the issue, and participate in or initiate meetings about this issue; consider teaming up with the constituents and communities being served by the effort.
› Prepare material for presentation to inform others about an issue.
› Observe and work in partnership with a legislative lobbyist.
› Track local, state, or federal legislation regarding an issue pertinent to the problems of the community.
› Identify global policies pertinent to the problems of the community.

Engagement Assignments

The next group of assignments addresses engagement across units of attention for individuals, families, groups, organizations and communities. Assignments that provide student experience in engagement may include asking the student to do the following:

- Outreach to community members and service recipients by telephone, in writing, or e-mail to set up appointments for interviews or to provide connections to the services available.
- Prepare an online outreach effort targeted for a specific population or issue.
- Practice a script that explains the student's role and reasons for initiating contact.
- Prepare for a first contact by tuning in to the issues facing the individual and attempting to anticipate perceptions of needs and feelings about seeking help, conduct a review of how these issues affect others in the community and may represent broader issues of need.
- Seek out and use existing sources of data, including case records.
- Use a justice-based framework in work with individuals and communities that requires consideration of varying worldviews and existing strengths and potential barriers to service.
- Write recordings that describe the process of beginning work and the feelings associated with helping. If it is an individual session, write a detailed recording of the first 20 minutes and the final 15 minutes of an interview to provide a unique view of this phase of contact. For a recording of more macro assignments, write a reflection on initial perceptions of the assignment and skill set initially anticipated for this assignment.
- Compare the differences between contracting for mandated or involuntary services and contracting for voluntary or self-referred services.
- Prepare for providing services by considering the dimensions of difference or similarities between those served and the student.

- Collaborate with collateral contacts and collaborate on interdisciplinary teams.
- Plan an initial interview with a family; take into consideration different roles, ages, and developmental levels of family members; think about ways of differentially engaging the family; consider the effect of authority issues, boundary structures, identities and communication patterns.
- Seek a mutual contract with families in clear, specific terms; elicit from members their perceptions of the problems to work on, prior attempts made in working on the problem, and the conditions, resources, and supports needed for solutions.
- Observe a group, prepare a recording on the group that focuses on stages of group development, dynamics within the group, the group climate, and efforts to build cohesion, diversity issues, leadership patterns, productively managing group conflict, and other interventions that facilitate group process.
- Prepare an outline on a specialized topic area to present to a group that is currently running.
- Prepare a proposal for planning a group.
- Implement the steps involved in developing a group, devising objectives and goals, conducting outreach, deciding on membership criteria, and advertising.
- Learn about the broad range of community services available or evaluate the lack of community services.
- Examine the setting's official mission statement, established goals and objectives, strategies for achieving goals, and recommended policy changes. Develop alternative or contingency plans to achieve an objective or recommended policy change.

Assessment Assignments

Assignments across units of attention that provide student experience in assessment may include asking the student to do the following:

- Gather information that helps inform a well-rounded assessment, including data on the following:
  - Individual functioning
  - Family relationships and roles

- Social dimensions of identity
- Language abilities and preferences
- Spiritual beliefs and practices
- Financial status and economic conditions
- Education and employment history
- Medical history and health status
- History of victimization and survival (trauma, violence, abuse, oppression) and daily microaggressions
- The presence or absence of support networks and activities

› Write a clinical formulation or biopsychosocial assessment following an initial contact or intake session. Distinguish between external and internal stresses such as discrimination, oppression, historical and current trauma, unemployment, homelessness, and institutional inadequacies versus intrapsychic, interpersonal, physiological, or psychological challenges.

› Anticipate ways to uncover reasons for seeking contact and hopes for change.

› Identify strengths and vulnerabilities, coping and adaptation skills, resiliency, capacities, opportunities, and motivation for change.

› Draw eco maps to identify the major systems involved, including the transactions among these systems, or prepare genograms and cultural genograms (Congress & Kung, 2005; McGoldrick, 2016) to assess family patterns, intergenerational transmission, and cross-cultural experiences.

› Consider how a justice-based perspective aids understanding of a system's struggle for change; and consider the problems that require attention from the perspective of whether these problems represent larger societal problems also needing to be addressed.

› Conduct intake or referral services.

› Make a recording of a family session, describe verbal and nonverbal communication patterns among members, or videotape or use two-way mirrors.

› Consider family system dynamics, including the family's history, culture and language, structure and roles, resources, physical environment, and economic and social supports.

- Facilitate or co-lead a support group; discuss the differences in leadership styles between the co-leaders and the strengths and limitations of each style.
- Discuss how conflict in leadership styles can be addressed. Add an analysis of how the dimensions of identity in the group—and between the co-leaders—affect group roles and interventions.
- Prepare a needs assessment questionnaire to determine interest in a group.
- Discuss the types of communication patterns of a group and ways to promote mutual aid environments.
- Identify the developmental stage of the group and consider the group's movement forward.
- Define the tasks and activities of various roles, positions, or programs in the setting, include the development of a job description for newly created positions or programs.
- Acquire and analyze the departmental organizational chart; decipher the organizational structure with experience of communication lines that do not appear on paper.
- Prepare an analysis of a meeting; assess how effective interventions were in moving through the agenda and facilitating communication.
- Review the setting's relationships in the community and interagency and community collaborations; propose ways of strengthening these collaborations and implementing some proposed ideas.
- Examine the setting's stage of multicultural organizational development using the literature on this topic; propose ways of moving along the continuum of a multicultural organization.
- Identify the criteria necessary for assessment of employee performance.
- Assess the setting's role in promoting justice; propose ways to implement some ideas.
- Consider how U.S. health policy affects service users' situations.

Intervention Assignments

All assignments provide experience in a range of interventions; students may be asked to do the following:

- Provide ongoing and regular supportive counseling
- Contract for services
- Implement a contract and treatment plan
- Define treatment modalities appropriate for the population assigned
- Help individuals apply for government benefits and needed services, such as public assistance, Medicaid, public housing, food stamps, or day care; in addition, research eligibility requirements, and locate needed documentation
- Work with people in crisis and learn the skills of crisis intervention
- Assess what is needed to promote the resiliency of group members and plan techniques and rituals needed to help the group end well
- Advocate, lobby, or implement steps for social change for and with service users
- Consider factors in the community that support or isolate the system's efforts and eventual success for change
- Examine different family therapy approaches and relevant evidence-based treatment models ensuring that they are culturally relevant, determine the models best suited for a certain family, and provide a rationale for those chosen
- Design an orientation program for newly hired employees or next year's social work interns
- Design and implement an in-service training program on a specific topic of concern to staff and assess department assets and needs
- Prepare press releases and online or media notices about activities for newspapers or newsletters.
- Use various planning tools (e.g., census data and community directories)
- Initiate a planning process that includes the participation of appropriate groups, community leaders, and members (e.g.,

citizen groups, boards, target groups, religious leaders, and residents)
- Forecast potential developments for a series of planning objectives, review prior attempts to solve community problems
- Prepare a time schedule for a comprehensive community-based planning process, use a range of planning tools such as the program evaluation review technique (PERT) and Gantt charts
- Form a problem-solving task group from diverse programs or consumer interest groups, community leaders, and residents
- Serve as a participant on a task force
- Collaborate with staff members or volunteers to manage an aspect of a unit, department, or program
- Initiate contact with a group or organization for purposes of cooperation and collaboration
- Develop and help implement an agreement to coordinate services with other agencies
- Prepare documents and proposals for negotiating sessions with funding sources
- Participate in lobbying efforts on local or state levels, include community leaders and members
- Organize a speaker's bureau
- Consider the implications of termination at each level of attention, plan for the termination, transfer or referral of assignments

Evaluation Assignments

Following are some assignments to give students that provide experience in evaluation.
- Create a feedback survey to be completed at the midway point of service and following service
- Anticipate ways to build conversations into the work that explore feedback
- Use recordings to examine progress made toward change on various levels of attention
- Use a single-subject research project (See previous discussion, "Research-Informed Practice and Practice-Informed Research" in this chapter.)

- Contribute to a community evaluation of services
- Monitor the changes that take place in groups from session to session and over the life span of the group such as goal determination and pursuit of goals, values and norms, roles, communication, conflict resolution, and attraction or cohesion (Glassman, 2009; Shulman, 2012)
- Evaluate the financial resources of a project, review the setting's resource needs and allocations over a 3- to 5-year period
- Include an evaluation of services as an ongoing effort and as part of termination
- Implement a participatory action research methodology in evaluating needs with community stakeholders

CHAPTER 8

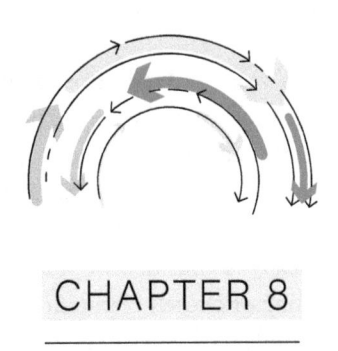

Promoting Reflection Through Process Recordings

Mirrors and Windows

The basic premise of process recording in social work education rests on the notion that a written account by the student concerning transactions with clients can be an effective medium to enhance learning. There are several important values that can be achieved by such a written document. Among them is the focus that it can provide for student/field instruction conference sessions where the student's work is dynamically processed. The recording allows the agency-based instructor a window on the student's practice. (Black & Feld, 2006, p. 139)

Reflection is critical to professional development and learning from experiences.... Reflection allows students to identify links between theory and practice, as well as uncover other issues that concern or puzzle them. Reflective assignments provide students an avenue to support their learning by transforming tacit knowledge into explicit, codified knowledge to be shared with others and to inform future decisions. (Cord & Clements, 2010, p. 289)

Recordings of students' work and reflections across levels of practice are among the best tools in field education for promoting self-assessment and evaluation. Combined with opportunities for direct observation of our students, these recordings also help us see and experience where students are in their thought processes and skill development. It is important to note that they offer a means to consider the student's intentions as well as actions. During the recording of chosen interactions and interventions, students are encouraged to wonder, ask questions, raise doubts, and reevaluate and reimagine. In this way, students become the leaders of their own learning; they present their work and permit our review. We offer our responses to explore how best to tackle the issues brought forward and expand the conversation on issues of importance.

Many field instructors use recordings as opportunities for a do-over, meaning students get to write about what they wish they had said or done in a practice situation. Consequently, recordings easily lend themselves to reflection on actions; students are also encouraged to include questions that relate to the CSWE's (2015a) nine competencies. For example, in learning how to engage a new group of adolescents in a community center, a student might reflect on what is being learned about engagement of youths in a group; the goal in this situation and what might be tried next time; whether this situation was like others previously experienced, and how the student's actions here differ from work with an assigned committee and whether the student is getting better at a skill by coming to it more quickly, consistently, or in a more sophisticated way and what that suggests has been achieved.

Recordings also offer a bird's-eye view into our students' worldviews, understanding of justice, and how they experience the pernicious impact of inequities they witness. Formats can be custom built to respond to or direct the learning task. They build on each other and become a record that tracks progression toward competence, and they offer a way to see where justice-based practice can assist progress and ongoing work. In this way, recordings are an important tool for prompting a critical review of the student's work including examining assumptions and creating options for considering alternatives. Through the recording, the student truly begins to own learning that leads to mastery, and the field instructor is the supportive ally in that process.

Micro to Macro Recordings in Field Education Supervision

This chapter examines field education recordings across units of attention from several perspectives. The requirement of student recordings has a long tradition in field education for a variety of reasons. Mary Richmond introduced written recording as a major tool in the development of social work professionals and supervisory regulation in 1917; writing down what took place in an interview quickly became the most widely used teaching method for practitioners (Wilson, 1980). Although technological advances provide audiotapes, videotapes, and live observation of interviews through two-way mirrors that supplement or replace written formats, written recordings continue to be used in the full range of student activities, from research, program planning tasks, telephone calls, lobbying activities, collateral contacts, planning workshops, and committee meetings to interactions with individuals (Conroy, 2012).

Although students use many kinds of recordings associated with practice that contribute to their overall professional skills, recordings for field education are different from any other form of record keeping. In addition to providing supervisory oversight of the student's work, their prime function is educational. They are an important tool for tracking progress and the development of reflective practice (Ames, 1999; Black & Feld, 2006; Kagle, 1991; Neuman & Friedman, 1997; Papell, 2015; Urdang, 2010) and for critical thinking on issues of justice (Gursansky, Quinn, & Le Sueur, 2010; Robinson, Cross-Denny, Kyeunghae, Wekmeister, & Yamada, 2016; Wehbi & Straka, 2011).

Field education recordings provide students with a means to integrate their knowledge and to enhance their skills. A primary aim is to reflect on all that happens in the decision making, interaction, or process of work so that the writer has another opportunity to think about actions taken; like a mirror or a window, a different perspective is offered. Thus, in the process of writing down what takes place, the recording promotes a self-directed evaluation, and questions emerge that guide the student in a reflective analysis, which in turn, promotes the development of critical thinking. The emphasis differs from other agency-based recordings that are focused on summations that record provided services.

Throughout this chapter *student recordings* refers to the full range of recordings used across units of attention from micro- to macro-level assignments. Although formats vary according to these different aspects, their aims share similar objectives. Traditionally, student process recordings are detailed records of student interventions with individuals, pairs, families, or small groups. Among the various formats for process recordings, the most common form is the basic recalling of observations and verbal reporting, where "students retell the story of their work (as they remember it) to the supervisor" (Graybeal & Ruff, 1995, p. 171). In other words, the student listens to the individual's concerns and then organizes the verbal information on to paper. This written representation may closely approximate the actual experience, but it will also reflect the student's subjective perspective about the individual and situation being described. Although many process recording formats encourage a verbatim recall of the interaction, Urdang (2010) proposed that a process recording "is not a script; it is not a verbatim transcription" (p. 533). Instead, it is conceived of as a story being told by the student that provides the core of what happened, the thoughts and questions that were evoked, and possible next steps. The story is peppered with real dialogue or examples of actions that give context to and illustrate what the student is attempting to convey. This narrative format promotes greater use of the student's reflective skills as opposed to simply relying on recall. Finally, the most common form of recording for more macro assignments including community and organizational interventions or policy analyses are usually referred to as logs, or journals. Although these recording formats document key events, steps taken, progress made, and setbacks or problems, they are meant to be more than a list of tasks or events.

Whatever format the recordings take for micro-level and macro-level work, they are a method of communication between students and field instructors, providing a view on each student's work and mastery of competencies from micro clinical interactions to progress made on mezzo or macro projects. They focus the student's attention on the work, and they facilitate teaching. They encourage learning while also promoting accountability and enhancement of social service delivery. They serve as a running account of specific activities on assignments, starting with brief statements of goals and objectives, student roles, levels of responsibility, and initial and ongoing tasks. They also include students' impressions, reflections, and assessments of what they have accomplished in relation to the assignments, logical next steps, identified barriers, and progress or successes achieved. In this way, recordings provide the "raw material from which the instructor can understand what occurred, assess performance, and develop and direct the teaching process" (Hawthorne, 1987, p. 7). An important component is that these recordings are also a mirror and method of communication for students because they stimulate an internal dialogue that allows reflection on and rethinking of actions they have, or have not taken (Schön, 1983,1987). In these ways, the full range of recordings promote autonomous practice, critical thinking, and self-awareness, and they support the development of the student's growing professional identity.

Recordings provide us with a written account of the student's development of social work practice knowledge, skills, and values and become the basis for teaching and educational assessment over time (Fox & Gutheil, 2000; Videka-Sherman & Reid, 1985). They serve as an educational tool to be used purposefully with the competencies in mind; they illustrate the student's skills and provide multiple examples for teaching purposes. They also may be structured to emphasize an identified learning focus (Black & Feld, 2006; Bogo, 2010; Graybeal & Ruff, 1995). This can be particularly useful in addressing student progress in achieving competence over the full range of competencies.

The process of reconstructing the interactions that take place in work with an individual, family, group, or with collaborators or constituents in organizations or communities has many other benefits. The task of recording forces students to recall the details of the interaction or the process of engaging in tasks, spot gaps in memory, identify themes or patterns in the content, and point to areas of strength or difficulty. This helps students recognize the explicit ways they interpret and record information. It can also draw attention to details that may seem inconsequential but on second glance may be important to what is or is not taking place. This process orientation asks students to consider their affective experiences and impressions of the situation as well as physiological and cognitive reactions. Students are encouraged to be mindful and self-aware. Examining the details of the work provides one level of review and adding the expectation that students reflect on other dimensions takes students to deeper levels of analysis and development.

At this point it should be clear that recordings serve multiple purposes, and these purposes serve students and field instructors in complementary but somewhat different ways. The following lists summarize the purposes of student recordings first for students then for field instructors. Recordings assist the learning task of students and also do the following:

> Serve as instruments to guide learning
> Help clarify the purpose of the interview or activity
> Encourage students' abilities to tune in to themselves and others
> Further the understanding of needs and available resources

- Help balance problem solving and reflective approaches
- Stimulate communication, critical thinking, self-awareness, and reflection
- Develop observational and active listening skills and expand the power of recall
- Offer practice in providing systematic accountability for practice
- Provide evidence of developing mastery of generalist and specialized practice competencies
- Provide material for classroom assignments

Recordings assist the teaching task of field instructors, and they do the following:

- Provide direction and structure for teaching on content such as justice-based practice
- Identify patterns and themes
- Assist in assessment of student abilities on a range of issues and activities with various systems such as the extent to which students integrate knowledge and theory gained from previous field education supervisory sessions, course work, and outside readings; evidence regarding growth in professional identity and professional use of self; and progress in the mastery of the competencies
- Provide concrete examples to base feedback
- Provide data for practice research

Teaching From Micro to Macro Recordings

We have all gone through the exercise of producing student recordings, and we tend to use recording formats that we were trained in or that are familiar to us. This may make it difficult to add new components. Because some social work programs have specific recording requirements and formats outlined in their field education manuals, it is important to clarify the program's guidelines at the beginning.

Although the material is available in the field education manual, as field instructors we are responsible to guide students on how to do recordings and what practical aspects are required, such as the content to include, the format to use, how often recordings should be done, and the procedures to follow. Going over examples of recordings with students gives them a concrete format to follow and clarifies literacy and accuracy expectations. Explaining why recordings are requested allays anxieties and feelings related to exposure and risk. As we work with recordings, students see that we use what students provide and then build from there. Allowing time during field placement hours to do recordings provides structure and communicates the importance of recordings to the placement experience.

Different approaches to teaching from recordings concur that the identification of patterns and themes helps to focus and guide review of the work. Themes may be associated with a practice issue, competency, or theoretical orientation (Black & Feld, 2006). Using the following questions as we review the recording is a suggested means of approaching the task (Hawthorne, 1987):

> What issues are identified in this recording? How do these issues connect with each other?
> Which ones should be chosen as a priority for focus at this time and why?
> What connections to previous recordings are important to consider?
> Given previous recordings, what progress has been made? What issues remain?
> What should the student continue doing? What has the student omitted? What should the student do differently? What next steps should be taken?
> What progress is being made in the identification and attention to issues of rights and justice?
> What progress is being made in the development of self-awareness and issues of positionality?
> What implications emerge from the work, and how do they relate to progress made, or not made, on practice issues identified in the competencies?
> What constructive feedback can be given? What learning strategy might be applied?

Reviewing the entire recording before adding comments or questions helps to focus on the more important aspects of the session. This avoids getting mired in the details of any one interchange or aspect of the work. Gradually, it becomes easier to recognize the student's practice patterns, and we can do a detailed review with these patterns in mind from previous work. Hawthorne (1987) proposed, "Through the details of the process recordings, the educational issues of the learner become clear so that the instructor can plan a focus for teaching and the student can analyze and become aware of his or her own process" (p. 9). This point is also true for logs, journals, and written reflections. The questions we pose are geared to further student understanding of their developing professional practice, and we should give adequate attention to successful interventions. By being specific when identifying what students do well in practice, we encourage students' behaviors or skills to be repeated, consolidated, and understood in terms of why they worked.

There are several points of view regarding comments provided on student recordings (Urbanowski & Dwyer, 1988). Adding our comments serves as a form of teaching while recognizing and respecting the students' efforts and work. Try to identify and support good intentions, risk taking, and growth; tune in to student struggles and perceptions. What were students attempting to accomplish? Perhaps the delivery was off, but the students' intentions were on target.

Comments can be referred to during field education sessions, which can be helpful in evaluating progress and focusing on student learning objectives. Helping students name the skills they are using, identifying the competency being applied, and posing questions that prompt critical thinking are all possible suggestions. When comments are added to the recording, technological advances enable feedback and synchronous chat time so that a virtual conversation may occur; other technologies offer the opportunity for running comments.

The opposing argument to adding our comments to a student recording is that it tends to shape the discussion from our perspective before we understand the student's assessment of how the contact went or why certain interventions were chosen. Initially, the focus of comments should identify major issues or questions rather than getting stuck in the details of interventions made by students. Excessive comments on recordings may be confusing for students and may dilute their focus for learning. Too many comments can affect students' capacities to critique their own practice or to raise questions in field education supervisory conferences. The comments may also increase student anxiety over getting something wrong.

Letting students take the lead in analyzing their work provides a positive learning environment and helps build confidence. Testing the student's ability to engage in this activity provides clues for how active we need to be. Developmental stage models propose that we may need to assume greater initiative in the beginning stages of learning and gradually increase our expectations that students direct their own learning. The struggle is to balance commentary based on students' learning needs while at the same time increase students' professional autonomy (Dwyer & Urbanowski, 1965; Deal, 2004; Deal & Clements, 2006).

In summary, some of the pros of field instructor comments on recordings are that they

> serve as a form of teaching,
> recognize and respect students' work,
> focus the teaching content, and
> track progress and add to the process of evaluation.

Some of the cons of field instructor comments on recordings are that they

> focus on field instructors' concerns rather than students' concerns,
> too many comments may dilute the focus and confuse the student,
> can mobilize student resistance, and
> may point out mistakes or danger spots rather than providing a balance of strengths and progress.

Rather than using comments on a recording to prompt a student's ability to look at the work differently, another way is to read the passage aloud. Sometimes students take the role of the individual being served or a committee member while field instructors take the student role. This provides a different means to examine interactions and can be a powerful learning experience; students hear their voice in a new manner and context. It brings the interaction alive and into the field education conference for greater scrutiny. In these ways, review of the student's practice becomes the basis for the field education conference agenda.

Traditional and Familiar Formats for a Justice-Based Framework

Several examples of traditional and familiar recording formats can be found in the Chapter 8 Appendix. Each has been adapted to include questions or topic areas consistent with a justice-based framework. They include a general process recording format, an outline recording for group process, a log or journal outline, a reflective log outline, and a process recording format for policy practice. This section summarizes the predominant formats for micro- through macro-level work. Throughout we have added ways to take the recordings beyond the traditional focus on the precise interaction and reflections derived from these interactions by adding considerations of achievement of practice competencies and questions that shape attention on rights and justice (Belkin Martinez, & Fleck-Henderson, 2014).

Recordings for micro-level assignments. The following three examples describe the prime formats used for micro level work. Verbatim or accordion-style recordings, narrative recordings and summary recordings. *Verbatim recordings* or *accordion-style recordings* are also known as *I said, she said* process recordings or *script* recordings. This style asks students to recall and record in as much detail as possible all aspects of the encounter in a logical sequence (Neuman & Friedman, 1997; Wilson, 1980). This involves writing a verbatim transcript of the interaction using a format that consists of columns or sections that contain the following:

> interview content and dialogue that records the mutual connection between the actors
> the student's affective reactions or the increasing self-awareness of the students' thoughts, feelings, observations, and what the student has noticed about the service user's nonverbal communications
> notes on the competencies, theories, or skills used
> a running comment on rights being addressed, commentary on the differing positionalities between the actors, issues of structural oppression, and individual, social, and institutional factors of concern
> supervisory comments, feedback, or observations and shared self-awareness

As noted previously, verbatim recordings stressing recall alone are not the ideal format. If programs require this format, or if some field instructors prefer it, it is recommended to add a summation and reflective component. The student can be asked to add a reflective statement at the end of the recording that summarizes developing self-awareness, how dimensions of identity were at play, or what rights, justice, and structural oppressive forces were noticed. A request for something specific on one of the competencies is a useful way to pay attention to each competency over time during placement. For example, the student can be asked to identify an intervention that demonstrates skill in engagement and then to progress through the competencies that focus on each stage of the helping process as contact with the individual continues.

Narrative recordings, like verbatim recordings, ask students to recall as much as possible about the encounter, but the encounter is retold in a running commentary that gives the reader the experience of being there. Observations, thoughts, transitions, feelings, and comments are included as a part of the narrative, often in parentheses. Dwyer and Urbanowski (1965) advocated for structured narrative recordings that blend verbatim recordings with a process orientation. The student (a) briefly notes the purpose of the session before it occurs, (b) writes a narrative of observations, (c) describes the content of the session as closely as possible, (d) describes feelings experienced during the session, and (e) records impressions and thoughts for ongoing plans for the work. As observations are made in a running note in this format, it could easily be adapted to require a summarization of the student's impressions of what was achieved in the interaction or include a competency focus as noted earlier.

Summary recordings require students to summarize the major themes and content of sessions, and students can choose to provide details about selective interactions. This is usually done in narrative form, but it may also be in verbatim style. The difference from the previous formats is the amount of verbatim requested. The interactions that are chosen for discussion are the ones that students have concerns about, they want to identify underlying factors affecting the interactions, or the interactions are illustrative of an aspect of the work. For example, the student may choose, or as suggested in Chapter 7, we may ask a student, to summarize the beginning 20 minutes of an interaction and the final 10 minutes of the session. This provides a unique glimpse into beginnings and endings. Summary recordings may take less time than verbatim recordings, but the exercise requires choosing and prioritizing parts of the work for consideration. The analysis extends and enriches attention beyond the interaction to reflections, competencies, and implications for next steps (Urdang, 2010) and in a similar manner, a justice-based framework asks the student to comment on issues related to rights, justice, and structural oppression, and develop self-awareness regarding the differing positionalities between the intern and individuals in the interaction.

Recordings for mezzo- and macro-level assignments. The recordings that address mezzo and macro units of attention often take the form of logs or journals to keep a running track of progress made on the assignment. They are not intended to be simple to-do lists, and the formats can vary depending on the task or project. For example, recordings for group work sometimes take the form of verbatim interactions, narrative, or summary recordings as described previously while also addressing development of specific aspects of the dynamics in the group.

Recordings on groups take different forms depending on the type of group and focus for learning. An outline for recording group work is included in the Chapter 8 Appendix. The items focus on the group's goals, maintaining the group's purpose, content of the dialogue, and the process of the group's overall activity. Issues of setting a climate for work, developing group cohesion, identification of roles group members assume, and providing room for specific illustrations of group interactions are noted. Like the previous formats, the aim is to provide opportunities for students to display their skills, develop their self-reflective capacities, and increase their competence. Identification of issues related to oppression, rights and justice, varying positionalities among group members and facilitators, and developing student self-awareness and influential affective reactions are important factors.

Logs or journals are used for more macro level assignments to examine key elements that define the nature of the work; despite the differences from the other recordings previously mentioned, they share the defined purpose of review and promoting reflection as suggested in all student recordings. Logs tend to be presented in outline form, and journals are usually presented in a written running commentary, any mezzo or macro assignment may be reviewed through the lens of a detailed account of the interactions involved.

Relating to the nature of much mezzo and macro level work, logs and journals include the plan and objective or an aspect of the task targeted for review, any anticipated obstacles, and progress being made toward achievement of the stated goals and objectives. The specific activities engaged in since the previous supervisory session are recorded; the student is asked to assess the effectiveness of the activity, propose any revisions to the plan, anticipate barriers and pose questions for discussion. Comments on the student's affective reactions to the progress of the work can be added; equally, a justice focus may be added that identifies the assignment's goals as they relate to rights and justice-based program planning, advocacy, project management, and so on.

Recordings for policy practice often follow an outline for policy analysis. The Chapter 8 Appendix offers an outline for consideration. In addition, a format used by Medina (2010) that includes an accordion style format incorporates attention to goals and objectives, documentation of actions, and reflection on the dialogue or process. This format provides students with an opportunity to reflect in action and it "stimulates inductive learning and generative theory building" (Graybeal & Ruff, 1995, p. 171). Medina's model (2010) asks the student to address four core policy practice skills: "analytical, political, interactional and value clarifying" (p. 34). Analysis includes evaluation of the social problem and the political skills applied in the situation. These skills include the use of power to influence development and implementation of strategies for change, interactional skills that assume an ability to take initiative and enact a leadership role and value clarification which involves prioritization of issues and actions (Medina, 2010). Segments of the process or dialogue are examined through the lens of one or other of these core policy practice skills while the student records cognitive reactions, affective reactions, and reflections in separate columns of the format.

Any of these formats may include space for relevant comments, questions, and reactions from students and field instructors. Making space for identification of skills and demonstrated competencies provides a running notation on the student's progress. This includes ongoing dialogue about the content and skills as well as room for students to raise questions and concerns. Whatever format is used, the most important aspect is for students to communicate the process and content as accurately and precisely as feasible in a way that facilitates broader discussions about the work. Achieving this balance may take time and require some guidance on how to reflect on deeper levels of what seems to the student to be the obvious next task to complete.

Focusing Recording Tools to Fit Teaching and Learning Needs

Field education's designation as the signature pedagogy of social work education demands us to create educational opportunities that facilitate integration of students' field education experiences into their classroom learning. Likewise, we can learn from what students are focusing on in the classroom to align our requests for reflections or recordings. Despite preferences and familiar formats, adapting the format to fit the teaching need individualizes the help we offer as students move through the learning process. Asking students to record activities on all assignments may be somewhat overwhelming for them and is likely an unrealistic expectation in the current context of fast-paced practice settings. Therefore, having a focus for recordings is recommended (Walsh, 2002).

Once we have a sense of the students' skills and abilities, we can request recordings of only first meetings with constituents, difficult meetings, or selected assignments. For ongoing practice, students may be required to provide summary recordings or critical incident recordings. The decision about this progression varies, but the general rule is that recordings should be used to help students move toward greater self-reflection, self-awareness, self-regulation, proficiency and autonomy. The format chosen aims to focus attention on reaching the learning objectives, and a change of format may also provide a needed shift if a student is stuck or having trouble submitting work for review. The format shapes what is produced. We may choose to assign a recording that calls attention to students' reflections on a situation, issue, or interaction or we may assign a different type of recording that addresses underlying components of the competencies. Additional examples include the following.

In action, on action, and for action. Similar to recording a critical incident, in at least three paragraphs this request builds the student's capacity for reflection on (1) what the student did in an interaction or task undertaken and what the student was thinking as this interaction or task was taking place, (2) what thoughts and reactions emerge as the student looks back on the event, and (3) thoughts on implications for next steps or resulting action (Schön, 1983, 1987).

The first section represents the student's ability to recall what happened, including the student's thoughts and reflections in action. The second section asks the student to add thoughts, observations, and reasons for and reactions about the activity. The aim is to demonstrate the student's ability to reflect on action taken. The final section of the narrative records the importance of the actions and implications or questions that result for future action. This exercise strengthens students' capacities to identify the actions they take to develop self-reflection, self-awareness, and the ability to consider how reflection leads to review and informed action. It can help a student who is having difficulty providing a full recording on a session by giving the student practice on what a recording aims to achieve, that is, building abilities to consider how reflection on action points to the assumptions and theoretical frameworks used and the consequences that ensue or next steps and implications for action in the future.

The exercise also may help the student identify the components of decision making. Rather than reflecting on what action might follow, the review focuses on the process leading up to an action taken. The student identifies an action or a verbal response and reflects on the elements that went into taking the action or making the decision to intervene in a certain manner. The reflection on the action taken asks for thoughts, feelings, assumptions, implicit values, knowledge, and theoretical concepts the student associates with the intent of the action. This exercise heightens students' awareness on the process of decision making and how assumptions and judgments affect the actions we take.

Consider a specialized macro practice level student placed at a community center. She is assigned to supervise a team of volunteers working on programming for the center. In supervision the student finds it challenging to reflect on her decision making, to consider how she arrives at choices or how her choices relate to her goals for the group. Her log documents that in her next team supervision meeting she plans to choose certain cards from a game that prompt questions leading in a certain direction. Her aim was to promote more open communication among members. The cards she chose prompt discussion toward various levels of self-disclosure. The following week's log notes that she began the exercise and, following her first question, she turned the cards to a team member to choose the next question. Aiming to prompt self-reflection, the field instructor asks her student to produce a reflection on what prompted this in-the-moment change of plan. The student replied that she had noticed group members' reactions when she chose the first question and became self-aware about how taking the lead stood in the way of the group members' abilities to share in this experience. She recalled previous supervisory discussions regarding her goal of building cohesion and a work-focused team when she decided to turn over leadership of the process by handing the pack of questions to a team member.

This example shows that by supporting the student's exploration, the field instructor and the student saw a clear demonstration of the student's decision making and how she had used reflection as she was involved in action. Initially the student experienced the action she took as resulting from some discomfort of taking the lead; she had not connected it with a purposeful intervention in support of the goal for her group. Assigning this reflection marked a turning point for the student's curiosity to engage in reflection on her actions and to link her interventive choices with her goals and objectives. The student saw what was involved and more clearly understood the purpose for asking for this type of reflection. She proudly announced, "I see now that I was acting to improve group cohesion. I didn't see that in the moment."

Intersectionality. Rather than asking for a recording on an interaction with a specific individual, students could be asked to examine each of the different identities the service user possesses and identify the statuses of positionality—privilege, power, oppression, subjugation—associated with these identities. Further, it may then be possible to consider how this affects the student's understanding of the individual's problems and the possible paths for resolution (Robinson et al., 2016).

> Consider a generalist practice level student who is asked to produce a recording on how she might facilitate the setting's involvement in voter registration for the population it serves, that is, fathers in recovery from substance abuse. As the student reflected on the multiple identities possessed by the setting's population and as she educated herself on voter eligibility, she began to see the complexities that affect these fathers. Questions arose related to immigration status, residency, and history of unemployment and previous incarcerations of many of the fathers.

In this example, what was first seen by the student as a straightforward assignment became a nuanced exercise in educating herself and then intervening to respond to the fathers' questions about voter registration while also being sensitive to their multiple identities and rights.

The competencies. Each of the CSWE's (2015a) competencies may be addressed separately by asking students to examine an assignment, or a comparison of assignments, on one of the competencies such as focusing on the explicit or implicit issues of human rights and justice involved in the service user's situation or problem. For example, how is oppression witnessed or experienced, what power does the individual possess that might be tapped into for the work ahead, or are constituents included in planning the work, what power exists in the community, and what external barriers impede access to fulfillment of rights? Ask students to comment on how this examination has changed their views and how it has facilitated their understanding of the influence of advancing human rights and of possessing a justice lens in their work (Anderson, 2013; Wehbi & Straka, 2011).

> Consider a generalist practice level student who was asked to reflect on how he was advancing human rights in his setting. His work focused on veterans attending a work opportunity retraining program; the student was keen to serve veterans and had identified them as his preferred population for his first field education internship. In his reflection he noted that he did not see the veterans as oppressed, and he listed the

number of benefits they were receiving as evidence of his statement. This provided opportunities to examine the differing layers of oppression and devaluation, and the complexities of ensuring rights beyond access to governmental benefits.

In this example, what began as a rotation through the competencies revealed an underlying assumption not previously addressed in supervisory sessions regarding a student's work with a population.

Running reflections. Students can be encouraged to keep a weekly reflective entry on any of the previously mentioned questions to be submitted for review weekly or monthly depending on the student's learning needs. This works well for students who are adept at writing to-do lists but have difficulty reflecting on these activities. By starting where the student is, the field instructor can lead the student incrementally toward the use of reflection.

Consider a specialized macro practice level student who was having difficulty moving beyond a mere listing of weekly activities and next steps in his logs. This seemed to be related to feeling that the next steps were obvious and straightforward. To move this capable student to deeper levels of learning, the field instructor asked for a running reflection of moments of frustration, uncertainty, satisfaction, and clarity during the next week.

In this example the student's reflection prompted insight related to managing staff relations, instances of building support among colleagues, and decisions to involve others or to manage the task without support. The student managed these interactions well but had been carrying the emotions involved and making decisions without reflecting on his demonstrated skills, on considering other possible responses, or on identifying the underlying organizational issues.

Liberation health model. Using the liberation health model (Belkin-Martinez & Fleck-Henderson, 2014) as part of a separate recording, or as a component for all recordings, the student writes an assessment of the problem being addressed by reviewing the structural, personal, and cultural factors that propel an individual to seek help. This brings attention beyond the immediate appeal for help to consider the pushes and pulls of the individual's context and social environment. This model is easily adapted to more macro considerations.

> Consider a generalist practice level student who is placed in a community women's health clinic. In her consideration of services offered through the liberation health model, she reviewed access to gynecological services and asked, "Whom does this clinic serve and who is not visible, not eligible, and not accessing services?" She became curious about individuals beyond cisgender women in need of services.

What emerged was an interest in pursuing answers to these questions. The student sought support from her field instructor to pursue this line of enquiry with the goal of contacting local programs for LGBTQ+TS individuals to improve links for access to services at the clinic.

Agendas in Field Education Supervision

Asking for weekly student agendas for supervision is another way of working toward the assumption of greater responsibility for learning and building the student's abilities to keep a record of issues. Agendas include questions or topics for discussion about recordings, interventions, assessments, resources, and general practice concerns or learning needs. In this way, agendas are a dynamic representation of the work assigned; that is, they list not only the person the student is serving or the project the student is working on but also the issue or theme the student wants to address. This can be discussion of an ongoing issue or something new, clarification about the competencies involved, or a request for amplification on a skill or theory related to the work. Agendas are primarily student generated, but we can contribute additional topics for discussion. For example, we watch to ensure that issues of justice are not left off the agenda and mark this as an item that relates to the student's assignments.

In summary, agendas are valuable; they help students comment on their work and raise questions about their practice. This builds initiative and taking responsibility for learning needs. Agendas also address students' specific questions and model collaboration and mutual decision making. They prepare students for meeting organizational and professional expectations, they facilitate the development of planning, organizational, and prioritization skills, and finally, they support autonomous practice.

Binders or Electronic Binders, Portfolios, and E-portfolios

Keeping an e-binder and building an e-portfolio on a shared computer file in which students enter their agenda for supervision and recordings help organize material on important components of supervision. The shared file makes it available to the field instructor, and the binders or portfolios act as a resource for the purposes of ongoing evaluation. Many schools have platforms that ensure confidentiality of such e-version records.

Students can be asked to review their work before an oral review, the midterm or sixth-week review, and the end-of-year evaluation and to answer for themselves where did they begin, where are they now, where do they need to go, and what do they need to get there? For example, it may be helpful to ask specific questions, such as, "When you started placement, what was your practice in sustaining discussion of sad or painful feelings? In what ways has your practice changed in being able to engage in a discourse about work across difference or about identifying the underlying structural societal causes of expressed concerns?" Adding your expectation for students to begin to consider what is needed for them to improve their skills is an important component. Expecting students to illustrate these themes with examples from their recordings promotes student ownership of their learning.

Special Considerations

We have presented recordings in a positive frame attempting to balance anticipated challenges with the many advantages associated to promoting reflection and developing students' disciplined review of their work. This balanced view is sometimes more difficult to maintain in the face of student reluctance to put their thoughts and feelings down on paper. This section provides a cautionary note on several stumbling blocks so that they can be recognized, and their negative influence can be lessened or avoided. These include addressing the "drudgery" (Nichols, Nichols, & Hardy, 1990, p. 280) associated with the task, attending to the inherent risk-taking involved, tackling the mistrust of a written record, respecting the work involved in gaining expertise in this form of writing, and dealing with the logistics of time and confidentiality.

Graybeal and Ruff (1993) note that recordings, especially verbatim recordings, "are likely to elicit at least a few groans from an audience of social workers or social work students." (p. 169). Hawthorne (1987) gives an early warning that these "recordings are resisted and resented; misunderstood and misused; time consuming and anxiety provoking for both students and instructors" (p. 7). These commentaries are long-standing, still apply, and probably apply to any form of required recording. Despite these drawbacks, social work educators continue to promote the advantages of some form of detailed recording as a teaching tool (Black & Feld, 2006; Bogo, 2010; Conroy, 2012; Graybeal & Ruff, 1995; Urdang, 2010).

Finding ways to overcome the drudgery of required recordings falls on us. Discussions about the purposes of recordings and adapting their use in supervision goes a long way in helping students see the value of recordings and encouraging their commitment to produce them. Furthermore, because the structures of the recordings are malleable, we can shape the format to serve a need, and this may help shift the student's understanding of their relevance to learning. Some suggestions were provided previously in this chapter for engaging students in experiencing the power of reflection and the rewards of gained insight and understanding.

A certain amount of risk taking is inherent in recording one's work. Students are asked to go on record about their actions and thoughts, which may seem vague or confusing or show a lack of confidence. Effective recordings include information about actions, thoughts, feelings, and questions. The specific selections chosen for inclusion, or obvious glaring omissions, indicate how students think about their work and their assumptions about expectations and good professional practice. The inherent anxiety they have when showing their work to us should be acknowledged, and the courage that students show in trusting the process of learning should be validated. Still, it is inevitable for students to consciously and unconsciously screen the content recorded.

This prompts the question of whether student recordings can be trusted as a true report of what occurred. Because some students find recalling the details of what occurred challenging, some misrepresentations may occur (Bogo, 2015; Bogo et al., 2014). Students also may wish to present as positive a picture as possible and select segments that place them in a more favorable light than the reality of what happened might reveal. Creating open and trusting communication keeps this type of distortion or screening of content to a minimum. We encourage meaningful student recordings by taking the time to review them, giving balanced feedback, and being prepared to discuss the students' questions and concerns. Observations of students in interaction help balance this phenomenon. Ideally, we should balance direct observations with continuing to require recordings to promote the student's written expertise and reflective capacities in using them.

Developing an effective professional voice, written and verbal, is a vital component of social work education. Being able to write in a variety of formats for a range of different purposes is an essential skill for social work practice (Green & Levy Simon, 2012). Recording activities on assignments provides ways for students to develop these skills and to experience the power of their written voice. In addition, writing down what occurs objectifies the process and promotes reflection. However, it has been noted that a current teaching challenge is helping students write effectively and efficiently as they reflect on developing their practice knowledge and skills (Alter & Adkins, 2001; Green & Levy Simon, 2012).

A provoking view on how assessing student writing from an antiracist perspective considers any writing assignment as an opportunity to become "antiracist projects, ones about sustainability and fairness, about antiracist practices and effects" (Inoue, 2015, p. 4). Assessing how to respond to students whose writing abilities reflect their native tongue or culture but do not meet Eurocentric standards falls under the responsibilities of field education as well as the classroom. The students' challenges offer opportunities to have conversations about their experiences and to more accurately balance their expertise and abilities. Often if we focus solely on pointing out grammatical deficits, we miss an opportunity to discuss the concepts that underpin what the student is attempting to communicate. Providing a chance for students to discuss the challenges they face in responding to demands to adapt or fit in with Eurocentric standards is also important. Simply referring students to the university's writing center misses an opportunity to discuss this important aspect of their journey toward developing written and verbal proficiency. By enquiring about our students' experiences in this realm we use our positionality to permit questioning of dominant norms of writing, expressions of self-awareness, and ways of acquiring knowledge. This opens opportunities for including oral traditions in supervision where the student tells a story of an interaction, engages in blogging, creates a genogram, or draws an organizational dilemma that maps the stakeholders and challenges and opportunities.

Student resistance to handing in timely recordings may be a symptom of deeper problems; it may also signal the need to slow the pace of the work in supervision. If handing in recordings becomes an issue, it is critical to understand the nature of the student's hesitancy and underlying difficulties. The lack of production automatically slows the pace of teaching and learning. It may be more than discomfort and being overworked; the situation could be related to desire for more independence and autonomy or their fear of revealing microaggressions that are occurring or confusion and ambivalence about value conflicts and unmet needs they are witnessing. For whatever reason, if not addressed, a simple request for recordings can turn into a power struggle between us and our students. Likewise, the amount of time it takes the student to produce a recording should be monitored, which helps us assess the effort involved. Open discussion is needed to determine a response and whether an alternative format can be attempted.

Ideally, our meetings with students are based on previously submitted recordings and on an agenda prepared by the student that has been shared with us in advance. This type of preparation enhances teaching and learning. As students gain experience in how to use supervision, their ability to formulate their agenda for learning increases, and their comfort in providing recordings is also likely to increase. We can adjust formats of recordings to accommodate the learning as suggested earlier, and we also might create agendas with our students at the start of the meeting to give them practice for this task before we expect them to create a written agenda on their own.

Confidentiality is essential in all recordings. Students should be reminded that the federally mandated privacy rule of the HIPAA regulations apply to their recordings. It is important for students to understand that confidentiality is a professional ethical responsibility, and it is equally important for students to understand that there are laws protecting any information gathered in their work. Any information that would allow another to identify the person, persons, or organization must be changed or eliminated. This includes obvious things such as names, but it may also include other information that is unique to the person or situation, which could allow identification. Methods to protect privacy may consist of using codes or numbers to disguise identifying information, especially because students may take their recordings off the premises or use them in classroom discussions and papers.

Educational recordings are the student's property and belong to the students even after they are reviewed by field instructors and field liaisons. Students should be encouraged to keep copies for their own review, for use in class assignments, for planning interventions, and for measuring their own growth through every stage of the evaluation process. Field education recordings are distinguished from agency notes or required agency recording formats; they are teaching tools. Field education recordings are communications from students to us and should be available only to those directly involved with teaching the student, such as field liaisons and faculty. They are not part of the placement site's records (Kagle, 1991) and should not be kept in agency files. We may keep copies of student recordings for our own records and for reviewing student progress, but they are most useful to students.

Technology and Recordings

Here we consider the uses of technology in aiding efforts to review our students' work. These resources range from the use of videotaping, two-way mirrors, and listening devices in the students' ears for communication to electronic methods that use platforms for confidential sharing of recordings, host chatrooms or share documents for simultaneous review.

Although field education relies heavily on written recordings, other forms of recording student interactions include audiotaping, direct observation using two-way mirrors or closed-circuit television and videotaping. Graybeal & Ruff (1995) remind us that "hearing or seeing oneself on tape is often a powerful learning experience, as is realizing how difficult it is to recall details from memory or performing live before a field instructor" (p. 170). These supplemental tools can be valuable in providing direct data about student interactions, including the pacing, tone, and attitudes conveyed, which are challenging to detect in a written recording or from verbal recall.

Students must receive written permission from the person they wish to tape to use any audiotape or videotape of meetings or sessions, but the advantage of these forms of recording is that they provide the most accurate account of interactions. Then later with our students we see and hear how much or how little they talk and listen; the modulation, tenor, and emotion in voices are evident; and attitudes and subtleties, not available in written records, can more easily be identified. Tapes are also easy to use, readily available, and inexpensive, but reviewing them can be time consuming. Often, we are limited by time over how much of a meeting or session can be reviewed, and the audiotapes or videotapes supplement written recordings. Students can be asked to choose a segment of an interaction that they feel went well, a segment they experienced confusion over what should happen next, or a segment where they questioned their intervention. In this way, the student is given the lead to choose certain parts for review. The student may also choose passages that demonstrate mastery of a skill or competency. Our ability to analyze the work and to formulate a teaching focus may seem easier when we have a written recording to review rather than reviewing a tape, but seeing and hearing are powerful means of review. The achievement of assessing the work provides more accuracy based on the actual visualization or auditory representation of the interaction. In addition, competency-based education requires direct observation of students' abilities, and these methods ensure our abilities to more directly experience our students' skills. This is not to say that one method is more useful than another. On the contrary, they all have their purposes and are valuable resources that provide opportunities to enrich the learning experience.

The goal is to figure out how the methods and resources we use facilitate student learning and our teaching. For example, we should consider ways to enable students to document, measure, and reflect on their work; how we plan to teach from the methods chosen; how the method will promote development of the student's professional identity and professional use of self; how the method will enhance the student's ability to develop skills for critical analysis and reflection, and how evidence will be gathered.

There are many positive outcomes in incorporating social media and new technologies for student recordings. For example, technology

> - connects with current modes of communicating and relating;
> - complements and extends students' learning styles and ways they learn;
> - creates space for dialogue and connection across socially constructed barriers and boundaries;
> - builds and opens doors for local and global connections;
> - provides other ways of connecting, such as online chatrooms, as the student engages in the act of review;
> - prepares students to be successful in the future because technology is here to stay; and
> - provides students with an early sense of mastery because they are more likely to be familiar with or even experts in the medium—they can teach us.

Summary

Recordings—process recordings, logs, and journals—focus on the detail of interactions and tasks. Goals, purpose, review of actions, and next steps to be taken are part of supervisory discussions, and over time these areas have become separate and supplemental components built into the formats. Likewise, the skills, theories, and competencies used have been added as separate columns in an accordion-style format or as topics to be addressed at the end of a recording. This rolling add-on approach signifies the many purposes recordings serve in the learning and teaching agenda. However, the accumulating sequence of issues may result in overload, or any single aspect may get lost among the overall attempt to capture the multilayered reality of the task or interaction. In our attempts to grasp the total picture for teaching, we may render the students' task more challenging. In addition, what they hear from us as the focus leads their response, or in the absence of our direction, they may choose to focus on an aspect that comes more easily with only cursory attention to other aspects such as naming of skills, competencies, or theories. These items may be named in a general sense rather than identifying the skills or theory involved or explaining how this competency applies and what meaning is attached.

One suggestion to avoid this potential for overload is for us to vary recording requests and decide what the focus is with students so that we might go deeper into their reflections and thinking about an issue. Several potential topics of focused recordings were presented earlier in this chapter, such as rotating a focus on an individual competency; summarized or abbreviated reflections interspersed with longer narrative or verbatim recordings; or a focus on a theory such as intersectionality, an issue such as justice, or an analysis of the components in a student's decision-making process. These topics can be adapted for an individual, family, group, community, organization, or macro issue. Recordings can also be used to compare assignments. These abbreviated or focused recordings are not meant to replace a full recording on interactions and tasks but instead to provide opportunities to dig deeper and to highlight aspects as needed.

Recording that is thoughtful and demonstrates self-awareness and critical thinking is an acquired skill that improves with regular and consistent practice. Likewise, developing the ability to recall and communicate essential elements also improves over time. It will take time for most students to produce recordings that effectively meet their needs and learning objectives. Our role is to push students to use recordings beyond mere recall and description and include material that enables a sound critique of their work. The challenge is preparing students so that they may experience how mindfulness and reflection build their capacity for intentional competent practice.

Recordings aid our teaching task in several important ways and enhance abilities to

> reflect and think critically about work, promote the integration of theory, and move toward autonomous practice;
> trace skills demonstrated across units of attention and the helping process;
> examine how students conduct themselves in encounters across dimensions of identity and positionality;

- focus on decision making, judgments, critical thinking, and reflection;
- keep a pulse on the student's observational and active listening skills, the power of recall, and the ability to reflect on developing practice skills and knowledge;
- build a justice-based lens for identification of individual, social, and institutional factors related to rights and justice so they may question and change social structures of oppression; and
- track student growth and development over time.

CHAPTER 8 APPENDIX

This appendix presents a summary of tips for focusing our teaching through micro to macro recordings. Also presented is a range of recording formats including a general justice-based process recording format for micro-level work, a recording for group process, a log or journal outline, a reflective log recording format for a policy issue, and a process recording format for policy practice. Three recordings are included. One is a narrative recording of a student session with an individual, the second is a verbatim recording of the supervisory session with this student, and the third is an administrative log.

Focusing Teaching Efforts Through Recordings

The following questions focus our teaching regarding recordings. They promote an examination of the student's ability to accurately reflect content and feelings and to use purposeful interactions.

› Does the student produce recordings that contain meaningful substance? Does the student identify the purpose of sessions, contacts, or processes involved? Are the student's interventions or activities aimed toward achievement of goals? Do the student's written or verbal explanations reflect an understanding of role and function in the setting?

› Is the student following a personal agenda or the system's agenda? Is the student able to start where the individual or group or community is? To what extent is the student receptive to the system's frame of reference? Is the student able to hear what is being communicated? Is the student helping individuals or communities tell their stories and focus on their issues? Is the student moving from a personal agenda or from an understanding of the task involved?

› Is the student able to balance empathetic listening with appropriate responses? Is the student listening or attentive to nonverbal communications and underlying issues? Does the student maintain appropriate professional boundaries? Who does most of the work in the session, task meeting, or committee? Is the student able to delegate leadership and authority to the individual or others involved?

› What level of self-assessment and self-awareness is evident? Is progress observed on the student's ability to self-reflect and critically analyze issues involved? Is the student able to identify when judgments or biases appear in assessments? Is the ability to self-correct behavior in the work or in comments about the work demonstrated? To what extent is the student able to risk exposing mistakes, biases, and faux pas in a manner that facilitates learning?

› Which competencies are evident in the recording? To what extent are issues of rights, justice, oppression, and privilege identified as issues for intervention? Does the student demonstrate awareness and sensitivity to different dimensions of identity? Over time, does the student demonstrate skills across a range of competencies? What progress toward mastery is shown? What behaviors, interventions, or activities reflect movement in the development of which competencies?

A General Justice-Based Process Recording Format

The following items are included in the process recording format whether a verbatim accordion-style, narrative, or summary format. An outline of an accordion-style format is provided in Figure 8A.1.

1. Preengagement: This preparation examines how structural oppression may affect this situation before the contact happens and extends the traditional practice of tuning in. Students include a statement on their preparation for this encounter and address the questions: What were their expectations? Were any preconceptions identified? What implications do these considerations present for the work? What considerations of differences or similarities in power and positionality apply in this situation?

2. Objectives or goals: Include the reason for the session or meeting, source of the referral, the initial or presenting problems, brief statement of any specific goals to be achieved during the session, students' plans, and system's agenda.
3. Narrative: Include a description of what occurs in the session, including a narrative or word-for-word dialogue meeting interspersed throughout to illustrate the essence of the mutual dialogue, connection, and interaction. Both sides of the interaction including verbal and nonverbal communication should be included.
4. Students' feelings: Students are required to add their reflections in parentheses or in a notation in a column or margin on cognitive and affective reactions, unspoken thoughts, feelings, and reactions to the session with the individual or group while the session proceeds (e.g., "I began to feel uneasy. I felt that the authority of my role and whiteness was challenging to this Somali mother as she was attempting to manage her crying 2-year old child. I was uncertain about what to do.").
5. Critical self-reflection: Students examine their assumptions, reactions, and self-awareness about what is happening as the session progresses saying, for example, "I was the only woman in the room and I felt like I didn't have anything worthwhile to say. I did have things to say, but I couldn't find an entry and I felt so self-conscious" or "I am wondering if the verbal cisgender young man is limiting the younger LGBTQ+TS members in the group to share what they are feeling. As I am also a cisgender man, I wonder how I should have intervened."
6. Impressions: This is a summary of students' critical thinking and analysis of the entire recorded session. It includes consideration of dimensions of identity during the session and how power and privilege were displayed. It also includes students' attempts to self-critique interventions and responses and reflections on the demonstrated strengths in handling the session as well as areas needing improvement (e.g., "I think I could have been more direct in the group about what I was feeling and noticing. I would like to try to start off that way next time.").

Preengagement:

Goals and objectives:

| Narrative or running dialogue | Self-reflection, self-awareness, tuning in to positionality | Competencies and skills applied | Justice concerns and issues of oppression | Supervisory comments |

Theories applied:

Justice-based advocacy factors identified on individual, social, institutional, or global levels:

Impressions and questions:

Next steps:

Figure 8.1 A Justice-Based Recording Format

7. Issues related to rights and justice: The individual, social, and institutional or global factors that are influencing access to rights or issues of justice are identified so that possible avenues for intervention can be explored.
8. Plans and next steps: In this section, unfinished business, short- and long-term goals, possible service needs, and goals for the next session are identified. This section may also include considerations on how the student might prepare for the next session.
9. Questions: Students ask about what they want to discuss in field instruction. These questions may come from the actual

session, or they may arise from the experience of reflecting on the session.
10. Space is provided for supervisory comments. Comments are intended to focus attention on themes that emerge from an examination of the student's work and on priorities that focus the learning agenda. In a justice-based framework, supervisors share their impressions and reactions to promote authentic communication in supervisory sessions.
11. Other possible elements are identified learning goals, competencies addressed, or themes revealed in the recording. Asking students to address their overall impressions and evaluation of the work, perhaps addressing a different competency each week or a specific issue to consider such as the various dimensions of identity that emerged during an interaction with an individual or identifying justice, policy or research issues or skills, and theories applied, are a few possible items to consider.

Recording for Group Process

In group recordings, students focus more on the process of the group as it emerges in the session than on the content of what was said by each member (Glassman, 2009; Shulman, 2012). Verbal and nonverbal behaviors of specific members or passages in the group session provide the detail of interaction that furthers consideration of the process of group development. Student recording of group sessions may be guided by the following items and questions:

1. Preengagement: This preparation examines how structural oppression may affect this situation before contact and extends the traditional practice of tuning in. Students include a statement on how they prepared for this session. What were their expectations? Did they identify any preconceptions? What implications do these considerations present for their work? What considerations of differences or similarities in power and positionality apply in this situation?
2. Description of the setting and structure: Students describe the context, population, session number, and type of group. How does the group organize itself to accomplish its tasks?

What group rules emerge? What leader behaviors are displayed among the members? How are decisions reached? How is information treated? How do the dimensions of identity play out regarding who speaks and who sets the rules?

3. Climate: Students describe the psychological and emotional atmosphere of the group. How are feelings, as opposed to points of view, dealt with? What nonverbal behaviors indicate changes in the climate? How do members' voices convey feelings? Do the similarities and differences affect group dynamics?

4. Facilitation: How do group members influence the development of the group? Does the group process run itself? What group-building behaviors are used and by whom (e.g., involving silent members, harmonizing conflict, reinforcing participation)? How will the facilitator create space for dimensions of identity to be recognized?

5. Barriers to the work: What behaviors emerge that hinder the accomplishment of the group's task, for example, what antigroup behaviors are evident (e.g., blocking, recognition seeking, dominating, withdrawing)? What communication patterns develop that block group tasks? How do the members' dimensions of identity play out regarding the barriers that emerge? How might unspoken issues of positionality, rights, justice, oppression, or privilege be at play? How might the tasks and responsibilities identified by Hardy (2016, 2017) for having conversations across difference (see Chapter 2) apply to the work of the group? How are members responding to their privileged and subjugated identities?

6. Group's demand for work: How does the group move from independence to collective judgment? What behaviors promote agreement? What consensus-seeking behaviors are observed? What false consensus behaviors are displayed (e.g., "me too" or "I'll go along with that")? Do the members' dimensions of identity manifest themselves regarding this issue?

7. Assessment of next steps: What possible next steps would be recommended? What changes in plans might be feasible? Is there unfinished business?

8. Examples of progress: What student development occurred in the achievement of greater skill with group methods?
9. Broader issues of concern: If not already addressed, what competencies are exemplified in the work of this group? Are justice, human rights, policy, or research issues related to the material and concerns discussed?

Log or Journal Outline

This outline is provided as an overview of the key elements of a log or journal entry (Swenson, 1988). It may also be used for reflective journal entries or meeting assessment forms for specialized practice in macro and social administration methods of practice.

The entry begins with a brief description of assignment and consists of a few sentences that provide the background, origin, and context of the assignment.

1. Preengagement: This preparation examines how structural oppression may affect this situation and extends the traditional practice of tuning in. Students include a statement on how they prepared for this assignment. What were their expectations? Did they identify any preconceptions? What implications do these considerations present for their work? What considerations of power and positionality apply to this assignment?
2. Task plan: This is a description of the purpose of the assignment and the need being addressed. The steps or primary activities needed to complete the assignment should be listed in the order they occur, with projected completion dates, including any resources from in and outside the setting that are needed to complete the project. Items that represent priorities should also be identified.
3. Obstacles: Students provide initial thoughts about problems they anticipate. Who is defining the community members' problems or issues? Who is excluded from this definition?
4. Progress summary: Students include details of activities they have completed and report on their progress to date.
5. Assessment of activity: Students raise questions they have encountered while attempting to complete tasks. They also

provide a retrospective evaluation of how activities might have been improved.
6. Activity summary: Students describe what primary project activities were completed during the week, including problems or barriers encountered, decisions made, and the underlying components involved.
7. Revised task plan: Students note any modifications in the initial plan of work. Any timetable changes that occur because of problems encountered or unexpected experiences during the session also are noted. If there is a major revision, students describe the new plan.
8. Agenda: Students outline questions and issues for discussion in field instruction supervision.
9. Broader issues of concern: If not already addressed, students note which competencies are embedded in this assignment, and which justice, human rights, policy, or research issues are related to the material and concerns discussed.

Reflective Log Regarding a Policy Issue

This outline provides guidance on recordings that examine work regarding various aspects of policy practice. Students are asked to consider the issues under each heading relevant to their assignments.

Learning Objective 1: Define social policy issues. Identify the social condition or issue to be studied and the specific steps for analysis. Reflect on who is affected by the condition or its solution, the extent to which their interests are organized and reflected in the media and political processes, the consequences of alternative definitions of the problem in finding policy solutions, and the dimensions of the problem that are covered (and ignored) in the media, formal political processes, community activities, and so on. How are policies influencing the issue or problem? What structural barriers are there? How are individual, social, and institutional factors operating as barriers? Reflect on the problem definition process, the ability to influence outcomes, and areas for additional learning. Specify the justice, human rights, policy, or research issues related to the material and concerns. Self-assess mastery of skills and areas for additional learning in this practice area.

Learning Objective 2: Identify and analyze prior efforts. Record the initial research task, its relevance to the policy development process, and progress toward completion. Note and critically reflect on the role of historical research, opportunities, and difficulties with obtaining data and the use of their analyses for program development, strategic planning, or a policy initiative. Specify the justice, human rights, policy, or research issues related to the material and concerns. Self-assess mastery of skills and areas for additional learning in this area of practice.

Learning Objective 3: Locate, collect, and analyze relevant data. Record the initial data analysis, task, and progress toward completion. Critically reflect on the role of the problem analysis in policy development, difficulties encountered with locating or analyzing data, solutions developed, and the use of the data and analyses. Specify the justice, human rights, policy, or research issues related to the material and concerns. Finally, reflect on and assess the level of practice skills used in the data collection process, such as interview skills in acquiring salient data.

Learning Objective 4: Identify and analyze alternative options. Record the initial policy development and analysis task and steps taken to complete the assignment. Note and critically reflect on issues in choosing evaluation criteria, problems, or diverse viewpoints in the identification of policy options, the process for incorporating diverse views and the role of systematic analysis in building consensus, and the use (or nonuse) of systematic analysis in decision making. Consider how micro-service delivery and relevant policies coincide with each other in intention and implementation. Specify the justice, human rights, policy, or research issues related to the material and concerns. Self-assess the mastery of analytic skills, group process, decision-making skills, and areas for additional learning.

Learning Objective 5: Assess the feasibility of alternative policy options. Describe progress on activities relating to analysis of the administrative and political, social, and economic issues that arise with the adoption and implementation of new policies, projects, or programs. Describe and comment on understanding how implementation issues influence choices made about new initiatives. Specify the justice, human rights, policy, or research issues related to the material and concerns. Critically reflect on mastery of skills, strengths in these areas, and needs for additional learning and practice in this area.

Learning Objective 6: Prepare and present policy proposals. Throughout the year, as specific assignments for written and oral presentations of policy analyses are made, describe the nature of each assignment, and the steps for completion. The targeted audience is described, and the group's or individual's interests and potential uses of the material are analyzed. The ways the presentation is tailored to respond to these interests are described, and its effectiveness is assessed. Specify the justice, human rights, policy, or research issues related to the material and concerns. Practice skills used in presentations, and strengths and learning needs are identified, and self-assessed.

Learning Objective 7: Implement and evaluate policy recommendations. Describe specific assignments related to monitoring, advocacy, public education and related activities, and progress made toward completion. Describe and comment on understanding of the policy review and adoption process, the role of education and advocacy in influencing policy decisions, and the inclusion (or exclusion) of groups and interests in this process. Systematically evaluate policy recommendations. Specify the justice, human rights, policy, or research issues related to the material and concerns.

Critically reflect on mastery of skills, strengths, and needs for additional learning as a policy advocate.

Process Recording Format for Policy Practice

The following is a summary of a structured process recording format for policy practice described by Medina (2010) that examines the content and process involved in developing four policy practice core skills: analytical, political, interactional, and value clarifying skills.

The format includes an introduction describing the purpose of the session, the goals and objectives, and the context; the aim is to provide a brief explanation of the major reason or focus of the interaction, which usually involves an encounter between the student and a key stakeholder or stakeholders. This provides some history and aids understanding the student's role.

The columns, reminiscent of an accordion style process recording, provide a focus on three components of the competencies of (1) cognitive reactions, (2) affective reactions, and (3) reflections. A fourth column provides space for the field instructor's comments. The cognitive analysis "requires the student to examine the development of techniques and strategies used" (Medina, 2010, p. 40). The affective analysis provides an opportunity for students to demonstrate their understanding of the underlying emotive feelings operating for the student and stakeholders; it explains the possible subtext of the interaction. The reflective skills column or section offers students an opportunity to develop self-evaluative skills and future forecasting for possible next steps. The supervisor's comments section, like other forms of process recording, provides space for a focus on the themes that emerge from the interactions, strategies, interventions, and feedback on the use of skills for policy practice.

Sample Field Education Recordings

We include three sample recordings. The first is a narrative student recording that is followed by a verbatim recording of the supervisory session when the student's recording is discussed. The third example is an administrative student's log. After reading the recordings, consider the questions at the end of the scenarios.

Specialized Practice Level Student Narrative Recording

The student is placed in a small community hospital. Mr. X is a 46-year-old married electrician with two children age 10 and 12. He is an ex-Marine who returned from combat 2 years ago; he was admitted to the emergency room following an unexplained episode when he collapsed and fell unconscious, and when he came to, he was unable to move. His wife said she noticed her husband was having flashbacks over the previous few days, had been avoiding contact with his ex-Marine friends, and, uncharacteristically, was withdrawing from her and their children. She was not aware of any physical problems, but she is worried about his recurrent bouts of seemingly unprovoked anger.

Student's introduction: I was nervous about meeting with Mr. X. I knew that he was anxious to return home, but I also knew that his doctor doesn't think Mr. X is ready to be discharged. Although the tests on his heart were clear, other tests were needed and the doctor is concerned about possible underlying problems. I was not looking forward to the interchange. Also, the X family's problems are becoming worse rather than better. Mrs. X is worried about mounting bills, and she has been crying each time she visits her husband.

I met with Mr. X and his doctor together; when the doctor recommended that Mr. X remain in hospital for another few days, I could see Mr. X. tense up. The doctor left immediately, and I stayed to talk with Mr. X. He immediately burst out about the doctor's recommendation. I had difficulty responding to Mr. X's anger. I feel like I was unable to appease him or to help him.

Student's narrative: This is a snippet of the conversation I had with Mr. X after Dr. P. left.

I said to Mr. X, "I could see that you tensed up when Dr. P suggested that you stay in hospital a while longer. Am I correct that you may want to talk about this?" Mr. X let loose on Dr. P, on the hospital, on his wife (Where was she anyway?) and on me! He has been angry before, but this was *angry*! I listened and attempted to absorb his anger. I could see why (He was not expecting this news and was looking forward to going home). I interjected: "I understand your surprise. You know that Dr. P and his team do not consult me on this. They are the experts on what you need medically." (This seemed to only fuel his anger. So, I thought maybe I should step it up a little.) I said something like. "Mr. X., Dr. P has been a good doctor for you, he is making a recommendation for your health. He wants you to be fully ready for a return home and return to work. I know that you are disappointed, but we need to consider this plan. I want to help you. Let's talk about what your hopes are and what a miracle could look like" (Well, this didn't work either. I was uncomfortable; I noticed I ran away from his emotions. In fact, I see now that I was attempting to use Dr. P as the fall guy by using his positionality of expert and implying that I have nothing at all to do with this decision. I feel awful and stumped. I was trying to apply solution-focused therapy, I guess I didn't get it right. I feel that I have begun a good working relationship with Mr. X., and I was hopeful that we were on the right path with him and his wife. I know I should be thinking about next steps, but I am stuck. I know that I am still in the engagement phase but, now I need help with interventions.)

The session ended with my saying that perhaps the news of a stay in the hospital was a shock and that he needed time to think about this. I told him that I could call his wife, or perhaps he would prefer to call her. He replied that he didn't care. I told him I would call his wife and check back with him later.

Student questions for supervision: What should I do? Was I as far off target as it felt? I wondered about asking Dr. P to come back in but decided against it. Was that right? Now what?

Consider the following questions

> If you were the field instructor, how would you start the supervisory session on this process recording? What feedback would you provide? What is your prime concern from this

recording in setting a conducive environment for learning in supervision?
› What are the next steps for supervision, and what is your beginning learning focus? What competencies are embedded in this recording, and how do they support the learning focus you have identified?
› Does the information provided in this recording give you what you need to move forward in supervision with this student to set a conducive environment in supervision and guide learning objectives? If not, what information is missing? Would you adapt this format? If so, how? Are there other forms of recording you would like to use with this student? If so, what are they, and what are your reasons?

Verbatim Recording: Field Instruction Conference

The field instructor was eager to discuss the student's difficulties with Mr. X's feelings and to examine how she might have responded. She was concerned that the student seemed to assume that because the doctor had made a recommendation, exploring Mr. X's reactions to this could not be pursued. Although she thought about bringing the doctor back into the room, this seemed to be more about dealing with Mr. X's anger and to use Dr. P's authority rather than facilitate communication between Dr. P and Mr. X. or mediate a clearer explanation regarding Dr. P's recommendation. The field instructor was also worried that the student did not pursue Mr. X's underlying urge to go home and being discharged before clarity about his condition was gained. She wanted to make sure that the student had represented her interactions with Mr. X fully, or whether there might have been other parts of the conversation that she did not include in this narrative. She hoped to assist the student's understanding about Mr. X's seeming powerless and helpless situation and how this may be fueling his emotions about himself and his relationship with his wife. The field instructor also saw a need to clarify the student's use of solution-focused therapy, her decision making in general, and her understanding of the goals and purposes of contact she was pursuing with Mr. X. The following is a verbatim section of a field education supervisory session.

Field Instructor: There are several areas we need to cover. We need to spend some time on the specific goals and broader needs of Mr. X and his family and how we might explore how to support these needs while Mr. X.

focuses on getting well. We shouldn't forget that Mr. X is a veteran and how this may be playing a part in his illness and his coping. We also should review your decisions in this interaction and clarify the uses of solution-focused therapy in this situation for next steps. The student agreed, and we began going through her recording.

Student: Mr. X was so angry. I jumped in to defend myself, but I had a mixture of feelings here. First, I'm not sure that I agreed with the doctor's decision; why couldn't the tests be done on an outpatient basis? I felt like they were not being sensitive to the family's feelings of wanting Mr. X home.

Field Instructor: What else was going on in this situation? Let's break it apart. (The student could not tune in to Mr. X's range of emotions, nor was she taking all the information about Mr. X into account. We talked about this for a while.) I stated that it is also difficult to manage emotions over a decision we do not personally agree with. Was this part of what was going on for you and Mr. X?

Student: How do you handle that?

Field Instructor: It is challenging; feelings of being powerless get in the way, but I try not to let my own feelings interfere. I focus on the individual and family, stay with their feelings, allow them to get angry with me, and explore what other emotions or issues are operating but may be more difficult to express.

Student: I guess that is the other piece. I don't want him to be angry with me. I mean, I allowed him to express his feelings but with little encouragement on my part.

Field Instructor: I asked her how she could have stayed with Mr. X's expression of anger. We began to discuss anger, how uncomfortable it makes the student feel, and how she tries to avoid these feelings. We then moved to her attempt to shift the discussion with thoughts of applying solution-focused questions. I asked the student what she thought was happening here.

Student: Mr. X was getting very angry, and I did not relate to his anger.

Field Instructor: I suggested that the student seemed to be trying to neutralize Mr. X's anger.

Student: You're right! That's exactly what I did! I was trying anything to move away.

Field Instructor: We explored the risk of allowing Mr. X to become angry. (She thought about this and began to realize that she had an investment in being successful with the X family. It was the one family she felt had the most capacity to engage with, and she was eager to help them. We went on to discuss her desire to be successful and worthwhile, particularly in this environment that was intimidating to her (e.g., in a hospital, her chosen career goal, working in a host environment with an interdisciplinary team). She thought this would be her success case.)

Student: I'm beginning to understand. It makes it harder for me to risk their anger. I'm probably afraid they won't want to work with me. I remember how upset I was when Mr. X stated he did not need to see me any longer after I first met with him.

Field Instructor: (After establishing what was on the line with this family for the student, we went on to track the process in the remaining recording to see what was on the line for Mr. X.) I asked for clarification. It seems that because Dr. P. made a recommendation, you assumed that exploring Mr. X's reactions were only anger. Do you know why he is so eager to return home, or did you make some assumptions here?

Student: Well, he was certainly clear that he didn't want to be in hospital and he was making sure I heard! Looking at the recording she replied, "I can't believe it! Mr. X gets angry, says he doesn't care who calls his wife, and I jump in with skipping over it or attempting a clarification or intellectual explanation for why he is getting angry." The student laughed and said, "At least I'm consistent!"

Field Instructor: (We continued to identify the student's interventions that moved the discussion away from the anger being expressed, her assumption that Mr. X was angry at her instead of his situation, and went on to discuss how this self-preoccupation diverted her from considering the unexpressed guilt Mr. X. may be feeling knowing that his need for care was furthering his family's financial debt, the powerlessness he may be experiencing in relation to his illness, being subjected to an illness resulting from his military service, fearing something more was wrong, being hospitalized, not being able to work, and his wife's absence at the meeting) What else is he experiencing? What else needs attention?

Student: This is very helpful. My own feelings prevented me from exploring his or from looking at the broader needs of the situation! I'd like to watch for these digressions with my other families to see whether it looks and feels the same. I see that I was getting caught.

Field Instructor: Yes, I agree. Let's review your role here and let's revisit what your main purpose is in meeting with Mr. X. Let's also consider how more information from Dr. P might help.

(The student was meeting with the X family that afternoon, and we considered how she might work to catch herself, find an alternative way of managing the conversation, and make sure she is prepared with information on how to support this couple in considering the stresses affecting them, that is, clarification of Mr. X's condition, their finances, Mr. X's need for support, Mrs. X's need for support, and anything else they wish to discuss. In preparation for this shift of focus, we discussed the larger issues affecting this family and the lack of external supports. We looked up resources for returning veterans in the community, and the student made note of those that seemed suited to this family's needs. We did not clarify her use of solution-focused therapy in this session. I made a note to return to this.)

Discussion. The student's recording is focused on increasing awareness of managing difficult feelings. The field instructor is concerned about this factor in the student's work as it is clearly interfering with the student's ability to focus on identifying Mr. X's and his family's needs.

Here are some questions to consider:

1. Were there issues from the student's recording you identified as critical that were not addressed by the field instructor? Were there ways you might have intervened to address the student's preoccupation with managing Mr. X's anger? Did the field instructor miss opportunities to help the student consider her role with this individual and his family, her role in relation to the medical team, the possible implications of stigma regarding ableism and illness, and the probable need for continued health services, veteran care and services (excluding post-traumatic stress disorder as a possible underlying factor), unemployment services, and so on.
2. Consider the field instructor's efforts to broaden the student's perspective while not losing sight of the emotions expressed. How might the competencies and a rights- and justice-based framework support her attempts?
3. Does either recording format need adjustment for teaching purposes? What are the pros and cons of either format of these recordings? How might the format be improved for your task of review?
4. What would be the next step in this student's skill development to demonstrate progression toward competence? What other recording format or focus might be helpful to apply with this student?

An Administration Log Entry Example of a Specialized Practice Level Student

1. Brief Description of Assignment, Date of Log Entry, Week 4

   a. Overall assignment and connections to issues of rights and justice: The research project seeks to interview refugees from war-torn countries and document their needs. The relation to rights and justice seem clear to me.
   b. Specific tasks to be processed: continued progress on (a) literature review and (b) interviews with program participants.

2. Purpose and Need

   a. I am assigned to complete a literature review connected with the research project on asylum seekers and refugees from war-torn countries. The emphasis is on the methods they use to cope with the stresses of their situations. The literature review will give us information on identifying and assessing the coping strategies the population uses.
   b. New instruments must be found to manage the range of ages of the respondents. The focus is on finding ways to measure (at various age ranges) the relationship among social supports in times of forced displacement, such as for asylum seekers, unaccompanied minors, and such.
   c. Creation of workshops to help recruit participants. (One for service users and one for staff.)
   d. Additionally, I participate in data collection. Since my last entry, I interviewed a 19-year-old woman who sought asylum from Syria 4 years ago with her family. The interview lasted 2 hours and was conducted with my task supervisor.
   e. I am expected to contribute a social work perspective to my work, which is an ecological systems theory and a strengths-based perspective.

3. Task Plan

   a. Ongoing: Cofacilitate interviews with participants.
   b. Due in 2 months: Contact staff to brainstorm ways to increase recruitment, and a possible workshop has been proposed (to be held in 2 months). It is not clear what the

precise focus of this workshop should be. I have been thinking that a presentation about the aims of the project could be the focus, but some staff have suggested an educational trauma-informed workshop.
   c. Over 2 days this week: Work with other intern to format and compare literature review material.
   d. Ongoing: Follow up with individuals that expressed interest in participating in the study.

4. Necessary Resources

   a. Resources needed are mainly related to access to agency computers.
   b. I would like to be clearer about the conditions that prompted these individuals to leave their homes.

5. Considerations and Obstacles

   a. The main obstacles in this entry are the lack of participant participation and then the lack of follow-up after conducting the interview. The recruitment process is challenging; in addition to finding subjects, compliance with the institutional review board requires that to be eligible, the individual must be assessed to be at minimal risk. Although the people interviewed are minimal risk, they are coping with a lot. The material shared in the interviews is intense and represents the deep trauma they have experienced and continue to experience. The setting is so short staffed that it is difficult for the case managers to follow up in a timely way. This appears to be a major barrier for these individuals to cope better.
   b. More medical information and tools are being requested. I am having a hard time assessing what I should be focusing on as I am not sure what to include in the literature review. This week my task supervisor showed me how to add an additional setting on the computer program we are using. This will help in sorting the material. The age ranges of the respondents are also making the literature review difficult. The ages range from 18 to 65.
   c. The interviews themselves are challenging and time consuming.

6. Self-Assessment

a. I need some guidance on how to expand my literature search to include all the issues. Sometimes I wonder if instead I should be focusing my search before expanding it.
b. I need to do a better job of time management and setting work boundaries. I have been working outside my internship hours to complete the literature review as finding a computer in the setting on the days I am there is challenging. My course work is suffering. I also find myself thinking about the interviews I conduct quite a lot. The stories are horrifying.
c. I need to find ways to complete the literature review during placement times and have begun to see when the computers are free so that I can make a schedule to take advantage of this.
d. I am learning a lot. I am becoming more accepting of the challenges, and I believe I am more aware of my role. The interviews remain a challenge. In the latest interview my task supervisor noticed that I did not allow the respondent to tell her story, and I seemed to be trying to make her feel better by changing the subject. My task supervisor said I need to slow down and allow myself to listen more.

7. Progress and Next Steps

Literature review: Once the other intern and I compare notes, we will dedicate 1 day per week for the literature review.

a. Work to compile findings on the literature review in preparation for presentation.
b. Work with the other intern on literature review.

Recruit, follow up with participants

a. Brainstorm ideas to create workshops next semester.
b. Plan a recruitment workshop and a possible educational trauma-informed workshop.

Administrative

a. Update criteria for respondent eligibility.
b. Record interviews for review.
c. Find organizational tactics to become more efficient.

8. Agenda for Supervision

   a. What are ways to enhance my confidence in relation to the tasks I am assigned?
   b. How do I handle the pulls on my time and better balance expectations?
   c. How can I feel I am competent even though that I just began and am exposed to complex material and situations?
   d. I feel aware—almost too aware—of the issues of justice involved in this assignment and am somewhat overwhelmed about how and where to begin.

Consider the following questions:

1. If you were the field instructor, how would you start the supervisory session on this log? What feedback would you provide on this log? What is your prime concern from this log in setting a conducive environment for learning in supervision? Given that the work of the setting and this assignment provide opportunities to engage diversity and difference in practice and to advance human rights and justice, how would you focus the discussion to consider these competencies?
2. What are the next steps for supervision, and what is your beginning learning focus? What competencies are embedded in this recording and how do they support the learning focus you have identified?
3. Does the information provided give you what you need to move forward in supervision with this student to set a conducive environment in supervision and to guide learning objectives? If not, what information is missing? Would you adapt this recording format? If so, how? Are there other forms of recording you would like to use with this student? If so, what are they and what are your reasons?

CHAPTER 9

Shifting the Discourse

Beyond the Language of Challenges

Educating practitioners in our diverse, multicultural reality is a major challenge for social work educators. As such, we must continue to search for and develop new, creative, and alternative perspectives and means to train our students to work in an environment that is characterized by increased diversity. (Nadan, 2016, p. 54)

We social work educators are imperfect people who must never take for granted the extreme privilege and power inherent in the responsibility to impart professional knowledge, skills, and values to students. The question must be asked therefore: Can educators realistically multitask the disparate activities of teaching, mentoring, supervising, evaluating, and screening out students? There is no quick fix to the inherent ambiguity in the social work educator role. The best approach may be to recognize the responsibility to struggle honestly with the multidimensional identities of being a social work educator (Sowbel, 2012, p. 38).

This chapter examines how a justice-based perspective influences our ability to alter what we experience as problems in learning to seeing the potential in these obstacles as opportunities. Concepts such as noncompliance and resistance are examined and transformed into opportunities for understanding the contexts our students face as they tackle learning.

Those we teach, as with those we serve, are allowed space to explore fears, lack of confidence, and value conflicts that might stand in the way of educational success. Our efforts are bolstered by the clear outcome measures competency-based education provides to us and our students as we move together toward competent practice.

One of the major advantages of competency-based education is that it establishes a common agenda for teacher and student and makes clear and transparent what the end goals are and the work each party must do to accomplish them. In Chapter 3 we describe rubrics as "learning road maps" (p. 102). So it is not surprising for students and field instructors to get lost along the way. Many things interfere, from being unable to teach about a competence, missing the opportunity to teach students about a certain issue, the lack of assignments to encourage mastery of a competence, differences that make learning or teaching in a particular area more difficult, and personal reticence to talk openly about struggles. This is often when teaching and learning become derailed. In these instances, the competencies and the evaluative framework used can serve as much needed life preservers, reminding us and our students of our mutual agenda, the work we need to do to help each other, and the precious end goal of competence. The competencies avoid the personalization that can occur during particularly challenging times, and instead provide a shared mission.

Overcoming Obstacles: Creating Favorable Learning Environments

We argue that competency-based education provides support to the task of evaluating students because of the professionally agreed-on performance outcomes and the rubrics that guide our assessment. Everyone is working toward the same outcomes. Yet many challenges exist as we collaborate on the professional development and evaluation of students. Some of these difficulties relate to the complex nature of social work practice and the stresses of consistent change in the social environment, organizational structures, and higher education (Lager & Robbins, 2004; Sowbel, 2012). Other difficulties relate to our approaches to teaching, and some are connected to the students' journeys toward mastery. Perhaps it is the issue or our tolerance for certain behaviors or the length of time the issue goes on without change despite our efforts that spark difficulties. For one of us it is our frustration when suggestions are not followed; for another it is the student's ongoing reluctance to take initiative or the challenge of tackling learning needs. Our charge is to facilitate the creation of environments conducive to learning despite the external stresses placed on us by the realities of practice. Chapter 4 describes the conditions required for conducive learning environments. Although these characteristics may appear straightforward, they are often difficult to achieve. Obstacles exist; yet, each obstacle represents a potential opportunity to enrich learning. For example, how we use time and keep our commitment to have regular supervisory sessions on time rather than keeping students waiting or putting them off; how we negotiate setting time frames for work completion, distribute space, address our students, distribute resources; and the extent to which we include students in decision making are all ways to seize openings for teaching, balance power, and achieve mutuality. The challenge is to keep an eye on our goals and expectations while also recognizing that how we exercise our authority may engender feelings of powerlessness.

Pitfalls that inhibit achievement of a conducive learning environment may be related to inadequate time for supervisory sessions because expectations and demands conflict with the time needed for optimal student learning. Perhaps there is difficulty in achieving a balance between our professional role as gatekeeper and our role as supportive educator. Often conflict arises between the need to be flexible in being accommodating of the range of responsibilities students have, including those related to work, family, and school. We may fear that if we accommodate too much, we compromise control over the progress of the work, or the pressures of accountability and liability to the setting supersede what we can do in response to a student's need. We fear that making accommodations to meet student needs places professional standards in jeopardy, and it may seem that we are caught between these poles of obligation. Often, however, our dual responsibilities may be skillfully managed by considering a middle ground where we see that our role as educator is closely aligned with our other professional responsibilities (Bertrand Finch, Lurie, & Wrase, 1997).

Keeping an Eye on the Long-Term Goal of Autonomous Practice

Being one step away from direct service is likely to create inherent tensions and fears. After all, we are accountable for service delivery and have responsibility for the work assigned to students. Rather than allowing time for reflection and for students to identify possible next steps, it may seem easier and safer to tell students how to proceed in certain situations, both as a protection against something going wrong and as a time-saving device. Likewise, accelerating the pace of assignments to meet organizational demands or feeding students quick solutions to speed up the process to achieve a correct outcome are examples of an apprentice model that leads us to imply "This is the way I would do it," "Do it this way," or "I am more experienced than you, so follow my instructions carefully." Instead, helping students reach their own answers and allowing reasonable alternative approaches may take more time but is likely to yield longer term results and clearer assessments of strengths and growth points. Allowing a student to proceed with an intervention that is stylistically different from our own may seem to be risky or inefficient but allowing students to experiment and shape an authentic professional style aids in the development of their autonomy. Providing support during these explorations supports self-efficacy and encourages students' willingness to examine why something worked or didn't and to hone interventional skills.

We have a responsibility to provide an atmosphere where risk taking is expected and mistakes are tolerated and anticipated as part of the learning process. After all, discomfort does not always signal a bad learning experience. In fact, it often promotes self-reflection and results in powerful learning. Promoting an atmosphere where students can laugh and enjoy their efforts, including errors made, may help lessen discomfort and awkwardness. This is achieved by conveying patience, support, and positive expectations and communicating that we anticipate mistakes as a part of learning. It is impossible to offer reassurance that uneasiness will result in powerful learning, nor can we assume that all students will respond to our invitations for taking risks; therefore, we must continually reengage with the student's desire to proceed in the face of uncertainty. Creating opportunities for an environment that provides adequate structure, promotes risk taking, and allows students to test their ideas to develop their own practice style is essential. Of course, this requires careful oversight and tolerance for the missteps that are likely to occur.

Student satisfaction is frequently used as a measure of progress. Yet, satisfaction may be just as likely a signal that the student has remained in a comfort zone or is joyful about surviving with minimal changes or challenges. Likewise, students who take risks may experience embarrassment and discomfort as they tackle new learning, and their expressions of dissatisfaction are colored by this. However, risk taking and learning from mistakes should be valued; both have the potential for significant learning. This applies to us as well as our students.

False Expectations Resulting From Idealized Images

Students and field instructors have strong opinions about how each should respond and what they can expect from each other. Sometimes idealized pictures color perceptions and affect what we think is acceptable. Ideal images reverberate and inform current expectations (Goldstein, 1989; Navari, 1993). Research has shown that students' perceptions of good field instructors are largely dependent on availability, use of recordings, the amount of supervision, skill, and the quality of the learning experience (Bogo, 2010; Knight, 1996). According to Navari (1993), an ideal field instructor

> is the consummate provider of service, has a 6th sense, a mega-memory, is assertive, tactful, idealistic, pragmatic, has a strong sense of self, but is caring, sensitive, and empathetic. The Ideal Field Educator has a strong sense of justice, is organized in her brain...is comfortable working in two very different organizational environments—the academic and human service—and recognizes the strengths and weaknesses of both, genuinely enjoys students, teaching, and doing social work. In sum, the Ideal Type Field Educator can "leap tall buildings in a single bound." (p. 15)

Taking into consideration the other side of the coin, an ideal student

> lightens the field instructor's workload and can function autonomously with a minimum of supervision; looks up to the field instructor and validates his or her competence; is a source of pride and reflects well on the field instructor; appreciates the field instructor's time pressures and is mature enough to sometimes listen to the field instructor's concerns; learns easily, is organized and efficient, particularly in written documentation, and integrates theory and practice spontaneously; is open, self-aware and self-reflective but not inappropriately revealing, self-indulgent or self-centered; is empathic with, sensitive to, and caring about clients without being overly identified and showing poor boundaries with them; is confident in approaching clients but cautious in raising challenging or embarrassing questions in staff meetings; confides in the supervisor but does not expect the supervisor to lessen workload expectations and demands because of the student's personal problems; is committed to social work values and realizes that agency practice is valuable; helps clients and is good enough to be hired by the agency; and feels that the field instructor has been a wonderful role model. (Goldstein, 1989, pp. 12–13)

These idealized images may impede our management of the reality. Learning does not always occur in leaps and bounds. It does not always proceed in a linear fashion. Even students possessing many of these positive qualities and who make more than satisfactory progress can plateau or become stuck in any phase of field education. The plateau may be a stalemate instead of a normal progression in the learning process, and we are challenged by the task of assisting students to overcome these impasses or we may fear that our accommodations place professional standards in danger (Sowbel, 2012). Ongoing heightened anxiety, personality conflicts, or lack of growth and development as practitioners should concern us. These potential challenges often combine to create obstacles and frustration, and they need to be tackled when they impede progress. However, they should be viewed as indications that new learning may be stirring, and we should not be surprised by their appearance. In these situations, maintaining our trust in the process of education is threatened. Reframing concerns into thresholds and opportunities for learning is recommended as a way forward.

Reframing Challenges as Opportunities for Learning

Over time and as we gain experience in supervising students, we see that each individualized learning challenge offers a prospect for growth.

> Consider the student who, at the end of the year, brings the field instructor an oil painting he painted as a parting gift and says humbly, "I wanted you to have this. I know at times we had difficulties, and I was unable to demonstrate all I felt I was learning. I wanted to leave you this so that you might have more positive associations about my abilities." The interchange that followed invited a discussion of all that was implied in this student's disclosure and gift. Acknowledging the unspoken divide between the field instructor and student during the year and the many talents this student possesses but did not use during the placement were part of the conversation. This conversation provided an opportunity to hear the student's experience of feeling less than perfect, to affirm the student's talents, seen and unseen, and to acknowledge the student's accomplishments that allowed closure on a plane not previously possible. Or the student who was terminated from the program because of her continued difficulty in empathizing with the individuals she served writes a

thank-you note letting you know that she is working in a newsroom and finds the work interesting and rewarding. She states that she would not have found this career path if it had not been for the work you did with her to identify her talents and strengths alongside her growth points. Also consider the student who challenges you every step of the way, who asks for explanation after explanation on why a certain assignment must be done and who comes to placement one morning and says, "I have been thinking about some of the things you have said. I can see that I have been obstructive. I am not sure why, but I wanted you to know that I can see it now, and I am going to try to manage myself differently. I know you will help to keep me to this intention."

These students illustrate that the work can be hard for the student and for us but also that important lessons for teaching and learning may result. Learning may not proceed in a straight line, it is not necessarily instantaneous, and its effect is cumulative. Not only do we have idealized images of what a perfect student or field instructor looks like, we define success in varying ways. Not all students will be able to give us a chance to round out the experience, not all will be able to tell us about how their experiences have affected them, and not all the influences of the placement will be apparent or discernible when termination is required.

What appears as a conflict may signal that the student is on a new threshold of learning (Jones, 2008) or as students may come from other careers or have degrees in other fields, they may have different perspectives on professional values and behaviors that continue to cause confusion and potential conflict (Wise, 2005). The diversity among fields of practice, settings, and social work functions also may complicate perceptions of professional roles and behavior. For some students, the multiple strains related to employment, family, and school place enormous stress on them to perform efficiently and effectively; this is especially true for first-generation students. They struggle to juggle these competing and compelling responsibilities, which may erode their capacity or time for reflection on value conflicts and on how they should respond (Cataldi, Bennett & Chen, 2018; Oldfield, 2007). Other students may possess fixed ways of thinking, and unlearning may be necessary to progress. New learning that contradicts what life experience has proven otherwise to be true may be mistrusted or integrated more slowly; at these junctures transformative learning experiences may emerge (Jarvis, 2009, 2015).

Resistance or Responses to Learning?

The following excerpt from Shulman (1994) is an excellent example of how we can share our power and the authority of our expertise, overcome reluctance to learning, increase the demand for work, and be empathic and supportive all at the same time:

> I told Frank that I was expecting to get some of his material on his first interview, so we could discuss how he began. I hadn't received it and wondered why. Frank said he had been very busy that week. I told him I realized the load was heavy, but I thought he would have had time to [write] some notes on that interview. He paused and then said that he wasn't sure why it was necessary to do that. Frank had stiffened and looked quite defensive at that point. I told him that I had sensed that there might be some reluctance on his part to do it and that perhaps this would be a good time to discuss it. I asked why he felt it wasn't necessary. He said he couldn't see the purpose, and anyway he didn't think he could remember what went on at the sessions. I said that developing the skill of recall was a difficult one. I asked if he had ever written anything like this before. He said he had not. I told him perhaps I could have been more helpful in describing what I was asking for. I asked if he understood. He said he wasn't sure, so I explained that I did not want the whole interview but rather some brief comments about the conversation in the beginning, a summary of how the interview went, some more detail about any parts he was interested in discussing, and how it ended. I told him I thought it wasn't easy as a new student to share his work with me, but I wanted to reassure him that I wasn't asking to snoop or to be critical. I felt that if I had some of the detail of what he was saying and doing with his clients, I might be more helpful to him. I asked him if it was true that he had been concerned about what I would do with the records. He said he was, and that he felt that the first interview hadn't gone very well at all. He was embarrassed to present it. I told him that I didn't expect these interviews to go perfectly and that I thought by going over some of his work with clients I might be able to help him identify what he did that went well, as well as what he could do better. I then asked if he could recreate from memory some of the details of this first interview and I would try to show him what I meant. I said I was willing to work from his memory of the experience, this time, but that the next time I would be expecting a written record. (p. 35)

New learning often engenders tensions and emotions resulting from a challenge to familiar ways of looking at and experiencing the world. In the previous example, Shulman (1994) adeptly responds to his student's struggle with patience and empathy. He shares his part in the equation, finds ways to explain his reasons for his request, and reaches beyond the student's hesitancy to grasp the student's desire to learn. Resistance is an inherent response to learning, and anxiety related to the evaluation of performance is expected and normal. Resistance to learning can be reframed as simply a response to change and a protection against exposure; it emerges for various reasons that expand our understanding and abilities to respond (Brookfield, 1990), including viewing the struggle as an opportunity for identity reconstruction (Butin, 2005a, 2005b). These conceptions of the many sources of individualized responses to new learning help us to view this resistance in innovative ways.

Reframing Resistance

Reframing resistance or noncompliance as a response to facing the challenges of new learning provides a glimmer of hope and possible avenues for intervention. For example, a student's hesitation to take on an assignment may be misunderstood as resistance, whereas the hesitation may simply be a request for further explanation, a desire to request a different activity, or a sign of a lack of confidence. Some learners may have negative associations with learning. They may have struggled with undiagnosed learning challenges or may have been told they were too dumb to learn or will never graduate. They may come to field education with these encoded perceptions of themselves, and a fear of failure may inhibit their ability to tolerate moving ahead without clear and precise direction. Students may feel that asking questions is equated with being ignorant or foolish. Challenges to their values and differing dimensions of identity and worldviews may cause conflict and confusion. Past experiences may have shaped expectations about authority, disclosure, communication styles, and topics that should not be discussed (Brookfield, 1990). The following section adapts Brookfield's (1990) identified factors associated with resistance to new learning:

> Low opinion of oneself as a learner: Developing a self-image as a learner involves regarding oneself as someone who can succeed and is able to acquire new skills and knowledge. This is not always easy to achieve. If students are not used to having supports as they tackle new learning, they might assume that

we will approach them in the same unsupportive and exacting manner. Understanding their experience of receiving feedback in this context is essential.

- Managing uncertainty and ambiguity: Routine, habit, and familiarity are appealing and reassuring. Therefore, it can be expected that some students approach new learning situations by seeking set rules and guidelines. Some students are uncomfortable with the uncertainty and ambiguity inherent in professional practice, and we may need to provide guidelines and a well-defined structure before they can move into uncharted territory and before we can accurately assess their capacity to manage uncertainty.
- The ups and downs of learning: As we learn something new, we often find that a yearning to return to the comfortable certainties of the past follows an initial assumption of new ideas, attitudes, or actions. When the uncertainty or lack of structure becomes overwhelming, students naturally revert to known and comfortable ways of working or habits that have worked before. This return to familiar or safer ground may be misinterpreted as resistance to adopting new methods or ideas, but it is often temporary and is the second part of two steps forward and one step back.
- Lack of clear expectations: If students are unsure of what is expected of them or of the criteria that will be used to judge them, they may resist and be mistrustful. An explanation of actions and skills associated with the competencies provide support in this area. Still, we might assume that everything we have discussed is clear and understood. However, as new terms are introduced, students may not have reference points that help them to understand the terms. We should frequently ask students to tell us in their own words what we have just communicated to them to confirm their depth of understanding or to discover alternative meanings and interpretations they may have. For example, words such as *engagement, contracting, assessment,* and *use of self* may have alternative meanings to students. They may understand the concepts intellectually but find it difficult to apply them. It is useful to give students permission not to understand and to encourage dialogue until they do.

> Personal discomfort and objections: Field instructors or students may dislike each other for any number of reasons, and this can interfere with learning. For example, a clash in personal styles, such as a field instructor who is more structured and formal than a student who is very informal in style and approach, may create a level of discomfort that interferes with daily interactions. In addition to clashes in personal style, there may be identity differences including biases, prejudices, a host of isms, and power and privilege issues that contribute to the dislike or distance between field instructor and student intern. As stressed throughout this book, these issues should be addressed in the supervisory relationship; otherwise they will interfere with learning and the creation of a climate conducive to learning. However, students do not have to enjoy us to learn from us, and we do not have to enjoy students to teach them. Differences can become valuable learning experiences for students as they learn to work with people in their professional world. This may also apply to the setting; students may be less than pleased by their placement and feel they were not given their first choice. In these situations, we can assist students to examine adjustments that might produce a better fit. Students may need assistance to sort out what would create good enough learning experiences as opposed to what they define as characteristics of an ideal field education experience.

> A clash between learning and teaching styles or levels of expectation: Sometimes the mismatch is not related to personality differences but to how the content or material is presented and how students are expected to learn the new material. For example, an assignment related to the impending death of a child's mother may be too close to a student's personal experience over the recent loss of a close friend. This personal association may make the task of dealing with the subject matter difficult, discussions may focus on concepts of death and dying that are too abstract for the student to absorb, or perhaps the student does not feel able to express the emotional discomfort accompanying the assignment. Any one of these situations may heighten the student's distress and impede learning.

> Embarrassment or shame connected to not knowing: Most of us want to avoid looking foolish in public and want to do

things we know we can do well. We may resist learning activities that occur in overly public forums such as making presentations at staff meetings or co-leading groups with senior staff members. Fear of looking foolish can prevent students from trying new approaches or strategies. Yet trying new roles and experimenting with new interventions are important aspects of learning. Being encouraged to experiment under our guidance involves supporting students as they navigate the risk taking involved. Our role is to help students bridge the known with the unknown and provide opportunities to experience success that leads to the ability to tackle more and more complex learning.

> Lack of connection or engagement in the learning: If the assignments are not connected to their goals and career objectives, or if students are not helped to understand the meaning of the work as it relates to the competencies and their professional development, they may reject or resist them. Students want to feel that the learning is meaningful and that their efforts are relevant to their goals. This can be a heightened issue in today's climate as students accrue high levels of debt to obtain graduate education or when students work full-time, have family responsibilities, and carry a full-time academic load.
> Misjudging readiness for the task: Students who find no way of letting us know that the task is simply beyond their grasp will let us know through their reluctance to begin.
> Value conflicts: Student difficulties are frequently related to conflicts arising from clashes between personal and professional values. Students may feel as if their professional values were challenging their allegiance to their personal values, and a crisis may result.

As we discuss in Chapter 5, this last issue addresses reactions to new learning that require a change in perspective or value orientation, especially relating to "theoretically complex, politically volatile, and culturally debated educational issues" (Butin, 2005a, p. 110). According to Jones (2008), in Butin's view, there are "four prevalent conceptualizations of student resistance to social justice education and cross-cultural learning" (p. 69). These perspectives view the student's resistance as a "fixed response" (Butin, 2005b, p. 174). Such static positions might be perceived as intellectual inability to understand (failure), a lack of racial identity self-awareness (unknowing), a seeming desire to maintain a privileged status (uncaring), or a reaction against the norms being taught (alienation). These views emerge from a negative perspective of the student's response and do not offer avenues for productive dialogue. Instead, Jones explains Butin's alternative view of seeing resistance as "identity (re)construction" (Jones, 2008, p. 69). This alternative perspective offers a prospect for resolution. Instead of viewing the student's response as fixed, we see the student as being on a precipice. There is potential for movement, and our understanding of the student's reaction provides clues for how to approach the presumed stalemate.

Briefly, how we view a student's resistance creates mindsets that affect our responses. Seeing resistance as *failure* prompts concerns about the student: "This student just does not get it." (Jones, 2008, p. 69). Seeing resistance as *unknowing* suggests that the student is not developmentally prepared to fully understand the complexity of the issue: This student is just not ready. Viewing resistance as *alienation* refers to a student's refusal to accept a new perspective that is interpreted by the student as a threat: This student refuses to see the need to reconsider the position; she is stuck and unwilling to shift. Seeing resistance as *uncaring* refers to the student's avoidance of the issue, which is considered not real or not having merit: This student denies that oppression exists; he just will not accept that male White privilege is an issue; it just doesn't matter to him (Jones, 2008).

However, reframing resistance as a student's process of *identity reconstruction* suggests that the resistance is part of the ongoing and dynamic process of maintaining and reformulating our sense of ourselves. It is the outward manifestation of movement toward self-authorship. In this perspective, observing a student's negative reaction normalizes the response, recognizes it as a declaration of the student's state, and provides clues on how we might respond to assist the student's growth and movement. Butin (2005b) wrote,

> teaching for social justice should therefore be more accurately articulated as teaching for identity destabilization and reconstruction. The proposition is as follows: Identity destabilization enhances tolerance of ambiguity of selfhood; enhanced tolerance of ambiguity in turn widens the scope of openness to alternative and/or opposing perspectives of selfhood; openness to alternative perspectives offers the potential for the reconstitution and redeployment of one's identity. (p. 7)

The implication of this perspective for us is we recognize that our students courageously embark on a path of social work education that often touches them profoundly. They entrust themselves to us, and we are responsible to observe, respect, and respond in ways that encourage and support the development of their professional selves. Consider the following questions that heighten awareness of the natural responses to new learning that may create obstacles in the progression of learning:

> How intimidating is the placement setting? Are students given ample support if the setting involves performance that entails complex interactions with the public, complex institutional hierarchies, or challenging situations?
> How have students been helped to feel supported to take the risks involved in new learning? For example, have implications of success or failure been considered? Has our evaluative role been openly discussed? Has the student's mutual role in assessment been discussed? Have expectations been discussed? Has the student's understanding of the expectations been explored?
> How do students approach uncertainty and ambiguity? Are students supported in their right not to know the answers to their questions and in their requests for help? What guidance is provided to help manage the uncertainty and discomfort often associated with cross-cultural learning? Have we shared our own paths through this journey?
> Are students prepared for the inevitable conflicts that arise between their personal views of themselves and their multiple layers of identity, difference, and social location and those of the people and communities they serve? How are personal and professional value conflicts handled?
> What are the experiences of microaggression (racial, sexual, homophobic, transphobic, etc.) in the setting, social work program, community, or elsewhere that inhibit student learning and need attention?

Educational Learning Contracts When Obstacles Emerge

Educational learning contracts are a vital tool in facilitating alternative responses to the learning challenges that inevitably surface. Learning contracts are used when complications arise in establishing a targeted learning plan, or when our efforts to respond to the obstacles that arise do not have the anticipated result or the challenges continue, reappear, or worsen. The structures and resources associated with the educational assessment and final evaluation offer opportunities to make our concerns explicit, but when problems emerge that signal inadequate progress toward competency, it is important to spell out observed complications in the student's growth and development and to delineate reciprocal responsibilities toward seeking resolution of each stakeholder—field instructor, field liaison, task supervisor, and student. When used in the context of this type of problem solving, educational learning contracts contain all the same components of initial educational learning plans discussed in Chapter 3, but learning contracts focus on problem-solving strategies. Like general educational learning plans, a learning contract includes consideration of the student's assets, the goal of providing opportunities for the student to demonstrate success whenever possible, and defined strategies for achieving objectives. In addition, as difficulties prompt the need for a learning contract, a clearly defined learning need is specified, a description of the learning obstacle and what has already been attempted toward resolution is included, and strategies responding to the learning needs along with responsibilities and time frames for those involved are spelled out. In this situation the contract is written, it involves the field liaison, is often signed by everyone involved, and it becomes part of the student's academic record.

When a task supervisor is a member of the learning team, this individual plays an important role in understanding the full parameters of the student's performance challenges and also in helping implement the strategies devised. For these reasons, it is essential to consider how the task supervisor is best involved in this process.

In summary, the educational learning contract is an educational learning plan that is used when problems emerge that signal the student is having difficulties meeting expectations. The field liaison is involved in formulating the learning contract, which builds on the aims of an educational plan (see the Chapter 3 Appendix). Following are some things to keep in mind for the learning contract:

> The process parallels the reciprocal, collaborative process of contracting for services with service users. We are providing an educational service to student consumers, encouraging self-awareness and the student's assumption of responsibility for learning. Learning contracts are derived from a shared experience; that is, they require mutual participation, the

expectations and concerns of all parties concerned are made explicit, and strategies and recommendations are created together and involve all members of the learning team.
> Priorities are formulated by focusing on the specific challenges or identified obstacles and the best way to address them.
> Specificity is essential in describing the issue of concern to form a baseline for assessing progress and identifying gaps.
> Time frames are set to guide the work. The contract is focused and evolves over time and is bound by the opportunities and time available as not everything there is to learn can be achieved in the time allotted.
> Ongoing review and evaluation are essential. Recurrent review is required, and the contract is meant to be dynamic. If further obstacles surface, these need examination, and strategies may need adjustment. Negotiation and redefinition of the tasks occur as the work of field placement proceeds and the time involved is assessed. In fact, to support fluidity and natural evolution over time, we should create opportunities in weekly supervision to reflect on progress being made and provide the opportunity for adjustment as needed.
> Reciprocal accountability is built in to the process; that is, students are encouraged to take responsibility for learning so that field instructors, task supervisors, field liaisons, and students have individual, complementary, and shared (although not necessarily equal) responsibilities.

Those involved are encouraged to consider the following questions in relation to forming the learning contract when addressing observed obstacles in learning:

> Have the identified challenges or obstacles been explained?
> How clear are the stated goals and objectives? Are the competencies and associated required skills made clear and understood by the student?
> Are there areas the student and field instructor disagree on in these goals or objectives?
> How clear are the strategies for achieving what needs to be done?
> Are any barriers or constraints anticipated in achieving what is hoped for?

› Have the time frames and reciprocal responsibilities been made clear?

Program Policies and Procedures When Challenges Persist

Often prior to calling for an educational learning contract, several steps are taken when students experience difficulties in field education, including clarifying learning objectives, changing assignments, assigning remedial work, and setting clear expectations and time limits on requirements. These decisions are often made in consultation with the field liaison and are always part of our ongoing discussions and reviews with students. The end-of-term evaluations and the process leading up to them provoke a reexamination of progress made and provide another opportunity to tackle a student's individualized learning challenges; however, students should not be surprised with our concerns at the end-of-term evaluations. Prior dialogue should have occurred, and the ratings and written components of the evaluation reflect these prior discussions. This begins in the sixth week plan and our oral reviews.

Clearly, we should not wait until the evaluation is due to express our concerns, but it can happen as implied above, that in the final preparation of the evaluation we see the total picture differently and decide to reflect it in the evaluation. In these situations, it still holds true that the student should have no surprises in the final evaluation. We need to explain our thinking, make suggested modifications, allow time for students to consider our comments, and examine whether we have provided adequate learning opportunities. The major difference between written and oral evaluations is that students see in writing what has been verbally discussed over time. It sometimes happens that students do not hear our concerns in the way we mean to communicate them. Because the written word sometimes has a more powerful effect than either we or students anticipate, the student may not recognize having heard our concerns until we have concretized them in our written summaries on sixth-week reviews or end-of-term evaluations.

We usually have no difficulty in identifying students' strengths, describing our stars or neophytes to the profession, or praising students' accomplishments. We may have more difficulty critiquing the work, especially when the students seem unaware of continuing limitations in areas they have been working hard to improve on or when some extenuating circumstances have contributed to the limitations. Our avoidance of making verbally explicit or putting in writing the full extent of our concerns about the student's performance is another pitfall. We often express our discomfort in confronting students with a negative critique of their performance by saying, for example, "I did not want to write this down. I am afraid of the student's reaction, which will only make my work more difficult"; "I didn't think I spent enough time addressing grant-writing skills in field education, so I didn't feel it was fair to comment on the demonstrated lack of skill in this area"; or "There were so many difficulties in a regular flow of assignments, I didn't feel I had enough evidence to judge whether it was the student or the lack of opportunity for her to demonstrate greater competence." These comments reflect blocks in seeing feedback, ongoing review, and evaluation as important tools in our teaching. They also signal difficulties in the ability to confront challenges and concerns. One way to tackle these complications is to create a regular time in supervision to review progress made or not made and to self-reflect on our avoidance of conflict. If task supervisors are involved, including them and confirming their impressions are crucial.

If challenges continue, discussion on a change of placement or field instructor and extending the time in the placement may also be considered (Bogo, 2010; Kilpatrick, Turner, & Holland, 1994; Power & Bogo, 2002). These decisions are made in consultation with the field liaison, and as noted previously, an educational learning contract is a valuable tool in these situations.

Most social work programs have clear and precise procedures that recognize the rights of all parties concerned when discontinuing a placement or dismissing students. These policies and procedures are supports in the most difficult situations. Due process protects the student and provides a framework that offers the student every possible effort to succeed. Even when the complications seem evident, determining the legal basis for student dismissal from the placement setting or social work program is often required (Raymond & Sowbel, 2016). Certainly, the expression of questionable values or inappropriate or unethical behaviors that provoke questions about the student's suitability for the profession warrant working toward improved behavior. Questions about how the student was admitted to the social work program in the first place are futile. Once a student is admitted, it is essential to move toward assessment and document the cause for termination, which might include consistently poor academic or field performance, inappropriate or questionable behavior, inability to meet technical standards that interfere with meeting required performance expectations, or outright violations of the NASW Code of Ethics, which is a guide for behaviors that indicate cause for dismissal. However, learning about ethics is also a learning goal, and one breach of ethics during the learning process may not lead to automatic dismissal from a social work program. The seriousness of the incident or the pattern and duration of unethical conduct are causes for concern. Even situations that signal immediate removal involve following the program's specified due process.

Once a student demonstrates inability to modify actions or to shift toward performance improvements, the program's processes of review take precedence. Although the field instructor's input and professional evaluation of student competency are needed and valued, these processes usually do not involve the field instructor other than documentation and a detailed account of the steps taken to support the intern. These policies and procedures must be followed to protect students' rights, yet it is important to acknowledge that structural inequities permeate social work and field education just as they do in the rest of the world. This reality requires us to be watchful in protecting students' rights through the assessments and learning opportunities we provide. We do this while also protecting the process of education and our professional responsibilities.

Marginally Acceptable Performance

Grievous and serious actions on the part of students are more easily defined than those that signal marginal performance. Marginally acceptable competence is often characterized by uneven performance. That is, students show ability in some situations, and then it seems to disappear in others. They fail to demonstrate a consistent basic level of competence. Perhaps there is improvement, but the pace is slow. Some students' anxiety levels remain heightened over an extended period, or the anxiety prohibits appropriate progression in achieving learning goals and objectives. Students who are excessively anxious about their field performance are often reluctant to take the necessary risks for new learning and may seem stuck or unable to reach the next level of skill. Some may need an intensive level of oversight that seems appropriate at the start of placement but continues beyond expectations. We become task masters, and this wears on our ability to not be annoyed or disappointed or to question the student's ability to achieve a level of self-autonomous practice or to reach performance expectations for entry-level social work practice.

The obstacles that emerge often are unclear, inconsistent, and on the cusp between barely acceptable and unacceptable. These barriers are as varied as the students. Challenges may emerge that relate to a student's seemingly rigid approach, reluctance to take direction, or apparent lack of concern, motivation, or commitment to the task, which is often exasperating. Each of these issues requires careful consideration in an environment of ongoing assessment. Our efforts to address them and the student's responses should be reviewed with the field liaison to consider possible next steps. Meetings to craft a specific educational learning contract are often required.

Failure to Meet Field Education Performance Criteria

Behaviors that most often signal failing performance are ongoing open defiance; avoidance of learning; lack of communication; continued breeches in professional behavior; inability to self-regulate behavior, which directly affects progress; or failure to engage in self-reflection or to take responsibility for learning. These behaviors hamper our ability to teach. Some students demand continuous reassurance and expressions of positive regard from us, and they may not hear our warnings or direct expressions of concern. They may negatively interpret any attempt to provide constructive criticism as an attack on them. In these situations, it is often very helpful to have three-way conferences with field liaisons who can reinforce expectations regarding self-reflective practice and clarify roles and expectations. Field liaisons act as translators between us and our students to lessen the miscommunication that may occur. The involvement of the field liaison also removes us from the role of task master and shifts to a shared responsibility between the social work program and the setting, freeing us to reestablish a teaching focus over and above the struggles.

Despite focused efforts to overcome the teaching challenges presented, we may conclude with the field liaison that students either will not or cannot meet performance expectations. In these situations, it is essential to be aware of the social work program's policies and procedures for dealing with difficulties in student performance. Confronting students to clarify the extent or seriousness of the concerns involves affirming what students are proficient in while making clear the specifics of our concerns. The field liaison is a valuable resource in these discussions and deliberations. In the long run, we may feel relieved to terminate the placement, but we are often left with feelings of guilt, failure, or shame at not being able to help a student succeed in the placement.

On the other hand, field instructors report finding the gatekeeping role challenging and stressful (Bogo, Regehr, Power, & Regehr, 2007; Finch & Imogen, 2013). Several factors account for these difficulties and the resulting tendency to rate students higher than students might rate themselves or is demonstrated in their performance. Determining whether the student's performance is within an acceptable range is often "difficult, demanding and complex" (Brookfield, 1990, p. 132), and field instructors may have received little guidance on the role of gatekeeper (Miller & Koerin, 2012). Specific guidelines and criteria are often lacking, and this is an area where competency-based education can reinforce our work. The specified outcomes provide clear goals to strive for. The educational learning contract is an essential component in helping to determine failing performance.

When Disruption and Replacement Appear to Be Needed

Throughout this book we encourage a rethinking of approaches to teaching when identifying and attempting to meet students' learning needs. Removing students from placements is disruptive for all concerned and therefore is not considered the first choice of intervention when complications in field education arise. The recommendation for replacement is almost always connected to the attempts to fulfill the requirements of a learning contract. The challenge includes remaining committed to reflecting on how conditions might be improved and seeking alternative responses for resolution that may include consideration of each person's role (Ornstein & Moses, 2010). However, despite all good intentions and adjustments, it will happen that students' needs are not being met in the setting or by the field instructor's efforts. Sometimes it is challenging to discern where the obstacle is or even how to best resolve it.

A change of placement might be recommended by field instructors or field liaisons to evaluate student capabilities in a new and different learning environment. We may realize that the strategy for meeting a learning objective for the student requires a different setting that may more adequately meet specific learning needs (Ornstein & Moses, 2010). For instance, students who have difficulty focusing on crises or whose anxiety is heightened in certain situations may need a change to a setting that provides more of a balance between crises and ongoing work or between short- and long-term assignments. It may also happen that students change their educational focus and career goals during their studies. Students who initially want to work in a micro practice environment may decide that a macro practice environment is better suited to their professional development and career goals. Reflect on the following questions and issues when considering whether disruption of a placement is warranted:

> How clear are we about the type of setting or field education supervision needed for this student?

- Identify the different styles of learning and teaching between us and our students. Have these differences been discussed? How adaptable are we in our approaches to teaching? Can compromises be achieved? Are the differences of such a nature that a divide exists that cannot be managed?
- How are issues of power and authority understood in the supervisory relationship? How open has communication been between the student and field instructor? What processes have been modeled for the student in supervision? For instance, how is self-disclosure managed? How is curiosity and exploration of alternative perspectives on the work integrated into discussions?
- How different is this setting from what has been identified as more ideal? Are there ways the current setting might adapt to the needs identified?
- Is the setting a place where the student can learn and reach full potential? Does the student face daily microaggressions based on identity or dimensions of difference? To what extent is the student given an equal voice in evaluating what the issues are or the solutions chosen?
- Does the substantive area of work in this setting present challenges? Are there methods of teaching that may make them more tolerable? How flexible can the setting be in allowing different choices in assignments? How intimidating is the context of the field placement? Are students given ample support if the setting involves high-profile performance? If a task supervisor is involved, is it necessary to fine-tune the communication and support offered?
- How clear is the student about what is expected? How closely aligned are the learning goals and expectations with the student's expressed career goals? How clear have we been in explaining the rhythm of ups and downs in learning new skills?
- Have attempts been made to strategize with the field liaison? Has a specific educational learning contract been established that sets clear objectives, strategies, and responsibilities for the student, liaison, and field instructor?

When Disruption Occurs

When students struggle in their field placement experience for whatever reason, and they have to be replaced, future success is highly dependent on their transition to a new setting and support from the new field instructor. Even when replacement is needed for reasons other than questions about the student's performance, the reality is that often field education departments struggle to find field instructors who are available in the middle of a semester or who are willing to take a student who might need additional support to succeed. Replacement might take longer than usual, which further complicates the situation. How different might it be if the social work program is able to establish structures to serve these students?

Field education department administrators can prevent these additional complications by becoming proactive. They can expect that mismatches will occur, and planning for this inevitability signals good management. Recruiting field instructors who agree ahead of the crisis to accept a student who needs replacement preempts a crisis resulting from finding a placement and creates a cadre of field instructors with a special role and focus. These field instructors can be recruited and offered advanced seminars or workshops while they wait to receive a student. Content in these seminars includes defining the potential challenges and how to facilitate learning for students who have experienced discontinuance because of a range of factors. By implementing this form of support, field instructors are prepared, ready, and energized to take on this special role, and students experience this eagerness and attentiveness as support and feel welcome. Additionally, the replacement process is more immediate, and the field instructor has time to prepare the setting, staff, and other interns for a student who will begin later in the semester. This is just one example of how structural changes might support anticipated difficulties.

Other efforts might involve creating skill labs for students at social work schools before they enter their field settings, which might preempt difficulties and provide training on tasks that are often related to challenges such as conducting intakes, writing progress notes and summaries, biopsychosocial assessments, or the differences in various recordings for micro to macro assignments. Another may be to work with classroom professors who could accept temporary field placement assignments to bridge the gap before finding a suitable replacement setting. Attempted solutions need to be shared so that field education departments might better respond to disruptions and questions about performance.

Pitfalls That Signal We Are at the Root of the Difficulties

Sometimes we present obstacles that may include a gap between learning needs and our teaching style, lack of teaching skills and experiences, difficulties in responding to the student's worldview and lived experiences, adherence to certain practice perspectives, personality or value conflicts, or difficulties in maintaining a conducive learning environment. As we gain experience, we realize that we cannot teach in only one way and that our teaching style must adapt to different learning styles and patterns. Over time, we develop an understanding of our strengths and weaknesses, and this understanding guides our ongoing development of skills.

The process of becoming a field instructor involves several phases of development (Blair & Peake, 1995; Carroll, 2010b; Dearnley, 1985). New field instructors may become preoccupied with technique or may overteach by talking too much, providing all the answers, taking over the work, and even thinking for students. A tendency toward dictating behaviors or expecting students to do things our way may demonstrate a lack of confidence and may be interpreted by students as our lack of trust in their abilities and skills. The opposite may also happen, and we may opt for more unstructured teaching, which leads to a lack of focus, vague directives, and unclear expectations. Equally, we may begin with flexibility in our expectations but run out of patience when students do not respond and instead seem to take advantage of our kindness. It can also happen that task supervisors are faced with behaviors or performance difficulties before we become aware of these issues, there may be differences in our expectations of the student, or there may be subtleties in differing approaches to the problems that confuse attempts for a remedy.

Students may interpret our or the task supervisor's flexibility as a lack of concern about details and misinterpret intentions for acceptance and leniency. Students may say something like, "You always accepted my reasons for my being late; I never knew it was an issue," or "My task supervisor is not concerned about this." These are clues to be more direct in our communication, provide feedback, initiate open communication, and perhaps to be less conflict avoidant. These are opportunities for us to model behavior and responses. We might reply, "You are correct. I avoided being more direct with you about your late arrivals. Let's talk about this now so that we can move forward together with new understanding." Or if the problem concerns communications with the task supervisor, we might say, "Thank you for sharing this potential cause of the confusion. Let's figure out together now how we should address this and how we might share our views with your task supervisor going forward." If the concern had been previously addressed, we could say, "Let's review the last time you were late, and we discussed this together. I recall saying that timeliness is critical to practice and that I am concerned about the difficulties you were having in being on time. I am wondering what you heard in this communication." Are there issues related to this that we have not discussed and that make this a challenging expectation to meet? Can you help me understand what the challenges are so that we can move to clearer communication about the related difficulties and what adjustments may be needed?"

Students who are unsure about our positions or think we are uninformed about their worldviews and value orientations will feel uncomfortable talking to us about multiple dimensions of their identity and on how they connect with what is expected of them. As discussed in Chapter 2, our ability to open the dialogue to include discourse about difference and issues of power and privilege offers an avenue for meaningful exchange.

Finally, unethical behaviors can blur the boundaries and challenge the teaching-learning relationship. Students have various reactions to ineffective field supervision, ranging from passivity to outright hostility, and not all students will seek assistance. Students often suffer through inadequate field education rather than call attention to the situation and are reluctant to share thoughts and feelings with field liaisons or with us (Baum, 2011; Bogo et al., 2007; Knight, 2016; Litvak, Bogo, & Mishna, 2010).

Several studies of student reactions to their field experiences point to serious concerns. Incidents of insensitive, indifferent, authoritarian, accusatory supervision, abuse of power, and unprofessional behavior have been reported (Barlow & Hall, 2007; Baum, 2011; Ellis, 2017; Gelman, Fernandez, Hausman, Miller, & Weiner, 2007; Giddings, Vodde, & Cleveland, 2003). These contributions to the literature confirm our need to examine our behaviors and teaching expertise. Students are often aware of the misuse of power but feel helpless, vulnerable, and unsure of how to seek help. It is not uncommon for students to obtain advice from their faculty liaisons or the program's director of field education on how to manage complications in supervision, but others may feel caught and powerless to reach out (Litvak et al., 2010).

The Explicit and Implicit Power of Our Role

According to Foucault (1994),

> power is not evil. Power is games of strategy.... I see nothing wrong in the practice of a person who, knowing more than others in a specific game of truth, tells those others what to do, teaches them, and transmits knowledge and techniques to them. The problem in such practices where power—which is not in itself a bad thing—must inevitably come into play, is knowing how to avoid...domination effects. (p. 40)

Here Foucault hints at the potential dangers in the exercise of power of our role. Recognizing the inherent power differentials between us and our students is a start to how we enable our students to question authority, that is, us. This does not mean that we erase the authority of our role. Management of the explicit authority invested in us by our profession and the social work program provides an opportunity for students to practice and apply their growing understanding of the effects of oppression, dominance, and discrimination. After all, we are a required relationship.

As field instructors, we implicitly exercise our power in how we teach and how we communicate on a day-to-day basis with our students and colleagues. Remember, our students are not blank slates. They are developing their powers of observation, and they have their own lens to assess our approaches to them and to others. Students must become active and have dialogues with us, but it is incumbent on us to create the climate for this to occur and to invite students to accept their own part in creating and maintaining their role as active learners and teachers. Of course, not all may go smoothly.

It is not unusual for our students to come from historically marginalized, underrepresented, and oppressed populations. The majority are women, and a growing number are first-generation students or from communities experiencing economic stress. Our students bring their own expectations of how authority figures will respond to them and how multiple layers of identity will play in the mix. They will need permission to practice ways of identifying their own power and to apply new ways of sharing power (Granello, 1996; Litvak et al., 2010; Messinger, 2007; Newman et al., 2009; Ornstein & Moses, 2010; Schamess, 2006; Tew, 2006).

Guidelines for managing the explicit and implicit complexities of the power in our relationships with students relate simply to what has been said elsewhere: Recognize the reality and acknowledge the potential dangers with and for our students. When it comes to issues of authority and power, we apply a differential approach in understanding how it affects students depending on who they are and who we are. We accept that there are multiple layers of power not fully acknowledged, and we work to uncover these layers to justly balance our frames of reference and behaviors.

Teaching Before Evaluating

We need to guard against evaluating students before we have taught them. This statement may be confusing as we evaluate our students from the moment we meet them. After all, our first consideration is whether this individual will succeed in this setting. However, as we move into evaluating skill levels and before concluding that students are unwilling to learn or that the placement is not appropriate for them, we need to reflect on how best to help a student learn and how to adapt our teaching or whether the setting's parameters might be adapted to individual student needs. We may be pleasantly surprised that students can respond to a different teaching style or approach.

For example, excessive absences or lateness inhibit the flow of the educational experience and may signal more serious conflicts or performance obstacles. Sometimes absences or lateness indicate health or family concerns that interfere with the rigorous periods of study required by social work programs. Students may be experiencing their own trauma or have reactions to the setting or have value conflicts with the setting's mission and goals. Absences can also indicate a lack of commitment to the profession or reluctance to meet the demands of field education. Either way, excessive absences or lateness may prevent students from remaining focused on their work. Before snags arise in this area, we need to review our students' understanding of time and attendance requirements and the cultural and value orientations that are involved in the meaning and adherence to time. For example, are our expectations built rigidly around perfection, a sense of urgency, or either-or thinking; that is, the student is either on time and responsible or late and irresponsible. What other frames of reference are there?

Timeliness is an organizational skill that must be learned, and not all students understand how this behavior demonstrates commitment to service, accountability, and identification with their professional role. They may view absences from their role as a student rather than as a social worker in training. This may also explain some students' lack of attention to communicating with us when they will be late or absent. Being explicit about the time commitment required to meet field placement expectations, aligning these expectations to their professional goals, the need for them to communicate with us regarding lateness or absences, how all this relates to their demonstration of professional behavior, and the direct relationship to achieving a satisfactory grade in field performance is essential. Yet achieving this may take some flexibility and adjustment for everyone. Inviting a conversation that explains the expectations may only go part of the way toward resolution. Talking about the student's responsibilities and values regarding time may go further. Through a justice-based lens, it may then become clear that the problem might be solved if the setting could adapt to a later start to the student's day, making juggling the student's responsibilities easier. With this environmental change, the student may have no obstacles to demonstrating commitment and meeting expectations as required.

Other factors or special concerns that may need to be addressed include students' persistent judgmental attitudes expressed toward individuals or the community served, perfectionist habits that interfere with the ability to get the job done, or students who are frozen and overwhelmed by the nature and complexity of the work they encounter. Each of these factors indicates learning needs; however, the pattern, extent, and duration of the behaviors indicate whether the student is failing to achieve adequate self-regulation. In any of these situations, when blocks arise or if they persist, the field liaison can be helpful in reinforcing expectations, mediating difficulties, and formulating educational learning contracts that target these behaviors. When we conclude that students are not performing within defined performance expectations, due process and careful documentation are essential.

Early attention to difficulties that arise in field education is crucial and so is seeking the support of the social work program as soon as we recognize these difficulties. Most of us find it difficult to fail students, and we often extend ourselves beyond the call of duty to save or rescue them (Parker, 2010; Sowbel, 2012). When we collude with our students, fail to confront them, and do not report difficulties to field liaisons, we relinquish our gatekeeping function. Just as alarming, we fail to provide hope that the situation might change, our student might meet the challenge of increased performance, or we might improve our teaching repertoire. A cardinal rule is to remember that success as field instructors is not dependent on student success. Likewise, our student's failure is not necessarily a reflection of inadequate teaching abilities. This is particularly difficult to remember in the throes of dealing with these challenges and because we recognize they are connected. Our teaching affects learning, and students' learning needs affect our choice of teaching techniques.

Differences Between Treating and Teaching

According to Shulman (1994),

> supervisors must be empathic about the strains faced by students who are experiencing personal issues and be sensitive to the effects these can have on their work.... However, it is not helpful to stop making expectations of students or to try to cover for a student who is having a hard time. It is better for the supervisor to maintain expectations about the work and thus help troubled students to function effectively in the agency, which, in turn, can help them deal with their personal problems—and ultimately those of the client. (pp. 35–36)

The "practice of social work is inextricably related to the life-experience of the learner, so that it is impossible to isolate the learning experience from study of its effects" (Towle, 1954, p. 24). This emotional learning experience presents challenges on how we facilitate learning without crossing the boundary into therapy or treatment. Yet to frame the question as "teach or treat" (Schamess, 2006, p. 428) bifurcates how these functions connect with each other. Keeping a balance involves setting a framework and structure that permits discussions of personal feelings and experiences as they relate to the work while at the same time respecting how this may be differentially manifested. The supervisory relationship we create may communicate confusion in how we invite self-disclosure and thereby complicate our purposes in open and authentic communication (Knight, 2012; Ornstein & Moses, 2010). Practice perspectives on this issue are evolving from a traditional position of needing to be a stoic mirror to understanding the benefits for authentic communication with those we serve based on a respectful, purposeful, and "thoughtful assessment" of need (Knight, 2012, p. 303). This applies equally in supervisory relationships. The relational approach to supervision "defined by mutuality, shared and authorized power, and the co-construction of knowledge" offers guidance because of its emphasis on "affective processes and mutual self-reflection" (Ornstein & Moses, 2010, p. 103).

For example, students engaged in new learning often become preoccupied with themselves or their lack of skill. Their energies become directed toward their discomfort rather than toward the issues and questions of the people and communities they serve. In these expected situations, we acknowledge the discomfort, clarify the emotions involved, and normalize the anxiety; it then becomes possible to reestablish a focus on the reality of constituents' needs, the facts of their situations, and methods and techniques that further the work. This is done instead of focusing on the student's discomfort, but it cannot be ignored either. Normalizing anxiety by sharing understanding from our own experiences and purposefully focusing on the work connects the student to the desire to serve and this often shifts the student back into a more stable state. The result is a return to a work-centered agenda for greater learning. Maintaining this balance can be a challenge. The aim is to avoid solely delving into a student's internal conflicts or concerns. Pursuing personal issues in field education supervision is never an end goal. The aim is always to integrate the student's experience and to advance learning and the work.

Acknowledging that the nature of social work practice and developing increased self-awareness requires us to pay attention to how our judgments are formed and provides an entry to discussing why it is necessary for us to explore inner thoughts and feelings evoked by the work. This is also why we require recordings and written reflections that involve students in examining their thought processes and affective reactions and that provide paths for considering new ways of looking at situations. These considerations may lead to discussions that provoke a disorienting event for the student. Something is said or proposed that positions a new way of viewing the situation. This in turn provokes transformations in how the situation is seen. While experiencing this disequilibrium, the student requires support and guidance in exploring cognitive and affective reactions to promote the aimed-for developmental change (Carroll, 2010a, 2010b; Mezirow, 2000; Moen et al., 2016). In these instances, the practice situation provokes a challenge, and field education supervision is the space where the student can navigate the quagmire of emotions and thoughts involved.

In other words, an essential part of our role is to help students figure out when the self is blocking learning during practice situations, in field education supervision, or in interactions with colleagues. We facilitate students' self-awareness in the context of an educational focus. Teaching students about ways that increase self-awareness aids their ability to build on strengths, assume greater responsibility in sharing concerns, identify potential blocks, and assess their own practice. Our goals are to facilitate the progression toward autonomous functioning, recognition of limitations, and to teach how to seek and obtain additional help when needed. One of our primary tasks is to build capacities for tolerance of ambiguity in the innate complexity of practice. Without this tolerance, learning is limited to the student's current capacity (Franks, 2013). We do this in various ways:

> Acknowledge the importance of feelings, legitimize students' rights to have feelings about the work and respectfully explore these affective reactions
> Provide clear explanations on why affective reactions are important, their influence on reasoning and why we are sensitive to students' reluctance or readiness to examine feelings and reactions
> Acknowledge that the work may engender feelings of fear, focus on feelings as they affect specific aspects of students' practice and provide ways for students to protect themselves
> Link feelings, thoughts, and actions with self-awareness, self-reflection, and self-regulation because evaluating decision making involves understanding the interaction among these realms
> Move selectively, time interventions when patterns emerge, and give specific examples of how the work is being influenced by affective reactions, their uses and associated potential pitfalls
> Acknowledge the effects of exposure to historical and current trauma (Walters et al., 2011) and compassion fatigue, and provide self-care methods that guard them from these effects

Basic practice skills such as understanding the elements involved in the establishment of a trusting relationship, neutral methods of exploration and clarification, the importance of probing, and the power of initiating change by posing questions that challenge assumptions are directly applicable to teaching students. These skills in field education supervision are applied to our role as teachers, not counselors (Bogo & Vayda, 1987; Congress, 1996; Ellis, 2010; Knight, 2016). Field education is about teaching students, not treating them, but because of the sensitive and complicated nature of the issues addressed and the powerful feelings that are often evoked, it is often necessary for us to explore students' innermost thoughts and feelings. Student self-disclosures are important primarily when they relate to the work. The skill is in establishing a trusting relationship that enables students to disclose work-related feelings while maintaining clear boundaries. Walking this delicate line between treating and teaching entails emphasizing the differences between developing practitioner self-reflection and self-awareness and learning more about oneself over time through a therapeutic relationship (Barretti, 2007; Grossman et al., 1990; Moen et al., 2016; Urdang, 2010; Weatherston, Weigand, & Weigand, 2010). We are concerned with examining how best to help students become self-aware, critical thinkers who can integrate theory into their practice. It follows that we are invested to find approaches that help us achieve this goal (Bogo, 2015; Caspi & Reid, 2002; Gambrill, 2013; Gitterman, 1988; Granello, 2010; Graybeal & Ruff, 1995; Knight, 2016; Neuman & Friedman, 1997; Simmons & Fisher, 2016; Urdang, 2010). According to Ganzer & Ornstein (2004),

> furthermore, [in a co-constructed, mutually derived relationship] the supervisee has the power to limit the focus on his or her issues, whereas the supervisor ensures that the supervisee's personal issues, aside from the treatment of the client, do not co-opt the supervision. In other words, the degree and level with which the exploration of personal issues are discussed with the supervisee is negotiated between the participants and authorized by the supervisee. (p. 439)

Self-development and growth are part and parcel of the learning goals for students and are integral to the development of the professional self. Ambivalence, regression, and resistance are normal and to be expected when adult learners confront new ways of looking at familiar situations. As stated earlier, taking on new roles can be threatening to the adult self. Learning entails risk, like the risk of admitting that one does not know something or the risk of exposing oneself as vulnerable and dependent. These are natural outcomes to learning and must be understood from this perspective (Grossman et al., 1990; Knight, 2016). Some teaching involves helping, and some helping involves teaching, but our focus is on the student's work and what the student needs to learn about social work practice. If students need more help in dealing with feelings evoked by their practice, we should not take it upon ourselves to take on a therapeutic role or to refer a student for counseling but instead sensitively involve the student's field liaison, who can provide school resources for student counseling (Bogo, 2010; Bonosky, 1995; Plaut, 1993).

This does not mean a total avoidance of attention to personal discussions or to personal issues that affect progress. The importance of this balance suggests that attending to aspects of a student's personality, or work style, when things are going well and when work falters is an essential part of field instruction; attention to these issues is vital, and delays in addressing them should be avoided. As Boyd Webb (1988) stated,

> becoming a social worker involves the integration of professional and personal identity via the various formal and informal socialization experiences that comprise social work education.... One learns to use aspects of

one's personality and style in a conscious deliberate way, according to the needs of a given client or situation. This conscious use of self is the mark of a true professional; the field instructor has a pivotal role in modeling this aspect of professional identity. (p. 40)

Because the boundaries between therapy and education are sometimes vague and permeable, the following guidelines are offered:

> - Establish professional boundaries by consciously and appropriately using physical space, work environment, body language, attire, communication skills, time, attitude, respect for multiple layers of identity, and issues of power and privilege.
> - Respect students' reluctance to disclose personal material, set appropriate and relevant boundaries, and be mindful to connect students' personal experiences and narratives to teaching points related to the work.
> - Be clear about the reasons for pursuing the student's personal experiences as they relate to the learning agenda and the work.
> - If the personal issues raised are taking over field education supervision, move the focus back to students' learning needs; check in with students to ensure they understand the reasons for the shift in focus. In negotiating the shift, make sure whatever personal issues raised are heard and responded to so that resources, if needed, can be found. Remember that the student is a partner in developing boundaries that are most conducive to professional development and learning.
> - Be conscious and purposeful in what we disclose to students about personal experiences, why we are doing so, and who is benefiting from the self-disclosure. Assess what is relevant and beneficial to student learning and involve the student in deciding on these boundaries; the boundaries themselves are influenced by the dimensions of identity of both parties.
> - Know ourselves; our own areas of sensitivity, predispositions, and biases; and how issues of power, oppression, and privilege play out in our relationships. It is our responsibility to acknowledge what ongoing personal work we need to do to ensure we are providing relevant field education supervision attuned to the individual before us.

Pitfalls That Signal the System Is at the Root of the Difficulties

Structural limitations represent barriers in the system beyond the actors involved. We have already addressed how programs might facilitate a student's need for replacement by identifying field instructors who serve in the capacity of accepting students after displacement. Other situations that may benefit from structural supports include students whose abilities require mandated accommodations, incidents of sexual discrimination or harassment that often place students and field instructors between policies and procedures of the agency and those of the social work program and supporting LGBTQ+TS students dealing with homophobia (see following discussion regarding these situations). Others who may require structural supports are international students who arrive without adequate preparation and serving gifted students who meet performance expectations early and require adjustments to the placement setting to enhance their learning and growth.

Mandated Accommodations

Section 504 of the Rehabilitation Act of 1973 prohibits discrimination of a person with special abilities in any program or activity that receives federal financial assistance solely based on need, if otherwise qualified; this section includes protections in postsecondary education (see https://www.eeoc.gov/eeoc/internal/reasonable_accommodation.cfm#_Toc531079192). The Americans with Disabilities Act (ADA, 1990), which builds on these protections and was amended in 2008, affirms that people with special abilities can work and be active members of their communities; it provides broad nondiscrimination protections in employment, public services, and public accommodations. Section 504 and the 2008 ADA Amendments Act protect the right to receive reasonable accommodations that support performance in defined essential functions (http://www.apa.org/pi/disability/dart/legal/section-504.aspx; http://www.apa.org/pi/disability/dart/legal/ada-basics.aspx).

Reasonable accommodations or modifications are adjustments that remove ability-related barriers for full participation. Students must be registered with the social work program's designated university office to receive the accommodations. If difficulties arise but the student is not registered with the university, the student is not eligible for accommodations but may apply for assessment. It is possible that some learners may not know they have needs until field instructors bring these difficulties to their attention. In these instances, students can be referred to the appropriate university office so that evaluation and services can be offered. However, even in these situations, the ADA (2008) does not shield these students until they are assessed as eligible for protection. Some programs will assess the student's needs at the time of identified problems, and depending on the need, accommodations may be offered; however, assessing for need may take time, and the student may proceed without protections or may take a leave of absence pending determination of accommodations.

Examples of the types of accommodations eligible students may receive in field education include providing computer access so that students are not penalized for spelling errors on reports, allowing extra time to produce written materials including recordings, allowing service or emotional support animals at the setting, allowing shorter time periods in field education rather than full 8-hour days, or providing telephone devices that amplify sound. Most of these modifications are straightforward, but in some situations, they may create difficulties. For example, program administrators may be able to organize shorter days for the student but not if it extends beyond existing constraints, for example, if the placement cannot be extended beyond the end of the usual academic semester (middle to end of May) to make up for the shorter days. It may also happen that the setting cannot offer more days during the week because of the lack of office space. In these types of circumstances, setting administrators may determine that they are not able to respond to the accommodation request.

A determination that an accommodation is not reasonable should be discussed with the social work program administration. Certain criteria must apply. For example, it must be shown that the accommodation would place a financial burden on the setting, the request is of a personal nature that requires the setting to assist with such basic needs as restroom visits or eating, or that the accommodation would fundamentally change the program's requirements. Program administrators have a duty to explore possible alternatives and to exercise their professional judgment regarding whether these accommodations would give the student an opportunity to complete the program without jeopardizing the integrity of the program's requirements.

Since the passage of the ADA, greater clarity on issues of implementation has been achieved. In addition, the latest guidelines on the required "interactive process" between students and universities clarify the various responsibilities in the accommodations process (U.S. EEOC, n.d., Section IV. C). Still, the rights protected under the ADA remain challenged by covert discrimination and unreasonable fears about working with people with special learning, emotional, mental, or physical abilities. These fears often interfere with the protected student's field placement and may also interfere with the evaluation of the student's field performance. As a result, we are often at the forefront of practice in this arena (Bial & Lynn, 1995; Cole, Christ, & Light, 1995; Paven & Shore, 2015; Raymond & Sowbel, 2016; Reeser, 1992).

In response to these challenges, offices of field education have been instrumental in establishing technical standards that stipulate essential requirements and abilities required of all students with or without technical accommodations. The standards protect students' rights and maintain the integrity of educational standards for students with or without technical accommodations. The areas addressed include behavioral, professional, and intellectual standards that are guides to basic requirements beyond the academic requirements of each program. The standards cover such areas as oral, written, and listening communication skills; acceptance of diversity and respect for differences in others; self-awareness and ability to be self-reflective; cognitive skills including short and long-term memory and inductive and deductive reasoning; integrity; professional behavior; interpersonal skills, and motor and sensory abilities that permit participation in class and field education.

Social work programs are not allowed to identify students' special mental or physical abilities or to notify a prospective field placement unless students give permission because it could be construed as a violation of confidentiality and violation of HIPAA (U.S. DHHS, 2003) or the Family Educational Rights and Privacy Act (U.S. DOE, 1974). Under these protections, a field instructor cannot be told that the student has a learning ability or condition that will require accommodation, but the field instructor and setting administrators do need to know what accommodation is needed. Therefore, field liaisons discuss with the student how the field instructor will be made aware of any accommodations that are needed. This helps the setting prepare for securing the accommodations beforehand. For example, if students have been granted reasonable accommodation, although the field education office accepts responsibility for notifying the setting of these requirements and frequently facilitates acquisition of needed equipment through university services, this is done with the student's knowledge and permission. In sum, placement settings and social work programs must comply with ADA requirements, and in a climate of shared communication and decision making with the student, needs of students must be evaluated and responded to on a case-by-case basis (Reeser & Wertkin, 1997).

Sexual Harassment and Sex Discrimination

The current global spotlight on sexual harassment, sexual assault, and gender-based discrimination has exposed the pervasive nature of the various forms of sexual discrimination and harassment from constant joking or teasing to physical assault and rape. Students are vulnerable to these situations, and they may experience uncomfortable, hostile, or unsafe work environment. Sex discrimination and sexual harassment are violations of Title VII of the Civil Rights Act of 1964. In addition, operating requirements of Title IX of the Education Amendments of 1972, administered by the U.S. Education Department's Office for Civil Rights, also protect students from sexual discrimination and sexual harassment in federally funded education programs.

According to the *Code of Federal Regulations* (2018) and adapted for the context of higher education, sexual harassment includes unwelcome sexual advances, requests for sexual favors, and other verbal or physical conduct of a sexual nature when

a. submission to such conduct is made either an explicit or implicit term or condition of a person's employment or admission to and progress in an academic program,
b. submission to or rejection of such conduct is used as the basis for decisions affecting a person's employment status or academic standing, or
c. such conduct is so frequent and so severe that a hostile work environment is created. The purpose or effect substantially interferes with a person's performance on the job, in the classroom, or by creating an intimidating or offensive work or study environment. (CFR (2018), Section 1604.11)

Perpetrators of sexual harassment most often exert power over students, either in placements or in their academic program. This includes sexual harassment of students by field instructors, task supervisors, administrators, staff, or other students. On the other hand, field instructors may feel they are being harassed by students. These forms of sexual harassment are also unlawful.

Recent guidance on implementation of university responsibilities has resulted in directions on the management of reporting and protections for victims and respondents (Mangan, 2017; https://www2.ed.gov/about/offices/list/ocr/sexharassresources.html). These guidelines are not only under review in the Department of Education, but universities also may vary in their operating procedures regarding reporting and handling of investigations.

Changing federal guidelines regarding protections for transgender students are also a concern. Current federal guidelines have rescinded interpretations of Title IX protections (Somashekhar, Brown, & Balingit, 2017) that extend to claims of discrimination based on sex or gender identity. In response, many states have enacted laws protecting their rights. Each social work program has a policy about how to manage allegations of sexual harassment and how staff work with the university on investigations and postinvestigation reporting in compliance with Title IX regulations. Field instructors are advised to seek clarity from the social work program administration regarding explanations and advice needed on these complex issues. In addition, settings have protocols and procedures that also apply. We share responsibility with social work programs to ensure that students are trained to recognize sexual harassment when it occurs and to understand how it will be handled by their academic institution (Bradley & Buck, 2016; Fogel & Ellison, 1998).

Handling reports of sexual harassment. When students indicate the possibility or incidence of sexual harassment, we may feel caught between the setting's policies and the policies of the Office of Field Education. Although it may seem imperative to follow organizational protocols first, it is important to remember that the student is technically not an employee, and it is critical to collaborate quickly with the field liaison or director of field education to decipher the best way to proceed. This is an important discussion to have with task supervisors as they may be more closely tied to organizational policies and procedures and will need to be alerted to university protocols that apply. It is critically important for field instructors to refer to the social work program's field education manual or discuss the situation with the program's field liaison for guidance. Field instructors must comply with the academic program's guidelines; complying with agency procedures and policies are not an adequate response. To help reduce the confusion that may result, do the following:

> - Determine educational and organizational policies and protocols that apply.
> - Contact the Office of Field Education or the field liaison.
> - Clarify with the field liaison who will speak to the parties involved to find out what happened.
> - Gather specific information about the allegations by asking clarifying questions.
> - Explain how you will proceed, and work closely with the student throughout the process.

› Provide support to the student to learn how this individual wants to handle the situation.
  > If students ask you to do nothing, explain that you cannot do nothing.
  > Students should not handle the situation themselves, even if they say they want to.
  > Give students the option of writing down what happened.
  > Be supportive and neutral and avoid labeling anyone's behavior.

Common mistakes in handling sexual harassment include the following:

› Not seeking consultation from the director of field education or the field liaison
› Viewing the complaints purely from the setting's perspective
› Trying to pretend nothing happened
› Not giving students an adequate hearing of their complaints
› Moving too fast or ahead of the student's pace
› Overreacting to complaints by punishing before investigating
› Having preconceived ideas about those involved
› Not educating students about possible options and legal responses to complaints
› Not clarifying with the field liaison on how to approach the accused about the specific complaints
› Not giving the accused a chance to respond to the complaints
› Interfering with an investigation because the accused is a friend or someone powerful in management

Sexual discrimination, homophobia, and transphobia. Sex discrimination includes treating an individual unfavorably because of that person's sex, sexual orientation, or gender identity and includes sexist remarks and unfair treatment. Discrimination can target students of either gender or LGBTQ+TS students who may require our support in challenging these behaviors and building support against homophobic spaces (Messinger, 2007; Newman et al., 2009).

As with all issues of prejudice, discrimination, and bias, it is appropriate and necessary for us to take a proactive role in reducing racism, sexism, heterosexism, or other isms in the placement setting. Sexist behaviors that are tolerated in the setting are toxic for students and require our attention. Students need our support to know that we will pay attention and be open to hearing their concerns. We need to identify and position ourselves as allies with our students and create a safe space for concerns to be shared and addressed.

Homophobia can be reduced or eliminated when people with heterosexual privilege challenge and correct misinformation about LGBTQ+TS community members and colleagues. Heterosexual students and staff can be made more aware of the homophobic ways they behave and the environment this creates whether it is expressed in heterosexually, heteronormative privileged attitudes and policies such as only binary-gender restrooms. This negative environment may relate to staff reactions to gay and lesbian students' gender expressions, including mindful awareness of personal disclosure and use of pronouns. It may also mean taking an active role in intervening with homophobic statements or heterosexist and heteronormative behaviors exhibited by staff members and community members. Furthermore, students should not be put into the position of being spokespeople for the LGBTQ+TS community, particularly if they feel unsupported and alone in the agency, similar to Latinx, Asian, African, Alaska Native, Native Hawaiian, and American Indian or First Nation students who are expected to speak for all individuals encompassed by these broad racial, indigenous, and ethnic categories.

When entering a new setting, LGBTQ+TS students may harbor anxiety over hiding and feeling unsafe in their field placements, and they may have concerns and experience confusion about managing personal disclosure of their sexual orientation (Messinger, 2004). The burden should not be on students but on settings and field instructors to be aware of heteronormative homophobic structures that are biased, stereotypical, and oppressive against members of the LGBTQ+TS community (Newman et al., 2009). Safety can be facilitated or inhibited by the field instructor's openness to the student's personal narratives and experiences. It is important to accept that students may not feel safe or prepared to discuss the issue and may need time to build trust in the field education supervisory relationship. Creating an inclusive environment that embraces and affirms all identities through participating as allies and establishing safe spaces for authenticity are essential. Openness and a willingness to learn and teach are basic to good practice and inclusive justice-based field education.

Increasing International Admissions

Although schools are increasing international student admissions, these students are often not given support to reduce the adjustments involved in studying and interning in a very different cultural environment. Field education departments can take the lead in developing a variety of supports for international students to ensure their success, which include providing an immersion course dealing with information on the local culture and on the broader societal issues and social welfare policy and systems, information on the social work profession and the profession's code of ethics, and opportunities to consider comparisons and similarities of issues and perspectives here and in the student's country of origin. If this sort of immersion experience is not available, field education departments can organize special orientation sessions for international students where these content areas could be addressed in addition to the orientation sessions all other students attend.

Ideally, support should continue beyond the usual first few weeks dedicated to orientation. Some programs delay fieldwork for a semester to facilitate adjustment and provide course work that examines the issues previously mentioned in more depth. This gives students an opportunity to visit their upcoming placement later in the semester and perhaps ease into a full-time internship. In addition to ensuring a global and inclusive perspective in the setting, affirming the voices of our international students should be encouraged to counter feeling that their experiences are not valued in the U.S. context. They bring global realities and perspectives into the setting and community and offer possibilities to enrich discussions and service perspectives.

Field instructors could be recruited if interested in serving an international student, and an advanced seminar in field instruction could be conducted for this group of field instructors. The content of this seminar should include the special issues and rewards associated with working with this population of students and the cross-cultural issues involved such as differences in approaches to learning, language challenges, and value orientations.

An interesting example is described by Tedam (2011), who introduced a training model for international Black social work students from Africa attending social work programs in England and Wales to buttress their learning and performance in field education. The students' needs for help to bridge understanding were accepted and acknowledged; the model starts from this acknowledgment and incorporates familiar values from the students' home countries to help make the bridge to their current local contexts. The students were not left on their own to find the links, but rather the education model incorporated the links, thereby facilitating their adjustment to their new context. More models like this could and should be designed and tested.

Achieving Competence Early

Gifted or experienced students who reach competency early or who demonstrate considerable capabilities can present specific sets of challenges. We may feel as if we have nothing to teach these students, and they may feel understimulated. Likewise, students may be content to remain in their comfort zone. The setting may be unable to enhance assignment offerings, and it is tempting to accept the level of competence gained rather than push for new levels of achievement. It can also happen that settings take advantage of the student's achievements and begin to treat the student as a member of staff, accelerating the workload and reducing the amount of supervision and oversight.

Ideally in these situations, there are opportunities to increase teaching and learning expectations by going beyond the status quo of regular service delivery. We may devise additional learning opportunities or find unique ways to build on students' experiences. For example, it may be possible to extend the repertoire of services to include family, group, community, or research assignments to provide learning experiences for those who are otherwise unchallenged by the usual range of service delivery in the setting. Maintaining the demand for work may involve expanding our own repertoire of knowledge and skills or finding task supervisors with specialized knowledge to stimulate the student's learning. These situations may present challenges, but it is equally rewarding when we are able to look beyond the norm of satisfactory field performance and find unique learning and teaching opportunities that take these students into new realms of learning. These adjustments also benefit us, our settings, and those served.

Summary

We serve as evaluators of our students, and together with field education departments, we act as gatekeepers for the profession. Not enough can be said about the significance of the evaluation process to emphasize the field instructors' importance in the process of social work education. The competencies guide us, and the program's procedures support our evaluation of students' abilities to enter the profession. Still, we are frequently the first to raise concerns about a student's field performance, and it falls on us to inform faculty field liaisons when students are performing or progressing in ways that signal they are at risk of not meeting performance expectations (Bogo, 2016; Sowbel, 2012).

Resources are in the form of theoretical perspectives on adult learning, transformative learning, and experiential learning theory, and styles, stages, and developmental models of learning. These perspectives offer direction on how to tackle the complications we confront. Once static is experienced, we know that fine tuning is needed; also, obstructive behaviors signal the need to assess the broader picture of what might be going on with the student. Are the setting, the supervisory relationship, and the social work program places where the student feels accepted and heard? Does the student feel that it is possible in these environments to learn? These considerations must be balanced by the realities of performance and the resulting assessment of student capabilities.

Handling the range of inherent pitfalls and challenges in field education in some ways is the essence of our work. Learning and teaching social work practice is complex, and much is involved in managing the difficulties and finding ways around the challenges that emerge; each choice brings its own consequences and opportunities for resolution. The scope of the difficulty, it's pervasive nature and persistence indicate danger in the learning enterprise. The field liaison is a collaborator and guide to reaching clarity on ways to proceed in the search for enhancing the learning experience.

CHAPTER 9 APPENDIX

This appendix contains tips on overcoming students' resistance to new learning, and five student scenarios that signal obstacles discussed in this chapter.

Tips: Overcoming Students' Resistance to the Changes Inherent in Learning

There are many ways to help students to identify, evaluate, and overcome learning difficulties. Consider these suggestions adapted from Brookfield (1990):

> Recognize that resistance is a normal response to new learning.
> Involve students in all aspects of educational planning, including seeking solutions on assignments, work management, and in-service training.
> Identify learning difficulties and possible solutions, allowing time and space for airing fears and confusion. Solutions evolve and emerge over time.
> Ask yourself whether the resistance is reasonable or understandable given the context.
> Talk to your students about multiple layers of social identity while reflecting on how these affect the student and field instructor relationship. This is an ongoing process that involves helping students make connections among the multiple threads in their lives that may be influencing their responses to learning.
> Explain your intentions and expectations early in the field education process. Do not assume that student compliance means consent or agreement. We sometimes must explain why a learning issue is important so that solutions and collaboration can emerge.

- Create situations where students can succeed, including partializing and breaking down complex practice concepts or demands into smaller, understandable components.
- Do not push students too fast or beyond their capacity. Allow consolidation and testing of new concepts. Provide time for them to integrate and reflect on what is being taught.
- Build trust with students and prepare them to hear constructive criticism and to ask for clarification on expectations they feel are too high or confusing.
- Recognize that we are joined with our students through their desire to learn and our desire to teach. However, it is also useful to acknowledge a student's right to resist new learning. Not all students will display a passion for learning.
- Seek clarification on why students seek to embark on a social work career and the expectations and goals they set for themselves as social work professionals. By hearing their motivations, it may be possible to see how available learning opportunities and expectations will help them achieve their goals.
- Encourage peer learning and teaching by using the support of the learning community. Field instructors can help students establish peer support groups in the placement setting, which is a powerful resource for normalizing the learning process and consolidating learning. This is also a useful adjunct to individual and group field education supervision.
- Finally, we can help students overcome difficulties in performance by finding ways to enable them to think differently about the work, situation, or placement setting. Reframing the work from a different viewpoint can shift students' perspectives to more positive outlooks.

Scenarios

The five student scenarios in this section consider situations that challenge student progress in field education. The first three scenarios deal with issues of sexual assault, sexual harassment, and homophobia experienced in the field setting, whereas the fourth and fifth scenarios consider obstacles to the student's learning and performance.

Scenario 1

A specialized governmental practice level student reported to her field liaison that she had been sexually assaulted while in placement. The student had been successful in fighting off the individual, but she was shaken and frightened that it could occur again. The person accused was a high-ranking individual in the office. The field liaison's initial instinct was to immediately replace the student. Instead, with the student's knowledge and involvement, guidance on the university's protocol was sought, and the field instructor was informed. The student declared her wish to remain in placement. "Why should I lose this learning opportunity because he is a predator?" she asked. The three of them developed a plan. Representatives of the university and the setting resolved to take steps to ensure the student understood her rights and time frames regarding her rights to file charges. Understanding was also reached regarding how the accusation would be managed. The student was relocated to a different office but kept under the supervision of the same field instructor. She kept two assignments that continued her learning but did not involve collaboration with staff from the initial office setting; all other work was provided at the new site. She received counseling support from the university, an active presence in the setting was provided by the field liaison, and the student went on to have a productive year. The university maintained an ongoing evaluation of the setting and the setting's response to the allegations.

> If you are the field instructor, what are the issues to be considered?
> How might this situation change if it occurred in your setting?
> What ongoing concerns might exist?

Scenario 2

A 27-year-old student alleges that a 32-year-old male student accosted her in the agency elevator. The male student asked her for a kiss, and when she said she did not want to kiss him, he kissed her anyway. She felt embarrassed and frightened in the situation. In addition, she recounts several other incidents when he "pushed" himself onto her. She is angry with him and is frightened to be alone with him. She asks her field instructor for advice.

> What are the first steps to be taken?
> Should the field liaison be informed of this incident?
> If a task supervisor is involved, how would the field instructor proceed?
> What information does the field instructor need to know to move forward?
> What advice should the field instructor give the student?
> What action, if any, should be taken regarding the male student?
> How would this situation change if the student accused a staff member in the placement? If so, specify in what way.

Scenario 3

A 24-year-old student placed in a well-known child guidance agency informs her field instructor that she is a lesbian and wants to be open and transparent with staff and the individuals she will be serving. She states that her identity is important to her as a social worker, and she believes she may also serve as a model and ally for others who do not feel safe. The field instructor is surprised by this student's request because she never questioned the student's sexual orientation. Knowing there has been limited incorporation of LGBTQ+TS awareness in the setting, the field instructor is somewhat concerned about how others in the setting will take this student's disclosure. The field instructor responds by saying that the staff in this setting are rather traditional and conservative. She explains that such an announcement may be counterproductive and may interfere with the student's professional relationships. The student seems to accept the field instructor's advice in the moment.

During a supervisory session, the student tells her field instructor that she wants to start a discussion group for adolescents who are questioning their sexual orientation. She wants to provide an opportunity for them to discuss their concerns and to process their questions about their sexual identities in a safe place. She asks for support to raise this idea at the next staff meeting.

The field instructor finds herself discouraging the student from such a course of action, stating that the staff would not be receptive to the idea. However, the student is convinced that the adolescents need this service, and she urges the field instructor to let her bring up this group idea with other staff. The field instructor is upset and angry that the student is so adamant and is suspicious that the student may have an ulterior motive in wanting to bring this issue to the staff's attention.

> As a field instructor, how would you assist this student in being her authentic self in a potentially unsafe, heterosexual, and heteronormative environment? What are some issues that might appear in your work with the student and the organization on heterosexism and homophobic microaggressions?
> What practice and organizational issues are operating in this situation? What are the field instructor's responsibilities in dealing with personal and agency homophobia, heterosexism, and heterosexual privilege as well as the heteronormative environment of the setting?
> How could the field instructor support integration of the competing demands in this scenario?
> If a task supervisor is involved, how would the field instructor proceed?
> What are the opportunities for learning about sharing power and authority in this situation?
> What are the civil and human rights issues in this situation? What are the ethical issues? How do they connect?

Scenario 4

A first-generation generalist practice level student begins the term by attending her setting dressed in an unkempt manner. The field instructor points to the student's attire asking whether the student could wear more business-appropriate attire in the future. The student apologizes stating that she had come straight to field education from work as a night care assistant, and as she was running late, she decided not to return home first to change. She stated that she would be able to adjust her attire in the future. The placement proceeds, and the student seemed to be adjusting to her role, but a pattern of late arrivals ensues, and other issues begin to emerge that prevent this student from fully engaging in the work of her field placement. During field instruction, the student explains that she lives with her mother who has decided to return to her home in Central America within the next few weeks. Her mother lost her job and has been too depressed to look for other work. The student explains that this means she is uncertain where she will live and that she may have to move in with relatives. The field instructor expresses concern and appreciation for the student's attempts to focus on her work under these circumstances. They go over what needs to be done at placement and anticipate a reduced schedule to accommodate the student's need to move. During the next few weeks, the student does not submit recordings and is found to be preoccupied and unable to focus on her work. The student states that she has noticed this in her classes also. At placement, she is frequently found on her cell phone when she is scheduled to be in meetings or sessions with individuals she is assigned to be working with. The field instructor continues to be supportive about the changes in the student's life and has attempted to balance the situation by discussing the student's behavior and inattention to her responsibilities at the setting. The day following another attempt to help the student focus on her work responsibilities, the student calls in to state she will not be attending field placement and asks the office secretary to phone the individuals the student is scheduled to meet with that day to cancel their meetings. When the field instructor learns of this, she places a call to the program's field liaison to arrange a meeting to include the student.

> As the field instructor, how would you proceed? What would you focus on in your discussion with the field liaison? In what competencies does the student's performance indicate cause for concern?
> What issues and concerns are operating in this scenario?
> What could the field instructor have done differently?
> Does what you would do change if a task supervisor is involved?

The field liaison agrees to a meeting and asks the field instructor to first explain her concerns to the student and to set the meeting's agenda with the student. A meeting with the student and field liaison to create a learning contract is scheduled for the following week.

> Given this scenario, identify the issues that need addressing and create strategies that might be included to address each issue.
> Include roles for each member of the learning team, in this case, the student, the field instructor, and the field liaison.

Over the next 4 weeks the following activities are agreed on to support the student's efforts.

The student will demonstrate professional behavior and remain focused on her role and responsibilities in this setting during field instruction hours. She will check in with her field instructor's secretary when she arrives at placement. She will arrive on time and alert the office secretary if she will be late. She will not use her cell phone when she is scheduled to be in meetings or when she is scheduled to meet with individuals in the setting. If there is an emergency she must respond to, she will seek consultation with her field instructor. She will keep track of meetings scheduled with individuals and note whether and when they need to be rescheduled or canceled and by whom. She will demonstrate that she is focused on learning by handing in timely recordings to her field instructor as agreed on together in supervision. The recordings will be handed in no later than 2 days before scheduled supervision.

The field instructor will be available for regular field education supervision with the student. The student's recordings will be reviewed, and comments will be provided on them for the student's review. They will be returned no later than the day before scheduled supervision. Each supervisory session will make the expectations clear regarding the student's next recording and assignments. The field instructor will be available to meet with the student if an emergency arises. If she is not able to meet with the student, she will respond via e-mail or phone.

The field liaison will arrange to meet with the student during the next week. They will review resources the student might need to manage her other responsibilities including her course work and sorting out her move. The student may also request a meeting as needed. The liaison will remain in contact with the field instructor, review a student recording over the next 4 weeks, and return for a follow-up meeting at the end of this 4-week period.

> Do these items deal with the concerns in the scenario adequately? How could they be improved?
> What concerns remain unaddressed, and how should they be dealt with in a learning contract?

Scenario 5

A 32-year-old generalist practice level student placed in a program serving latency-age children in need of case management services asks for a special session with her field instructor during the second week of placement to discuss some concerns.

During this session the student brought up one issue after another. She has lived with special learning abilities all her life and is registered with the university's office that deals with students with special abilities. She has received some accommodations for the classroom, but none for field placement. She is frightened she will fail the program and field education. Sometimes it takes her three times to read something to understand what she is reading. She has difficulty taking notes in class because she needs to listen, and she cannot write that fast. She was married the previous year and is hoping to become pregnant but then what will happen if she has morning sickness and cannot keep her field placement hours? She does not believe that this is the best setting for her. She would like a more clinical setting. She is particularly interested in cognitive behavioral therapy and hopes to start a private practice after she graduates. She does not feel that she is making good contacts with the children in this setting, and they do not seem to want to discuss their issues. She is having difficulty getting to placement as her husband is driving her, and she is wondering whether she can change her days and hours. She does not understand how to use the computers in the setting and would like help with how to use the system. She does not believe she will get what she needs from this placement.

The field instructor tried to interrupt the student to slow down the litany of concerns, but this seemed to only further agitate the student. The student eventually was able to get to a point of self-exhaustion and settled back in her chair and asked, "What do you think I should do?" The field instructor replied, trying to lighten the atmosphere, "Perhaps we should choose one issue at a time. Which would you would like us to talk about first?" The student laughed and replied, "Yes, I do seem to have a lot on my mind." The field instructor commented that she had mentioned issues in her personal life and several relating to her education. Although they seem interconnected, it was important for them to attempt to focus on what might be impeding her progress in field education. The field instructor asked the student if she agreed and whether they could consider the field education issues in more detail. Then they could make sure that the student has a plan to deal with the other personal and academic issues.

The student concurred, and they were able to come to an agreement on how to proceed with the field placement concerns. They arranged to work together over the next few weeks on her engagement with the children, link her with a staff member who could explain the setting's computer system, set a more suitable schedule, and examine how the student was managing the placement's recording requirements. The field instructor said that they would discuss how this placement will serve her career goals. They agreed this would remain an issue for discussion in supervision. The student was linked with her field liaison and faculty adviser to address her concerns about managing the program academically. They discussed her knowledge about the university's counseling resources for support on her other concerns.

As the placement progressed, the student was assigned to work with several children and to work on a program with another staff member. Her work with the children resembled her manner of talking with others; that is, her thoughts raced, her conversation jumped around, and the children were disinterested in conversing with her. The task supervisor she was working with found the student "endearing," but was beginning to resent the student's constant interruptions for help with this or that.

In supervision, her field instructor slowed the student down, helped her focus, and was able to make some progress in helping her think about her role and goals with the children. The student remained convinced that the placement was not serving her needs. The field instructor addressed this concern by identifying the skills she was working on that linked to what she was learning in practice class. That led to a running joke between them. The student responded, "Yes, I know. I want yesterday what I will learn tomorrow."

The field instructor was direct about pointing out how the student's manner of jumping from one subject to the other affected her engagement with the children. The student recognized this, and ways of slowing down were discussed. The field instructor also addressed her work in the setting and asked the student to identify areas she found she needed additional help with so that they might discuss possible responses to them. The student needed frequent reassurance and would sometimes end the session by turning to the door but sitting down again with additional questions or repeating questions gone over previously. Again, the field instructor patiently responded and pointed out to the student that these were issues previously discussed. The field instructor asked the student to return to her office, write down what she required further help with, and provide this to the field instructor so that they could examine what remained unclear. The student agreed. The following week the field liaison called to say that the student had asked to be replaced and asked for the field instructor's opinion.

› What issues are operating in this scenario?
› What could the field instructor do differently?
› How should the task supervisor be involved?

- What are the civil and human rights issues in this situation? What are the ethical issues? How do they connect?
- How would you as the field instructor, respond to the field liaison's request?
- What do you believe would be achieved by replacing this student?

CHAPTER 10

Evaluations, Endings, and Taking Stock: Pulling It Together

A liberatory consciousness enables humans to maintain an awareness of the dynamics of oppression characterizing society without giving in to despair and hopelessness about that condition, to maintain an awareness of the role played by each individual in the maintenance of the system without blaming them for the role they play, and at the same time practice intentionality about changing the systems of oppression. A liberatory consciousness enables humans to live "outside" the patterns of thought and behavior learned through the socialization process that helps to perpetuate oppressive systems.... The awareness...means making the decision to live our lives from a waking position. It means giving up the numbness and dullness with which we have been lulled into going through life.... Living with awareness means noticing what happens in the world around you. (Love, 2013, pp. 601–602)

Our failure to engage in progressive conversations about race makes it difficult to address or transform antiracist practices in a thoughtful and productive manner.... Being a good steward of effective racial conversations requires one to "know thyself," particularly in terms of the relative power and privilege that one holds in a relationship. (Hardy, 2012, p. 138)

A justice-based lens provides opportunities to link our experiences and gives us another chance to effect change in people's lives during periods of transitions, termination, and evaluation. These phases provoke a range of emotions and are unique occasions for reflection and review that make sense of our experiences in different ways. The principles of a justice-based perspective also take account of how endings are differentially defined. Evaluations include and respond to the voices of those we serve, ensure that constituents own the success of what has been achieved, identify to what extent the process of ending is tied to unfinished work, and ensure that personal and external resources are explored to support the continuing work ahead. At the same time, competency-based education assumes that at the end of the field education experience the student has mastered the basic CSWE (2015a) competencies for our profession. If the job is done well, student and field instructor can identify, articulate, describe, and provide examples of growth in every one of the nine competency areas. Students can also say what they hope to learn more about, refine, and further deepen as they begin their professional careers. If we have done our jobs, the prize at the end is an aware, newly minted, competent social worker eager to pursue justice and to push themselves and our profession forward toward this goal.

Like all endings, this chapter marks an end and at the same time signals the start of a new phase. It considers the work of termination with our students, what is involved in assisting their ability to review and evaluate their work and prepare them for their impending transition of moving forward in their education or the choices they make after graduation. The work of pulling the threads together helps to keep an accounting of all that has occurred and been achieved. The role of field liaisons is discussed in previous chapters and is examined more closely here. We review field education supervision and the need to evaluate our supervisory practice so that we might hone our skills further. Finally, we pause to reflect and summarize the main thrusts of this book.

Evaluation, Terminations, and Transitions

Termination is another critical component of the helping and teaching process. Like assessment and evaluation, the process of termination is ongoing and begins as soon as we start our work; each contact contains its own ending, and in that sense, we are starting and ending repeatedly. The fragility of time demands our attention to the ending of each contact to provide an experience that pays respect to the past, holds to present concerns, and attends to what is anticipated going forward. The aim is to be clear about the boundaries of time, the goals we set, and how we will judge our efforts.

Evaluation is a process as well as a product. Chapter 3 examines the evaluation process as it relates to student progress and the product of end-of-term evaluation formats. Here we consider the reciprocal relationship between evaluation and termination. Termination shapes evaluation and vice versa. Evaluations help determine whether and when termination of service is needed, and preparing for termination involves a summation of the work that is enhanced through the work of evaluation. Interestingly, various iterations of the helping process name the final stage by placing evaluation and termination together (Hepworth, Rooney, Rooney, Gottfried, & Larsen, 2017), others name the final stage *ending* and include evaluation as part of a working or implementation phase (Cournoyer, 2017; McClam & Woodside, 2012), and others place evaluation in a space by itself separate from the final stage of termination (Morgaine & Capous-Desyllas, 2015). The CSWE (2015a) competencies incorporate termination into interventions, and evaluation is the final competency, which sets the process of termination as an integral part of our interventional choices and gives evaluation a place of its own for our full attention.

Termination is addressed in the competencies by noting that "social workers ... facilitate effective transitions and endings that advance mutually agreed-on goals" (CSWE, 2015a, p. 9). Termination is integral to the natural outcome of our plans and aims. The competency dealing with evaluation describes our responsibilities as being able to "select appropriate methods ... apply knowledge and theoretical frameworks in evaluation ... critically analyze, monitor, and evaluate intervention and program processes and outcomes; and apply evaluation findings to improve practice effectiveness at the micro, mezzo and macro levels" (CSWE, 2015a, p. 9). Evaluation's relationship to each phase of our work is given prominence, and although placed as the last competency, the implication of the identified tasks is that evaluation is ongoing throughout the student's work. Consider gauging student performance on their ability to evaluate practice. The competency dealing with evaluation states,

> social workers understand that evaluation is an ongoing component of the dynamic and interactive process of social work practice with, and on behalf of, diverse individuals, families, groups, organizations and communities. Social workers recognize the importance of evaluating processes and outcomes to advance practice, policy, and service delivery effectiveness. Social workers understand theories of human behavior and the

social environment, and critically evaluate and apply this knowledge in evaluating outcomes. Social workers understand qualitative and quantitative methods for evaluating outcomes and practice effectiveness. (p. 9)

As a practical guide, this discussion is a beginning; we require additional specificity to identify and recognize these activities as they unfold in practice, teach students the intent of the competency, prompt activities that involve these skills, and observe the performance of competent actions. The descriptors mentioned previously remain abstract and require further translation to relate to our contexts and chosen assignments in the setting where the teaching and learning occurs.

Evaluation and Ongoing Review

Competency in evaluation requires students to experience more than reviewing their own progress with us. (Refer to assignments suggested in Chapter 7 under research and evaluation.) They are required to practice skills of evaluation in their assignments and examine the outcomes they have achieved and assist their constituents' assessments of what they have experienced and achieved. This involves helping them choose methods to apply, exploring which theoretical perspectives help, keeping track of progress being made, and knowing how this information shapes the work going forward. Addressing the major tasks and issues while enabling students to deal with their own feelings about the process prepares them for how they will achieve the same thing with those they serve. Excitement over progress made and disappointment over hopes not met are part of the work.

As in other areas addressed in the text, our work with students provides a model for their work in our settings. Through the ongoing work of review, summation, and evaluation, we keep track of the levels of growth accomplished in the context of the goals and objectives. The ongoing work in supervision that prepares students for review and evaluation also prepares them for their need to incorporate review and evaluation into their assignments. Enabling students to apply these approaches to their work with constituents and communities is facilitated by their experience and participation in the work of review and evaluation of their own progress. When asked to conduct a review with their constituents for evaluation, they have an automatic model to work from.

Questions that lead to discussions in field education supervision that help us keep on track with review and evaluation include prompting recall of how students began the year and anticipating the next phase of learning ahead. This provides a natural comparison and documentation of progress made and how to prepare for what is ahead. If we identify gaps, we might ask the following questions:

> What is needed so that we can address the gaps that we identified?
> What have you learned about your strengths and growth points? How have you used yourself as a justice-based practitioner, and what does this tell you about the progress you have made?
> What is going well and why? What is going less well and why? Is there something we might do differently to increase progress in achieving our goals? If so, what and why?
> Where are we in relation to our aims? How will we know when we get there?

These questions are a means to assess and plan for next steps as we look back while looking forward (Carroll, 2010b). Additionally, the following items are useful to consider:

> Identify what students rely on from us during supervision. This promotes awareness of what they may require as they navigate toward greater autonomy.
> Review written and oral evaluations and supervisory agendas, process recordings, logs, or journals that provide evidence of professional growth and areas for future work. This review is best done with the student.
> Recall and share experiences that triggered strong emotional reactions and ultimately resulted in professional growth and self-awareness. This provides a meaningful way to recall and record developmental milestones and prepares students for an autonomous review of their abilities (Bennett & Deal, 2009; Bogo 2010; 2015; Grossman et al., 1990; Woods & Hollis, 2000).
> Acknowledge the uncertainty of leaving their work before a well-rounded ending has been accomplished. This enables more realistic expectations for closure.

When applying these questions to their work, we must ensure that students understand the importance of considering ways to evaluate progress from the system's point of view (Fortune, 2015). This means understanding the system's needs and methods that fit. This is an often neglected but important aspect of practice and essential from a justice-based perspective (Ishizuka & Husain, 2015). Another important aspect is paying equal attention to termination issues across units of attention (Harrigan, Fauri, & Netting, 1998; Knight, 2014).

Regarding the final point, because groups are small communities, their endings are unique and merit different attention from endings with individuals or families. Members of groups may have to deal with the concurrent ending of three different relationships: with the group leader, with the work of the group, and with each other. Not only the needs of individual members but also their attachment to the dissolving community of supportive others must be considered. When groups have been successful, members have formed ties that may not be easily replicated (Knight 2014; Walsh, 2007). The type of group and phase of its development may have relevance to the timing of the student's leaving. For instance, consider what the reason is for terminating the group. In addition, consider whether the group was organized as time limited or ongoing, the group's membership was closed or open, the group continues but the leader or cofacilitator is changing or moving on, and whether the termination is natural or premature. Given these considerations, what rituals can be used to enhance a healthy good-bye (Shulman, 2012)? Task groups, committees, or peer group experiences for students may possess similar issues and represent particularly powerful learning experiences requiring thoughtful termination discussions.

> Consider a generalist practice level student working with adolescents in groups who was eager to learn how the youths experienced their work together. She was working toward termination with the group, and she was not sure that asking for their verbal assessments would yield what they really felt. She wanted to give them a way to tell her whether the group experience had been helpful and to protect their identity, but she did not believe asking them to write something on their last session would work either. She struggled over whether she should approach asking for their opinions from the point of view of their willingness to contribute to her developing practice or from the notion of giving them an opportunity to think through what worked for them during the duration of the group. She decided to tackle the question with the youths and prompted a discussion with them about the value of evaluation for whom

and for what. The youths were intrigued and engaged in the discussion; one of them asked whether she could send a survey and a reminder that they could choose to respond to. The student created an anonymous electronic form titled "#Answer this!" The responses were brief but pointed to the value of the group for the respondents. It was clear that this exercise provided a valuable interchange between the student and the youths beyond the simple completion of an evaluation form, yet the student saw that although hearing their opinions was valuable, the effort was an insufficient way to evaluate the group's effectiveness. She became curious about how she might include a way of tracking behaviors next time and engaging in the discussion about evaluation with the group sooner. She learned the importance of allowing space and time to obtain opinions about the service we provide and was ready to build on this experience to incorporate evaluation into her work in the future.

How different might have been this student's experience and level of competency achieved if the field instructor had introduced the importance of evaluation early in the placement? Planning and exploration about ways to evaluate the group's effectiveness and the youths' experience of the student's interventions could have been integrated in to the expectations of this assignment.

Our work with students therefore entails keeping tabs on time and preparing them for reviews, evaluations, transitions, and terminations in their work with us and with constituents over the course of the academic year. We are working at both in parallel time. Keeping track of the thresholds monitors the journey, marks the goals and accomplishments achieved, and identifies unfinished business. Evaluation and endings are tied together, and each supervisory session provides its own opportunity to review and anticipate these markers for our work with students and their work in the setting.

Terminations and Transitions

Termination is a transition, but not all transitions are total terminations. Both involve change and loss and all the complex individual emotions and responses that endings raise in us (Bennett & Deal, 2009). Terminations and transitions require reorientation as we try to adapt to change, welcome or unwelcome, planned or unplanned. A student's departure from placement marks several different terminations, for example, with their work assignments, with the placement setting, and with us. Leaving the field placement also marks a transition and is connected to the excitement of moving on to an anticipated next phase, but if there is uncertainty, students can be left feeling they are in limbo (Baum, 2004, 2011; Gelman, 2009).

Students in their first field education setting end their roles as students at the placement site and are in transition to a new phase. This may include continuing to another placement or perhaps choosing a different path. Either way, they are also involved in attempting to make sense of what they have achieved in the generalist practice year. Specialized practice level students are ending their role as students and moving on to becoming our colleagues. For some, this may be the end of financial impoverishment and the end of non-professional jobs. Each case entails negotiating a transition in relationships with classroom peers and faculty, and with students' specific relationship to the field education placement, task supervisor, field liaison, field instructor, staff, constituents and communities served. Some may be eager to finish and move on, often thinking that school is almost over and they need to find a job, or they are exhausted and need a break. The reverse is also true, with students lamenting that no matter how hard they tried, they did not get to where they had hoped, or if only they had had more time. They see that even the achievement of a planned transition, or the identification of a new goal, involves some loss of comfort and increased anxiety associated with ending a phase that enabled attainment of a new plateau or beginning something new.

The reactions to termination are further complicated when the ending is unplanned, unanticipated, or premature. Perhaps the end of term seems to have come too quickly (Baum, 2004; Gelman, 2009). The length of the education placement sets a structure for the work with students that may not match the extent or nature of the work assigned (Gelman, 2009). This applies to any placement. Not all that is attempted may be possible to achieve in the time set by the academic calendar. In addition, studies have reported that student-determined terminations create an atmosphere of guilt for leaving work undone; this is combined with students being in a "temporary role exit" (Baum, 2004, p. 165) and feelings of being on uncertain ground when in transition. These reactions are differentiated from agreed endings or those determined by service users.

Our own reactions may be different. We may feel relief for the break from the added responsibilities of having a student, and we may be more focused on questions about our performance (Baum, 2006). Although the literature suggests that as we terminate with our students, we model the termination process for them, Baum (2006) proposes that the differences in our reactions from our students complicate the ability to model how to manage the termination process.

In short, teaching students the termination process is an opportunity to build on students' understanding of the components involved in endings and in supporting their ability to give adequate attention to this phase from the start of their work. This can be achieved by being watchful about time, evaluating progress made on an ongoing basis, keeping an eye on next steps, and managing the emotions involved. Preparing for the actual ending can be a complicated phase of work to manage. Yet, it is also an opportunity to teach from a holistic view of practice, incorporating authentic responses regarding its meaning for us, our students, and the people and communities we serve. Terminations and transitions are opportunities to incorporate evaluations into the process as an integral component to examine achievements and longed-for promises.

Teaching Tasks Associated With Termination

As crucial and complex as termination and endings can be, they are often neglected, whether in helping students end their work well or dealing with the end of field education and field supervision (Baum, 2011; Gelman, 2009; Grossman et al., 1990; L. Shulman, 1994; Wall, 1994; Walsh, 2007). At the same time, even if preparing for termination is addressed in an ongoing manner, when the ending comes it may not be given enough or comprehensive attention, or the attention comes too late to manage the complexity of ending well. Considerations for termination and processes of evaluation start with the choice of student assignments. The reality of the status as a student automatically delineates a time frame for working relationships. We help students work under a time-limited contract at any level of service where ending is part of the initial goal-setting and contracting phase and where the rhythm of work is kept in context (Baum, 2006; Feiner & Couch, 1985; Gelman et al., 2007; Sherby, 2004; Wall, 1994).

Social work literature has historically focused on negative or difficult reactions to the terminations we experience, such as denial, indirect or direct anger, regression, avoidance, bargaining, mourning, and depression. Within this frame, not giving voice to the negative emotions associated to abandonment is viewed as avoidant behavior (Garland, Jones, & Kolodny, 1976; Northern, 1988; Palombo, 1982). However, more recent strengths-based and resiliency-oriented theoretical perspectives have pointed to the positive reactions associated with termination such as achieving growth and maturity, positive advancement, increased self-reliance, celebration for what has been accomplished, and hope for the future (Corey, 2016; Fortune, 1987, 2015; Morgaine & Capous-Desyllas, 2015; Shulman, 1994, 2012; Siebold, 2007; Woods & Hollis, 2000). In these ways of thinking about endings, the expressions of sadness and regret that a valued relationship will not continue are viewed as positive, healthy responses to connections that have personal meaning rather than as problematic or regressive responses (Walsh, 2007). Tackling the obstacles provides examples of how to manage other experiences of change, crisis, and chaos. The lessons learned from coping, managing, enduring, and prevailing through these daily realities are acknowledged and celebrated. In this respect, teaching culminates during the termination phase. We help students to anticipate reactions to endings, transitions, and change from all the systems they have been working with and, of course, their own reactions to this process. It also demands that we be mindful of our reactions too. An ongoing balanced appraisal is essential to this process.

Each ending experience presents challenges and opportunities for growth and learning for us, students, and the individuals and systems served through field placement assignments. Our role is to prompt students to identify the range of feelings involved, navigate them when they become uncomfortable, instill curiosity about when and why they move away from these feelings, critically analyze how the gains or barriers to change have been influenced by their efforts, increase their capacity to develop and grow personally and professionally through this ending phase of the work, and provide an inclusive and fair evaluation of the work achieved and work left to be done.

Enabling students to identify their feelings about endings. Reflecting on the range of emotions, reactions, defenses, and behaviors—positive as well as negative—in ending helps students prepare for the work of this phase of the helping process (Fortune, 2015; Gelman, 2009; Siebold, 2007; Woods & Hollis, 2000). Whether the assignment being terminated involves work on the micro, mezzo, or macro levels, reactions to ending will emerge; processing these reactions is part of the development of a professional stance for the task of terminating well and promotes meaning and learning. The following is a guide to the work of terminating:

> Review whether content on anticipating endings has been incorporated into discussions about the work. Establish how prepared the student is in tackling endings and how the student has prepared those being served.

- Enable a discussion of the meaning of endings for students derived from their own multiple dimensions of identity. Acknowledge that ending means different things to different people (Fortune, 2015), and facilitate the differentiation of these meanings and rituals from our own and those of the individuals and communities they have been working with. The implications of gift giving, hugging, and shaking hands is useful material for discussion.
- Promote reflection on students' personal needs as they relate to the work (e.g., to be needed, liked, or in control) and anticipate how these may affect the termination process.
- Assess the student's capacity to manage the feelings and conflicts associated with discussing potentially painful, uncomfortable material; continue to teach in ways that increase that capacity.
- Review process recordings, journals, and logs as a foundation for discussions of termination. Check for omissions, missed opportunities to address the issue, insufficient time spent on issues, and a lack of depth or evidence of conflict and discomfort. Suggest a written reflection on the termination process. Use these materials to access the student's assumptions and feelings about termination. Resolve blocks or barriers to identifying these assumptions so that the student will be able to do the same with the individuals and communities served (Woods & Hollis, 2000).
- Talk about the best ways to introduce rituals, activities, and interventions that facilitate dealing with feelings about endings. Some examples in the context of group work include a simulated toast to each person saying what members learned from each other, exchanges of mementos with special meaning such as group photos or certificates of completion, or a potluck supper with each person contributing a personal favorite (Fortune, 2015).
- Share our own feelings about termination to help further the discussion (Shulman, 1994, 2012). Modeling, promoting reflection, and keeping present are critical.

Planning for the future. To move on to new ground, students need to acquire an understanding of the progress and process of their learning achievements as well as the learning goals they have identified for the next stage of their professional development. This is how the process of ongoing review and evaluation assists our work. We can identify where we have been and where we need to go. Planning for next steps includes processing information and experiences that inform and anticipate what likely lies ahead. This provides foresight on how to proceed and places social work experiences in the context of lifelong learning.

In the way that we prepare service users for future problem solving, we prepare our students to be their own bridge from one learning experience to the next. The aim is to help students own their achievements while identifying what they still need to work on in their future practice. It is not enough for us to understand the students' strengths and growth points, it is essential to ensure that our understanding is transmitted so students can own this knowledge as their own. This confirms how much they have learned and identifies what they should continue to work on. It clarifies possible misconceptions regarding the work they accomplished. We assist and facilitate the learning effort, but students do the work. Students may need support to identify what they have contributed and what is left behind as they exit the setting such as specific programs, projects just getting started, new ideas, new services, and so forth. Spending time to consider how to sustain the initiatives they have introduced provides important learning regarding organizational change and sustainability.

We should also introduce some rituals to mark the end of student placements that reflect relevance for this stage of work. Rituals acknowledge the importance of the experience for all involved—students, staff, and us. We are responsible for making sure that the student's last day is acknowledged. Rituals also highlight the importance of closure to our student's experiences in the placement. Even if an agencywide formal good-bye is planned, encourage students to take an active role in their termination by scheduling private final conversations with staff members who have been important to their field placement experience (Sweitzer & King, 2009). This prepares students for their eventual entry into the professional arena and the reality that at graduation, students and staff may become colleagues and collaborators. This may be particularly important when a task supervisor has been available during the student's placement. In these situations, it may be helpful to arrange a three-way meeting for the student, the task supervisor, and field instructors so the learning can be reviewed. Each situation is different, and each requires some planning regarding what is needed to respond to the student's individualized needs.

Field Liaisons

Field liaisons have a special role to play in determining how best to respond to the various questions and concerns that occur throughout the stages of a student's field education experience. In most social work education programs, full-time or adjunct faculty are assigned to advise students regarding field performance and to coordinate with the student's field instructor. Each program's structures and expectations of this role may differ, but there are some common expected responsibilities. Field liaisons are a partner and part of the team assigned to support each student's learning experience. They may select sites and place students as representatives of the social work program's field education faculty and staff; provide support to placement settings, field instructors, and students; and they act as a bridge or connection between the academic institution and the field education components of social work education. In general, liaisons are primarily advocates for and guardians of the student's educational field placement experiences in the broadest sense. That is, they are part of the social work program's connection to the practice community, and they serve as administrators and monitors of the reciprocal relationship that maintains and promotes program renewal and the professionalization of practice.

Consider the skills and roles required in the following.

> An Asian American student is placed in a setting where the staff and community served are predominantly Black. She approaches her field liaison stating that she feels invisible. How should the liaison respond, and how should they proceed in discussing this with the field instructor?

> A student arrives late for the meeting with her liaison and field instructor at the placement setting in an underresourced community. She explains that she had difficulty hailing a taxi that morning. After further discussion the liaison learns that the student has fears about traveling to the agency's neighborhood, and the field instructor told her that she might want to change her placement, or she can take a taxi every day, which the student has been doing ever since. How should the liaison respond, and how should the implied issues of bias against the community and the potential financial burden for the student be raised while responding to the concerns of safety?

> A Black field instructor has two White social work students. They feel that the field instructor is unprofessional and does

not know what she is doing. They approach the field liaison together and express their views about many areas where the setting has not met the needs of the community including an unkempt waiting area. Additionally, the students are upset and complain to the liaison that the setting does not have adequate work space for them. How should the liaison respond, and how might the issues of race, White privilege, and dominant world values play a part in their reactions?

› A generalist practice level male student served 25 years in prison. He was open about this on his admission forms, and he is articulate about his experience and the effect it has had on his determination to serve. As settings often require background checks before confirming a placement, it was difficult finding a setting that would accept this student. He was eventually placed in a special project working with people who were formerly incarcerated assisting them in their transitions from prison to community life. The student's own adjustment was not going smoothly, he admits to feeling behind in the world, he is having difficulty using technology, and is challenged in keeping up with e-mails and timely communications with his field instructor, field liaison, and classroom professors. His field instructor is supportive but is concerned that she may be adjusting her expectations because of her sensitivity to this student's needs, which are like those of the individuals served in the setting. The liaison questions whether it was fair to this student and field instructor to place the student in this program. How does the liaison deal with these concerns with the student and the field instructor? How should the field liaison support this student and field instructor? How does management of the concerns raised change depending on the racial identities of those involved?

Responsibilities and Roles of Field Liaisons

The responsibilities discussed here and mentioned in the scenarios throughout this book incorporate several features of the field liaison's roles of administrator, advocate, adviser, instructor, mediator, and evaluator (Bogo, 2010; Moen et al., 2016; Raphael & Rosenblum, 1987, 1989). Although the responsibilities of liaisons may blend and overlap, this section describes the main responsibilities contained in these roles.

Administrative responsibilities. Offices of field education use field liaisons for establishing contact with potential settings, recommending sites for use as a placement, and for monitoring the setting's relationship with the university. They are responsible for several administrative components including ensuring that placement setting applications are reviewed, student grades are submitted, evaluation forms are completed, and student time sheets are received. They also match students for placement, monitor the student's experience, and approve the students' sixth week reviews and final evaluations. The methods used by the social work program for implementing these duties vary and can include visiting, phone contacts, and electronic connections. Placement matching may be implemented through individual or group sessions or be primarily based on paper or electronic assessments. Methods used are often relate to the stresses of managing remote locations, ratios of students to liaisons, and the liaisons' general administrative workload.

The administrative role also includes the important part liaisons play in maintaining the program's relationship with the practice community. They keep a check on issues affecting the practice community and bring these issues back to the program faculty for discussion and possible incorporation into the curriculum or continuing education programs. Thus, they create bridges and share information back and forth to contribute to program renewal and to the professionalization of the practice community.

Educational responsibilities. Field liaisons may offer seminars on supervision and may be teachers of SIFIs. They provide clarification of a social work education program's procedures and the school's performance outcomes. This valuable information helps students and field instructors know what is expected of them in field education regarding the program's generalist and specialized practice level competencies and requirements. The field liaison also assists in the development of a better match between a student's style of learning and a field instructor's style of teaching and instilling respect for the inherent differences. This may involve becoming active in explaining teaching methods and approaches, offering specific strategies to achieve learning objectives, or providing supplemental contact with students to support achievement of learning objectives. Additionally, bolstering the integration of theory and practice is another area where the field liaison can be a resource for students and field instructors; some programs' field liaisons run seminars with the students they monitor. Liaisons also keep track of learning opportunities that expand student workloads. For example, Tully (2015) points to the liaison's role in ensuring that students have opportunities working with group methods so that they may build group-work skills and integrate learning about groups through direct experience.

Advisory responsibilities. Field liaisons provide consultation, advice, and suggestions to students and field instructors, and they provide resources to the educational endeavor. They may offer suggestions on modifying teaching methods and assignments, and they may add perspectives that lead to improved management of teaching and learning. They add their own time, effort, and expertise to increase the viability of the placement and learning experience. For example, liaisons provide an important link among field instructors, placement, and schools of social work over issues that may need smoothing out to provide a more favorable learning environment for students. Situations that include a task supervisor and off-site field instructor may require coordination (Zuchowski, 2015). The field liaison's involvement in establishing specific educational learning contracts when complications emerge are also part of their advisory responsibilities.

Mediation. Liaisons are concerned primarily with promoting optimal learning situations; they seek to strengthen the educational relationships between field instructors and students, promote communication, and identify and clarify any learning issues needing attention. Liaisons are particularly vital when obstacles arise or when students or field instructors seek consultation to strengthen the supervisory or learning experience. Modeling the creation of a conducive environment for learning and making it possible to raise otherwise avoided discussions is a major function of the field liaison. This means that field liaisons need to have the capacity to initiate and facilitate the challenging conversations and questions that emerge on multiple and overlapping dimensions of identity discussed throughout this book. Those who have experience and training in conducting challenging conversations offer a special resource to engaging, assessing, and intervening when issues arise. Field liaisons can be very helpful in assisting our work, setting guidelines and teaching strategies, completing performance appraisals, evaluating outcomes, and reframing challenges in learning opportunities. They are also important resources for students who may need assistance in resolving communication blocks between themselves and members of the learning team. Extra support may be needed for any member of the learning team, such as students who feel caught between field instructors and the task supervisor, the task supervisor who may not be as informed about the social work program's requirements, or the field instructor in managing the extra responsibilities of a new role.

Evaluative responsibilities. The final determination of the field education grade is submitted to directors of field education by field liaisons after reading student evaluations. They review the field instructor's recommendations and they independently gather information on student learning opportunities and field performance evaluations. Field liaisons also evaluate field placements. They provide information to the field education office on the type of learning experience field instructors provide to students and on the learning opportunities available in each setting.

Contacts With Liaisons

Field liaisons maintain contact with field instructors and placement settings to monitor the learning experience provided to students. As the structures of field education change, so does the range of programmatic arrangements surrounding how field liaisons fulfill their monitoring responsibilities. Some programs that place students in distant block placements hire field liaisons who are located near the placement. This facilitates closer contact with the student and placement but places potential strains for the liaison's connection with the academic program. Other programs hire liaisons regardless of their location and use technological advances to conquer geographical distances. Regardless of these programmatic differences, contact with liaisons provides a means for monitoring and access to needed resources.

Usually the means of contact include a three-way conversation with the liaison, field instructor, and student. Placements that use a task supervisor may include this person as an additional contributor. Any member of the collaboration—students, field instructors, task supervisors, and field liaisons—may initiate a request for contact as the need arises. As there are many more field instructors and students than field liaisons, field instructors need not wait until liaisons arrange a contact or a visit (Dalton, Stevens, &Maas-Brady, 2011; Ligon & Ward, 2005).

The field liaison usually leads the conversation. Conducting this meeting is a method in itself, and schools are accountable for providing the training and support needed to meet the responsibilities of the field liaison's role (Power & Bogo, 2002). Although tasks and the nature of field liaison contacts or visits during the academic year vary, unless called for a specific purpose, the contact or visit's timing often defines the focus and task. For example, a contact or a visit at the beginning of student placements will by necessity focus on the educational task ahead and on an evaluation of the educational opportunities being made available to students. As the semester proceeds, it is then possible for field liaisons to begin an appraisal of student learning needs and competencies. Contact or visits that take place during subsequent semesters incorporate the achievements of the previous semester and encourage anticipation of end-of-year goals. If a contact or visit is close to the end of the program, the student's preparedness for entering the field is affirmed, and the field instructor's contributions to the student's learning is placed in the context of preparing the student for entry-level practice. This final contact may also be used as a job application rehearsal for students to articulate what their education has prepared them for and the special skills and attributes they possess.

Visits scheduled to mediate an emerging problem or create an educational learning contract focus on defining the problem and seek solutions or strategies to address the identified concerns. Chapter 9 discusses these circumstances.

Regardless of the reason for the visit, students are meant to take an active role in the conversations by defining their goals and reflecting on progress toward these goals. Liaisons and field instructors encourage students to take an active part in the discussions by eliciting their contributions. In this way, the contact provides an opportunity for the integration of theory and practice, evaluation of students' developing professional identity, and their ownership of competency mastery and learning needs. It is an opportunity for field instructors to provide feedback to students and to restate issues needing emphasis. It is another opportunity to discuss power differentials that may occur based on identity differences to create a safe space for students to learn and grow in the process. In whatever format these contacts occur, field liaisons offer support and guidance, and they provide a source of additional consultation, a third set of ears, about teaching and learning issues in field education.

Field Education Supervision: Lifelong Learning

Throughout this book we present the field education supervisory relationship as a primary ingredient in achieving a conducive learning environment; the intent has been to reinforce perspectives of a justice- and competency-based lens. We have argued how important field instructor training and awareness to working with diverse students are to improve supervisory practice and to contribute to the preparation of a competent diverse workforce (Walters et al., 2016).

Two recent contributions to the literature on supervision deserve special note; one presents a model of cross-cultural student supervision (Lee & Kealy, 2018) and the other addresses a model for engaging in "critical conversations" in supervision (O'Neil & del Mar Fariña, 2018, p. 298). Both articles support the tenets of this text and argue for supervisors to "bear the responsibility for introducing culture and other social justice issues in supervisory conversations" (Lee & Kealy, p. 310). Likewise, O'Neil and del Mar Fariña argues for our need to "gain capacity to engage and explore inevitable dynamics of racial and social injustice, prejudice, power and privilege that emerge in social interactions, particularly in the supervisory triad (supervisor, supervisee and client(s))." (p. 307). Additionally, a number of theoretical frameworks support this work including transformative teaching perspectives (Fazio-Griffith, & Ballard, 2016; Shohet, 2011; Siebold, 2007; Weld, 2012), reflective supervision (Scott Heller & Gilkerson, 2009; Weatherston et al., 2010), mindfulness techniques (Epstein, 2003; Tomlin, Weatherston, & Pavkov, 2014), attachment theoretical perspectives applied to supervision (Bennett, 2008; Bennett & Deal, 2009; Bennett, Mohr, Szoc, & Saks, 2008; Bennett & Saks, 2006), and a relational perspective (Knight 2012; Ornstein & Moses, 2010; Schamess, 2006). These perspectives represent efforts to facilitate self-awareness and reflection and encourage development of the student's attention to existing power differentials and an understanding that field education supervision is a place to model authentic relationships. These approaches support taking every opportunity to talk about dimensions of identity and issues of power and privilege as part of our regular work together and for supporting our intentions to remain aware of the realities that surround us and our students (Love, 2013).

Some self-evaluation tools are provided in the Chapter 10 Appendix, and we refer you to Murdock, Ward, Ligon, and Jindani (2006) for an assessment tool that describes various aspects of our role. Although this tool was developed prior to competency-based education, it is easy to follow, and it is possible to add some items that focus on work with the competencies.

Summary and Concluding Thoughts

This book differs considerably from the previous two editions because of the 14 years that separate the publication of the first edition and this one, the ways social work practice has responded to the social and global changes during this period, and the critical effects of competency-based social work education on teaching and practice. Although competency-based education was an issue being discussed when we were writing the first edition, it had been discussed for some time before, and its approval in 2008 was not on our horizon in 2005. The power of this change continues to reverberate, and one of its effects has been the focus of this text, which is that the mandates to teach the designated CSWE (2015a) competencies touch everything to do with social work education. The goals we set, the assignments we choose, our educational assessments, the methods we use to get our students to where they need to be, and the very focus of our teaching are all affected. Finally, the process of preparing for and writing this book has had a powerful effect on us.

We have taken the mandates of the CSWE (2015a) EPAS beyond ensuring we address each competency. We have embraced our profession's global mission to work for justice and translated this to the processes of field education as the signature pedagogy of social work education. We propose that when field educators take up this mantle, the efforts of our colleagues in academe will be bolstered and supported to the full intent of what social work education needs to be. Together we can work toward our quest for justice and for competence of those we teach. This book begins the dialogue and sets a path for this phase in our journey.

The first edition was based on work begun in a committee of field educators responsible for administering SIFIs in the New York Schools of Social Work Consortium. We collaborated on the materials we were using to teach new field instructors and compiled these into an enhanced curriculum that became the foundation of the book's first edition. The text achieved its goal for being a primer for new field instructors and a guide for experienced field instructors as they continued their professional growth and development. We saw then that the work did not cover everything one needs to know about field education or being a field instructor; it was a beginning effort to consolidate knowledge and experience on field education. We declared it as a work in progress and designated field instructors as equal partners in the educational endeavor and situated at the core of students' learning; we acknowledged that field instructors cannot achieve all that needs to be done in isolation and that much depends on the support received from the placement setting and the social work program. As the challenges and critical part field instructors play demand respect and recognition, we have argued for enhanced SIFIs and seminars for experienced field instructors on special topics to enrich their teaching. None of this has changed.

What has changed is at the essence of our work. Our roles as teachers of practice and translators of the realities of practice have been affected by competency-based education. The CSWE (2015a) competencies provide goalposts, and we teach and translate the practice principles embedded in them.

In hindsight, the second edition in 2008 did not fully address the needs of field instructors as they faced competency-based education. We saw that the transition toward what competency-based education could fully offer us and our students required a shift to generalist practice. We altered our examples to include more mezzo and macro practice stressed in the 2008 EPAS (CSWE, 2008). The major thrust of change in the second edition drew special attention to social and economic justice and the need to facilitate our students' understanding and preparedness to incorporate human rights into their practice. We took the position that we cannot teach social work practice without teaching students about the struggle for human rights and social and economic justice here and around the world, and we offered ways to weave human rights into supervisory discussions. Furthermore, we suggested that field education should model a human rights framework.

We saw that this position had ramifications for field instructors and field placements. Our sight was on the need for new models for field education. We envisioned agencies, social work programs, and community leaders working in partnership with those served to develop new models of field education that better respond to persistent social problems. This conception moves us toward placement settings and contexts that bring us closer to constituents' needs. We saw this as a bold position, but we felt confident in proposing it. This is the second way that our perspective has changed.

What has emerged in this third edition moves more firmly to a justice-based framework for field education. This framework supports our profession's pursuit of justice. It fortifies field instructors as they take hold of the CSWE (2015a) competencies to improve their teaching. It targets our aims toward preparing students for competent practice in an increasing globalized world with human rights and justice at the forefront of their minds; it "means making the decision to live our lives from a waking position" (Love, 2013, p. 602). A direct implication results for the field instructor and student relationship and is the third area where our perspectives have evolved. We underscore that as Freire (1993) suggested, social work is praxis: critical consciousness with social action. Field instructors teach and mentor students not just to be knowledgeable and skilled but also to be competent advocates, organizers, managers, counselors, and activists for social change that includes being awake to justice and rights.

Informed by the first two editions of this text, this third edition has embraced but moved beyond equality to embrace equity and inclusion and liberation. We ask our readers to consider what it would take for us to use the field instruction supervisory relationship to not only ensure equitable and inclusive relationships but also to be committed as a professional mandate to work always side-by-side or behind those we serve to support the taking down of the structures and barriers that privilege, oppress, and continue to maintain the status quo. We support the move from mere tracking of numbers that monitor our movement toward diversity on identity politics to a move that considers ways that shift and influence institutional transformation. We emphasize the urgency for each of us to understand our place in our profession's mission of justice and the work we need to do to develop consciousness and capacity to empathize, engage, assess, intervene, evaluate, and transform.

Field instruction is a challenging and important part of social work education. We train our own, and each of us has a hand in preparing the future workforce in the profession by passing on the history, values, ethics, and philosophy of social work. We do this in settings ranging far and wide, across a region or state, around a large metropolitan city, or in an international agency. We do this from the boundaries of our local contexts while responding to the reality that those we serve bring the world with them as they walk through our doors. We teach in myriad fields of practice, each with a unique mandate and organizational culture. We teach across methods, units of attention, and international boundaries—all of which intersect with each other. We teach with a historical and structural analysis of the systems of power and privilege, oppression, and dominance that have created and continue to create so many of the problems faced by the individuals, families, and communities we serve. This understanding keeps us and our students alert about how we sometimes serve as gatekeepers for maintaining the status quo. This means we need to support each other as we work to stay vigilant about this possibility, and we teach our students to do the same. In Tuck's and Yang's terms we do this to keep each other vigilant and alert to missteps along our way (2012).

We teach students about person in environment and about strengths and resiliency. We understand that teaching from a perspective of person *in* environment requires concentration on the person *and* the environment. More and more it seems the reality we respond to is people in hostile environments; therefore, we must also recognize these conditions so that remediation and reparation is possible. Concentrating on promoting a person's resiliency is strengthened by equal attention to assessing structures and conditions that require people to be resilient. Instead of orienting ourselves to the individual's problem or need, focusing on rights brings "issues of social inequity, discrimination, oppression and social injustice" forward (Kam, 2014, p. 734), and it becomes more possible to attend to the problems rooted in the environment and structures that surround the individual. How else are strategies for support appropriately identified? Aiding our students' appreciation of this fact pushes our profession forward and ensures that advancing rights and justice and social change are incorporated into the minds and hearts of those entering our field. Individuals are not divorced from the realities of their environments and contexts.

To achieve this goal, we teach students about social work as mindful practice, requiring persistent collaboration with many disciplines. Instilling collaboration and building coalitions are how we achieve success. As important, we need to teach our students about self-care and the impact of retriggering historical trauma and secondary trauma in our daily work. We are in this for the long haul, and our students benefit from the early development of means and methods to sustain themselves through the challenges ahead.

This third edition builds on the experience of working with the CSWE (2008, 2015a) competencies and our resolve to provide a justice-based framework for field education. The focus on justice builds purpose in field education supervision to engage in challenging dialogues and to build our capacity to have these conversations with each other, our colleagues, and those we serve. These conversations promote a deeper understanding of injustice, offer strategies for change, and inspire a desire to intervene to advance rights and make a difference in people's lives and in the communities where they live.

In addition to recommending strengthening SIFIs for new and experienced field instructors, we recommend the formation of communities of practice to support field educators as they engage in challenging dialogues with students. This will not only sustain their work, it will add resources and energy by sharing strategies and stories of triumph. This work is strengthened through sharing and collaboration. Collaboration will also enhance how we teach to those competencies that take us outside our normal and usual way of tackling service delivery. If these learning communities also include our colleagues from academe—classroom faculty and field liaisons—the conversations will build a stronger bridge between class learning and field learning.

We hope this book will ease the trek toward justice by providing a clearer view of the practice principles embedded in the CSWE (2015a) competencies, how to embrace them in our teaching, and tools that begin the work of engaging in meaningful communication with our students regarding the pernicious effects of privilege and oppression. This is a beginning. Next steps include continuing this discussion while advancing practice, igniting commitment, and improving our students' capabilities as change agents. ¡Ándale!

CHAPTER 10 APPENDIX

This Appendix contains several items related to the topics covered in this chapter, including issues involved in preparing for termination and three termination scenarios from the field instructor's and student's perspective, topics to cover in meetings with field liaisons, a description of a field instructor's educational journal, questions that prompt the field instructor's self-evaluation of teaching techniques, and self-assessment forms for field instructors and students.

Preparing for Termination

Consider the following:

> How do the similarities or differences among dimensions of identity influence the experience of this placement and supervision?
> Were the inherent differences between you and your student addressed? If so, in what ways were you able to find productive ways to work with these differences? If not, what made it difficult, and how did you go about navigating the course through the challenges?
> How have you changed? You may also share how the work with your student has affected you and your capacity as a field educator. How has the nature of field education supervision changed as you became more familiar with your role? How is this experience different from other supervisory experiences?
> Are you direct with the student in identifying what makes this experience positive or less than what was hoped for? If learning goals have not been fully achieved, have the factors that hindered goal achievement been discussed?
> How clear have you been in outlining your student's progress? Were you able to facilitate the student's integration of classroom and field learning? How might you achieve greater

clarity or improve the student's integration between theory and practice even in the final meetings?
- What are some of the rewards of your experience as a field instructor? What aspects of your role would you like to change? What further support or training do you need?
- Are your ideas about field education or social work education changing? If so, in what ways?
- How could your role be better supported by the social work educational program? By your agency?
- Will you be a field instructor again?
- What can the program or setting do to retain field instructors? To whom can you communicate your thoughts about this?

Termination Scenarios

The following scenarios are provided to prompt dialogue between field instructors and students about different perspectives on termination.

Scenario 1: Student's Perspective: "I've applied for a job here, maybe I won't need to terminate."

Your field instructor told you 2 weeks ago to begin termination with the individuals and the project committee you have been working with, but you have not begun to do this yet. It is a difficult topic to discuss, especially in relation to one task group you feel very attached to. Besides, you have applied for a job in the agency, and you hope you will get the job, so you may not have to terminate with this project at all.

Field Instructor's Perspective

You told your student 2 weeks ago, to begin terminating with individuals and projects assigned, but to date progress on this has not been raised in supervision. The process recordings and logs submitted this week again show no mention of the topic. In field education supervision, the student asked you to keep several cases open and active, but you think they are appropriate for termination. The student has not begun to prepare the work committee on a project he is involved in for transition to another worker. This student has also applied for a job in the agency. Although he has done adequately as a student, you and your director think you can find a better candidate for the job. You do not plan to hire him, but you have not yet told him.

Scenario 2: Student's Perspective: "Oh no, how can I leave this individual?"

Your field instructor told you 2 weeks ago to begin termination with Mrs. Jones, your favorite case assignment, who unfortunately still has many unresolved problems. You meant to discuss termination the previous week and this week, but both times Mrs. Jones raised very important issues before you could get to it. This week she learned that her mother has a life-threatening illness, and she is very upset about it. You are tempted to give Mrs. Jones your home phone number because she seems so upset. How can you possibly tell her you are leaving? How will she ever last until a new worker can be assigned? What are you going to tell your field instructor?

Field Instructor's Perspective

You told your student 2 weeks ago to begin termination with Mrs. Jones, the student's favorite case assignment, who unfortunately still has many unresolved problems. Mrs. Jones will be placed on a waiting list for another worker. The student's process recordings show no evidence that she has raised the issue of termination and the reality of the waiting list. You are preparing to confront the student in supervision this week about her continued failure to raise this topic with the individuals she sees.

Scenario 3: Student's Perspective: "I have worked so hard, they will understand that I just didn't have time to get everything done in time."

You have been anticipating the end of your field placement for months and have been planning a trip immediately after your last day of placement. You have worked harder at this placement than you ever imagined possible. You have learned a lot and feel satisfied with your achievements. You have been so busy with all that needs to be done that you have not had a chance to fully prepare for your trip. Everything is in place for the end of your placement, and the important community event happening as the culmination of this semester's work is going well. You know that you will have a busy last week in placement and that there is a lot still to do, but you also know that the promise of your trip is what is keeping you going. You have worked extra hours, and you are waiting for your field instructor's response to your request to end a day early so that you can prepare for your trip. You are sure she will agree.

Field Instructor's Perspective

Your student has been intensely involved in planning a major community event scheduled for the last week of her field education placement. She has been working hard, but she seems preoccupied as the year comes to an end. You have been working with her to complete the planning of the event, and this has gone fairly well. However, it has come to your attention that she has not begun to prepare the final report, nor has she included time in her schedule for the postevent evaluation that is required. These are tasks that were included in your student's agenda related to this assignment. Because the event has required some overtime, your student has asked to terminate her placement a day early as compensation for the time involved. You do not see how she will be able to finish all that needs to be done without that extra day.

Consider the following positions and how they affect the above scenarios:

> You sense your student's reluctance about having to terminate work. You have gone slowly as you see that the student becomes anxious when you identify the additional administrative tasks associated with ending. You fear that conflict over what is required will ensue and you have perhaps gone slower than the reality of time will allow.
> You have been attempting to model what is involved in termination to allow the student time to anticipate what is involved before having to implement the skills and tasks required. You see now that your student is having more difficulty than you anticipated.
> You have ensured that you and your student have engaged in ongoing evaluations of progress made in the work, and what still needs to be achieved. A structure for the work of termination has been part of regular discussions within supervision.

Meetings With Field Liaisons

The following are topics to cover in meetings with field liaisons:

> Context and nature of actual and anticipated assignments that illustrate the learning opportunities and skill areas provided by the placement
> Issues related to field education itself, including how time is allotted, teaching methods used, the student's use of the field education relationship and supervisory process, and possible additional learning opportunities to enhance the learning experience
> Student progress in demonstrating skill attainment related to the competencies, clarification on any competency components, and achievements and challenges to date
> The student's growing understanding of our professional mission and values
> Opportunities for integration between field education and the social work program's curriculum
> How teaching and learning in a justice- and competency-based model has affected the experience and capability to engage in challenging conversations on difference and to engage in advancing rights
> The climate and skills needed to further discussions on inclusion, equity, power, privilege, and oppression
> Goals and objectives for the remaining academic term or next steps toward progress in the program, graduation, or career choices
> Clarification of the roles and responsibilities between the field instructor and task supervisor
> Any other issues or concerns

The Field Education Journal

Keeping a journal of our teaching, including the challenges, satisfactions, and dilemmas of this role, is recommended (Brookfield, 1990; Rogers & McDonald, 1992). Over time, the journals reflect how we develop as field instructors and how our students respond to our teaching. Using reflective journals to monitor our own growth parallels teaching students how to use recordings as a self-reflective tool in field education supervision. Not only are we modeling professionalism by our receptiveness, honesty, and openness we are also creating an environment for learning, self-reflection, and professional growth. Journals aid reflection on the process of learning by keeping track of critical episodes and by recording the actions and processes that enhance or hinder us (Brookfield, 1990). They serve as reflective and restorative tools that help us evaluate our growing capacities in engaging in and facilitating challenging dialogues in supervision.

Journal entries about critical incidents in our teaching and conversations with colleagues for feedback and consultation can help break the isolation that often surrounds teaching (East & Chambers, 2007). Videotaping supervisory sessions for SIFI training is another useful method (Rogers & McDonald, 1992). Edited sequences that represent excellence, a specific skill or, a problematic situation provide a rich perspective to help us and others increase supervisory proficiency.

We can promote the creation of supportive structures to improve our teaching practice by "bringing isolated individuals [field instructors] together to share experiences, by building communities of support, by finding voice in the public realm, and by developing alternative rewards" (Palmer, 1998, p. 824). This exists in the format of SIFIs; however, the challenge is to extend these supports to our community of field instructors beyond this initial injection of support.

After reviewing the teaching techniques in Appendix A, field instructors may wish to observe themselves for a week to assess the variety of techniques used in teaching. In the following weeks, adding one new teaching technique per week may be incorporated into their repertoire.

Responses to the following questions can be included in the field instructor's reflective journal. Remember to use this self-evaluation form at the end of a field placement experience to review whether your repertoire of teaching skills has expanded over the course of your work with students.

> Which teaching techniques have I used? Which competencies do I focus on? Which teaching methods are most useful in assisting my current students?
> Have I noticed reliance on one teaching method over another? Do I cover all the competencies, or are there some I need to incorporate more frequently?
> How have I begun to extend myself into a new aspect of teaching or range of techniques?

- Do my students' comments about how supervision is meeting their learning needs suggest they are ready for a change or should I continue what I am doing?
- How am I helping my students become more self-aware and confident in their practice?
- Am I supporting my students and myself to engage in challenging conversations to support justice-based practice? Do we work in such a way that increases the capacities of both of us to do so?
- How am I guiding students to find their professional style to work with the target population?
- Which new technique will I introduce into my repertoire, and how does this new technique fit my teaching style?
- Would Skype or online chatting as an alternative to face-to-face supervision facilitate the work? What other forms of technology might enhance the work?

Field Instructor's Self-Assessment Form (for Use Throughout the Academic Year)

	Yes	No	Somewhat
Was I prepared for what my student discussed today?			
Did I model self-awareness and reflective practice?			
Did I model how to share power and authority in this session?			
Was I in touch with my own feelings?			
Did I listen, and did I teach rather than lecture?			
Were my questions inquiring rather than leading?			
Did I avoid challenging dialogues or conflict?			

	Yes	No	Somewhat
Did I convey interest in my student's agenda?			
Did I prevent interruptions, and did I allow enough time for my student to talk?			
Did I apply a justice framework to the practice and policy issues discussed?			
Did I explore my student's cognitive and affective reactions and judgments?			
Did I engage the student in an analysis of power in the issues presented?			
Did my questions encourage critical thinking skills and student self-reflection?			
Did I encourage elaboration and invite questions?			
Did I provide balanced feedback?			
Did I provide the opportunity to link theory with practice?			
Did I supplement dominant theories with those that represent the communities and cultures of those served? Was a global perspective added?			
Did I link the competencies to my student's skill performance?			
Did I identify issues or patterns in the student's practice or in my teaching?			
Did I invite my student's self-reflection and self-evaluation?			
Is there any unfinished business left for our next session?			

	Yes	No	Somewhat
An area where I would like to see more improvement in my teaching is _____			
An area where I have noticed improvement in my teaching is _____			

Student's Self-Assessment (Used Intermittently During the Academic Year)

	Yes	No	Somewhat
Was I prepared for field education today?			
Did I prepare an agenda of my concerns?			
Was I preoccupied?			
Did I prevent interruptions to our session?			
Did I share my views and reactions freely?			
Am I pleased with how I communicated?			
Did I voice my questions and concerns?			
Did I listen?			
Was I able to link theory with practice?			
Was I able to ask for explanations when I was unclear?			
Was I in touch with my own feelings?			
Did I avoid challenging dialogues and areas where conflict may arise?			
Did I apply a justice and rights framework to the practice and policy issues discussed?			

	Yes	No	Somewhat
Did I avoid invitations to analyze existing issues of power?			
Do I understand how my performance relates to the competencies?			
Were my questions and concerns addressed?			
Was I able to incorporate theories and a global perspective in my work?			
Did I provide feedback?			
Did I engage in critical analysis or in self-reflection?			
What issues or patterns emerged in my learning or my practice?			
Is there any unfinished business left for our supervisory next session?			
An area where I have noticed improvement in my practice or understanding is _____			
An area where I would like to see more improvement in my practice or understanding is _____			

Part Three

Moving Forward

Chapter 11 stands alone in this section. It considers the connections among field education, the practice community, and academe and the importance of a combined response to shape our profession's future. The chapter presents an ambitious agenda. We articulate how we understand our past and status quo to master our future. We ask what should our strategic plan entail, what are our aspirations for the future of our profession, and how will they influence social work education in general and field education specifically? In response we consider current struggles from a justice-based perspective and examine signals that predict needed change, recognize existing opportunities, and point to promising initiatives rising in support of the individuals and communities we serve. The challenge is to forge forward to meet the challenges in front of us while examining and reviewing long-relied-on ways of working so that we might respond to meet current contexts and needs. Consequently, the central question becomes what social work educators, and especially those engaged in field education, must do to fulfill the obligation to produce social workers who can competently pursue justice.

CHAPTER 11

The Future of Social Work Education

The third edition of *Learning to Teach, Teaching to Learn* was written and published at a specific historical moment. Nearly every social issue that concerns social workers—immigration, health and mental health care, youth development, education, community violence, mental and physical abilities, women's rights, employment, the courts and criminal systems, housing, and the environment—is being reviewed and reconsidered at the highest levels of government. The future of long-established social benefits, including Medicaid, Social Security, food stamps, and public housing, is in doubt. Commitments to justice, the poor, inclusion, and safety, which social workers hold dear and are embedded in our Code of Ethics (NASW, 2017), are routinely challenged. Battles and renewed struggles for greater equity have been refueled for affirmative action, for civil rights, and government protections. Social workers will need strengthened fervor and effective strategies to continue to pursue justice. But there are hopeful signs including new initiatives, sustained efforts, and impetus emerging from activists who are building movements and joining forces to effect change. We see this particularly among youths.

The Millennial generation is large and diverse. According to a report from the Brookings Institute, there are 75 million millennials, and 44% of them are from underrepresented groups (Frey, 2018). Polls suggest they have greater comfort with racial and gender diversity, and they report a concern about racism as one of the top three most important problems in the United States (Cohen, Fowler, Medencia, & Rogowski, 2017). Millennials seem to be civically engaged at a rate not seen since the 1960s. Generation Z follows the Millennials, and this new cohort exhibits a similar passion for civic engagement. Members of Generation Z, which began roughly in the mid-1990s (*Chronicle of Higher Education*, 2018; Williams, 2015), have already arrived on college campuses, and it is anticipated that their zeal will affect what they expect—and receive—from their experience in higher education (Rickes, 2016). Certainly, it is encouraging to see today's high school students lead the fight for gun control and safety, which has already begun to result in increased awareness and positive change.

A survey of the current landscape reveals that these times are not for the cowardly or the foolhardy. The issues before us demand new strategies and tools targeted for change in today's context. Perhaps it is not the creation of new strategies but more about honing and making solid those that can be adapted to the demands of a global context and to the advances in technology to advance our goals. That realization framed our idea that this book must embrace the profession's pursuit of justice as a raison d'être. The obligation of social work education is to educate for the competent pursuit of justice. Throughout the book, we have used these two frames—justice and competence—to describe the details of field education practice. In this chapter we discuss how social work education fully becomes just and inclusive so that we can create the context to produce competent and diverse practitioners.

As we said in Chapter 1, the mission of social work is to competently, diligently, and persistently pursue justice and that every social work thought and action, from our respectful and attentive work with individuals to mass organizing, policy practice, and research agenda and protocols, are focused on and calculated to advance rights and justice. The role of social work education is to educate those who will have this responsibility. As educators in the classroom and in the field, our purpose is to educate students, who at graduation and beyond will be able to competently pursue justice at every system level.

If we are to achieve change, we must begin now. The Millennials with their experience in and expectation for justice are already most of our students and are entering the profession. We already have Generation Z in our classrooms. These generational cohorts, with their passion for civic engagement, will be called to serve consumers who are facing great need, a constricted human service environment, and an unresponsive and often punitive political and increasingly global environment. Let us be mindful that many students will have needs themselves, and there is a fine line between those who serve and those who are served. As a modest beginning, we suggest four broad areas for transformation that will need our careful and thoughtful attention: the workforce, the school environment and culture, the social work curriculum, and field education.

Transforming the Workforce

Demographers agree that the U.S. population will be an increasingly diverse one. Consider these predictions:

> By 2060, 44.3% of the U. S. population will be non-Hispanic White, which represents a minus 9.6% change from 2016 (Vespa, Armstrong, & Medina, 2018).
> The biracial population is expected to increase by 200%, and the Asian and Latinx populations will double. Additionally, if immigration trends continue, by 2028 the percentage of foreign-born people will be larger than at any time since 1850 (Vespa et al., 2018).
> The majority of newcomers are predicted to be Asian and Latinx. According to the U.S. Census Bureau, by 2045 non-Hispanic Whites will no longer make up the majority of the U.S. population (Vespa et al., 2018).

These forecasts are probably some of the reasons for such a great effort to halt immigration with increasingly more rigid and oppressive immigration protocols for some populations. Increasingly, newcomers arriving from European countries do not receive the same scrutiny and expulsion policies. Social workers must and do challenge these restrictive policies as policy advocates, community organizers, and direct practitioners, but the strains and stressors experienced by new immigrants and asylum seekers persist.

Emerging populations will contribute new resources, build new communities, begin new initiatives, and will also likely have new needs our society must respond to. As equity rather than equality is a primary principle of justice, the professional workforce of every profession ought to reflect this changing national profile. It is not enough for a profession to replicate the proportional racial composition of the nation, although in most cases that alone would be an improvement. Instead, professions must consider holistic institutional and structural transformations to surmount practices that perpetuate injustice (Carten et al., 2016). This includes seeking equity in representation among those who practice and lead. For example, if a profession had an equitable racial distribution, we would expect to see relatively equal numbers of practicing doctors, lawyers, and social workers from every racial group. But although gender equity appears to have made dramatic gains in formerly male-dominated professions like law and medicine, there are still wide discrepancies among racial groups in both professions (Law School Admissions Council, 2016).

Social work has compelling reasons to ensure our ranks are diverse and inclusive. Were all things equal, we would expect Blacks, Latinx, Whites, Asians, and indigenous populations to be consumers of social work consistent with their percentage of the population; that is, we would expect our consumers to be about 13% Black, 18% Hispanic, 6% Asian, 1% American Indian and Alaska Native, and 77% White (U.S. Census Bureau, 2016). Yet unlike other professions, we work primarily with women and people of color in all sectors and in most locations. Many, if not quite all of us, work with those who are economically disadvantaged, and this almost always entails working with people of color as poverty is strongly associated with race (Poverty USA, 2016).

Anecdotally, every social worker understands that because of the historical legacy of genocide, racism, slavery, and continued structural oppression, most of our service users are people of color, but we may not know the degree to which that is true. Further evidence of the interface among social workers and people of color can be found in our fields of practice.

According to Figure 3 in the Nationwide Workforce Initiative the population groups served by MSWs working as social workers as main clients are the following: 39% work with children and families, 21% in mental health care, 15% in health care, 7% in school social work, and 6% work with people with substance abuse issues (Salsberg, Quigley, Aquaviva, Wyche, & Sliwa, 2018). Women, people of color, and members of the LGBTQ+TS population are heavily represented in these service sectors.

Examining these numbers more closely, consider the following:

› In the child welfare system 54% of children in care are children of color with overrepresentation of African American, Hispanic (of any race), American Indian/Alaska Native, and children of two or more races (Child Welfare Information Gateway, 2018).
› According to a report from the Henry J. Kaiser Family Foundation, 55% of nonelderly uninsured are people of color despite the coverage gains under the Patient Protection and Affordable Care Act, leading to significant disparities in access and use of health care (Artiga, Damio, & Garfield, 2015).

- A disproportionate number of people of color manifest higher rates of asthma, diabetes, heart disease, and HIV/AIDS (Artiga et al., 2015); Walters et al. (2011) gives testimony to the links between experiences of historical trauma to the manifestation of poor health at "disproportionately high levels" among American Indian and Alaska Native populations (p. 180).
- Whereas rates of mental illness in communities of color are similar to those of the general population, only one in three African Americans who need mental health care receives it (Carson & Anderson, 2016).
- Black students are three times more likely than their non-Black peers to be diagnosed with an emotional disturbance and more than twice as likely to be placed in separate settings (i.e., special education classes) (U.S. Department of Education, 2016).
- Black people with mental health conditions are more likely to be incarcerated than people of other races (Carson & Anderson, 2016). African Americans are imprisoned at 5.1 times the rate of Whites, and Latinx are imprisoned at 1.4 times the rate of Whites (Nellis, 2016). The Statista (n.d.-a) website estimates that 41% of homeless people are African American.

Other populations at risk include members of the LGBTQ+TS community, who are also overrepresented as consumers of social services, particularly in health care (Ard, 2016), suicide (Ahuja et al., 2015), and those who experience violence and bullying (see Office of Disease Prevention and Health Promotion: https://www.healthypeople.gov/2020/topics-objectives/topic/lesbian-gay-bisexual-and-transgender-health). Additionally, social workers are more likely to work with women than men. New and important work is taking place with men, but because of biases and challenges of successful outreach and because women are more likely to experience economic hardship, it is likely that women will continue to dominate social work caseloads (Statistica, n.d.-a; n.d.-b). Regarding this reality, Mersky, Janczewski, and Nitkowski (2013) reports that

- "according to the World Health Organization (2013) approximately 30% of women globally experience interpersonal partner violence (IPV) during their lifetime" (p. 15).
- 1 in 10 women in the United States experiences sexual IPV, 1 in 4 experiences serious physical IPV, and nearly 1 in 2 experiences psychological IPV (Breiding, Chen, & Black, 2014).

> Besides the consequences for individuals, IPV affects whole families and communities; it is connected with mental health problems, partner alcohol use, poverty, crime, and housing insecurity (Capaldi, Knoble, Shortt, & Kim, 2012; Crane, Godleski, Przybyla, Schlauch, & Testa, 2016; Dillon, Hussain, Loxton, & Rahman, 2013; Lagdon, Armour, & Stringer, 2014; Wildeman et al., 2012).

Our commitment to a just professional future requires the social work workforce to reflect the communities served and in need. This is not only because we are committed to the well-being of society and its more vulnerable members. It enhances the consciousness needed for and greater affinity with the experiences of service consumers, and our profession and our purposes benefit from diverse perspectives and world views. Finally, because the profession should represent and be led by those it serves, that is, people of color, women, indigenous peoples, and members of the LGBTQ+TS community. We are far from that aspiration today. Although there are limitations in the data, the National Workforce Initiative (Salsberg et al., 2017) reports that according to the American Community Survey, only "9.5% of active social workers with a master's degree or higher are Hispanic or Latino" (p. 17). This same source reports more optimistic numbers for African Americans as representing "active social workers, 25.7% of the BSWs and 19.1% of the MSWs" (p. 18). The absence of American Indian and Alaskan Native social workers is particularly egregious given their overrepresentation in the child welfare system (Cross, Day, Gogliotti, & Pung, 2013).

The CSWE (2018c, 2018d) data for students and faculty in 2017 provide ample evidence, at least on the issue of gender, that students and faculty are currently well matched to the individuals we work with. Nonetheless, we must invest in best practice strategies to recruit and retain men and create mentors and environments where they can thrive and engage with male youths and men of color (Walters et al., 2016; Gandhi and Johnson, 2016; Schilling, Morrish & Liu, 2008). Women make up more than 80% of part-time and full-time students at the BSW and MSW levels, and more than 75% of total enrollment of PhD students. More than 72% of full-time faculty and more than 76% of part-time faculty are women (CSWE, 2018c.) On the issue of race equity, however, the data for students and faculty is far less impressive. Figure 11.1 presents data compiled from the 2017 *Statistics on Social Work Education Appendix* (CSWE, 2018c).

Given the percentage of those in the systems we serve who are people of

	African American (%)	Latino[a] (%)	Asian/Pacific Islander (%)	American Indian/Native American (%)	White (%)	Unknown/ Multiple/ Other (%)
BSW Full-time students	22.8	15.4	2.4	1.0	47.5	11
BSW Part-time students	26.3	16.5	1.9	1.3	39.7	14.3
BSW graduates	19.3	14.9	2.3	0.9	48.8	14.0
MSW Full-time students	18.2	13.1	3.9	0.7	50.8	13.3
MSW Part-time students	23.4	13.4	3.2	0.9	48.9	9.5
MSW graduates	16.6	12.3	3.7	0.8	49.5	17.1
Practice doctorate students	36.1	5.7	2.3	0.9	39.5	13.9
Practice doctorate graduates	23.0	9.2	[b]	[b]	55.2	0
PhD students	20.1	7.1	12.7	1.0	47.4	11.6
PhD graduates	16.1	5.9	13	[b]	52.7	9.2
Full-time faculty members	16.7	5.8	7.4	1.0	63.6	5.4
Part-time faculty members	16.0	8.0	3.6	0.5	60.8	11.2

Note. From 2017 Statistics on Social Work Education in the United States: Appendix (CSWE, 2018c, pp. 1–19)

[a] Puerto Rican, Chicano/Mexican Americans, and other Latinos combined
[b] Excluded because number of individuals was fewer than five

Table 11.1: Social Work Education in 2017 for students and faculty by race (CSWE, 2018a, p. 1–19).

color, the data on students, graduates, and faculty are disappointing. Students of color are slightly more present in part-time programs than in full-time programs and in practice doctorates than in PhD doctorates. American Indian, Alaska Native, and Asian and Pacific Island/Hawaiian Native populations remain invisible or nearly invisible in too many categories. Diversity among faculty is disheartening and inexcusable. This is particularly true for part-time faculty. Predictions of demographic change indicate that we will need to be even more diverse soon, and it is disturbing that we are now so far behind where we should be.

There are little data on the presence of LGBTQ+TS people either as students, faculty, or members of the social work workforce (Chinell, 2011). To seek equity, we should at the very minimum ask students and faculty to self-identify as members of these populations so we can track how we are doing in recruiting and maintaining LGBTQ+TS people in our profession. However, because of issues surrounding bias and safety, such tracking itself is complicated. The data that exist provide indicators for action. The National Social Work Workforce Study (Salsberg et al., 2018) reports that the respondents who identified as lesbian, gay, or homosexual were higher in number among PhD and DSW students than among BSW and MSW students, whereas the number of those who identified as bisexual or "something else" was higher among BSW and MSW than PhD and DSW students (p. 31). Taking these groups together, 14.7% of BSW graduates, 16.2% of MSW graduates, and 20.6% of PhD and 16.7% of DSW graduates identified with these categories. There are cautions and narratives from LGBTQ+TS faculty members who describe their experiences of marginalization in academe (Gates, 2011; LaSala, Jenkins, Wheeler, & Fredriksen-Golsdsen, 2008; Turner, 2015). Reports of how this climate affects faculty members should turn us also toward creating inclusive policies and practices that focus on ensuring an affirming and proactive environment for all historically oppressed student populations (Dentato, Craig, Lloyd, Kelly, Wright, & Austin, 2017). We address some of these needed changes in the following section.

In summary, if we compare ourselves to those we serve in the health and mental health systems, in child welfare and in schools, in the criminal justice system, and the economically disadvantaged populations in general, the people who make up the social work profession currently at every level do not correspond. If we aspire to professional equity, we must focus on the disparity between our whiteness and the people of color we work with, and we must seek change. The Nationwide Workforce Initiative (Salsberg et al., 2018) offers important information to help guide us forward. It is no longer excusable to demand our practice community to diversify its workforce recruitment strategies if we do not act in a corresponding manner to improve our recruitment and retention in social work education programs.

The CSWE's (2010) last strategic plan for 2010–2020 alluded to the need to transform the profession's workforce. The fifth goal pledges to "promote the preparation of social work graduates who can practice effectively in an increasingly diverse and global practice environment" (para. 5). The most effective way of transforming our professional composition is to transform the pipeline at the BSW and MSW level. Students not only become the future workforce but also can be encouraged, recruited, mentored, and engaged as doctoral students and eventual faculty members and leaders of human service agencies. We should not, however, wait until the pipeline is strengthened to diversify doctoral programs and faculty. The goal for professional equity must be embraced by each of the major social work organizations (i.e., the CSWE, the NASW, National Deans and Directors of Social Work, Association of Baccalaureate Social Work Program Directors, Society of Social Work Research, Group for the Advancement of Doctoral Education in Social Work, and the ASWB) and become central to their strategic planning. We need a shared strategic goal to reach for professional equity by 2030. The task is complex.

For example, Chin Hawkins, Krings, Peguero-Spencer, and Gutiérrez (2018) investigate diversity in U.S. social work doctoral education to "examine how dynamics of power influence training the next generation of social workers" (p. 2). The authors conclude with a recommendation to shift our focus from only considering singular dimensions of social difference (such as race) to expand our view to examine the way doctoral programs engage with multiple dimensions of difference. The authors call for an examination of the barriers to retention and success and identification of the structures that support career trajectories. This examination will assist our efforts in seeking the change we need.

To accomplish this goal, in support of the Nationwide Workforce Initiative (Salsberg et al., 2018) in addition to examining what barriers exist once the PhD candidate enters the program, we must go beyond waiting for applications and open houses or sending admissions staff to recruitment fairs. Online recruitment and webinars have provided more options for many applicants. We must stimulate interest in social work among high school students by reaching into high schools that serve a range of populations, engage undergraduates, and create partnerships with agencies.

One promising trend is this generation's commitment to justice issues, especially regarding immigration, gun control, and police violence. Millennials have led many of the recent movements, including Occupy Wall Street, Black Lives Matter, and United We Dream. Generation Z Parkland students have been effective at winning gun control victories since the shooting at a Florida high school in February 2018 (Holpuch, 2018). These movements are frequently led by people of color and members of the LGBTQ+TS community, who have been quick to acknowledge the inherent racism in these issues and incidents and have embraced an inclusive organizing strategy. These young activists are a hopeful and important pool for social work education. How do we reach them?

Social work educators might borrow some of the techniques that have been used by other professions to generate interest among high school students. Although we address field education placements later, each of the suggestions in this section might be considered as potential field education settings and placement opportunities that serve the purposes of educating generalist and specialized practice level social work students as well as providing connections between schools of social work and settings that offer access to potential recruits for the profession. For example, school-based social workers should be encouraged to create programs such as those created by the physicians, scientists, accountants, engineers, and bankers who have promoted career interest among high school girls by forming special clubs, organizing activities, and having students visit campus for science, technology, engineering, and math programs (Diekman, Weisgram, & Belanger, 2015). If social work students are placed in districts where such social service clubs do not exist, field instructors may be approached to incorporate these ventures as a learning opportunity for their social work students. Those in the field of public health have also tried innovative strategies to diversify their student bodies (Kreuter et al., 2011). Social workers can develop community service projects, and field instructors can develop assignments in which middle and high school students work alongside social workers and learn about the root causes of problems and proposed solutions. One example is to form an after-school basketball team for high school youths and youths from a local family homeless shelter to encourage interconnections and understanding beyond basketball to learning about homelessness. Social workers can also collaborate in established programs such as the Children's Defense Fund's (2018) Freedom Schools that bring in college students and young adults as staff to help deliver its summer and after-school reading program. These programs focus learning and activities on justice-related topics including documentaries, readings, and guest speakers. The fund also sponsors youth development programs that host recognition celebrations for high school students who overcome adversity (Beat the Odds), train young advocates in leadership, or that engage college students to promote health outreach. Each is a vibrant example of providing avenues for schools of social work to form partnerships and invest in youth development with an eye to inspiring these young advocates' interest in social work. Other possibilities include mentoring programs like Big Brothers Big Sisters and immigrant support services.

College is a time when most students discover their career interests, but social work is often not very visible during the period when students select their majors. Contact with social workers during the application phase and freshman and sophomore years should be maximized. For example, placements on campus can be developed to engage social work students as links to career and advising services or to admissions staff to serve as admissions ambassadors and college tour guides. Beyond the placement opportunities on campus, social work faculty and staff should be present in various peer programs, service-learning projects, and student groups. Likewise, reaching student clubs such as those serving the LGBTQ+TS student community may be possible in our campus community clubs and organizations as well as linking with community organizations active in providing mentorship programs. We return to this discussion later when considering university-community enterprises to form field placement partnerships.

Social work departments could work with field instructors to launch speakers series, movie nights on social work themes, and online book clubs that appeal to students. Probably most important are partnerships with majors that often lead students to choose a social work career, such as the Departments of Sociology, Psychology, Political Science, Forensic Science and Forensic Psychology, Criminal Justice, Women's Studies and Gender Studies, and departments representing racial and ethnic identities. Social work faculty can seek opportunities to engage undergraduate students in these departments beyond the occasional lecture, perhaps by teaching or coteaching a course in other departments or working with these departments to credit social work electives in other curricula. We could work with faculty in opportunity programs, Black male initiative programs, sororities and fraternities, student clubs, churches, professional associations based on social identity, and historically Black colleges and universities and Latinx-serving institutions to broaden and deepen our recruitment of students of color and other underrepresented groups. Although schools of social work are already taking advantage of many of these opportunities, we propose that schools of social work may benefit from intentional and purposeful outreach to other departments on their campuses, other institutions of higher learning, and our practice community to collaborate on the broader purpose of connecting with the student body in civic engagement and service. Social workers have much to offer in terms of expertise in service learning and also have much to gain in forging these connections.

It is especially important for social work to develop close relationships with community colleges, which represent an important resource for social work recruitment because they have historically been the educational portal for students of color and first-generation college students. In 2016, 48.5% of Black students, 50.8% of Hispanic students, and 44% of students from low-income communities were enrolled in 2-year colleges (Community College Research Center, n.d.). Consequently, 2-year colleges offer a significant opportunity to transform the social work workforce.

The other major pipeline for diverse students is large agencies whose staff members are often of historically oppressed identities and do not possess a social work degree. These agencies are often public and provide services to children and families (e.g., child protection services) or seniors and people with mental and physical abilities (e.g., home health or care coordination), or health (e.g., peer navigators). In some areas such as home care, for example, it is particularly important to couple community college partnerships with employment strategies, so employees can enter at the community college level and seamlessly complete their bachelor's and master's degrees. Such an initiative would pay off in promoting women and people of color from low-paying jobs with limited prospects to clinical and management positions with better pay and more hope for promotion. For example, education and nursing programs have been effective at recruiting students in 2- and 3-year models that allow community college students to enter and complete master's degrees efficiently. Seamless admissions processes engage and advise students early and help with retention.

Transforming School Environments and Culture

If justice is the mission, then merely having a diverse student body is insufficient to achieve it. Drew Faust, president of Harvard University, said that "simply gathering a diverse mixture of extraordinarily talented people in one place does not in itself ensure the outcome we seek" (Rosenberg, 2015, para. 1). We must create environments where people of various identities do not experience daily microaggressions. As noted previously, we must also address the situations that obstruct retention in our programs (Chin et al., 2018).

Departments of social work must have a strategic approach to shifting their climate from assimilation to inclusion and affirmation, thereby creating organizational contexts and transforming structures where all thrive and reach their full potential. In the EPAS (CSWE, 2008) the importance of learning environments was acknowledged by including a requirement to assess the "implicit curriculum." (p. 10). An implicit curriculum is "what a school teaches because of the kind of place it is" (Bruner, 1996, p. 98). Frequently referred to as the *hidden curriculum*, the term recognizes that students absorb lessons that are not a part of the formal curriculum but are from the unspoken academic, social, and cultural messages, even from the physical environment and decor (Great Schools Partnership, 2015). These factors communicate welcome and safety or disrespect and risk. We support the CSWE's attention to the learning environment and believe that the future of social work will require us to pay even greater attention to our organizational cultures.

We have considered the importance of creating a conducive environment in this text and the internal and external factors we must pay attention to as part of our field instruction responsibilities. Here, we consider the social work program's responsibilities to consider the reality that as predominately White dominant organizations, social work educational programs can be uncomfortable, if not alienating, environments that far too often perpetuate dominant worldviews. Faculty and students of color or those with any historically oppressed or marginalized identity usually get the message that they are required to assimilate into the current structure if they want to fit in. The literature suggests, and we have confirmed this in talking with many students of color, that they experience microaggressions in and outside the classroom, feel unsafe with faculty and their peers and are pained and even retraumatized when asked to represent their communities in class discussions. Field instructors often learn about these occurrences, and we share a responsibility to talk with students about whom they can talk to in the program about what they are experiencing. If they cannot identify someone, we must suggest they consult with their field liaison. Schools of social work must rigorously assess the program's implicit curriculum, identify needed changes, and implement them. There are several areas where we can begin.

Faculty Support

It is imperative to have faculty members of color from a range of groups in our departments and support their inclusion. For example, the special strains, barriers, and challenges to surviving and thriving in often toxic and detrimental academic environments are examined from the unique status of American Indian and Alaska Native faculty (Walters, Casey, Evans-Campbell, Valdez, & Zambrana, in press). "As members of sovereign nations and their relationship as Tribal Peoples to settler colonialism may pose particular challenges" (p. 2). Creating understanding, and endorsing emerging strategies toward success, are essential for our efforts to promote and maintain these faculty members.

Faculty members of color and LGBTQ+TS faculty members must be compensated for the extra, often unrecognized, work they do to support students seeking mentorship and support. Cluster hiring creates additional sponsorship for these faculty members because they are often the only one in their role and they have few mentors. Programs that convene doctoral students and emerging scholars of color can provide advice and encouragement from a peer network. One particularly notable program is Black Administrators Researchers and Scholars (https://www.socialwork.pitt.edu/researchtraining/bars), a group for African Americans in social work education academia. This group's goal is to provide guidance for navigating administrative or faculty positions. It has held four formal summits convening African American faculty members, and it has the potential to be of tremendous assistance to the profession in preparing and promoting African American faculty members to thrive in their environments. For an example of an event, see https://www.bc.edu/bc-web/bcnews/nation-world-society/social-work/ssw-hosts-bars-event.html (private communication with Dr. L. Larry Davis, personal communication, June 18, 2018). This group offers us a model for replication to address the concerns expressed here.

Student Support

As our programs become more inclusive, we must shift our focus to retention and graduation, develop better systems of care for students, and give greater attention to their needs rather than our rules. We also should assume that many will have financial needs and time constraints and that life issues may interfere with their continuous matriculation. It will therefore be a priority to provide greater flexibility in course scheduling and sequencing and in field education options. The data indicate that students of color are more enrolled in part-time programs, so it makes sense for us to develop cogent and doable part-time curricula. This may require relinquishing some of our preferences for corequisites and one-model-fits-all field education placements. Online and hybrid courses have helped make degree completion more flexible, but because these programs are financed in partnership with private companies that administer aspects of them, the degrees often come at considerable expense. We must consider more flexible or even perhaps individualized plans of learning that allow students to suspend their matriculation when necessary and to complete in their own time frames, either gradually taking courses or in an accelerated fashion as needed. This also applies to arrangements for field education placements. Recent consideration of program responses to these realities demonstrates that these suggestions do not represent the norm. The CSWE (2015b) *State of Field Education Survey* reports:

› Uniquely designed field experiences, "such as modified block placements, international, out-of-state, or out-of-sequence placements" (p. 9), existed for less than 6% of students as reported by 81.9% of respondents.
› Students who "completed field experiences involving nonweekday business hours" (p. 9) were also at 6 % or lower, reported by 54.4% of respondents.
› Likewise, of 71.2% respondents, less than 6% of students used "field experiences in their workplaces" (CSWE, 2015b, p. 9).

We will need to create mechanisms for students to easily reenter a program after an absence. Field education hours may need to be extended to accommodate students' working schedules or completed in intensive time periods to allow faster time to graduation. We must take a fresh look at the requirement that restricts social work students' places of employment and supervisors from qualifying as internships and perhaps create a new model that embraces these potential learning environments while simultaneously enriching on-site independent learning. Program flexibility meets the needs of students who see "learning as one continuous, multi-faceted, completely integrated experience—connecting social, academic and professional interests" (Barnes & Noble College, 2016, p. 6).

Most important, we will have to strengthen student support, notably academic and career advising, making it attentive to retention, helping students choose their best options, and removing obstacles toward degree attainment (Finch, 2015). For example, the campus experiences of first-generation students are shaped by socioeconomic forces and the lack of familial mentorship in understanding what to expect from college. Challenges in managing their responsibilities at home and college expectations are frequently reported (Cataldi et al., 2018; Coffman, 2011; Oldfield, 2007).

One such potential area for needed support is related to writing skills. It is particularly important to deliver assistance with writing and tutoring respectfully, in ways that value the different forms of expression in diverse cultures. Our approaches must consider diverse students' linguistic and cultural identities (Inoue, 2015). We must support students and communicate our belief in their abilities and their capacity to succeed. We encourage schools to offer a range of writing assignments that acknowledge learning styles and opinions such as journals, creative writing, and the use of social media and pictures. At the Columbia University School of Social Work, the conversation about writing begins with discussions about how people of diverse backgrounds value the exchange of ideas and thoughts through different methods while questioning dominant standards of writing and grading. Further, writing should not be channeled into writing and tutoring programs but included as a form of expression integral to all learning and the competent execution of our practice.

We must identify and direct financial aid to students who arrive through these pathways, as well as establish support such as stipends for books and supplies, free mass transportation cards, and aid programs for the inevitable crises that occur for students with limited financial resources. Although more are needed, opportunities do exist. The National Association of Black Social Workers and the National Association of Puerto Rican Hispanic Social Workers are two of several affinity organizations aligned with the aims espoused here. General advancement of students and some scholarship funds have been an important goal for these organizations, and both are important collaborators as we recruit, sustain, and support students of color. The CSWE Minority Fellowship Program for doctoral and graduate students is a model program aiming to reduce health disparities, improve behavioral health outcomes, and recruit students who are interested to serve racially and ethnically diverse populations (see https://www.cswe.org/Centers-Initiatives/Initiatives/Minority-Fellowship-Program.aspx). The CSWE is one of seven organizations that support the administration of this program. Although social work program faculty usually provide a student's recommendation, field instructors have an important role to play by bringing these opportunities to students' attention, mentioning our support to the field liaison, and backing our students through the application procedures.

Students themselves must be encouraged and assisted in creating support networks in our programs and placement settings that provide alliances to strengthen their efforts and bolster their purpose to persevere. There are models, such as Al1gn (Alliance for the Low Income and First Generation Narrative), a student movement that focuses on connecting low-income and first-generation students across the nation and that has hosted an annual conference since 2017.

There is ample evidence that students express a growing need for mental health services and university services are struggling to expand in response to these needs. Reported highlights from the Center for Collegiate Mental Health (2018) noted anxiety and depression as the most common concerns of students. Average rates of student self-reported anxiety and depression continue to increase, whereas other areas of self-reported distress remain flat or are decreasing. Lifetime prevalence rates of 'threat-to-self' characteristics "increased for the eighth year in a row," and 54.4% of those seeking counseling have had prior counseling, which represents an "upward trend for the last three years" (p. 4). These factors signal that we will be faced with circumstances requiring us to make accommodation in our programs for the realities of our students' lives, rather than expecting them to conform to an inflexible set of requirements.

Retention

Finally, far too often students who drop out of our programs or are counseled out during an academic review process are students of color. Committees on academic performance review, ethics committees, and disciplinary committees are too often ignorant about the various experiences of students when making decisions about perceived misconduct. They may not understand how difficult it is for some students to fit into the dominant culture of social work education and education in general. That ignorance can have very bad outcomes. For example, a classroom professor who uses race data throughout the semester to make a point about disproportionality in child welfare frequently asks a male Black student, the only one in the class, about his experience working in that system. The student responds with silence and is subsequently absent. Without exploring the reason for the absences or talking directly to the student to understand his behavior and withdrawal, the classroom professor reports the student for academic review without considering the differential effects of the material presented.

Disciplinary procedures are often biased and unhelpful in getting students to graduation. The Social Care Workforce Research Unit at King's College London examined these situations and trends to better understand how to ensure retention and continuous matriculation (Hussein, Moriarty, & Manthorpe, 2009). It benefits every program for administrators to evaluate its outcomes and procedures each year, checking for bias and for how the forces of power and oppression influence outcomes (Chin et al., 2018). In a similar way, offices of field education might track demographics of students required to complete a learning contract during the academic year. This information would enable field departments to identify students who find the requirements of field education the most challenging, fall below expectations, are unable to improve their demonstration of competence through this process, or are helped by the process to succeed. We strongly urge the CSWE to require programs to track and report that data as part of the reaccreditation process, so we can understand this critical aspect of our educational systems.

We must find ways of supporting our students through to graduation rather than creating systems that discourage and prevent it, particularly in cases where the internship is disrupted, and the student's academic performance is reviewed. Students of color appear to perform better when they are learning among peers (Furness, 2012; Parker, 2010). There is some evidence that the involvement of a second reviewer, a transparent and solution-focused review process, and peer support for those experiencing difficulties may make a difference. To be a just profession, social work educators must develop and test programs that ensure successful completion of their program (Parker, 2010).

Transforming the Curriculum

If the central tenet of social work is the pursuit of justice, then the curriculum must ensure that students are competent to apply themselves to this task. Additionally, if we are to attract a new population of students, our curricula need to reflect and involve these students' interests and experiences.

The information that graduates must understand and master to practice competently today has expanded and will continue to do so. There are new practice specializations and global venues; new populations that require greater cultural, racial, religious, sexual, and gender consciousness insights and sensitivity; new evidence about practice effectiveness; and new technology. Social work's grand challenges features 12 areas to promote family well-being, a more strengthened social fabric, and a more just society (American Academy of Social Work & Social Welfare, 2018). Many more challenges could be identified. Social workers practice in these areas at every level, from case manager to policy maker and from prevention to treatment and evaluation; they engage in activities as far ranging as child protection to working for environmental and racial justice on an international scale, and everything in between. They work with increasingly diverse populations including American Indians and Alaska Natives in the West and various Pacific and Mountain states, to Somali and Hmong populations in the Midwest, to Bhutanese and Nepalese in Pennsylvania to Bukharin and Uzbekistani in New York City. This breadth and need for currency create new demands on our curricula.

When schools of medicine and dentistry faced their own set of challenges because of scientific advances and greater complexity of practice, they created specializations requiring additional education that extended the school year. Given the social work student population and its burgeoning loan debt, lengthening the time of education is unlikely to be successful. Larger schools have the resources to mount specializations and subspecializations, but because many of the social work programs are small (on average 136 full- and part-time BSW students and less than 300 MSW students; CSWE, 2018d), that does not seem feasible for many departments unless collaboratives or online options are created. So what strategies can we use to help students gain competence given the complex realities of today's profession?

Again, models exist. Many programs are providing models for others to follow, such as the School of Social Work, University of Illinois (2018), whose initiatives in engagement and workforce development list a range of collaborations. Among several initiatives listed is the Social Work Healthcare Education and Leadership Scholars Program (Social Work HEALS), awarded to 10 schools of social work by the NASW and the CSWE to develop social work health-care leaders. Other grants and efforts aim to improve access to quality care and strengthen the workforce such as the Health Resources & Services Administration grants (see https://www.hrsa.gov/grants/index.html). Community labs and campus and community collaboratives are other possible models. Additionally, faculty and student loans and scholarships recruit, sustain, and improve needed representation of underserved and underrepresented populations in the fields of health, mental health, and substance abuse. The challenge is maintaining success in these areas and finding new collaboratives that support our aims.

Pursuit of Justice as a Focus

The competent pursuit of justice must be a serious and significant part of social work education. Further, the CSWE requires students to master skills that pursue justice on broad community and societal levels and within a historical systemic analysis. If we are serious that the pursuit of justice is our professional responsibility, we must educate graduates to understand the global as well as local political and economic systems that influence our work so they have the capacity to assist in affecting large-scale changes.

We encourage social work programs to design significant experiences for students to learn and demonstrate skills in pursuing justice (Steen et. al., 2017). Online social work programming that includes introducing opportunities to reach across the world for educational and international practice advances are ways to connect students across cultures in real time. These experiences are compatible with Generation Z student preferences for projects that can lead to social change (Seemiller & Grace, 2016). The learning and demonstration of competency can be embedded in policy courses, practice labs, generalist practice courses, and integrated seminars redesigned to include action for change or planned for extracurricular student activity. At Stony Brook University we have embedded this teaching into policy classes for BSW seniors, first-year MSW generalist practice, and second-year specialization students. The students come together in the fall for policy change projects that culminate in poster board sessions in the spring.

Course work can be designed to deliver several goals at once, a strategy we will need if we are to cover the breadth of social work today. The idea of embedding teaching additional skills into existing courses extends and deepens what students can master during their education. For example, assignments may require students to focus on a population or issue relevant to their field education settings and skills in professional writing and digital literacy can be embedded into existing courses. If we want students to learn to write for professional practice (e.g., case notes, editorials, reports for the courts, project proposals, etc.) or for digital literacy (e.g., using technology for servicer user support, to garner coalition support, or to meet organizational needs), we can develop content and annotated bibliographies and assignments that teach and assess those skills as part of the regular curriculum. Policy classes may include an assignment to write an editorial, practice courses may include writing a succinct case note or a research proposal. Faculty may object to the requirement to oversee students' writing, but the faculty member need not deliver the content. Instead it can be taught in partnership with university writing centers or online by others with greater proficiency in writing and linked to regular course content. This approach has the added advantage of delivering writing content for all students rather than for only the students who may require writing assistance.

One challenge we face is that as courses in civics disappear from high school curricula, students are often less knowledgeable about the U.S. government and economic system, the purposes and responsibilities of each and how they operate. An understanding of these issues is fundamental to discussions of policy and change; such a course should be a pre- or corequisite for matriculation in BSW and MSW programs. Of course, the content must be from the perspective of the people's history; that is, one written from the perspective of ordinary people and rooted in an analysis of power, oppression and racism, and decolonization (Tuck & Yang, 2012; Zinn, 1980). Of course, many schools have a required course that teaches this material and already use this as an attractive feeder into social work programs. Educators often need support in the skills needed to teach this content and just as we advocate for field instructors to be supported in the face of this challenging work, faculty also must be supported in their efforts to facilitate the challenging and needed dialogues in the classroom. Too often social work education isolates this content in courses in social policy and courses in social change, electoral activism, mobilization, and community organization. Likewise, while some students may have internships that involve policy change and organizing, many do not. Many programs include a lobby day experience that provides students with a brief policy experience, but it does not expose them to other forms of social change action including mobilization and organizing that may have greater effect. Introducing programming into more micro focused placements provides students with the experience of creating and serving constituents on a broader basis. These skills can lead to new found interests and talents that propel students into alternative strategies for change.

These experiences and courses build on the antiracist and antioppressive practice courses by giving students skills and actionable work to pursue real concrete change. To truly embrace and educate students to pursue justice, these subjects and experiences should be studied and taken together and supported by faculty able to manage the difficult conversations that will emerge. To effectively pursue change, vulnerable and underrepresented populations have little choice but to employ organizing strategies; and tangible and sustainable large-scale change is only possible through the enactment of policy. Change efforts also require the capacity to conduct challenging conversations with one another and with one's constituents. Consequently, organizing must be about policy change, and policy change must happen through competent organizing; both must occur in the context of understanding how to conduct oneself from a framework of authenticity, mutuality, and respect, which must be merged for learning and skill development.

Supporting Lifelong Learning and Building Credentials

Still, the breadth of our field and the necessity to provide students with education for the competent pursuit of justice will need strategies in addition to embedding content or supporting the content with experiential learning. We will need a way to extend content during traditional education and during professional careers.

The CSWE (2008) EPAS required evidence of lifelong learning, and although many members believed in the merit of the competency, it was difficult, if not impossible, to document evidence of it at graduation. To approach the challenge of providing more evidence-based, specialized, and continuously updated content, social work education might borrow from the emerging non-credit-bearing credential movement that has taken hold most firmly in the field of business. These noncredit credentials frequently take the form of digital badges (Carnavale, Rose, Hanson, 2012). The literature suggests that Millennial students prefer this type of credential, which offers them a tangible sense of accomplishment, directly explains knowledge and skills gained, specifically demonstrates the value of the curriculum, and provides evidence to potential employers of skill sets (Overland, 2016). These certificates do not replace degree education. Instead, they are evidence of deepening and certifying learning in chosen areas. Fain (2018) explored how alternative credentials may help more Americans to obtain work, gain a promotion, or succeed in making a career change. It is likely that Gen Z students will continue with interest in and seeking of these credentials.

Similarly, schools and departments of social work have already begun to establish a set of credentials in a particular area of practice to indicate that a social worker has special skills and knowledge that range across populations and fields of practice beyond the normal expectations for a graduate, such as in child welfare (Cash, Mathieson, Barbanell, Smith, & Graham, 2006) or gerontology (Euster, 1999). Content for these credentials may be included in courses, embedded in experiences in internships, or as part of in-service training or in out-of-classroom experiences. For example, students may receive a credential in recovery behavioral health strategies if they have taken certain course work, interned in organizations using a recovery model, and completed papers on social policy and research related to recovery. The idea of offering noncredit credentials can help us as a profession to get serious about lifelong learning. Noncredit credentials can help social workers carefully map their learning over the length of their career. It augments and gives greater purpose to the continuing education requirements for licensing renewal.

Discovering and Using Active Teaching Methods

As the student population changes, new student learning needs and economic forces will force us to rethink what happens in the classroom. Rickes (2016) writes,

> the paradigm may be shifting to a focus on curriculum and delivery, technological skills, and continuous learning in support of an educated populace that will find meaningful careers. What has worked in the past will not necessarily work in the future. (p. 30)

Social work education has been at the forefront of using the classroom for group learning. Now we may need to strengthen our techniques for increased individualized and focused active learning approaches. In addition to the benefits of observing student performance discussed in following text, the use of simulated practice also offers promise in providing active and individualized approaches to learning (Bogo, Regehr, Katz et al., 2011; Bogo, Regehr, Logie, 2011; Logie, et al, 2013).

Much of the direct teaching may be done virtually, with lectures, videos, or reading discussions outside the classroom. Fronek, Boddy, Chenoweth, and Clark (2016) report on their use of podcasts as a way of augmenting the curriculum. Class then becomes precious time for peer interaction where students engage in problem solving on an issue, with the instructor offering support and answering questions (Williams, 2015). These methods are being used now. How do they match what students are experiencing in their field placements? How can what we learn about expanding our methods be shared? We must routinely and carefully train the instructors who are delivering this critical content, and we propose a clear and intentional use of the time and contexts so that we focus with our students on building competence in the pursuit of justice.

We recognize the educational system has been controlled by the experiences of dominant scholars. As we encourage and include more students of color, we must be vigilant that we are producing and including literature that is relevant to their historical and current cultural experiences. For all students it is critical that bibliographies reflect the voices of indigenous scholars, LGBTQ+TS scholars and scholars of color in assigned readings, documentaries, and other supportive resources. This helps ensure access to voices and experiences that do not target people as problems. Neither should the classroom perpetuate experiences that create barriers for students. Students must be freed from continued microaggressions embedded in the manner their histories and experiences are portrayed (Daniel, 2011). The CSWE's Center for Diversity and Social & Economic Justice (2018), made possible through the support of the University of Texas at Austin Steve Hicks School of Social Work, provides educator resources, invites contributions, and seeks to enhance justice-based practice effectiveness.

These are just a few of the possible strategies social work educators employ to broaden and contemporize the competence of social workers, and we encourage sharing and adding to this list. Examples abound regarding how different programs are integrating various content across the curriculum, providing external experiences to the curriculum in support of what is being taught and various methods of using the skills of faculty in coteaching or participating in composite modules. Facilitating our ability to share this information is critical.

Transforming Field Education

In 2015 the CSWE surveyed field directors and field coordinators about such issues as administrative program models, staffing, and resources to determine the range of program responses to field demands and the influence of these differences on the quality of field education and learning (CSWE, 2015b). Recommendations emerged (2018b) that indicate the need for additional research to examine

> › how to support community partners to promote student learning and which structures support integration of student learning;
> › which structures promote field education leadership and respond to the diverse needs of students;
> › how to ensure adequate levels of resources for field departments;
> › the influence of program size on concerns related to staffing and overall program stressors; and
> › how to support the integration of field education departments with the social work program's curriculum.

In response to these concerns, this section of the chapter focuses on four topics: the implications of field education's status as the signature pedagogy of social work, rethinking models and settings for field education, university and community partnerships, and field education supervision.

Implications of Being the Signature Pedagogy of Social Work

The CSWE (2008) EPAS designated field education as the signature pedagogy of social work. According to L. S. Shulman (2005), a signature pedagogy is the teaching that "organizes the fundamental ways in which future practitioners are educated for their new professions" (p. 52). Shulman further states that a signature pedagogy has three dimensions: a surface structure, a deep structure, and an implicit structure. The surface structure includes procedures used to teach, including those we have tried to describe in detail in this book, such as preparation for assignments, the use of various kinds of recording that capture practice, and the process of evaluation. Deep structures reflect a set of assumptions about how best to impart a certain body of knowledge and know-how. We have endeavored to describe this as the work that occurs in the partnership between learner and teacher and that is modeled for and then mirrored between the student and the service user. Finally, Shulman includes the implicit structure of a signature pedagogy, which is the moral dimension comprising a set of beliefs about professional attitudes, values, and dispositions. We have addressed those moral dimensions directly as the field instructors' commitment to a justice-based model of field education.

It was not without reason that field education was given the distinction of being named the profession's signature pedagogy. It is likely that the most intimate teaching and learning occurs in the dyad between student and field instructor. The student-instructor relationship lasts longer and has frequent interaction, generally lasting over two semesters and with several contacts a week. The field instructor is often privy to the students' deepest concerns, personal history, triumphs, long-held biases, daily challenges, and most rewarding experiences. The field instructor usually knows the student more completely than anyone in the educational enterprise. It requires enormous trust, authenticity, and a high level of consciousness and skill to create a climate of safety for such an intimate relationship to be successful. This approach to field instruction correlates with academic success, and perhaps most important, models how students should work with those they serve.

Although it is understandable that field education has been given this prominent role, it is also clear there is increasing pressure on field education and on field instructors to deliver the goods. The CSWE (2015a) EPAS requires at least one assessment measure to be based on "demonstration of the competency in a real or simulated practice situation" (p. 18). For most programs, that means competency will most often be measured in field education.

In this regard, promising work is being tested to share the burden by placing more direct observation in the classroom and providing standardized case scenarios to gauge the quality of student responses (Bogo, Regehr, Katz et al., 2011; Bogo, Regehr, Logie, 2011). Likewise, simulation laboratories have been used to provide opportunities for students to obtain exposure to "objective structured clinical examinations" (Logie, Bogo, Regehr, & Regehr, 2013, p. 67). Like the models that are used for assessment of performance outcomes in medical education and other health professions, these simulations go beyond the frequently used role plays with classmates and instead employ actors in the role of "standardized clients" (Logie et al., 2013, p. 67). We might also consider the use of direct observation in field education, beginning with students' observations of field instructors and requiring students to reflect on these observations, to be followed by direct observation of students in interaction with individuals or groups before moving them into work on their own. This observation process works against concerns regarding misrepresentations frequently connected with self-reporting in student recordings and self-assessments in verbal reports of interactions in supervisory sessions. These simulated and direct observations are thus more "consistent with evidence-based teaching practices" (Bogo, 2015, p. 320).

As we have stressed throughout this text, although the field instructor–student relationship is core to learning, many more factors play crucial roles. The designation of field education as the profession's signature pedagogy places broader demands on social work education to consider a range of solutions to the many concerns identified in the State of Field Education Survey. For example, as we look to needed resources to meet student needs and as we expand field partnerships, directors of field education will play an increasingly important role. They are positioned at the threshold between schools of social work and the practice community, and they serve as a link to both (George, Silver, & Preston 2013; Lyter, 2012; Pierce, 2008). Those of us who have served in this role understand the rewards associated with bringing practice realities to the attention of social work education while also engaging in the professionalization of service delivery. Clearly, as field education moves to center stage as the signature pedagogy, the role of directors of field education will need to be more fully understood, they must be encouraged to innovate, and the means to help them with their increased responsibilities must be supported, a point poignantly made clear in the CSWE (2018b) field education survey report:

> If institutions were to consider carefully and evaluate the resources afforded to field education, as well as the integration of field within the

curriculum, and how the needs of the practice environment are reflected in both, the tenets of field education as signature pedagogy would likely become more fully realized. Similarly, clearly identifying the director or coordinator of field education as a member of the program's management team, with influence on decision making, would strengthen the role of field education in the curriculum and in the functioning of the program. (p. 33)

Rethinking Placement Models and Settings

Moreover, if social work is to educate for the competent pursuit of justice, then field education must respond to the learning needs of the student population, shape field education placement models, create innovative internships that capture the needs of the changing practice landscape, and introduce responsive ways of teaching, learning, and assessment. As Preston, George, and Silver (2014) propose that

> agency-based field education may actually reinforce the very neoliberalism that we critique and seek to resist in our classrooms. We further contend that most field education currently occurs with program or agency-based practice learning, in settings that have become depoliticized due to government funding restrictions, potential funding loss, or overall increased service delivery workloads (Baines, 2010; Ferguson, 2007; Webb, 2006). As such, students potentially face a myopic experience that neglects the social, political, and economic context of practice, and that limits the opportunity for broader practices that challenge norms, build alliances, and work towards a transformative social agenda. (p. 64)

If we are doing our job, the new student population that we addressed earlier in this chapter will be more diverse and more representative of those we serve. We have considered responding to these students' needs when focusing on recruitment, retention, and the curriculum. Here we draw attention again to the implications of how students' lives and needs will influence field placement. They are probably working while in school and may have more emergent needs. The model of completing field hours during full-time study will probably not be sustainable for many. Online models of field education are emerging, and the research on the efficacy of this approach is still coming in. Cummings, Chaffin, and Cockerham (2015) summarized findings and reported on their own research, concluding that "online part-time students received significantly higher ratings in 6–8 field competency ratings" and that "online students were more satisfied with faculty accessibility, helpfulness, and advising." (p. 109). Despite these and other program's promising findings, Cummings et al. concluded that the results are likely related to what others have found as the expected link between student characteristics with the program's intended audience. That is, the online model suits those who choose this method of delivery, and they do well with it. Interestingly, these reports do not mention how supervision is provided for students, and the literature is scant on guidance about online supervision methods and models. Results suggest that supervisory methods may require some adjustments for the participants, but the benefits suit those who adapt and become comfortable with the online delivery (Antczak, Mackrill, Steensbaek, & Ebsen, 2017; Csiernik, Furze, Dromgole, & Rishchynski., 2006; Suler, 2000). Csiernik et al. (2006) compares responses on experience with online supervision from BSW, MSW, and professional social workers and find the younger participants, who are more adept at online communications in general, to be more comfortable and satisfied with their online supervisory group experience. This finding is echoed in earlier accounts (Stofle & Hamilton, 1998).

Although we are in a period of transition incorporating innovations and finding ways to evaluate their effectiveness, we propose that the signals of change discussed here require us to have a healthy skepticism about our reliance on aspects of field education that may need adjustment to meet the needs of the current context. Just as we need to consider adjustments in our classroom teaching methods, we will have to consider more feasible ways for students to complete their internships and methods of supervising their competence. To do this, we will have to think differently about internships, less about the completion of hours, and more about the learning and mastery of competence.

Social work education holds many assumptions about field education: Only a specific and substantial number of hours makes learning significant and necessary to achieve competency, the hours are best completed concurrent with practice classes, and the student's current employment responsibilities and supervisor are frequently not sufficient for learning and therefore the places of employment and their supervisors are not explored as potential field education sites and resources unless certain, although underresearched, criteria are met. The CSWE (2018b) confirms this reality. Instead of being a proactive choice, developing unique and individualized placement experiences in programs with increasing student enrollment may be a reactive choice connected to "the complexity of students' needs and requests related to field education" (p. 29). These long-held positions about field learning must be studied with the goal of proving their efficacy in educating students for the competent pursuit of justice. These findings can then be placed in the context of student learning needs rather than attempting to fit them into the older box of untested requirements. Competency-based education suggests that students may reach mastery in different time frames or in different ways. Are we ready to have these seemingly heretical conversations? Certainly, in the context of competency-based education and the possibilities of more easily comparing outcomes, we may be closer than previously in being able to begin these conversations.

For example, examining the number and time frames for internship hours is needed. Although there are often fears that reducing the hours below 2 days a week weakens the field education experience, Raskin, Wayne, and Bogo points out that the "number of field hours necessary for a student to demonstrate competency has never been empirically tested" (as cited in Bradley & Buck, 2016, p. 35). This is an important question as it is likely that some students may be able to complete extended hours supplemented with periods of intensive work based on their work schedules. This may combine the measure of flexibility and intensity that students and educators seek.

Some flexibility in requirements for completion of field placements that help working students or students with families are already being tested. Many schools have long allowed students with experience who are currently employed in social work roles to complete fewer internship hours. Likewise, block placements where students complete their hours in intensified time periods sometimes complete these placements along with practice classes and sometimes not; these long-standing options provide opportunities to study the efficacy of these arrangements. These block placements usually occur over the summer when students may be able to take time off from work. They work especially well for students who are employed in school systems; however, problems sometimes occur in finding field instructors during the summer because staff members are on vacation. In these cases, field instructors might be able to provide coverage for each other during vacation periods and share the supervision of a student.

Restrictions on placements making use of the student's employment should be revisited. Field educators have been concerned about the possible collusion between and among the student worker and supervisor or field instructor and the demands of the setting in this model. Of course, there are possible conflicts and collusion in all placements where students, faculty members, and agencies have interests. Many other programs, including master's in business administration and residency programs in medicine, use the students' jobs as venues to teach and learn. We have insisted on a separation between employment and internship rather than viewing the students' ongoing work as a rich environment for learning and where programs of social work may have a role in professionalizing the service. Instead, we must ask what resources can be added to the work environment that might strengthen the learning there. Can we add sessions like medicine's grand rounds, group supervision, or other educational enrichments? Can we teach our practice classes at the placement location to make it easier for students to attend classes and to strengthen the connection between the internship and classroom? It is important to pilot and study these approaches to ensure their effectiveness in teaching and learning for competency.

One example involved a group of metropolitan schools of social work that moved their students from the public child welfare agency to complete their placements in resettlement neighborhoods for new immigrant families based in schools, hospitals, and child protective agencies. The public child welfare agency financially helped their staff members to matriculate as social work students. The initiative created an innovative educational model for students that included shared learning opportunities through ongoing seminars, an intersession course, and clinical consultations. The model was evaluated to examine its success in preparing the MSW students for preventive practice with these immigrant families. The benefits for families served and for student learning were substantial despite the many institutional challenges involved (Carten & Bertrand Finch, 2010).

Community–University Partnerships

We have mentioned community–university partnerships in relation to recruitment, and the previous example provides a glimpse of the benefits afforded students, constituents, and settings through these collaborations. Here we discuss the need to work with employers to strengthen the workforce through employee-supported field education placements. University–community partnerships show their joint interest in generating a competent workforce, and these interests forge the impetus to work together (Bogo, 2015; Hussein et al., 2009; Strolin, McCarthy, & Caringi, 2006). Such partnerships have the potential for breaking down the vexing silos between field and classroom learning (Clapton et al., 2008; Manthorpe, Harris, & Hussein, 2102; Mirabito, 2012). Also known as place-based learning, school and agency partnerships have many positive outcomes. They also can take many forms (Pierce,

McGuire, & Howes, 2015). First, the partners can provide education for employees who may not otherwise be able to attend school. If classes are held on site, it makes it easier for students to attend and move seamlessly from class to field. The incentive to obtain an education makes it easier for human service organizations to recruit employees. Closer relationships are possible between school and field staff; they can more easily work together to fine-tune and diversify student assignments and individualize supervision. Group supervision, in-service training, and providing coverage for supervision all become more viable. Class projects also are easier to implement. Conversations about research opportunities, partnerships, and coteaching between academics and practitioners are more likely to occur. Classroom and field teachers can ameliorate the gap between research-informed practice and practice-informed research, and integration of learning is enhanced (Clapton et al., 2008) and where possible, workers and students benefit from the educational resources such as videos and libraries. In sum, the organization develops a culture of learning, and students benefit from the direct practical application of learning to practice. Perhaps most important, everyone benefits from the collaboration to create a quality field education learning environment; and the partnership also allows the school and the setting to implement, reinforce, and integrate principles of justice throughout the setting and student training.

Strategies that have worked provide scholarships for employees as a retention strategy (Rheaume, Collins, & Amodeo, 2011) and place-based learning that include courses taught on site at the setting or through distance technology. However, the inherent challenges need to be acknowledged and ongoing renewed commitment to these partnerships is required.

Rheaume et al. (2011) report on child welfare agencies' strong support for these programs; however, the history of university partnerships in child welfare departments demonstrate that these collaborations require ongoing commitment and creative solutions for familiar problems related to organizational change and renewal, staff retention, financial constraints, and ways to measure benefits to the workforce and constituents (Anderson & Briar-Lawson, 2015; Deglau et al., 2015). This is also true in the United Kingdom. Although schools of social work and public social service agencies in the United Kingdom reported benefits of these partnerships, research that explored why this model, referred to as Grow Your Own (GYO) (Noble, Harris, & Manthorpe, 2009), was not used more frequently found underlying questions regarding whether the effort was a means of "developing the profession or filling workforce demands" (Manthorpe et al., 2002, p. 648). This confusion then manifested itself further in questions regarding the suitability of some of the candidates, whether funding education was the best use of public or agency funds, or to what extent individual commitment to education was enhanced if students contributed financially to their own education. The GYO model may have been applauded by those involved, but the inherent underlying ambivalence over these core questions undercut the willingness to collaborate and fund such efforts (Manthorpe et al., 2012). These findings confirm embedded challenges and point to the work of consensus building among stakeholders, clarifying aims, and building effective mutually beneficial partnerships.

There are promising attempts to identify innovative venues for placement that reach new populations and expand field experiences and hours. People often seek help in familiar contexts and in trusted relationships outside the human service system; problems are often presented and identified in non-social-worker contexts by teachers, police, doctors, and other professionals. Building on this reality, several schools have been active in developing placements in settings like libraries, transit systems, urgent care centers, fire and police stations (Hek, 2012), and in offices of elected officials, private law firms, primary care physicians, veterinary offices, and financial managers. This is despite extensive criterion recommended to maintain quality sites (Hunter & Poe, 2016). The new venues are critically important because they provide assistance to individuals who might not otherwise get help, build support and relationships with other disciplines, and expand opportunities (and possibly upgrade the salaries) for social work employment. Because most of these settings are operational on weekends and evenings when many human service agencies are closed, we can potentially offer students more flexible internship hours. However, these nontraditional settings may have difficulties. Although some schools contract with the setting to hire and provide field instruction, often there are challenges in acquiring field instructors in these settings. Another challenge is to ensure that courses cover content and that we are teaching subjects relevant to these new venues, including assertive outreach, engagement of reluctant consumers, and working with colleagues from other disciplines. Being introduced to interdisciplinary practice is critical in working to achieve justice; these settings offer daily exposure to the rewards of collaboration and the benefits of viewing situations from varying disciplinary perspectives.

There are also arguments for field placements that are no longer agency based but focus on an issue or community where field instructors shift from individual teaching responsibilities to encourage the activism of the field unit on specific issues or community problems. These placements are viewed as a way of confronting neoliberalism in social work (George, Silver, & Preston,

2013; Preston, George, Silver, 2014; Steen et al., 2017). Placements based in the social work program have also been established in research, grant development, and admissions. Some programs have formed student units to provide services to agencies by writing grants, developing or evaluating programs, serving the needs of specific populations, and supporting organizing efforts (Garcia, Mizrahi, & Bayne-Smith, 2010; Pinto, McKay, & Escobar, 2008).

Field Education Supervision

This book attempts to address the best practices of field instruction using the competent pursuit of justice as its mission. We have devoted much attention to the central and core role of the field instructor in student learning and integration. To confront the challenges of the future, however, supervision itself must be examined. Are we ready to examine whether one-to-one and face-to-face supervision is the preferable method to achieve the competence required by the EPAS (CSWE, 2015a)? Our commitment to competency and the pursuit of justice will require us to consider whether alterations are needed, and which competencies for student supervision best support our aims. Many of the issues raised throughout this chapter and in our consideration of new placement models and settings point to this need.

First, we assert that departments of field education must provide field educators with seminars to help them to engage in challenging dialogue on race, class, gender, sexual orientation, and intersecting identities to support all students in justice-based practices. Field instructors are a vital resource for students, and it is critical for them to engage students in these most difficult topics; this mandate extends with equal attention to improving classroom faculty's abilities in this arena.

Second, considering the burgeoning science and evidence-based interventions in practice, it is unlikely that one field instructor can teach and evaluate all that must be learned by students today. This is an especially important task given the responsibility of field education to attest to the nine CSWE (2015a) competencies at the generalist and specialist levels of practice. The NASW (2017) Code of Ethics has addressed this issue since 1996, stating that field instructors "should provide instruction only within their areas of knowledge and competence and should provide instruction based on the most current information and knowledge available in the profession" (Standard 3.02). The profession's longstanding one field instructor to one student model as the sole method of instruction is already threatened because of inadequate supports, current workplace demands, and the costs involved. It is essential for us to find ways to examine core essentials related to field education supervision, consider how these core essentials can be provided, and support field instructors' efforts to offer what is required or to ensure that the total package of the placement experience contains all that is required. Without responding to these realities, one-on-one field instruction will emerge as a method that is out of reach, impractical, idealistic, or outdated.

New models are being developed that assemble and engage multiple teachers and students. Beyond designating an *anchor instructor* for each student and finding a task supervisor who can provide additional support to the student, we must find other ways to meet the demands of the current practice context to protect the important role of field education supervision in social work education. Multiple teachers, perhaps through rotations or virtual teaching or field instructor teams, are possibilities. Technology may also be used in creative ways to support field education. Webinars, TED talks, podcasts, videos, and blogs can be developed and used by social work field educational staff to teach content across their areas of expertise. Although students may start off with the traditional model of field instruction in the first semester, as they progress through the program, they might be exposed to more instructors with different expertise and more group and peer supervision. This may be an advantage over the current model that relies on one setting, which may limit the student's exposure to the range of methods and modalities needed for practice, or that rely on one field instructor who is unable to provide all the oversight and instruction needed.

Recruiting a more diverse population of students will mean that agency staff may not always be ready to respond to the diverse learning needs that will emerge. Any one setting or field instructor may not possess the range of expertise needed. In certain areas this is already true. Certainly, Millennial students know a great deal about the use of technology. They may also be more current, knowledgeable, and comfortable with the thinking and language about gender and race and how it affects relationships. Respect for student expertise suggests that group supervision, where everyone is a learner and a teacher, could become more the norm. Peer groups can be empowering learning experiences that increase confidence and a sense of independence; students voice their concerns about their learning or validate the field placements' strengths and limitations and garner support and guidance from each other regarding these issues (Golia & McGovern, 2015; Zeira & Schiff, 2010). We stress the need to examine the efficacy of a flipped model in which the primary field instructor offering group supervision is the norm, and individual supervision is the supplement. We do not see this model as lessening the critical role of the field instructor in field education; on the contrary, this model requires even greater clarity regarding the field instructor's role, skills, and expertise. We support envisioning our future with practice for justice at the forefront. We also support these trends in ensuring greater equity in the field education experience for ourselves and our students by recognizing where the current flaws are and addressing needed remedies. How we educate for competence is our driving concern, and as such, our role as field instructor and partner in these educative innovations requires our full attention. We hope the next generation of field instructors and field education faculty and staff members will take this challenge on to develop and test innovations and collaborations that expand the learning opportunities for students and appreciate the potential of contributions of collaboration among field instructors.

Summary and Final Note

We have tried to describe some of the changes in social work education that we believe are at the cusp of practice demands and require our response to help us more effectively educate students for the competent pursuit of justice. We have proposed that perspectives of equity and liberation must guide our interventions, and we have suggested that understanding how the legacy and remnants of settler colonialism impede our progress is also essential. In this regard, we have not gone far enough. That is, the opening paragraph of this chapter acknowledges that a response is needed to match a time when seemingly "every social issue that concerns social workers...is being reviewed and reconsidered at the highest levels of government." As we conclude our thoughts, a critical U.S. midterm election resulted in a large voter turnout giving congressional seats to more than 100 women, including two American Indians and two Muslims. The effect of these firsts on the political process is as yet unknown, but the promise and hope of the presence of voices not previously at the table will now unfold. Boundaries are being spanned and tested.

We have suggested that as our understanding and experience increase, our understanding of justice evolves. Similarly, our own professional challenge will be to consider how a justice framework that includes the premises of equity, liberation, and decolonization might lead the way for the recruitment, retention, and success of students who more closely reflect representation of the populations we serve. As our profession digs deeper into the work of liberation, restorative justice, and contemplative methods toward healing, we will be propelled further into how field education must support students' understanding that liberation is not just a word. This trajectory will move us toward their greater participation, inclusion, and affirmation as future leaders of the profession. As we end this text, we see that we are on the edge of new frontiers in the pursuit of justice. The trends suggested in this chapter will change and influence the work of social work education; students will grow to expect expertise from those we seek to represent. They will look to field education faculty members to assist in creating unique and flexible placement options, seek faculty scholars able to support their exploration of practice demands, and demand course bibliographies that reflect their diverse concerns. We have suggested that we need to begin now. In this chapter we also have attempted to emerge from a silo that considers only issues affecting field education. This reflects the reality that separating field education or the practice community from academe do not serve the needs of social work education. This is not a new concept, but we have attempted to show how interconnected and interrelated the issues and concerns are. Much of what we describe present challenges.

First, some of the recommendations will require additional resources. The recruitment strategies we have discussed to build new pipelines to reach more students who will diversify our student population will require additional people power. We have argued that more attention must be given to student services, likely resulting in the expansion of advising and other student support mechanisms. These new expenditures will come at a time when many universities are shrinking budgets and asking departments to do more with less. Universities across the nation are already experimenting with 24-hour, 7-day-a-week, Web-based technological advising applications to serve these needs. We must persuade university administrators that these expenditures will result in critical outcomes: more students, more diversity in the student body, and better retention and graduation rates. It is incumbent on us to collect the data that offer evidence of these outcomes.

Second, change will require all actors in the educational system—faculty members, administration, admissions, student services staff, students, and field educators in schools and agencies—to interact and work together. We cannot admit a new and inclusive student body without developing a better advising system, creating a more fair and inclusive culture that does not marginalize students, adding and updating our curriculum in significant ways, and creating field education models that support these new realities. We cannot change field education without faculty members, advisers, liaisons, and leaders who support those changes. The curriculum reform will require faculty members to stretch their teaching into new content areas and to give up autonomy over their courses. We have advocated for some of the most sacrosanct requirements in social work education to be reviewed and tested. The field education changes will necessitate a review of current CSWE (2015a) accreditation policies and ask more of human service agencies during times of fiscal constraint. Those of us who have worked in social work education will not underestimate the challenges in such a transformative process. We know that everyone comes to the table with different views, experiences, and interests. If we are to coalesce around such a major task, the focus must be on what the social work profession and those we serve will gain by tackling how we have always functioned. Only a renewed commitment to justice and inclusion can serve as the mission for such an undertaking.

Not all of what we suggest here are new concerns; most of the changes are long overdue and many are being or can be implemented incrementally. If not yet begun, they have perhaps not been implemented because such innovation challenges some of our most historical and dearly held beliefs about the best way to educate newcomers to our field. It is important to balance our interest in change with the necessity for competence and excellence in graduating the next generation of social workers, who will be responsible for the future pursuit of justice. It will take time, patience, and a deep commitment to a rational process of planning and evaluation to move us ahead. We will have to agree to experimentation and evaluation at every juncture, so we can purposefully chart the most effective path for student outcomes and the most productive paths for our departments. We urge the CSWE to take the next step in incorporating an innovation task force within one of the existing CSWE centers and initiatives or establish a separate initiative charged with collecting and disseminating results of experiments being undertaken in social work field departments and providing support for their evaluation across social work education. The need for action and sharing is so great that the task force should use communication media that promote interchange.

The same charge can be given to social work programs. We must share what field instructors are trying and achieving with the program's total cadre of field instructors. Too often one field instructor in one setting attempts something new in crafting an assignment, introducing a teaching method, or reshaping the field placement experience; it may work, but the creativity does not go beyond that field instructor and that student. We have the tools to share and we have the need. We must learn what is working and how to replicate and evaluate wider applications.

Despite these real challenges, we cannot refuse to confront the essential tasks of educational reform. If we are to remain relevant and effective and committed to justice, there is no other course. We recognize CSWE's (2018a) initiative currently underway to examine the relationship between changing practice contexts and the concurrent impetus of technological resources and advances. A similar rethinking of our premises and responses in the context of societal realities and demands is overdue. Examining the implications for social work field education is essential to this conversation.

So we end with a challenge to ourselves and to the profession. Let us seek and nurture the new workforce our profession requires. Let us honor, value, and learn to follow our community colleagues, activists, and faculty members from currently underrepresented and indigenous populations who can influence and teach us about how we can contribute to justice. Perhaps when offering a justice-based framework to field education in the social work profession we should have started here. Instead, we have ended here with hopes that we have somehow, through this text, increased capacity to listen to the voices calling for justice and for guidance on developing strategies of liberation and decolonization across all levels of practice. And we hope that this listening and attention to the future helps ensure a willingness and commitment to continuing to do the difficult, unsettling work involved. Finally, we hope this book will offer a boost to this important dialogue.

APPENDIX A

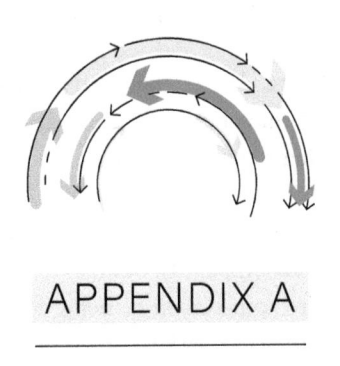

Teaching Methods and Tools for Use in Supervision

In this appendix we share methods and approaches we have found helpful in our supervision of students. This is not meant to be an exhaustive list but as building blocks and an addition to your repertoire of techniques and tools. A variety of methods and approaches are presented. These are not new approaches, but we stress how these approaches help support student learning.

Didactic Methods

Didactic methods are frequently used in situations where the information is likely new to the students and the aim is to succinctly convey information. In this approach, the field instructor is the expert who offers information, guidance, practice wisdom, and suggestions primarily through a lecture format. Students are directed to pay attention, take notes, and recall the information transmitted. Yet, as Shulman (1984) warns us, this method presumes that students learn by assuming a passive posture:

> The teaching and learning process in supervision, as in educational settings, has been profoundly affected by acceptance of the myth that teaching essentially involves transmitting existing ideas to learners who somehow absorb them and make the ideas as their own. (p. 161)

Referring again to Freire (1993), the disadvantages of this approach include our maintaining the role of expert in such a manner that the student's expertise is excluded. Other drawbacks include overwhelming students with too much information all at once, expecting them to follow suggestions to the letter, preventing them from developing their own approach to assignments, and not allowing time to absorb, apply, or analyze and synthesize the information. Many students are accustomed to being fed information, and they like this method because they can gather a great deal of information quickly and then move on to something else. It is also easier to listen than to think creatively.

Power clearly rests with the field instructor or teacher in this hierarchical approach to teaching, but there are ways to ameliorate negative effects. Anticipating the dangers of perpetuating students as passive learners and speaking to students directly about this, provide a means to confront the power imbalances in our relationships with them. Articulating our desire to bring their voices forward offers a powerful teaching vehicle and model for the cultivation of effective relationships with diverse families, groups, and individuals. Hair and O'Donoghue (2009) said, "It is by acknowledging these contexts that social work stands out as a political and moral enterprise, challenging the power relationships that place individuals, families and communities [and students] in positions of distress, marginalization and oppression" (p. 73).

Attending to these potential pitfalls provides some assurances that the use of a didactic method achieves its intended purposes, especially if students are expected to evaluate and apply what is presented to them rather than merely absorb and retain it. Choosing to deliver the information in a didactic manner can be enhanced by using active learning methods such as small-group discussions, problem-solving exercises, case studies, and projects that increase participation, reflection, and discussion with us and among our students. The aim is to stimulate growth and progression in the student's stage of learning.

Still, other challenges emerge when a student asks a direct question seeking a direct answer. In these situations, we are often drawn to a more didactic approach in response. What should the response be in these situations? Jarvis (1995) proposes that rather than using a didactic approach,

> perhaps the teacher should encourage the students to seek an answer as well; secondly, it is the questioning process that facilitates independent learning and so, perhaps a good teacher leads students from question to question rather from answer to answer. (p. 109)

Likewise, "Just as problems invite solutions, questions invite answers" (Witkin, 2014, p. 595). The conclusion drawn from this is that measuring our success by the number of questions rather than the number of facts the students are left with might enable students to live with the uncertainties of professional practice.

We can be selective in how much didactic content to offer students and how many experiential, concrete experiences to structure into field instruction that offer ideas, suggestions, and hunches on how the work gets done. We can select from a combination of teaching methods that include auditory or visual technologies, podcasts, Web sites, distance learning, interactional and participatory face-to-face activities, and methods that use all senses in learning. As we increase our confidence in our supervisory abilities and gain clarity on our student's needs, we are freer to try new methods and techniques, which are then added to our repertoire and incorporated into our toolbox. The ways of promoting learning are as myriad as our creativity allows.

Additional Methods

The following methods are examples of ways to instigate skill development. The aim is to identify which underlying values are operating, discern what knowledge is being drawn on or is missing in the equation, and provide practice in critical thinking, examining affective reactions, and assessing judgments. Each method supports and prompts several of these components, which in turn encourages development of our students' abilities and skills through discussion and activities.

Achieving a Questioning Stance

Engaging students to be reflective and to think critically is often a challenge. "Creating a culture of thoughtfulness" (Gambrill, 2013, p. 594) is developed and sustained through numerous ways including open, honest discussions that do not avoid conflict. This can be achieved by involving students in clarifying their thinking processes, which leads to an assessment of their values (Deal, 2003; Paul, 1992). For example, a learning atmosphere that encourages critical thinking and self-awareness is developed by questions that probe assumptions, evidence, and implications. Careful phrasing of questions supports our teaching and provides a model for our students. Seeking clarification, probing assumptions, and seeking reasons and evidence as distinguished from inferences provide opportunities for logical reasoning, critical thinking, and reflection to develop. This is most productive if our questions are posed in a thoughtful, curious, but nonjudgmental manner and phrased in a way that facilitates development of insight from unarticulated thought patterns and reactions. This means promoting a questioning approach to theories and intervention strategies by looking at the context of practice and asking questions such as, "Why might this be so? Who says? Under what circumstances? Who has been advantaged by it?" (Hartman, 1997, p. 224) and "How do these services fit the needs of those being served? What else might be needed to better respond to this situation? and What questions are not being asked?" (Ortiz and Jani, 2010, p. 184).

Questions that seek clarification may help students deepen their understanding of the issues such as, "Could you put it another way?" or "Could you give me an example?" Questions that probe assumptions or seek reasons and evidence provide an opportunity to explain how certain conclusions are made, for example, "How did you determine that he did not want to go to the job interview?" or "What made you think the little girl was afraid of her mother?" In a process parallel to student-consumer interactions, we seek answers to these questions for clarification of thought processes and to explore unspoken values and assumptions. Being careful not to begin these questions with "Why did you?" avoids the potential of questioning students' reasoning and placing them on the defensive. It is easier to respond to a how, when, or what question.

Similarly, questions that probe for implications and consequences such as, "What effect would that have?" or "If this and that are the case, what else might also be true?" and "What would it mean to you if that were the case?" help students become more reflective and discerning as practitioners. By responding to students' questions with questions, we increase their abilities to arrive at their own answers. For example, tell them, "To answer your question, what questions would we have to answer first?" or "When we break this question down into smaller components, what issues emerge?" or "Before I answer your question, can you help me understand what might be underlying your concern about this particular issue? This will help me to respond to your concerns more fully."

Analogies and Metaphors

Some students respond well to analogies and metaphors that help make connections between their experiences and unspoken content such as in the following: "It seems like you are expecting yourself to act as a kind of Wonder

Woman or superhero! Let's consider your need to fix this community's problems single-handedly" or "You appear to be describing this part of the group process as an out-of-control freight train" or, "You are describing the committee meeting as if you were a lion tamer. Can you comment more on what was happening at this point?" The possibilities are endless. Creating analogies that are relevant to the specific experience and relate to the target population, setting, or community context can be helpful when students are feeling overwhelmed and need to connect the reality of the situation to feelings that may be underlying their actions. It helps students tune in and understand the reasons why they or the individuals they are working with might be reacting as they do. It gives voice to the often-unspoken thoughts involved and promotes reframing the situation for considering an alternative approach.

Metaphors provide additional avenues for promoting reflective thinking (Drew & Hinkle, 2018). Gladding (2011) provides examples of exercises to introduce in supervision to unblock progress or to provide a means to unleash creativity. For example, asking students to take a photograph of an object from different angles and to bring these to supervision releases an awareness of how our perspective on an object is affected by the angle we assume, the perspective we take, and the focus of our view. This type of exercise promotes new ways of seeing and viewing the world and enhances the development of a student's creativity and capacity for reflection.

Brainstorming and Heartstorming

Brainstorming and heartstorming are neutral means to invite experimentation and playful consideration of the possible options operating in a situation. Inviting a value-free list of issues often yields ideas and solutions not otherwise recognized for consideration. In processing these ideas, learning may emerge. Brainstorming provides an open space for students to contribute an idea they may have considered previously but felt inhibited or restricted to raise in field education supervision. The brainstorming effort adds excitement to the interchange as we seek the best possible range of solutions to a pressing or complex problem.

An equally important request is to ask the student to heartstorm, which calls for attention to affective aspects that might influence the situation. The invitation to heartstorm taps into the student's feelings, emotive thoughts, and hopes for the situation rather than sticking more closely to issues or problem-solving aspects frequently involved in brainstorming, for example: Let's list the unspoken hopes you have in this situation. Now, let's list what hopes have been voiced by the members of this family." By giving voice to hopes and feelings, other aspects of the work are possible for consideration. Active engagement with the student's affective reactions to the work is given attention.

Concept and Mind Mapping

Mapping tools enable diagramming complex relationships among information, ideas, and concepts. Although software tools exist, it is possible to engage students in an informal mapping exercise without technological support. According to Davies (2011), "Mind mapping allows students to imagine and explore associations between concepts; concept mapping allows students to understand the relationships between concepts and hence understand those concepts themselves and the domain to which they belong" (p. 280). Mind mapping is an informal and spontaneous technique that displays associations and branches of critical domains of importance to the subject. It puts form into a simple brainstorming effort, and the student starts to build relationships of the ideas presented; similar explorations may benefit from using a concept mapping framework that aims to examine the relationships among ideas more deeply. Rather than depicting branches, a hierarchical structure is often applied. A concept map usually begins with a question that focuses on answers such as "What leads to, or results from, or is part of this or that?" For example, a student may seek an answer to "How do I effectively engage with this disfranchised youth?" The student wants to answer what leads to, results from, or is part of effective engagement. Concept mapping requires more familiarity with the concept being explored than a simple brainstorming or mind mapping exercise. Brainstorming might lead to mind mapping as a first step; concept mapping can be used later in the academic year.

Argument mapping is a tool that "allows students to display inferential connections between propositions and contentions, and to evaluate them in terms of validity of argument structure and the soundness of argument premises" (Davies, 2011, p. 280). The aim of argument mapping is to explore the structure of arguments; it is also more focused and structured than either mind or concept mapping. Each of these tools are linked to an increase in critical thinking and promotion of deep learning; they are methods to engage students in new ways of looking at a topic.

Feedback

Students need feedback on how they are doing. They need to hear that they are doing what is needed, and they need guidance on how to improve their efforts. Frequent feedback or learning reviews help students recognize achievements, see where they are in reaching learning goals, and identify learning difficulties or gaps in their knowledge. Feedback also guides change in thinking, attitudes, and behaviors in desired directions. In a very real way, feedback is an integral component of ongoing learning reviews and evaluation of field performance. Each builds on and enriches the other. We could say, "You have achieved good rapport with this group of chronic mentally ill patients. Let's look at the specific ways you accomplished this" or "You were not afraid to accept the reality of this individual's anger and hostility. This led to an effective containment of her emotions and provided a deeper connection with her. What was going through your mind as she raged at you that helped you to keep focus and self-regulate?" or "You were extremely efficient getting the personnel manual done, but you are having trouble getting this work group started. Let's brainstorm together about the differences and similarities between these two assignments to understand this more together." These examples illustrate the provision of feedback and using this feedback to build additional understanding.

In these ways, we focus our student's concentration on a specific aspect of practice. Feedback is more than saying they did something well, it involves engaging the student in understanding the specifics of what went well or not so well and to consider what was involved. Formulating a balanced expression of things that are going well in the context but that may need improvement helps students to think more deeply. Reaching for students' own review gives us a sense of how close we are to their perception of their abilities. This allows us to begin where they are, but not leave them with an unrealistic positive or negative vision of their performance.

Linking Concepts and Skills to Examples in Practice

As many of the learning outcomes associated with the CSWE (2015a) competencies include identifying and applying theories that support chosen intervention strategies, we are called on to help students understand and operationalize theoretical concepts encountered in practice. This can be done by linking concepts to examples that bring the concepts to life and facilitate a deeper understanding of theories they are using.

Recording formats often require identification of theories or models but students frequently have difficulty completing this task, or they may repeat the most familiar theory they encounter. The classroom is no longer the only place where discussion of theory and models should be introduced. Having a sense of the student's course work and theoretical perspectives being taught in the classroom are helpful in achieving integration of theory and practice. This also means being informed about the theories that apply to the work assigned. Providing time to address how the student is experiencing the relevance of theory to practice identifies how the student is integrating this knowledge.

Similarly, labeling or naming the skills and identifying the specific methods used are helpful teaching techniques. Students often do more than they know, and they need our assistance in identifying their intuitive or learned skills and techniques. As suggested earlier, it is helpful to ask students to link learning about intervention strategies from their class discussions or readings to the competencies.

Modeling

According to Gitterman and Miller (1977),

> workers are particularly influenced by a supervisor who demonstrates skill in practice, maintains high standards, and shows excitement, curiosity, and openness to differing perspectives and possibilities. What effective supervisors "say to do" needs to be congruent with what they actually "do." (p. 106)

Barretti notes that it is commonly accepted that "[W]hat is caught" is as important as "what is taught" (Barretti, 2007, p. 221; Shulman, 2012), and as field instructors, we are role models for students across the broad spectrum of professional values and behaviors. The task of teaching values is supported through modeling. Students are provided with a visual and lived experience that bolsters adoption of these behaviors and attitudes. Consider the following ways we directly influence our students through the modeling we provide (Bertrand Finch et al., 2003):

> - Listening, conveying a nonjudgmental attitude, and being open to students' thinking processes, such as, responding to questions and not being afraid to say, "I don't know!" or "Let's find out!"
> - Accepting criticism

- Taking our responsibilities seriously
- Addressing the importance of openly discussing multiple and overlapping dimensions of identity in our work and field education supervision
- Having the same expectations for ourselves as for our students, for example, as we expect our students to be timely in their work submissions, we make certain that recordings are reviewed in a timely manner and we submit timely written materials required by the social work program such as midterm or sixth- to eighth-week reviews, educational learning contracts or end-of-semester written evaluations
- Demonstrating the importance of consistency and structure by ensuring a regular time for field education supervision that is negotiated with the student
- Initiating difficult dialogues in a direct and straightforward manner
- Managing the power differentials between ourselves and our students with respect and mutuality

Modeling is being used, if not explicitly then implicitly, throughout the field placement. Explicitly we may choose to demonstrate a skill, approach, or technique. Much can be gained through this method, but as experienced professionals we may forget that demonstrating a challenging skill with ease without breaking down the components of that skill may appear daunting to the novice. As with any of these techniques and methods, being aware of the pitfalls provides a safeguard. Simply allowing ourselves to think out loud in front of our students shows our thought processes. This models openness, how we think through a situation, and our ability to be self-reflective. Perhaps saying something like the following may be enough to free students from feeling that they must know how to do something just as you have: "I know I may have made it seem simple, but now that I have shown you what I mean, let's try to break down what just happened; can you explain what you observed?" or "Are there ways of tackling this that might fit more closely with your personality or way of talking?" Of course, the opposite is also true. By demonstrating a skill, we may be presuming that our student does not have a better way of approaching the task.

Implicitly, we are role models for students in all that we do. The influence of our professional behavior and demeanor is particularly important to our students' development of ethical and professional behavior. This reality provides many unspoken teachable moments for us to use in our conversations and reflections with our students. Openly reflecting on an interaction may demonstrate more than we might ever hope to achieve through a didactic interchange. It provides a shared experience to reflect together and to share perceptions and beliefs about what was intended and what was experienced.

Being aware of this phenomenon means that we can become purposeful in our actions and choices of topics for analysis with our students, for example, "Let's take a moment to examine what just happened at this morning's staff meeting. I took a very firm stance in opposition to the proposal presented. What happened next? What prompted a change in the process that resulted in a modified response and eventual adoption of the proposal?" Or, "I have been thinking about our meeting last week, I can see that my own reactions to this challenging situation may have affected how we talked about it and how you felt about it. Let's take some time now to review what happened between us so that we can progress in our work together on this issue."

Observation

Observation is an excellent way of teaching throughout the field placement. Opportunities for students to observe as well as to be observed provide straightforward ways of assessing how our students view and reflect on what they see and for assessing their performance (Bogo, 2015).

Assigning students to observe is especially useful in the first few weeks of placement or when introducing a new method. By being purposeful and assigning an observation of a specific situation, we provide opportunities to model aspects of practice and professional relationships. In the beginning stages of field education, we may ask students to report on observations of staff meetings, interactions with individuals served, team meetings, and community or board meetings. These observations provide practice for reflections and for recordings; they record the student's understanding of interactions such as who sits next to whom, who speaks, and so on. Students also may be asked to be outside observers of themselves as they perform their work, as if they were following themselves around the agency, and then write about it. This begins the process of developing student self-awareness and reflection in and on action. Their observational skills and their assessment of and reflections on what they see and experience are developed. Opportunities for dialogue in supervision may focus on pieces that can be examined together, and foundations can be set for further exploration.

As the semester progresses, we examine our own accumulating observations of students in their interactions, and, of course, students are involved in observing whether we ask them to or not. Students see and hear us while practicing their observational and assessment skills. Gaining access to these observations and reflections simply requires an invitation for students to share them with us. These various ways of using observation taps into assessing the students' ability to analyze their reactions to what they have observed or experienced. Discussing these observations facilitates growth of self-awareness by drawing attention to the process and discerning suppositions from the evidence presented. This is a critical aspect of several competencies that emphasize self-awareness, reflection, self-regulation, and critical thinking. Directly observing students beyond what we experience in supervision adds an important component to our assessments of their skills. This can be achieved in several ways depending on our settings and work assigned. Finally, in the way that observations at the start of placement give us clues to our student's perceptions, asking for students to observe interactions again at the end of placement give them and us the chance to assess how their perceptions have developed.

Partializing

Partializing, or breaking down a concept or task into manageable parts, helps students understand and appreciate complex ideas or interventions. For example, you could say, "Assessment involves data gathering, evaluation of the data, and plans for intervention. Let's start with data gathering. What do you need to know to carry out this assignment, and how will you go about finding it out?" By breaking the process into its relevant pieces, students are supported in understanding the complexity. Clarity about the various components emerge.

Problem Posing

Problem posing draws student participation in to critical thought and multicultural learning. The method defines learning as "problem-posing rather than problem-solving" (Shor, 1992, p. 43). It aims to create a bridge between the student's lack of organized critical thought and the educator's experience with societal issues of historical and systemic oppression. This applies a model of learning that begins with, and resides in, the student's own experience. It draws first from the student's understanding—an inside-out approach. Shor introduces three themes: generative, topical, and academic. Each is positioned as closer or farther from the student's direct experience. A generative theme is directly connected to the student's lived experience, whereas the academic theme is more distant and more associated with an intellectual activity. Although applied in a classroom context, these approaches have applicability for field education supervision as well.

A generative theme is drawn from the student's lived experience and is an unresolved social issue that relates to the essence of the work, derives from discussions with students, relates to the population or issue being addressed, and is drawn from students' perspective. Social location, power and privilege, issues of justice, and historical and systemic racism are central issues of concern. In an example of work with a Mexican youth referred for outbursts of anger in school, a generative theme might ask the social work intern to consider the reason for the youth's referral for services and the context of this youth's experience of being Mexican in this school and community. The question asks the intern to link personal knowledge with experience of oppressed or marginalized youths. The student's understanding and experience regarding the issues and aims to promote understanding are drawn on, much like the task of tuning in.

A topical theme from this situation introduces an important social question relevant to the work. It is an issue the student has some acquaintance with but is less directly applicable to the student's experience—for example, how contemporary issues regarding threats to Mexicans crossing the U.S. southern border and immigration police raids in the local immigrant community are pertinent to the work with this youth. The student is invited to consider this topical theme and to talk about it from the wider societal and global context; the discussion promotes critical thought about the direct implications of this seemingly external issue for work with this youth and immigrant youths in general.

An academic theme from this example is an issue that is brought forward by the field instructor based in formal bodies of knowledge or theories the field instructor wishes to introduce for the student's consideration. This theme is the furthest from the student's own lived experience. The way to introduce an academic theme is to pose it as a problem. Using the same case scenario, an academic theme might be the engagement process, asking, "What is engagement?" and "What theoretical approaches might help us?" followed by, "What are the special issues for engagement with Mexican youths in this community, and how might this reality affect your building rapport and establishing a treatment alliance with this youth?" In a problem-posing model, introducing an academic theme still requires student participation and demands students to work at translating the new knowledge into their own language and understanding so that they are more able to apply it to their work.

Role Playing

Role playing is a useful teaching method, especially when we reverse roles with our students so that we alternately play the individual served or the worker. This technique can be effective in helping students experience an interaction in a different manner and in developing empathy. It can also help plan strategies on how to approach difficult situations and deal with complex and sensitive material. Role playing encourages students to pose their own responses and questions rather than repeating what we might say. The exercise allows students to figure out and plan an approach to their work, increases the development of critical thinking as students ponder next steps out loud, and it promotes reflection on the process.

Some students feel awkward when asked to role-play because it places them in an unknown and imaginary space. In these situations, it is important to explain our aims for the exercise and to explain the importance of play and experimentation in learning. A period of debriefing, even if the role play seems to have progressed smoothly, provides time for the student to share any unspoken feelings about exposure or embarrassment. As noted in Chapter 8, sometimes using the exact interchange that has been recorded by the student in the role play provides a bridge to other views of the interaction and to other responses and interventions.

Strengths Assessment Framework

An assessment framework using the strengths perspective (see Figure A.1) applies two axes that consider environmental factors versus help-seeker factors and strengths versus obstacles (Anderson, 2013). These axes create four quadrants that provide attention to internal personal resources and barriers as well as those strengths and barriers that exist in the environment and target system.

This structure categorizes aspects of a situation that may sometimes be missed or only seen in one quadrant rather than recognizing the possibility that some factors fit on both sides of a continuum. The axes also enable discussion of consequences of oppression and factors that promote resilience and stamina in the face of obstacles encountered. The framework forces consideration of all four quadrants and thereby influences a more inclusive view of the situation.

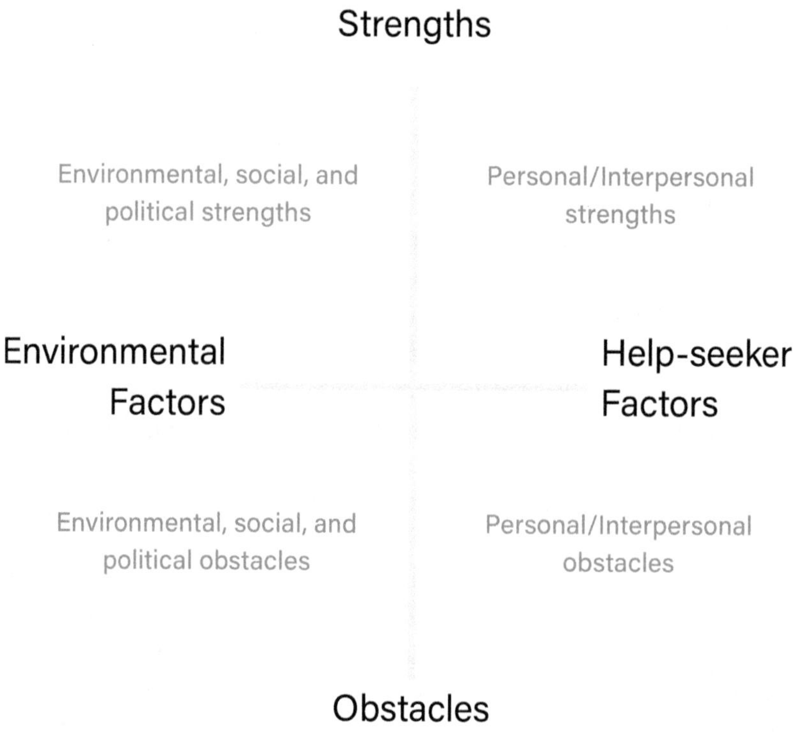

Strengths

| Environmental, social, and political strengths | Personal/Interpersonal strengths |

Environmental Factors   Help-seeker Factors

| Environmental, social, and political obstacles | Personal/Interpersonal obstacles |

Obstacles

Figure A.1 Assessment framework (*Note.* Adapted from Cowger, Anderson, & Snively, 2006, p. 108)

Applying this framework in field education supervision assists in identifying strengths that already exist in the situation and clarifying avenues for interventions. It also points to obstacles that underpin the challenges for change. By requiring this concrete listing of factors, a discussion emerges regarding each element, and sometimes something a student initially sees as an obstacle can be reframed into a potential strength and vice versa. Also, listing the items in this way enables students to see the situation in an alternative format. A visual depiction supports their comprehension on a deeper level.

Technology

Technological advances provide many opportunities for our teaching. The use of videos and podcasts that support our teaching, Web sources for information, and research findings and data available on the Web are all resources that support our work. The options might overwhelm us.

The use of technology and online learning in social work education has rapidly increased in the classroom and in field education. This is reflected in the emerging literature on its uses in practice and education (Ayala, 2009; Dennis, 2016; McElrath & McDowell, 2008; Petracchi & Patchner, 2000; Siebert, Siebert, & Spaulding-Givens, 2006; Singer & Sage, 2015; York, 2008). Schools of social work are testing new ways of educating field instructors, educational coordinators, and advisers through online seminars (McElrath & McDowell, 2008). Some field education departments are using technology to match and place students. It is becoming common practice for program staff to communicate with their field partners through interactive television, e-mails, Blackboard, electronic records, websites that contain field education forms, and online evaluation formats. Some schools have full-time online MSW programs, whereas other programs are only slowly venturing into this arena because of limited resources. This reality affects placement settings as well. As programs and organizational practice become more familiar with the advances and applications available, the approach to technology naturally evolves to greater and greater inclusion and adaptation to the benefits technology makes possible.

Students are increasingly exposed to learning management systems (English & Duncan-Howell, 2008) such as Blackboard and other online discussion groups in and outside the classroom with field instructors, field liaisons, and other students. These online conversations can take the form of informal chats or grand rounds and virtual case conferences, with students posing or responding to questions and consulting on each other's cases. This is often combined with some form of face-to-face connection in a blended format (Bogo, 2005, 2010; Birkenmaier et al., 2005). Social networking tools are also increasingly used in a variety of ways to engage students and to encourage a community for learning that might not otherwise have been possible (Barnett, Harwood, Keating, & Saam, 2002; English & Duncan-Howell, 2008; Wretman & Macy, 2016). Likewise, there is an increasing use of e-portfolios, virtual learning environments for capstone projects students undertake at the end of their program, and macro-level recording methods for social administration and policy practice (Voshel, 2008). These forms of communication may be used when placements are at a distance from the university, such as in rural areas, or where sites are spread across wide distances or cross state boundaries. Technological innovations can make international field placements possible by using online communities, webcams, Skype, e-mail, and videoconferencing in field education supervision and advising (Panos, 2005).

Likewise, Web sources unquestionably increase our field education supervision offerings to students. For example, the Web offers new avenues to teach advocacy tactics and skills and outreach using social media applications. Blogs, wikis, videocasts, apps, and so forth may advance communication, collaboration building, and sharing information (Edwards & Hoefer, 2010). Web-based tools are being used in a range of areas including, dialectical behavioral therapy and cross-cultural trainings (Lopez, 2015; Nadan, 2016). In addition, some social work programs have introduced useful sites for public use. For example, Jonathan Singer, associate professor at Loyola University Chicago, has been recognized for his work in initiating the *Social Work Podcast* (http://socialworkpodcast.blogspot.com/), which offers a range of relevant topics on all things social work. The University at Buffalo School of Social Work also offers a podcast series that features interviews with social work professionals on various topics and helpful resources including interviews with social work experts on aspects of social work practice (http://socialwork.buffalo.edu/resources/our-podcast-series-insocialwork.html). Of note for supervisors is an interview with Larry Shulman on supervision models (see http://www.insocialwork.org/episode.asp?ep=5). The site also has made available a Web-based self-care resource for students and professionals.

As we benefit from the use of technology in practice and supervision, we should also exercise caution in the protection of confidentiality and ensuring that our students are introduced to reliable sources for guidance. Helping students become informed explorers and users of the readily available information is an important component of our work with them. The podcasts and other Web tools can be brought into supervision. Similarly, technology standards (NASW, ASWB, CSWE, & Clinical Social Work Association, 2017) are available for our work in supervision.

Summary

In addition to the numerous tools of effective communication used in social work practice, an exhaustive range of methods can further our educative purposes. We may choose from lecturing on specific topics, discussing assigned articles or viewing videotapes together, using case material or current events to stimulate discussions, requiring weekly journals, or teaching from student recordings. Remember that we do not have to do all the teaching. Besides using staff or professionals in the placement setting, other students also can be involved. It can be helpful to have a variety of avenues for learning in addition to field education supervision such as grand rounds, in-service training programs, conferences, collaborating with a colleague to act as a task supervisor, group meetings for students in your setting or neighboring settings, field trips, and films, and so on.

The content, approach, and activities we apply facilitate our student's efforts toward increased competency. In Chapter 1 we address the importance of identifying our own values and purposes for becoming a field educator and recognizing the special talents we bring that connect with a chosen teaching style and approach. The approaches may be adjusted to the student's stage of learning. Some also might be more useful for beginning-level students than students in a more advanced stage. Specifically, three learning activities significantly associated with student satisfaction and perception of field placement quality of first-year MSW students were found to be con-joint work, explanations by field instructors, and feedback on recordings (Fortune, McCarthy, & Abramson, 2001). However, a different combination of methods was identified for second-year MSW students. For this group, explanations from the field instructor, being asked to critique one's own work, making connections to theory, and observing others in professional roles emerged as significant (Fortune et al., 2001). This research was conducted prior to the introduction of competency-based education, and it would be interesting to see whether the results would change in this new era of social work education.

APPENDIX B

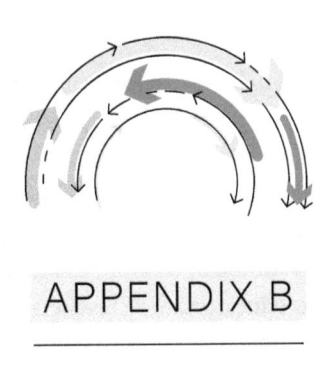

A Justice-Based Seminar in Field Instruction (SIFI)

SIFI facilitates the role transition for first-time field instructors by providing support while acknowledging the special challenges of this role. The task for each seminar participant is to achieve ownership of expertise in a new role, to acknowledge individual capabilities, to transfer skills to the teaching of skill development, and to mobilize the energies of the group to help each other make this professional shift. (Bertrand Finch & Feigelman, 2008, p. 210).

Led by experienced field instructors or faculty members with a special interest in field education, SIFIs are designed to help field instructors acquire the necessary knowledge, skills, and values in field teaching (Bogo, 1981; Rogers, 1996; Saari, 1989). The following outline is based on the justice-based framework outlined in the third edition of *Learning to Teach, Teaching to Learn*. This book can be used as a support to these seminars to help new or experienced field instructors apply a justice-based framework in their work with students and for facilitating challenging dialogues with students on issues of social location, power, privilege, oppression, equity, and liberation. SIFIs also support new field instructors as they adapt to the demands of their role, and experienced field instructors benefit from advanced seminars that highlight unique aspects of field education, such as teaching students about managing value conflicts and offering group supervision or continued refinement to engage in challenging dialogues.

SIFIs cover the material field instructors will need as they respond to the various phases of the academic year and what will be required in preparing their students for the demands of entry-level social work practice. As field educators engage in their relationships with students, they model, or parallel, their students' engagement in their work; as they work together in the seminar, they contribute to collaborative problem solving, evaluation of students, and to evaluation of themselves as educators. SIFI teachers emphasize that the collegial and mutual support possible among participants is particularly important in learning how to teach others about what we do as social workers. The partnerships created and the mutual learning made possible in these seminars offer rich learning opportunities and the possibilities of building new professional connections (Bertrand Finch, & Feigelman, 2002, 2008; Wenger, 1998).

Purposes of SIFIs

Educating social workers involves learning and teaching about our professional mission and achieving competent practice. Together these purposes frame the work of field education, and they are the basis of the SIFI. That is, SIFIs prompt the development of a teaching philosophy based on our professional mission that guides the field instructor's approach to teaching social work practice and they support new field instructors as they educate students in accordance with the program's performance expectations and delineated learning outcomes related to the competencies. Additionally, SIFIs are meant to be a supportive place where new field instructors may discuss teaching concerns, support each other in finding ways to promote student success, and engage in finding alternative solutions for special circumstances and situations.

SIFIs for new field instructors emphasize the following goals and objectives:

> Facilitate the development of a teaching philosophy based in our professional mission of justice and competency-based social work education
> Assist new field instructors in the assumption of their role to prepare students who are competent to pursue justice as entry-level social work practitioners
> Assist new field instructors to become familiar with competency-based social work education, its benefits and requirements, and to evaluate students on the performance

behaviors of the social work program where their student is matriculating
- Balance teaching in the context of agency practice while linking this to the broader professional issues that apply
- Familiarize field instructors with the purposes and methods of conducting challenging dialogues with students on issues of justice so that students increase their capacity to do the same with those they serve
- Consider the beginning, middle, and end phases of the field instructor and student relationships and the parallels for the student's work
- Provide mutual support and assistance to peers to engage in authentic and meaningful dialogue to promote a conducive learning environment.

Structure of SIFIs

SIFIs have a long history in the profession, and in some areas, there is a collaborative or consortium of social work education programs that develops and maintains a uniform SIFI curriculum with set standards and requirements (Fishbein & Glassman, 1991). This allows programs to exchange affiliations and establish reciprocity. For example, once certified as a field instructor for one program, the participant may be a field instructor for any other social work education program in the consortium.

The CSWE (2015a) EPAS requires field instructors of MSW students to "hold a master's degree in social work from a CSWE accredited program and have 2 years of post-master's master's social work practice experience"; field instructors of BSW students must "hold a baccalaureate or master's degree in social work from a CSWE accredited social work program and have 2 years post social work degree practice experience in social work" (p. 13). The individuals demonstrate an interest in broadening their professional expertise and have the general support of their settings to undertake this new and important responsibility. SIFI participants are new field instructors who are concurrently assigned social work students, whereas advanced SIFIs are for experienced field instructors.

Advanced seminars contribute to the conceptualization of the art and science of field teaching and are often topic focused and geared to meeting interests and needs beyond those linked with beginning processes. For example, an advanced SIFI could be organized on special issues that address continuing needs to develop skills in conducting challenging dialogues with students, how to craft assignments that incorporate the CSWE (2015a) competencies, how to introduce group or peer supervision in placement settings, or to teach group supervisory skills for field instructors who want to develop more expertise in this area. These advanced workshops could be offered at agency sites and broaden the audience to more than just field instructors.

As SIFIs are developed across the country, in Canada and internationally a variety of models exist. One way to deliver a SIFI is to offer 10 to 12 two-hour sessions on a weekly basis in one semester or every other week through the academic year. SIFIs can also be offered in day-long sessions, just a few times a semester or spread out over two semesters. A growing number of programs are also offering distance education formats and online versions to take advantage of technological advances and to conquer the challenge of connecting over wide geographical areas. In whatever format the SIFI is delivered, it generally begins by reviewing the purposes, structure, and requirements of the SIFI, including methods used for teaching and learning, such as active participation, readings, videotapes, and small-group exercises. A SIFI outline, provided on p. 499 at the end of this appendix, adapts the framework of this text into 12 units; the outline can be adjusted to the chosen format for delivery. Scenarios and worksheets throughout chapter appendixes may be used as supportive material for the sessions. Additionally, experiential exercises and examples from field education are used to facilitate a learning environment that promotes meaningful exchanges across various identities and positions of power. Assignments are created to assist integration of the material; four sample assignments are also provided with the outline on p. 503.

Early in the SIFI, discussion takes place about confidentiality policies for seminar participants and between field instructors and students. This sets the foundation for creating a safe space for discussion and exploring new ways of working and considering what is involved in educating students that might be different from what they experienced in their own professional training. Confidentiality extends to all SIFI participants regarding any oral or written material shared about students, settings, those served, or faculty. Field instructors are supported to raise confidential or ethical issues and to discuss any field education experiences and concerns. Thus, SIFIs are professional forums bound by rules of confidentiality and mutual respect.

In the best circumstances, the first session of the SIFI takes place before the arrival of students at the field agencies. This allows SIFI participants to be introduced to the importance of their role before students arrive, which is particularly important given the need to begin our work with students with justice as a focus and as integral for setting the stage for all that follows. Beginning the SIFI before students are in placement also prepares for orientation programs and the field instructor's role as architect of student assignments. If participants in the seminar represent several different social work programs, SIFI teachers should be prepared to discuss the specific requirements established by each social work education program represented by the participants. Last, a review should be conducted of the requirements for SIFI certification as a field instructor (e.g., attendance, participation, and assignments).

The focus of SIFIs is to facilitate the participant's transition to the role of field instructor, including the development of a teaching philosophy that guides their assumption of this role. Participants come from a range of settings and therefore represent the broad range of social work perspectives and roles and functions in our profession. A justice-based SIFI seminar offers the opportunity for participants to practice challenging dialogues among colleagues and to examine their own power, privileges, and dimensions of identities to support their work with students. Having a variety of perspectives available provides an opportunity to learn the overarching principles that guide social work education and not just agency practice. This creates a vibrant interchange and consideration of how our profession's values and mission are implemented across modalities and units of attention. Teaching for justice and positive change emerge as critical considerations in participants' discussions.

Distance-Learning SIFIs

SIFIs can be delivered through distance learning or through Internet formats that can be accessed more locally, on the job, or even from home. This relieves some of the added pressure on field instructors who must travel to the social work education program's location for a SIFI. Technology can also add a new learning dimension to traditional field instruction and SIFI formats with such opportunities as online curricula, discussion boards, and individual and group assignments in between face-to-face sessions. Whether to enhance or to provide ready access, technology can become an important tool for SIFI teachers. They can be conducted at several different locations and with several cohorts of field instructors synchronously, simultaneously, and live. This technology is evolving, and it is now possible to conduct distance-learning sessions through a variety of platforms that do not require elaborate television studio-like equipment such as Adobe Connect, Zoom, or some form of video or teleconferencing. The major advantage of such technology is that field instructors can have real, live interactions with each other and the instructor, just as if they were face-to-face in the same location. Some collegiality or spontaneity may get lost in transmission, but participants at different sites tend to bond quite well with each other and appreciate the conveniences in saving time. In addition, managing the technology may take practice, and glitches can delay smooth running of a session. There are pros and cons to distance learning, but without a doubt it can provide easier access across large areas and will probably change the ways SIFI content is delivered in the future.

Online SIFIs

Another technological advance allows field instructors to access SIFI materials, SIFI teachers, and other field instructors entirely or at least partially through the Internet. By logging on to the SIFI's Web page, field instructors can review a lecture, a small-group discussion topic, a vignette, or an assignment, and they can respond instantly or at their leisure to a discussion occurring online with other field instructors. They can also have access to the SIFI instructor directly and privately for consultation. Discussions can take place during scheduled slots and anywhere participants have access to the Internet. Materials can be accessed at any time (late at night or early in the morning, from home or from the field instructor's place of employment). Individual choice has many advantages; chief is access to consultation with colleagues when and if it is needed.

Online courses can be taught entirely over the Internet, or SIFI teachers can blend the use of a combination of live seminars and online chat sessions to improve the delivery of the SIFI content. In between SIFI sessions, field instructors can collaborate with each other and SIFI teachers on aspects of their field instruction experience, including asking questions about the social work education program's requirements, dealing with issues in the setting or in supervision, exchanging best teaching practices, or consulting with each other on field evaluations. When used properly, this online consultation can be extremely beneficial and can act as an extension of the seminar as SIFI teachers filter the discussions and bring them to the seminar for additional collaboration.

In summary, as this book emerged from a group of field educators who were responsible for establishing SIFIs in the New York School of Social Work Consortium, our intention has always been to help develop the knowledge and skills of excellent field instructors of professional social work practice and to support the development of the SIFI.

A Justice-Based Outline for a SIFI

The following SIFI outline is based on a 12-week post-master's certificate program for field instructors who will be teaching social work students for the first time. Field instructors are required to attend a minimum of 10 sessions of the 12 sessions offered, submit required assignments, and share their evolving teaching styles and approaches as part of the seminar format. If a different time format is used, the units presented here may be adjusted and combined to suit the method used. This outline can be adapted to an online version, either synchronous or asynchronous. The text provides supportive material for the topics and can be expanded to the specific context as needed. After completion of the SIFI requirements, field instructors receive a Certificate in Field Instruction. Where applicable, it may be possible to achieve approval from the granting institution for continuing education credits that apply to field instructors' licensing requirements.

Objectives

1. To assist SIFI participants with acquiring competence as field instructors in relevant educational principles and methods associated with a justice-based framework for field education, teaching CSWE (2015a) competency expectations, and understanding the social work education program's performance outcomes and criteria for evaluation of field education performance in meeting competency requirements.
2. To provide a forum for learning and a mutual exchange of ideas and concerns related to acquiring the role, knowledge, and skills of teaching for entry-level social work practice.

Sample Outline

Unit 1. Introduction to the Justice-Based Field Education SIFI Curriculum: Justice, Competence, and Field Education

    A. Introductions to Each Other, Our Task, and SIFI
    B. Explaining Our Frames of Reference
        a. Competency-based social work education
        b. Justice-based field education
        c. Field education processes

C. Setting the Stage
   a. SIFI—Facilitating a community of practice
      i. Understanding our role and developing a teaching philosophy
      ii. What are challenging dialogues and what is their role in justice-based field education supervision?
      iii. Beginning with ourselves
      iv. Concepts of power and powerlessness
   b. Getting our settings ready for students
D. Requirements and Expectations for Successful Completion of the SIFI
E. Examples and Exercises

Unit 2. Preparing Ourselves and Our Settings for Our Students

A. Creating Conducive Learning Environments for Field Education Supervision
B. Challenging Dialogues: Digging Deeper
   a. Starting With Ourselves: Self-reflection and Self-awareness
   b. Starting the Conversation
      i. Introducing concepts of cultural equity and liberation
      ii. Introducing intersectionality
      iii. Introducing meta- and procedural competencies
      iv. Introducing the six components of the competencies: values, knowledge, cognitive and affective reactions, judgment and skills
   c. Challenging Dialogues: Tasks and responsibilities
   d. Special considerations: Dimensions of identity
C. Examples and Exercises

Unit 3. Teaching Competency-Based Practice: Rubrics, Assessment, Evaluation, and Integrating the Competencies in Supervision

A. Teaching in the Context of Competencies: Using a Rubric Framework
   a. The ongoing educational assessment process
   b. Understanding evaluation in a rubric framework
B. Our Role as Architects of Student Assignments

Appendix B   501

      a. Translating the competencies through the perspective of our settings
      b. Identifying a learning focus using the competencies
      c. Using assignments as the vehicles for achieving competence
  C. Examples and Exercises

Unit 4. Adult Learning: Individualizing Our Responses and Fine-Tuning Our Assessments

  A. Engaged Pedagogy: A Facilitative Approach to Teaching
  B. Creating an Individualized Environment for Learning in Field Education
  C. Learning Theories
      a. Transformational learning: Learning as change
      b. Experiential learning
      c. Developmental stages of learning
      d. Bloom's taxonomy
  D. Examples and Exercises

Unit 5. Promoting Reflective Practice Through Recordings

  A. A. Common Purposes of Recording Formats Across Units of Attention
  B. Types of Recordings in Field Education Supervision
      a. Promoting self-reflection, self-awareness, and self-regulation
      b. Promoting mindfulness and critical consciousness
      c. Processing the information and providing feedback
  C. Creating Formats to Individualize and Focus the Learning
  D. Examples and Exercises

Unit 6: Ethical and Professional Behavior: Personal and Professional Values

  A. Our Code of Ethics and a Justice-based Framework for Field Education
  B. Inherent Tensions: Societal, Professional, and Personal Values
  C. Examining Professional Behavior and Performance
      a. Reflective practice: Applications

b. Critical consciousness: Applications
D. Examples and Exercises

Unit 7. Advancing Our Skills as Field Educators

   A. Developing Supervisory Skills
      a. Exploring and expanding our teaching methods
      b. Responding to our students' diverse needs
   B. Models: Shared and Task Supervision, Group Supervision and Learning Teams
   C. Connections with Field Liaisons
   D. Examples and Exercises

Unit 8. Identifying Learning Opportunities Within Our Settings

   A. Understanding our Settings Through the Lens of Justice
      a. Responding to the societal and global concerns affecting service
      b. Ensuring that all competencies are addressed within our supervisory meetings with students
   B. Evaluating service provision—micro to macro
      a. From the voices of those served
      b. From the student's practice
   C. Examples and Exercises

Unit 9. Reviewing Ways of Tracking Progress: Taking Stock

   A. Preparing Ourselves and Our Students for Evaluation
   B. Exploring Outcome Performance Measures
   C. The Mutuality of Feedback
   D. Examples and Exercises

Unit 10. Shifting the Discourse

   A. From Noncompliance and Resistance to Learning, Potential and Possibilities
   B. Sharing Obstacles and Finding Opportunities for Growth
   C. Educational Learning Contracts: Best Practices
   D. Examples and Exercises

Unit 11. Evaluation of Field Performance: Process and Methods

- A. Evaluation of Student Field Education Practice
- B. Student Self-Evaluation in Achieving Competency in Justice-Based Practice
- C. Writing the Evaluation: Best Practices
- D. Field Instructor Self-Evaluation
- E. Examples and Exercises

Unit 12. Pulling It Together

- A. Ending and Termination: Assisting Ownership of Progress Achieved
    - a. Celebrating and honoring transitions and renewal
    - b. Identifying next steps forward
- B. Review and Concluding Thoughts
- C. Examples and Exercises

Sample Assignments

Four examples of assignments are provided. Be certain to maintain confidentiality with the student's and field instructor's information.

Teaching from field instructor and student recordings. Submit a student's recording of an individual, group, community organizing, or administrative assignment. Attach your recording of the field instruction conference when the specific assignment and recording are reviewed. Include your assessment or impressions of the conference, especially the teaching and learning that takes place. Discuss your attempts to link issues of justice and use of the competencies to teach the practice principles involved. List at least three questions or issues generated by this field instruction session. Selected parts of field instructors' recordings will be used in the SIFI with the field instructors' permission.

› Identify the student by program year (generalist practice or specialized practice) and by the student's specific focus specialization or concentration, if applicable.
› Identify the student's positionality and dimensions of identity and how these relate to your own.

- Briefly describe the agency's programs and services and the populations served. Describe how the setting is instituting a justice-based framework.
- Briefly describe the student's assignment and the educational rationale for the assignment.
- Include objectives for the field instruction conference.
- Cite some examples of verbatim content on important teaching moments.
- The focus of this assignment is to assess the teaching that takes place. What was effective and why? What might you might have done differently and why?

Educational assessment and teaching plan. Present an educational assessment of your student using the outline provided in the Chapter 3 Appendix. Be sure to include the student's demonstrated learning patterns and styles, specific learning and teaching goals associated with the competencies, teaching strategies including assignments chosen and teaching methods chosen, and the set priorities.

Critique of the student's field performance sixth-week plan or evaluation. Submit a copy of the student's sixth-week plan or an end-of-semester evaluation of a student's field performance. Critique the evaluation process using the structure of the rubric formulation and the written components of the evaluation format. Reflect on the student's efforts to grasp an identified learning issue and your teaching methods to deal with content areas in the evaluation. Provide a reflection on this process or direct excerpts. Attach a description of the student's assignments. This should include the nature of the work and learning anticipated with each assignment.

Self-evaluation of my evolution as a field instructor. Review your first experience as a field instructor and your experience of teaching using a justice- and competency-based social work practice framework. Report your initial expectations, anxieties, and concerns. What major transitions occurred in your field instruction role, and what goals have you set for your future development as a field instructor? How has a justice and competency-based framework affected your perspective on your role as a field instructor? Speak from your positionality and dimensions of your identity. How has your awareness of your privileges and power evolved? Provide an example that illustrates this from your supervisory practice with your student.

REFERENCES

Abram, F. Y., Hartung, M. R., & Wernet, S. P. (2000). The non-MSW task supervisor, MSW field instructor, and the practicum student: A triad for high-quality field education. *Journal of Teaching in Social Work, 20*(1/2), 171–185.

Abrams, L. S., & Moio, J. A. (2009). Critical race theory and the cultural competence dilemma in social work education. *Journal of Social Work Education, 45*, 245–261.

Adams, J. L. (2001). *Conceptual blockbusting: A guide to better ideas* (4th ed.). New York, NY: Perseus.

Adams, M., Bell, L. A., Goodman, D. J., Joshi, K. Y. (2016). *Teaching for diversity and social justice*. New York, NY: Routledge.

Adams, M., Bell, L. A., & Griffin, P. (Eds.). (2007). *Teaching for diversity and social justice: A sourcebook* (2nd ed.). New York, NY: Routledge.

ADA Amendments Act of 2008, PL 110-325 (2008).

Ahuja, A., Webster, C., Gibson, N., Brewer, A., Toledo, S., & Russell, S. (2015). Symposium proceedings: Bullying and suicide: The mental health crisis of LGBTQ youth and how you can help. *Journal of Gay & Lesbian Mental Health, 19*, 125–144.

Allan, J., Pease, B., & Briskman, L. (Eds.). (2009). *Critical social work: An introduction to theories and practices* (2nd ed.). New York, NY: Allen & Unwin.

Almeida, R., Hernandez-Wolfe, P., & Tubbs, C. (2011). Cultural equity: Bridging the complexity of social identities with therapeutic practices. *International Journal of Narrative Therapy and Community Work, 3*, 43–56.

Alschuler, M., Silver, T., & McArdle, L. (2015). Strengths-based group supervision with social work students. *Groupwork, 25*(1), 34–57. doi:10.1921/gpwk.v25i1.841

Alter, C., & Adkins, C. (2001). Improving the writing skills of social work students. *Journal of Social Work Education, 37*, 493–505.

Altmann, T. K. (2007). An evaluation of the seminal work of Patricia Benner: Theory or philosophy? *Contemporary Nurse, 25*, 114–123.

American Academy of Social Work & Social Welfare. (2018). *12 challenges*. Retrieved from grandchallengesforsocialwork.org/grand-challenges-initiative/12-challenges/

Americans With Disabilities Act, 42 U.S.C.A. § 12101 *et seq.* (1990).

Ames, N. (1999). Social work recording: A new look at an old issue. *Journal of Social Work Education, 35*, 227–237.

Anderson, G., Briar-Lawson, K. (2015). Guest editorial—Advancing 21st century university child welfare agency partnerships. *Journal of Social Work Education, 51*(Suppl. 2), S149–S152. doi:10.1080/10437797.2015.1074023

Anderson, K. M. (2013). Assessing strengths. Identifying acts of resistance to violence and oppression. In D. Saleebey (Ed.), *The strengths perspective in social work practice* (6th ed., pp. 182–202). Boston, MA: Pearson.

Anderson, L. W., & Krathwohl, D. R., (Eds.). (2001). *Teaching and assessing: A revision of Bloom's taxonomy of educational objectives*. New York, NY: Longman.

Anderson, M., & Collins, P. H. (2015). *Race, class and gender: An anthology*. (9th ed.). Boston, MA: Cengage Learning.

Andrade, H. G. (2005). Teaching with rubrics: The good, the bad, and the ugly. *College Teaching, 53*(1), 27–30.

Antczak, H. B., Mackrill, T., Steensbaek, S., & Ebsen, F. (2017). Online video supervision for statutory youth caseworkers—a pilot study. *Journal of Children's Services, 12*, 127–137. doi:10.1108/JCS-06-2017-0029

Aptekar, H. H. (1966). Education for social responsibility. *Journal of Education for Social Work, 2*(2), 5–11.

Arato, B., & Clemens, K. (2013). Frame safe spaces to brave spaces: A new way to frame dialogue around diversity and social justice. In Landreman, L. M. (Ed.), *The art of effective facilitation: Reflections from social justice educators*. (p. 135–150). Sterling, VA: ACPA–College Student Educators International and Stylus.

Ard, K. (2016). *Understanding the health needs of LGBT people*. Retrieved from www.lgbthealtheducation.org/wp-content/uploads/LGBTHealthDisparitiesMar2016.pdf

Arditti, J. A. (2005). Families and incarceration: An ecological approach. *Families in Society, 86*, 251–260.

Armour, M. P., Bain, B., & Rubio, R. (2004). An evaluative study of diversity training for field instructors: A collaborative approach to enhancing cultural competence. *Journal of Social Work Education, 40*, 27–38.

Aronson L. (2010). Twelve tips for teaching reflection at all levels of medical education. *Medical Teacher, 7*, 1–6.

Artiga, S., Damie, A., & Garfield, R. (2015). *Estimates of eligibility for ACA coverage among the uninsured by race and ethnicity*. Figure 1, Distribution of nonelderly uninsured by race/ethnicity, 2015. Retrieved from https://www.kff.org/disparities-policy/issue-brief/estimates-of-eligibility-for-aca-coverage-among-the-uninsured-by-race-and-ethnicity/

Austin, M. J. (2014). *Social justice and social work: Rediscovering a core value of the profession*. Thousand Oaks, CA: SAGE.

Ayala, J. S. (2009). Blended learning as a new approach to social work education. *Journal of Social Work Education, 45*, 277–288.

Bain, K. R., & Bass, R. J. (2012). Threshold concepts of teaching and learning that transform faculty practice (and the limits of individual change). In D. W. Harward (Ed.), *Transforming undergraduate education: Theory that compels and practices that succeed* (pp. 189–208). Lanham, MD: Rowman & Littlefield.

Baines, D. (2010). Neoliberal restructuring, activism/participation, and social unionism in the nonprofit social services. *Nonprofit and Voluntary Sector Quarterly, 39*(1), 10-28.

Banerjee, M. M. (2005). Applying Rawlsian social justice to welfare reform: An unexpected finding for social work. *Journal of Sociology and Social Welfare, 32*, 35–57.

Barker, R. L., & Branson, D. M. (2000). When laws and ethics collide. In. R. L. Barker & D. M. Branson, *Forensic social work: Legal aspects of professional practice* (2nd ed., pp. 99–114). Binghamton, NY: Haworth Press.

Barker, R. L. (2014). *Social work dictionary* (6th ed.). Washington, DC: NASW Press.

Barlow, C., & Hall, B. I. (2007). What about feelings? A study of emotion and tension in social work field education. *Journal of Social Work Education, 26*, 399–413.

Barnacle, R. (2009). Gut instinct: The body and learning. *Educational Philosophy and Theory, 41*(1), 22–33.

Barnes and Nobel College. (2016). *Getting to know Gen Z: Exploring middle and high schoolers' expectations for higher education*. Retrieved from https://next.bncollege.com/wp-content/uploads/2015/10/Gen-Z-Research-Report-Final.pdf

Barnett, M., Harwood, W., Keating, T., & Saam, J. (2002). Using emerging technologies to help bridge the gap between university theory and classroom practice: Challenges and successes. *School Science and Mathematics, 102*, 299–313.

Barretti, M. (2004). What do we know about the professional socialization of our students? *Journal of Social Work Education, 40*, 255–283.

Barretti, M. (2007). Teachers and field instructors as student role models: A neglected dimension in social work education. *Journal of Teaching in Social Work, 27*, 215–237.

Barsky, A., Reamer, F., & Hobdy, D., (2017). *The official national training of the new NASW Code of Ethics* (Online PowerPoint presentation. Course number NAT43032) Retrieved from https://naswinstitute.inreachce.com/Details/Information/8f90fed4-fd42-46d6-ab26-f8b0ee08c00c

Baum, N. (2004). Social work students' treatment termination as a temporary role exit. *Clinical Supervisor, 23*, 165–177.

Baum, N. (2006). Are they really the same? Supervisor and student responses at termination. *Arete, 30*, 58–74.

Baum, N. (2011). Social work students' feelings and concerns about the ending of their field work supervision. *Social Work Education, 30*, 83–97.

Baxter Magolda, M. B. (2009). The activity of meaning making: A holistic perspective on college student development. *Journal of College Student Development, 50*, 621–639.

Bay, U., & Macfarlane, S. (2011). Teaching critical reflection: A tool for transformative learning in social work? *Social Work Education, 30*, 745–758.

Belenky, M. F., Clinchy, B. M., Goldberger, N. R., & Tarule, J. M. (1986). *Women's ways of knowing: The development of self, voice, and mind*. New York, NY: Basic Books.

Belkin-Martinez, D., & Fleck-Henderson, A. (Eds.). (2014). *Social justice in clinical practice: A liberation health framework for social work*. New York, NY: Routledge.

Benner, P. (2001). *From novice to expert: Excellence and power in clinical nursing practice*. New York, NY: Prentice Hall.

Bennett, C. S. (2008). Attachment-informed supervision for social work field education. *Clinical Social Work Journal, 36*, 97–107.

Bennett, C. S., Mohr, J., Szoc, K. B., & Saks, L. V. (2008). General and supervision-specific attachment styles: Relations to student perceptions of field supervisors. *Journal of Social Work Education, 44*, 75–94.

Bennett, S., & Deal, K. H. (2009). Beginnings and endings in social work supervision: The interaction between attachment and developmental processes. *Journal of Teaching in Social Work, 29*(1), 101–117.

Bennett, C. S., & Saks, L. V. (2006). A conceptual application of attachment theory and research to the social work student–field instructor supervisory relationship. *Journal of Social Work Education, 42*, 669–682.

Berengarten, S. (1957). Identifying learning patterns of individual students: An exploratory study. *Social Service Review, 31*, 407–417.

Berger, B., Thornton, S., & Cochrane, S. (1993, March). *Communicating a standard of professional behavior: A model for graduate and undergraduate field education*. Presentation at the 39th Annual Program Meeting, Council on Social Work Education, New York, NY.

Bertrand Finch, J. (2016). Theoretical perspectives for transformation. In A. J. Carten, A. B. Siskind, & M. Pender Greene (Eds.). *Strategies for deconstructing racism in the health and human services* (pp. 101–124) New York, NY: Oxford University Press.

Bertrand Finch, J., Bacon, J., Klassen, D., & Wrase, B. J. (2003). Critical issues in field instruction: Empowerment principles and issues of power and control. In W. Shera (Ed.), *Emerging perspectives on anti-oppressive practice* (pp. 431–446). Toronto, Ontario: Canadian Scholars' Press.

Bertrand Finch, J., & Feigelman, B. (2002, October). *Training new field instructors: The power of mutual aid in the educational process*. In Carol S. Cohen, DSW (Chair), "Think group: Strength and diversity through group work." Conference conducted at the XXIV annual meeting of the Association for the Advancement of Social Work with Groups, Brooklyn, NY

Bertrand Finch, J., & Feigelman, B. (2008). The power of mutual aid in the educational process: A seminar for new field instructors of trainees. *Clinical Supervisor, 27*, 191–214.

Bertrand Finch, J., Lurie, A., & Wrase, B. J. (1997). Student and staff training: Empowerment principles and parallels. *Clinical Supervisor, 15*, 129–143.

Berzin, S. C., Singer, J., & Chan, C. (2015). *Practice innovation through technology in the digital age: A grand challenge for social work*. Retrieved from aaswsw.org/wp-content/uploads/2013/10/Practice-Innovation-through-Technology-in-the-Digital-Age-A-Grand-Challenge-for-Social-Work-GC-Working-Paper-No-12.pdf

Bial, M., & Lynn, M. (1995). Field education for students with disabilities: Front door/back door: Negotiation/accommodation/mediation. In G. Rogers (Ed.), *Social work field education: Views and visions* (pp. 437–451). Dubuque, IA: Kendall/Hunt.

Birkenmaier, J., Wernet, S. P., Berg-Weger, M., Wilson, R. J., Banks, R., Olliges, R., & Delicath, T. A. (2005). Weaving a web: The use of Internet technology in field education. *Journal of Teaching in Social Work, 25*(1/2), 3–20.

Bisman, C. (2004). Social work values: The moral core of the profession. *British Journal of Social Work, 34*, 109–123.

Bisman, C. (2014). *Value-guided practice for a global society*. New York, NY: Columbia University Press.

Black, J. E., & Feld, A. (2006). Process recording revisited: A learning-oriented thematic approach integrating field education and classroom curriculum. *Journal of Teaching in Social Work, 26*(3/4), 137–153.

Black, P., Hartley, E., Whelley, J., & Kirk-Sharp, C. (1989). Ethics curricula: A national survey of graduate schools of social work. *Social Thought, 15*(3/4), 141–148.

Blair, K. L., & Peake, T. H. (1995). Stages of supervisor development. *Clinical Supervisor, 13*, 119–126.

Blitz, L. V., (2006). Owning whiteness: The reinvention of self and practice. *Journal of Emotional Abuse, 6*, 241–263.

Bloom, B. S. (1956). *Taxonomy of educational objectives, Handbook I: The cognitive domain*. Philadelphia, PA: David McKay.

Blundo, R. (2001). Learning strengths-based practice: Challenging our personal and professional frames. *Families in Society, 82*, 296–304.

Bogo, M. (1981). An educationally focused faculty/field liaison program for first-time field instructors. *Journal of Education for Social Work, 17*(3), 59–65.

Bogo, M. (2005). Field instruction in social work: A review of the research literature. *Clinical Supervisor, 24*, 163–193.

Bogo, M. (2010). *Achieving competence in social work through field education*. Toronto, Ontario, Canada: Toronto University Press.

Bogo, M. (2015). Field education for clinical social work practice: Best practices and contemporary challenges. *Clinical Social Work Journal, 43*, 317–324. doi:10.1007/s10615-015-0526-5

Bogo, M. (2016). Evaluation of student learning. In C. A. Hunter, J. K. Moen, & M. S. Raskin (Eds.), *Social work field directors* (pp. 154–178). Chicago, Il: Lyceum Books.

Bogo, M. (2018). *Social work practice: Integrating concepts, processes, & skills* (2nd ed.). New York, NY: Columbia University Press.

Bogo, M., Globerman, J., & Sussman, T. (2004). The field instructor as group worker: Managing trust and competition in group supervision. *Journal of Social Work Education, 40*, 13–26.

Bogo, M., Katz, E., Regehr, C., Logie, C., Mylopoulos, M., & Tufford, L. (2013). Toward understanding meta-competence: An analysis of students' reflection on their simulated interviews. *Social Work Education, 32*, 259–273.

Bogo, M., Rawlings, M., Katz, E., & Logie, C. (2014). *Using simulation in assessment and teaching: OSCE adapted for social work*. Alexandria, VA: Council on Social Work Education.

Bogo, M., Regehr, C., Power, R., & Regehr, G. (2007). When values collide: Providing feedback and evaluating competence in social work. *Clinical Supervisor, 26*, 99–117.

Bogo, M., Regehr, C., Katz, E., Logie, C., Mylopoulos, M., & Regehr, G. (2011). Developing a tool to assess student reflections. *Social Work Education 30*, 186–195.

Bogo, M., Regehr, C., Logie, C., Katz, E., Mylopoulos, M. and Regehr, G. (2011). Adapting objective structured clinical examinations to assess social work students' performance and reflections. *Journal of Social Work Education, 47*, 5–18.

Bogo, M., & Vayda, E. (1987). *The practice of field instruction in social work: Theory and process*. Toronto, Ontario, Canada: University of Toronto Press.

Bogo, M., & Vayda, E. (1991). Developing a process model for field instruction. In D. Schneck, B. Grossman, & U. Glassman (Eds.). *Field education in social work: Contemporary issues and trends* (pp. 59–66). Dubuque, IA: Kendall/Hunt.

Bogo, M., & Vayda, E. (1993). *The practice of field instruction in social work: A teaching guide*. Toronto, Ontario, Canada: University of Toronto Press.

Bogo, M., & Vayda, E. (1998). *The practice of field instruction in social work: Theory and process* (2nd ed.). Toronto, Ontario, Canada: University of Toronto Press.

Boitel, C. R., & Fromm, L. R. (2014). Defining signature pedagogy in social work education: Learning theory and the learning contract. *Journal of Social Work Education, 50*, 608–622. doi:10.1080/10437797.2014.947161

Bonosky, N. (1995). Boundary violations in social work supervision: Clinical, educational, and legal implications. *Clinical Supervisor, 13*, 79–95.

Bowleg, L. (2012). Framing health matters: The problem with the phrase "women and minorities": Intersectionality—an important theoretical framework for public health. *American Journal of Public Health, 102*, 1267–1273.

Bowser, B. P., & Hunt, R. G. (Eds.). (1996). *Impacts of racism on White Americans* (2nd ed.). Thousand Oaks, CA: SAGE.

Boyd Webb, N. (1988). The role of the field instructor in the socialization of students. *Social Casework, 69*, 35–40.

Bradley, J. A., & Buck, P. W. (2016). Roles and responsibilities of the field director. In C. A. Hunter, J. K. Moen, & M. S. Raskin (Eds.). *Social work field directors* (pp. 23-40). Chicago, Il: Lyceum Books.

Bransford, J. D., Brown, A. L., Cocking, R. R. (Eds.). (2004). *How people learn: Brain, mind, experience and school*. Washington, DC: National Academies Press.

Braxton, J. M. (2009). Understanding the development of the whole person. *Journal of College Student Development, 50*, 573–575.

Breiding, M. J., Chen, J., & Black, M. C. (2014). *Intimate partner violence in the United States—2010*. Atlanta, GA: National Center for Injury Prevention and Control, Centers for Disease Control and Prevention.

Bressi, S. K., & Vaden, E. R. (2017). Reconsidering self-care. *Clinical Social Work Journal, 45*, 33–38. doi:10.1007/s10615-016-0575-4

Brookhart, S. M. (2013). *How to create and use rubrics*. Alexandria, VA: ASCD.

Brookfield, S. (1987). *Developing critical thinkers*. San Francisco, CA: Jossey-Bass.

Brookfield, S. D. (1990). *The skillful teacher: On technique, trust, and responsiveness in the classroom*. San Francisco, CA: Jossey-Bass.

Brookfield, S. (1995). Adult learning: An overview. In A. C. Tuinjman (Ed.), *International encyclopedia of education* (2nd ed., pp. 375–381). Oxford, UK: Pergamon.

Brookfield, S. (2014). Teaching our own racism: Incorporating personal narratives of Whiteness into anti-racist practice. *Adult Learning, 25*(3), 89–95.

Bubar, R., Cespedes, K., & Bundy-Fazioli, K. (2016). Intersectionality and social work: Omissions of race, class and sexuality in graduate school education. *Journal of Social Work Education, 52*, 283–296.

Bruner, J. (1996). *The culture of education*. Cambridge, MA: Harvard University Press.

Bundy-Fazioli, K., Quijano, L. M., & Bubar, R. (2013). Graduate students' perceptions of professional power in social work practice. *Journal of Social Work Education, 49*, 108–121.

Burack-Weiss, A., & Coyle Brennan, F. (2013). Styles of learning and teaching. In A. Burack-Weiss & F. Coyle Brennan (2nd ed.). *Gerontological supervision: A social work perspective in case management and direct care* (pp. 31–42). New York, NY: Routledge.

Burack-Weiss, A., & Coyle Brennan, F. C. (2008). *Gerontological social work supervision: A social work perspective in case management and direct care*. New York, NY: Haworth Press.

Butin, D. (2005a). Identity (re)construction and student resistance. In D. Butin (Ed.). *Teaching social foundation of education: Context, theories and issues* (pp. 109–126). Mahwah, NJ: Erlbaum.

Butin, D. (2005b). "I don't buy it": Student resistance, social justice and identity construction. *Invention, 7*, 1–12.

Capaldi, D. M., Knoble, N. B., Shortt, J. W., & Kim, H. K., 2012. A systematic review of risk factors for intimate partner violence. *Partner Abuse, 3*, 231–280.

Carnavale, A. P., Rose, S. J., & Hanson, A. R. (2012). *Certificates: gateway to gainful employment and college degrees. Executive Summary*. Retrieved from https://1gyhoq479uf d3yna29x7ubjn-wpengine.netdna-ssl.com/wp-content/uploads/2014/11/Certificates .ExecutiveSummary.071712.pdf

Carpenter-Aeby, T., & Aeby, V. G. (2013). Application of andragogy to instruction in an MSW practice class. *Journal of Instructional Psychology, 40*(1/4), 3–13.

Carroll, M. (2010a). Supervision: Critical reflection for transformational learning (part 1). *Clinical Supervisor, 28*, 210–220.

Carroll, M. (2010b). Supervision: Critical reflection for transformational learning (part 2). *Clinical Supervisor, 29*, 1–19. doi:10.1080/07325221003730301

Carson, E. A., & Anderson, E. (2016). *Prisoners in 2015*. Retrieved from https://www.bjs.gov/content/pub/pdf/p15.pdf

Carten, A. J., & Bertrand Finch, J. (2010). An empirically-based field education model: Preparing students for culturally competent practice with new immigrants. *Journal of Public Child Welfare, 4*, 365–385.

Carten, A. J., Siskind, B., & Pender Greene, M. (2016). *Strategies for deconstructing racism in the health and human services*. New York, NY: Oxford University Press.

Carter, R. T. (1995). *The influence of race and racial identity in psychotherapy: Toward a racially inclusive model.* New York, NY: Wiley.

Cartney, P. (2000). Adult learning styles: Implications for practice teaching in social work. *Social Work Education, 19,* 609–629.

Cash, S. J., Mathieson, S. G., Barbanell, L. D., Smith, T. E., & Graham, P. (2006). Education and partnerships in child welfare: mapping the implementation of a child welfare certificate program. *Journal of Social Work Education, 42,* 123–138.

Caspi, J., & Reid, W. J. (2002). *Educational supervision in social work: A task-centered model for field instruction and staff development.* New York, NY: Columbia University Press.

Cataldi, E. F., Bennett, C. T., & Chen, X. (2018). *Stats in brief: First-generation students: College access, persistence, and postbachelor's outcomes.* Retrieved from https://nces.ed.gov/pubs2018/2018421.pdf

Center for Collegiate Mental Health. (2018). *2018 annual report.* Retrieved from https://sites.psu.edu/ccmh/files/2019/02/2018-Annual-Report-2.11.18-FINAL-y2nw3r.pdf

Center for Social and Economic Justice. (2018). *Educator resource of the month.* Retrieved from https://cswe.org/Centers-Initiatives/Centers/Center-for-Diversity.aspx

Chang, C. Y., Hays, D. G., & Shoffner, M. F. (2003). Cross-racial supervision: A developmental approach for White supervisors working with supervisees of color. *Clinical Supervisor, 22,* 121–138. doi:10.1300/J001v22n02_08

Children's Defense Fund. (2018). *Programs.* Retrieved from https://www.childrensdefense.org/programs/programs/

Child Welfare Information Gateway. (2018, April). *Foster care statistics 2016. Numbers and trends April 2018.* The Child Welfare Information Gateway, Children's Bureau. Retrieved from https://www.childwelfare.gov/pubPDFs/foster.pdf#page=8&view=Race and ethnicity

Chin, M., Hawkins, J., Krings, A., Peguero-Spencer, & Gutiérrez, L. (2018), Investigating diversity in social work doctoral education in the United States. *Journal of Social Work Education,54,* 762–775. doi:10.1080/10437797.2018.1503127

Chinell, J. (2011) Three voices: Reflections on homophobia and heterosexism in social work. *Journal of Social Work Education, 30,* 759–773.

Chisom, R., & Washington, L. (1997). *Undoing racism: A philosophy of international social change.* New Orleans, LA: People's Institute for Survival and Beyond.

Chronicle of Higher Education. (2018). *The new generation of students: How colleges can recruit, teach and serve Gen Z.* Washington, DC: Author.

Civil Rights Act of 1964 § 7, 42 U.S.C. § 2000e et seq (1964).

Clapton, G., Cree, V. E., Allan, M., Edwards, R., Forbes, R., Irwin, M., ... & Perry, R. (2008). Thinking "outside the box": A new approach to integration of learning for practice. *Social Work Education, 27,* 334–340.

Clark, C. (2006). Moral character in social work. *British Journal of Social Work, 35,* 75–89.

Clifford, D., & Burke, B. (2005). Developing anti-oppressive ethics in the new curriculum. *Journal of Social Work Education, 24,* 677–692.

Code of Federal Regulations. (2018.) Retrieved from https://www.govinfo.gov/content/pkg/CFR-2018-title29-vol4/xml/CFR-2018-title29-vol4-subtitleB-chapXIV.xml#seqnum1601.4

Cohen, C. J., Fowler, M., Medencia, V. E., & Rogowski, J. C. (2017). *The "woke" generation? Millennial Attitudes on Race in the U.S.* Retrieved from https://genforwardsurvey.com/assets/uploads/2017/10/GenForward-Oct-2017-Final-Report.pdf

Cohen, M. B., & Garrett, K. J. (1995). Helping field instructors become more effective group work educators. *Social Work with Groups, 18,* 135–148.

Cohen, R. I. (2004). *Clinical supervision: What to do and how to do it*. Belmont, CA: Brooks/Cole.

Coffman, S. (2011). A social constructionist view of issues confronting first-generation college students. *New Directions for Teaching and Learning, 127*, 81–90.

Cole, B. S., Christ, C. C., & Light, T. R. (1995). Social work education and students with disabilities: Implications of Section 504 and the ADA. *Journal of Social Work Education, 31*, 261–268.

Cooper, M. G. (2006). Integrating single-system design research into the clinical practice class. *Journal of Teaching in Social Work, 26*(3/4), 91–102.

Cooper-Bolinskey, D., & Ketner, M. (2016). Does type of supervision impact the quality of social work field education? *International Journal of Education and Social Science, 3*(7), 34–40.

Community College Research Center. (n.d.). *Community college FAQs. Community college enrollment and completion*. Retrieved from https://ccrc.tc.columbia.edu/index.php?option=com_faqftw&view=printfaqs&tmpl=component&Itemid=476

Congress, E. P. (1996). Dual relationships in academia: Dilemmas for social work educators. *Journal of Social Work Education, 32*, 315–328.

Congress, E. P. (2000, February). *Dual relationships in academia: Results of a national survey*. Presentation at the Annual Program Meeting, Council on Social Work Education, Nashville, TN.

Congress, E. P. (2002). Social work ethics for educators: Navigating ethical change in the classroom and in the field. *Journal of Teaching in Social Work, 22*(1/2), 151–166.

Congress, E. P., & Kung, W. W. (2005). Using the culturagram to assess and empower culturally diverse families. In E. P. Congress & M. J. Gonzalez (Eds.), *Multicultural perspectives in working with families* (2nd ed., pp. 3–21). New York, NY: Springer.

Conroy, K. (2012). Student writing in field education. In W. Green & B. Levy Simon (Eds.), *The Columbia guide to social work writing* (pp. 85–113). New York, NY: Columbia University Press.

Constance-Huggins, M. (2012). Critical race theory in social work education: A framework for addressing racial disparities. *Critical Social Work, 13*(2), 2–6.

Cord, B., & Clements, M. (2010). Pathway for student self-development: A learning orientated internship approach. *Australian Journal of Adult Learning, 50*, 287–307.

Corey, G. (2016). *Theory & practice of group counseling* (9th ed.). Boston, MA: Cengage Learning.

Coulshed, V. (1993). Adult learning: Implications for teaching social work education. *British Journal of Social Work, 23*, 1–13.

Coulton, P, & Kimmer, L. (2005). Co-supervision of social work students: A model for meeting the future needs of the profession. *Australian Social Work, 58*, 154–166. doi:10.1111/j.1447-0748.2005.00200.x

Council on Social Work Education. (2008). *Educational policy and accreditation standards*. Retrieved from https://www.cswe.org/Accreditation/Standards-and-Policies/2008-EPAS.aspx

Council on Social Work Education. (2010). *2010–2020 CSWE strategic plan: Vision 2020: Strengthening the profession through research, education, and career advancement*. Retrieved from https://www.cswe.org/About-CSWE/Governance/Board-of-Directors/2010-2020-CSWE-Strategic-Plan

Council on Social Work Education. (2015a). *Educational policy and accreditation standards*. Retrieved from https://www.cswe.org/getattachment/Accreditation/Standards-and-Policies/2015-EPAS/2015EPASandGlossary.pdf.aspx

Council on Social Work Education. (2015b). *Findings from the 2015 State of Field Education Survey: Executive Summary*. Retrieved from https://www.cswe.org/getattachment/cabf3 e01-6800-4c2a-b14f-aaac4f84cdb5/Findings-From-the-2015-State-of-Field-Education -Su.aspx

Council on Social Work Education. (2018a). *Envisioning the future of social work: Report of the CSWE Futures Task Force April 2018*. Retrieved from https://cswe.org/About-CSWE/ Governance/Board-of-Directors/2018-19-Strategic-Planning-Process/CSWE-FTF -Four-Futures-for-Social-Work-FINAL-2.aspx?platform=hootsuite

Council on Social Work Education. (2018b). *State of field education survey*. Retrieved from https://www.cswe.org/getattachment/05519d2d-7384-41fe-98b8-08a21682ed6e/ State-of-Field-Education-Survey-Final-Report.aspx?_zs=CHWael&_zl=nc1F5

Council on Social Work Education. (2018c). *2017 statistics on social work education in the United States: Appendix*. Retrieved from
https://www.cswe.org/getattachment/News/General-News-Archives/2017-Annual-Stats -Social-Work-Education-Report/CSW

Council on Social Work Education. (2018d). *2017 statistics on social work education in the United States: A summary of the CSWE Annual Survey of Social Work Programs*. Retrieved from https://www.cswe.org/Research-Statistics/Research-Briefs-and-Publications/CSWE_ 2017_annual_survey_report-FINAL.aspxCournoyer, B. R. (2017). *The social work skills workbook* (8th edition). Boston, MA: Cengage Learning

Cowger, C. D., Anderson, K. M., & Snively, C. A. (2002). Assessing strengths: The political context of individual, family and community empowerment. In D. Saleebey (Ed.), *The Strengths perspective in social work practice* (4th ed., pp. 93-115). Boston, MA: Allyn & Bacon.

Cox, E. (2015). Coaching and adult learning: Theory and practice. *New Directions for Adult and Continuing Education, 148*, 27–38.

Crane, C. A., Godleski, S. A., Przybyla, S. M., & Schlauch, R. C., Testa, M. (2016). The proximal effects of acute alcohol consumption on male-to-female aggression: A meta-analytic review of the experimental literature. *Trauma Violence Abuse, 17*, 520–531.

Crenshaw, K. W. (1993). Mapping the margins: Intersectionality, identity politics, and violence against women of color. *Stanford Law Review, 43*, 1241–1299.

Crenshaw, K. W. (2010). Close encounters of three kinds: On teaching dominance feminism and intersectionality. *Tulsa Law Review, 46*, 151–189.

Crenshaw, K. W. (2011). Twenty years of critical race theory: Looking back to move forward. *Connecticut Law Review, 43*, 1253–1352.

Criss, P. (2010). Effects of client violence on social work students: A national study. *Journal of Social Work Education, 46*, 371–390.

Cross, S. L., Day, A., Gogliotti, L. J., & Pung, J. J. (2013). Challenges to recruit and retain American Indian and Alaskan Natives into social work programs: The impact on the child welfare workforce. *Child Welfare, 92*(4), 31–53.

Cross, W. E. (1978). The Thomas and Cross models of psychological nigrescence: A literature review. *Journal of Black Psychology, 4*, 13–31.

Csiernik, R., Furze, P., Dromgole, L., & Rishchynski, G. M. (2006). Information technology and social work—the dark side or light side? *Journal of Evidence-Based Social Work, 3*(3/4), 9–25.

Cummings, S. M., Chaffin, K. M., & Cockerham, C. (2015). Comparative analysis of an online and a traditional MSW program: Educational outcomes. *Journal of Social Work Education, 51*, 109–120. doi:10.1080/10437797.2015.977170

Daloz, L. A. (1986). *Effective teaching and mentorship: Realizing the transformational power of adult learning experiences.* San Francisco, CA: Jossey-Bass.

Dalton, J., & Crosby, P. (2008). Challenging college students to learn in campus cultures of comfort, convenience and complacency. *Journal of College & Character, 9*, 1–5.

Dalton, B., Stevens, L., & Maas-Brady, J. (2011). "How do you do it?": MSW field director survey. *Advances in Social Work, 12,* 276–288.

Daniel, C. (2011) Lessons learned. Pedagogical tensions and struggles with instruction on multiculturalism in social work education programmes. *Social Work Education, 3,* 250–265.

Danowitz, M. A., Tuitt, F. (2011). Enacting inclusivity through engaged pedagogy: A higher education perspective. *Equity & Excellence in Education, 44*(1), 40–56.

Davies, M. (2011). Concept mapping, mind mapping and argument mapping: What are the differences, and do they matter? *Higher Education, 62,* 279–301. doi:10.1007/s10734-010-9387-6

Davis, A., Mirick, R., McQueen, B. (2014). Teaching from White privilege: Reflections from White female instructors. *Affilia, 30,* 302–313.

Deal, K. H. (2000). The usefulness of developmental stage models for clinical social work students: An exploratory study. *Clinical Supervisor, 19,* 1–19.

Deal, K. H. (2002). Modifying field instructors' supervisory approach using stage models of student development. *Journal of Teaching in Social Work, 22*(3/4), 121–137.

Deal, K. H. (2003). The relationship between critical thinking and interpersonal skills: Guidelines for clinical supervision. *Clinical Supervisor, 22,* 3–20. doi:10.1300/J001v22n02_02

Deal, K. H. (2004). Understanding MSW student anxiety and resistance to multicultural learning: A developmental perspective. *Journal of Teaching in Social Work, 24*(1/2), 73–86.

Deal, K. H., & Clements, J. A. (2006). Supervising students developmentally: Evaluating a seminar for new field instructors. *Journal of Social Work Education, 42,* 291–306.

Deal, K. H., Hopkins, K. M., Fisher, L., & Hartin, J. (2007). Field practicum experience of macro-oriented graduate students: Are we doing them justice? *Administration in Social Work, 31*(4), 41–58.

Deal, K. H., & Hyde, C. A. (2004). Understanding MSW student anxiety and resistance to multicultural learning: A developmental perspective. *Journal of Teaching in Social Work, 24*(1/2), 73–86.

Dearnley, B. (1985). A plain man's guide to supervision—or new clothes for the emperor? *Journal of Social Work Practice, 2,* 52–65.

Degges-White, S., Colon, B. R., Borzumato-Gainey, C. (2013). Counseling supervision within a feminist framework: Guidelines for intervention. *Journal of Humanistic Counseling, 52,* 92–105.

Deglau, E., Ray, A., Conway, F., Carre-Lee, N., Waldman, W., Cunningham, K., ... Powell, T. (2015). Practice change in child welfare: The interface of training and social work education. *Journal of Social Work Education, 51*(Suppl., 2), S163–172. doi:10.1080/10437797.2015.1072402

Dennis, S. (2016). Advancing field education through technology. In C. A. Hunter, J. K. Moen, & M. S. Raskin (Eds.), *Social work field directors* (pp. 260–282). Chicago, Il: Lyceum Books.

Dentato, M. P., Craig, S.L., Lloyd, M. R., Kelly, B. L., Wright, C., & Austin, A. (2017). Homophobia within schools of social work: The critical need for affirming classroom settings and effective preparation for service with the LGBTQ community. *Social Work Education,35,* 672–692. doi:10.1080/02615479.2016.1150452

Dentato, M. P., Craig, S. L., Messinger, L., Lloyd, M., & McInroy, L. B. (2014). Outness among LGBTQ social work students in North America: The contribution of environmental supports and perceptions of comfort. *Social Work Education, 33*, 485–501. doi:10.1080/02615479.2013.855193

Dessel, A. B., & Rodenborg, N. (2017). An evaluation of intergroup dialogue pedagogy: Addressing segregation and developing cultural competency. *Journal of Social work Education, 53*, 222–239. doi:10.1080/10437797.2016.1246269

Dettlaff, A. J. (2003). *From mission to evaluation: A field instructor training program.* Alexandria, VA: Council on Social Work Education.

Diambra, J. F., Cole-Zakrzewski, K. G., & Booher, J. (2004). A comparison of internship stage models: Evidence from intern experiences. *Journal of Experiential Education, 27*, 191–212.

DiAngelo, R. (2018). *White fragility: Why it's so hard for White people to talk about racism.* Retrieved from https://www.nbcnews.com/think/opinion/white-people-are-still-raised-be-racially-illiterate-if-we-ncna906646

Diekman, A. B, Weisgram, E. S., & Belanger, A. (2015). New routes to recruiting and retaining women in STEM: Policy implications of a communal goal congruity perspective. *Social Issues and Policy Review, 9*(1), 52–88.

Dillon, G., Hussain, R., Loxton, D., & Rahman, S. (2013). Mental and physical health and intimate partner violence against women: a review of the literature. *International Journal of Family Medicine,* Article 313909. doi:10.1155/2013/313909

Dominelli, L. (2017). *Anti-racist social work* (4th ed.). Basingstoke, Hampshire, UK: Palgrave Macmillan.

Dreisbach, G., & Böttcher, S. (2011). How the social-evaluative context modulates processes of cognitive control. *Psychological Research, 75*, 143–151.

Drew, M., & Hinkle, M. (2018, April 13). *Creative strategies to enhance supervisee professional & clinical development.* Presentation at the meeting of the Adelphi University School of Social Work, Networking Breakfast, Sagamore Children's Center, Dix Hills, NY.

Dreyfus, H. (1980). *A 5-stage model of the mental activities involved in directed skill acquisition.* Berkeley, CA: Office of Science Research, University of California.

Drisko, J. W. (2000). Play in clinical learning, supervision and field advising. *Clinical Supervisor, 19*, 153–165.

Drisko, J. W. (2014). Competencies and their assessment. *Journal of Social Work Education, 50*, 441–426.

Du Bois, W. E. B. (1903). *The souls of Black folk.* Chicago, Il: A. C. McClurg.

Dunn, R., Callahan, J. L., Farnsworth, J. K., & Watkins, C. E. Jr. (2017). A proposed framework for addressing supervisee-supervisor value conflict. *Clinical Supervisor, 36*, 203–222. doi:10.1080/07325223.2016.1246395

Dwyer, M., & Urbanowski, M. (1965). Student process recording: A plea for structure. *Social Casework, 46*, 283–286.

East, J., & Chambers, R. (2007). Courage to teach for social work educators. *Social Work Education, 26*, 810–826.

Edwards, H. R., & Hoefer, R. (2010). Are social work advocacy groups using Web 2.0 effectively? *Journal of Policy Practice, 9*, 220–239. doi:10.1080/15588742.2010.489037

Ellis, M. V. (2010). Bridging the science and practice of clinical supervision: Some discoveries, some misconception. *Clinical Supervisor, 29*, 95–116. doi:10.1080/07325221003741910

Ellis, M. V. (2017) Narratives of harmful clinical supervision. *Clinical Supervisor, 36*, 20–87.

English, R., & Duncan-Howell, J. (2008). Facebook goes to college: Using social networking tools to support students undertaking teaching practicum. *MERLOT Journal of Online Learning and Teaching, 4*, 596–601.

Epstein, R. M. (1999). Mindful practice. *JAMA, 282*, 833–839.

Epstein, R. M. (2003). Mindful practice in action (II): Cultivating habits of mind. *Families, Systems & Health, 21*(1), 11–17.

Euster, G. L., (1999). Gerontology field education experiences of graduate social work and gerontology certificate students. *Journal of Gerontological Social Work, 31*(3/4), 29–47. doi:10.1300/J083v31n03_03

Everett, J. E., Miehls, D., DuBois, C., & Garran, A. (2011). The developmental model of supervision as reflected in the experiences of field supervisors and graduate students. *Journal of Teaching in Social Work, 31,* 250–264.

Fain, P. (2018, September 19). *On-ramps and off-ramps: Alternative credentials and emerging pathways between education and work.* Retrieved from https://www.insidehighered.com/content/alternative-credentials-and-emerging-pathways-between-education-and-work

Falender, C.A. (2009). Relationship and accountability: Tensions in feminist supervision. *Women & Therapy, 22*(1/2), 22–41.

Fazio-Griffith, L., & Ballard, M. B. (2016). Transformational learning: Theory and transformation teaching: A creative strategy for understanding the helping relationship. *Journal of Creativity in Mental Health, 1,* 225–234.

Fazzi, L., & Rosignoli, A. (2016). Reversing the perspective: When the supervisors learn from their trainees. *British Journal of Social Work, 46,* 204–221. doi:10.1093/bjsw/bcu112

Feiner, H. A., & Couch, E. H. (1985). I've got a secret: The student in the agency. *Social Casework, 66,* 268–274.

Ferguson, I. (2007). *Reclaiming social work: Challenging neo-liberalism and promoting social justice.* London, UK: SAGE.

Finch, J. (2015). Running with the fox and hunting with the hounds: Social work tutors' experiences of managing failing social work students in practice learning settings. *British Journal of Social Work, 45,* 2124–2141.

Finch, J., & Imogen, T. (2013). Failure to fail? Practice educators' emotional experiences of assessing failing social work students. *Social Work Education, 32,* 244–258.

Finn, J. L. (2016). *Just practice.* (3rd ed.). New York, NY: Oxford University Press.

Fishbein, H., & Glassman, U. (1991). The advanced seminar for field instructors: Content and process. In D. Schneck, B. Grossman, & U. Glassman (Eds.), *Field education in social work: Contemporary issues and trends* (pp. 226–232). Dubuque, IA: Kendall/Hunt.

Fogel, S. J., & Ellison, M. L. (1998). Sexual harassment of BSW field placement students: Is it a problem? *Journal of Baccalaureate Social Work, 39*(2), 17–29.

Fook, J. (2008). *Social work: Critical theory and practice.* Los Angeles, CA: SAGE.

Fook, J., & Gardner, F. (2007). *Practising critical reflection: A resource handbook.* Maidenhead, Berkshire, UK: Open University Press.

Fortune, A., McCarthy, M., & Abramson, J. S. (2001). Student learning processes in field education: Relationship of learning activities to quality of field instruction, satisfaction and performance among MSW students. *Journal of Social Work Education, 37,* 111–124.

Fortune, A. E. (1987). Grief only? Client and social worker reactions to termination. *Clinical Social Work Journal, 15*(2), 46–53.

Fortune, A. E. (2015). Terminating with clients. In K. Corcoran & Albert R. Roberts (Eds.), *Social worker's desk reference* (3rd ed., pp. 697–703). Oxford, UK: Oxford University Press.

Foucault, M. (1980). *Power/knowledge: Selected interviews and other writings, 1972–1977.* New York, NY: Pantheon.

Foucault, M. (1994). The ethics of the concern for the self as a practice of freedom. In P. Rabinow & N. Rose (Eds.), *The essential Foucault* (pp. 25–42). New York, NY: New Press.

Fox, R. (2011). *The use of self: The essence of professional education.* Chicago, IL: Lyceum Books.

References

Fox, R., & Gutheil, I. A. (2000). Process recording: A means for conceptualizing and evaluation practice. *Journal of Teaching in Social Work, 20*(1/2), 39–55.

Fox, R., & Zischka, P. C. (1989). The field instruction contract: A paradigm for effective learning. *Journal of Teaching in Social Work, 3*(3/4), 103–116.

Franks, C. (2001). *On becoming White: The relationship between White racial identity and self-esteem* (Unpublished doctoral dissertation). Columbia University School of Social Work, New York, NY.

Franks, C. (2013). *Self, social and global awareness: Personal capacity building for professional education and practice. Orientation curriculum.* New York, NY: Columbia University Mailman School of Public Health.

Franks, C., Hess, M., Sheiman, E., Walters, K., Wernick, L., & Wheeler, D. (1996). *Self-awareness for practice in a multicultural world. Orientation curriculum.* New York, NY: Columbia University School of Social Work.

Franks, C., & Insel, S. (2008). *Cultural self-awareness day: Personal capacity building for professional practice. Orientation curriculum.* New York, NY: Columbia University School of Social Work.

Franks, C., & Riedel, M. (2008). Privilege. In T. Mizrahi & L. Davis (Eds.), *Encyclopedia of social work* (20th ed.). New York, NY: Oxford University Press.

Franks, C., & Yoshioka, M. (2008). *Skills and strategies for facilitating challenging dialogues on diversity-related content in the classroom.* Unpublished manuscript.

Freire, P. (1993). *Pedagogy of the oppressed* (M. B. Ramos, Trans.). New York, NY: Continuum. (Original work published 1970)

Frey, W. H. (2018). *The Millennial generation: A demographic to America's diverse future.* Retrieved from https://www.brookings.edu/research/millennials/

Fronek, P., Boddy, J., Chenoweth, L., & Clark, J. (2016). A Report on the use of open access podcasting in the promotion of social work. *Australian Social Work, 69*, 105–114. Retrieved from http://dx.doi.org/10.1080/0312407X.2014.991338

Funge, S. (2011). Promoting the social justice orientation of students: The role of the educator. *Journal of Social Work Education, 47*, 73–90.

Furness, S. (2012). Gender at Work: Characteristics of "failing" social work students. *British Journal of Social Work, 42*, 480–499.

Gandhi, M., & Johnson, M. (2016). Creating more effective mentors: mentoring the mentor. *AIDS and Behavior, 20*, S294–S303

Gambrill, E. (2013). *Social work practice: A critical thinker's guide.* New York, NY: Oxford University Press.

Ganzer, C., & Ornstein, E. D. (2004). Regression, self-disclosure, and the teach or treat dilemma: Implications of a relational approach for social work supervision. *Clinical Social Work Journal, 32*, 431–449.

Gardner, H. (2011). *Frames of mind.* New York, NY: Basic Books.

Garcia, M. L., Mizrahi, T., & Bayne-Smith, M. (2010). Education for interdisciplinary community collaboration and development: The components of a core curriculum by community practitioners. *Journal of Teaching in Social Work, 30*, 175–194.

Garland, J., Jones, H., & Kolodny, R. (1976). A model of stages of group development in social work groups. In S. Bernstein (Ed.), *Explorations in group work: Essays in theory & practice* (pp. 17–71). Boston, MA: Charles River Books.

Garran, A., Kang, H., & Fraser, E. (2014). Pedagogy and diversity: Enrichment and support for social work instructors engaged in social justice education. *Journal of Teaching in Social Work, 34*, 564–574.

Garran, A. M., & Rasmussen, B. M. (2014). Safety in the classroom: Reconsidered. *Journal of Teaching in Social Work, 34*, 401–412.

Gates, T. G. (2011). Coming out in the social work classroom: Reclaiming wholeness and finding the teacher within. *Social Work Education, 30*, 70–82. doi:10.1080/02615471003721202

Garvin, C. D., Gutiérrez, L. M., & Galinsky, M. J. (2004). *Handbook of social work with groups.* New York, NY: Guilford Press.

Gelman, C. R. (2004). Anxiety experienced by foundation-year MSW students entering field placement: Implications for admissions, curriculum and field education. *Journal of Social Work Education, 40*, 39–54.

Gelman, C. R. (2009). MSW students' experience with termination: Implications and suggestions for classroom and field instruction. *Journal of Teaching in Social Work, 29*, 169–187.

Gelman, C. R., Fernandez, P., Hausman, N., Miller, S., & Weiner, M. (2007). Challenging endings: First-year MSW interns' experiences with forced termination and discussion points for supervisory guidance. *Clinical Social Work Journal, 35*, 79–90.

George, P., Silver, S., & Preston, S. (2013). Reimagining field education in social work: The promise unveiled. *Advances in Social Work, 14*, 642–657.

Giddings, M. M., Vodde, R., & Cleveland, P. (2003). Examining student-field instructor problems in practicum: Beyond student satisfaction measures. *Clinical Supervisor, 22*, 191–214.

Ginwright, S., & Cammarota, J. (2002). New terrain in youth development: The promise of a social justice approach. *Social Justice, 29*, 82–88.

Gitterman, A. (1988). Teaching students to connect theory and practice. *Social Work with Groups, 11*, 33–41.

Gitterman, A., & Knight, C. (2016). Promoting resilience through social work practice with groups: Implications for the practice and field curricula. *Journal of Social Work Education, 52*, 448–461.

Gitterman, A., & Miller, I. (1977). Supervisors as educators. In F. Kaslow (Ed.), *Supervision, consultation and staff training in the helping professions* (pp. 100–114). San Francisco, CA: Jossey-Bass.

Gladding, S. T. (2011). *The creative arts in counseling* (4th ed.). Alexandria, VA: American Counseling Association.

Glassman, U. (2009). *Group work: A humanistic and skills building approach* (2nd ed.). Thousand Oaks, CA: SAGE.

Goldstein, E. (1989, December). *The field instructor as master teacher.* In Judith Lemberger (Chair), The seventh annual field instructor symposium. Featured speaker at the annual meeting of the Greater New York Area Schools of Social Work, New York University School of Social Work, New York, NY.

Goldstein, H. (2001). *Experiential learning: A foundation for social work education and practice.* Alexandria, VA: Council on Social Work Education.

Golia, G. M., & McGovern, A. R. (2015). If you save me, I'll save you: The power of peer supervision in clinical training and professional development. *British Journal of Social Work, 45*, 634–650. doi:10.1093/bjsw/bct138

Goodman, H., & Munoz, M. (2004). Developing social work group skills for contemporary agency practice. *Social Work with Groups, 27*, 17–33.

Granello, D. H. (1996). Gender and power in the supervisory dyad. *Clinical Supervisor, 14*(2), 53–67.

Granello, D. H., (2010). Cognitive complexity among practicing counselors: How thinking changes with experience. *Journal of Counseling & Development, 88*, 92–100.

Graybeal, C. T., & Ruff, E. (1995). Process recording: It's more than you think. *Journal of Social Work Education, 31*, 169–181.

Great Schools Partnership. (2015). *The glossary of education reform*. Retrieved from https://www.edglossary.org/hidden-curriculum/

Green, M. S., & Dekkers, T. D. (2010). Attending to power and diversity in supervision: An exploration of supervisee learning outcomes and satisfaction with supervision. *Journal of Feminist Family Therapy, 22*, 293–312. doi:10.1080/08952833.2010.528703

Green, W., & Levy Simon, B. (Eds.). (2012). *The Columbia guide to social work writing*. New York, NY: Columbia University Press.

Grossman, B., Levine-Jordano, N., & Shearer, P. (1990). Working with students' emotional reactions in the field: An educational framework. *Clinical Supervisor, 8*, 23–39.

Gursansky, D., Quinn, D., & Le Sueur, E. (2010). Authenticity in reflection: Building reflective skills for social work, *Social Work Education, 29*, 778–791.

Hair, H., J., & O'Donoghue, K. (2009). Culturally relevant, socially just, social work supervision: Becoming visible through a social constructionist lens. *Journal of Ethnic and Cultural Diversity in Social Work, 18*, 70–88. doi:10.1080/15313200902874979

Hamilton, N., & Else, J. (1983). *Designing field education: Philosophy, structure and process*. Springfield, IL: Charles C Thomas.

Hardina, D. (2013). *Interpersonal social work skills for community practice*. New York, NY: Springer.

Hardy, K. V. (2016). Antiracist approaches for shaping theoretical and practical paradigms. In A. J. Carten, A. B. Siskind, & M. Pender Greene (Eds.), *Strategies for deconstructing racism in the health and human services* (pp. 125–140). New York, NY: Oxford University Press.

Hardy, K. V. (2017). *Of walls and wars: Tips, tactics and strategies for talking about race*. New York, NY: Columbia University.

Harriet W. Sheridan Center for Teaching and Learning. (2018). *Diversity & Inclusion Syllabus Statements*. Retrieved from https://www.brown.edu/sheridan/teaching-learning-resources/inclusive-teaching/statements

Harrigan, M. P., Fauri, D. P., & Netting, F. E. (1998). Termination: Extending the concept for macro social work practice. *Journal of Sociology and Social Welfare, 25*(4), 61–80.

Hartman, A. (1997). Power issues in social work practice. In A. Katz, A. Lurie, & C. Vidal (Eds.), *Critical social welfare issues* (pp. 215–226). New York, NY: Haworth.

Hartung, R. J. (1982). The practicum instructor: A study of role expectations. *Journal of Sociology and Social Welfare, 9*, 662–670.

Hawthorne, L. (1987). Teaching from recordings in field instruction. *Clinical Supervisor, 5*(2), 7–22.

Haynes, D. T. (1999). A theoretical integrative framework for teaching professional social work values. *Journal of Social Work Education, 35*, 39–51.

Heffron, M. C., Reynolds, D., & Talbot, B. (2016). Reflecting together: Reflective functioning as a focus for deepening group supervision. *Infant Mental Health Journal, 37*, 628–639. doi:10.1002/imhj.21608

Heft LaPorte, H., & Sweifach, J. (2011). MSW foundation students in the field: Reflections on the nature and quality of group work assignments and supervision. *Journal of Teaching in Social Work, 31*, 239–249.

Hek, R. (2012). Is it possible to develop and sustain non-traditional placements? An evaluation of the development of practice learning opportunities in partnership with the police and probation services in the West Midlands. *Social Work Education, 31*, 512–529.

Helms, J. E. (1990). *Black and White racial identity: Theory, research and practice*. Westport, CT: Greenwood.

Helms, J. E. (1995). An update of Helms's White and people of color racial identity models. In J. G. Ponterotto, J. M. Casas, L. A. Suzuki, & C. M. Alexander (Eds.), *Handbook of multicultural counseling* (pp. 181–198). Thousand Oaks, CA: SAGE.

Henderson, K. J. (2010). Work-based supervisors: The neglected partners in practice learning. *Social Work Education, 29*, 490-502. doi:10.1080/02615470903156352

Hepworth, D. H., Rooney, R. H., Rooney, G. D., Strom-Gottfried, K., & Larsen, J. (2017), *Direct social work practice: Theory and skills* (10th ed.). Belmont, CA: Brooks/Cole.

Ho, M. K., Rasheed, J. M., & Rasheed, M. N. (2003). *Family therapy with ethnic minorities* (2nd ed.). Thousand Oaks, CA: SAGE.

Holpuch, A. (2018, March 26). Six victories for the gun control movement since the Parkland massacre. *The Guardian*. Retrieved from https://www.theguardian.com/us-news/2018/mar/26/gun-control-movement-march-for-our-lives-stoneman-douglas-parkland-builds-momentum).

hooks, b. (1994). *Teaching to transgress: Education as the practice of freedom*. New York, NY: Routledge.

hooks, b. (2000). *Where we stand: Class matters*. New York: NY: Routledge.

hooks, b. (2010). *Teaching critical thinking: Practical wisdom*. New York, NY: Routledge.

Horejsi, C. R., & Garthwait, C. L. (2002). *The social work practicum: A guide and workbook for students* (2nd ed.). Boston, MA: Allyn & Bacon.

Houston-Vega, M. K., Nuehring, E., & Daguio, E. (1997). *Prudent practice: A guide to managing malpractice risk*. Washington, DC: NASW Press.

Hughes, M. (2013). Enabling learners to think for themselves: reflections on a community placement. *Social Work Education, 32*, 213–229.

Hunter, C. A., & Poe, N. T. (2016). Developing and maintaining partnerships with practice settings. In C. A. Hunter, J. K. Moen, & M. S. Raskin (Eds.), *Social work field directors* (pp. 65–82). Chicago, Il: Lyceum Books.

Hussein, S., Moriarty, J., & Manthorpe, J. (2009). *Variations in progression of social work students in England: Using student data to help promote achievement: Undergraduate full-time students' progression on the social work degree*. Retrieved from http://www.kcl.ac.uk/sspp/policy-institute/scwru/pubs/2009/husseinetal2009Variations.pdf

Hutchings, M., & Quinney, A. (2015). The flipped classroom, disruptive pedagogies, enabling technologies and wicked problems: Responding to "the bomb in the basement." *Electronic Journal of e-Learning, 13*, 105–118).

Hytten, K., & Bettez, S. C. (2011). Understanding education for social justice. *Educational Foundations, 25*(1/2). 7–24.

Inoue, A. B. (2015). *Antiracist writing assessment ecologies: Teaching and assessing writing for a socially just future*. Fort Collins, CO: WAC Clearinghouse.

Ishizuka, K., & Husain, A. L. (2015). Anti-oppressive practices. In K. Corcoran & Albert R. Roberts (Eds.), *Social worker's desk reference*. (3rd ed., pp. 969–980). Oxford, UK: Oxford University Press.

Jacobs, C. (1991). Violations of the supervisory relationship: An ethical and educational blind spot. *Social Work, 36*, 130–135.

Jani, J. S., Osteen, P., & Shipe, S. (2016). Cultural competence and social work education: Moving toward assessment of practice behaviors. *Journal of Social Work Education, 52*, 311–324. doi:10.1080/10437797.2016.1174634

Jani, J. S., Pierce, D., Ortiz, L. O., & Sowbel, L. (2011) Access to intersectionality, content to competence: Deconstructing social work education diversity standards. *Journal of Social Work Education, 47*, 283–301.

Jani, J. S., & Reisch, M. (2011). Common human needs, uncommon solutions: Applying a critical framework to perspectives on human behavior, *Families in Society, 92*(1), 13–20.

Jansson, B. S. (2018). *Becoming an effective policy advocate* (8th ed.). Belmont, CA: Thompson Brooks/Cole.

Jarvis, P. (1995). *Adult and continuing education: Theory and practice* (2nd ed.). New York, NY: Routledge.

Jarvis, P. (2009). Developments in learning theory. *International Journal of Continuing Education & Lifelong Learning, 2,* 1–14.

Jarvis, P. (2010). *Adult education and lifelong learning: Theory and practice* (4th ed.). London, UK: Routledge.

Jarvis, P. (2015). Learning expertise in practice: Implications for learning. *Studies in the Education of Adults, 47*(1), 81–94.

Johnson, B. (2005). Overcoming doom and gloom: Empowering students in courses on social problems, injustice and inequality. *Teaching Sociology 33,* 44–58.

Jones, J. M. (1997). *Prejudice and racism* (2nd ed.). New York, NY: McGraw-Hill.

Jones, S. R. (2008). Student resistance to cross-cultural engagement: Annoying distraction or site for transformative learning? In S. Harper (Ed.), *Creating inclusive environments for cross cultural learning and student engagement* (pp. 67–86). Washington, DC: National Association of Student Personnel Administrators.

Kadushin, A., & Harkness, D. (2002). *Supervision in social work* (4th ed.). New York, NY: Columbia University Press.

Kagle, J., & Giebelhausen, P. (1994). Dual relationships and professional boundaries. *Social Work, 39,* 213–220.

Kagle, J. D. (1991). Teaching social work students about privileged communication. *Journal of Teaching in Social Work, 4*(2), 49–65.

Kam, P. W., (2014). Back to "social" of social work: Reviving the social work profession's contribution to the promotion of social justice. *International Social Work, 57,* 723–740. doi:10.1177/0020872812447118

Kanno, H., & Koeske, G. F. (2010). MSW students' satisfaction with their field placements: The role of preparedness and supervision quality. *Journal of Social Work Education, 46,* 23–38. doi:10.5175/JSWE.2010.200800066

Keeling, R., & Dungy, G. J. (Eds.). (2004). *Learning reconsidered: A campus-wide focus on the student experience.* Retrieved from https://www.naspa.org/images/uploads/main/Learning_Reconsidered_Report.pdf)

Kellerman, B. (2007, December). What every leader needs to know about followers. *Harvard Business Review,* 1–8.

Ketner, M., Cooper-Bolinskey, D., & VanCleave, D. (2017). The meaning and value of supervision in social work field education. *Field Educator, 7*(2). Retrieved from http://www2.simmons.edu/ssw/fe/i/17-175.pdf

Kilpatrick, A. C., Turner, J. B., & Holland, T. P. (1994). Quality control in field education: Monitoring students' performance. *Journal of Teaching in Social Work, 9*(1–2), 107–120.

King, P. M. (2009). Principles of development and developmental change underlying theories of cognitive and moral development. *Journal of College Student Development, 50,* 597–620.

Kirst-Ashman, K. K., & Hull, G. H., Jr. (2015). *Empowerment series: Understanding generalist practice.* (7th ed.). Stamford, CT: Cengage.

Knight, C. (1996). A study of MSW and BSW students' perceptions of their field instructors. *Journal of Social Work Education, 32,* 399–414.

Knight, C. (2000). Engaging the student in the field instruction relationship: BSW and MSW students' views. *Journal of Teaching in Social Work, 20*(3/4), 173–201.

Knight, C. (2012). Social workers' attitudes toward and engagement in self-disclosure. *Clinical Social Work Journal, 40*(3), 297-306. doi: 10.1007/s10615-012-0408-z.

Knight, C. (2014). Teaching group work in BSW generalist social work curriculum: Core content. *Social Work with Groups, 37,* 23–35.

Knight, C. (2016). Training and supporting field instructors. In C. A. Hunter, J. K. Moen, & M. S. Raskin (Eds.), *Social work field directors* (pp. 105–129). Chicago, Il: Lyceum Books.

Knowles, M. S. (1972). Innovations in teaching styles and approaches: Based upon adult learning. *Journal of Education for Social Work, 8*(2), 32–39.

Knowles, M. (1975). *Self-directed learning: A guide for learners and teachers.* Englewood Cliffs, NJ: Prentice Hall/Cambridge.

Knowles, M. (1984). *Androgyny in action: Applying modern principles of adult education.* San Francisco, CA: Jossey-Bass.

Knowles, M., Holton, E. F., & Swanson, R. A. (1998). *The adult learner: The definitive classic in adult education and human resource development* (5th ed.). Woburn, MA: Butterworth-Heinemann.

Kohi, H. K., Huber, R., & Faul, A. C. (2010). Historical and theoretical development of culturally competent social work practice. *Journal of Teaching in Social Work, 30,* 252–271.

Kolb, D. (1984). *Experiential learning: Experience as the source of learning and development.* Englewood Cliffs, NJ: Prentice-Hall.

Kreuter, M. W., Griffith, D. J., Thompson, V., Brownson, R. C., McClure, S., Scharff, D. P., ... & Haire-Joshu, D. (2011). Lessons learned from a decade of focused recruitment and training to develop minority public health professionals. *American Journal of Public Health, 101*(Suppl., 1), S188--S195.

Kumashiro, K. (2004). *Against common sense: teaching and learning toward social justice.* New York, NY: Routledge.

Kurland, P. (1989). Viewpoint/process recording: An anachronism. *Social Casework, 70,* 312–314.

Lagdon, S., Armour, C., & Stringer, M. (2014). Adult experience of mental health outcomes as a result of intimate partner violence victimisation: A systematic review. *European Journal of Psychotraumatology 5*(1), Article 24794. doi:10.3402/ejpt.v5.24794

Lager, P. B., & Robbins, V. C. (2004). Guest editorial—Field education: Exploring the future, expanding the vision. *Journal of Social Work Education, 40,* 3–11.

Laird, J. (2001). Theorizing culture: Narrative ideas and practice principles. *Journal of Feminist Family Therapy: An International Forum, 11*(4), 99–114. doi:10.1300/J086v11n04_08

Landon, P. S., & Feit, M. (1999). *Generalist social work practice.* Dubuque, IA: Eddie Bowers.

LaSala, M. C., Jenkins, D. A., Wheeler, D. P., & Fredriksen-Goldsen, K. I. (2008) LGBT faculty, research, and researchers: Risks and rewards. *Journal of Gay & Lesbian Social Services, 20,* 253–267. doi:10.1080/10538720802235351

Lavoie, C. (2012). Race, power and social action in neighborhood community organizing: Reproducing and resisting the social construction of the other. *Journal of Community Practice, 20,* 241– 259.

Lazar, A., & Eisikovits, Z. (1997). Social work students' preferences regarding supervisory styles and supervisors' behavior. *Clinical Supervisor, 16,* 25–37.

Law School Admissions Council. (2016). *Admitted applicants by race/ethnicity & sex.* Retrieved from https://www.lsac.org/lsacresources/data/ethnicity-sex-admits

Lee, E., & Kealy, D. (2018). Developing a working model of cross-cultural supervision: A competence- and alliance-based framework. *Clinical Social Work Journal, 46,* 310-320. doi:10.1007s10615-018-4

Lee, J. J., & Himmelheber, S. A. (2016). Field education in the present moment: Evaluating a 14-week pedagogical model to increase mindfulness practice. *Journal of Social Work Education, 52,* 473–483.

Lemberger, J., & Marshack, E. F. (1991). Educational assessment in the field: An opportunity for teacher–learner mutuality. In D. Schneck, B. Grossman, & U. Glassman (Eds.), *Field education in social work: Contemporary issues and trends* (pp. 187–197). Dubuque, IA: Kendall/Hunt.

Lewis, H. (1987). Teaching ethics through ethical teaching. *Journal of Teaching in Social Work, 1,* 3–14.

Ligon, J., & Ward, J. (2005). A national study of the field liaison role in social work education programs in the United States and Puerto Rico. *Social Work Education, 24,* 235–243.

Litvak, A., Bogo, M., & Mishna, F. (2010). Understanding the emotional impact of field experiences on MSW students. *Journal of Social Work Education, 46,* 227–241.

Logie, C., Bogo, M., Regehr, C., & Regehr, G. (2013). A critical appraisal of the use of standardized client simulations in social work education. *Journal of Social Work Education, 49,* 66–80. doi:10.1080/10437797.2013.755377

Lopez, A. (2015). An investigation of the use of Internet-based resources in support of the therapeutic alliance. *Clinical Social Work Journal, 43,* 189–200.

Love, B. J. (2013). Developing a liberatory consciousness. In Adams, M., Blumenfeld, J., Castañeda, C., Hackman, H. W., Peters, M. L., & Zúñiga, X. (Eds.), *Readings for diversity and social justice* (3rd ed., pp. 601–611). New York, NY: Routledge.

Lusk, M., Terrazas, S., & Salcido, R. (2017). Critical cultural competence in social work supervision. *Human Service Organizations: Management, Leadership & Governance, 41,* 464–476.

Lyter, S. (2012). Field note: Potential of field education as signature pedagogy: The field director role. *Journal of Social Work Education, 48,* 179–187.

Lyter, S. (2016). Safety and risk management. In C. A. Hunter, J. K. Moen, & M. S. Raskin (Eds.), *Social work field directors* (pp. 218–238). Chicago, Il: Lyceum Books.

MacCleave, A., Eghan, F. (2010). Use of cultural styles or repertoires of experience to guide instruction: What difference does it make? *Interchange, 41,* 233-253.

Maidment, J., & Cooper, L. (2002). Acknowledgement of client diversity and oppression in social work student supervision. *Social Work Education, 21,* 399–408. doi:10.1080/02615470220150366

Mangan, K. (2017, September 22). What you need to know about the new guidance on Title IX. *Chronicle of Higher Education.* Retrieved from https://www.chronicle.com/article/What-You-Need-to-Know-About/241277?cid=RCPACKAGE

Manthorpe, J., Harris, J., & Hussein, S. (2012). Employers' experiences and views of grow your own social work programmes: A qualitative interview study. *Social Work Education, 31,* 637–650. doi:10.1080/02615479.2011.584525

Manuel, T. (2008). Envisioning the possibilities for a good life: Exploring the public policy implications of intersectionality theory. *Journal of Women, Politics & Policy, 28,* 173–203.

Marino, G. (2004, February 20). Before teaching ethics, stop kidding yourself. *Chronicle of Higher Education,* B4–B5.

Marshack, E. F., Ortiz Hendricks, C., & Gladstein, M. (1994). The commonality of difference: Teaching about diversity in field instruction. *Journal of Multicultural Social Work, 3,* 77–89.

Massey, M. G., Kim, S., & Mitchell, C. (2011). A study of the learning styles of undergraduate social work students. *Journal of Evidence-Based Social Work, 8,* 294–323.

Mattsson, T. (2014). Intersectionality as a useful tool: Anti-oppressive social work and critical reflection. *Affilia, 29,* 8–17.

Maynard, S. P., Mertz, L., & Fortune, A. E. (2015). Off-site supervision in social work: What makes it work? *Journal of Social Work Education, 51,* 519–534. doi:10.1080/10437797.2015.1043201

McAuliffe, D., & Chenoweth, L. (2008). Leave no stone unturned: The inclusive model of ethical decision-making. *Ethics and Social Welfare, 2*(1), 38–49.

McClam, T., & Woodside, M. (2012). *The helping process: Assessment to termination.* Belmont, CA: Brooks/Cole.

McElrath, E., & McDowell, K. (2008). Pedagogical strategies for building community in graduate level distance education courses. *Journal of Online Teaching and Learning, 4,* 117–127.

McGoldrick, M. (2016). *The genogram casebook: A clinical companion to genograms: Assessment and intervention.* New York, NY: Norton.

McIntosh, P. (1989). White privilege: Unpacking the invisible knapsack. *Peace and Freedom,* 10–12. Retrieved from https://nationalseedproject.org/white-privilege-unpacking-the-invisible-knapsack

Medina, C. K. (2010). The need and use of process recording in policy practice: A learning and assessment tool for macro practice. *Journal of Teaching in Social Work, 30,* 29–45.

Merriam, S. B. (2008). Adult learning theory for the twenty-first century. *New Directions for Adult and Continuing Education,* 119, 93–98.

Merriam, S. B, & Caffarella, R. S. (1999). *Learning in adulthood.* San Francisco, CA: Jossey-Bass.

Merriam, S. B., & Kim, Y. S. (2008). Non-Western perspectives on learning and knowing. *New Directions for Adult and Continuing Education,* 119, 71–81.

Mersky, J. P., Janczewski, C. E., & Nitkowski, J. C. (2018). Poor mental health among low-income women in the U.S.: The roles of adverse childhood and adult experiences. *Social Science & Medicine, 206,* 14–21. doi:10.1016/j.socscimed.2018.03.043

Messinger, L. (2004). Out in the field: Gay and lesbian social work students' experiences in field placement. *Journal of Social Work* Education, *40,* 187–204.

Messinger, L. (2007). Supervision of lesbian, gay, and bisexual social work students by heterosexual field instructors: A qualitative dyad analysis. *Clinical Supervisor, 26,* 195–222.

Metzl, J. M., & Hansen, H. (2014). Structural competency: Theorizing a new medical engagement with stigma and inequality. *Social Science & Medicine, 103,* 126–133.

Mezirow, J. (1978). Perspective transformation. *Adult Education Quarterly, 28*(2), 100-110.

Mezirow, J. (1991). *Transformative dimensions of adult learning.* San Francisco, CA: Jossey-Bass.

Mezirow, J. (1997). Transformative learning: Theory to practice. *New Directions for Adult and Continuing Education,* 74, 5–12.

Mezirow, J. (2000). *Learning as transformation: Critical perspectives on a theory in progress.* San Francisco, CA: Jossey-Bass.

Miehls, D., Everett, J., Segal, C., du Bois, C. (2013). MSW students' views of supervision: Factors contributing to satisfactory field experiences. *Clinical Supervisor, 32,* 128-146.

Miehls, D., & Moffat, K. (2000). Constructing social work identity based on the reflexive self. *British Journal of Social Work, 30,* 339–348.

Mildred, J., & Zúñiga, X. (2004). Working with resistance to diversity issues in the classroom: Lessons from teacher training and multicultural education. *Smith College Studies in Social Work, 74,* 359–375.

Miller, J., Donner, S., Fraser, E. (2004). Talking when taking is tough: Taking on conversations about race, sexual orientation, gender, class and other aspects of social identity. *Smith College Studies in Social Work, 74,* 377–392.

Miller, J., & Garran, A. M. (2017). Confronting racism in agencies and organizations. In J. Miller & A. M. Garran, *Racism in the United States* (2nd ed., pp. 257–274). New York, NY: Springer.

Miller, J., Hyde, C. A., & Ruth, B. J. (2004). Teaching about race and racism in social work: Challenges for White educators. *Smith College Studies in Social Work, 74,* 409–426.

Miller, J., & Koerin, B. B. (2012). Gatekeeping in the practicum. *Clinical Supervisor, 20,* 1–18.

Miller, J., Kovacs, P. J., Wright, L., Corcoran, J., & Rosenblum, A. (2004). Field education: Student and field instructor perceptions of the learning process. *Journal of Social Work Education, 41,* 131–146.

Miller, J., & Rodwell, M. K. (1997). Disclosure of student status in agencies: Do we still have a secret? *Families in Society, 78,* 72–83.

Miller, S. E. (2010). A conceptual framework for the professional socialization of social workers. *Journal of Human Behavior in the Social Environment, 20,* 924–938.

Mirabito, D. M. (2012). Educating a new generation of social workers: Challenges and skills needed for contemporary agency-based practice. *Clinical Social Work Journal, 40,* 245–254. doi:10.1007/s10615-011-0378-6

Mishna, F., Bogo, M. (2007). Reflective practice in contemporary social work classrooms. *Journal of Social Work Education, 43,* 529–541.

Mishna, F., Bogo, M., Root, J., Sawyer, J., & Khoury-Kassabri, M. (2012). "It just crept in": The digital age and implications for social work practice. *Clinical Social Work Journal, 40,* 277–286. doi:10.1007/s10615-012-0383-4

Mizrahi, T., & Davis, L. E. (Eds.). (2008). *Encyclopedia of social work* (20th ed.). Washington, DC: NASW Press.

Moen, J. K., Goodrich Liley, D., Dennis, S. R. (2016). Facilitating student learning between classroom and field. In C. A. Hunter, J. K. Moen, & M. S. Raskin (Eds.), *Social work field directors* (pp. 130–153). Chicago, Il: Lyceum Books.

Morgaine, K. L., & Capous-Desyllas, M. (2015). *Anti-oppressive social work practice: Putting theory into action.* Thousand Oaks, CA: SAGE.

Morley, C. (2013). Teaching critical practice: Resisting structural domination through critical reflection. *Social Work Education, 27,* 407–421.

Mullaly, B. (2002). *Challenging oppression: A critical social work approach.* New York, NY: Oxford University Press.

Mullaly, B. (2010). *Challenging oppression and confronting privilege* (2nd ed.). Ontario, Canada: Oxford University Press.

Munson, C. (2001). *Handbook of clinical supervision* (3rd ed.). New York, NY: Haworth.

Murdock, V. Ward, J., Ligon, J., & Jindani, S. (2006). Identifying, assessing, and enhancing field instructor competencies. *Social Work Education, 12,* 165–183.

Nadan, Y. (2016). Teaching note—Revising stereotypes: Enhancing cultural awareness through a Web-based tool. *Journal of Social Work Education, 52,* 50–56.

Narayan, U. (1997). *Dislocating cultures: Identities, traditions and third world feminism.* New York, NY: Routledge.

National Association of Social Workers. (1996). *Code of ethics.* Retrieved from https://www.socialworkers.org/LinkClick.aspx?fileticket=YkFrOi8Vu-0%3d&portalid=0

National Association of Social Workers. (1999). *Code of ethics.* Retrieved from https://www.socialworkers.org/LinkClick.aspx?fileticket=0Jvdnd6

National Association of Social Workers. (2001). *NASW standards for cultural competence in social work practice*. Retrieved from http://catholiccharitiesla.org/wp-content/uploads/NASW-Cultural-Competence-in-Social-Work-Practice.pdf

National Association of Social Workers. (2007a). *Indicators for the achievement of the NASW standards for cultural competence in social work practice*. Washington, DC: Author.

National Association of Social Workers. (2007b). *Institutional racism & the social work profession: A call to action*. Retrieved from https://ncwwi.org/files/Cultural_Responsiveness__Disproportionality/Institutional_Racism_and_the_Social_Work_Profession.pdf

National Association of Social Workers. (2008). *Code of ethics*. Retrieved from https://www.socialworkers.org/LinkClick.aspx?fileticket=KZmmbz15evc%3d&portalid=0

National Association of Social Workers. (2013). Association of Social Work Boards (ASWB) 2013. *Best Practice Standards in Social Work Supervision*. Retrieved from https://www.socialworkers.org/LinkClick.aspx?fileticket=GBrLbl4BuwI%3d&portalid=0

National Association of Social Workers. (2015). *Standards and indicators for cultural competence in social work practice*. Retrieved from https://www.socialworkers.org/LinkClick.aspx?fileticket=7dVckZAYUmk%3d&portalid=0)

National Association of Social Workers. (2017). *Code of ethics*. Retrieved from https://www.socialworkers.org/About/Ethics/Code-of-Ethics/Code-of-Ethics-English

National Association of Social Workers. (2019). *Ethical standard of the month*. Retrieved from https://www.socialworkers.org/About/Ethics/Ethics-Education-and-Resources/Ethical-Standard-of-the-Month

National Association of Social Worker & Association of Social Work Boards. (2013). *Best practice standards in social work supervision*. Retrieved from https://www.socialworkers.org/LinkClick.aspx?fileticket=GBrLbl4BuwI%3d&portalid=0

National Association of Social Workers, Association of Social Work Boards, Council on Social Work Education, & Clinical Social Work Association. (2017). *Standards on technology in social work practice*. Retrieved from https://www.socialworkers.org/includes/newIncludes/homepage/PRA-BRO- 33617.TechStandards_FINAL_POSTING.pdf

Navari, S. (1993, March). *The essence of a field educator*. Paper presented at the Annual Program Meeting of the Council on Social Work Education, New York, NY.

Nellis, A. (2016). *The color of justice: Racial and ethnic disparities in state prisons*. Retrieved from https://www.sentencingproject.org/publications/color-of-justice-racial-and-ethnic-disparity-in-state-prisons/

Nelson, J. (1974). Teaching content of early fieldwork conferences. *Social Casework, 55*, 147–153.

Netting, F. E., Kettner, P. M., & McMurtry, S. L., & Thomas, M. L. (2017). *Social work macro practice* (6th ed.). London, UK: Pearson Education.

Neuman, K. M., & Friedman, B. D. (1997). Process recordings: Fine-tuning an old instrument. *Journal of Social Work Education, 33*, 237–243.

Newell, J. M. (2017). *Cultivating professional resilience in direct practice: A guide for human service professionals*. New York, NY: Columbia University Press.

Newell, J. M., & Nelson-Gardell, D. (2014). A competency-based approach to teaching professional self-care: An ethical consideration for social work educators. *Journal of Social Work Education, 50*, 427–439.

Newman, P., Bogo, M., & Daley, A. (2009). Breaking the silence: Sexual orientation in social work field education. *Journal of Social Work Education, 45*, 7–27. doi:10.5175/JSWE.2009.200600093

Nichols, W. C., Nichols, D. P., & Hardy, K. V. (1990). Supervision in family therapy: A decade of restudy. *Journal of Marital and Family Therapy, 16,* 275–286.

Nisivoccia, D. (1990). Teaching and learning tasks in the beginning phase of field instruction. *Clinical Supervisor, 8,* 7–22.

Noble, J., Harris, J., & Manthorpe, J. (2009). *Grow your own social workers: A tool kit.* Retrieved from https://www.kcl.ac.uk/sspp/policy-institute/scwru/pubs/2009/nobleetal2009tool kit.pdf

Northern, H., & Kurland, R. (2001). *Social work with groups* (3rd ed.). New York, NY: Columbia University Press.

Nussbaum, M. C. (2011). *Creating capabilities: The human development approach.* Cambridge, MA: Harvard University Press.

Oldfield, K. (2007, January–February). Welcoming first-generation poor and working-class students to college. *About Campus,* 2–12.

O'Leary, P., Tsui, M., & Ruch, G. (2013). The boundaries of the social work relationship revisited: Towards a connected, inclusive and dynamic conceptualisation. *British Journal of Social Work, 43,* 135–153.

O'Neill, P., & del Mar Fariña, M. (2018). Constructing critical conversations in social work supervision: Creating change. *Clinical Social Work Journal, 46,* 298–309. doi:10.1007s10615-018-0681-6

Ornstein, E. D., Moses, H. (2010). Goodness of fit: A relational approach to field instruction. *Journal of Teaching in Social Work, 30,* 101–114. doi:10.1080/08841230903479615

Ortiz, L., & Jani, J. (2010). Critical race theory: A transformation model for teaching diversity. *Journal of Social Work Education, 46,* 175–193.

Ortiz Hendricks, C. (2013). Patients with lupus: An overview of culturally competent practice. In N. L. Beckerman & C. Auerbach (Eds.), *Psychosocial impact of lupus: Social work's role and function* (pp. 77–88). New York, NY: Routledge.

Osteen, P. J. (2011). Motivations, values, and conflict resolutions: Students' integration of personal and professional identities. *Journal of Social Work Education, 47,* 423–444.

Oşvat, C., Marc, C., Makai-Dimeny, J. (2014). Group supervision in social work: A model of intervention for practitioners. *Revista de Asistență Socială, 1,* 17–26.

Overland, S. (2016). *Pioneering study reveals more than 90 percent of colleges and universities embrace alternative credentials.* Retrieved from https://upcea.edu/pioneering-study-reveals-90-percent-colleges-universities-embrace-alternative-credentials/

Palmer, P. (1998). *The courage to teach: Exploring the inner landscape of a teacher's life.* San Francisco, CA: Jossey-Bass.

Palombo, J. (1982). The psychology of the self and the termination of treatment. *Clinical Social Work Journal, 10,* 15–27.

Panos, P. T. (2005). A model for using videoconferencing technology to support international social work field practicum students. *International Social Work, 48,* 834–841.

Papell, C. P. (1980). *A study of styles of learning for direct social work practice* (Unpublished dissertation). Yeshiva University, New York, NY.

Papell, C. P. (2015) Process recording revisited: An essay on an educational artifact as a cognitive exercise, *Social Work with Groups, 38,* 345–357.

Papell, C. P., & Skolnik, L. (1992). The reflective practitioner: A contemporary paradigm's relevance for social work education. *Journal of Social Work Education, 28,* 18–26.

Parker, J. (2010). When things go wrong! Placement disruption and termination: Power and student perspectives. *British Journal of Social Work, 40,* 983–999. doi:10.1093/bjsw/bcn149.

Pashler, H., McDaniel, M., Rohrer, D., & Bjork, R. 2008. Learning styles: Concepts and evidence. *Psychological Science in the Public Interest, 9*, 106–119

Pathy Solett, E., & Koslow, D. R. (2015). *Multicultural perspectives on race, ethnicity and identity.* Washington, DC: NASW Press.

Paul, R. (1992). *Critical thinking: How to prepare students for a rapidly changing world.* Sonoma, CA: Foundation for Critical Thinking.

Paven, J. A., & Shore, M. (2015). *College for students with disabilities: We do belong.* Philadelphia, PA: Jessica Kingsley.

Pease, B., & Fook, J. (1999). *Transforming social work practice: Postmodern critical perspectives.* New York, NY: Routledge.

Petracchi, H. E., & Patchner, M. A. (2000). Social work students and their learning environment: A comparison of interactive television, face-to-face instruction, and the traditional classroom. *Journal of Social Work Education, 36*, 335–335.

Petracchi, H. E., & Zastrow, C. (2010a). Suggestions for utilizing the 2008 EPAS in CSWE-accredited baccalaureate and masters curriculums—reflections from the field, part 1: The explicit curriculum. *Journal of Teaching in Social Work, 30* 125–146.

Petracchi, H. E., & Zastrow, C. (2010b). Suggestions for utilizing the 2008 EPAS in CSWE-accredited baccalaureate and masters curriculums—reflections from the field, part 2: The implicit curriculum. *Journal of Teaching in Social Work, 30*, 357–366.

Pierce, B., McGuire, L. E., & Howes, P. (2015). Ready, set, go . . . again: Renewing an academy-agency child welfare partnership. *Journal of Social Work Education, 51(Suppl. 2)*, S239–S251. doi:10.1080/10437797.2015.1072424

Pierce, D. (2016). History, standards, and signature pedagogy. In C. A. Hunter, J. K. Moen, & M. S. Raskin (Eds.), *Social work field directors* (pp. 5–22). Chicago, Il: Lyceum.

Pimpare, S. (2011). Hopeful, active realism: A pedagogy of critical social policy, In J. Birkenmaier, A. Cruce, J. Wilson, J. Curley, E. Burkemper, & J. Stretch (Eds.), *Educating for social justice: Transformative experiential learning* (pp. 99–110). New York, NY: Lyceum Books.

Pinderhughes, E. (1983). Empowerment for our clients and ourselves. *Social Casework, 64*, 331–338.

Pinderhughes, E. (1989). *Understanding race, ethnicity and power: The key to efficacy in clinical practice.* New York, NY: Free Press.

Pinto, R., McKay, M., & Escobar, C. (2008). "You've gotta know the community": Minority women make recommendations about community-focused health research. *Women and Health, 47*(1), 83–104.

Plack, M. M., Greenberg L. (2005). The reflective practitioner: Reaching for excellence in practice. *Pediatrics, 116*, 1546–1552.

Plaut, S. M. (1993). Boundary issues in teacher student relationships. *Journal of Sex & Marital Therapy, 19*, 210–219.

Pomeroy, E., & Steiker, L. (2011). Paying it forward: On mentors and mentoring. *Social Work, 56*, 197–199.

Pompeo, A. M., Levitt, D. H. (2014). A path of counselor self-awareness. *Counseling & Values, 59*(1), 80–94.

Poole, J. (2010). Perspectives on supervision in human services: gazing through critical and feminist lenses. *Michigan Family Review, 14*(1), 60–70.

Postma, T. C. (2015). Self-regulation: The key to progress in clinical reasoning? *African Journal of Health Professions Education, 7*, 201–207.

Poulin, J., & Matis, S. (2015). Social work competencies and multi-dimensional assessment. *Journal of Baccalaureate Social Work, 20*(1), 117–135.

Poverty USA. (2016). *The population of poverty USA: Who lives in poverty USA?* Retrieved from https://povertyusa.org/facts

Power, R., & Bogo, M. (2002). Educating field instructors and students to deal with challenges in their teaching relationships. *Clinical Supervisor, 21*, 39–58.

Powers, M., & Faden, R. (2006). *Social justice: The moral foundations of public health and health policy.* New York, NY: Oxford University Press.

Preston, S. George, P. and Silver, S. (2014). Field education in social work: The need for reimagining. *Critical Social Work, 15*(1), 57–72. Retrieved from http://www1.uwindsor.ca/criticalsocialwork/field_education_SW

Pyke, K. D. (2010). What is internalized racial oppression and why don't we study it? Acknowledging racism's hidden injuries. *Sociological Perspectives, 53*, 551–572.

Raphael, B. F., & Rosenblum, A. F. (1987). An operational guide to the faculty field liaison role. *Social Casework, 68*, 156–163.

Raphael, B. F., & Rosenblum, A. F. (1989). The open expression of difference in the field practicum: Report of a pilot study. *Journal of Social Work Education, 25*, 109–116.

Raymond, G. T., & Sowbel, L. R. (2016). Gatekeeping. In C. A. Hunter, J. K. Moen, & M. S. Raskin (Eds.), *Social work field directors* (pp. 181–199). Chicago, Il: Lyceum Books.

Reamer, F. G. (2013a). Social work in a digital age: Ethical and risk management challenges. *Social Work, 58*, 163–172.

Reamer, F. G. (2013b). *Social work values and ethics* (4th ed.). New York, NY: Columbia University Press.

Reeser, L. C. (1992). Students with disabilities in practicum: What is reasonable accommodation? *Journal of Social Work Education, 28*, 98–109.

Reeser, L. C., & Wertkin, R. A. (1997). Sharing sensitive student information with field instructors: Responses of students, liaisons, and field instructors. *Journal of Social Work Education, 33*, 347–362.

Regehr, C., Bogo, M., Donovan, K., Anstice, S., & Lim, A. (2012). Identifying student competencies in macro practice: Articulating the practice wisdom of field instructors. *Journal of Social Work Education, 48*, 307–319.

Reisch, M. (2002). Defining social justice in a socially unjust world. *Families in Society, 83*, 344–354.

Reisch, M. (2011). Defining social justice in a socially unjust world. In J. Birkenmaier, A. Cruce, J. Wilson, J. Curley, E. Burkemper, & J. Stretch (Eds.), *Educating for social justice: Transformative experiential learning* (pp. 11–28). New York, NY: Lyceum Books.

Reisch, M. (2013). Social work education and the neo-liberal challenge: The US response to increasing global inequality. *Social Work Education, 32*, 715–733.

Reisch, M. (2016). Why macro practice matters. *Journal of Social Work Education, 52*, 258–268.

Reisch, M. (2017). *Social policy and social justice: Meeting the challenges of a diverse society* (2nd ed.). San Diego, CA: Cognella.

Reynolds, B. C. (1942). *Learning and teaching in the practice of social work.* New York, NY: Russell & Russell.

Rheaume, H., Collins, M. E., & Amodeo, M. (2011). University/agency IV-E partnerships for professional education and training: Perspectives from the states. *Journal of Public Child Welfare, 5*, 481–500, doi:10.1080/15548732.2011.617261

Richan, W. C. (1989). Empowering students to empower others: A community-based field practicum. *Journal of Social Work Education, 25*, 276–283.

Rickes, C. (2016). Generations in flux: How Gen Z will continue to transform higher education space. *Planning for Higher Education Journal, 44*(4), 21–45.

Robbins, S. P., Chatterjee, P., & Canda, E. R. (2012). *Contemporary human behavior theory: A critical perspective for social work.* New York, NY: Allyn & Bacon.

Robbins, S. P., Coe Regan, J. R., Williams, J. H., Smyth, N. J., & Bogo, M. (2016). The future of social work education. *Journal of Social Work Education, 52*, 387–397

Robinson, M. A., Cross-Denny, B., Kyeunghae Lee, K., Wekmeister, L. M., Yamada, A. (2016). Teaching Note—Teaching intersectionality: Transforming cultural competence content in social work education. *Journal of Social Work Education, 52*, 509–517.

Roche, S. E., Dewees, M., Trailweaver, R., Alexander, S., Cuddy, C., & Handy, M. (1999). *Contesting boundaries in social work education: A liberatory approach to cooperative learning and teaching.* Alexandria, VA: Council on Social Work Education.

Rogers, G. (Ed.). (1995). *Social work field education: Views and visions.* Dubuque, IA: Kendall/Hunt.

Rogers, G. (1996). Training field instructors British style. *Journal of Social Work Education, 32*, 365–276.

Rogers, G., & McDonald, L. (1992). Thinking critically: An approach to field instructor training. *Journal of Social Work Education, 28*, 166–177.

Rosenblatt, A., & Mayer, J. E. (1975). Objectionable supervisory styles: Students' views. *Social Work, 20*, 184–190.

Rosenberg, J. S. (2015, September 2). Risk forgiveness. *Harvard Magazine* Retrieved from https://harvardmagazine.com/2015/09/harvard-president-faust-on-diversity

Rosenthal Gelman, C. (2011). Field instructors' perspectives on foundation level students' preplacement anxiety. *Journal of Teaching in Social Work, 31*, 295–312.

Rosenthal Gelman, C., & Lloyd, C. (2008). Foundation-year MSW students' preplacement anxiety: A follow-up study. *Journal of Social Work Education, 44*, 173–183.

Saari, C. (1989). The process of learning in clinical social work. *Smith College Studies in Social Work, 60*, 35–49.

Salsberg, E., Quigley, L., Aquaviva, K., Wyche, K., & Silwa, S. (2017). *Profile of the social work workforce.* National Workforce Initiative. Retrieved from https://www.cswe.org/Centers-Initiatives/Initiatives/National-Workforce-Initiative/SW-Workforce-Book-FINAL-11-08-2017.aspx

Salsberg, E., Quigley, L., Aquaviva, K., Wyche, K., & Sliwa, S. (2018). *New Social workers: Results of the nationwide Survey of 2017 Social Work Graduates.* Retrieved from https://cswe.org/Centers-Initiatives/Initiatives/National-Workforce-Initiative/Survey-of-2017-SW-Grads-Report-FINAL.aspx

Sandars J. (2009). The use of reflection in medical education: AMEE Guide No. 44. *Medical Teacher, 31*, 685–695.

Sanford, N. (1967). *Where colleges fail: A study of the student as a person.* San Francisco, CA: Jossey-Bass.

Schamess, G. (2006). Therapeutic processes in clinical supervision. *Clinical Social Work Journal, 34*, 427–445. doi:10.1007/s10615-005-0038-9

Schilling, R., Morrish N. J., & Liu, G. (2008). Demographic trends in social work over a quarter-century in an increasingly female profession. *Social Work, 53*, 103–114.

School of Social Welfare, Office of Field Education. (2017). *MSW advanced generalist second year graduate student field education evaluation.* Stony Brook, NY: Stony Brook University. Unpublished document.

Schön, D. A. (1983). *The reflective practitioner: How professionals think in action.* New York, NY: Basic Books.

Schön, D. A. (1987). *Educating the reflective practitioner.* San Francisco, CA: Jossey-Bass.

School of Social Work, University of Illinois. (2018). *Engagement and workforce development*. Retrieved from http://socialwork.illinois.edu/about-ssw/engagement-initiatives/

Scott Heller, S., & Gilkerson, L. (Eds.). (2009). *A practical guide to reflective supervision*. Zero to Three. Washington, DC.

Section 504 of the Rehabilitation Act of 1973, 34 CFR Part 104 (1973).

Seemiller, C., & Grace, M. (2016). *Generation Z goes to college*. San Francisco, CA: Jossey-Bass.

Sen, A. (2009). *The idea of justice*. Cambridge, MA: Harvard University Press.

Sensoy, O., & DiAngelo, R. (2014). Respect differences? Challenging the common guidelines in social justice education. *Democracy & Education, 22*(2), 1–10.

Shen Ryan, A., & Ortiz Hendricks, C. (1989). Culture and communication: Supervising the Asian and Hispanic social worker. *Clinical Supervisor, 7*(1), 27–40.

Sherby, L. B. (2004). Forced termination: When pain is shared. *Contemporary Psychoanalysis, 40*, 69–90.

Shohet, R. (Ed.). (2011). *Supervision as Transformation: A passion for learning*. London, UK: Jessica Kingsley.

Shor, I. (1992). *Empowering education: Critical teaching for social change*. Chicago, IL: University of Chicago Press.

Shulman, L. (1984). *Skills of supervision and staff management*. Itasca, IL: Peacock.

Shulman, L. (1994). *Teaching the helping skills: A field instructor's guide* (2nd ed.). Alexandria, VA: Council on Social Work Education.

Shulman, L. (2005). The clinical supervisor-practitioner working alliance: A parallel process. *Clinical Supervisor, 24*, 23–47.

Shulman, L. (2012). *The skills of helping individuals, families, groups, and communities* (7th ed.). Belmont, CA: Brooks/Cole.

Shulman, L. S. (2005). Signature pedagogies in the professions. *Daedalus, 134*(3), 52–59.

Siebert, D. C., Siebert, C. F., & Spaulding-Givens, J. (2006). Teaching clinical social work skills primarily online: An evaluation. *Journal of Social Work Education, 42*, 325–336.

Siebold, C. (2007). Every time we say goodbye: Forced termination revisited, a commentary. *Clinical Social Work Journal, 35*, 91–95.

Simmons, C., & Fisher, A. K. (2016). Promoting cognitive development through field education, *Journal of Social Work Education, 52*, 462–472.

Simoni, J. M., Meyers, T., & Walters, K. L. (2001). Heterosexual identity and heterosexism: Recognizing privilege to reduce prejudice. *Journal of Homosexuality, 41*(1), 157–172.

Singer, J. B., & Sage, M. (2015). Technology and social work practice: Micro, mezzo and macro applications. In K. Corcoran & Albert R. Roberts (Eds.), *Social worker's desk reference* (pp. 176–198). Oxford, UK: Oxford University Press.

Siporin, M. (1982). The process of field instruction. In B. W. Sheafor & L. E. Jenkins, *Quality field instruction in social work: Program development and maintenance* (pp. 175–197). New York, NY: Longman.

Slavich, G. M., Zimbardo, P. G. (2012). Transformational teaching: theoretical underpinnings, basic principle, and core methods. *Educational Psychology Review, 24*, 569–608.

Smith, M. K. (2002). *Malcolm Knowles, informal adult education, self-direction and andragogy*. Retrieved from http://www.infed.org/thinkers/et-knowl.htm

Smith, L., Foley, P. F., & Chaney, M. P. (2008). Addressing classism, ableism and heterosexism in counselor education. *Journal of Counseling & Development, 86*, 303–309.

Soheilian, S. S., Inman, A. G., Klinger, R. S., Isenberg, D. S., & Kulp, L. E. (2014). Multicultural supervision: supervisees' reflections on culturally competent supervision. *Counselling Psychology Quarterly, 27*, 379–392. doi:10.1080/09515070.2014.961408

Solas, J. (1990). Effective teaching as construed by social work students. *Journal of Social Work Education, 26*, 145–154.

Solo, C. (2018). Supervising students in emerging adulthood: Modeling use of self in developmentally informed supervision. *Clinical Social Work Journal, 47,* 72–78. doi:10.1007/s10615-018-0674-5

Somashekhar, S. Brown, E., & Balingit, M. (2017, February 22). Trump administration revokes protections for transgender students in public schools. *Washington Post*. Retrieved from https://www.washingtonpost.com/local/education/trump-administration-rolls-back-protections-for-transgender-students/2017/02/22/550a83b4-f913-11e6-bf01-d47f8cf9b643_story.html?noredirect=on&utm_term=.ad68609246b9

Southern Poverty Law Center. (2017). *Let's talk: Discussing race, racism and other difficult topics with students*. Retrieved from https://www.tolerance.org/sites/default/files/2017-09/TT-Lets%20Talk-2017%20Final.pdf

Sowbel, L. (2012). Gatekeeping: Why shouldn't we be ambivalent? *Journal of Social Work Education, 48*, 27–44.

Statista. (n.d.-a). *Estimated numbers of homeless people in the United States in 2017, by race*. Retrieved from https://www.statista.com/statistics/555855/number-of-homeless-people-in-the-us-by-race/

Statista. (n.d.-b). *Poverty rate in the United States in 2016 by race and gender*. Retrieved from https://www.statista.com/statistics/233154/uspoverty-rate-by-gender/

Steen, J., Mann, M., Restivo, N., Mazany, S., & Chapple, R. (2017). Human rights: Its meaning and practice in social work field settings. *Social Work, 62*, 9–17.

Sternberg, R. J., & Zhang, L. F. (Eds.). (2000). *Perspectives on cognitive, learning, and thinking styles*. Mahwah, NJ: Erlbaum.

Stofle, G. S., & Hamilton, S. (1998). Online supervision for social workers. *New Social Worker, 5*(4). Retrieved from http://www.socialworker.com/feature-articles/field-placement/Online_Supervision_for_Social_Workers/

Stoltenberg, C. (1981). Approaching supervision from a developmental perspective: The Counselor complexity model. *Journal of Counseling Psychology, 28*, 59–65.

Strolin, J. S., McCarthy, M., & Caringi, J. (2006). Causes and effects of child welfare workforce turnover: Current state of knowledge and future directions. *Journal of Public Child Welfare, 1*(2), 29–52.

Sue, D. W. (2010). *Microaggressions in everyday life: Race, gender, and sexual orientation*. New York, NY: Wiley.

Sue, D. W., & Sue, D. (2012). *Counseling the culturally diverse: Theory and practice* (4th ed.). New York, NY: Wiley.

Suler, J. (2000). *Myths and realities of online clinical work. Psychotherapy and clinical work in cyberspace*. Retrieved from http://www.rider.edu/%7Esuler/psycyber/myths.html

Sullivan, E., & Johns, R. (2002). Challenging values and inspiring attitude change: Creating an effective learning experience. *Journal of Social Work Education, 21*, 217–231.

Sussman, T., Bogo, M., & Globerman, J. (2007). Field instructor perceptions: Establishing trust in group supervision through managing group dynamics. *Clinical Supervisor, 26*, 61–80.

Sweitzer, H., & King, M. A. (2009). *The successful internship: Personal, professional, and civic development* (3rd ed.). Belmont, CA: Brooks/Cole.

Swenson, C. R. (1988). The professional log: Techniques for self-directed learning. *Social Casework, 69*, 307–311.

Taylor, E. W. (Ed.). (2006). The challenge of teaching for change. *New Directions for Adult and Continuing Education, 109*, 91-95.

Taylor, E. W. (2007). An update of transformative learning theory: A critical review of the empirical research (1999–2005). *International Journal of Lifelong Education, 20*, 173–190.
Taylor, E. W. (2008). Transformative learning theory. *New Directions for Adult and Continuing Education*, 119, 5–14.
Taylor, M. F. (2007). Professional dissonance: A promising concept for clinical social work. *Smith College Studies in Social Work, 77*, 89–99. doi:10.1300/J497v77n01_05.
Tedam, P. (2011) The MANDELA model of practice learning: An old present in new wrapping? *Journal of Practice Teaching & Learning 11*(2), 60–76. doi:10.1921/175951511X661219
Tew, J. (2006). Understanding power and powerlessness: Towards a framework for emancipatory practice in social work. *Journal of Social Work, 6*, 33–51.
Thyer, B. A., Artelt, T. A., & Shek, D. T. L. (2012). Using single-system research designs to evaluate practice: Potential applications for social work in Chinese contexts. *International Social Work, 46*, 163–176.
Title IX, Education Amendments of 1972 (PL No. 92-318, 86 Stat. 373)
Tomlin, A. M., Weatherston, D. J., & Pavkov, T. (2014). Critical components of reflective supervision: Responses from expert supervisors in the field. *Infant Mental Health Journal, 35*(1), 70–80.
Towle, C. (1954). *The learner in education for the professions as seen in education for social work.* Chicago, IL: University of Chicago Press.
Tsui, M., & Cheung, F. C. H. (2009). Social work administration revisited: A re-examination of concepts, context and content. *Journal of Social Work, 9*, 148–157.
Tuck, E., & Yang, K. W. (2012). Decolonization is not a metaphor. *Decolonization: Indigeneity, Education and Society, 1*(1), 1–40.
Tully, G. (2015). The faculty field liaison: An essential role for advancing graduate and undergraduate group work education. *Social Work With Groups, 38*(1), 6–20.
Turner, G. (2015). A coming out narrative: Discovering my queer voice, my social worker superpower. *Reflections, 21*(4), 40–50.
United Nations. (1948). *Universal declaration of human rights.* Retrieved from http://www.un.org/en/udhrbook/pdf/udhr_booklet_en_web.pdf
United Nations. (2007). *Declaration on the rights of indigenous peoples.* Retrieved from https://www.un.org/esa/socdev/unpfii/documents/DRIPS_en.pdf
University of Buffalo School of Social Work. (2019). *Our self-care starter kit.* Retrieved from https://socialwork.buffalo.edu/resources/self-care-starter-kit.html
Urbanowski, M. L., & Dwyer, M. M. (1988). *Learning through field instruction: A guide for teachers and students.* Milwaukee, WI: Family Service of America.
Urbanowski, M. L., & Dwyer, M. M. (1989). Counterpoint/in defense of process recording. *Social Casework, 70*, 312–314.
Urdang, E. (1999). Becoming a field instructor: A key experience in professional development. *Clinical Supervisor, 18*, 85–103.
Urdang, E. (2010). Awareness of self: A critical tool. *Social Work Education, 29*, 523–538.
U.S. Census Bureau. (2016). *Quick facts: Population estimates July 1, 2018.* Retrieved from https://www.census.gov/quickfacts/fact/table/US/PST045216U.S.
U.S. Department of Education. (1974). *Family educational rights and privacy act.* Retrieved from https://www2.ed.gov/policy/gen/reg/ferpa/index.html
U.S. Department of Education Office of Special Education and Rehabilitation Services. (2016). *Racial and ethnic disparities in special education: A multi-year disproportionality analysis by state, analysis category and race/ethnicity.* Retrieved from https://www2.ed.gov/programs/osepidea/618-data/LEA-racial-ethnic-disparities-tables/disproportionality-analysis-by-state-analysis-category.pdf

U.S. Department of Health and Human Services. (1996). *Health insurance portability and accountability act of 1996* (HIPAA). Retrieved from https://aspe.hhs.gov/report/health-insurance-portability-and-accountability-act-1996

U.S. Department of Health and Human Services. (2003). *Summary of the HIPAA privacy rule*. Retrieved from https://www.hhs.gov/sites/default/files/privacysummary.pdf

U.S. Equal Employment Opportunity Commission (n.d.) *Reasonable accommodation procedures, Section IV c. The interactive process*. Retrieved from https://www.eeoc.gov/eeoc/internal/reasonable_accommodation.cfm#_Toc531079192

Van Gelder, T. (2005). Teaching critical thinking: Some lessons from cognitive science. *College Teaching, 53*(1), 41–46.

Van Soest, D., & Garcia, B. (2008). *Diversity education for social justice: Mastering teaching skills* (2nd ed.). Alexandria, VA: CSWE Press.

Van Soest, D., & Kruzich, J. (1994). The influence of learning styles on student and field instructor perceptions of field placement success. *Journal of Teaching in Social Work, 9*(1/2), 49–69.

Vespa, J., Armstrong, D. M., & Medina, L. (2018). *Demographic turning points for the United States: Population projections for 2020 to 2060: Population estimates and projections*. Retrieved from https://www.census.gov/content/dam/Census/library/publications/2018/demo/P25_1144.pdf

Videka-Sherman, L., & Reid, W. (1985). The structured record: A clinical educational tool. *Clinical Supervisor, 3*(1), 45–62.

Voshel, H. (2008). E-portfolios. *University of Michigan School of Social Work, field work manual*. Ann Arbor, MI: University of Michigan.

Wagner, A. E. (2005). Unsettling the academy: Working through the challenges of anti-racist pedagogy. *Race, Ethnicity and Education, 8*, 261–275.

Wall, J. C. (1994). Teaching termination to trainees through parallel processes in supervision. *Clinical Supervisor, 12*(2), 27–36.

Walsh, J. (2007). *Endings in clinical practice: Effective closure in diverse settings*. (2nd ed.). Chicago, IL: Lyceum.

Walsh, T. (2002). Structured process recordings: A comprehensive model that incorporates the strengths perspective. *Journal of Social Work Education, 21*, 23–34.

Walter, C. A., & Young, T. M. (1999). Combining individual and group supervision in educating for the social work profession. *Clinical Supervisor, 18*, 73–89.

Walters, K. L., Mohammed, S. A., Evans-Campbell, T., Ramona, B. E., Chae, D. H., & Duran, B. (2011). Bodies don't just tell stories, they tell histories: Embodiment of historical trauma among American Indians and Alaska Natives. *Du Bois Review, 8*(1), 179–189.

Walters, K. L., Simoni, J. M., Evans-Campbell, T., Udell, W., Johnson-Jennings, M., Pearson, C. R., ... & Duran, B. (2016). Mentoring the mentors of underrepresented racial/ethnic minorities who are conducting HIV research: Beyond cultural competency. *AIDS and Behavior, 20*, S288–S293. doi:10.1007/s10461-016-1491-x

Walters, K. L., Casey, M. L., Evans-Campbell, T., Valdez, R., & Zambrana, R. E. (In press). "Before they kill my spirit entirely": Insights into the lived experiences of American Indian/Alaska Native faculty at research-extensive universities. *Race Ethnicity and Education*.

Wayne, J., Bogo, M., & Raskin, M. (2016). Nontraditional field models. In C. A. Hunter, J. K. Moen, J. K., & M. S. Raskin (Eds.), *Social work field directors* (pp. 41–59). Chicago, Il: Lyceum Books.

Wayne, J., & Cohen, C. S. (2001). *Group work education in the field*. Alexandria, VA: Council on Social Work Education.

Weatherston, D., Weigand, R. F., & Weigand, B. (2010). Reflective supervision: Supporting reflection as a cornerstone for competency. *Zero to Three, 31,* 22–30.

Webb, L. M., Allen, M. W., & Walker, K. L. (2002). Feminist pedagogy: Identifying basic principles. *Academic Exchange Quarterly, 6,* 67–72.

Webb, S. (2006). *Social work in a risk society: Social and political perspectives.* Basingstoke, Hampshire, UK: Palgrave Macmillan.

Wehbi, S., & Straka, S. (2011). Revaluing student knowledge through reflective practice on involvement of social justice efforts. *Social Work Education, 30,* 45–54.

Wehlburg, C. W. (2010). Thriving in academe: Assessment, teaching, and learning. *National Education Association: The Advocate, 28*(2), 5–7.

Weick, A. (2000). Hidden voices. *Social Work, 45,* 395–402.

Weld, N. (2012). *A practical guide to transformative supervision for the helping professions.* London, UK: Jessica Kingsley.

Wendt, S., & Seymour, S. (2010). Applying post-structuralist ideas to empowerment: Implications for social work education. *Social Work Education, 29,* 670–682.

Wenger, E. (1998). *Communities of practice: Learning, meaning, and identity.* New York, NY: Cambridge University Press.

Wildeman, C., Schnittker, J., & Turney, K. (2012). Despair by association? The mental health of mothers with children by recently incarcerated fathers. *American Sociological Review, 77,* 216–243.

Williams, A. (2015, September 18). Move over, Millennials, here comes Generation Z. *New York Times.* Retrieved from www.nytimes.com/2015/09/20/fashion/move-overmillennials-here-comes-generation-z.html

Williams, B., Brown, T., & Etherington, J. (2013). Learning style preferences of undergraduate social work students. *Social Work Education, 32,* 972–990.

Williams, P. (1991). The death of the profane. In *The alchemy of race and rights: Diary of a law professor* (pp. 44–51). Cambridge, MA: Harvard University Press.

Willingham, D. T. (2007). Critical thinking: Why is it so hard to teach? *American Educator, 31*(2), 8–17.

Willingham, D. T. (2009). Why don't students like school? Because the mind is not designed for thinking. *American Educator, 4*(9), 12–13.

Wilson, S. J. (1980). *Recording guidelines for social workers.* New York, NY: The Free Press.

Wise, E. H. (2005). Social responsibility and the mental health professions. *Journal of Aggression, Maltreatment and Trauma, 11*(1/2), 89–99.

Witkin, S. L. (1998). Human rights and social work. *Social Work, 43,* 197–201.

Witkin, S. L. (2014). Change and deeper change: Transforming social work education. *Journal of Social Work Education, 50,* 587–598. doi:10.1080/10437797.2014.947897

Wolfsfeld, L., Haj-Yahia, M. M. (2010). Learning and supervisory styles in the training of social workers. *Clinical Supervisor, 29,* 68–94. doi:10.1080/07325221003742066

Woods, M., & Hollis, F. (2000). *Casework: A psychosocial therapy* (5th ed.). New York, NY: McGraw-Hill.

World Health Organization. (2013). *Global and regional estimates of violence against women: Prevalence and health effects of intimate partner violence and non-partner sexual violence.* Geneva, Switzerland: WHO Press.

Wretman, C. J., & Macy, R. J. (2016). Technology in social work education: A systemic review. *Journal of Social Work Education, 52,* 409–421.

Wronka, J. (2014). Human rights as pillars of social justice. In M. Reisch (Ed.). *The Routledge international handbook of social justice* (pp. 216–226). London, UK: Routledge.

Yan, M. C., & Wong, Y. (2005). Rethinking self-awareness in cultural competence: Toward a dialogic self in cross-cultural social work. *Families in Society, 86,* 181–188.

York, R. O. (2008). Comparing three modes of instruction in a graduate social work program. *Journal of Social Work Education, 44,* 157–172.

Yorks, L., & Kasl, E. (2009). Toward a theory and practice for whole-person learning: Reconceptualizing experience and the role of affect. *Adult Education Quarterly, 52,* 176–192.

Zeira, A., & Schiff, M. (2010). Testing group supervision in fieldwork training for social work students. *Research on Social Work Practice, 20,* 427–434. doi:10.1177/1049731509332882

Zinn, H. (1980). *A people's history of the United States.* New York, NY: HarperCollins.

Zuchowski, I. (2015). Being the university: Liaison persons' reflections on placements with off-site supervision. *Social Work Education, 34,* 301–314.

INDEX

Figures and tables are indicated by f and t following page numbers.

A

Ability. *See* Mental and physical ability
Ableism, 95–96
Abram, F. Y., 35
Absences, 373
Accommodations, 95–96, 380–382, 396–399
Accordion-style recordings, 310, 312
Accreditation standards. *See* Educational Policy and Accreditation Standards
Active learning, 114
Active teaching methods, 459–460
Activism, 445–446
ADA (Americans with Disabilities Act, 1990), 380–382
ADA Amendments Act (2008), 380–381
Administration assignments, 284
Administration log, 342–346
Administrative responsibilities, 414–415
Adult learning, xxiii–xxiv, 141–175
  Bloom's taxonomy on, 161–163
  critical thinking and, 163–167
  developmental stages of learning and, 156–161
  experiential learning and, 151–161
  individualized learning approaches and, 155–156
  Kolb's four dominant learning patterns and, 153–155, 154–155f
  Kolb's learning cycle and, 151–153
  resistance to learning. *See* Resistance to learning
  teaching approaches for, 170–175
  theory of, 141–146, 173–175
  transformational learning and, 146–151, 150f, 169, 173–175, 353
Advisory responsibilities, 415–416
African Americans, 442, 443t, 448, 450
Agendas, 318
Alaska Natives, 442–444, 443t, 450. *See also* Indigenous peoples

Alienation, 359
American Community Survey, 442
American Indians, 442–444, 443t, 450. *See also* Indigenous peoples
Americans with Disabilities Act (ADA, 1990), 380–382
Analogy and metaphor use, 478–479
Anchor instructors, 470
Anderson, L. W., 162
Andragogy. *See* Adult learning
Antioppression perspectives and practice, xvi–xvii, 54, 83, 457
Anxiety of students
  group work assignments and, 282
  learning obstacles and, 352, 355
  marginally acceptable performance and, 365
  normalizing, 376
  replacement placement settings for, 367
  safety practices and, 145
  starting field education and, 226, 246
Aptekar, H. H., 29–30
Argument mapping, 480
Asian and Pacific Island/Hawaiian Natives, 443t, 444. *See also* Indigenous peoples
Assessments
  across units of attention, 284
  assignments for, 294–296
  of competencies, 102, 119–129, 462
  creating, 132–135
  educational assessment process, 108–118, 110f
  strengths assessment framework, 487–488, 488f
  tools for, 120
Assignments. *See* Student assignments
Assimilation, 449
Association of Social Work Boards (ASWB), 31–32
Authentic dialogue, 244
Authenticity in learning environments, 145
Authority. *See* Power

537

B

Barker, R. L., 6
Barretti, M, 482
Basic human needs, xvii, 49
Baum, N., 408–409
Belkin-Martinez, D., 80
Benchmarks for assessment, 109–111, 110f
Benner, P., 159
Berengarten, S., 152
Best practice standards, 31–32, 276
Biases, 16, 51, 189–190, 444
Bilingual skills, 264
Bisman, C., 181–182
Black Administrators Researchers and Scholars, 450
Block placements, 417, 465
Bloom, B. S., xxiii, 142, 161–163, 166
Boddy, J., 459
Bogo, M., 32, 130, 151–153, 169, 465
Boundaries and dual relationships, 207–208, 210–211, 215–217
Boyd Webb, N., 378–379
Brainstorming, 479–480
Brookfield, S. D., 58, 168, 355, 390–391
Burnout, 199
Butin, D., 358–359

C

Carroll, M., 169
Center for Collegiate Mental Health, 453
Chaffin, K. M., 464
Challenging dialogues, xxii, 47–99
    avoiding, 52, 81–82
    basic assumptions and, 85–86
    faculty support for, 449–450, 469
    identity theory and intersectionality, 75–78
    literature on, 428–429
    power in communities and, 74–75
    power in supervisory relationships and, 71–74
    practice competence and, 49–54
    process recording and, 96–99
    self-evaluation and, 57–64
    starting conversations and, 64–69
    structured interviews and, 88–89
    student scenarios to promote, 89–96
    tasks and responsibilities in, 69–71
    terminology and, 78–80
    tips for, 87–88
Chambers, R., 37
Chenoweth, L., 459
Children's Defense Fund, 446
Chin, M., 445
Civic engagement, 437–438
Civil discord, 50
Civil rights, xvi–xvii, 7
Civil Rights Act (1964), 383
Clark, J., 459
Class, 76–77
Clients, 207–208, 214–215, 441. *See also* Communities
Cockerham, C., 464
Code of ethics. *See* National Association of Social Work Code of Ethics
Code of Federal Regulations (2018), 383
Coe Regan, J. R., 169
Cognitive and affective reactions, 123–124
Cognitive disequilibrium, 148
Collaboration in learning environments, 144, 150–151, 168
Collective leadership, 22
Collective learning, 22
Comfort zones, 350, 356
Communication, 370–371. *See also* Challenging dialogues
Communities
    civil discord and fear in, 50
    organization and planning for, 283
    orientation to, 234–235
    power in, 74–75
    practice assignments, 277, 282–283
    rural, 215
    safety issues and, 242–243
    terminating field education and, 406
    university partnerships, 466–469
Community colleges, 448
Compassion fatigue, 199
Competency-based education and practice
    adult learning and, 142
    advancing, 9–16
    assessment of, 102, 119–129, 462. *See also* Assessments
    benefits of, 101
    characteristics of, 9–10, 10f
    expectations for, 402
    future of social work education and, 438
    justice-based framework for. *See* Justice-based field education
    placement settings and, 247–248, 250–256, 260
    student assignments for. *See* Student assignments
    teaching approaches for. *See* Teaching approaches
    teaching challenges and, 367
    time frames for, 465
Concept and mind mapping, 480
Confidence, 157–158, 160–161, 265, 308, 355
Confidentiality
    disclosure to prevent harm to others and, 207, 214–215
    ethics and, 213–215
    physical abilities and, 382

process recordings and, 322
professional values and, 185
of SIFI participants, 496
technology use and, 207–208, 214, 490
Conflicts of interest, 203–206, 207, 241
Constructive criticism, 34, 366
Contexts, as key concept of justice-based field education, 48–49
Continuing education, 213. *See also* Seminar in Field Instruction
Cooper, L., 57
Cooper, M. G., 277
Corcoran, J., 151
Co-supervision, 36
Council of Social Work Education (CSWE). *See also* Educational Policy and Accreditation Standards
   on basic human needs, 50–51
   Center for Diversity and Social & Economic Justice, 460
   competency-based education and. *See* Competency-based education and practice
   on critical thinking, 164–165
   data on students and faculty, 442
   on diversity and difference, 50, 117
   on ethical behavior, 183
   on evaluation, 403–404
   field education survey report, 463
   future of justice-based field education and, 473–474
   on learning environments, 449
   Minority Fellowship Program, 452
   process recordings and competencies of, 316–317
   on research needs, 460–461
   State of Field Education Survey, 450
   Statistics on Social Work Education Appendix, 442, 443*f*
   on terminations and transitions, 403
   on workforce transformations, 445
Credentials, 458–459
Crisis-oriented service assignments, 266
Critical consciousness, 71
Critical incident recordings, 313–314
Critical pedagogy, 18–19
Critical race theory, 54
Critical thinking
   adult learning and, 163–167, 169
   competence and, 11
   holistic evaluations and, 13–14
   policy practice assignments and, 279
   process recordings and, 303
   professional behaviors and, 183
   questioning stance as teaching method, 477–478

on racism, 63
role playing and, 487
Crosby, P., 148
Cross-cultural interactions and relationships, 52–54, 76, 85–86
Cross-cultural learning, 358–359
Cross-cultural student supervision, 418–419
Csiernik, R., 464
CSWE. *See* Council of Social Work Education
Cultural awareness, 79, 206
Cultural competence, 78–80, 206
Cultural equity, 54, 79–80
Cultural identity, 452, 459
Cultural values, 181–182
Culture of schools, 448–454
Cummings, S. M., 464
Cumulative learning, 24
Curiosity in learning environments, 145
Curriculum
   active teaching methods for, 459–460
   implicit or hidden, xv, 102, 143, 229, 449
   integration of field practice into, 231
   justice as focus of, 456–458
   for lifelong learning and credentials, 458–459
   rubric framework of, 103–108, 105*f*
   transforming, 454–460, 473

D

Daloz, L. A., 149, 150*f*
Dalton, J., 148
Davies, M., 480
Davis, L. Larry, 450
Deal, K. H., 159–161
Decision making
   about learning, 144
   emotional reactions and, 169
   in practice, 153
   process recordings and, 314–315
   professional values and behavior in, 180, 183, 217–219
Declaration on the Rights of Indigenous Peoples (UNDRIP), xvii, 49–50, 271
Defensiveness, 145
Developmental stages of learning, 156–161, 168–169
DiAngelo, R., 145
Didactic teaching methods, 475–477
Directors of field education, 462–463
Disability. *See* Ableism; Mental and physical ability
Discrimination
   gender and, 383–384
   homophobia, 383, 385–386
   NASW Code of Ethics on, 5
   racial. *See* Race and racism

sexual, 94–95, 229, 383–386
Dismissals from placement settings, 364–365
Disruption of field placements, 367–369
Distance-learning SIFIs, 497–498
Diversity
　CSWE competency on, 50, 117
　equity and, 48–49
　faculty support and, 449–450
　in learning environments, 448–454
　student assignments on, 272–273
　student support and, 450–453
　teaching approaches and, 57
　of U.S. population, 439
　of workforce, 439–448, 443*t*
Diversity training model, 57
Dreyfus, H., 159
Dual relationships and boundaries, 207–208, 210–211, 215–217
DuBois, C., 156–157
Du Bois, W. E. B., 55
Due process, 364–365
Duty to warn laws, 213
Dwyer, M., 155, 311

E

East, J., 37
Economic justice, 273–275
Educational assessments. *See* Assessments
Educational learning contracts, 109, 116, 360–369, 454
Educational learning plans, 112–113, 135–136, 242
Educational Policy and Accreditation Standards (EPAS)
　on basic human needs, xvii
　competency-based education and, 9–10
　on credentials of instructors, xxx–xxxi, 495
　on critical thinking, 165
　on demonstrating competencies, 102
　on ethical behavior, 180
　on field education as signature pedagogy, 17, 461–463
　on field education standards, 17–18
　on field placement, xv
　on implicit curriculum, 143, 229, 449
　on lifelong learning, 458
Education Amendments (1972), 383
Electronic binders, 319
E-mail communications, 214
Empathy, 199
Employment, 241, 425–426, 448, 466
Ending field education. *See* Terminations and transitions
End-of-term evaluations, 116–118, 137–139, 363
Engaged pedagogy, 18–21

Engagement assignments, 284, 293–294
Environmental justice, 273–275
Environments. *See* Learning environments
EPAS. *See* Educational Policy and Accreditation Standards
E-portfolios and binders, 319, 489
Epstein, R. M., 192–193
Equity
　cultural, 54, 79–80
　defined, 7
　diversity and inclusion, 48–49
　equality vs., 53
　justice and, 439
　professional, 444–445
　race and underrepresented populations, 439–440
Ethical dilemmas, 184, 198, 209, 220–222, 243
Ethics. *See* National Association of Social Work (NASW) Code of Ethics; Professional values and behavior
Ethnicity. *See* Race and racism
Evaluation. *See also* Process recordings
　across units of attention, 285
　assignments for, 298–299
　CSWE competencies on, 403–404
　educational assessment process and, 108–118, 110*f*
　end-of-term, 116–118, 137–139, 363
　example of, 106–107
　field liaison responsibility for, 416–417
　holistic perspective of, 13
　mutual, 21
　orientation to processes of, 237
　power in supervisory relationships and, 72
　rubric framework for, 103–108, 105*f*
　student competency in, 403, 404–407
　teaching before, 373–374
　written, 363–364
Everett, J. E., 156–157
Evidence-based practice, 275–276
Experiential learning, 151–161, 167
Experts, 19, 72, 237, 476
Explicit power, 372–373

F

Failure. *See* Resistance to learning
Fain, P., 458
Families, cultural values and, 182
Family Educational Rights and Privacy Act (1974), 382
Faust, Drew, 448
Feedback, 105–106, 113–114, 117, 481. *See also* Assessments; Evaluation
Field education
　administration of, 232

adult learning and. *See* Adult learning
assessment and evaluation of. *See* Assessments; Evaluation
assignments in. *See* Student assignments
assumptions about, 464–465
challenging dialogues in. *See* Challenging dialogues
competency-based. *See* Competency-based education and practice
defined, xxx
ending. *See* Terminations and transitions
future of. *See* Future of social work education
instructors for. *See* Field instructors
justice-based framework for. *See* Justice-based field education
liaisons for. *See* Field liaisons
placement settings. *See* Field placements; Starting field education
recordings in. *See* Process recordings
research needs in, 460–461
as signature pedagogy, 17–37, 313, 461–463
student orientation to, 231, 257–258
student support in, 450–453
Field education journals, 428–430
Field instructors. *See also* Teaching approaches; Teaching challenges
alternative arrangements for, 33–37
assignment creation and. *See* Student assignments
challenging dialogues and, 57–64, 469
credentials of, xxx–xxxi, 495
defined, xxx–xxxi
development of, 370
diversity, program inclusiveness and, 449–450
dual relationships and boundaries, 210–212
end-of-term evaluations and, 117
engaged pedagogy and, 18–21
ethical dilemma scenarios for, 220–221
evaluative role of, 108
evolving roles of, 29–31
gatekeeping role of, 202, 349, 366
group supervision and, 33–37. *See also* Group supervision
idealized images of, 351–352, 357
lifelong learning and, 418–419, 458–459
mentoring and, 30–31
microaggressions and, 59–63
modeling of. *See* Modeling
power in supervisory relationships and, 20, 23, 57–58, 71–74, 211–212, 245
professional mission and, 21–24
reflection, promotion of. *See* Process recordings
self-assessment forms for, 430–432
shortage of, 33, 369, 417
SIFIs for. *See* Seminar in Field Instruction

statistical data on, 442–444
student needs, diversity of, 25–29, 380–382
student professional values and, 180
supervisory responses to stages of learning, 160
supervisory skill development, 31–33, 469
terminations with students, 408–409
unethical behavior of, 371
Field liaisons
administrative responsibilities of, 414–415
advisory responsibilities of, 415–416
challenging dialogues and, 60–63
contacts with, 417–418
educational assessment process and, 109–110
educational learning contracts and, 116, 361, 364
educational responsibilities of, 415
evaluative responsibilities of, 416–417
mediation responsibilities of, 416
meetings with, 428
microaggressions and, 59–63
placement settings and, 229
skills and roles of, 213, 227, 413–414
student performance criteria and, 366
teaching challenges and, 374
Field placements. *See also* Starting field education
dismissals from placement settings, 364–365
flexibility and student support in, 451
mismatches in, 369
orientation to, 233–238, 258
placement models, 463–466
placement setting staff and, 229–230, 236–237
replacement placement settings, 367–369
restrictions on, 466
rethinking for student needs, 463–466
shortage of field instructors for, 33
student assignments and. *See* Student assignments
student challenges in, 116, 118
Financial assistance, 452, 455
Finn, J. L., 48–49, 53
Fleck-Henderson, A., 80
Foucault, M., 372
Freire, Paulo, 18, 65, 71, 421, 476
Fronek, P., 459
Future of social work education, 437–474
curriculum transformations and, 454–460
field education transformations and, 460–471
school environments and culture transformations, 448–454
workforce transformations, 439–448, 443*t*

G

Ganzer, C., 378
Garran, A., 147, 156–157
Gatekeeping role, 202, 349, 366

Gender
  challenging dialogues and, 94–95
  consumers of social work services and, 440
  discrimination and, 383–384
  identity or expression of, 5, 383–384
  student and faculty data and, 442
  violence and, 441–442
Generalizations, 78
Generation Z, 437–438, 445–446, 456, 458
George, P., 463
Gifted and experienced students, 240–241, 387–388
Gitterman, A., 281, 482
Gladding, S. T., 479
Global issues, xxxi, 75, 272
Globalization, 182
Goals. *See* Learning goals and objectives
Goldstein, E., 146–147
Grants, 455
Graybeal, C. T., 319, 323
Greenberg, L., 163
Group supervision
  adult learning theory and, 173–175
  collective learning and, 22
  overview, 33–37
  process recordings and, 331–332
  reflective stance for, 42–46
  shortage of field instructors for, 33
  student expertise and, 470–471
  successful facilitation of, 35
Group work assignments, 277, 281–282
Group work process recordings, 312
Grow Your Own (GYO) model, 468
Gutiérrez, L., 445

H

Hair, H. J., 476
Haj-Yahia, M. M., 155
Handicapping behaviors, 194
Hardy, Kenneth V., 57–58, 69–71, 87
Hartung, M. R., 35
Hate crimes, 50
Hawaiian Natives. *See* Asian and Pacific Island/Hawaiian Natives
Hawkins, J., 445
Hawthorne, L., 307–308, 319–320
Health Insurance Portability and Accountability Act (HIPAA, 1996), 213–214, 322, 382
Health Resources & Services Administration, 455
Heartstorming, 479–480
Hidden curriculum. *See* Implicit curriculum
Historical trauma, xvii, 53
History, as key concept of justice-based field education, 48–49
Homophobia, 53, 385–386

hooks, b., 17
Hospital emergency room setting assignments, 266–267
Human rights
  CSWE competency on, 50–51
  justice-based framework for education and, xvi–xvii, 7
  social justice and, 6
  student assignments on, 273–275
  Universal Declaration of Human Rights (UN), xvii, 49–50, 271
Humility, 191
Hybrid courses, 451

I

Identity. *See also* Intersectionality
  challenging dialogues and, 63, 67
  class and, 76–77
  cultural, 452, 459
  diversity and difference, 50, 272
  professional, 181, 378–379
  racial, 52, 76–77
  reconstruction of, 147, 359
  resistance to learning and, 358–359
  sexual, 53–54, 76
  starting field education and, 227–228
Identity theory, 75–78, 272
Immigration status, 5, 439
Implicit curriculum, xv, 102, 143, 229, 449
Implicit power, 372–373
Inclusive perspectives, 144
Indigenous peoples
  Declaration on the Rights of Indigenous Peoples (UNDRIP), xvii, 49–50, 271
  decolonization and, 54
  defined, xxx
  faculty support and, 450
  historical trauma of, xvii
  justice-based framework for education and, xvi–xvii, 7
  representation of scholars in curriculum, 459–460
  student and faculty data and, 442–444, 443*t*
  Two Spirit. *See* LGBTQ+TS people
Individualized learning approaches, 155–156, 242, 363
Informality of learning environments, 143
Institutional racism, 4–5, 53, 73
Instructors. *See* Field instructors
Integration of theory and practice model (BOGO & Vayda), 151–153
Internal dissonance, 148
International students, 386–387
Internet searches of clients, 207–208, 215
Interpersonal partner violence (IPV), 441–442

Intersectionality
  challenging dialogues and, 54, 75–78
  diversity and difference, 50
  justice-based education and, 7
  process recordings and, 315–316
  student assignments on diversity and, 272
Intervention assignments, 266, 285, 297–298
I said, she said process recordings, 310
ITP model (BOGO & Vayda), 152–153

J

Janczewski, C. E., 441–442
Jarvis, P., 151, 476
Jindani, S., 419
Jones, S. R., 147, 358–359
Journals
  for field education, 237, 428–430
  for mindfulness, 193
  process recordings and, 311–313, 317, 332–334
Judgments, examining, 125, 374
Justice-based field education, xxi, 3–46. *See also* Challenging dialogues
  competence in practice and, 9–16, 10*f*, 15*f*
  curriculum for, 456–458
  engaged pedagogy and, 18–21
  field instructor role and, 29–31
  future of, 438, 472–474
  group supervision and learning teams, 33–37
  introduction to, 3–8
  justice, defined, 6–8
  key concepts of, 48–49
  professional mission and, 21–24
  reflective posture for, 38–46, 51
  SIFI on. *See* Seminar in Field Instruction
  as signature pedagogy, 17–37, 313, 461–463
  student needs and, 25–29
  supervisory skills, development of, 31–33

K

Knight, C., 32, 281
Knowing in action, 153
Knowles, Malcolm, 142, 143
Kolb, D., xxiii, 142, 151–155, 154–155*f*
Kovacs, P. J., 151
Krathwohl, D. R., 162
Krings, A., 445

L

Laird, J., 19
Latinx, xxix, 442, 443*t*, 448
Learning
  adult. *See* Adult learning
  challenges vs. opportunities in, 352–360
  conflicts in, 353

cumulative, 24
developmental stages of, 156–161, 168–169
educational learning contracts and, 109, 116, 360–369
educational learning plans and, 112–113, 135–136, 242
educational plans using competencies, 118–129
environment for. *See* Learning environments
experiential, 151–161, 167
individualized learning approaches, 155–156, 242, 363
multicultural, 161
obstacles to. *See* Teaching challenges
opportunities for, 134, 352–360
peer learning and, 22, 37. *See also* Group supervision
resistance to. *See* Resistance to learning
structural barriers to, 380–388
student patterns of, 133
styles of, 151–156, 154–155*f*, 357
teaching approaches and. *See* Teaching approaches
transformational, 146–151, 150*f*, 169, 173–175, 353
Learning environments
  adult learning and, 142–146
  for challenging conversations, 55, 64, 72
  collaboration in, 144, 150–151, 168
  competency assessment and, 102
  culture and diversity of, 448–454
  implicit curriculum and, 449
  for justice-based field education, 23–24
  microaggressions and, 448, 449
  process recording evaluation and, 308
  teaching challenges and, 348–352
Learning goals and objectives
  autonomous practice as, 349–350
  educational assessments and, 131, 134–135
  educational learning contracts, 109, 116, 360–369
  educational learning plans, 112–113, 135–136, 242
Learning management systems, 489
Learning reviews, 481
Learning styles, 151–156, 154–155*f*, 357
Learning teams, 33–37
Levitt, D. H., 190–192
LGBTQ+TS people
  as consumers of social work services, 441
  defined, xxx
  discrimination and homophobia, 383, 385–386
  faculty support and, 450
  microaggressions and, 58. *See also* Microaggressions

representation of scholars in curriculum, 459–460
social movements and, 445–446
student and faculty data, 444
teaching challenges and, 393–394
transphobia, 385–386
Liberation, 53, 79–80
Liberation health model, 317–318
Lifelong learning, 21, 275, 418–419, 458–459
Ligon, J., 419
Literature reviews, 275–276
Logs. *See* Journals

M

Macro-level assignments, 265–266, 282–283, 311–313
Macro-level practice, 210, 265, 282–283
Maidment, J., 57
Manuel, T., 77
Mapping tools, 480
Mar Fariña, M. del, 418–419
Marginally acceptable performance, 365–366
Meaning, as key concept of justice-based field education, 48–49
Mediation, 416
Medina, C. K., 312–313, 336
Mental and physical ability, 5, 95–96, 206, 380–382, 396–399
Mentorships, 30–31, 450
Mersky, J. P., 441–442
Metacompetence, 11–12
Metaphor use, 478–479
Mezirow, J., 147–148
Mezzo-level assignments, 311–313
Mezzo-level practice, 210
Microaggressions
  avoiding, 53
  bias and, 189–190
  challenging dialogues and, 58–63
  embedded in curriculum, 460
  learning environments and, 448, 449
  power differentials and, 211
  in student assignments, 264
Micro-level assignments, 265–266, 281, 310–311
Micro-level practice, 210, 265, 284
Micro research assignments, 276–277
Miehls, D., 156–157
Millennials, 437–438, 445, 458, 470
Miller, I., 482
Miller, J., 151
Mindfulness, 191–194
Mind mapping, 480
Misrepresentations, 320, 462
Mistakes, 350, 357–358
Modeling
  authentic relationships, 245
  mindfulness, 193
  open feedback and communication, 370–371
  power differentials and, xix
  self-awareness and reflection, 23, 65
  as teaching method, 482–484
  teamwork, 21
  terminations with students, 408–409
Multicultural learning, 161
Multiple intelligences, 155
Murdock, V., 419
Mutuality
  authentic dialogue and, 244
  challenging dialogues and, 64
  dual relationships and boundaries, 211
  learning environments and, 55, 146
  professional mission and, 21

N

Narayan, U., 81
Narrative recordings, 310–311
National Association of Black Social Workers, 452
National Association of Puerto Rican Hispanic Social Workers, 452
National Association of Social Work (NASW)
  best practice standards created by, 31–32
  on cultural competence, 79
  on professional mission, 4
  on self-care practices, 199
  Standards and Indicators for the Achievement of Cultural Competence in Social Work Practice, 78
  on structural racism, 4
National Association of Social Work (NASW) Code of Ethics (1996), 4–5, 210
National Association of Social Work (NASW) Code of Ethics (2017)
  on basic human needs, xvii, 49, 271
  challenges to, 437
  on cultural awareness, 79
  Cultural Awareness and Social Diversity (Standard 1.05), 79
  on discrimination, 5
  on education and training (Standard 3.02), 210–213
  on field instruction, 470
  on injustice, 5–6
  main standards of, 206, 209–210
  Preamble of, 5
  Social Workers' Ethical Responsibilities to Clients (Standard 1), 209
  technological advances and, 206, 207–208
  violations, terminations from placement settings and, 364
National Social Work Workforce Study, 444

Nationwide Workforce Initiative, 440, 442, 444, 445
Native Americans. *See* American Indians
Navari, S., 351
Newell, J. M., 199–200
Nitkowski, J. C., 441–442
Nussbaum, Martha, 6

O

Observation, 462, 484–485
O'Donoghue, K., 476
Off-site field instructors, 33, 35
O'Neill, P., 418–419
Online SIFIs, 498
Online social work programs, 456, 459, 464
Openness about learning, 144–145
Oppression. *See also* Power
  basic assumptions of, 85–86
  challenging dialogues and, 56, 87–88, 91–92
  critical thinking and, 165
  CSWE competencies on, 50–51
  justice and, 6
  in placement settings, 229
  structural barriers and, 53, 204
Oral reviews, 113–116, 135–136, 363
Organizational research assignments, 277–278, 284
Organizational skills, 373
Orientation
  to community being served, 234–235
  to competencies, 247–248, 250–256, 260
  to evaluation processes, 237
  to field education, 231, 257–258
  to field education supervision, 243–247, 259–260
  individualized pace of, 225
  to placement settings, 233–238, 258
  to student's professional role, 238–243, 258–259
Ornstein, E. D., 378
Otherize, 193

P

Papell, C. P., 152
Partializing, 485
Part-time programs, 451, 464
Peer groups, 34–35, 470–471
Peer learning, 22, 37. *See also* Group supervision
Peguero-Spencer, C., 445
People's Institute for Survival and Beyond, 63
People with disabilities. *See* Mental and physical ability
Performance behaviors, 14–16, 104, 106–109
Performance criteria, 366–367
Performance expectations, 117–118
Personal biases. *See* Bias
Personal values, 182, 184–188, 358

Perspective transformation, 147–149, 169
Physical ability. *See* Mental and physical ability
Physical comfort in learning environments, 145
Pinderhughes, Elaine, 56, 85–86
Placement settings. *See* Field placements
Plack, M. M., 163
Policy
  advocacy assignments on, 292
  analysis research assignments on, 277
  curriculum on, 456–458
  limitations of, xviii
  restrictions on access to services and, 50
  on sexual harassment, 384
Policy manuals, 233
Policy practice, 278–280, 291–292, 334–336
Political social work assignments, 292
Pomeroy, E., 30–31
Pompeo, A. M, 190–192
Portfolios, 319
Possibilities, as key concept of justice-based field education, 48–49
Power differentials. *See also* Privilege
  basic assumptions of, 85–86
  challenging dialogues and, 56, 87–88
  in communities, 74–75
  critical thinking and, 165
  didactic teaching method and, 476
  explicit and implicit, 372–373
  justice and, 6
  as key concept of justice-based field education, 48–49
  learning environments and, 146
  modeling collaborative relationships and, xix
  sexual harassment and discrimination, 383–384
  shared in engaged pedagogy, 19
  in supervisory relationships, 20, 23, 57–58, 71–74, 211–212, 245
Practice-informed research, 11, 275–278
Practice principles, 34, 41, 102–103. *See also specific principles*
Practice protocols, xviii
Preston, S., 463
Privacy, 185, 207–208, 213–215. *See also* Confidentiality
Privilege. *See also* Power
  challenging dialogues and, 56, 69–71, 91–92
  gender and, 77
  heteronormative attitudes and, 386
  socialization and, 63
  transformational learning and, 147
Privilege and Subjugated Task (PAST) Model, 69–71
Privileged communication, 213–215
Problem posing, 485–487
Procedural competence, 12

Process recordings, xxvi–xxvii, 301–346
  agendas in supervision, 318–319
  challenging dialogues and, 56–57, 96–99
  focusing recording tools for, 313–318
  focusing teaching efforts through, 327–328
  group process and, 331–332
  justice-based process recording format, 328–331, 330*f*
  log or journal outline, 332–336
  micro to macro recordings, 303–306
  for mindfulness, 193
  for policy practice, 336
  sample field education recordings, 336–342
  special considerations for, 319–322
  specialized practice level student, log entry example of, 342–346
  teaching from micro to macro recordings, 306–322
  technology and, 303, 323–324
Professional equity, 444–445
Professional identity, 181, 378–379
Professional mission, 4, 9, 21–24, 420, 438
Professional values and behavior, xxiv–xxv, 179–222
  conflicting perspectives of, 353, 358
  conflicts of interest, resolving, 203–206
  dual relationships and boundaries, 215–217
  ethical dilemmas and, 184, 198, 209, 220–222, 243
  mindfulness, promotion of, 191–194
  NASW Code of Ethics, 206–213
  overview, 181–183
  privacy, confidentiality, and privilege communication, 213–215, 322
  reflective practice and, 188–192, 190*f*
  self-care and safety, 199–203
  self-regulation, promotion of, 194–199
  student assignments on, 270–272
  teaching challenges and, 394–396
  tension between personal and professional values, 182, 184–188, 358
  terminations from placement settings and, 364–365
Professional voice, 320–321
Program requirements, field assignments and, 231–232
Psychological disequilibrium, 148

Q

Questioning stance, 477–478

R

Race and racism
  challenging dialogues and, 56, 69–71, 92–93
  class and, 76–77
  consumers of social work services and, 440–441
  conversations on, 52–54
  faculty support, 450
  institutional racism and, 4–5, 53, 73
  microaggressions and, 58. *See also* Microaggressions
  Millennials and, 437
  in placement settings, 229
  privilege and, 77
  recruitment and retention strategies, 444–448, 453–454
  representation of scholars in curriculum, 459–460
  socialization and, 63–64
  social movements and, 445–446
  student support, 450–453
  Undoing Racism training, 63
  white supremacy, 58
  workforce transformations and, 439–440
  writing assessment and, 321
Racial identity theory, 76
Rapid assessment instruments, 276–277
Raskin, M., 465
Rasmussen, B. M., 147
Record-keeping practices, 207, 213, 240, 322
Recruitment strategies, 444–448, 469, 472–473
Reflection. *See* Journals; Process recordings; Self-awareness and reflection
Reflection in action, 153
Reflective practice, 24, 188–192, 190*f*
Rehabilitation Act (1973), 380
Reisch, M., xvii, 6, 209–210
Religion, 58, 89–91
Research assignments
  community organization, 277
  group work, 277
  micro, 276–277
  organizational, 277–278
  peer groups for, 34–35
  policy analysis, 277
  practice-informed, 275–278
Research-informed practice, 11, 275–278
Research needs, 460–461
Resistance to learning
  educational learning contracts and, 109, 116, 360–369
  overcoming, 19, 354–355, 390–391
  process recordings and, 321
  reframing, 355–360
  scenarios for, 391–399
Respect in learning environments, 144
Retention strategies, 444–448, 453–454
Reynolds, B. C., xvii, 157–158, 226
Rheaume, H., 467

Richmond, Mary, 303
Rickes, C., 459
Risk taking
  in learning, 145, 357–358, 378
  process recordings and, 320
  student autonomy and decision making, 350
Robbins, S. P., 169
Rogers, G., 29
Role models. *See* Modeling
Role playing, 487
Rosenblum, A., 151
Rubric framework, 103–108, 105*f*
Ruff, E., 319, 323
Running reflections, 317
Rural communities, 215

S

Saari, C., 158–159
Safety and safe spaces. *See also* Microaggressions
  adult learning and, 145
  for challenging dialogues, 64–65
  communities and, 242–243
  learning environments and diversity, 449
  for LGBTQ+TS people, 444
  for LGBTQ+TS students, 386
  placement settings and, 245
  self-care and, 199–203
Sandars, J., 188
Sanford, N., 149
Scaffolding, 161
Scholarships, 455
Schön, D. A., 30, 153, 188
Script recordings, 310
Secondary trauma, 199
Self-awareness and reflection. *See also* Professional values and behavior
  critical thinking and, 164, 166–167
  on difference, identity, and social location, 87–88
  journals for, 428–430. *See also* Journals
  justice-based field education and, 38–46, 51, 71
  metacompetence and, 12
  modeling, 23, 65
  personal biases and, 16, 51
  professional behaviors and, 183, 271
  questioning stance as teaching method, 477–478
  reflection in action and, 153
  reflective practice, promotion of, 188–192, 190*f*
  resistance to, 366
  risk-taking and mistakes, 350
  teaching challenges and, 375–377
Self-care, 199–203
Self-consciousness, 157–159
Self-determination, 185, 204

Self-disclosure, 375–377
Self-regulation, 194–199
Self-review, 109, 120
Seminar in Field Instruction (SIFI), 493–504
  distance-learning, 497–498
  justice-based outline for, 499–504
  online, 498
  purposes of, 494–495
  sample assignments for, 502–504
  structure of, 495–497
Sen, Amartya, 6
Sensoy, O., 145
Sexual harassment and discrimination, 94–95, 211, 229, 383–386, 392–393
Sexual orientation, 53–54, 76
Shared supervisory model, 35
Shulman, Larry S., 209–210, 282, 354–355, 375, 461, 475, 490
Silver, S., 463
Singer, Jonathan, 490
Single-system research design, 276
Sixth-week plans, 363
Skill labs, 369
Skill performance, 14–16
Smythe, N. J., 169
Social action, 71
Socialization, 63
Social justice, 6–7, 273–275
Social location, 76–77
Social media, 208
Social movements, 445–446
Social networks, 489
Social Work Healthcare Education and Leadership Scholars Program, 455
Social Work Podcast (Singer), 490
Social work skills, 125–129. *See also* Competency-based education and practice
Social work values and knowledge, 123–124. *See also* Professional values and behavior
Standards and Indicators for the Achievement of Cultural Competence in Social Work Practice (NASW), 78
Starting field education, xxv, 223–260
  learning while serving, 232–248
  orientation to competencies, 247–248, 250–256, 260
  orientation to field education supervision, 243–247, 259–260
  orientation to setting, 233–238, 258
  orientation to student's professional role, 238–243, 258–259
  self-evaluation for, 227–228, 257
  settings for, 228–232
  social work education programs, 257–258
  stage setting for, 224–232, 255–260

548 Index

State of Field Education Survey, 462
Statistics on Social Work Education Appendix, 442, 443*t*
Steiker, L., 30–31
Stereotyping, 78
Sternberg, R. J., 155
Stony Brook University, 106–107
Strengths assessment framework, 487–488, 488*f*
Structural barriers to learning, 380–388
Structural inequality, 8, 53, 204, 365. *See also* Institutional racism
Structured Interview on Dimensions of Difference, Identity, and Social Location, 88–89, 244
Student assignments, xxv–xxvi, 261–300
　competencies and, 262–264, 263*f*
　designing, 264–269
　engage, assess, intervene, and evaluate practice, 280–285, 293–299
　engaging diversity and difference in practice, 272–273
　ethical and professional behavior, 270–272
　human rights, advancing, 273–275
　learning styles and, 156–157
　policy practice, 278–280, 291–292
　practice-informed research and research-informed practice, 275–278
　research. *See* Research assignments
　sample assignment summaries, 287–299
Student learning outcomes, 15–16, 103, 112
Student recordings. *See* Process recordings
Students
　academic records of, 116
　anxiety of. *See* Anxiety of students
　assessments of. *See* Assessments
　autonomy of, 349–350
　challenges in placement settings, 116, 118
　challenging dialogues, scenarios to promote, 89–96
　competency-based education and, 11
　developmental stages of learning, 156–161, 168–169
　dismissals from placement settings, 364–365
　diverse needs of, 25–29, 380–382, 463–466, 470–471
　diversity, program inclusiveness and, 450–453
　educational learning contracts for, 109, 116, 360–369
　educational learning plans for, 112–113, 135–136, 242
　ethical dilemma scenarios for, 221–222
　evaluation of. *See* Evaluation
　gifted and experienced, 240–241, 387–388
　group supervision of. *See* Group supervision
　idealized images of, 351–352, 357
　informing clients of student status, 212, 214
　international, 386–387
　learning and. *See* Adult learning; Learning
　mental health services for, 453
　power in supervisory relationships and, 20, 23, 57–58, 71–74, 211–212, 245
　professionalism of. *See* Professional values and behavior
　reactions to field experiences, 371
　reflection of. *See* Process recordings; Self-awareness and reflection
　resistance of. *See* Resistance to learning
　responsibility for learning, 114
　satisfaction, measurement of, 350
　self-assessment forms for, 432–433
　self-review of, 109, 120
　starting field education. *See* Starting field education
　statistical data on, 442–444
　terminations and. *See* Terminations and transitions
Success coach, 289
Summary recordings, 311, 312
Supervisory skill development, 31–33

T

Tardiness, 373–374
Task supervisors, 35–37, 115, 247, 361, 370, 412
Teaching approaches and methods, xxii–xxiii, 101–139
　active teaching methods, 459–460
　for adult learning, 170–175
　analogy and metaphor use, 478–479
　brainstorming and heartstorming, 479–480
　challenging dialogues and, 56–57
　competency-based framework and, 102–103, 103*f*
　concept and mind mapping, 480
　didactic methods, 475–477
　educational assessment process, 108–118, 110*f*
　engaged pedagogy, 18–21
　feedback, 481
　learning focus using competencies, 117–129, 118–129
　learning styles and approaches, 155–156
　linking concepts to skills and examples, 481–482
　for meta and procedural competencies, 11–12
　modeling, 21, 482–484
　observation, 484–485
　outlines and tools for evaluations, 132–139
　partializing, 485
　problem posing, 485–487
　process recordings and, 306–322. *See also* Process recordings
　questioning stance, 477–478

Index **549**

role playing, 487
rubric framework for, 103–108, 105*f*
strengths assessment framework, 487–488, 488*f*
technology for, 488–490
for terminations, 409–412
transformative teaching and supervisory techniques, 150–151
Teaching challenges, xxvii–xxviii, 347–400
 diversity and oppression, teaching, 57
 educational learning contracts for, 109, 116, 360–369, 454
 explicit and implicit power, 372–373
 failure to meet criteria, 366–367
 gifted and experienced students, 387–388
 international admissions, increasing, 386–387
 learning environments, 348–352
 mandated accommodations, 380–382
 marginally acceptable performance, 365–366
 opportunities for learning and, 352–360
 program policies and procedures for, 363–365
 removal from placements, 367–369
 scenarios for, 391–399
 sexual harassment and discrimination, 383–386
 structural barriers to learning and, 380–388
 teaching before evaluating, 373–374
 tips for overcoming, 390–391
 treating vs. teaching, 375–379
Teaching styles, 357
Teamwork, 20–22
Technology
 access issues, 207
 confidentiality and, 207–208, 214, 490
 distance-learning and online SIFIs, 497–498
 Internet searches of clients and, 207–208, 215
 online social work programs, 456, 459
 process recordings and, 303, 323–324
 revisions to NASW Code of Ethics and, 206, 207–208
 to support field education supervision, 470
 teaching approaches and, 488–490
Technology-assisted social work practice, 206
Tedam, P., 387
Terminations and transitions, xxviii, 401–434
 CSWE competencies on, 403
 enabling students to identify their feelings about, 410–411
 evaluation and ongoing review, 404–407
 field education journals, 428–430
 field education supervision and, 418–419
 field liaisons and, 413–418, 428
 overview, 407–409
 planning for the future, 411–412
 preparing for, 424–425
 scenarios for, 425–427

self-assessment forms for instructors, 430–432
self-assessment forms for students, 432–433
teaching tasks associated with, 409–412
Terminology, xxix–xxxi
Thyer, B. A., 277
Timeliness, 373–374
Title IX protections, 383–384
Towle, C., 225
Training
 challenging dialogues and, 83
 diversity training model, 57
 skill labs for field education preparation, 369
 Undoing Racism training, 63
Transformational learning, 146–151, 150*f*, 169, 173–175, 353
Transgender people, 383. *See also* LGBTQ+TS people
Transphobia, 385–386
Trauma, xvii, 53, 199
Trust
 challenging dialogues and, 63
 in learning environments, 145–146
 process recordings and, 320
 self-disclosure and, 377
 student–teacher relationships and, 23–24, 32, 245, 377, 386
 transformative learning and, 149
Tuck, E., 53–54, 422
Tully, G., 415
Two Spirit. *See* LGBTQ+TS people
Typecasting, 264

U

Undoing Racism training, 63
United Nations (UN)
 Declaration on the Rights of Indigenous Peoples, xvii, 49–50, 271
 Universal Declaration of Human Rights, xvii, 49–50, 271
University–community partnerships, 466–469
Unknowing, resistance as, 359
Urbanowski, M., 155, 311
Urdang, E., 304

V

Values. *See* Personal values; Professional values and behavior
Vayda, E., 151–153
Verbatim recordings, 310, 319
Violence, 441–442

W

Wagner, A. E., 23
Walters, K. L., xvii, 441
Ward, J., 419

Wayne, J., 36, 465
Weick, A., xvii
Werner, S. P., 35
Whites, 52–54, 76, 443*t*, 444
White supremacy, 58
Williams, J. H., 169
Within-group differences, 91–92
Wolfsfeld, L., 155
Workforce transformations, 439–448, 443*t*
Work–study students, 241

Worst-case scenarios, 243
Wright, L., 151
Writing skills, 320–321, 452, 456
Written evaluations, 363–364

Y

Yang, K. W., 53–54, 422

Z

Zhang, L. F., 155

ABOUT THE AUTHORS

Jeanne Bertrand Finch, DSW, LCSW-R, is a part-time field instructor and coordinator of a shared supervision unit of 15 students for the School of Social Welfare, Stony Brook University. She previously served in various leadership roles in the School of Social Welfare including interim assistant dean for academic affairs, director of the MSW program, and assistant dean of field education. Dr. Finch has also been a faculty liaison, educational coordinator, and SIFI teacher.

Ovita F. Williams, LCSW-R, is associate director of field education at Columbia School of Social Work, where from 2013–2015 she served as interim director of field education. She co-convenes the decolonizing social work foundation course and conducts workshops on justice-based practice. Ms. Williams is an instructor for the social work practice lab on anti-oppressive practice and a student in the doctoral program at the Silberman School of Social Welfare at Hunter College, City University of New York. She has been a field instructor, field liaison, and advanced SIFI teacher on facilitating challenging dialogues in supervision.

Jacqueline B. Mondros, DSW, is dean of the School of Social Welfare and assistant vice president of social determinants of health at Stony Brook University. She is past president of the National Deans and Directors of Social Work. The second edition of her widely used co-authored text, *Organizing for Power and Empowerment*, will be published soon. She has served as director of field education, associate dean, and dean of several schools of social work. She is a committed community activist working to bring the resources of academia to effect change in urban neighborhoods throughout the country.

Cheryl L. Franks, PhD, LMSW, is a faculty member and administrator in the Percy Ellis Sutton SEEK Department, John Jay College of Criminal Justice, City University of New York, where she manages the social work internship program. She served 22 years at Columbia School of Social Work in various leadership roles including assistant dean; director of field education; and executive director of diversity, human rights, and social justice. She has been a field instructor, faculty liaison, and educational coordinator and developed advanced SIFI seminars on macro practice and the skills for facilitating challenging dialogues on diversity-related content.